CompTIA® Linux+ XK0-005 Cert Guide

Companion Website and Pearson Test Prep Access Code

Access interactive study tools on this book's companion website, including practice test software, review exercises, Key Term flash card application, a study planner, and more!

To access the companion website, simply follow these steps:

1. Go to **www.pearsonitcertification.com/register**.
2. Enter the **print book ISBN: 9780137866885**.
3. Answer the security question to validate your purchase.
4. Go to your account page.
5. Click on the **Registered Products** tab.
6. Under the book listing, click on the **Access Bonus Content** link.

When you register your book, your Pearson Test Prep practice test access code will automatically be populated with the book listing under the Registered Products tab. You will need this code to access the practice test that comes with this book. You can redeem the code at **PearsonTestPrep.com**. Simply choose Pearson IT Certification as your product group and log in to the site with the same credentials you used to register your book. Click the **Activate New Product** button and enter the access code. More detailed instructions on how to redeem your access code for both the online and desktop versions can be found on the companion website.

If you have any issues accessing the companion website or obtaining your Pearson Test Prep practice test access code, you can contact our support team by going to **pearsonitp.echelp.org**.

CompTIA® Linux+ XK0-005 Cert Guide

Ross Brunson

Pearson

Hoboken, New Jersey

CompTIA® Linux+ XK0-005 Cert Guide

ISBN-13: 978-0-13-786688-5

ISBN-10: 0-13-786688-7

Library of Congress Control Number: 2023913510

1 2023

Trademarks

Warning and Disclaimer

Special Sales

For information about buying this title in bulk quantities, or for special sales opportunities (which may include electronic versions; custom cover designs; and content particular to your business, training goals, marketing focus, or branding interests), please contact our corporate sales department at corpsales@pearsoned.com or (800) 382-3419.

For government sales inquiries, please contact governmentsales@pearsoned.com.

For questions about sales outside the U.S., please contact intlcs@pearson.com.

Vice President, IT Professional
Mark Taub

Director, ITP Product Line Management
Brett Bartow

Executive Editor
Nancy Davis

Development Editor
Ellie Bru

Managing Editor
Sandra Schroeder

Senior Project Editor
Mandie Frank

Copy Editor
Bill McManus

Indexer
Ken Johnson

Proofreader
Jennifer Hinchliffe

Technical Editor
Casey Boyles

Publishing Coordinator
Cindy Teeters

Designer
Chuti Prasertsith

Compositor
codeMantra

Pearson's Commitment to Diversity, Equity, and Inclusion

Pearson is dedicated to creating bias-free content that reflects the diversity of all learners. We embrace the many dimensions of diversity, including but not limited to race, ethnicity, gender, socioeconomic status, ability, age, sexual orientation, and religious or political beliefs.

Education is a powerful force for equity and change in our world. It has the potential to deliver opportunities that improve lives and enable economic mobility. As we work with authors to create content for every product and service, we acknowledge our responsibility to demonstrate inclusivity and incorporate diverse scholarship so that everyone can achieve their potential through learning. As the world's leading learning company, we have a duty to help drive change and live up to our purpose to help more people create a better life for themselves and to create a better world.

Our ambition is to purposefully contribute to a world where

- Everyone has an equitable and lifelong opportunity to succeed through learning

- Our educational products and services are inclusive and represent the rich diversity of learners

- Our educational content accurately reflects the histories and experiences of the learners we serve

- Our educational content prompts deeper discussions with learners and motivates them to expand their own learning (and worldview)

While we work hard to present unbiased content, we want to hear from you about any concerns or needs with this Pearson product so that we can investigate and address them.

Please contact us with concerns about any potential bias at https://www.pearson.com/report-bias.html.

Contents at a Glance

Online Elements

Table of Contents

About the Author

Ross Brunson has more than 30 years of experience as a Linux and open-source trainer, training manager, and certification architect, and is the author of the now-classic *LPIC-1 Exam Cram 2*, several iterations of the *CompTIA Linux+ Cert Guide*, and dozens of technical courses for major organizations.

Ross is currently the Education Architect at Grafana Labs (www.grafana.com), where he focuses on building a learning framework and training offerings that help employees and customers make the best use of Grafana to observe, troubleshoot, and maintain their environments.

Previously, Ross was a Senior Technical Training Engineer for NGINX, where he completely redid the Fundamentals learning track, authored a number of Getting Started guides, and taught a number of customer engagements to help new NGINX customers take full advantage of the platform.

Before NGINX, Ross enjoyed a few years at Linux Academy/A Cloud Guru where as a Senior Training Architect, he authored the SUSE Certified Administrator and Engineer courses, did the Red Hat Certified System Administrator Labs, created many additional courses on systemd, VIM and the screen command, and wrote and reviewed way too many exam questions.

Ross has also put in a tour of duty as the Certification Architect at SUSE, where he helped redesign and modernize the entire certification program. He has also spent five years as the Director of Member Services for the Linux Professional Institute, where he contributed to placing several LPI courses into the Cisco Networking Academy, conducted dozens of train-the-trainer sessions, and provided sales enablement support for the worldwide Master Affiliate network, spanning more than 100 countries and nearly a million certified professionals.

Ross holds a number of key IT certifications and is author of several successful technical books and dozens of technical courses for major organizations (including the first U.S. LPI Certification Bootcamps). He is skilled at both contributing to and building community around IT products.

Ross lives in Paradise Valley, Montana, with his family and enjoys traveling far and wide, participating in hiking, winter sports, photography, and playing the drums with great vigor (although not everyone around him appreciates it).

Dedication

My heartfelt thanks to all of my mentors and friends who have helped me get where I am: Andres Fortino, Arnold Villeneuve, Ken Haug, Ted Jordan, Edward Denzler, and many more. I am eternally grateful for the love and support of my wife and daughter, who understand what it means when "daddy is writing" and still love me anyway.

I also want to shout out to all our previous edition readers who made this book likely and possible. I love the emails and photos of you all and your certifications; it really makes a difference when we get something that lets us know we are somehow making even a tiny difference in someone's career and life.

I want to hear from YOU. Let me know what you liked, what I can improve, and how you're doing. Please send pics of you and your study tools, you and your certification, and so on...

—Ross E. Brunson, July 2023

Acknowledgments

This book is a result of the concerted efforts of many dedicated people, without whom this book would not be a reality. I would like to thank the technical reviewer, Casey Boyles, whose efforts and patience made this a better book for all to use, and to Chris Cleveland, who helped me navigate the adjustments to new CompTIA Linux+ versions over the years.

Much thanks to William (Bo) Rothwell for the courseware and writing MACHINE that he is, and for being a great author and technical editor over these many years—I couldn't have done it without you, buddy!

Thanks also to Nancy Davis, Executive Editor, for her help and continuous support during the development of this book. I wish to also express my appreciation to Mary Beth Ray, executive editor at Pearson/Cisco Press (retired), for her confidence in me throughout years of working on book projects.

Much thanks to Ellie Bru for both her superb editorial skills and acumen, but especially her good humor and geek-wrangling skills; it is a pleasure to work with her on every book!

In addition, many thanks to Dr. James Stanger for being such a great supporter of the world of Linux and open source. He's a good friend and a hugely relevant person in the world of getting our customers and attendees the skills they need!

It has been a huge undertaking to pull together all the pieces of this project. It is due to the dedication of those mentioned above that this book is not only large in scope but high in quality. It is my sincerest hope that our combined efforts will help you, the readers and users of this book, achieve your goals in an IT career.

About the Technical Reviewer

Casey Boyles started working in the IT field more than 28 years ago and quickly began to work with distributed application and database development. Casey later moved on to technical training and development; he specializes in full stack Internet application development, database architecture, and systems security. Casey typically spends his time smoking cigars while "reading stuff and writing stuff."

We Want to Hear from You!

As the reader of this book, *you* are our most important critic and commentator. We value your opinion and want to know what we're doing right, what we could do better, what areas you'd like to see us publish in, and any other words of wisdom you're willing to pass our way.

We welcome your comments. You can email or write to let us know what you did or didn't like about this book—as well as what we can do to make our books better.

Please note that we cannot help you with technical problems related to the topic of this book.

When you write, please be sure to include this book's title and author as well as your name and email address. We will carefully review your comments and share them with the author and editors who worked on the book.

Email: community@informit.com

Reader Services

Register your copy of *CompTIA Linux+ XK0-005 Cert Guide* at www.pearsonitcertification.com for convenient access to downloads, updates, and corrections as they become available. To start the registration process, go to www.pearsonitcertification.com/register and log in or create an account*. Enter the product ISBN 9780137866885 and click Submit. When the process is complete, you will find any available bonus content under Registered Products.

*Be sure to check the box that you would like to hear from us to receive exclusive discounts on future editions of this product.

Introduction

In mid-2022, CompTIA released a new version of the Linux+ certification exam, labeled XK0-005. To throw a monkey wrench is to goof up or confuse or sabotage. The gears of other content authors may be messed up by this change, but I remain unaffected.

In particular, the new exam version has more DevOps-related and cloud-specific topic areas, allocates more space to Git and containers, and adds the revised Troubleshooting domain, which covers significant space on the exam and comprises approximately 28% of the scoring.

Most of the Linux+ exam will be multiple choice, much like the previous exams. However, you should also be prepared for a handful of scenario questions in which you will be asked to answer some questions based on a particular situation. In addition, you'll encounter some simulation questions, where you're running what appears to be a command-line terminal and you have to answer the question by actually typing the right commands and so forth. (Please note, you can use the **commandname help** option for *all* of these simulation questions, which will really help you puzzle out what the questions require!)

Use this book as a reference to all of the key exam-testable topics. This book provides an excellent roadmap on your journey to learning Linux and passing the Linux+ certification exam.

Study hard and study well. Pore over the exam objectives, and if you don't know something, I guarantee that you will see it on the exam, so make sure to locate the topic or term in this book's TOC or index and read the relevant material.

Good luck!

—Ross E. Brunson, July 5, 2023

Goals and Methods

The number-one goal of this book is a simple one: to help you pass the CompTIA Linux+ XK0-005 certification exam.

Because the CompTIA Linux+ certification exam now stresses problem-solving abilities and reasoning more than memorization of terms and facts, my goal is to help you master and understand the required objectives for the exam.

To aid you in mastering and understanding the Linux+ certification exam objectives, this book uses the following methods:

- **Opening topics list:** The list at the beginning of each chapter defines the topics to be covered in the chapter, followed by identification of the corresponding CompTIA Linux+ objective.

- **Foundation Topics:** The body of the chapter explains the topics from both hands-on and theory-based standpoints, including in-depth descriptions, tables, and figures that help you build your knowledge so that you can pass the Linux+ exam. The chapters are broken down into several topics each.

- **Key Topics:** Key Topics icons indicate important figures, tables, and lists of information that you should know for the exam. They are interspersed throughout the chapter and are listed in table format at the end of the chapter.

- **Key Terms:** Key terms without definitions are listed at the end of each chapter. Write down the definition of each term and check your work against the key terms in the glossary.

- **Review Questions:** These quizzes and answers with explanations are meant to gauge your knowledge of the subjects covered in the chapter. If an answer to a question doesn't come readily to you, be sure to review that portion of the chapter.

- **Practice Exams:** The practice exams are included in the Pearson Test Prep practice test software. These exams test your knowledge and skills in a realistic testing environment. Take them after you have read through the entire book. Master one, then move on to the next.

The Linux+ Domains and Objectives

The Linux+ XK0-005 exam consists of the following domains and objectives:

1.0 System Management (32% of the exam)

1.1 Summarize Linux fundamentals

1.2 Given a scenario, manage files and directories

1.3 Given a scenario, configure and manage storage using the appropriate tools

1.4 Given a scenario, configure and use the appropriate processes and services

1.5 Given a scenario, use the appropriate networking tools or configuration files

1.6 Given a scenario, build and install software

1.7 Given a scenario, manage software configurations

2.0 Security (21% of the exam)

2.1 Summarize the purpose and use of security best practices in a Linux environment

2.2 Given a scenario, implement identity management

2.3 Given a scenario, implement and configure firewalls

2.4 Given a scenario, configure and execute remote connectivity for system management

2.5 Given a scenario, apply the appropriate access controls

3.0 Scripting, Containers, and Automation (19% of the exam)

3.1 Given a scenario, create simple shell scripts to automate common tasks

3.2 Given a scenario, perform basic container operations

3.3 Given a scenario, perform basic version control using Git

3.4 Summarize common infrastructure as code technologies

3.5 Summarize container, cloud, and orchestration concepts

4.0 Troubleshooting (28% of the exam)

4.1 Given a scenario, analyze and troubleshoot storage issues

4.2 Given a scenario, analyze and troubleshoot network resource issues

4.3 Given a scenario, analyze and troubleshoot central processing unit (CPU) and memory issues

4.4 Given a scenario, analyze and troubleshoot user access and file permissions

4.5 Given a scenario, use systemd to diagnose and resolve common problems with a Linux system.

Be sure to visit CompTIA's web page at https://certification.comptia.org/certifications/linux to ensure that you have the latest information for the CompTIA Linux+ exam.

How This Book Maps to the Exam Objectives

All exam objectives are covered in this book and each chapter is devoted to a specific exam objective. But, in the interest of presenting a logical learning path, the order of the content in each chapter does not exactly match the order of the topics listed within the corresponding objective. To help you focus on the exam objectives for which you might need some additional learning and preparation, this table shows you which chapters cover the various exam objectives:

Chapter	Exam Objective(s) Covered
Chapter 1, "Understanding Linux Fundamentals"	1.1
Chapter 2, "Managing Files and Directories"	1.2
Chapter 3, "Configuring and Managing Storage"	1.3
Chapter 4, "Managing Processes and Services"	1.4
Chapter 5, "Using Network Tools and Configuration Files"	1.5
Chapter 6, "Building and Installing Software"	1.6
Chapter 7, "Managing Software Configurations"	1.7
Chapter 8, "Understanding Linux Security Best Practices"	2.1
Chapter 9, "Implementing Identity Management"	2.2
Chapter 10, "Implementing and Configuring Firewalls"	2.3
Chapter 11, "Using Remote Connectivity for System Management"	2.4
Chapter 12, "Understanding and Applying Access Controls"	2.5
Chapter 13, "Automating Tasks via Shell Scripting"	3.1
Chapter 14, "Performing Basic Container Operations"	3.2
Chapter 15, "Performing Basic Version Control Using Git"	3.3
Chapter 16, "Understanding Infrastructure as Code"	3.4
Chapter 17, "Understanding Containers, Cloud, and Orchestration"	3.5
Chapter 18, "Analyzing and Troubleshooting Storage Issues"	4.1
Chapter 19, "Analyzing and Troubleshooting Network Resource Issues"	4.2
Chapter 20, "Analyzing and Troubleshooting CPU and Memory Issues"	4.3
Chapter 21, "Analyzing and Troubleshooting User and File Permissions"	4.4
Chapter 22, "Analyzing and Troubleshooting Common Problems Using Systemd"	4.5

Book Features

To help you customize your study time using this book, the core chapters have several features that help you make the best use of your time:

- **Foundation Topics:** These core sections of each chapter explain the concepts that are important to the chapter.

- **Exam Preparation Tasks:** This section lists a series of study activities that you should do at the end of the chapter:

  - **Review All Key Topics:** The Key Topic icon appears next to the most important items in the "Foundation Topics" section of the chapter. The "Review All Key Topics" activity lists the key topics from the chapter, along with their page numbers. Although the contents of the entire chapter could be on the exam, you should definitely know the information listed in each key topic, so be sure to review them.

  - **Define Key Terms:** Although the Linux+ exam is unlikely to ask an open-ended question such as "Define this term," the exam does require that you learn and know a lot of industry-related terminology. This section lists the most important terms from the chapter, asking you to write a short definition and compare your definition to the glossary definition at the end of the book.

  - **Review Questions:** Confirm that you understand the content that is covered in the chapter by answering these questions and reading the answer explanations.

- **Web-Based Practice Exams:** The companion website includes the Pearson Cert IT certification test engine, which allows you to take practice exams. Use it to prepare with a sample exam and to pinpoint topics where you need more study.

What's New?

If you are used to the objectives of the older Linux+ exam and the content of the previous version of this book, you should read the following which describes how both the exam objectives and the layout of this book have changed.

For more information about how the CompTIA Linux+ certification can help your career or to download the latest official objectives, access CompTIA's Linux+ web page at https://www.comptia.org/certifications/linux.

As the Linux+ objectives are now presented in an order that makes sense from a learning perspective, this book is patterned with each chapter taking on an objective topic in its entirety. (Thanks, CompTIA!)

However, as a long-time technical instructor who likes things to make sense even within a chapter, I have taken some liberties with the in-chapter order of each objective's contents, to ensure that everything flows nicely as you read and study so that you truly understand the subtopics.

You might be wondering how different the current Linux+ exam compares to the previous version.

As mentioned earlier in this Introduction, the main changes are

- An expanded focus on DevOps and cloud topics
- The new Troubleshooting section

Finally, as with most other CompTIA exams, you can expect a handful of scenario questions. In many cases, you will be asked to configure or manage a system using several steps or to describe a collection of Linux features and how they relate to each other. Note this that is not new, but worth mentioning.

In addition, look for the newer simulation questions, which are just like a Linux terminal session, and if you don't already know how to do these, you will by the end of this book!

The rest of the questions will be multiple-choice questions that require you to choose one, choose two, choose three, or choose all that apply.

Who Should Read This Book?

The CompTIA Linux+ certification exam will verify the successful candidate has the knowledge and skills required to configure, manage, operate, and troubleshoot Linux on-premises and cloud-based server environments, while using security best practices, scripting, containerization, and automation.

The level of knowledge and skills expected of the examinee is equivalent to at least 12 months of hands-on experience working with Linux servers in a junior Linux support engineer or junior cloud/DevOps support engineer job role. Additionally, CompTIA does specifically mention that having the experience of passing the A+, Network+, and Server+ exams is considered a recommended prerequisite for taking the Linux+ exam.

This book is for you if you are attempting to attain a position in the IT field or if you want to keep your skills sharp or perhaps retain your job if your company mandates that you take the latest Linux+ exam.

Strategies for Exam Preparation

Strategies for exam preparation will vary depending on your existing skills, knowledge, and equipment available. The ideal exam preparation would consist of building a few virtual machines from scratch and installing and configuring the operating systems covered.

The next best step you can take is to read through the chapters in this book, jotting notes down with key concepts or configurations on a notepad. Each chapter contains a quiz near the end of the chapter that you can use to test your knowledge of the chapter's topics.

Try *all* of the commands you see, look through the configuration files, experiment on your virtual machines, and use the snapshot and rollback feature that is on every virtualization software's toolbar these days—it'll make for a much more pleasant experience when you can try out commands and then revert to a previous snapshot.

After you have read through the book, take a look at the current exam objectives for the CompTIA Linux+ certification exam, listed at https://www.comptia.org/certifications/linux. If there are any areas shown in the certification exam outline that you would still like to study, find the appropriate sections in this book and review them.

When you feel confident in your skills, attempt the practice exams included on this book's companion website. As you work through a practice exam, note the areas where you lack confidence and review those concepts or configurations in the book. After you have reviewed the areas, work through the practice exam a second time and rate your skills. Keep in mind that the more you work through the practice exams, the more familiar the questions will become.

After you have worked through each practice exam a second time and feel confident with your skills, schedule the real CompTIA Linux+ (XK0-005) exam through Pearson VUE (https://home.pearsonvue.com/). To prevent the information from evaporating out of your mind, you should typically take the exam within a week of when you consider yourself ready to take the exam.

My usual advice for all my certification classes and courses stands: Drink a liter of water and have a nice ripe banana before you go take the exam. The exam is a long one, and you need your brain to function well; the water will help keep that computer in between your ears humming along, and the nutrients (particularly the niacin) in the banana will help you concentrate.

I can't tell you how many pictures of readers I have been sent with their liter of water, a banana, a newly achieved certification, and a BIG SMILE!

In fact, look me up on LinkedIn, at https://www.linkedin.com/in/rossbrunson/, and message me with your picture of your water, banana, and certification! I'll be sure to include you in any giveaways of book copies and so forth.

Companion Website

Register this book to get access to the Pearson IT certification test engine and other study materials, as well as additional bonus content. Check this site regularly for new and updated postings written by the author that provide further insight into the more troublesome topics on the exam. Be sure to check the box indicating that you would like to hear from us to receive updates and exclusive discounts on future editions of this product or related products.

To access this companion website, follow these steps:

Step 1. Go to www.pearsonitcertification.com/register and log in or create a new account.

Step 2. Enter the ISBN: **9780137866885**.

Step 3. Answer the challenge question as proof of purchase.

Step 4. Click the Access Bonus Content link in the Registered Products section of your account page to be taken to the page where your downloadable content is available.

Please note that many of the companion content files—especially image and video files—are very large.

If you are unable to locate the files for this title by following these steps, please visit www.pearsonITcertification.com/contact and select the Site Problems/Comments option. Our customer service representatives will assist you.

Pearson Test Prep Practice Test Software

As noted previously, this book comes complete with the Pearson Test Prep practice test software, including two full exams. These practice tests are available to you either online or as an offline Windows application. To access the practice exams that were developed with this book, please see the instructions below.

How to Access the Pearson Test Prep (PTP) App

You have two options for installing and using the Pearson Test Prep application: a web app and a desktop app. To use the Pearson Test Prep application, start by finding the registration code that comes with the book. You can find the code in these ways:

- You can get your access code by registering the print ISBN (9780137866885) on pearsonitcertification.com/register. Make sure to use the print book ISBN, regardless of whether you purchased an eBook or the print book. After you register the book, your access code will be populated on your account page under the Registered Products tab. Instructions for how to redeem the code are available on the book's companion website by clicking the Access Bonus Content link.

- Premium Edition: If you purchase the Premium Edition eBook and Practice Test directly from the Pearson IT Certification website, the code will be populated on your account page after purchase. Just log in at pearsonitcertification.com, click Account to see details of your account, and click the digital purchases tab.

NOTE   After you register your book, your code can always be found in your account under the Registered Products tab.

Once you have the access code, to find instructions about both the PTP web app and the desktop app, follow these steps:

Step 1.   Open this book's companion website as shown earlier in this Introduction under the heading, "Companion Website."

Step 2.   Click the **Practice Exams** button.

Step 3.   Follow the instructions listed there for both installing the desktop app and using the web app.

Note that if you want to use the web app only at this point, just navigate to pearsontestprep.com, log in using the same credentials used to register your book or purchase the Premium Edition, and register this book's practice tests using the registration code you just found. The process should take only a couple of minutes.

Customizing Your Exams

When you are in the exam settings screen, you can choose to take exams in one of three modes:

- **Study Mode:** This mode allows you to fully customize your exams and review answers as you are taking the exam. This is typically the mode you use first to assess your knowledge and identify information gaps.

- **Practice Exam Mode:** This mode locks certain customization options in order to present a realistic exam experience. Use this mode when you are preparing to test your exam readiness.

- **Flash Card Mode:** This mode strips out the answers and presents you with only the question stem. This mode is great for late-stage preparation, when you really want to challenge yourself to provide answers without the benefit of seeing multiple-choice options. This mode does not provide the detailed score reports that the other two modes provide, so it is not the best mode for helping you identify knowledge gaps.

In addition to these three modes, you can select the source of your questions. You can choose to take exams that cover all of the chapters, or you can narrow your selection to just a single chapter or the chapters that make up specific parts in the book. All chapters are selected by default. If you want to narrow your focus to individual chapters, simply deselect all the chapters then select only those on which you wish to focus in the Objectives area.

You can also select the exam banks on which to focus. Each exam bank comes complete with a full exam of questions that cover topics in every chapter. You can have the test engine serve up exams from all four banks or just from one individual bank by selecting the desired banks in the exam bank area.

There are several other customizations you can make to your exam from the exam settings screen, such as the time allowed to take the exam, the number of questions served up, whether to randomize questions and answers, whether to show the number of correct answers for multiple-answer questions, and whether to serve up only specific types of questions. You can also create custom test banks by selecting only questions that you have marked or questions on which you have added notes.

Updating Your Exams

If you are using the online version of the Pearson Test Prep software, you should always have access to the latest version of the software as well as the exam data. If you are using the Windows desktop version, every time you launch the software while connected to the Internet, it checks if there are any updates to your exam data and automatically downloads any changes that were made since the last time you used the software.

Sometimes, due to a number of factors, the exam data might not fully download when you activate your exam. If you find that figures or exhibits are missing, you might need to manually update your exams. To update a particular exam you have already activated and downloaded, simply select the Tools tab, and click the Update Products button. Again, this is only an issue with the desktop Windows application.

If you wish to check for updates to the Windows desktop version of the Pearson Test Prep exam engine software, simply select the Tools tab and click the Update Application button. Doing so enables you to ensure that you are running the latest version of the software engine.

Credits

Figure 4-1-Figure 4-3, Figure 4-5, Figure 5-5: Linus Torvalds

Figure 5-6, Figure 5-7: Wireshark Foundation

Figure 6-1, Figure 7-3, Figure 15-9, Figure 15-10, Figure 18-1-Figure 18-17, Figure 19-2-Figure 19-6, Figure 20-1, Figure 22-1: Canonical Ltd

Figure 6-2: Debian

Figure 6-3-Figure 6-10, Figure 7-1: SUSE

Figure 7-2: Microsoft

Figure 13-2: The GNOME Project

Figure 13-3-Figure 13-6: KDE

Figure 14-1-Figure 14-4: Red Hat, Inc

Figure 15-7-Figure 15-8: Atlassian

Figure 18-18: Gparted

Cover credit: Quardia/Shutterstock

This chapter covers the following topics:

- Filesystem Hierarchy Standard
- Basic Boot Process
- Boot Loaders and Files
- When Kernels Panic
- Device Types in **/dev**
- Installing Software from Source
- Storage Concepts
- Listing Hardware Information

The exam objective covered in this chapter is as follows:

- **Objective 1.1:** Summarize Linux fundamentals

## CHAPTER 1

Understanding Linux Fundamentals

Linux is a great operating system, useful for a large variety of tasks and replete with a lot of tweakable and configurable options, although some of them are not well documented or easy to understand.

Using Linux is like buying a car off the car dealer's lot, if you just start it up and drive it, it's pretty simple, just avoid crashing and keep the fluids full and you'll be okay for a while.

The real fun begins when something doesn't work right and you have to pop the hood and start figuring out what went awry or what needs to be changed. Linux can be very easy to use, but it also allows you to dive as deep under the hood into the inner workings as you could possibly want to.

This chapter is all about the essentials of Linux system management, including information about what the Filesystem Hierarchy Standard is; where files and directories are located in the filesystem and what they contain; particulars about the **/dev** directory and its contents; the basics of storage management, including types of storage, partition types, RAID, and FUSE; the boot process of a Linux system; and constructing software packages from source.

We'll also look at what happens when the Linux kernel panics or crashes occur, and how to investigate what hardware your system contains.

"Do I Know This Already?" Quiz

The "Do I Know This Already?" quiz enables you to assess whether you should read this entire chapter or simply jump to the "Exam Preparation Tasks" section for review. If you are in doubt, read the entire chapter. Table 1-1 outlines the major headings in this chapter and the corresponding "Do I Know This Already?" quiz questions. You can find the answers in Appendix A, "Answers to the 'Do I Know This Already?' Quizzes and Review Questions."

Table 1-1   "Do I Know This Already?" Foundation Topics Section-to-Question Mapping

Foundation Topics Section	Questions Covered in This Section
Filesystem Hierarchy Standard	1
Basic Boot Process	2
When Kernels Panic	3
Device Types in **/dev**	4
Installing Software from Source	5
Storage Concepts	6
Listing Hardware Information	7

CAUTION   The goal of self-assessment is to gauge your mastery of the topics in this chapter. If you do not know the answer to a question or are only partially sure of the answer, you should mark that question as wrong for purposes of the self-assessment. Giving yourself credit for an answer you correctly guess skews your self-assessment results and might provide you with a false sense of security.

1. The set of firm suggestions that most distribution vendors follow about what files and directories are where and what they contain is?

   a. Data Positioning Standard

   b. File and Directory Protocol

   c. Filesystem Hierarchy Standard

   d. None of these answers is correct.

2. In order to format a filesystem on a newly installed disk device on a Linux system, what must be done?

   a. Mount the device

   b. fsck the device

   c. Defrag the device

   d. Partition the device

3. If your system has encountered an internal error and is unable to continue processing, which of the following has occurred?

   a. Stop error

   b. Green screen of death

   c. Kernel panic

   d. Init zero

4. Which of the following is not a valid device type that you would typically find in the **/dev** directory on a Linux system?

   a. **tty**

   b. **zero**

   c. **urandom**

   d. **tmp**

5. If you want to compile a software package on your system, which of the following commands must you run first in order to customize the makefile for your system?

   a. **make conf**

   b. **setup**

   c. **conf makefile.c**

   d. **configure**

6. Which directory is the beginning of the virtual filesystem?

   a. **/**

   b. **/vert**

   c. **/sys**

   d. None of these answers is correct.

7. Which command gives an overview of all the hardware and drivers in the system, including the ports used to talk to the CPU?

   a. **lspci**

   b. **lsdev**

   c. **lsusb**

   d. **sysinfo**

Foundation Topics

Filesystem Hierarchy Standard

The filesystem's structure starts with the root of the filesystem, which is denoted by the forward slash character (/). Every item on the filesystem is accessible by a single unique path off the root of the system, such as **/usr/local/bin/foobar**, no matter which device that file is stored on.

Unix evolved its own set of traditions as to where certain files would go. The fragmentation of the commercial and academic Unixes led to differences in conventions depending on which flavor of Unix you were using.

Linux borrows practices from many different Unixes and has fragmentation of its own in the form of different distributions. The community started working on a standard for filesystem layout called the Filesystem Hierarchy Standard (FHS) to make it easier for both people and software to know where files can be found.

The latest FHS version is 3.0, released in 2015, and is available from the Linux Foundation.

The FHS isn't exactly a standard but a firm set of suggestions that most, but not all, Linux distribution vendors follow. The FHS describes where particular types of files are to be placed, which helps maintain consistency across different distributions. The CompTIA Linux+ exam will include questions about the FHS.

What Goes Where in the FHS

The Linux+ exam makes somewhat of a big deal about what the proper directories and locations are for Linux files, but few things are more vexing than to be asked what should positively be in the root (/) directory, or what can be stored elsewhere. This means you should at least do a cursory read-through of the FHS; it's good information and will help you understand Linux systems even better.

The Root of the Filesystem

The existence of a filesystem, and indeed the actual system being a functional Linux computer, begins with the / (root) directory and its *subdirectories*, which also can contain files and subdirectories, all the way down to the lowest-level files on the system.

Table 1-2 lists and describes the common top-level subdirectories of the / directory.

Table 1-2 Common Top-Level Subdirectories off the Root (**/**) Directory

Directory	Description
bin	Binaries for all users
boot	Kernel, system map, boot files
dev	Device files
etc	Configuration files for the host
home	Home directories for users
lib	Necessary shared libraries/modules
media	Mount points for removable media
mnt	Temporary mount point for the systems administrator
opt	Third-party application software
proc	Kernel and process information
root	The root user's home directory
sbin	System binaries needed for boot
sys	Server-specific and service-related files
tmp	Temporary data
usr	Sharable, read-only data and programs; no host-specific data
var	Variable data, logs, Web, FTP, and so on

The exam will pose questions designed to determine if you know the purpose of the most common directories on your Linux system. You may encounter a question about which directories are listed as optional, so again, I encourage you to peruse the table of contents of the FHS and be sure you are aware of those.

Where to Put Programs

The FHS does not allow programs to create their individual named directories in the **/usr** directory tree. This tree is where programs or binaries are normally kept that are not core applications for the running of a Linux system—those go in **/bin** and **/sbin**, typically.

The following subdirectories are allowed to exist directly under the **/usr** directory:

- **bin:** Contains most user commands
- **lib:** Contains libraries
- **local:** Contains local/sharable programs (may be empty)

- **sbin:** Contains nonvital system binaries

- **share:** Contains architecture-independent data

The FHS discourages having individual application directories in the **/usr** root (in that directory), but instead wants them stored in a subdirectory off of **/usr**, or in one of its allowed subdirectories.

Basic Boot Process

Booting a Linux system isn't just a matter of turning on the system and having it eventually present you with a login prompt. Rather, it's a set of events that results, if all goes well, in your being presented with that login prompt.

In this section we look at the boot process as a set of tasks performed to get a system to the point where it can enter the default runlevel, where things can become complex due to the various methods of configuring, starting, and managing system services or processes.

We cover these topics:

- **BIOS:** Basic Input/Output System

- **UEFI:** Unified Extensible Firmware Interface

- **Boot commands:** Such as **mkinitrd, grub2***, and **dracut**

- **GRUB2:** Grand Unified Bootloader 2

- **Boot sources:** PXE, USB, and ISO booting

What Is the Boot Process?

The *boot process* for Linux is the process by which a system progresses from the power-on of the hardware (or virtual hardware) until the chosen operating system is at the desired state of functionality. Thanks to the popularity of systemd, Upstart, and other initialization methods, there are a number of pathways to achieving a running system.

The Linux boot process can be broken up into four distinct stages:

1. Boot loader phase

2. Kernel phase

3. Early user space

4. Init process

System Boot Options

There are a number of ways to boot a system. Some require installation of software and configuration on the local disk, some allow for using a boot or installation server, and some allow you to boot from remote filesystems across the network.

initrd and initramfs

Linux runs on an extremely wide range of hardware, and many of the distributions use a fairly standard Linux kernel image for compatibility and depend on the detection of each system's individual hardware and the loading of needed kernel modules to properly accommodate that hardware during the installation and subsequent system initializations.

Because of the incredible range of possible boot methods, styles, and types of hardware involved, there is a bit of a "chicken-or-egg" problem: The system must boot off hardware with a generic Linux kernel image, but where is the root filesystem, and how can you let the generic image know its location?

Rather than take the inelegant option of compiling into the kernel the modules that are required for a given hardware configuration, an early user space temporary filesystem is used. The temporary filesystem is located on disk, and the location is known to the firmware or boot loader. The temporary filesystem is accessed and mounted, and an array of possible modules are made available for use during the booting process. The kernel and the early user space filesystem's image are loaded into RAM, and the kernel is informed of the location in memory of the image so that it can detect its format—either **initrd** or **initramfs**.

The *initrd* method, which is quite old, is effectively an image of a filesystem that is represented as the **/dev/ram** device and gets mounted as the temporary root filesystem for the kernel to use. The disadvantage of this method is that the kernel must have a compiled-in or hard-coded reference to the driver for this filesystem. This is possibly problematic if the disk is changed, such as through swapping out a disk, changing the size or geometry of the disk, or modifying the partition containing the file.

The command traditionally used to create an initial RAM disk is the **mkinitrd** command, followed by the initrd image to be created and the kernel it is being created for, as in this example:

```
# sudo mkinitrd --preload=/boot/initrd.img-5.11.0-37-generic
5.11.0-37-generic
```

If there is a particular module that should be loaded so that the kernel can find and access the disk with the initrd image on it, you can specify it by using the **--preload** option followed by the module name, as shown here:

```
# sudo mkinitrd --preload=/boot/initrd.img-5.11.0-37-generic
5.11.0-37-generic
```

The more commonly used option for providing an early user space filesystem is the *initramfs* method. This method uses an initial root filesystem that is unpacked from a particular type of archive file (cpio) and gets mounted in RAM as the temporary root filesystem. A distinct upside of this method is that there is no need to have special modules precompiled or included in the kernel, so it is generic and compatible with many system configurations.

Constructing an initramfs image initially involves using the **mkinitrd** command, which is also used in the initrd method. However, the **dracut** command is almost immediately involved in the construction of the initramfs image, which it attempts to create with the least possible dependency on hard-coded scripts. The **dracut** framework relies on udev (the device manager in the kernel) to tell it what devices are detected and mounted, and when the proper device is mounted, the system switches the root filesystem over to that device.

A main advantage of **dracut** is its wide support of boot devices, including devices that use RAID and LVM and more esoteric device types, such as remote devices via Internet Small Computer Systems Interface (iSCSI) and Network File System (NFS).

Creating an initramfs image with **dracut** is fairly simple. If you run the command alone, the system attempts to create a functional initramfs image for the currently running kernel. This causes an error message, as this is an attempt to overwrite the current initramfs image.

To create an initramfs image without overwriting the current image, simply specify another image name, and then you can inspect the format of the resulting initramfs image:

```
# dracut some-image-file-name.img
```

Booting with UEFI

The problem child for most Linux installations these days is the Unified Extensible Firmware Interface (UEFI). The portion of the UEFI that makes installation so much more difficult for Linux distributions is called Secure Boot. Secure Boot is ostensibly designed to make it as hard as possible for bad folks to corrupt, change out, or alter your boot manager image and thereby gain inappropriate access to your computer.

In reality, because initially all UEFI Secure Boot images had to be signed by an official signing authority, and the only authority was Microsoft, installing Linux was made much more difficult, requiring distribution maintainers to either go to Microsoft to get a boot image signed off on or create their own completely alternative signing authority and get that approved through the UEFI process.

The best solution, and one that still currently works, is to simply turn off UEFI Secure Boot in the preboot system configuration and avoid the whole issue from the beginning. To be very clear, you only need to disable the Secure Boot portion of the UEFI process, and there are great reasons to continue to use UEFI. On the whole, it's a definite improvement over the master boot record (MBR) method.

The **/boot/efi** directory is not always present in every distribution, but if it's there, typically it's used when you must dual-boot a system, as the UEFI system wants a UEFI partition to be available.

NOTE   In the system examples in this chapter, the Ubuntu machine has no **/boot/efi** directory, and the CentOS machine has a **/boot/efi/EFI** directory that contains only an empty directory named **centos**.

If a system were configured to use EFI for booting, there would be a FAT32 partition (an EFI system partition) mounted on **/boot/efi** that would contain the boot files for the various operating system boot options on the system, with the extension .efi, as in the following file, which is an EFI boot image:

```
/boot/efi/EFI/arch/vmlinuz-linux.efi
```

The file may also be named simply **linux.efi**.

Booting via PXE

The Preboot Execution Environment (PXE) requires a client to have a PXE-capable network interface card (NIC) and, on the server side, a Dynamic Host Control Protocol (DHCP) server that supports PXE booting.

The PXE server side is more complex than the client side, requiring several protocols to be supported in the right combination, including having a valid network boot program (NBP) available to be transferred to the client after it has its networking configured via DHCP.

The process of booting up a PXE-capable client computing device goes something like this:

Step 1.   The client device is powered on, and the PXE boot option is chosen from the BIOS/Startup interface.

Step 2.   The client sends out a DHCPDISCOVER broadcast that has built-in PXE options that let the DHCP server know what type of a request it is.

Step 3.   The PXE-capable DHCP server returns a DHCPOFFER broadcast that contains all the networking information needed for the PXE client to set up its networking stack and contact the DHCP server's Trivial FTP (TFTP) service.

Step 4.   The PXE client finishes its network setup and initiates a TFTP transfer of the NBP image and stores it in the client's RAM.

Step 5.   Finally, the client boots with the NBP and, depending on the operating system, requests additional boot files from the TFTP server or from other network resources, such as an NFS server.

Booting via NFS

We have already looked at using TFTP and DHCP servers to distribute networking configuration and network boot programs. It's now reasonable to consider booting systems from files contained on an NFS share on the network.

Booting a running system from NFS is a little different from PXE booting a system, which is normally used for installation (though not restricted to that function).

For an example of booting from NFS, we'll use the scenario of a diskless workstation, where the entire operating system is downloaded and mounted to the PXE-capable system from an NFS server.

Here is an overview of what needs to happen to enable a diskless workstation to boot and mount its root filesystem over NFS:

Step 1.   Select a server and install/enable DHCP and TFTP services.

Step 2.   Configure TFTP to support PXE booting.

Step 3.   Copy the appropriate image to the TFTP boot directory.

Step 4.   Ensure that the DHCP/TFTP server's firewall allows the traffic.

Step 5.   Configure the DHCP server to support PXE booting.

Step 6. Create a root directory that contains a full Linux system for sharing across NFS. Various distributions recommend using rsync or using the YUM option **--installroot**.

Step 7. Configure the appropriate kernel that the diskless workstation will be booting from.

Step 8. Create and set the permissions on the initrd method and copy it into the TFTP boot directory.

Step 9. Share out the diskless root directory by adding it to the **/etc/exports** file and either restart the NFS daemon or use the **exportfs** command.

Step 10. Boot the diskless workstation and choose the **PXE Boot** option, and when the system presents a menu of boot options, choose the one that was just configured. The system mounts the remote root filesystem as its own **/** filesystem, and the system is now a functioning system.

Booting via ISO

Booting from an ISO file (a disk image of a Linux distribution installation optical disc) is relatively simple to set up. The main reason for doing so is to have an on-disk rescue environment in case the distribution installed to disk has a problem or password recovery is needed.

The only things really needed are an ISO of a Linux distribution optical disc, a free partition big enough to hold the optical disc's contents, and the ability to edit the **grub.cfg** file to point one of the menu entries to the ISO file on the partition you copied the ISO file to.

There are multiple ways to boot a rescue system from ISO, and this is a relatively simple method for doing so:

Step 1. Choose a Linux distribution and download an installation optical disc.

Step 2. If you are installing Linux to the system for the first time, create the rescue partition during the install, making sure to label it something obvious like RESCUE, and create an MS-DOS filesystem on the partition.

Step 3. If you are modifying an existing and running Linux system, you can use **parted** or **gparted** to resize the current partitions and free up room for a rescue partition. (This is far beyond the scope of the Linux+ exam.)

Step 4. Copy the ISO file to the disk and note the name of the file.

Step 5.   Update the **grub.cfg** file to include a boot stanza that uses the MS-DOS partition as the root partition and then mounts as a loopback device the ISO file of the Linux distribution.

Step 6.   Boot the system and test the configuration.

There are dozens of tutorials online that can walk you through all the various aspects of this process, which differs on the various distributions. The main concept here is that you can boot from an ISO file that's contained on a disk device.

Boot Loaders and Files

When a computer boots up, it doesn't know how to talk to all its peripherals or even how to load applications. But each computer has a ***Basic Input Output System (BIOS)*** that gives it just enough intelligence to read and write to local disks and write some text to the screen.

After a computer boots up, it transfers control to the BIOS, which initializes the hardware and reads the first block—512 bytes—from the boot disk. This block contains the first part of the boot loader that loads the boot manager from disk and runs it. This special sector on the disk is called the ***master boot record (MBR)***.

The Linux boot block can be placed in the first block of the Linux partition if an existing operating system already occupies the MBR. In this case, the first boot manager needs to be told to pass control over to the Linux boot manager. It's complicated, but this multi-booting allows two different operating systems to coexist on the same computer.

The boot manager displays a menu offering different operating system choices. Usually a default is chosen if no input is received within a short period of time, which allows a computer to boot unattended. Boot managers can also pass parameters to the kernel, such as to initialize hardware differently, disable problematic features, or alter the boot sequence.

Several boot managers are available, but most distributions have standardized on the ***Grand Unified Bootloader (GRUB)***, which is currently in version 2, aka GRUB2.

NOTE   The Linux+ exam will focus on GRUB2, but it's important to know where GRUB came from, and what the differences are between the original GRUB and the newer GRUB2.

GRUB Legacy

In the early days of Linux, the boot manager was simple: You would boot a kernel either from an existing Microsoft DOS system through **LOADLIN.EXE** or directly with the Linux Loader (LILO). The latter was fairly inflexible. While it had a basic menu system, any changes that needed to be made required rewriting the boot manager to disk. Even the location of the kernel blocks on disk needed to be known beforehand. LILO would have to generate a list of blocks containing a kernel and write them to a known place so that it could piece the kernel back together on boot.

Eventually the GNU Foundation started work on GRUB. This boot manager is more flexible than others because it offers an interactive menu that can be easily changed and adapted to boot many operating systems. GRUB understands different filesystems, and it can read the kernel from disk as if it were a file instead of needing to know where the individual blocks are.

GRUB uses a temporary boot volume, **/boot** by default, to store kernels and the GRUB configuration. A BIOS might not be able to see the whole disk, so putting the boot manager in a safe area means that it can boot a kernel that has the functionality to read the entire disk.

GRUB2

GRUB2 is the version of GRUB currently in use, and it has been the default for most distributions since about 2010. GRUB2 started out as a core rewrite for stability and features and quickly became what is now known as GRUB2. Those who are familiar with GRUB will quickly understand GRUB2's syntax, commands, and structure; they are fairly similar, aside from a few filename and location changes and a number of important and handy features.

Changes Made for GRUB2

One of the core changes in GRUB2 is the name of the configuration file, which has changed from **menu.lst** or **grub.conf** in GRUB to **grub.cfg** in GRUB2. In addition, in GRUB2 the main configuration file (**/boot/grub2/grub.cfg**) is generated by the **grub-mkconfig** command or the installation routine. Because of how system updates are currently done, your **/boot/grub2/grub.cfg** file may be regenerated by a kernel or another system update, so to be safe, there are two locations where customizations can safely be stored so they are available after any automated changes to the **/boot/grub2/grub.cfg** file. Those two locations for any customizations (entries or parameters) are the **/etc/grub.d/40_custom** file and the **/boot/grub/custom.cfg** file. These files are read by the **grub-mkconfig** command and used when generating the **/boot/grub2/grub.cfg** file.

Another change from GRUB to GRUB2 is a change in how partitions are numbered. GRUB used fd/hd to denote disks, and the first hd on a device was labeled hd0; the first partition on that device would be referred to as hd0,0. This has changed in GRUB2 so that partitions start with the numeral 1, while devices still start with 0.

In addition, the filename **/etc/grub2.cfg** is a symbolic link to the **grub.cfg** file for compatibility purposes.

GRUB2 Command Names

A quick mention of the command names for GRUB2 is in order. While the documentation may leave the **2** designation off the commands (for example, **grub-install** vs. **grub2-install**), some distributions use the version number in the command names, and others don't. For example, Ubuntu doesn't use the **2** in the command names, but Fedora and CentOS do. The easiest way to find out what a distribution ("distro") uses is to type the **grub** portion of the command and press the **Tab** key twice to get output like that shown in Example 1-1.

Example 1-1   Example of the **grub**-Related Commands on a System

```
root@tuxix:/boot# grub
grub                    grub-mklayout
grub-bios-setup         grub-mknetdir
grub-editenv            grub-mkpasswd-pbkdf2
grub-file               grub-mkrelpath
grub-fstest             grub-mkrescue
grub-glue-efi           grub-mkstandalone
grub-install            grub-mount
grub-kbdcomp            grub-ntldr-img
grub-macbless           grub-probe
grub-menulst2cfg        grub-reboot
grub-mkconfig           grub-render-label
grub-mkdevicemap        grub-script-check
grub-mkfont             grub-set-default
grub-mkimage            grub-syslinux2cfg
```

As you can see, this distro doesn't use the **2** version designation behind the **grub** portion of the command.

> **NOTE**   The different distributions handle command names differently, which can be confusing to the poor soul who just wants to follow a set of instructions to accomplish something. For example, the update-grub command is a front-end or "stub" that will really execute the grub-mkconfig command in the background to generate a GRUB2 config file. You may also see this command specified as grub2-update, grub-update and update-grub2.
>
> Additionally, you may find that the Linux+ Objectives list grub2-update, but what they are referring to is the update-grub2 command previously mentioned.

Installing GRUB2

The first step in getting GRUB2 installed is to have the tool write itself to the master boot record as follows:

```
[root@localhost ~]# grub2-install /dev/sda
Installing for i386-pc platform.
Installation finished. No error reported.
```

This copies the boot sector image to disk and the remaining files to **/boot**. If your bootable partition is not **/boot**, you can override this default setting, such as **/mnt/ tmpboot** in Example 1-2.

Example 1-2   Installing GRUB2 to an Alternate Location

```
[root@localhost ~]# grub2-install --boot-
directory=/mnt/tmpboot/dev/sda
Installing for i386-pc platform.
Installation finished. No error reported.
[root@localhost ~]# tree -d /mnt/tmpboot/
/mnt/tmpboot/
|--- grub2
| - - fonts
| - - i386-pc
|--- locale
 4 directories
```

In Example 1-2 the GRUB2 files are installed to **/mnt/tmpboot**, and the **tree** command shows the directories created for the boot manager. The GRUB2 image and related modules are in the **i386-pc** directory.

This alternate boot disk option is most often used for making boot disks on an existing system, where you will have an image of the disk temporarily mounted.

Using the GRUB2 Command Line

Your first interaction with the GRUB2 command line is during the boot process. When you boot a computer, you see the **GRUB2** menu offering a list of kernels to boot and an option to enter the **c** character to get to the command line. Pressing this gets you to a simple command prompt:

```
grub>
```

If you can't boot normally, you can use the GRUB2 command line to inspect your running system and get a kernel booted. You can look at the list of devices with the **ls** command:

```
grub> ls
(proc) (hd0) (hd0,gpt2) (hd0,gpt1) (hd1) (cd0)
```

The syntax of the partitions is similar to the Linux partition naming syntax. It's important to remember that disks are counted from 0, but partitions are counted from 1. So the first partition on the first disk is hd0,gpt1, which corresponds to sda1 in Linux. It is often difficult to know which partition contains the files you want, so you can inspect each. The shell does not provide wildcards, though you can press the **Tab** key as a substitute:

```
grub> ls (hd0,msdos1)/vml<TAB>
```

Possible files are

```
vmlinuz-0-rescue-1bc6a0e5dd394f63b228657b634ba252
vmlinuz-3.10.0-862.14.4.el7.x86_64
```

> **NOTE**   If you are new to Linux, you might find these naming inconsistencies confusing. Linux tools are developed by different people with different ways of doing things. Devices in the Linux kernel are fairly consistently named, but GRUB overall is developed by a completely different set of people with a different set of goals. GRUB/GRUB2 was designed to boot different operating systems, so some concepts don't line up directly with the way things are done in Linux.

Pressing the **Tab** key causes the system to look on the device for any files beginning with **vml**, which are kernel files. Two are shown here. If you know, based on the name, that the second file is the kernel to boot, you can give GRUB enough information to boot it by supplying the name of the kernel and the name of the corresponding initial RAM disk. The initial RAM disk, abbreviated initrd, contains the extra drivers necessary to boot the kernel on the specific hardware the kernel is running on.

By using the **Tab** completion, you can discover your way to the proper kernel and initramfs to use, and then when those are set, you can type **boot**, and it should boot properly. Here is an example:

```
grub> linux (hd0,gpt2)/ vmlinuz-5.4.0-91-generic
  genericroot=/dev/mapper/fedora-root ro
grub> initrd (hd0,gpt2)/ initrd.img-5.4.0-91-generic
grub> boot
<boot process output truncated>
```

While several parameters are involved in booting the kernel, they are already in the **grub.cfg** file, which you can view by using the **cat** command or searching on the Internet. The kernel can take many parameters, but it is important to pass the path to the root filesystem (**root=**), and that filesystem should initially be booted read-only (**ro**).

In the early days of Linux, a problem with a boot manager meant that you needed to find a CD or floppy disk containing Linux so that you could boot and begin recovery. GRUB2's command line means that you can still get into your system and fix it up more quickly.

Demystifying Kernel Images

You can't spend much time in the realm of kernel booting configuration without encountering two apparently random versions of the kernel: **vmlinuz** and **vmlinux**.

In short, the **vmlinux** file is an uncompressed and statically linked kernel image file. This file was used primarily in earlier kernel days. The file is fairly small and can be loaded into the free space in lower RAM. Having to load into lower RAM limits the size of the image to 512KB, as it has to fit in the lower 640KB of RAM.

The **vmlinuz** and **vmlinux** files are created by compiling the kernel using the **zImage** option, which produces a kernel that is designed to be uncompressed into that lower 640KB of RAM.

As the kernel grew in its capabilities and features, the kernel images also grew in size, and they quickly could not fit into the space available in lower RAM; thus, the **vmlinuz** method was adopted. The kernel is compiled with the **bzImage** option, which sounds like it's related to **bzip2** but isn't. This produces a compressed kernel image, which is uncompressed shortly before it's booted. This also means that the image will not fit into the lower RAM, so it must be loaded into higher memory (that is, above 1MB).

Configuring GRUB2

GRUB2's configuration file is called **grub.cfg** (or **grub2.cfg** on some distributions). In this file, you find the configuration that sets up the menus you see when the system boots.

> **NOTE** GRUB uses **menu.lst** and **grub.conf** for configuration. The syntax changed between GRUB and GRUB2, and your distribution's default may look more like code than a configuration file.

Configuring GRUB2 is more complicated than configuring GRUB. Whereas with GRUB you edit **grub.conf** and are done, with GRUB2, **grub.cfg** is generated with a script, and you must look to the scripts to see how to make your changes. The **grub-mkconfig** command generates the configuration file for you, optionally receiving a path to the output file. If you don't specify a file, the output goes to your screen, as demonstrated in Example 1-3.

Example 1-3   grub-mkconfig Command Output

```
# grub2-mkconfig -o /boot/grub/grub.cfg
Sourcing file '/etc/default/grub'
Sourcing file '/etc/default/grub.d/init-select.cfg'
Generating grub configuration file ...
Found linux image: /boot/vmlinuz-5.4.0-91-generic
Found initrd image: /boot/initrd.img-5.4.0-91-generic
Found linux image: /boot/vmlinuz-5.4.0-80-generic
Found initrd image: /boot/initrd.img-5.4.0-80-generic
Adding boot menu entry for UEFI Firmware Settings
done
```

The inputs to **grub-mkconfig** are **/etc/default/grub** files are in **/etc/grub.d/**. The former sets various defaults; the latter is a series of shell scripts:

```
# ls /etc/grub.d/
00_header  05_debian_theme  10_linux  10_linux_zfs  20_linux_xen  30_
uefi-firmware  30_os-prober  41_custom
40_custom  README
```

Each script is run in order, and all their outputs are concatenated into the master output. If you want to add a custom section to your boot manager menu, look at the file named **40_custom**, for example, and either extend what you find there or add your own.

Common Commands at Boot Time

When booting Linux, you often want to change an option at the beginning of the process, such as changing the default *runlevel* or *target*, disabling or enabling specific hardware capabilities, or setting a particular mode for hardware that allows Linux to load properly.

NOTE   The parameters typed at the command prompt or boot options prompt are passed directly to the kernel upon initialization. These prompts are typically at the beginning of the boot process and give you the first opportunity to enter any parameters. Some distributions are configured to show a splash screen or logo, and you have to find out what keystroke allows for the entry of boot parameters.

The following are some common Linux boot options:

- **vga:** Enables you to set the framebuffer's resolution to a given mode, such as **vga=2**, which was historically used for difficult laptop LCDs.

- **apm:** APM (Automated Power Management) is on by default. Declaring **apm=off** or **noapm** at the beginning of the boot process enhances the system's compatibility. This should be done only when indicated by a vendor or FAQ from a distribution provider.

- **init:** Specifying **init** at the start causes the **/sbin/init** process to be the first process to run on the system. This may not work properly on initialization schemes where **init** is not present.

- **panic=#seconds:** The kernel does not reboot by default after a panic error occurs, which can cause a system to sit disabled until a technician can reach it physically. If a panic occurs, the kernel waits the specified number of seconds and then reboots and attempts to load normally.

- **single or 1:** These options cause the system to skip a full initialization to a default runlevel, and instead the system goes into a troubleshooting state or simple root-level state, where you are the root user and have minimal processes running.

- **2, 3, 4, or 5:** These options can be entered at the GRUB prompt to cause the system to initialize and then move to the specified runlevel or, in the case of systemd, move to the specified target that matches the runlevel number indicated.

- **ro or rw:** The **ro** option causes the root filesystem to be mounted in read-only mode so that **fsck** can be run on the root filesystem if errors occur. The **rw** parameter ensures that the root filesystem is mounted read/write, which is the default state.

- **mem=xxxxM:** This old system boot parameter simply sets the amount of memory that can be accessed by the about-to-be-booted system. You can use it when you suspect that a memory bank is bad or to test a system with a specific amount of memory, such as when testing a set-top box configuration or other limited-hardware device.

NOTE You have to look at the boot parameter documentation for your given distribution and boot manager to find out exactly which options are appropriate.

When Kernels Panic

The Linux kernel is a complex set of software and services. Things don't always go smoothly. For example, something related to hardware, a driver, or a software package might misbehave, or memory addresses might be overwritten inappropriately.

Much as an ejection seat can get you safely out of a malfunctioning jet fighter, the kernel is designed to panic, or stop its operations, when a condition or conditions have occurred that make continuing normal processing impossible.

Identifying a Kernel Panic

You can usually tell a *kernel panic* has occurred based on several symptoms. The most common symptom is that the system shows a kernel panic message that typically consists of trace information about what was running at the time of the panic. Another common indication is mysterious reboots, often obscured to the systems administrator (sysadmin) unless the log files contain helpful information about the issue.

Because of the severity of the issue that causes a kernel panic, it's normally not possible for the system to continue functioning normally, so either the system has the panic and displays the tracing information to the console and stops otherwise functioning, or it reboots itself. Either way, one of the last things a system does in a panic situation is to attempt to write to the logs that a panic has occurred.

Getting More Information

If you are experiencing multiple kernel panics, one step you can take to try to get more information is to look in your system logging configuration and try removing the leading - from any of the targets (log files) so that logging disk writes are not cached or stored in a queue to allow other, more important disk writes to finish first.

Kernel Panic Causes

What causes a kernel panic? Unfortunately, there are many possibilities, including the following:

- Corrupted hard disk sectors
- Incomplete or corrupted or truncated kernel modules
- File or directory permissions problems
- References to invalid or nonexistent memory addresses
- References to memory addresses that contain key codes
- Hardware failures, especially defective or failing RAM
- CPU failure or unhandled bugs
- Insertion or removal of hardware that causes conflicts or attempts to load defective or incomplete modules

A cause that is often missed but occurs often enough to deserve special mention is system overheating; with either the hardware with a host OS on it or the underlying hardware for a virtualization or containerized system, physical overheating or cooling can cause the system to panic or halt to avoid further damage.

Device Types in /dev

The **/dev** directory includes files that serve as device access points for physical devices. When the system is booted, the kernel and its subprocesses look through the BIOS and find the attached physical devices and then match those real devices to the appropriate special files in the **/dev** directory. "Special files" refers to the fact that these are not simple files or directories; they have a special meaning in that they are a connection point to real or pseudo devices on the system.

Device directory files are broken up into four main types: block, character links and subdirectories. The main difference between block and character special files is how they send and receive data from what is attached to them.

A *block device* is communicated with by a driver, and when doing so sends or receives an entire block of data at a time, a typical example being a disk, optical disc, or other storage device, or something that has a filesystem on it, as those are made up of data blocks.

A *character device* sends and receives a single character at a time, and is characterized by such devices as a scanner or a keyboard, things that communicate in non-block modes.

(sub)*Directory* files in the **/dev** directory usually lead to groups of special files that all are of a given type, an example being the **/dev/input** directory that contains special files that pertain to devices that generate events, such as mouse pointers with their *x-y* coordinate events.

As the name suggests, *link files* in the **/dev** directory are files that are symbolic links or pointers to other files elsewhere on the system. For example, the **/dev/cdrom** file on my test system points to **/dev/sr0** or the first SCSI-type optical disc detected on the system.

There are several pertinent (and testable!) individual files that exist in the **/dev** directory, including:

- **/dev/null:** Known as the "bit bucket" or the "black hole" of the system, this file literally is a way to throw away output such as unwanted errors generated (in great quantities) by the **find** command etc. This file is used only to discard either standard output or standard error.

- **/dev/zero:** This file exists to provide an endless series of null characters or whitespace noise for the purposes of sending non-content data to a source for testing purposes, or for initializing a device with character data that doesn't have any content. The **/dev/zero** special file is different than the **/dev/null** special file in that you can conduct read *and* write operations with **/dev/zero**, while **/dev/null** can accept *only* write operations (i.e., it cannot be read from).

- **/dev/urandom:** This file produces cryptographic-level random number data for use when randomization of data is needed. The more noise gathered from various hardware sources (fan noise variances, mouse movements, thermal noise, or anything that can be used to feed randomness to the generator), the better, as it adds to the pool of available randomness. The numbers generated by **/dev/urandom** can be used to feed randomness into cryptographic key generation or anything that needs a steady supply of random characters.

In summary, there are a number of files in the **/dev** directory, the main types of which are character and block special files (such as **/dev/sda1**), and some of the more important or key special files are **/dev/null, /dev/zero**, and **/dev/urandom**, which are commonly used in command line processes.

Installing Software from Source

Source code is the heart of all computing, and access to that source is the linchpin of Linux and open source software. Without access to the source, you can't inspect the code for bugs, security issues, or other flaws.

When programmers produce source code, they typically "tar it up," or create a compressed archive called a tarball. *Tarballs* are typically created with the **tar** command and some switches; then the software is made available on the Internet so others can try it and report bugs.

The following are advantages of installing programs via source code:

- It allows inspection of code for flaws, bugs, and security issues.

- It's available earlier than binary packages.

- Compiling optimizes the resulting program for the current system.

- It feeds that cutting-edge need. (Beta testing can be fun!)

Typically, you don't see a program that's under heavy development in any format other than a source tarball. It's time-consuming and unwieldy to make a package out of the source code until it's at least of release or late beta stability.

After you've installed a program from source, you'll be more comfortable with the process, so start with small programs and work your way up. For example, you might download and install rdesktop (http://www.rdesktop.org) and see the whole process in a couple minutes, including compile time.

The other end of the scale would be installing Apache or Samba from source, which is a much longer and more complex process.

The following are disadvantages of installing programs via source code:

- It requires a more complex installation.

- The necessary dependencies might not exist or might be very difficult to resolve.

- It's often poorly documented, sometimes with only a readme or an install file available.

- Uninstalling source packages can be difficult, particularly if the package's makefile doesn't have an uninstall routine, which means you need to manually discover and remove the package files.

When installing from source, a number of conflicts and dependency problems can occur. Until a package is released by the various distribution vendors as a part of their products, it's typically not for the faint of heart. If your goal is stability, wait for the eventual release; otherwise, you might spend hours searching for missing libraries and other needed files.

You should use source code installs when needed for performance and security.

Components of a Source Code Install

Source code tarballs typically include the following:

- **Configure script:** This script checks out the system and configures the makefile.

- **Makefile:** This file governs the installation location, parameters, and other variables.

- **Source files:** These are the actual directories of the source files.

- **Readme:** This file contains important information about the installation process.

- **Install:** Typically, this file contains the actual installation instructions; it's not present in all source installs.

- **Install script:** This is often a single script that can be run to perform the installation.

The Makefile

A *makefile* is a set of instructions and compiling parameters that makes the installation possible. After the makefile is updated by the configure script, typically the **make** command and then the **make install** command are run to compile and install the software.

To quote the man page for make, "The purpose of the **make** utility is to determine automatically which pieces of a large program need to be recompiled, and issue the commands to recompile them."

A makefile typically contains the following sections:

- **Platform:** The platform of the system

- **Debug:** How to handle errors

- **Optimize:** Items that are customized by **.configure**

- **Source:** Where the source files are found

- **Targets:** All, install, clean, dist, and so on

Targets of the makefile deserve a little attention because some confusion exists about what they consist of. The **make** command by itself usually compiles the source code but does not do anything else. Running the **make** command with the clean target usually removes any temporary files from a previous attempt to compile the code. If you run the **make** command with the install target, it puts the compiled code into the right directories in the path, continuing until the proper software has been installed.

A typical makefile has the following paths and variables (though this can vary from program to program):

```
install-prefix = .
bin_dir = $(install-prefix)/bin
uparm_dir = $(install-prefix)/lib/uparm
include_dir = $(install-prefix)/include
```

These instructions tell the installation and other targets where to put the various pieces of the program. **$(install-prefix)** indicates that, when it is compiled, the software is stored in the subdirectories of the current directory—for instance, **./bin**, **./lib/parm**, and **./include**.

Example of a Compilation of Source Code

In this example, a simple program is compiled and installed on a default Linux system. (You must have the gcc compiler and related development tools and libraries installed to compile source code.) Here's how you do it:

Step 1.   Open a browser and go to **http://www.rdesktop.org**.

Step 2.   Click the **Download** link.

Step 3.   Click the latest stable version.

Step 4.   Choose the location that's closest to you from the list of download links, and then click the small page icon under the Download column at the right of the page.

Step 5.   When prompted, put the source code in your user's home directory. Usually all you have to do is click the **Save** button in the browser you're using.

Step 6.   Open a shell session or an xterm client.

Step 7.   Navigate to the directory that contains the compressed file.

Step 8.   Unpack the archive file.

Step 9.   After the scrolling stops, change to the source directory:
```
cd sourcedir
```

Step 10.   Run an **ls** command and notice what files are present.

Step 11.   Run the configure script with the following command:
```
./configure
```

Step 12.   Run the **make** command to compile the software.

Step 13.   When the software is finished compiling, install the program with the **make install** command.

These are the basic steps needed to install an app or a command from source code. To prepare for the Linux+ exam, you don't necessarily need to do an installation from source; just ensure that you are aware of the steps in a typical source installation, as shown here.

Storage Concepts

Before users can use a disk to store their information, a systems administrator must perform a few typical tasks:

Step 1.   Install the device.

Step 2.   Partition the device.

Step 3.   Make a filesystem on the partition(s).

Step 4.   Make or choose a mount point (directory).

Step 5.   Mount the filesystem.

Step 6.   Configure the filesystem to be mounted on boot.

Step 7.   Set the permissions.

Linux devices are associated with a device file in the **/dev** directory. There are many preexisting files in this directory. As you saw earlier in this chapter, a hard drive has a corresponding device file similar to **/dev/sda**. This hard disk is referred to as a "raw device." The device is partitioned into one or more partitions, such as **/dev/sda1**. A filesystem is applied to the partition, and then the device is grafted onto the rest of the filesystem to make the storage usable. Finally, the permissions are configured to allow the necessary people to access it.

Partitions

On most modern systems, there are two partition schemes you will use: the master boot record (MBR) and the GUID Partition Table (GPT). There are several differences between these two technologies, but the most important one is generally considered to be the partition structure itself.

NOTE   On the Linux+ exam you can expect to encounter a scenario where you must identify the type of partition scheme being detailed and choose that answer from a list, or conversely, be told you're using a particular type and have to identify its characteristics from a set of available answers.

MBR

Disks on systems that use master boot record can have up to four primary partitions per disk, and in cases when you need more than four, you can exchange one of the primary partition slots for an extended partition. You can then divide the extended partition further into more partitions, called *logical partitions*.

Only one extended partition can be used per disk. The extended partition can hold an unlimited number of logical partitions, although warnings abound to hold the number down to 12 or so.

The logical partitions inside an extended partition are virtually identical to a primary partition; they just happen to live only inside an extended partition. No perceivable difference exists between a primary partition and a logical partition except in the numbering, the position on disk, and the fact that the boot files for a Linux machine should exist on a primary partition.

Logical partitions exist to get around the four-partition MBR limitation.

GPT

The MBR partitioning scheme has been around for a very long time and provides a workaround to the x86 architecture limitation of four primary partitions. Modern systems support a newer partitioning scheme called GPT. Unlike with MBR, with GPT there is no limitation of four primary partitions. As a result, there is no need for extended or logical partitions.

With GPT there is only a limitation of 128 partitions. Note that some older partitioning tools, such as the **fdisk** utility, do not support GPT.

Data Storage Methods

Most computer systems offer the same general methods of storing data on storage devices. The names of the methods may vary among computer systems, but the underlying concepts and a lot of the practices are the same.

To summarize these methods, they are as follows:

- Block storage
- File storage
- Object storage

Block Storage

Filesystems have traditionally used blocks, or block storage, to store data on disks or storage media. Blocks are treated individually, each assigned an identifier that uniquely addresses that block and makes it easier to distribute or store data either in contiguous, noncontiguous, or even cross-platform or cross-media fashion.

Blocks make it so that the data is stored wherever it is, and the storage subsystem on the computing device tracks blocks, accesses the blocks in the right order and from the proper location, and makes the data on those blocks available for the higher-level storage mechanisms on the device.

Block storage, because of its efficiency and reliability, is often associated with storage area network (SAN) devices and is almost always accessed via an access point by a client. Block storage is often used by attaching or "fronting" it with a server system that users will attach to, mount shared filesystems from, and use for their remote network storage.

Block storage is read and written as a block, doesn't handle metadata except at a very basic level, and is great for large chunks of data access, such as very large media files and databases. Block storage can be quite expensive, as well.

File Storage

File storage is a higher layer of storing data than block storage, in that a disk may be made up of blocks, evenly sized units of storage, and a filesystem will exist on top of a portion or all of that block storage and contain what we are used to seeing as files, directories, and hierarchical structures of these.

Files and directories are very familiar to us because they have analogs in the physical world, files being analogous to pieces of paper and directories being analogous to file folders or drawers in a storage cabinet. File storage, or a filesystem full of files and directories, will appear to be a single structure that we can navigate, access data from, and make changes to, but that structure may actually consist of multiple filesystems that are built on top of multiple different block devices, and may not even be remotely physically near each other or the system they make up the hierarchical structure of.

File storage allows for files to be changed, updated, and modified at a very detailed level, such as updating a single word or many pages in a file, whereas a block would have to be changed as a block. File storage is good for reasonable-size data sets, but for very large data sets, block storage is better and faster.

Object Storage

Object storage is a much more complex and featureful method of storing data than either block storage or file storage. Object storage contains the most *metadata*—specific and actionable information about what it's storing. Let's use the example of a media file that has a number of different access levels for how people access that file, but also may contain metadata about where that media file was produced, the software used, the author, and much more. The metadata is associated with the object.

Objects in this type of storage are almost completely self-contained, so where they are physically located is much less important than how they interrelate or fit together with other objects.

Object storage is typically accessed on an as-needed basis, making it cost-effective, and it's a favorite storage type of off-premises cloud providers. Files and directories are very familiar to us because they have analogs in the physical world, files being analogous to pieces of paper and directories being analogous to file folders or drawers in a storage cabinet.

Objects are only modifiable by writing or overwriting the entire object, and they don't play very well in mixed database environments because they are accessed and written to in very different manners.

FUSE (Filesystem in Userspace)

Traditionally (which is a way of saying "some time ago!"), filesystems had to be dealt with mostly or only in the kernel area of the operating system, which made it very difficult for a user to create their own filesystem. If the goal was absolute control over what happened on, say, a server system, then this scheme was likely to be a way to achieve a safer system, and therefore one that would be less likely (in theory) to crash because of some rash or ill-advised action of a user.

Why Use a FUSE?

FUSE, or *Filesystem in Userspace*, is a way to allow filesystems to be created, as the name suggests, in the userspace, or under the control of a standard user. Whereas a server system should be as predictable as possible for the sake of making sure it's up and available as much as possible, many Linux systems are in the hands of end users, developers, and many other types of users, and enabling them to create and manage filesystems is very handy and powerful for many scenarios.

Handling FUSE User Requests

FUSE filesystems are governed by a program (a handler) that is the intermediary for all actions that occur with the filesystem being created, managed, or read and written upon. The handler program must be known to and interact with the kernel, and when the user interacts with the filesystem, the user request to the filesystem is sent from the kernel to the handler program, which then interacts with the handled filesystem, and when the filesystem sends a response back to the user, it goes back through the kernel and then is given to the user or process making the request.

Possible FUSE Applications/Uses

The list of possible applications or uses of a FUSE includes but is not limited to the following:

- NTFS (Windows Filesystem)
- LTFS (Linear Tape File System)
- Layered filesystems (overlay of a FUSE on a given filesystem)
- Virtual compressed filesystems
- Backup and archival filesystems
- Remote filesystems (e.g., JuiceFS, MooseFS, SSHFS, etc.)
- Distributed filesystems (e.g., Lustre Clustering, GlusterFS, ObjectiveFS, etc.)
- Many other filesystems with widely varied uses

NOTE   FUSE is also available for several uses on Windows systems, but that will not be a topic for the Linux+ exam!

RAID

RAID, or *Redundant Array of Independent (or Inexpensive) Disks*, is an important feature for server operators who need disk and storage to be as consistently available as possible for use on their systems. When a hard disk fails, typically all of the data on the disk is lost. Data recovery professionals might be able to recover some of the data, but that can be time-consuming and expensive, and ultimately the professionals might not be able to recover the data that you really need.

RAID is a technology that was originally designed to provide a solution to the problem of hard disk failure. The original RAID (now called RAID 1) mirrored data between two hard disks. As a result, if one hard disk failed, the data still was available on the second hard disk.

RAID Levels

Since the original RAID was created, several other RAID levels have been created. The following list only includes the levels in common practice:

- **RAID 0:** This level provides no redundancy but rather increases available storage by merging multiple hard disks (or partitions) into a single device. For example, three hard disks of 30GB each can produce a RAID 0 device with 90GB of storage space. Data is written to each physical device (hard disk/partition) in stripes, which results in the requirement of each physical device being the same size to avoid wasting storage space. RAID 0 can improve the performance of reading data from the devices.

- **RAID 1:** This level is where two drives are mirrored and identical data is written to both devices, requiring two writes, but when data needs to be read from the RAID, then on spinning-disk storage the disk that has a read-write head closest to the data location is used, which can noticeably speed up data reads. The data volume is limited to the size of the least disk, and will not use additional space on mismatched disks.

- **RAID 3:** This level stripes data across several disks, with a dedicated disk that provides parity or data that can be used to keep the volume operational if a disk fails. This type of RAID has some significant drawbacks, as it requires disks to be in synchronicity and store data in the same locations on each disk. It's great for large, contiguous, uncompressed sets of data, but less than ideal for smaller read and write operations of a more random nature.

- **RAID 5:** This level provides more efficient use of the physical storage devices. Unlike RAID 1, which completely mirrors all data to all physical storage devices, or RAID 3 which stripes across several devices, RAID 5 writes different data to each physical storage device with the exception of one device, which is used to store parity data. In the event that a physical storage device is lost or damaged, the data on that device can be restored by using the parity data and the real data on the other storage devices. RAID 5 requires at least three storage devices and can have a negative impact on system performance, so software RAID (RAID performed by the kernel) is not commonly used. However, hardware RAID (RAID performed by a separate processing chip) is fairly common on high-end servers.

RAID devices are created by using the **mdadm** command, which is covered elsewhere. In terms of the current topic (device mapper and device file location), you should be aware that specific device names are associated with RAID devices. These device names begin with **/dev/md** and have a numeric value between 0 and 31. When you use the **mdadm** command, you assign your RAID to an "MD device," such as **/dev/md0** or **/dev/md1**. (Note that *md* in this case stands for *metadata*.)

Mirroring

In the world of RAID, *mirroring* equates to RAID 1, where you have two disks that are configured to appear as if they are a single disk, or a volume, often via software but also via hardware. As an example, two disks configured to appear as a volume would be partitioned, then have filesystems written on them, and each disk in the volume would contain exactly the same filesystem and data, or what is called a *mirror*.

Mirroring is very safe, since an entire disk can fail and there is an exact duplicate that can be used with little or no reconfiguration. Mirroring disks has the effect of slowing down writes, as it requires two write functions, one per disk, for each write to the volume or wherever the data is stored. Mirroring has the opposite effect on reads from the disks, as the system will read from whichever disk is going to produce the fastest access to the data desired.

NOTE   Mirroring works slightly differently on SSD (solid-state drive) disk storage, but the concept of mirroring is effectively the same on either type of device used.

Striping

The concept of *striping* is where you store segments or stripes of data across multiple devices, so that any given stripe of data blocks can be read more efficiently by issuing multiple reads or writes through the disk controller to the devices that are storing the stripes of data.

Like mirroring, striping was invented and implemented primarily on spinning-platter disk storage devices; it's less noticeable or effective on SSDs, since they do not have spinning platters or read-write heads that can be in any position. Reading and writing data from SSDs is a matter of issuing the read or write request for the location where the data exists or will exist.

Another use for striping is to take two disks and combine their aggregate storage space into a single volume or make them appear to be a single disk that is the size of their combined individual sizes minus the usual space dedicated to format structure.

Striping (or RAID 0) can result in a larger virtual or apparent disk (N+N, or adding the cumulative storage amounts) and can also result in faster access times because of the multiple possible reads or writes occurring simultaneously or closely in parallel. The main danger of striping across multiple disks to build a larger volume is that the loss of any of those devices will result in the loss of access to the entire volume. Imagine a bridge with three main supports spanning a river and one of those main supports is removed—it makes no difference if the other two remain, because the integrity or ability to use the bridge (volume) is lost.

Parity

Now that we have both mirroring and striping defined and (hopefully) demystified somewhat, let's put them together with the concept of *parity*, where at least one disk is used to provide fault tolerance for a RAID volume or the use of at least a third disk or device to contain enough of each of the first two to maintain access to the volume that contains the filesystem and data.

The concept of parity would be to have three disks in a system and use all three in a RAID 3 arrangement. Disk 1 and Disk 2 would store the volume and data, and Disk 3 would be calculated to hold enough of both Disk 1 and Disk 2 data to maintain access to and the integrity of the data volume if one of them were to fail.

As a more complex example of parity, a RAID 5 disk arrangement would include both striping of data across the involved disks and storing parity data so that any of the three disks could fail and the data volume would still exist and be usable.

> **NOTE**   RAID can go from simple to very complex in short order, so keep in mind the various levels as you are preparing for the Linux+ exam. You'll likely encounter questions that refer to the RAID levels described in this chapter, 0, 1, 3, and 5. Other levels likely won't appear. RAID 2, 4, and 10, in particular, are very specialized and not commonly used.

Listing Your Hardware Info

Your running Linux system contains a treasure trove of important information, and you can easily query that information using a set of commands commonly known as the **ls*** commands.

The primary source for the information about a running Linux system is the **/proc** directory, but it's a very large, hierarchical tree of files, directories, and cryptic numbers, so the ls* commands are a great way to mine that set of information.

The Proc Filesystem

Unix has a philosophy that "everything is a file," and this means, in part, that hardware information and state information for both the system and processes are exposed on the filesystem. In Linux this started off as *procfs*, which is usually mounted on **/proc**. In this directory, you find that each process on the system has a directory containing information about itself. Features that must keep state to work, such as a firewall that tracks network connections being handled by the system, also expose their information through **/proc**.

In addition, **procfs** contains details about the hardware in the system. Files such as **/proc/ioports, /proc/dma**, and **/proc/interrupts** can show an investigating user or a sysadmin a lot of pertinent information about the system's configuration.

Incidentally, **procfs** is called a pseudo-filesystem. It looks like a device but doesn't exist on any real hardware. It's simply a way of exposing kernel information to the user in a well-defined format.

When errors or conflicts occur, a number of commands are essential to resolving the conflicts shown in the output. Viewing information straight from the **/proc** directory is accomplished with the following commands:

```
cat /proc/interrupts
cat /proc/ioports
cat /proc/dma
cat /proc/usb
cat /proc/pci
```

In addition, a series of commands beginning with **ls*** gather the same information and present it in a more human-readable format.

> **NOTE**   The Linux+ exam expects you to know three main utilities to list hardware information, `lsusb`, `lspci` and `dmidecode`, but it's very important to know *all* the commands that are able to show you information about your system, so this section presents the rest of the notable ones as well.

Notable ls* Commands

The pertinent commands are as follows:

- **lscpu:** Provides details about the CPU, such as the number and speed of each socket and core.

- **lspci:** Shows a lot of information about the PCI bus and devices. It can identify devices on the bus that the kernel doesn't know about and provides addressing information for configuring them.

- **lsscsi:** Shows information about the SCSI devices on the system, if the system supports SCSI. This tells you whether the system can see the disk.

- **lsdev:** Shows the devices recognized by the system.

- **lsraid:** Displays the RAID devices on the system.

- **lsusb:** Displays the USB information and devices for the system.

- **lsblk:** Displays the block devices (disks) attached to the system.

- **dmesg:** Displays the "kernel ring buffer," which is a collection of messages that were created during the boot process. This is a great tool for determining what devices were recognized by the system during booting.

Friends of procfs

Mining the **/proc** directory and its contents (mounted via the **procfs** filesystem) is the most popular way to expose kernel information to users, but there are more options. The files under **/proc** are unstructured and contain information about both processes and devices. The goal of *sysfs* is to solve some of these shortcomings by migrating device data to **/sys**. Data still can exist in both locations, and the device tools such as **lspci** still use **/proc**.

The dmidecode Command

The **dmidecode** command works primarily with the **/sys** directory and its contents, and is one of the commands you are likely to see on the Linux+ exam, so let's look at what it is, where it gets its information, and what you can do to better display all of this amazingly detailed and voluminous system information.

Displaying DMI Table Information

The **dmidecode** command is designed to query the *DMI* (Desktop Management Interface) table, which contains information that is gathered from the system BIOS and represented in an in-memory table (or set of tables) that allows processes and commands to access that information without having to resort to a direct hardware query.

To better understand what's being queried and displayed by the **dmidecode** command, think of most of the information being returned as following this format:

```
Handle, Type, Size
Decoded Value
```

The following is an example of an entry the **dmidecode** command would return:

```
Handle 0x0005, DMI type 16, 23 bytes
Physical Memory Array
        Location: System Board Or Motherboard
        Use: System Memory
        Error Correction Type: None
        Maximum Capacity: 4 GB
        Error Information Handle: Not Provided
        Number Of Devices: 1
```

As you can see, the first three items are on the first line, with the handle being a unique identifier in the table, the type showing where the information came from, and the size indicating how much information is in that entry in the table.

A great way to familiarize yourself with what is displayed by the **dmidecode** command (and what's in your system's DMI table) is to funnel the 100+ lines of output that **dmidecode** typically returns through a pager like the **less** command, such as running this command:

```
$ sudo dmidecode | less
```

This will display the information gathered from the DMI table in the context of the less pager, where you can scroll up and down, use PGUP and PGDN, Home and End, and do some searching if that suits your needs.

NOTE   It is very important to remember when a command can be run as a standard user and when it must be run as either the root user or via a privilege elevation mechanism such as the **sudo** command. The Linux+ exam writers are aware of the difference between running a root-level command as a standard user and as a root-level user, so watch closely for that distinction on the exam!

Summary

In this chapter we cover some of the basics that affect users of Linux systems including introductions to the Filesystem Hierarchy Standard, how the boot process works overall, what devices you'll see in **/dev** and how software is installed from source.

Additionally, we discussed the main storage concepts and how to get hardware information from your system.

Exam Preparation Tasks

As mentioned in the section "Goals and Methods" in the Introduction, you have a couple of choices for exam preparation: the exercises here, Chapter 23, "Final Preparation," and the exam simulation questions in the Pearson Test Prep Software Online.

Review All Key Topics

Review the most important topics in this chapter, noted with the Key Topic icon in the outer margin of the page. Table 1-3 lists these key topics and the page number on which each is found.

Table 1-3 Key Topics for Chapter 1

Key Topic Element	Description	Page Number
Paragraph	The Root of the Filesystem	6
Table 1-2	Common Top-Level Subdirectories of the Root (/) Directory	7
Paragraph	initrd and initramfs	9
Paragraph	GRUB2 Command Names	16
Section	Kernel Panic Causes	23
Section	Components of a Source Code Install	26
List	Makefile sections	26
Paragraph	Sysadmin tasks required before users can use a disk to store information	28
Paragraph	Block Storage	30
Paragraph	File Storage	30
Paragraph	Object Storage	31
Paragraph	Possible FUSE Applications/Uses	32
Paragraph	RAID Levels	33
Paragraph	Mirroring	34
Paragraph	Striping	34
Paragraph	Parity	35
Paragraph	Notable **ls*** Commands	36
Paragraph	Friends of **procfs**	37
Paragraph	Displaying DMI Table Information	37

Define Key Terms

Define the following key terms from this chapter and check your answers in the glossary:

> subdirectories, initrd, initramfs, Basic Input Output System (BIOS), master boot record (MBR), Grand Unified Bootloader (GRUB), kernel panic, source code, tarball, makefile, logical partition, metadata, object storage, FUSE, RAID, mirroring, striping, parity, procfs, sysfs, DMI

Review Questions

The answers to these review questions are in Appendix A.

1. To change the configuration of the GRUB boot loader, which of the following files would you edit?

   a. **/grub/grub2.config**

   b. **/etc/boot/grub**

   c. **/etc/sysconfig/grub/boot**

   d. **/boot/grub2/grub2.cfg**

2. Your Linux server installs correctly, but when you try to boot it, you cannot see the specialized disk subsystem that it installed to. Which of the following commands will be helpful in fixing this situation? (Choose two.)

   a. **zImage**

   b. **dracut**

   c. **mkinitrd**

   d. **initramfs**

3. You are looking for the numbered set of directories that represent your system's running processes. Which of the following directories would most likely contain them?

   a. **/sys**

   b. **/proc**

   c. **/run**

   d. **/tmp**

4. Your server system seems fine, it's backed up often, and its power is provided via UPS (uninterruptible power supply), but upon inspecting your logs and system uptime, you determine that it's rebooting at least once a day. Which of the following best describes what is happening?

   a. Scheduled updates

   b. Compromised security

   c. Kernel panic

   d. System of a Down

5. Which of the following is an advantage of using source code instead of packaged software to install your system software?

   a. Ease of updating software

   b. Software version control

   c. More compatible

   d. Specific configuration control

6. There is a set of in-memory tables that contain information gathered from the system BIOS and allow processes and commands to access that information without having to resort to a direct hardware query. Which command would you use to display these tables?

   a. **dmidecode**

   b. **lspci**

   c. **lsusb**

   d. **lsdev**

7. What type of data storage allows for files to be changed, updated, and modified at a very detailed level, such as updating a single word or many pages in a file?

   a. Block storage

   b. Object storage

   c. Line storage

   d. File storage

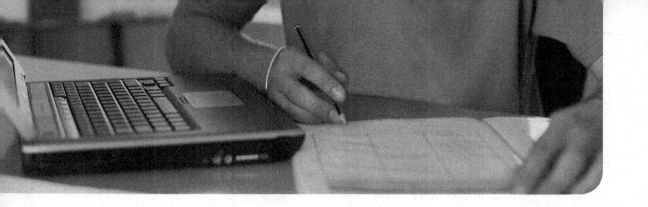

This chapter covers the following topics:

- File and Directory Operations
- File Metadata and File Types
- Soft and Hard Links
- File Compression, Archiving, and Backup
- Copying Objects Between Systems
- File Editing

The exam objective covered in this chapter is as follows:

- **Objective 1.2:** Given a scenario, manage files and directories

## CHAPTER 2

Managing Files and Directories

Management of files and directories is very important on a Linux system, as literally every single thing on a Linux system is a file of some kind, and directories are files of the type directory.

Properly managing these files includes many tasks, such as displaying information about the files to know more about what you are managing, contents of the files, creating, altering the details editing the contents of the files, determining file types, and gaining insight by displaying deeper information than normally shown.

The concept of editing files being part of managing them is not as odd as it might seem; you definitely have to manage files when you are doing a lot of editing, and many times you must be aware of file creation, deletion, transforming files, and displaying those files differently than they currently exist.

Managing files also includes the important step of copying or moving them from system to system, typically without losing their important attributes such as permissions, ownership, and other critical details.

Knowing how to compress, uncompress, and back up your files is a management skill that can make your day, or break your career, depending on what the situation is. Data in files can be mundane, have little or no value, or be the expression for intellectual property or national secrets that have immense importance, all located in a lowly text or formatted file. Losing important data is, at the very least, inconvenient, and at the very worst it can cause loss of revenue, loss of business opportunities, or even result in life-changing circumstances.

"Do I Know This Already?" Quiz

The "Do I Know This Already?" quiz enables you to assess whether you should read this entire chapter or simply jump to the "Exam Preparation Tasks" section for review. If you are in doubt, read the entire chapter. Table 2-1 outlines the major headings in this chapter and the corresponding "Do I Know This Already?" quiz questions. You can find the answers in Appendix A, "Answers to the 'Do I Know This Already?' Quizzes and Review Questions."

Table 2-1   "Do I Know This Already?" Foundation Topics Section-to-Question Mapping

Foundation Topics Section	Questions Covered in This Section
File and Directory Operations	1
File Metadata and File Types	2
Soft and Hard Links	3
File Compression, Archiving, and Backup	4
Copying Objects Between Systems	5
File Editing	6

CAUTION   The goal of self-assessment is to gauge your mastery of the topics in this chapter. If you do not know the answer to a question or are only partially sure of the answer, you should mark that question as wrong for purposes of the self-assessment. Giving yourself credit for an answer you correctly guess skews your self-assessment results and might provide you with a false sense of security.

1. You are currently in the directory **/home/user1/subdir1** and need to navigate to the directory **/home/user3**. Which of the following commands will accomplish this? (Choose two.)

    a. **cd home/user3**

    b. **cd ~/user3**

    c. **cd ../../home/user3**

    d. **cd ../../../home/user3**

2. Which command will show you the three file dates and times kept in metadata when used on a file or directory?

    a. **file**

    b. **ls -li**

    c. **stat**

    d. **info**

3. Which of the following situations would prevent you from creating a hard link?

    a. The link spans filesystems.

    b. The source of the link is a hidden file.

    c. The source of the link is a device file.

    d. The source of the link is a directory.

    e. The destination contains special characters.

4. You want to display the contents of a **.tar.gz** compressed file. Which of the following commands would show you the contents, along with the file particulars, as if you had displayed them with the **ls** command?

    a. tar -czvf file1.tar.gz

    b. tar - xzvf file1.tar.gz

    c. tar -tzvf file1.tar.gz

    d. tar -lzvf file1.tar.gz

5. You want to copy a file in your local directory to the home directory of the mortimer user on a remote system. Which of the following commands would result in this action?

    a. scp ~file1 @192.168.10.10:mortimer

    b. scp ./file1 mortimer@192.168.10.10/home/mortimer:

    c. scp file1 mortimer@192.168.10.10:~

    d. scp mortimer:file1 < scp @192.168.10.10

6. In the **vim** editor, instead of using the up and down arrow keys, you can use what keys?

    a. k for up and **j** for down

    b. j for up and **k** for down

    c. Ctrl+D for down and **Ctrl+U** for up

    d. j for up and **h** for down

Foundation Topics

Linux (and its antecedent, Unix) systems are almost exclusively constructed of files, be they regular files such as text, graphics, databases, device files such as block or character types, binary program or executable script files, and let's not forget a very important type of file, directory files.

System operators who deal with files and systems made up of files for most of their work life must know how to properly do a large number of file- and directory-related tasks, including creating, modifying, deleting, listing, displaying the contents of, viewing, changing and setting permissions on, archiving, unarchiving, compressing, and transforming files.

Additionally, system operators need to be able to create empty files; edit many different types of files to change their contents; navigate all around their systems using the tools available, such as the **cd** command and the directory indicators (. and ..); and view their file and directory structures in helpful and efficient ways using such utilities as the **tree**.

File and Directory Operations

NOTE   The Linux+ objectives list the topics in an order that is simply not the best flow for what we have to discuss here, since we are loosely following the objectives on a by-chapter basis. With that in mind, I have thoughtfully rearranged the topics to flow naturally and make the most sense.

Being able to properly work with files and directories on a Linux system is as important as any other task, as a major amount of any time spent with a Linux system is spent working at the command line. As a good sysadmin, you are expected to know how to create, delete, edit, set permissions, display, move, copy, link and unlink, find and locate, determine the type of files and programs, and even determine the differences between two sets of files and directories.

Tips for Working with Linux Files

Because most users and sysadmins come from a Windows or other OS background, a quick set of recommendations for less-experienced Linux sysadmins can be of help here:

- **Hidden files aren't really hidden:** They just begin with a ., such as the **.bashrc** and **.bash_profile** files. They are normally not visible unless you explicitly ask for them to be displayed, and they aren't deleted by commands such as **rm -f *.***.

- **Filenames can contain multiple periods or no period characters:** The filenames **this.is.a.long.file** and **thisisalongfile** are perfectly reasonable and possible.

- **Spaces in filenames look nice but are a pain to type:** Use an _ or a - instead of spaces because it's neater and easier than prefixing all spaces with a \. (To display a space in a filename, the system shows a space prefixed with a backslash.)

- **File extensions aren't mandatory:** However, they are useful for sorting, selection, and the **copy/move/delete** (cp/mv/rm) commands, as well as for quickly identifying a file's type.

Basic Navigation

The command to change the current working directory, **cd**, is used frequently, and knowing how to move around the filesystem is a main focus of the Linux+ exam.

The following command simply moves you from wherever you are in the filesystem to the **/etc** directory. This type of move uses *absolute pathnames* and can be used from within any directory.

```
# cd /etc
```

The path is called *absolute* because it defines a path starting at the root of the filesystem. You can quickly see that a path is absolute if it starts with a slash (**/**).

Moving from the current directory to a subdirectory is quick and easy. For example, here is how you can change into the **/etc/samba** directory from your current position in the **/etc/** directory:

```
# cd samba
```

This is referred to as a *relative path* because the option you pass to the **cd** command is relative to the current directory. You are in **/etc**, and moving to **samba** gets you in **/etc/samba**. If you were in **/home** and ran **cd samba**, it would not work unless **/home/samba** also existed.

If you get confused about where you currently are, use the **pwd** command to print the working (current) directory:

```
# pwd
/etc/samba
```

By itself, the **cd** command takes you back to your home directory, wherever you happen to be. The tilde (~) also means "home directory," so **cd ~** takes you to your home directory, and **cd ~sean** takes you to Sean's home directory.

Advanced Navigation

It's good to get experience with some complex relative path situations. For example, say that you are in the directory **/home1/user1** and want to move into the directory **/home2/user2**:

```
# tree /
/
|-- home1
|  `-- user1
`-- home2
   `-- user2
```

Which command would you use?

Remember that you aren't using absolute pathnames, just relative pathnames. The answer is

```
# cd ../../home2/user2
```

Each of the .. pairs takes you up one level: The first takes you to **/home1**, and the second puts you at the root. From there, it's relative pathnames. Practice this method and remember that going up one level in this exercise only gets you to the **/home1** directory. This is a relative path because the path does not start with a **/**. The directory where you end up depends on where you started.

Although this example of relative and absolute pathnames demonstrates changing directories, it applies to any situation where you're prompted for a filename.

Additionally, you can use the single dot character (.) to denote the current directory, such as if you are trying to run a **find** command that uses the current directory as the path portion of the **find** command's arguments, like the following:

```
# find ./ -iname "*.txt"
```

This command starts searching in the current directory, wherever that is, and extends its search below the current directory.

The . character is also extremely helpful when copying or moving something to the current directory, such as the following command that would copy the **/etc/hosts** file to the current directory:

```
# cp /etc/hosts .
```

As you can probably imagine, there are any number of command situations where being able to refer to the current directory is very helpful, so remember not only .. for the upper-level directory, but . for the current directory.

Listing Files and Directories

The **ls** command is used for listing directories or files or both.

If you use the **ls** command to see multicolumn output of the current directory, only the file or directory names are shown, not other details about the file:

```
# ls
file1 file2 file3 file4
```

Use the **-l** (long) listing option to see all the details of a particular file or directory or set of files or directories in a single column, like so:

```
# ls -l
total 0
-rw-r--r-- 1 root root 0 Jan 24 18:55 file1
-rw-r--r-- 1 root root 0 Jan 24 18:55 file2
-rw-r--r-- 1 root root 0 Jan 24 18:55 file3
-rw-r--r-- 1 root root 0 Jan 24 18:55 file4
```

Using the **-l** option is the only way to use the **ls** command and see the permissions, ownership, and link counts for objects. The only other command that can give such information is the **stat** command (covered later in the chapter), which shows a single filesystem object at a time.

Other examples of using the **ls** command include

- **ls /home/user:** Shows a plain listing of the specified directory.

- **ls -a:** Lists all files, including hidden . files.

- **ls -d foo:** Lists just the directory called **foo** and not the contents.

- **ls -i:** Lists the inode number for the target file or directory. Linux uses inodes to represent files on disk; inodes are discussed later in this chapter, in the section "Copying Files and Directories."

- **ls -l:** Shows permissions, links, and date, group, and owner information. *Permissions* dictate who can access the file and are discussed in detail in Chapter 12, "Understanding and Applying Access Controls."

- **ls -lh:** Shows human-readable output of file sizes, in kilobytes, megabytes, and gigabytes, along with file details.

Chaining together the options produces useful results. For example, if you needed to see all the files (including hidden ones) in the current directory, their permissions, and their inode numbers, you would use the following command:

```
# ls -lai
290305 drwxr-x--- 13 root root 4096 Jan 24 18:55 .
2 drwxr-xr-x 20 root root 4096 Jan 24 17:56 ..
292606 -rw-r--r-- 1 root root 1354 Jan 21 00:23 anaconda-ks.cfg
292748 -rw------- 1 root root 3470 Jan 24 18:16 .bash_history
290485 -rw-r--r-- 1 root root 24 Jun 10 2000 .bash_logout
290486 -rw-r--r-- 1 root root 234 Jul 5 2001 .bash_profile
290487 -rw-r--r-- 1 root root 176 Aug 23 1995 .bashrc
290488 -rw-r--r-- 1 root root 210 Jun 10 2000 .cshrc
```

Touching Files

The **touch** command seems odd at first, but it comes in handy often. You give it the name of one or more files, and it creates the files if they don't exist or updates their timestamps if they do.

There are various reasons to use the **touch** command, such as to create a new blank log file or update a file's modification time to use as a reference, such as to know the last time a job was run.

To create a new file, you can use the relative pathname for creating one in the current directory:

```
# touch filename
```

Or you can use the absolute pathname to create the file, such as shown here:

```
# touch /home/ross/filename
```

As you prepare for the Linux+ exam, expect to see **touch** for log file creation, along with the use of a reference file to mark the last backup. In other words, if a log file is created from a successful backup, that file can be used as a date and time reference file because it occurred at a desirable time.

When you use **touch** on an existing file, the default action is to update all three of the file's times:

- **access:** The last time a file was written to/read from

- **change:** The last time the contents of the file were changed or that the file's *metadata* (owner, permission, inode number) was changed

- **modify:** The last time the file's contents were changed

A programmer preparing a new release of a software package would use the **touch** command to ensure that all files have exactly the same date and times. Therefore, the release could be referred to by the file date, given multiple revisions.

Setting a file's date is relatively easy; the following command sets **file1**'s date to a particular date and time:

```
# touch -t 202201010830 file1
```

The time format used here is *yyyymmddhhmm*, or a four-digit year, two-digit month, two-digit day, two-digit hour, and two-digit minute.

Reference files are useful, particularly when you just want to have a file or set of files updated to a particular date/time rather than to the current date/time. You could use the following:

```
# touch -r reffile file2update
```

The date/time of **reffile** is applied to the **file2update** file date/time.

Copying Files and Directories

One aspect of copying an object is that the act creates a new file with a separate inode, which is literally a number assigned by the filesystem from a table and effectively is the system's method of referring to the file; the friendly filename is really for the understanding of humans.

NOTE An inode is a pointer to a file on a disk. An inode is created along with all the other files as a part of the filesystem and, depending on the filesystem, it can be either finite in number or auto-generated as needed. An inode essentially equates to the presence of a file on the system, for a file cannot exist without its own inode or a reference to one.

All of this means that the operating system sees the new file as being separate from the old one. Contrast this to a move operation, where it's the same file (that is, the same inode, as long as it's on the same filesystem) with a new name.

When you create an object in a filesystem, it gets its own permissions. **cp** doesn't always copy the permissions over to the new file. This can be done, but it requires the use of the **-p** option to preserve the permissions and ownership. The root user is the only user that can change the *ownership* of a file; therefore, regular users using this option always own the copied files, no matter who the original owner was.

A normal copy is simple to perform and essentially causes the file to be replicated to the new location:

```
# cp file1 /dir1/file2
```

A few options that make life easier for copying files include

- **-d:** Doesn't follow symbolic links; copies a link instead. A link points one file to another (see the section "Linking Files," later in this chapter).
- **-f:** Forces overwriting existing files.
- **-i:** Interactively asks before overwriting.
- **-l:** Creates a hard link to the source file.
- **-r or -R:** Recursively traverses directories (copying everything).
- **-s:** Creates a symbolic link (symlink) to the source file.
- **-u:** Updates the copy only when the source is newer than the target or the target doesn't exist.
- **-x:** Doesn't traverse to filesystems mounted from other devices.

Copying an existing directory to a new one is simple:

```
# cp -r dir1 dir2
```

The **-r** option is necessary because the **cp** command doesn't process directories by default. As long as the target directory does not exist, the previous command makes an identical copy of the source and all subordinate files and directories in the target directory.

Copying a source directory to an existing target directory doesn't involve an overwrite; it involves making the source directory into a new subdirectory of the target. For example, if you are in the **/test** directory and have the following structure, you might assume that issuing **cp -r dir1 dir2** would overwrite **dir2**—or at least prompt you to do so:

```
# tree .
|-- dir1
| |-- file1
| `-- subdir1
`-- dir2
```

When you issue the **cp -r dir1 dir2** command, the filesystem (along with the **cp** command) notices the existing **dir2** entry and automatically drops the source directory into **dir2** as a subdirectory, like this:

```
|-- dir1
|  |-- file1
|  `-- subdir1
`-- dir2
  `-- dir1
  |-- file1
  `-- subdir1
```

The correct way to copy the contents of **dir1** into **dir2** and mirror **dir1** exactly is to focus on the word *contents*. By suffixing the source (**dir1**) with a forward slash and an asterisk (that is, **dir1/***), you tell the **cp** command to ignore the directory entry and focus on the filenames inside the directory.

With the same initial setup, if you issue the command **cp -r dir1/* dir2**, you get the correct results:

```
# tree .
|-- dir1
|  |-- file1
|  `-- subdir1
`-- dir2
  |-- file1
  `-- subdir1
```

The Linux+ exam will test your ability to properly copy a directory and its contents. In addition, if you see a source directory with only a trailing forward slash but no asterisk, such as **dir1/**, this is identical to using **dir1**. In other words, to copy just the contents of a directory, you have to address them specifically with the forward slash and asterisk (**dir1/***).

Two special characters used in relative directory naming are often used when copying files. The current directory is represented by a single period (.) and the parent directory by two periods (..). For example, if you are currently in the **/home/rossb** directory and want to copy a set of files from the **/home/lukec** directory, you can avoid typing the full path of the current directory by using the . character. Both of these commands perform the same action:

```
# cp /home/lukec/*.mp3 .
# cp /home/lukec/*.mp3 /home/rossb
```

Moving Objects

Whereas the **cp** command copies a file by creating a new file, inode, and data, the **mv** command simply changes which directory file contains the file or directory entry or alters the entry in the file if it stays in the same directory. When you change just the metadata that points to the file, you can quickly move a file on the same device. If the file move happens across two devices, the file is copied to the new device and deleted from the old one.

Create a file named **file1** and then run the **stat** command on it to check the details, as shown in Example 2-1.

Example 2-1   Running the **stat** Command on **file1**

```
# touch file1
# stat file1
 File: 'file1'
 Size: 0 Blocks: 0 IO Block: 4096 regular empty file
Device: fd00h/64768d Inode: 2261179 Links: 1
Access: (0664/-rw-rw-r--) Uid: (500/sean) Gid: (500/sean)
Access: 2015-02-03 21:47:46.000000000 -0600
Modify: 2015-02-03 21:47:46.000000000 -0600
Change: 2015-02-03 21:47:46.000000000 -0600
 Birth: -
```

Now move the file to a new name with the **mv** command, as shown in Example 2-2.

Example 2-2   Moving a File to a New Name

```
# mv file1 file2
# stat file2
 File: 'file2'
 Size: 0 Blocks: 0 IO Block: 4096 regular empty file
Device: fd00h/64768d Inode: 2261179 Links: 1
Access: (0664/-rw-rw-r--) Uid: (500/sean) Gid: (500/sean)
Access: 2015-02-03 21:47:46.000000000 -0600
Modify: 2015-02-03 21:47:46.000000000 -0600
Change: 2015-02-03 21:48:41.000000000 -0600
 Birth: -
```

Because the device and inode stayed the same in Example 2-2, you know this is the same file as before. The change time is modified to reflect the fact that the file was renamed.

When you move a file, the **mv** command overwrites the destination if it exists. This command supports an option, **-i**, that first checks the target to see whether it exists. If it does, **mv** asks whether you want to overwrite the target. Some distributions make **-i** a default option with a shell alias.

Another quirk of the command is the lack of an **-r**, or *recursive*, option. This is because when you move a directory or a file, you're just changing the directory entry for the file. The directory continues to point to the same files, so there is no need to move the files themselves.

You can avoid the overwriting of newer target files or directories by using the **-u** option, which preserves the latest copy of an object.

Examples of moving files and directories include moving a single directory to another directory name, as shown here:

```
# mv -f dir1 dir2
```

This merely changes the directory entry **dir1** to the new name **dir2**. The -f option also omits the "are you sure?" prompt.

Just as with the **cp** command, moving directory contents requires a correctly formed command; otherwise, you'll move a directory not to the new name but to a subdirectory of the existing directory. For example, consider the **/test** directory again, which has a structure similar to the following:

```
# tree .
|-- dir1
|  |-- file1
|  `-- subdir1
`-- dir2
```

If you were a Windows administrator, it would make sense to run the following command to move **dir1** to **dir2**:

```
# mv dir1 dir2
```

If you do this on a Linux system and then run the **tree** command, you see the following output:

```
# tree .
`-- dir2
 `-- dir1
 |-- file1
 `-- subdir1
```

This moves **dir1** under **dir2** because **dir2** already existed. To properly move the contents of the source **dir1** to the target **dir2**, you don't need to use the nonexistent **-r** option. (Remember this for the Linux+ exam.) You can just use a forward slash and an asterisk to refer to the files under **dir1**, like this:

```
# mv dir1/* dir2
```

NOTE   The * wildcard operator doesn't match hidden files because they begin with a period. Handling this case is actually quite complicated and beyond the scope of the Linux+ exam.

If you run the **tree** command, you see the following output:

```
# tree .
|-- dir1
`-- dir2
 |-- file1
 `-- subdir1
```

Finally, the directories you pass to the **mv** command don't always have to be under your current directory. You can use absolute pathnames, such as **mv /dir1 .** to move **dir1**, which is off the root directory, into the current directory. You can also run **mv /dir1 /tmp** from anywhere in the system to move that same directory into the temporary directory.

Creating and Removing Directories

A basic task in file management is to be able to create and remove directories, which sometimes means creating or removing whole trees at once. To create a directory named **dir1**, you use **mkdir dir1**. To create a directory named **subdir1** in the **dir1** directory, you use **mkdir dir1/subdir1**.

Always think of the last segment of any directory path as the object being created or removed and think of the rest of the items in a path as supporting or parent objects. The **mkdir** and **rmdir** commands are similar in features and options, including the capability of **mkdir** to create a deep subdirectory tree from scratch in a single command (using the **-p** or **parent** option to create any subdirectories needed to create that last subdirectory):

```
# mkdir -p /home/user1/dir1/dir2/dir3/dir4
```

One of the quirks about the **rmdir** command is that it can remove only empty directories. For example, the last directory of the chain **/dir1/dir2/dir3/dir4** is the real target for this command, and only if that directory is empty (containing no regular or directory files) can it be removed:

```
# rmdir -p /home/user1/dir1/dir2/dir3/dir4
```

By using the **-p** or **parent** option with **rmdir**, you can remove the tree starting with the last subdirectory all the way back to the top one—but only if the sole entry in any directory was the one just removed. One option to the **rmdir** command does allow it to remove directories that have files and so on in them. It's called **--ignore-fail-on-non-empty** and is the longest option I know of in Linux. I'd rather type **rm -rf targetdir** 20 times than use this beast.

Removing Objects

You typically want to remove objects after creating or copying them, which is done with the **rm** command for most objects. **rmdir** can also be used.

Deleting files with the **rm** command is a matter of choosing the target to be removed and the options that work best.

If you want to remove a particular file and never be prompted by confirmation messages, the command is **rm -f target**.

To remove a directory and all its contents, without getting a confirmation message, the command is **rm -rf /full/path/to/target**.

File Metadata and File Types

Since everything on a Linux system is really a file, it's very important to know that files come in different types, what those are, and how to identify what you are looking at, which we will do in this section.

Determining File Types

With no absolute requirement for extensions on Linux files, a tool for easily determining file types is essential. The **file** command can be used to read a file's headers and match that data against a known set of types.

The file Command

The **file** command uses several possible sources, including the **stat** system call, the magic number file (**/usr/share/magic**), and a table of character sets, including ASCII and EBCDIC. Finally, if the file is text and contains recognizable strings from a given programming or other language, it is used to identify the file.

The output can be used, manipulated, and filtered to show useful things. For example, simply using the **file** command on a given file shows the type:

```
$ file file1
file1: ASCII text
```

Running the **file** command against a known binary shows various elements about the architecture and layout of the file, as shown here:

```
$ file /bin/ls
/bin/ls: ELF 32-bit LSB executable, Intel 80386, version 1 (SYSV),
dynamically linked (uses shared libs), for GNU/Linux 2.6.32, stripped
```

Running the **file** command against a directory full of files is useful for viewing the possible types, but the real gold lies in filtering the output using the pipe operator (|) and the **grep** command to see only the results that contain a particular word, such as **empty**:

```
$ file /etc/* | grep empty
/etc/dumpdates: empty
/etc/exports: empty
/etc/fstab.REVOKE: empty
/etc/motd: empty
/etc/printconf.local: empty
```

This is one way of finding empty files that are littering your system. They are probably required in the **/etc** directory but only clutter temporary directories such as **/tmp**.

Displaying File Metadata

If all you know how to do is use the **ls** command and its various options, you are missing out on many important and significant pieces of information that will prove useful to you. Along with the **file** command, which uses the **stat** system call but not much else that it provides, you can do wonders with the actual **stat** command.

The stat Command

The **stat** command is quite useful even by itself, showing a multitude of different file information items, and as previously mentioned it can work in conjunction with other commands to unveil even more details.

Using **stat** is fairly simple; just invoke it with a file or filesystem object as its argument and you'll see what it has to offer:

```
$ stat file1
  File: file1
```

```
  Size:0     Blocks:0    IO Block:4096    regular empty file
Device: 801h/2049d     Inode: 259418    Links: 1
Access: (0664/-rw-rw-r--) Uid:(1000/ ubuntu)Gid:(1000/  ubuntu)
Access: 2022-01-14 19:32:09.307094382 -0700
Modify: 2022-01-14 19:32:09.307094382 -0700
Change: 2022-01-14 19:32:09.307094382 -0700
 Birth: -
```

As you can see, you get so much more than simple **ls -l** output, you even get the type of the file as if you had used the file command.

Information the **stat** command shows:

- **File:** This shows the filename as it exists on the filesystem.

- **Size:** The file is an empty file, one that has 0 bytes of data in it.

- **Blocks:** The file takes up 0 blocks of space.

- **IO Block:** The file occupies or is associated with a 4096-byte block.

- **File Type:** There is no label for this information, because the file is a regular empty file, similar information as shown by the **file** command.

- **Device:** This is the device the file's block is located on.

- **Inode:** This is the inode # associated with the file.

- **Links:** This is a regular file, no hard links exist to the same inode. If there are hard links, the value will be greater than 1.

- **Access:** This shows the permissions and user/group ownership for the file.

- **Access:** This is the date/time of the last file contents read.

- **Modify:** This is the last date/time the file metadata (name, size, permissions) was changed.

- **Change:** This is the last date/time the actual file contents were changed.

- **Birth:** This field is only used by certain filesystems such as ext4, and is there to be a separate and static initial birth date/time for the file.

The **stat** command can also be used to display any number or order of the supported *format sequences*, such as **%i**, **%A**, and so on, which can be found in the man page for the **stat** command. These are short codes for specifying what individual piece of **stat** output you want to display, and putting them into a particular order can be very helpful, or allow you to send that output to other commands for further processing.

As an example, you could issue the following command:

```
$ stat -c %i file1
  259461
```

The use of **-c** followed by **%i** restricts **stat** output to just the inode number of the file. To output several format sequences all together, surround them with single quotes like this:

```
$ stat -c '"%n",%i,"%F",%h' file1
"file1",259461,"regular file",1
```

The use of double quotes to surround possible filenames or descriptions that have spaces or commas in them, and separating the output with commas is so that items that have spaces in that field will not cause problems, and whatever is inside the double quotes will be taken as that field's contents. This will make it very easy to generate something truly useful like a filesystem contents report that contains the fields you want to report on in the right order to use them in a spreadsheet, and so forth.

NOTE You should also be (slightly) aware of the **-printf** format sequence option, which would allow you greater control by interpreting backslash escapes, such as trailing newlines with **\n** and more.

Having this knowledge about the multiple uses of the **stat** command should be useful both in your daily work and to help you answer any questions about file metadata you encounter on the Linux+ exam.

Soft and Hard Links

Links are very useful for several purposes, the main one is so that users don't have to navigate all over the system just to access a file or run a command.

Linking Files

Links come in two varieties: symbolic (or soft) and hard links. Each has its own set of advantages and disadvantages. Sysadmins use links for a multitude of purposes; chief among them is to make shortcuts on a system for users to access data without having to navigate multiple directory levels.

If you have users on your Linux systems, you may need to have a single mount point that is accessible to multiple users. The options include having users navigate to the **/mnt/somemount** directory to save data and putting a link to that mount point in each user's home directory. You're much better off using a link for this task.

Symbolic Links

A symbolic link is primarily used to make a shortcut from one object to another. A *symbolic link* creates a tiny file with its own inode and a path to the linked file. Symlinks can span filesystems and drives, primarily because a symlink has its own inode. Figure 2-1 shows the relationship between a symlink and a target file.

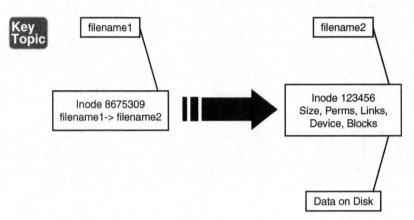

Figure 2-1 Symbolic link detail

For example, you might mount an external disk on the **/mnt/projdata** mount point and want each user to be able to access that remote share from their own home directory. You simply have to issue the following command in each user's home directory to accomplish this:

```
# ln -s /mnt/projdata projdata
# ls -l projdata
lrwxrwxrwx 1 root root 13 Jan 26 12:09 projdata -> /mnt/projdata
```

Notice that the listing for the new symlink shows exactly where the link points, and the permissions are set to the maximum to avoid interfering with the permissions on the target object.

Symbolic links always look like they have the same permissions, but they don't try to change them. Changing permissions on a symlink changes the permissions on the target permissions instead.

To unlink a symbolic link, you simply delete the file that is the symbolic link, which removes the reference to the original file. Removing that symbolic link file may seem scary, but by default doing so does not remove the target linked file.

Hard Links

A *hard link* is normally used to make a file appear in another place. A hard link is simply an additional name in a directory that points to exactly the same inode and shares every aspect of the original file except the actual name (although the filename could be identical if it were in a different directory). Figure 2-2 shows the relationship between a hard link and the target file.

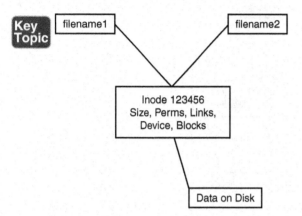

Figure 2-2   Hard link detail

For an example of using a hard link, consider the need to ensure that a frequently deleted file is easily restorable for a given user. The user, Jaime, travels a lot, but when he's in the office, he seems to delete things a lot and claim that the system has eaten his files. When Jaime is traveling, you don't have any issues, so the problem must be the user's actions.

To anchor or back up an important file, such as the company contact list, in Jaime's home directory, you first must create a backup directory, such as **/backup**. Then you create a hard link from Jaime's **ccontactlist.txt** file to a file in the **/backup** directory, like so:

```
# cd ~jaime
ln ccontactlist.txt /backup/home_jaime_ccontactlist.txt
ls -l ccontactlist.txt
-rw-r--r-- 2 jaime users 0 Jan 26 13:08 ccontactlist.txt
```

Notice that the file appears normal, but the number **2** for the link count lets you know that another name entry for this file exists somewhere.

Also notice that the listing for the new hard link doesn't show the target file and doesn't seem to refer to it in any way. Running the **stat** command on this file won't show you the other filename or seem to be aware of it except for the higher link count.

The name and location of a file are the only things about the file that are not stored in the inode. You will see questions about this on the Linux+ exam.

Hard links can't be created if the target is on another filesystem, disk, or remote object. The need to associate multiple names to the same inode makes such remote creation impossible.

Be careful when changing the permissions and ownership on hard-linked files because all name entries point to exactly the same inode. Thus, any changes are instantly made to what would appear to be multiple files but what, in reality, are only filenames.

Deleting a file that has multiple hard links requires the removal of every hard link or the multiple names. While it would appear that you are unlinking the files, since they are all exactly the same inode and data with different names in the filesystem directory files, you have to remove all the files that point to the original file to successfully perform an "unlink" from the original file.

In addition, to find all the links for a file, run the following command:

```
# ls -i ccontactlist.txt
17392 ccontactlist.txt
find / -inum 17392
/home/jaime/ccontactlist.txt
/backup/home_jaime_ccontactlist.txt
```

When you have found all the links to the file by querying the common inode number, you can delete all the undesired links to the original file, but you need to take great care not to remove *all* the links to the file; that is, do not delete the file entirely!

NOTE For the Linux+ exam, remember that a symlink is another actual file with its own inode. A large number of symlinks can therefore cause a problem for a filesystem, such as one that contains users' home directories. Using too many inodes can restrict you from using the storage space available. Run the **df -i** command to see what the statistics are.

File Compression, Archiving, and Backup

Archiving and restoring files have come a very long way since the days of Mountain ™ tape drives and putting disk packs from mainframes into a case to be taken off-site by a delivery driver.

System operators who will be dealing with files and systems made up of files for most of their work life must know how to properly archive, list, unarchive, compress, and transform files.

Being able to competently design and implement a system backup and recovery scenario is one of the most critical tasks besides making sure the servers are serving files and providing services. Without a good backup and recovery scheme, a business that suffers a crippling systems crash may risk going out of business. I often say that most small businesses are one hard drive crash and a missed pay cycle from extinction.

It is important to take your organization or personal data security, safety, and integrity very seriously by backing up the data, using proper storage, and making certain what you have backed up can be restored properly.

Using tar

The **tar** command is the workhorse of the archival world. The name, which comes from the term **tape archive**, goes back to the time when most backup was done to a local tape drive. You can think of **tar** as a pipeline that takes in a series of files and outputs a single file that is meant to be streamed to tape, but this output could be sent to a file on disk as well.

As the data goes through the pipeline, you can do some transformations on the files, such as chop up the output into something that fits across multiple tapes, exclude files that weren't recently changed, or rewrite the directory names stored in the archive.

tar also provides extraction options. You can run a **.tar** file, also called a *tarball*, through **tar** to get back a copy of the original files. It is possible to extract only certain files and manipulate the filenames.

The **tar** command can also be used with special option characters to make use of various *compression* commands, particularly the **gzip/gunzip**, **bzip2/bunzip2**, and **xz/unxz** commands. This has the effect of creating a compressed archive file, typically named **.tar.gz** for **gzip**-compressed files, **.tar.bz2** for **bzip2**-compressed files, and **.tar.xz** for **xz**-compressed files.

tar commands have a slightly unusual syntax. The command is **tar**, followed by a dash (-), and then all the options concatenated together, such as **xvjf**. After this is a list of zero or more filenames; the meanings depend on the options you choose.

The **tar** command can act on files or **tar** archives in three main ways; each has a corresponding letter that must be the first letter in the list of options:

- **c:** Creates an archive.
- **t:** Tells you the contents of an archive.
- **x:** Extracts files from an archive.

A number of other options are available, including the following:

- **v:** Be verbose by giving a list of files as they are processed.

- **j or z:** Compress or decompress with **bzip2** or **gzip**, respectively.

- **f:** The next word is the name of the file to operate on.

Figure 2-3 shows the choices graphically. Next, we'll look at examples of these options.

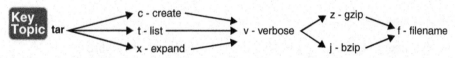

Figure 2-3   Picturing the **tar** options

When you're creating an archive with **tar**, you should think about what you want to archive, where you want the resulting archive to be created, and what compression, if any, you want to use.

To create a simple **tar** archive, the options you need are as follows:

```
tar -cf archive.tar /foo
```

In this example, the **-c** option signals **tar** to create the file specified after the **-f** option and specifies the directory you are archiving, which is the **/foo** directory. Note that you have to add the **.tar** suffix. By default, the operation is recursive, so if you specify a directory as the target, it archives that directory and all its subdirectories and files in that tree.

To create a **tar** archive and see the filenames as they are processed, use the **-v** option:

```
tar -cvf archive.tar /foo
```

This produces the following output:

```
tar: Removing leading '/' from member names
foo/
foo/install.log
foo/install.log.syslog
foo/.bash_logout
```

If given an absolute directory name to archive, **tar** strips the leading **/** from the full path of the objects in the archive. It would not be good if you could overwrite files in your **/usr** directory by extracting a file in an unrelated directory!

You can pass more than one directory or file to **tar**. For example, **tar -cf foo.tar bin var** creates an archive called **foo.tar** that contains both the **bin** and the **var** directories.

> **NOTE** The **tar** command does not compress the files it places into an archive file. Even though the entirety of the files on disk and the file size might be slightly different, there's no real compression happening.

Using Compression Utilities

Due to the toolset mentality of Linux and Unix commands, where everything does one thing really well and works well with other commands, you can use compression utilities with the **tar** command to get much smaller archive file sizes.

The Linux+ exam objectives mention three commonly used compression commands: **gzip**, **bzip2**, and **xz**. These three commands are accompanied by corresponding decompression utilities: **gunzip**, **bunzip2**, and **unxz**.

All three of these utility pairs share a similar command-line syntax, and they are perfect companions to the **tar** command, which doesn't really compress files and directories, but it puts them into an archive file and leaves the compression up to the commands we are discussing now.

By default, the **gzip/gunzip, bzip2/bunzip2**, and **xz/unxz** commands act on individual files, which is almost exactly the opposite of the **tar** command's behavior.

For example, if you have three files, **file1**, **file2**, and **file3**, in the current directory, you could use the **tar** command on them to produce a **tar** archive file that contains all three of these files. Conversely, using any of the three compression utilities against these files will result in each of the individual files being compressed and *replaced* by a file that has the same name but ends now in either **.gz**, **.bz2**, or **.xz**.

To create the same archive with **gzip** compression, you simply insert a **-z** option and use **.gz** as the filename suffix:

```
# tar -czf archive.tar.gz /foo
```

The result will be a **gzip**-compressed file named **archive.tar.gz** in the current directory.

To create the same archive with **bzip2** compression, you simply insert a -j option and use **.bz2** as the filename suffix:

```
# tar -cjf archive.tar.bz2 /foo
```

The result will be a **bzip2**-compressed file named **archive.tar.bz2** in the current directory.

To create the same archive with **xz** compression, you simply insert a **-J** option and use **.xz** as the filename suffix:

```
# tar -cJf archive.tar.xz /foo
```

The result will be an xz-compressed file named archive.tar.xz in the current directory.

The following is an example of listing all three of these archive files:

```
tar -tzf archive.tar.gz
tar -tjf archive.tar.bz2
tar -tJf archive.tar.xz
```

Keep in mind that the appropriate archive option character *must* be paired up with the corresponding compressed archive file, or it will fail.

The output of the listing is affected by the use of the **v** option:

```
-rw-r--r--rossb/rossb 34 2019-03-22 08:34
compressfiles/ld.so.conf
-rw-r--r--rossb/rossb 552 2019-03-22 08:34
compressfiles/pam.conf
-rw-r--r-- rossb/rossb 14867 2019-03-22 08:34
compressfiles/ltrace.conf
```

Without the **v** option, you would simply see a listing of the filenames, not the longer listing just shown:

```
compressfiles/ldso.conf
compressfiles/pam.conf
compressfiles/ltrace.conf
```

Using tar with Compression Utilities

You will likely see questions on the Linux+ exam that test your knowledge of which compression command has the highest compression. In my testing, the order of highest compression to lowest compression effectiveness is

- Highest = **xz**
- Medium = **bzip2**
- Lowest = **gzip**

Another command, **zip**, is an interesting utility, in that it was developed on Unix but was most used on the PC platform. The **zip** command is accompanied by the **unzip** command, similar to the other compression command pairings. While this is a fine utility set, it's not as commonly used as the three sets previously mentioned.

You are most likely to use **zip** and **unzip** on Linux when you receive an archive file in that format and you need to unarchive the file's contents.

zip and **unzip** work slightly differently than the other three commands mentioned previously, in that **zip** doesn't automatically replace a file with a compressed version of itself, like the other three do; it works more like a combination of **tar** and a compression utility.

NOTE   If you grew up using **pkzip** and **pkunzip** or **winzip**, you'll immediately recognize how **zip** and **unzip** work. The **tar** and **gzip/bzip2/xz** utilities may seem strange to you.

Let's look at how to create a compressed archive with **zip**. To zip up a set of files in a directory, such as the current one, you use this command:

```
# zip somefile.zip file1 file2 file3
```

Or you could zip up all the files in the directory with this command:

```
# zip somefile.zip *
```

This command zips up everything in the current directory, including subdirectories, but very importantly, it does not include the files in those subdirectories unless you specify the **-r** (recursive) option.

Say that you have the following directory and file tree:

```
 file1
 file2
 subdir1
  file3
  file4
1 directory, 4 files
```

Running **zip** does not, as you might think it would, get the contents of the **subdir1** directory. Instead, it produces a zip file that has **file1**, **file2**, and **subdir1** in it:

```
# zip somefilenor.zip *
 adding: file1 (stored 0%)
 adding: file2 (stored 0%)
 adding: subdir1/ (stored 0%)
```

To properly zip up the current directory and all its subdirectories and their files, you would run

```
$ zip -r somefilewithr.zip *
 adding: file1 (stored 0%)
 adding: file2 (stored 0%)
 adding: somefilenor.zip (stored 0%)
 adding: subdir1/ (stored 0%)
 adding: subdir1/file3 (stored 0%)
 adding: subdir1/file4 (stored 0%)
```

Before you unzip a zip archive, it's considered elegant and reasonable to list the archive contents, since you probably don't want 3,000 loose files in the current directory. Listing the contents of a zip archive is easy:

```
# unzip -l somefile.zip
Archive:   somefilewithr.zip
Length      Date          Time       Name
---------   ----------    -----      ----
   20       2019-07-11    12:16      file1
   26       2019-07-11    12:18      file2
  488       2019-07-18    11:41      somefilen.zip
    0       2019-07-18    11:37      subdir1/
   20       2019-07-18    11:34      subdir1/file3
   26       2019-07-18    11:34      subdir1/file4
---------                           -------
  580                               6 files
```

Notice that the files are listed according to whether they are at the root of the archive file or in a subdirectory, which is the case with **file3** and **file4**. The **-l** option does not unarchive the zip file; it simply iterates through the contents of the file.

Performing an unzip on a zipped file is pretty simple:

```
# unzip somefile.zip
Archive: somefilewithr.zip
replace file1? [y]es, [n]o, [A]ll, [N]one, [r]ename:
```

This message is asking if you want to overwrite an existing set of files that match some or all of the contents of the zip archive. If you were to answer with the A character for "overwrite all," this would be the result:

```
 extracting: file1
 extracting: file2
 extracting: somefilenor.zip
```

```
extracting: subdir1/file3
extracting: subdir1/file4
```

There are a number of other options available for the **zip/unzip** command pair, but you already know all you need to know for the Linux+ exam.

Taking Pity on the Unarchiver

It's considered proper and elegant to create **tar** archives by specifying a directory that contains the files to be archived, not just a bunch of files that are in the current directory. This means that when the files are untarred, they show up in a single directory instead of in the current directory.

For example, create an archive of the **/etc** directory contents with the following command:

```
# tar -cf etc.tar /etc
```

When you unarchive the **tar** file, by default it creates an **etc** directory in the current directory, which contains the entirety of the **/etc** directory you archived.

Contrast this with the nightmare that happens when you navigate to the **/etc** directory and create the archive from there with this command:

```
# tar -cf /root/badetc.tar *
```

This archive file contains the same files as the previous one, but they aren't contained in a top-level **etc** directory; rather, everything is in the top level of the archive. Imagine what would happen to your system if you were to unarchive this file in the root user's home directory. You will spew approximately 2,400 files directly into the root user's home directory!

It really does matter where you are in the filesystem and which path options you use when you create or expand an archive file. It's best practice to use absolute pathnames.

To solve the problem of 2,400 files polluting your root user's home directory, use the following command, where **badetc.tar** is the offending archive file:

```
# tar -tf badetc.tar | xargs rm -rf
```

This command produces a list of the paths and filenames of files in the archive and uses the **xargs** command to feed each line of output as a filename specification to the **rm -rf** command, removing all the files and directories expanded from the **badetc. tar** file.

Useful Creation Options

A number of options can be used for creating **tar** archives. Here is a list of the ones that are most useful and most likely to appear on the Linux+ exam:

- **-b:** Sets the block size to fit the media to which you are archiving. This is necessary for some tape devices.

- **-M:** Specifies multiple archive targets or spreads a large archive across multiple tapes or media.

- **-g:** Creates a new format incremental backup (only files that have changed since the last full or incremental backup).

- **-l:** Stays on the local filesystem; it's used to prevent backing up the entire NFS network by accident.

- **-L:** Sets the tape length so multiple tapes can be used for an archive. It is followed by a number that indicates the number of kilobytes, so, for example, **-L 500** equals 500KB.

- **--remove-files:** Removes the specified files from the filesystem after they have been added to the archive. This option is dangerous!

Listing Archive Files

Listing is underrated. It's something you're likely to do after you don't get the results you want or realize what you've just done and want to confirm how hard it is going to be to clean up.

You can learn the contents of a **tar** archive by using the following command:

```
# tar -tf archive.tar
```

This produces the following output:

```
etc/
etc/sysconfig/
etc/sysconfig/network-scripts/
etc/sysconfig/network-scripts/ifup-aliases
etc/sysconfig/network-scripts/ifcfg-lo
```

To list an archive that uses compression, simply insert the necessary letter between the **-t** and the **-f** options, such as the **bzip2 -j** option shown here:

```
# tar -tjf archive.tar.bz2
```

This produces the following output:

```
etc/
etc/sysconfig/
etc/sysconfig/network-scripts/
etc/sysconfig/network-scripts/ifup-aliases
etc/sysconfig/network-scripts/ifcfg-lo
```

To list an archive and see the file details for its contents, add the **-v** option to the existing command to see output listing the details:

```
# tar -tvjf archive.tar.bz2
```

This returns output similar to the following:

```
drwxr-xr-x root/root 0 2015-02-10 03:46 etc/
drwxr-xr-x root/root 0 2015-01-31 10:09 etc/sysconfig/
drwxr-xr-x root/root 0 2014-11-10 22:13 etc/sysconfig/
network-scripts/
```

When you create an archive with the **-v** option, a list of the files being archived is shown onscreen. When you unarchive an archive with the **-v** option, you see a similar list of the files being unarchived. It's only when you list an archive with the **-v** option that you get the type of output that approximates an **ls -l** command being run on the archive contents. This is a Linux+ exam topic, so be ready for it.

Using cpio

The **cpio** command doesn't appear much in the Linux+ exam objectives. The exam might ask you about the **cpio** command at only the simplest levels. For example, you need to know that the command exists, how it works in general terms, and whether it can be used to back up a Linux system.

All the **cpio** command actions treat the filesystem as the home base. If you are copying out, it's from the filesystem out to another file. The same is true with copying in: you copy in from a file into the filesystem.

The **cpio** command has three options for acting on files and filesystems:

- **-o or --create:** This copies files to an archive, using a list of files typically created by the **find** command.

- **-i or --extract:** This copies files into the filesystem from an archive or a list of the archive contents.

- **-p or --pass-through:** This copies files from one directory tree to another without the use of an archive, essentially performing the same function as the **cp -r** command.

The **cpio** command accepts a list of files in a one-file-per-line format and uses this list to send the archived files to either the standard output or an archive file you specify.

cpio supports a variety of archive formats, including binary, ASCII, crc, and **tar**.

The following example creates a **cpio** archive from the files in the current directory:

```
# find . "*" | cpio -o > archive.cpio
```

This command outputs the list of files found by this particular **find** command, and the **cpio** command sends all the files to the **archive.cpio** file by redirecting standard output to the file.

The **cpio** command doesn't accept a list of files to archive on the command line, as do the other utilities you've seen so far. Instead, it reads the names of the files from the standard input or console. So be aware that you need to use either the **find** command or the **ls** command to feed **cpio** a list of filenames.

For example, if you needed to archive all the files that have the extension **.txt** in the current directory to a **cpio** archive named **txt.cpio**, you would use the following command:

```
# ls *.txt | cpio -o > txt.cpio
```

Notice that this command redirects the output of **cpio** to a file rather than letting it write the file itself. Therefore, the filename is up to you, and if you want a **.cpio** file extension, you need to add it yourself.

Using the dd Command

The **dd** command is useful for a variety of tasks, not the least of which is creating backup images, called ISO files, of CDs or DVDs. The two main formats **dd** interacts with are the raw device file and the full path of a file or an object on the system.

For example, when creating a new boot disk, the **.img** binary file is read block by block from the optical disc (as a file) and written to a USB disk raw device as a set of blocks:

```
# dd if=/mnt/cdrom/images/boot.img of=/dev/sdb
```

Creating an image of an optical disc involves reading the raw USB device block by block and creating a file on the filesystem that contains all those blocks:

```
# dd if=/dev/sdb of=/root/usb.img
```

To duplicate a USB device named sdb to another USB device named sdc, the command is

```
# dd if=/dev/sdc of=/dev/sdc
```

The **if** keyword means to input file, and the **of** keyword means to output file. The exact order is unimportant, but as you can imagine, mixing up the in and out files can cause terrible problems such as overwriting parts of your hard drive!

dd, unlike most other Unix utilities, does not use dashes for its options. Options are specified in the format *option=value*.

The **dd** command is also often used to duplicate a drive or a partition of a drive to another object. For example, to copy the first partition from the **/dev/sda** disk to the same location on the second hard drive on the system, you use the following command:

```
# dd if=/dev/sda1 of=/dev/sdb1
```

You can also copy an entire disk device to another device on the system by leaving off the partition numbers:

```
# dd if=/dev/sda of=/dev/sdb
```

This works only if the second device is as large as or larger than the first; otherwise, you get truncated and worthless partitions on the second one.

Backing up the MBR is another trick that **dd** does well. Remember that the MBR contains the indexes of all the partitions on that drive, and thus it is very important. To create a disk file that contains only the first 512 bytes of the first hard drive in the system, use this command:

```
# dd if=/dev/sda of=/root/MBR.img count=1 bs=512
```

The **count** keyword sets the number of reads from the input file you want to retrieve, and the **bs** keyword sets the block size.

If you don't set the count and block size on this command to back up the MBR, you'll be copying the entire device's blocks to the filesystem—a snake-eating-its-own-tail operation that is guaranteed to fill up the partition quickly and crash the system.

The restoration procedure is just the opposite:

```
# dd if=/root/MBR.img of=/dev/sda count=1 bs=512
```

Compression Tools

Whereas the **tar** command is used to gather files and put them in a container, the **gzip**, **bzip2**, and **xz** commands are used to compress that container. Used by themselves, they act on each file they find and replace that file with a compressed version that has an extension indicating that the file is compressed.

The **gzip** and **bzip2** compression utilities compress files and are similar in their functions and operations. The main difference is that **bzip2** offers slightly better compression than **gzip**, but **gzip** is much more widely used. The **xz** utility offers better compression than either of the other two and is enjoying a growing user base.

These commands replace the original file with a new file that has an additional extension, so don't delete the **.gz** or **.bz2** files that you create. They are the original files in a compressed wrapper!

To compress all the files in the current directory with **gzip**, use this command:

```
# gzip *
```

This replaces all the regular files (not the directories or their contents) in the current directory with the original filenames plus a **.gz** extension. So, if you had two files named **file1** and **file2** in the directory, they would be replaced with

```
file1.gz
file2.gz
```

To uncompress these files, just do the opposite of the compression:

```
# gunzip *
```

This restores the original files.

Using **bzip2** produces the same sort of results. You can issue the following command in the same directory:

```
# bzip2 *
```

You would then have the following two files:

```
file1.bz2
file2.bz2
```

To uncompress these files, issue this command:

```
# bunzip2 *
```

This restores the files to their original states.

xz is a newer option for compressing files than **bzip2** and **gzip**. In some cases it has better performance than **bzip2**, but at a cost of more memory. Files are compressed with **xz, xz -z**, or **xz --compress** and decompressed with **unxz, xz -d, xz --uncompress**, or **xz --decompress**.

The **.xz** file extension indicates that a file was compressed with **xz**. To uncompress **foo.xz**, for example, you would run **xz -d foo.xz** and would be left with an uncompressed file called **foo**.

Watch for Linux+ exam questions that ask about why you would use either **gzip**, **bzip2**, or **xz** for a particular compression task.

Backing Up Is Hard to Do

If there's anything that is more important than a good backup, it's a successful restore! Backups are useless without the ability to restore the data properly and in a timely manner.

> **NOTE** For the sake of simplicity, this section discusses backups in a manner that is detached from the actual media (disk, tape, DVDs, and so on).

There are many considerations for backup scenarios. The following sections lay out the different methods and discuss why you would use them—either singularly or with each other.

Backup Types

There are three basic types of backups:

- **Full backup:** This is the most basic method of backup, in which the operator initiates a full copy of the dataset to a backup location. An advantage is that a single-step restore is possible because all the data is there. Disadvantages are long backup times and an ever-growing amount of storage needed for the backups.

- ***Incremental* backup:** This type of backup is a real time-saver, as it backs up *only* new data since the last backup operation, whatever type it was. Advantages are a quick backup time, compared to a full backup, and the most efficient use of space, since it only includes data since the last operation. Disadvantages include an increasing number of valid backups to do a successful restore, and if one fails, you lose all that data from the restore.

- ***Differential* backup:** This method strikes a balance between a full backup and an incremental backup in that it includes all data from the last full backup. The advantage is that you need only two backups to do a restore at any point: the last full backup and the last differential backup (which includes all data changed since the last full backup). The disadvantage is that the backups take an increasing amount of space because the time between the current date and the last full backup increases.

Other Backup Types

There are a couple of other types of backups to mention: snapshot clones and images.

The Linux+ exam objectives used to say "snapshot clones," but VMware and other vendors use the terms *snapshots* and *clones* separately.

A snapshot is used primarily with a virtual machine (VM), where the initial state of the VM is the baseline. A snapshot is essentially an incremental backup of what's changed with the VM since the last snapshot.

For example, if you have a VM that you set up for software testing or experimentation and you don't want to go through the whole setup routine again, you can snapshot it, or create a backup of the current state of the VM, and then you will be able to restore to that point at any time in the future.

Another great use of a snapshot, or series of snapshots, is when you are testing lab steps and want to be able to quickly take the machine back to or up to any level of changes.

A clone, on the other hand, is essentially a full backup of a VM. It can be used to test new software, OS updates, and so on—on what is effectively the production VM.

A clone is heavy because it is really another VM like the original, except for the name, IP address, and other identifying information.

Benefits of snapshots are that you can start off with a clean setup, do a snapshot, do almost anything to the VM, revert to the clean setup with a couple of mouse clicks or commands, and start the process again.

An image is effectively a clone that occupies a single file, and the software that manages the image backup can do a number of things with it, including restore to dissimilar hardware, pull individual files and sets of files out of the image and restore to another device, and a lot more.

Another use of image backups is to build a VM, with all the software and services it needs to immediately perform a given service or function and then deploy it across a network, in virtualization environments such as Docker, Kubernetes, and so on.

Copying Objects Between Systems

Whereas the **cp** command is used to copy files to different locations on the same filesystem or between filesystems on the same machine, the **scp** command is used to copy files between computers.

Using the scp Command

The **scp** command, which is part of the Secure Shell (SSH) suite of protocols and utilities, authenticates between the source and target systems in the same way as **ssh**, using the public/private key mechanisms.

Copying a file from **systema** to **systemb** using **scp** has a couple more components to the command line than a standard **cp** command from one directory to another on the same machine. To copy the file **foobar.txt** from **systema** to **systemb**, for example, you need to specify which user you want to be on the remote system; otherwise, it will use the default username on the source system.

For example, in the following command, say that you are root on **systema** but want to copy **foobar.txt** to the **ross** home directory on **systemb**:

```
# scp foobar.txt ross@systemb:~
ross@systema's password:
foobar.txt 100% |**********************| 1379 00:00
```

Following password entry and any other prompts, the file is copied to the remote system and placed in the **/home/ross** directory.

Another fun feature of the **scp** command is the ability to copy from another system to yours, just by reversing the order of the command. For example, this is how you copy the file **tarfoo.txt** to the **ross** home directory on **systema** from **systemb**'s root user home directory:

```
# scp root@systemb:~/tarfoo.txt ross@systema:~
root@systema's password:
tarfoot.txt 100% |**********************| 1379 00:00
```

The **scp** command also has a useful ability to copy from **systemb** to **systemc** from the user's vantage point on **systema**. Linux simply uses the tunneling aspect of the SSH protocol and creates a tunnel for the command to work from **systemb** to **systemc**; it's just as if you were on **systemb** copying the file to **systemc**, only you are really on **systema**:

```
# scp root@systemb:~/blahwoof.txt ross@systemc:~
root@systemc's password:
blahwoof.txt 100% |**********************| 1379 00:00
```

NOTE   The **scp** command is very versatile, and while this section has introduced you to its main tricks and capabilities, there is much more to explore and learn by reading the man pages for **scp** and **ssh**.

Everything and the Kitchen rsync

While we are on the topic of copying objects around systems and even between systems, it's important to include a discussion of the **rsync** command.

The **rsync** command is an extremely powerful command that we can't begin to cover fully, but let's look at it and see what it's most known for and probably most used for.

rsync is similar to the **copy** command in that you can use **rsync** to copy a file from one place to another, one file to another, and even one directory tree to another—all functions that the **copy** command can do.

So what exactly are the real reasons to use the **rsync** command? It is useful for its speed of operation, efficiency in just copying what's changed, and its ability to be used inside SSH for better security.

A main aspect of the **rsync** command that makes it so useful is that **rsync** can make a copy of a set of files and directories, and it can also be used to copy just the changes between files, directories, and trees of files and directories. This makes **rsync** much faster and more efficient than a traditional **copy** command, as it can just copy over and update the changes to files and directories.

To make a mirror of a directory and all its descendants, use the following command:

```
# rsync -ar ./somedir /data/someotherdir
datafile1
datafile2
datafile3
<output truncated>
```

This makes an exact mirror copy of every file and directory from the source (**somedir**) to the target (**/data/someotherdir**), including all contents, ownership, file permissions, and timestamps for the files, as mentioned.

A major feature of **rsync** is its capability to perform copying and mirroring functions across systems. It can be used in a similar fashion to the **scp** command:

```
# rsync -avzh /home/ross/datafiles ross@192.168.10.20:~
datafile1
datafile2
datafile3
<output truncated>
```

This command opens a connection to the remote system and transfers the directory **/home/ross/datafiles** to the remote machine and makes or updates the **/home/ross/datafiles** directory on that system.

Another key feature of **rsync** is the capability to conduct all of its otherwise normal operations over the SSH protocol, such as this copy of a directory tree from the local system to a remote system:

```
# rsync -avzh datafiles -e 'ssh -p 22' ross@192.168.10.20:~
datafile1
datafile2
datafile3
<output truncated>
```

Not all your operations with **rsync** will be quick. Some will likely contain many megabytes or, more likely, multiple gigabytes of data. A very useful option for determining the operation's progress is the **--progress** option, and you can add the **--delete** option as well so that you can be certain that the target directory will be a mirror of the source:

```
# rsync -avzh test --progress --delete ross@10.0.0.41:~
Password:
deleting test/etc2/xrdb/Xaw.ad
deleting test/etc2/xrdb/Tk.ad
deleting test/etc2/xrdb/Motif.ad
deleting test/etc2/xrdb/General.ad
deleting test/etc2/xrdb/Emacs.ad
deleting test/etc2/xrdb/Editres.ad
deleting test/etc2/xrdb/
deleting test/etc/mailcap.order
deleting test/etc/magic.mime

sent 97.42K bytes  received 124.60K bytes   63.43K bytes/sec
total size is 6.57M  speedup is 29.60
```

As you can see, this command has done what you wanted: removed various files and directories that don't exist on the source and given some statistics about the transfer to the remote system, including the amount of data sent and received in the transfer and the total data size transferred.

In short, **rsync** is a very useful command and a key part of any awesome sysadmin's kit of tools. It's a lot like a merging of the **copy** command and **scp**, with a few other great options.

The nc Command

The man page of the nc command (also referred to as the netcat command) provides an excellent summary of the nc command:

> The nc (or netcat) utility is used for just about anything under the sun involving TCP or UDP. It can open TCP connections, send UDP packets, listen on arbitrary TCP and UDP ports, do port scanning, and deal with both IPv4 and IPv6. Unlike telnet(1), nc scripts nicely and separates error messages onto standard error instead of sending them to standard output, as telnet(1) does with some.

There are quite a few uses for the nc command. For example, suppose you want to know whether a specific port is being blocked by your company firewall before you bring online a service that makes use of this port. On the internal server, you can have the nc command listen for connections on that port:

```
# nc -l 3333
```

You should end up with a blank line below the nc command. Next, on a remote system outside your network, you could run the following nc command to connect (replacing server with the resolvable hostname or IP address of the local system):

```
# nc server 3333
```

If the connection is established, you see a blank line under the nc command line. If you type something on this blank line and press the Enter key, then what you typed appears below the nc command on the server. Actually, the communications works both ways: What you type on the server below the nc command appears on the client as well.

The following are some useful options to the nc command:

- **-w**: This option is used on the client side to close a connection automatically after a timeout value is reached. For example, nc -w 30 server 333 closes the connection 30 seconds after it is established.

- **-6**: Use this option to enable IPv6 connections.

- **-k**: Use this option to keep the server process active, even after the client disconnects. The default behavior is to stop the server process when the client disconnects.

- **-u**: Use this option to use UDP connections rather than TCP connections (the default). This is important for correctly testing firewall configurations as a TCP port might be blocked, while the UDP port might not be blocked.

You can also use the nc command to display open ports, similar to the way you use the netstat command:

```
# nc -z localhost 1000-4000

Connection to localhost 3260 port [tcp/iscsi-target] succeeded!
Connection to localhost 3333 port [tcp/dec-notes] succeeded!
```

The -z option can also be used for port scanning on a remote host.

NOTE   There is one feature of the nc command that I don't expect you will see on the exam; however, it is a useful technique for transferring all sorts of data. Assuming that the transfer is from the client to the server, on the server, you use the following format:

```
# nc -l 3333 | cmd
```

And on the client, you use this format:

```
# cmd | nc server 3333
```

For example, you can transfer an entire /home directory structure from the client to the server by using the tar command by first executing the following on the server:

```
# nc -l 333 | tar xvf -
```

Then on the client, you execute the following command:

```
# tar cvf - /home | nc server 333
```

The client merges the contents of the /home directory structure into a tar ball. The "-" sign tells the tar command to send this output to standard output. The data is sent to the server via the client's nc command, and then the server's nc command sends this data to the tar command. As a result, the /home directory from the client is copied into the current directory of the server.

This is just one technique of many for using this powerful feature of the nc command.

File Editing

Editing files in a Linux environment is a very important skill, as almost everything on a Linux system is a file, and nearly, if not all configuration files are text-based.

Linux server systems, rather they are physical or virtual machines, are typically text-based, with the GUI (Graphical User Interface) not even installed, or not typically running.

Because you're typically working on a text-based system, on text files, a working knowledge of the default text editor is critical to your success when setting up, configuring, or administering those Linux systems.

Let's begin with the most common editor, **vim**.

One of the most confusing things about **vim** is the presence of modes, or states, in the editor. It has three modes:

- Command

- Insert

- LastLine, also called "ex" mode

Each of these modes is used for different purposes. *Command mode* is used for moving the cursor around and doing operations on text. *Insert mode* is used to add text to your document. *LastLine mode* is used to invoke more complicated modes, such as search and replace, or to manipulate split window panes.

The Message Line

The bottom of the **vim** screen contains a number of pieces of information that can help you, varying to suit the situation and actions just completed. This section details some of the messages that can appear.

If you've just entered **vim file1**, when the editor opens the file, the message line should contain something similar to the following:

```
"/home/rbrunson/file1" 57L, 1756C 18,1 Top
```

The numbers 18,1 on the right side of the message line are the current line and column numbers, and the Top text is the current position of the cursor. This changes to Bot if you entered the last half of the file. The other value possible is All, which simply means that all the contents of the file are currently on the screen.

A new file (one invoked with **vim file1**) would show the line

```
"file1" [New File] 0,0 All
```

If you are in Insert mode, the message line shows

```
-- INSERT -
```

Editing in vim

vim always starts in Command mode, unless you specify differently. True editing (where you type a character, and that character appears on the screen) takes place in Insert mode.

The keys you commonly use to invoke Insert mode from Command mode are

- **i:** The most common method of moving into Insert mode is to press the **i** key, which leaves the cursor at the current position. All typing from that point pushes existing text to the right. Think of this as "insert here."

- **I:** The uppercase **I** key moves to the beginning of the current line and from there acts like the **i** key. Think of this as "Insert at the beginning of the line."

- **a:** The second-most-common method is to press the **a** key, which moves the cursor one character to the right and essentially behaves like an **i** key after that. Think of this as "append after current position."

- **A:** The uppercase **A** moves to the end of the current line and from there acts like an **a** key. Think of this as "Append to the end of the line."

- **o:** Use this key to open a new line under the present line. For example, if you're on line 3 in Command mode, pressing **o** drops line 4 down to become 5 and opens a new line 4 that's empty. Think of it as "Open a new line below."

- **O:** The uppercase **O** opens a new line at the current line. For example, if you're on line 3, pressing **O** drops line 3 down to become line 4 and opens a new empty line 3 for editing. Think of it as "Open a new line above."

Getting back to Command mode is easy: Press the **Esc** key at least once; many people double-press it just to make sure they're really there. At any time, you can return to Command mode from Insert mode by pressing the **Esc** key.

Opening a File for Editing

To create a new file in the current subdirectory, you type **vi** *filename*.

To create a new file in a particular directory, use the full path: vi */full/path/to/file*.

Sometimes you will want **vim** to open a file with a search string and put the cursor on the first found instance of that string. To accomplish this, enter **vi +/string filename**.

Other times, you'll want to edit a file and have the cursor jump to a particular line when the file is opened, such as the **initdefault** line in **/etc/inittab**. In this case, you would enter **vi +18 /etc/inittab**.

> **NOTE**   Expect Linux+ exam questions about opening files with particular options, searching a file upon opening it, and starting the **vim** editor in other ways. The **+** command-line option tells **vim** to run that particular command once the file is open.

Navigating Within a File

The **vim** editor allows you to use the following keystrokes to move left, right, up, and down, but if you have cursor keys, you can use them, too:

- **h:** This functions as the **Left Arrow** key; it's easy to remember because it's the leftmost key in the four-key set.

- **j:** Use this for the **Down Arrow** key.

- **k:** Use this for the **Up Arrow** key.

- **l:** Use this for the **Right Arrow** key.

Figure 2-4 illustrates how these keys work.

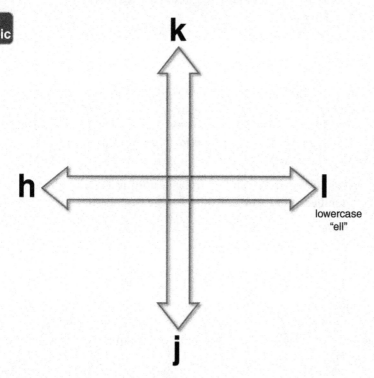

Figure 2-4 Cursor key directions

As you can see in Figure 2-4, one of the ways to remember the keyboard cursor keys is to just look down at the home row and remember that **h** is the leftmost, **j** goes jown (down), **k** goes kup (up), and **l** is on the right. Makes perfect sense, right?

NOTE You'll see questions on the Linux+ exam about the movement keys. The arrow keys are a favorite topic, whereas the **Ctrl** keys don't get much love. Know those arrow (**h, j, k, l**) movement keys!

You can also move around in **vim** by using Ctrl key combinations:

- **Ctrl+F:** Moves forward a page.

- **Ctrl+B:** Moves backward a page.

- **Ctrl+D:** Moves forward a half-page.

- **Ctrl+U:** Moves backward a half-page.

- **G:** Moves to a particular line, such as **12G** to go to line 12. Without a number, **G** takes you to the end of the file.

Force Multipliers

The concept of force multiplication comes from the military world and it's where you use technology or hardware to increase the amount of force or effect a given action has. Being able to rapidly get more troops to the scene of a battle and overcome the opposition by using helicopters is a *force multiplier*, as is using certain types of munitions that produce a larger than normal effect.

I use this to describe the ability to have vim help you by performing nearly any keystroke or action a given number of times by prefixing it with a number.

For example, from Command mode, to move down 5 lines, you would type **5j**. Moving 12 words to the right is accomplished with **12W**.

A lot of editing, inserting, and escaping back can sometimes leave the message line without some pertinent information showing, such as the name of the file being edited. When you get confused about where you are or under which filename you saved a particular iteration of a file, you can press Ctrl+G while in Command mode to see the filename, total number of lines, and current position expressed as a percentage of the total lines in the file.

Undo Operations

The undo operations are a useful and largely unknown set of options. You press **u** in Command mode to undo a single operation or the latest in a series of changes. If you opened a file, made 30 changes, and then pressed the **u** key 30 times, you would end up with exactly the same file you originally opened.

Don't bother trying to use **U** to undo all changes; that's not what it's for. **U** undoes all the changes on a single line. Instead, use the **:e!** keystroke combination to undo all changes since the last disk write to the file. The **:** takes you to LastLine mode, and the **e!** command reloads the current file, discarding all unsaved changes.

Saving Files

The most straightforward way to save a file in **vim** is to enter **:w** in Command mode. This saves the file and allows you to continue to edit it. To remember the **w**, think of "write."

Quitting **vim**

When you've made changes to a document, **vim** doesn't let you quit normally, such as with **:q**. One of the most frustrating situations every **vim** user faces is the dreaded "E37: no write since last change (add ! to override)" message. This error can be fixed only by using the correct additional **!** character. To exit a file that is read-only or that you don't want to save the changes to, you must use the keystrokes **:q!**. This is known as *qbang*, or "quit dammit."

> **NOTE** If I had a dollar for each time a student got stuck in **vim** and had to use the **:q!** option to get out of the session, I would be very rich.

Saving and quitting a given file is simple, too. In Command mode you enter **:wq**. Think of "write, quit" to remember this command. If you are editing a file, such as a configuration file, as the root user, this file might lack the write permission, which means the **:wq** command would fail. Entering **:wq!** forces the file to be written, as long as the only barrier is a missing write permission.

Two additional methods of saving and quitting a file are available. The first is to enter **:x** to save and exit. The second is to press **ZZ** (hold down the Shift key and press the **Z** key twice); this is my personal favorite and is easy to remember. Because **:x** starts with a colon, the **x** is a LastLine command (as is **wq**). **ZZ** is a Command mode command. The **x** LastLine command has the added benefit of not saving a file that's already been saved, which makes exiting much faster on large files.

> **NOTE** Read Linux+ exam questions carefully, especially when they ask about saving and/or exiting the **vim** editor. Many test takers have mentioned that the question's syntax is critical to getting it right. For example, the question "Which of the following saves and exits a file in **vi**?" is very different from the question "Which of the following can be used to save or exit a file in **vi**?"

Changing or Replacing Text

A number of options are incredibly useful when you're altering an existing file and need to change a character, a line, a sentence, or just a word. For example, the **c** command changes text, and you can add additional modifiers after the command to indicate to **vim** how much text to change. Use the following options to change or replace text:

- **cw:** Changes a single word from the current cursor position. To change a whole word, you put the cursor on the first character of the word.

- **c$:** Changes from the current cursor position to the end of the line, even if that line is wrapped to appear as another line on the screen.

- **r:** Replaces the character under the cursor.

- **R:** Replaces text on the same line as you type until you press **Esc**, but it doesn't change text on the next line.

> **NOTE**   Remember to use the force multipliers in the appropriate places. You can easily change multiple words by using **5cw**, or you can replace ten characters with **10r**. Some commands don't accept the force multipliers, such as **R**, and some behave differently than you might expect. For example, **10O** accepts text and then repeats it nine more times.

Deleting Text and Lines

You can use **vim** to remove or delete characters, words, or even lines. Be careful to check your deletions and changes. Also keep in mind that you can press the **u** key to get things back to normal and try it again. These options are available for deleting text and lines in **vim**:

- **x:** Deletes a single character under the cursor.

- **X:** Deletes a single character before the cursor.

- **dw:** Deletes a single word that's currently under the cursor, from the cursor position onward.

- **dd:** Deletes the current line entirely, regardless of the cursor position in the line.

- **D:** Deletes all text from the current cursor position to the end of the line.

- **dL:** Deletes all text from the cursor to the end of the screen.

- **dG:** Deletes all text from the cursor to the end of the file.
- **d^:** Deletes all text from the beginning of the line to the cursor.

NOTE When you delete in **vim**, **vim** stores the cut or deleted string of text in the unnamed buffer for future use. This buffer's contents will be overwritten by any further cuts or deletions.

NOTE For the Linux+ exam, it is important to know how to delete. If asked to delete from the current position to the end of the line, don't pick or type the keys that delete the whole line; there are no partial credits on the exam!

Searching in vim

To search for text in Linux utilities, you typically need to follow a common convention. With the **less**, **more**, and **vim** commands, a forward slash followed by a search term searches forward in the file from the current cursor position or the top of the file, highlighting found strings. Initiating a backward search from the cursor position is done with a question mark followed by the string to search for, such as **?*sometext*.**

NOTE Searches are performed only in Command mode, so remember to press the **Esc** key to get back to Command mode before searching.

Finding the next occurrence (whether a forward or backward search) is usually accomplished by pressing the unshifted **n** key to search in the same direction as the original search. You press **Shift+N** for a search in the opposite direction of the original search.

Searching and Replacing

When you want to search a document for a given string or character to replace it, you commonly use either **vim** while editing a given file or the **sed** command on a large set of data. **vim** and the **sed** command share a common search-and-replace syntax, with small differences that won't confuse you if you use both. Indeed, learning to search and replace in one will equip you to use it in the other.

The search-and-replace syntax is as follows:

```
action/tofind/replacewith/modifier
```

For example, the following string in **vim** replaces just the first instance of the string **bob** in the current line with the string **BOB**:

```
:s/bob/BOB/
```

To replace all instances of the string **bob** with **BOB** in the current line, you would use this line:

```
:s/bob/BOB/g
```

The **g** stands for *global*, or doing the action on every found instance of the string.

To replace all instances of **bob** with **BOB** in the entire file, no matter how many exist or how many changes are made to each line, you would use this:

```
:%s/bob/BOB/g
```

> **NOTE** It's critical that you read a multiple-choice Linux+ exam question and all its answers to see exactly what is being asked for. A percent symbol (%) in front of the search-and-replace string causes **vim** to search the entire file rather than just the current line.

nano, nano

In the past 20 or so years, we have seen a sea change from the use of more powerful editors like **vim** and **EMACS** to ones like **nano**. **nano** is quick and easy to use, gives you onscreen clues about what keystrokes are available, and edits files quite nicely.

As a bit of historical perspective, computers used to have very limited RAM and disk space, so it was essential not to load them up with extra packages when very usable packages already existed on the system by default.

Many times I have rolled up to someone else's computer—whether a desktop, a server, or remotely—and edited a file in **vi** or **vim**, without a thought about any other editors. The only places I haven't been able to use **vi/vim** were on a couple of network edge systems that were embedded OS versions. This shows you how consistently **vi/vim** is deployed and available.

Why nano and Not Pico?

nano is almost an exact clone of the Pico editor, which has existed for a long time. Pico, a non-free software-licensed program that has existed for many years on Unix and Linux, was originally a part of the Pine email program. (It was the editing part, which makes sense.)

For many reasons, Linux distribution maintainers did not want to include the Pico editor with all the other programs in a Linux distribution. Mixing free licensed software and non-free licensed software is problematic and inelegant and will generally get you frowned upon in the world of Linux and open source.

Chris Allegretta created **nano** in an attempt to make a virtual clone of Pico that was easily distributable under appropriate free software licensing. However, it has grown to include a number of features that have taken it far beyond Pico's capabilities, earning it respect in its own right.

nano's Interface

Unlike **vi/vim**, which has a very sparse interface, **nano** gives you some onscreen clues about useful keystrokes. Instead of requiring you to use action keys and Last-Line commands such as **:wq**, **nano** allows you to use the **Ctrl** key with another key. Figure 2-5 illustrates the user interface with the **nano** command invoked.

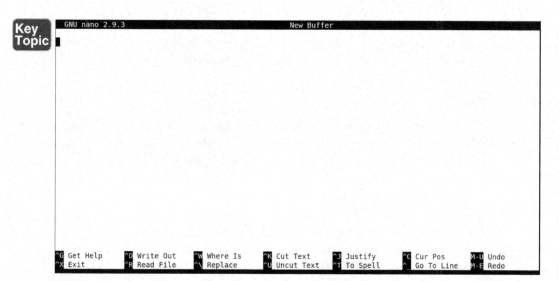

Figure 2-5 The **nano** command interface, showing the **Ctrl**-key editing and formatting options onscreen

As you can see, the last two lines of the **nano** interface are devoted to 14 useful commands and provide hints about what to press. The ^ character denotes the **Ctrl** key, and it is followed by the character you would then press while holding down the **Ctrl** key, such as **Ctrl+X** to exit the file or buffer if there is no file you are editing (at which point you are prompted to save or discard anything done in your nano session).

The interface is a little misleading in that the characters that follow the ^ character in the interface are uppercase letters. However, you do not have to use **Ctrl-Shift-X** to exit the editor; **Ctrl-Shift-x** also does the trick. Uppercase letters likely are used for readability purposes, but their use is notable because the rest of Linux and command-line interactions are very specific about uppercase/lowercase distinctions.

In addition to the **Ctrl** key combinations, you can use the Meta key, which is mapped variously but is universally accessible by pressing the **Esc** key plus the keystroke character indicated. For example, after entering some text, you could tap the **Esc** key and then press the **U** key to invoke the Undo function, and then tap **Esc** again and press the **E** key to restore what you just undid.

> **NOTE**   nano allows for the use of **Esc** as the Meta (M) key, but it also might—depending on your computer's OS, how it's configured by the user, and other factors—allow you to use the **Windows** key on the keyboard of a PC or the **Cmd** or **Apple** key on a Mac system.

You can also use the mouse to select, cut, copy, and paste text inside nano, even on a non-GUI session, if the mouse is recognized by the text terminal you are operating in.

That's a Wrap

nano is a little more self-explanatory than **vi/vim** is, but if you want to know more, see the help documentation, accessible by pressing **Ctrl+G** and using the navigation keys to find out all about **nano**'s features and key combinations.

Feeling a Bit (awk)ward

The **awk** command, whose name comes from the three originators of the command (Aho, Weinberger, and Kernigan) is another amazingly useful and somewhat terrifyingly powerful text processing command.

The design goals of **awk** are to allow you to process text files to select some lines of text and drop the rest, find bits of text and act on them (leaving the rest untouched), perform data validation, and generate meaningful reports from large amounts of text.

Much of **awk**'s functionality is well beyond the scope of the Linux+ exam and objectives, but a few useful examples will serve to drive home the usefulness and functionality of **awk** for nearly all system administrators.

At its very simplest, an awk command uses this syntax:

```
awk pattern { action }
```

Another way to look at the awk command line structure is:

```
awk options program file
```

The **grep** and awk commands can be used almost identically in a simple search. For example, both of the following commands find and print or display to stdout the lines the search string is on:

```
# grep vagrant README.md
```'vagrant up'''
```'vagrant halt'''


# awk /vagrant/ README.md
```'vagrant up'''
```'vagrant halt'''
```

Another (sort of) easy-to-understand example would be to use **awk** to reorder the fields in the **/etc/passwd** file, such as:

```
# awk -F: `{print $1"\t""ID #"$3"\t""In the role of""\t"$5}' /etc/
passwd
```

The output might look like this:

```
gnats ID #41 In the role of Gnats Bug-Reporting System (admin)
nobody ID #6553 In the role of nobody
kernoops ID #106 In the role of Kernel Oops
Tracking Daemon,,,
lightdm ID #110 In the role of Light Display Manager
speech ID #117 In the role of Speech Dispatcher,,,
ross ID #900 In the role of Ross,,,
```

Here, the **/etc/passwd** file is a colon-delimited file, so you use **-F:** to tell **awk** that the fields are separated by that character. Then you rearrange the file columns in between the curly brackets ({}) by using the **print** statement.

Here is what each element of the preceding example does:

- **awk:** This is, obviously, the command.

- **-F:** This is the previously mentioned option that tells the awk command the field delimiter character—in this case the colon (:) character.

- **'{:** This starts the transformation section.

- print: This is the action taken; it prints everything that follows.

- **$1:** This is the first field of the /etc/passwd file, the username.

- **"\t":** This denotes an inserted tab between the $1 and the next element.

- **"D #":** This is a string of text.

- **$3:** This is the third field of the /etc/passwd file, the UID.

- **"\t":** This is another inserted tab between elements.

- **"In the role of":** This is another descriptive string of text.

- **$5:** This is the fifth field of the /etc/passwd file, the description.

- **}':** This ends the transformation section.

This is a relatively simple example of how you can use **awk** not just to transform a file but to use the file's fields and information to produce a report that is more informative than just a listing out of an **/etc/passwd** file.

The printf Function

The printf function is either provided by the built-in version in BASH or is a separate command that is installed on the system. You use printf for formatting output in a particular sequence or method.

The use of printf is rather complex, because this function has a large number of format specifiers or ways to show output from the command line. The following is a simple example of using printf to display a formatted line:

```
# printf("the %s rose over the %s, %d time a day",
"sun","horizon", 1);
```

This would print the following to the standard output:

```
the sun rose over the horizon 1 time a day
```

The printf built-in or external command has many options and is used extensively in outputting text from programs and scripts. The way printf is used varies slightly according to the programming language it's implemented through—Perl, Java, and so on.

Summary

In this chapter you learned about a large amount of file- and directory-related tasks that affect the daily operations of a system. You learned about files and directories, how to manage them, how to get more information about your system's files, and how to use commands like **file** and **stat** to get much more info of a useful nature and format it. You also learned about links, both hard and soft (symbolic), all about how files are compressed, how to use the **tar** command and how to backup data.

Additionally, you learned how to use the **scp** command and its options to send data between systems, and finally you learned how to edit files on Linux systems with my personal favorite editor, **vim**, as well as nano.

Exam Preparation Tasks

As mentioned in the section "Goals and Methods" in the Introduction, you have a couple of choices for exam preparation: the exercises here, Chapter 23, "Final Preparation," and the exam simulation questions in the Pearson Test Prep Software Online.

Review All Key Topics

Review the most important topics in this chapter, noted with the Key Topic icon in the left margin of the page. Table 2-2 lists these key topics and the page number on which each is found.

Table 2-2   Key Topics for Chapter 2

Key Topic Element	Description	Page Number
Section	Tips for Working with Linux Files	46
Section	Touching Files	50
Paragraph	The **tree** command (advanced navigation)	56
Section	Determining File Types	57
Section	The **stat** Command	58
Figure 2-1	Symbolic link detail	61
Figure 2-2	Hard link detail	62
Figure 2-3	Picturing the **tar** options	65
Paragraph	Creating an archive with **xz** compression	67
Section	Using **cpio**	72
List	Backup Types	76
Section	Everything and the Kitchen **rsync**	79
List	Keys used to invoke Insert mode in **vim**	84
Figure 2-4	Cursor key directions	85
Section	Quitting **vim**	87
Section	Searching and Replacing	89
Section	Why nano and Not Pico?	90
Figure 2-5	The **nano** command interface, showing the **Ctrl**-key editing and formatting options onscreen	91

Define Key Terms

Define the following key terms from this chapter and check your answers in the glossary:

absolute pathname, relative path, permissions, metadata, ownership, recursive, format sequence, symbolic link, hard link, archiving, tarball, compression, incremental, differential, Command mode, Insert mode, LastLine mode, force multiplier

Review Questions

The answers to these review questions are in Appendix A.

1. You are currently located in the directory **/etc/nginx/conf.d** and want to return to the home directory for your user in the fewest number of typed characters. Which of the following will accomplish this?

   a. **cd .**

   b. **cd ~**

   c. **cd**

   d. **cd $$**

2. Which of the following commands will consult a reference set of data types and report back information on each file it is used on?

   a. **stat**

   b. **ls -lT**

   c. **file**

   d. **info**

3. Which of the following is a characteristic that distinguishes a symbolic link from any other type?

   a. It has a different inode number.

   b. You can change its permissions easily.

   c. The linked file shares the same name.

   d. It cannot span across filesystems.

   e. Deleting one link has no effect on the other.

4. You find a backup file that has an extension of **.bz2**. Which of the following commands was this file likely created with?

   a. **tar -czvf**

   b. **tar -cyvf**

   c. **tar -cjvf**

   d. **tar -cbvf**

5. You are trying to copy a local directory and all of its contents to a remote system but are getting an error. What is the most likely option to include to the **scp** command to get the result you want?

   a. **-x**

   b. **-r**

   c. **-z**

   d. **-f**

6. You are using **vi** or the VIM text editor to write a technical article for your organization's website, and after typing a couple of lines of content, you want to save and exit the file. Which of the following keystrokes will accomplish saving and exiting the file? (Choose two.)

   a. **ESC**

   b. **:wq**

   c. **:F1**

   d. **:save**

   e. **ZZ**

This chapter covers the following topics:

- Determining Storage Hardware
- Performing Disk Partitioning
- Inspecting and Managing Software RAID
- Using Logical Volume Manager (LVM)
- Mounting Local and Remote Devices
- Monitoring Disk Space Usage
- Filesystem Management
- Storage Area Networks/Network-Attached Storage

The exam objective covered in this chapter is as follows:

- **Objective 1.3:** Given a scenario, configure and manage storage using the appropriate tools

## CHAPTER 3

Configuring and Managing Storage

Outside of the actual computing via the processor and availability from a network interface, storage is arguably the most important characteristic for any server-class Linux system.

The life of a storage device begins with it being attached to a system, either temporarily or permanently. A system operator will want to be able to use the available utilities to determine what the hardware is that is available and then take the steps to prepare that hardware to be available for use by users and the system for storing data.

In short, a system operator will take those steps, in the proper order, making the necessary decisions about the function, format, and local or remote availability, and then implement the storage so that it performs the desired function.

Storage management is a big part of a system operator's job. Users are constantly demanding more disk space because data is "magically and inexplicably" disappearing, mostly because of their own actions, and the need for consistent and persistent availability of shared and network-attached drives and data can cause system operators to dedicate a lot of time and energy to storage management.

The principles and practices in this chapter will help you immensely to make the right decisions and perform the appropriate actions to ensure that your storage devices appear where and how they are supposed to in support of your goals.

"Do I Know This Already?" Quiz

The "Do I Know This Already?" quiz enables you to assess whether you should read this entire chapter or simply jump to the "Exam Preparation Tasks" section for review. If you are in doubt, read the entire chapter. Table 3-1 outlines the major headings in this chapter and the corresponding "Do I Know This Already?" quiz questions. You can find the answers in Appendix A, "Answers to the 'Do I Know This Already?' Quizzes and Review Questions."

Table 3-1   "Do I Know This Already?" Foundation Topics Section-to-Question Mapping

Foundation Topics Section	Questions Covered in This Section
Determining Storage Hardware	8
Performing Disk Partitioning	1
Inspecting and Managing Software RAID	2
Using Logical Volume Manager (LVM)	3
Mounting Local and Remote Devices	4
Monitoring Storage Space and Disk Usage	5
Filesystem Management	6
Storage Area Networks/Network-Attached Storage	7

CAUTION   The goal of self-assessment is to gauge your mastery of the topics in this chapter. If you do not know the answer to a question or are only partially sure of the answer, you should mark that question as wrong for purposes of the self-assessment. Giving yourself credit for an answer you correctly guess skews your self-assessment results and might provide you with a false sense of security.

1. Which of the following is *not* a valid command for disk partitioning or disk information gathering?

     a. **partprobe**

     b. **diskinfo**

     c. **parted**

     d. **blkid**

     e. **fdisk**

2. To view your RAID configuration on your server, which of the following files would you display the contents of?

     a. **/etc/raid/info**

     b. **/sys/mdconf**

     c. **/proc/mdstat**

     d. **/media/redund**

3. Which command removes a PV from a VG?

     a. **vgremove**

     b. **pvremove**

    c. vgreduce

    d. pvreduce

4. You want to confirm that what you think is mounted on your system is correct, you have the output of the **mount** command. Which file does the mount command gather its information

    a. /etc/disks

    b. /dev/mnted

    c. /proc/mounts

    d. /sys/devbyid/sd

5. You want to verify the list of mounted filesystems on your server, including the space available in a friendly format, percentage used, and the type of filesystem on that device. Which of the following options to the **df** command will produce this output? (Choose two.)

    a. -h

    b. -s

    c. -T

    d. -f

6. You are looking at a script that uses the **e2fsck** utility, but want to run it on ext3 and ext4 filesystems. Which versions will this command work on?

    a. ext2

    b. ext3

    c. ext4

    d. All of these filesystem types

7. Which of the following characteristics helps define a storage area network?

    a. Ease of setup and administration

    b. Typically less expensive than local storage solutions

    c. Uses Ethernet, TCP/IP

    d. Requires special hardware

8. Which of the following commands would you use to display the storage devices on your system?

    a. lsdev

    b. lsstorage

    c. lspci

    d. lsscsi

Foundation Topics

In this chapter we'll cover the various ways that you can figure out what storage devices are attached or mounted to your systems, do the necessary tasks to prepare those devices for use, and then put a filesystem or advanced volume scheme (such as Logical Volume Management or LVM) on those devices.

We'll also cover how you can manage those filesystems, growing them as needed by adjusting the filesystems, as well as the volumes that underly them as appropriate, monitoring their utilization and the growth of your data and how it affects your storage needs.

Additionally, we will look at the concepts of RAID implementation; storage area networks and network-attached storage; and using SMB or CIFS (Samba) filesystems shared out for use by SMB clients.

I will take my usual liberties with the order of the subtopics in this exam objective so that they flow well and make sense.

Determining Storage Hardware

Before you can decide what you will be able to do with the hardware that you have, you need to determine what that hardware is! Often enough, you will find that the hardware you thought you had does not show up on your newly created Linux system, which is why you need to know how to query your Linux system using the array of information-gathering utilities that Linux provides.

Viewing SCSI Device Information

If you have just created a filesystem, it will likely be easy to remember which. Recall that Chapter 1, "Understanding Linux Fundamentals" introduced the **ls*** utilities, one of which is the **lsscsi** command, which you can use to determine which SCSI-related devices you may have on your system.

Using **lsscsi** is relatively easy; just run it as any user to view the devices that are currently recognized on the system:

```
# lsscsi
[0:0:0:0]    disk    QEMU    QEMU HARDDISK    2.5+    /dev/sda
```

The information **lsscsi** shows is arranged to give you everything you need to know about the storage item on one line. The line begins with four numbers that are separated by three colon characters and enclosed in brackets. The first number is the "host" number, the second is the "controller" number, the third is the "target" number, and the last number is the logical unit number (LUN), all of which are standard numerals or integers.

NOTE For NVMe devices, the numbers are slightly different, with the "N" taking over the "host" number position, aka the 1 in the name **/dev/nvme1**. The **lsscsi** man page has much more about this difference, but a lot of Linux systems translate this into the more normalized **/dev/sdX** format.

The **lsscsi** command puts several pieces of information from different sources, mainly the **/sys** and **/dev** directories, and you can tailor what information you get back as output by using some of the more common options, such as the following (long equivalents are in parentheses):

- **-b (--brief):** This option is designed to pack a lot of info into a single line, but may not contain enough details for your needs.

- **-l (--long):** This option gives you another line's worth of information, including any attributes and their values.

- **-L (--list):** This option displays the storage item's info in a block, with the normal **-b** output followed by a listing of attributes in an attribute=value per line format. You can also use **-lll** to get the same type of information as the **-L** or **--list** option.

- **-n (--no-nvme):** This option will mask out the NVMe device and controller information.

- **-s (--size):** This option shows the storage item's size in human-readable formats, such as 5.36GB.

Viewing Partition and Filesystem Device File Information

If you have just created a filesystem, it will likely be easy to remember which device file was used to access the filesystem. The following sections will explore commands that will provide useful information about partitions and filesystems so you don't need to remember which device file was used.

The **lsblk** Command

If you forget which device files are available, however, you can execute the **lsblk** command. The following command was performed on a native virtual machine, hence the device names **vda**, **vda1**, and **vda2**:

```
# lsblk
NAME            MAJ:MIN    RM  SIZE   RO TYPE MOUNTPOINT
vda             252:0       0  254G    0 disk
|[en] - vda1    252:1       0  250G    0 part /
|--vda2         252:2       0    4G    0 part [SWAP]
```

Another way to see this information is to view the contents of the **/proc/partitions** file:

```
# cat /proc/partitions
major minor   #blocks   name

  252         0   266338304 vda
  252         1   262144000 vda1
  252         2     4193280 vda2
```

You may also find that the information in the **/sys/block** directory is useful. Each block device (hard drive, partition, and so on) has a directory within the **/sys/block** directory. Within the block device subdirectory is a collection of files that provide information about the block device.

For example, considering the following output:

```
# ls /sys/block/vda
alignment_offset  device             mq         ro        subsystem
bdi               discard_alignment  power      serial    trace
cache_type        ext_range          queue      size      uevent
capability        holders            range      slaves    vda1
dev               inflight           removable  stat      vda2
```

From this output, you can tell that the **/dev/vda** device has two partitions (from the **vda1** and **vda2** directories in the output). Additional files and directories provide more information about the device.

The **blkid** Command

When you are mounting a filesystem, you need to be able to tell Linux how to find the device. There are different ways to do this. The first is to refer to the device filename, such as **/dev/sda1**. This works on a small scale, but if you add or remove hardware, the device names can change.

To get around this unpredictable naming, information can be stored inside the superblock of the filesystem to identify that particular filesystem. The two elements used are the filesystem label and the universally unique identifier (UUID). The label is a human-generated name that should be unique across all disks, and the UUID is generated when the filesystem is made and should always be unique.

You can see your label and UUIDs with the **blkid** command:

```
# blkid
/dev/sda1: UUID="4d2b8b91-9666-49cc-a23a-1a183ccd2150" TYPE="ext4"
/dev/sda3: LABEL="mars" UUID="bab04315-389d-42bf-9efa-b25c2f39b7a0"
TYPE="ext4"
/dev/sda4: UUID="18d6e8bc-14a0-44a0-b82b-e69b4469b0ad" TYPE="ext4"
```

Here, you can see that each filesystem has a UUID to identify it, and the second one is assigned the label **mars**. You won't ever change the UUID, but you may want to change the label. This can be accomplished by using the **e2label** command:

```
# e2label /dev/sda3 pluto
# blkid
/dev/sda1: UUID="4d2b8b91-9666-49cc-a23a-1a183ccd2150" TYPE="ext4"
/dev/sda3: LABEL="pluto" UUID="bab04315-389d-42bf-9efa-b25c2f39b7a0"
TYPE="ext4"
/dev/sda4: UUID="18d6e8bc-14a0-44a0-b82b-e69b4469b0ad" TYPE="ext4"
```

You may also find it useful to use the contents of the **/dev/disk** directory to see devices by UUID, label, and so on:

```
# ls /dev/disk
by-label  by-uuid
# ls -l /dev/disk/by-uuid
total 0
lrwxrwxrwx 1 root 10 Oct 25 22:06 14872d7d-bd78-49a2-a179-
8d5c168310ca -> ../../vda1
lrwxrwxrwx 1 root root 10 Oct 25 22:06 a1345ce8-384a-4a25-8170-
a066a147c53c -> ../../vda2
```

cd / include

The following are valid ways to specify devices:

- **id:** Symbolic links to device files using filenames that are based on the serial number of the hardware.

- **uuid:** Symbolic links to device files using filenames that are based on the UUID of the device.

- **path:** Symbolic links to device files using filenames that are based on the hardware path to the device (the hardware path from the CPU to the device).

■ **multipath:** Symbolic links to device files using filenames that are based on the multipath assigned to the device. (See Chapter 18, "Analyzing and Trouble-shooting Storage," for information on multipath.)

The (Non-Linux) fcstat Command

The Linux+ exam development crew at CompTIA have a habit of letting at least one command slip through into the objectives that either isn't a Linux command *at all* or is in such limited and narrow use as to basically not matter to any practicing sysadmin. Such is the case with the **fcstat** command in objective 1.3.

Thankfully, I recognize this command from my work with AIX while teaching a number of times at IBM's Boulder facility. All you basically need to know is that the **fcstat** command—were it to be in wide availability on Linux and somehow you could find a repository that provided it—would show you Fibre Channel statistics for your devices.

Performing Disk Partitioning

Disk partitioning is the process of dividing a physical storage device, such as a hard disk drive (HDD) or solid-state drive (SSD), into separate, isolated sections or partitions. Each partition functions as an independent unit with its own filesystem, data, and directory structure. Disk partitioning is a fundamental concept in computer storage management and is commonly used for various purposes, including organizing data, improving performance, and enabling multiple operating systems to coexist on a single disk. The standard disk tool is the **fdisk** utility. Nearly every system has a copy of **fdisk** that can be used to create or alter the partition table. The **fdisk** utility is limited to MBR-based partitions, so you should also know how to use the **parted** utility to create and modify GPT and MBR partition tables. You'll also need to know the role and scope of the **partprobe** command in refreshing partition information in the kernel.

fdisk

fdisk is a handy command-line tool for managing the master boot record (MBR). A key concept with **fdisk** is that your changes are not written to disk until you tell it to save. This means you can manipulate your partition table without fear of making any permanent changes until you're ready.

Starting the **fdisk** tool to partition a drive is easy; just remember to specify the device file that contains the partition table you want to edit, as shown in the following example:

```
fdisk /dev/sda
```

NOTE   If you want to practice using these partition tools and you are using a virtual machine (VM), consult your VM software documentation regarding how to add additional disk devices.

The following steps show you how to create a quick layout of three partitions on a new disk with **fdisk**, including setting a swap partition and viewing your handiwork afterward:

Step 1.   Start the **fdisk** program, passing the name of the device (in this case, **sdb**):

```
# fdisk /dev/sdb
Welcome to fdisk (util-linux 2.25.2).
Changes will remain in memory only, until you decide to write
them.
Be careful before using the write command.

Device does not contain a recognized partition table.
Created a new DOS disklabel with disk identifier 0x25fd25d2.
```

Step 2.   Even though there are no partitions (according to the previous message), enter the **p** command to view the device details:

```
Command (m for help): p
Disk /dev/sdb: 8 GiB, 8589934592 bytes, 16777216 sectors
Units: sectors of 1 * 512 = 512 bytes
Sector size (logical/physical): 512 bytes / 512 bytes
I/O size (minimum/optimal): 512 bytes / 512 bytes
Disklabel type: dosDisk identifier: 0x25fd25d2
```

Step 3.   Verify that you're using the right disk. The message says it's an 8GB drive, which is what's expected here. If there were partitions, you could clear them out with the **d** command.

Step 4.   Create a new partition by pressing the **n** key, and then press the **p** key to make it a primary partition. After that, specify that it's the first partition:

```
Command (m for help): n
Partition type
p primary (0 primary, 0 extended, 4 free)
```

```
e extended (container for logical partitions)
Select (default p): p
Partition number (1-4, default 1): 1
```

Step 5.   When you are prompted to lay out the partition on disk in terms of the starting and ending sectors, accept the defaults for the starting sector, which is 2048 in this example:

```
First sector (2048-16777215, default 2048): 2048
```

Step 6.   You can then enter a value like **+1G** to indicate that you want the partition to be 1GB:

```
Last sector, +sectors or +size{K,M,G,T,P} (2048-16777215,
default 16777215): +1G
Created a new partition 1 of type 'Linux' and of size 1 GiB.
```

Step 7.   Press **p** to verify that the partition was created, as shown in Example 3-1.

Example 3-1   Verifying That a Partition Was Created

```
Command (m for help): p
Disk /dev/sdb: 8 GiB, 8589934592 bytes, 16777216 sectors
Units: sectors of 1 * 512 = 512 bytes
Sector size (logical/physical): 512 bytes / 512 bytes
I/O size (minimum/optimal): 512 bytes / 512 bytes
Disklabel type: dos
Disk identifier: 0x2178bc7b

Device Boot Start End Sectors Size Id Type
/dev/sdb1 2048 2099199 2097152 1G 83 Linux
```

Step 8.   Create another partition for primary partition number 2 the same way you did for the first, as shown in Example 3-2.

Example 3-2   Creating a Partition for Primary Partition Number 2

```
Command (m for help): n
Partition type
 p primary (1 primary, 0 extended, 3 free)
 e extended (container for logical partitions)
Select (default p): p
Partition number (2-4, default 2): 2
```

```
First sector (2099200-16777215, default 2099200): 2099200
Last sector, +sectors or +size{K,M,G,T,P} (2099200-16777215, default
16777215): +2G

Created a new partition 2 of type 'Linux' and of size 2 GiB.

Command (m for help): p
Disk /dev/sdb: 8 GiB, 8589934592 bytes, 16777216 sectors
Units: sectors of 1 * 512 = 512 bytes
Sector size (logical/physical): 512 bytes / 512 bytes
I/O size (minimum/optimal): 512 bytes / 512 bytes
Disklabel type: dos
Disk identifier: 0x2178bc7b

Device Boot Start End Sectors Size Id Type
/dev/sdb1 2048 2099199 2097152 1G 83 Linux
/dev/sdb2 2099200 6293503 4194304 2G 83 Linux
```

Step 9. Allocate the rest of the disk to primary partition 3. Perform these steps on your own, and for the last step, just press the **Enter** key to accept the default. After completing this step, the last part of the **p** command looks as follows:

```
Device Boot Start     End       Sectors    Size Id Type
/dev/sdb1      2048    2099199   2097152    1G   83 Linux
/dev/sdb2      2099200 6293503   4194304    2G   83 Linux
/dev/sdb3      6293504 16777215  10483712   5G   83 Linux
```

Step 10. The final two columns, **Id** and **Type**, are worth noting. Id **83** is for a regular Linux partition. If you want to use swap or LVM, you need to explicitly set the partition type with the **t** command. For example, you can set the second partition to swap, using ID **82**:

```
Command (m for help): t
Partition number (1-3, default 3): 2
Hex code (type L to list all codes): 82
Changed type of partition 'Linux' to 'Linux swap / Solaris'.
```

Step 11. Use the third partition as an LVM physical volume, which is Id **8e** (in hexadecimal):

```
Command (m for help): t
Partition number (1-3, default 3): 3
```

```
Hex code (type L to list all codes): 8e

Changed type of partition 'Linux' to 'Linux LVM'.
```

Step 12.   Double-check your work with the **p** command:

```
Device Boot Start End Sectors Size Id Type
/dev/sdb1 2048 2099199 2097152 1G 83 Linux
/dev/sdb2 2099200 6293503 4194304 2G 82 Linux swap / Solaris
/dev/sdb3 6293504 16777215 10483712 5G 8e Linux LVM
```

Step 13.   Write your changes by pressing the **w** key, and then press **Enter**:

```
Command (m for help): w
The partition table has been altered.
Calling ioctl() to re-read partition table.
Syncing disks.
```

Step 14.   To confirm that you correctly partitioned the disk layout after a system is running or viewing the partition tables, run the following command:

```
fdisk -l
```

Partitioning with parted

The MBR partition table format is long in the tooth. There are a few limitations:

- 2TB limit on a partition size

- Only four partitions allowed (though extended and logical partitions are a hack to get around this)

- No checksums, so a single bit error can render a disk useless

parted is the Swiss Army knife of disk partitioning tools. It can manage partition tables in both GPT and MBR formats and modify partition flags and sizes. Start **parted** by passing the device on the command line:

```
# parted /dev/sdb
GNU Parted 3.2
Using /dev/sdb
Welcome to GNU Parted! Type 'help' to view a list of commands.
```

The command to create a partition is **mkpart**, and you can specify all the parameters on one line. Example 3-3 shows how to create a partition with the label MyData that goes from the beginning of the drive to the 7GB marker.

Example 3-3 Creating a Partition with the Label MyData That Goes from the Beginning of the Drive to 7GB

```
(parted) mkpart MyData 0.0 7G
Warning: The resulting partition is not properly aligned for best
performance.
Ignore/Cancel? ignore
(parted) p
Model: ATA VBOX HARDDISK (scsi)
Disk /dev/sdb: 8590MB
Sector size (logical/physical): 512B/512B
Partition Table: gpt
Disk Flags:

Number Start End Size File system Name Flags
 1 17.4kB 7000MB MyData
```

Curiously, one thing that **parted** doesn't do is set the filesystem type. As it turns out, Linux doesn't care much about those IDs; for example, you can overwrite an LVM partition with a swap filesystem, and Linux won't complain. Consider the partition IDs to be suggestions to someone who is reading the partition table, not strict rules that must be followed.

partprobe

The *partprobe* command is very useful for several reasons, not the least of which is its ability to let the kernel know that the partition table has changed, without the need for a reboot.

While not very complex, **partprobe** is a great way to see what exists as partitions before doing any actual partitioning, and then to confirm what has happened after you have made changes.

For example, if you run the **partprobe** command on your system to gather your partition information, it might look like this:

```
# sudo partprobe -s
/dev/sda: gpt partitions 15 1
/dev/vda: msdos partitions
```

The previous output is about the most you'll get from **partprobe**; it's telling you that there is a **/dev/sda** partition that has a gpt boot section and two partitions, 1 and 15. If you look further with other tools such as **fdisk -l**, you can see the particulars of those partitions.

Think of **partprobe** as a cleanup tool to use after you have completed your partitioning tasks, to refresh the kernel's knowledge of what those partitions are now.

Inspecting and Managing Software RAID

One of the first things you'll do in managing your RAID is to create a RAID device.

Creating and Inspecting a Software RAID

To create a software RAID device, execute a command like the following:

```
# mdadm -C /dev/md0 -l 1 -n 2 /dev/sdb /dev/sdc
mdadm: array /dev/md0 started.
```

This command uses the following options:

- **-C:** Use this option to specify the device name for the RAID device.

- **-l:** Use this option to specify the RAID level.

- **-n:** Use this option to specify the number of physical storage devices in the RAID.

Inspecting a Software RAID Device

After creating the RAID device, you can see information about the device by viewing the contents of the */proc/mdstat* file:

```
# more /proc/mdstat
Personalities : [raid1]
md0 : active raid1 sdc[1] sdb[0]
      987840 blocks [2/2] [UU]
unused devices: <none>
```

The **mdadm --detail** command can also be useful for displaying information about a software RAID device.

After you create the RAID devices, you can treat **/dev/md0** as if it were a partition. For example, the next steps would be to create a filesystem and then mount the filesystem under a mount point directory.

Using Logical Volume Manager (LVM)

LVM is a relatively new way of doing things for some folks, so the first goal of this section is to ensure that everyone has a high-level understanding of what LVM is and how it's intended to work. After that, you will leave how to create and manage LVMs.

Overview of LVM

Over time, the shuffling of physical disk partitions to keep up with demand gets tiring. What happens if you need a **/home** drive that's bigger than a single disk? Do you just throw away your older disks when you add more space?

Enterprise Unixes solve this problem with *Logical Volume Manager (LVM)*, based on ideas from enterprise Unixes. With LVM, system physical disks are combined into smaller sets of pools, and the partitions themselves are built from those pools.

Figure 3-1 shows the basic components of LVM and how they fit together.

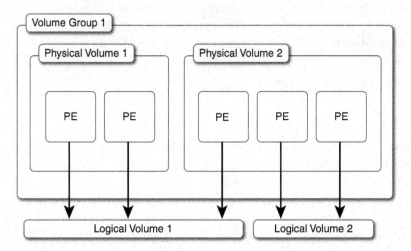

Figure 3-1   Logical volume concepts

The base unit of storage in LVM is the ***physical volumes (PVs)***. A PV corresponds to a hard disk partition such as **/dev/sda1** or some kind of block storage device coming from a dedicated storage system called a storage area network (SAN), introduced later in this chapter. One or more physical volumes are combined to form a pool of storage called a ***volume groups (VGs)***. Under the hood, the physical volume is chopped up into a series of *physical extents* (*PEs*) to make allocations easier.

The administrator then carves up the volume group into a series of ***logical volumes (LVs)***. Each logical volume holds a filesystem that is used by the operating system.

Many interesting things can happen when the filesystem on the logical volume is thoroughly abstracted from the exact placement on disk. If you need more disk space on a logical volume, you can take it from anywhere in the volume group. If the volume group is low on space, simply add another physical volume to the volume group, and the new physical extents are available to any logical volume.

Filesystems can be grown and shrunk by adjusting the size of their underlying logical volume as long as the filesystem supports it. The LVM system takes care of allocating the physical extents to the logical volume, so you don't have to worry about shuffling around partitions on disk anymore.

Snapshotting is now possible in an LVM enhanced system. A snapshot takes a point-in-time copy of a logical volume and makes it available as another disk while still allowing writes to happen to the original filesystem. This allows you to back up the snapshot image without needing to take the files or database offline; you can continue to work and change the files for later backup.

Because a logical volume acts as a partition (where you create a filesystem and mount it), it needs to have a device name. When you run the commands to create volume groups and logical volumes, you need to provide names for these things, as shown in the following examples:

```
# vgcreate vg1 /dev/sdb /dev/sdc
# lvcreate -n lv1 -L 10G vg1
```

The upcoming section "Managing LVM" provides more details about the various commands. For now, focusing on the previous commands, the volume group is named **vg1** and the logical volume is named **lv1** (and placed within the **vg1** volume group). As a result, the following file is created:

```
/dev/vg1/lv1
```

You can use this device name to refer to the new logical volume. However, you will discover that this isn't really a device name but rather a symbolic link to the **/dev/mapper/vg1_lv1** file. The device mapper is a component of the kernel that generates new device files (technically block device files). It creates these files under the **/dev/mapper** directory and, in the case of LVM, creates symbolic links that are backward compatible with older LVM technologies.

Understanding Multipath

Some storage devices are available only through the network, which creates a point of failure: the network itself. If you lose network access to a remote storage device—perhaps because a router went down or a new firewall rule was implemented—applications on your system may fail to function properly.

The idea of multipath is to create different network paths to a remote storage device. This requires additional network setup, including configuring different routes to the network storage device.

Details regarding configuring multipathing are beyond the scope of the Linux+ exam and are not covered in this book. However, the term *multipath* is included in the exam objectives, so be prepared to answer questions regarding the purpose of multipathing.

Managing LVM

The following steps are how you would create an LVM device, which would then hold a filesystem of your choice.

To create a new LVM device, perform the following steps:

Step 1.   Use the **pvcreate** command to convert physical devices into physical volumes.

Step 2.   Use the **vgcreate** command to merge PVs into a single volume group.

Step 3.   Use the **lvcreate** command to create a logical volume using the space provided from a VG.

For example, to convert the hard disks **/dev/sdb** and **/dev/sdc** into PVs, use the following command:

```
# pvcreate /dev/sdb /dev/sdc
  Physical volume "/dev/sdb" successfully created.
  Physical volume "/dev/sdc" successfully created.
```

The **pvs** command is a utility used to display information about physical volumes. To display the physical volumes that have been created, use the *pvs* command.

```
# pvs
```

To use these new PVs to create a new VG, use the following *vgs* command:

```
# vgcreate vg0 /dev/sdb /dev/sdc
  Volume group "vg0" successfully created
```

The **vgs** command is a utility used to display information about volume groups. To display the volume group that has been created, use the *lvs* command

```
# vgs
```

To create an LV from the new VG, use the following command:

```
# lvcreate -L100 -n lv0 vg0
  Logical volume "lv0" created.
```

The lvs command is a utility used to display information about logical volumes. To display the logical volumes that have been created, use the command

```
# lvs
```

After you create the LV devices, you can treat the new device file, **/dev/vg0/lv0**, as if it were a partition.

Remember that **/dev/vg0/lv0** is actually a symbolic link. The mapper file in **/dev/ mapper** points to the real device name.

Additional LVM commands that you should be aware of include the following:

- **vgremove:** Deletes a VG. The VG must not have any LVs.

- **vgreduce:** Deletes a PV from a VG.

- **vgextend:** Adds a PV to an existing VG.

- **vgdisplay:** Displays information about a VG.

- **pvdisplay:** Displays information about a PV.

- **lvdisplay:** Displays information about an LV.

- **lvextend:** Extends the size of an LV. (Note that this only resizes the LV, not the filesystem that resides within the LV. Use the **resize2fs** command to resize the filesystem.)

- **resize2fs:** Resizes the underlying ext2, ext3, or ext4 filesystem.

- **lvchange:** Changes Logical Volume attributes.

- **lvresize:** Resizes the Logical Volume, either by taking more space from the Volume Group or giving space back to the Volume Group.

NOTE There is more to know about logical volumes, but this section has covered more than you need to know for the Linux+ exam. Be sure to experiment with creating and displaying LVM volumes, and take care to do some extending and resizing of the volumes *and* the filesystems on them.

Mounting Local and Remote Devices

Making a device available to the Operating System is called mounting a device. Before we get into how you can *mount* devices, you need to understand the files involved and how they interact.

The Filesystem Table

The filesystem table, which is stored in the *etc/fstab* file, is a configuration file that defines the parameters needed to mount each filesystem. While an administrator can always mount a filesystem manually, having the mount described in the **/etc/fstab** file allows for automatic mounting during the boot process.

An added bonus of the **/etc/fstab** file is that when you provide only the mount point or device name when manually mounting, the **/etc/fstab** file is consulted to determine the rest of the information, including mount options.

The following is an example of an **/etc/fstab** file:

```
LABEL=/ / ext3 defaults 1 1
LABEL=/boot /boot ext3 defaults 1 2
LABEL=/data /data ext3 defaults 1 2
none /proc proc defaults 0 0
none /dev/shm tmpfs defaults 0 0
/dev/sr0 /cdroms ext2 defaults 0 0
/dev/sda3 swap swap defaults 0 0
/dev/sdb1 /mnt/media auto noauto,user 0 0
/dev/cdrom /mnt/cdrom iso9660 noauto,users,ro 0 0
```

The column contents (from left to right) are as follows:

- **Device:** This is any device; local dev files, NFS shares, or UUID or partition labels.

- **Mount point:** This is any directory where the device's filesystem will be attached. This directory should initially be empty.

- **Filesystem type:** This is a valid filesystem type.

- **Options:** Options are separated by commas. The **defaults** option is made up of **rw**, **suid**, **dev**, **exec**, **auto**, **nouser**, **async**, and any filesystem-specific options.

- **Dump:** If this value is **0**, the **dump** command doesn't act on it; a **1** indicates that the filesystem should be dumped on demand. Note that the **dump** command is rarely used on modern Linux distributions, so this value is almost always **0**.

- **fsck:** This causes the filesystem with a **1** to be checked first and then those with a **2** and so on to be checked next. A value of **0** means "don't perform **fsck** on this filesystem."

Filesystems are defined in the **/etc/fstab** file, one filesystem per line. Any mounted filesystem, whether or not it is in the **/etc/fstab** file, is automatically stored in **/etc/ mtab**. This information (or most of it) is also in the **/proc/mounts** file.

Type the **mount** command to see the current list of filesystems. Here's an example:

```
$ mount
/dev/sda1 on / type ext4 (rw,errors=remount-ro)
proc on /proc type proc (rw,noexec,nosuid,nodev)
sysfs on /sys type sysfs (rw,noexec,nosuid,nodev)
udev on /dev type devtmpfs (rw,mode=0755)
devpts on /dev/pts type devpts (rw,noexec,nosuid,gid=5,mode=0620)
tmpfs on /run type tmpfs (rw,noexec,nosuid,size=10%,mode=0755)
/dev/sda3 on /mnt/data type ext4 (rw)
/dev/sda4 on /mnt/timemachine type ext4 (rw)
```

Compare this to the contents of **/etc/mtab**:

```
$ cat /etc/mtab
/dev/sda1 / ext4 rw,errors=remount-ro 0 0
proc /proc proc rw,noexec,nosuid,nodev 0 0
sysfs /sys sysfs rw,noexec,nosuid,nodev 0 0
udev /dev devtmpfs rw,mode=0755 0 0
devpts /dev/pts devpts rw,noexec,nosuid,gid=5,mode=0620 0 0
tmpfs /run tmpfs rw,noexec,nosuid,size=10%,mode=0755 0 0
/dev/sda3 /mnt/data ext4 rw 0 0
/dev/sda4 /mnt/timemachine ext4 rw 0 0
```

You can get the same view of the mounted disks through **/proc/mounts**:

```
$ cat /proc/mounts
rootfs / rootfs rw 0 0
sysfs /sys sysfs rw,nosuid,nodev,noexec,relatime 0 0
proc /proc rw,nosuid,nodev,noexec,relatime 0 0
udev /dev devtmpfs rw,relatime,size=1980172k,nr_
inodes=495043,mode=755 0 0
devpts /dev/pts devpts rw,nosuid,noexec,relatime,gid=5,mode=620,
ptmxmode=000 0 0
tmpfs /run tmpfs rw,nosuid,noexec,relatime,size=404804k,mode=755 0 0
/dev/disk/by-uuid/309b3416-5a59-4954-b4a6-f2c105d9aac5 / ext4
rw,relatime,errors=remount-ro,data=ordered 0 0
/dev/sda3 /mnt/data ext4 rw,relatime,data=ordered 0 0
/dev/sda4 /mnt/timemachine ext4 rw,relatime,data=ordered 0 0
```

All three outputs show roughly the same information except that the information in **/proc/mounts** is the most detailed. The first two examples omit any default options, but **/proc/mounts** shows all mount options, whether they're default or provided.

Manually Mounting Filesystems

If a filesystem isn't configured in the **/etc/fstab** file, it can be mounted manually by using this syntax:

```
# mount -t type -o option device mountpoint
```

The following example of a manual mount includes the type, an option, the device, and a mount point:

```
# mount -t iso9660 -o exec /dev/cdrom /mnt/cdrom
```

With this **mount** command, the system's optical disc is mounted, allowing users access to the contents. The **exec** option also means that files on the disk can be executed, such as if the optical disc included a software installation file.

The following are important mounting options:

- **-a:** Mounts all filesystems listed in **/etc/fstab**
- **-r:** Mounts the filesystem read-only
- **-w:** Mounts the filesystem in write mode
- **-L:** Mounts a filesystem with a given label instead of using the device filename

Unmounting Filesystems

The unmounting command **umount** works similarly to the **mount** command, acting on the label, mount point, or device listed in the **/etc/fstab** entry.

For example, to unmount the **/mnt/cdrom** device, use either of the following commands:

```
# umount /mnt/cdrom
# umount /dev/cdrom
```

The **umount** command doesn't let you unmount any device that is currently in use, including a device that has a user accessing it via a file manager, a shell session, or a file in use on that device. If you don't know who is using the filesystem, you can use the **fuser** command:

```
# fuser -m /mnt/data/
/mnt/data: 1929c
```

The **-m** option denotes a mounted filesystem and returns a list of all processes with open files on that device. In this case, **/mnt/data** is being used by process 1929, and the **c** indicates that the process is using it as its current directory. The process needs to be killed or the user needs to move out of the directory before the device can be unmounted.

Using systemd to Mount

Among the amazingly large number of other things that systemd does, you can use it to mount filesystems when and where you wish. As you are likely aware, systemd uses unit files (basically a config file) to encompass the instructions and details for a given "unit" of configuration.

The *systemd.mount* objective 1.3 item refers to the command that you can use to have a filesystem be mounted as a part of systemd's starting up of your system. Unit files have all sorts of options for configuring and handling dependencies, allowing for a particular unit—in this case a filesystem mount—to be performed either before another unit or service is run or started, after, or on demand, to name but a few of the available options.

An example of a **.mount** unit file in systemd is the one for configuring snap, shown in Example 3-4.

Example 3-4   Example of the snap-bare-5.mount Man Page

```
# cat snap-bare-5.mount
[Unit]
Description=Mount unit for bare, revision 5
Before=snapd.service
After=zfs-mount.service

[Mount]
What=/var/lib/snapd/snaps/bare_5.snap
Where=/snap/bare/5
Type=squashfs
Options=nodev,ro,x-gdu.hide,x-gvfs-hide
LazyUnmount=yes

[Install]
WantedBy=multi-user.target
```

In the **snap-bare-5.mount** unit file, the **Before=** and **After=** directives enable you to specify explicitly what order the unit files should be executed. Traditionally, you'd have your mount unit's action be performed after the software driver that is needed has been invoked.

Once you have determined when something is performed and what dependencies there are, you can then specify exactly what you want to have happen when this mount unit is invoked, mostly in the **[Mount]** section of the unit file.

> **NOTE** The **/etc/crypttab** file which is used to describe the encrypted filesystems that are decrypted during the boot process.

Linux Unified Key Setup (LUKS)

Encrypting your disks and data is an excellent deterrent or safeguard if a disk or machine with critical data on it is lost, stolen, or compromised. *Linux Unified Key Setup (LUKS)* was invented to provide a more consistent and more understandable way to set up disk encryption, primarily on Linux systems.

The brainchild of Clemens Fruhwirth, LUK is designed to make the usual experience of using encryption on disks less frustrating and less likely to end up with inaccessible volumes due to loss of passwords. The mismatch of update cycles between encryption tool versions and the in-place encrypted volumes those tools acted upon.

As the name suggests, LUKS was primarily begun as a way to have less trouble with encrypted volumes and access to the data thereon. Another key feature of LUKS is the ability to have multiple passwords associated with any encrypted volume, allowing for multiple user access and the ability to securely change those passwords at will.

Monitoring Storage Space and Disk Usage

There are several methods of determining the space used by data on a system. It's important to know when to use each command because they all act differently and display different information.

Using iostat

The **iostat** command provides input/output statistics on devices, including partitions. When executed with the **-d** option, it provides a variety of information:

```
#iostat -d egrep "Device|sd"
Device    tps    kB_read/s    kB_wrtn/s    kB_read    kB_wrtn
sda      1.62        17.05        12.08     969749     686696
```

```
sdb        0.02       3.76       0.00       213643         88
sdc        0.01       0.11       3.59         6239     203860
```

The values of this output include the following:

- **Device:** The device filename of the storage device

- **tps:** Transactions per second

- **kB_read/s:** Kilobytes of data read from the device per second

- **kB_wrtn/s:** Kilobytes of data written to the device per second

- **kB_read:** Total kilobytes of data read from the device

- **kB_wrtn:** Total kilobytes of data written to the device

This data can be useful when trying to determine if the read/write actions on the device create a load that is too great. You need to monitor this information over time, as it is difficult to determine if there are issues by reading this output only once. Output must be compared to data from other points in time to determine if there is an issue.

 Using du

To see the space used by a set of files or a file tree, you use the *du* command. This command is configurable to show file and directory sizes, including summarization and human-readable output (in KB, MB, and GB).

To summarize the disk usage, in blocks, for each file and directory within the current directory, use the following command:

```
# du *
8 a_directory
4 go
4 sharing
```

This command descends into directories. The value reported next to the name of the directory or file is the number of blocks in the file or in all the files under that directory.

To see the current directory and all directories below it with "human-readable" output (in KB, MB, and GB), use the following command:

```
# du -h
24K ./.gconfd
8.0K ./.gstreamer
8.0K ./.gconf/desktop/gnome/applications/window_manager
12K ./.gconf/desktop/gnome/applications
```

```
8.0K ./.gconf/desktop/gnome/file_views
24K ./.gconf/desktop/gnome
28K ./.gconf/desktop
... Output removed
```

To view a summary of space used by all files on a given directory tree, such as the **/home** user's tree, use this command:

```
# du -sh /home
```

Typical output would look like this:

```
404 MB /home
```

 Using df

The **df** command is different from the **du** command in that it operates on filesystems rather than files and directories.

The *df* command displays used and available disk space for all mounted filesystems, on a per-filesystem basis (shown here with the **-h** human-readable output option):

```
# df -h
Filesystem     Size  Used Avail Use% Mounted on
udev           453M     0  453M   0% /dev
tmpfs           98M  1.1M   96M   2% /run
/dev/sda1      4.7G  2.0G  2.8G  41% /
tmpfs          486M     0  486M   0% /dev/shm
tmpfs          5.0M     0  5.0M   0% /run/lock
```

Notice that **df** works only on mounted filesystems. Each line of output describes one filesystem, and the output includes the following information:

- The name of the partition where the filesystem is stored
- The size of the filesystem
- The amount of space used in the filesystem
- The amount of space available in the filesystem
- The percentage of space used
- Where the device is mounted

> **NOTE**   The **df** command also features the *very* helpful **-T** option, which shows the filesystem type for each entry in the **df** command output. For example, you might issue the following command to show the filesystem type:
>
> ```
> # df -hT
> Filesystem      Type        Size   Used   Avail   Use% Mounted
> udev            devtmpfs    453M      0   453M    0%  /dev
> tmpfs           tmpfs        98M   1.1M    96M    2%  /run
> /dev/sda1       ext4        4.7G   2.0G   2.8G   41%  /
> tmpfs           tmpfs       486M      0   486M    0%  /dev/shm
> tmpfs           tmpfs       5.0M      0   5.0M    0%  /run/lock
> ```

Filesystem Management

The filesystems on your machines are relatively robust but need some care and attention now and then. You can use various tools to check the filesystems, configure settings that affect their performance, and debug their operations.

Filesystem Checker

When a filesystem is broken or has errors, a filesystem check is in order. When you run the **fsck** tool, you're really delegating the work to the appropriate filesystem check tool:

- **e2fsck:** Shortcut for checking the ext (ext2, ext3, and ext4) filesystems

- **dosfsck:** Used for all varieties of the DOS/FAT filesystem

- **fsck.btrfs:** Used for the Btrfs filesystem

> **NOTE**   The **fsck** command does not check XFS filesystems; you must use the **xfs_repair** command instead (as described in the upcoming section "XFS Commands").

Sometimes the **fsck** utility is automatically executed during the boot process. The mount count and maximum mount count are how the system knows when to execute the **fsck** command automatically at boot. (See the section "Tuning ext Filesystems," later in this chapter, for more on mount counts and using **tune2fs**.)

If the filesystem was shut down cleanly, such as through the **shutdown** or **halt** commands, then the **fsck** command doesn't need to check anything. When a filesystem is properly unmounted, any data cached in memory is flushed to disk, and the disk is considered to be "clean." If the computer was shut down abruptly, it's possible that some of this cache is lost and that the filesystem may be missing data. It is the job of **fsck** to fix any damage caused by such missing data.

If there is damage that is too great to fix automatically during the boot process, the system presents you with a message similar to "Ctrl+D to continue, otherwise enter the root password to perform a filesystem check." If you enter the root password, you see the shell prompt and a helpful message that tells you which filesystem needs to be checked.

NOTE   Run **fsck** only on unmounted or read-only mounted filesystems. This is mandatory; otherwise, **fsck** might perform an operation on a file a user has open, causing corruption.

Example 3-5 shows a sample of a check on a filesystem.

Example 3-5   Sample Check on a Filesystem

```
# fsck -v /dev/sda1
fsck from util-linux 2.25.2
e2fsck 1.42.11 (09-Jul-2014)
/dev/sda1 is mounted.
e2fsck: Cannot continue, aborting.
# umount /dev/sda1
# fsck -v /dev/sda1
fsck from util-linux 2.25.2
e2fsck 1.42.11 (09-Jul-2014)
/dev/sda1: clean, 430/128016 files, 182615/512000 blocks
```

EXT2/3/4 Tools Overview

One of the characteristics of this family of filesystems is the extensive set of tools the versions share.

The easiest way to see all of these tools is to do a quick search of the man pages, such as:

```
# man -k ext[2,3,4]
```

This will display about 20 or so utilities that you can use on various versions of the ext2, 3, 4 filesystem family.

Tuning ext Filesystems

The **tune2fs** command is used to set parameters after a filesystem is created. For example, the maximum mount count dictates how many times a filesystem can be mounted before an **fsck** is forced on it. This number is set to **20** by default unless you set it at filesystem creation or change it afterward with **tune2fs**. The following example sets the mount count to **40** for an ext3 journaling filesystem:

```
# tune2fs -c 40 /dev/sda1
```

In addition to using **tune2fs** to set the mount count, you can use the command to alter error checking. For example, if you use **tune2fs -e**, the system does one of three things when a filesystem error is detected by the kernel:

- **Continue:** Continues normally

- **remount-ro:** Remounts the filesystem read-only, ready to **fsck**

- **Panic:** Causes the kernel to panic, which stops the system (and is not recommended unless you're a system tester)

The reserved percentage associated with the root user (that is, the space available only to the root user) can also be associated with a system group with the **-g** option, as in this example:

```
# tune2fs -g admins /dev/sdb1
```

Btrfs Tools

The *Btrfs* filesystem is relatively new and has a lot of tools that you can use to manage it, but it also has a particular feature that sets it apart from other filesystems in that it is usable as an overall command, with subcommands that mirror the **btrfs-*** utility commands.

Traditionally, filesystems haven't included an overall utility to manage them. For example, the ext filesystem family just has a lot of utilities that begin with **ext***.

The **btrfs** command exists as an overall command toolbox that helps you manage your Btrfs filesystems. There is also a large number of related tools that begin with **btrfs-***, a list of which you can see by using the following command:

```
# man btrfs
```

Then, take a look at the COMMANDS section, which is easy to find while viewing the Btrfs man page with the following internal command:

```
/^COMMANDS
```

This **man** command searches forward to find the COMMANDS section, because it looks for the string COMMANDS at the very first position of a line.

In this section, you'll see a full listing of the commands that the **btrfs** command will accept as subcommands. For more information on each of these, look at the recommendation for the matching command-line tool, such as the pairing shown in Example 3-6.

Example 3-6   Man Page Entry for a Btrfs Subcommand

```
COMMANDS
        check
            Do off-line check on a btrfs filesystem.


            See btrfs-check(8) for details.
```

Inspecting the man page for the **btrfs-check** tool will give you the appropriate details for that command and its usage.

There are two quick methods for finding all the available **btrfs** specific tools on a system. The first is to use tab completion, where you type **btrfs-** and then press the **Tab** key twice, which will show all the **btrfs-*** tools in your path on the screen.

The second method is to run a similar **man -k** command as we did in our search for the **ext*** tools, such as that shown in Example 3-7.

Example 3-7   Output of the **man -k btrfs** Command

```
# man -k btrfs-
btrfs-balance (8)     - balance block groups on a btrfs...
btrfs-check (8)       - check or repair a btrfs filesystem
btrfs-convert (8)     - convert from ext2/3/4 or reiserfs...
btrfs-device (8)      - manage devices of btrfs filesystems
btrfs-filesystem (8)  - command group that primarily does...
btrfs-find-root (8)   - filter to find btrfs root
btrfs-image (8)       - create/restore an image of the filesystem
btrfs-inspect-internal (8) - query various internal information
btrfs (5)             - topics about the BTRFS filesystem (moun...
btrfs-map-logical (8) - map btrfs logical extent to physical...
btrfs-property (8)    - get/set/list properties for given...
btrfs-qgroup (8)      - control the quota group of a btrfs...
btrfs-quota (8)       - control the global quota status of a...
```

```
btrfs-receive (8)       - receive subvolumes from send stream
btrfs-replace (8)       - replace devices managed by btrfs with...
btrfs-rescue (8)        - recover a damaged btrfs filesystem
btrfs-restore (8)       - try to restore files from a damaged bt...
btrfs-scrub (8)         - scrub btrfs filesystem, verify block...
btrfs-select-super (8) - overwrite primary superblock with a...
btrfs-send (8)          - generate a stream of changes between t...
btrfs-subvolume (8)    - manage btrfs subvolumes
```

NOTE   Keep in mind that the Linux+ exam objectives merely list "Btrfs tools," so you really only need to know that they exist, where to get more information on them, and that the **btrfs** command has subcommands that match or mirror these separate command-line tools.

XFS Commands

The ext filesystems may get most of the attention, but you shouldn't ignore XFS. It is now the default filesystem for some enterprise Linux systems because it offers high performance for large files and advanced journaling and online backup features.

Example 3-8 demonstrates how to make an XFS filesystem.

Example 3-8   Making an XFS Filesystem with **xfs**

```
# mkfs -t xfs -f /dev/sdb1
meta-data=/dev/sdb1 isize=256 agcount=4, agsize=427245 blks
 = sectsz=512 attr=2, projid32bit=1
 = crc=0 finobt=0
data = bsize=4096 blocks=1708980, imaxpct=25
 = sunit=0 swidth=0 blks
naming =version 2 bsize=4096 ascii-ci=0 ftype=0
log =internal log bsize=4096 blocks=2560, version=2
 = sectsz=512 sunit=0 blks, lazy-count=1
realtime =none extsz=4096 blocks=0, rtextents=0
```

Many of the parameters are best left at defaults. One parameter to note is **log**, which identifies where the journal will go. By default, it goes on the same device as the filesystem, but you can choose to place it on a dedicated device, if needed for performance.

You can also use the **xfs_info** command to see these same details that the **dumpe2fs** command provides for ext filesystems.

Some advanced commands are different between ext4 and XFS. Instead of using **fsck** to look for and fix problems, you use **xfs_check** to look for problems, and you use **xfs_repair** to fix the problems. If a repair fails, you may need to use the **xfs_metadump** command and call a vendor for support. This command puts debugging information into a file that helps the vendor diagnose the problem.

An interesting thing about XFS is that you can grow the filesystem with **xfs_growfs**, but you can't shrink it. This is not because of technical reasons but because the project hasn't implemented it! It would be a lot of work to implement this feature, and that effort could be better spent on other features that people use more often.

A final feature of XFS is that it supports online defragmentation (called *reorganization* in XFS lingo) through the **xfs_fsr** command. Over time, the blocks comprising a single file might be placed in different parts of the disk, which means the file becomes fragmented; lower performance results because the disk heads need to do more seeking. Reorganizing, or defragmenting, the file involves copying it to a new spot where it's in a contiguous series of blocks.

Storage Area Networks/Network-Attached Storage

The Linux+ exam objectives are rather specific regarding what you need to know about using remote (or external) storage devices. You are required to know what types of servers and remote storage devices are connected to your Linux system and how they are connected. You'll need to know what SANs and NAS are and how they differ. You'll also need to know a certain amount of information about the typical filesystems that would allow you to store and access data on those remote devices.

SAN vs. NAS

While not the most misunderstood set of terms in all of computing, there exists a *lot* of confusion as to what is a ***storage area network* (*SAN*)** and what is a ***network-attached storage* (*NAS*)** device. A SAN is a specialized high-speed network that connects various storage devices (such as disk arrays) to multiple servers and computing systems. A NAS is a specialized file-level storage device or appliance that is connected to a computer network and provides data storage and file-sharing capabilities to multiple users and client devices over that network. Unlike a SAN, which provides block-level storage, NAS operates at the file level, making it a convenient solution for sharing files across different platforms and devices.

Table 3-2 shows the simplest and most direct definition of these two important technologies that I can provide, and also slightly more than you need to know for the exam.

Table 3-2   Differences Between NAS and SAN Implementations

Network-Attached Storage (NAS)	Storage Area Network (SAN)
1. Simple to set up and maintain	1. More difficult to set up and maintain
2. Relatively inexpensive	2. More expensive
3. Uses a TCP/IP network and address(es)	3. Requires specialized Fibre Channel cards and switches
4. Volumes are mounted across the IP network	4. Mimics direct-attached storage or local disk
5. Users experience the volumes as file storage	5. Users experience the storage device as a block device
6. Good for smaller environments and lower numbers of users	6. Better for professionals or high volumes of users and data
7. Can reach an upper limit unless higher-end NAS devices are used	7. Scales up and out using more controllers and storage arrays
8. May have single points of failure (SPOFs), such as power supplies on the lower end	8. Fault tolerance built in for network and systems; considered much more reliable

Multipathing with multipathd

One of the underlying concepts that you need to understand about using a SAN or NAS device in your environment is how multipathing works.

Multipathing means to set up multiple physical or virtual pathways from a server device to the same storage device, such as having a server with both a Fibre Channel card and pathway and an iSCSI connection over the conventional network to the same storage device.

There are two basic reasons to use multipathing:

- Fault tolerance
- Load balancing

One of the best results of having multipathing set up is the automatic detection and isolation of the faulty path and automatic rerouting of the requests and responses between the server and storage device.

Also of note is the ability of the multipathing daemon/configuration to detect the restoration and health of the previously failed pathway and to place it back into service for use if another pathway fails, or as a valid pathway when you desire to use multiple pathways in a round-robin fashion, such as for load balancing.

Typical Network Filesystems Used by SAN/NAS

The most common two network filesystems in wide usage are NFS and Samba or CIFS.

- **NFS:** *Network File System* (*NFS*) is primarily designed to share files between Linux or Unix systems (sometimes referred to as **Nix systems*). There are some non-*Nix client programs available, but they are not commonly used. NFS lacks a lot of the modern security features found in other file servers, but given that it is normally used only on a LAN, these security issues are not a big concern. Unlike with FTP or SFTP, users typically don't initiate access to an NFS server. An administrator mounts an NFS share to make the share available via the filesystem structure on the client system, or makes the system automount the share on the client system if configured to act that way.

- **Samba:** Samba is a service that runs on a server and can share both files and printers as well as provide and connect to Windows domains. It is designed to share files in a manner that allows Microsoft Windows clients to access the shares that are provided either via the older *Server Message Block* (*SMB*) file-sharing protocol, or the newer *Common Internet File System* (*CIFS*). Samba can also be integrated with a Microsoft Server domain, so it is a good solution in an environment that has a mix of operating systems. To access a Samba server, an individual user could initiate the access via a Samba client program, but an administrator can also configure access via a mount point (a directory available in the filesystem).

Samba vs. SMB and CIFS

Some confusion exists about Samba, SMB, and CIFS. In the early days of Samba, it was called "SMB Server," but that name had to be changed due to name conflicts. It's been called Samba for many years now.

Samba is a service that runs on a server, whereas both SMB and CIFS are file-sharing protocols. The main difference between SMB and CIFS is that the SMB protocol is much older than CIFS and CIFS incorporates many of the features of the older SMB protocol.

Summary

In this chapter you learned a great deal about how to identify your storage using command-line tools and how to partition your disks. You also learned some RAID basics and details about the critically important Logical Volume Manager.

Additionally, you learned about mounting and unmounting remote and local file-systems; monitoring your disk and filesystem usage; the various tools to use for managing your filesystem; the differences between remote storage systems and how multipathing works with those systems; and the more common network filesystems in wide usage.

Exam Preparation Tasks

As mentioned in the section "Goals and Methods" in the Introduction, you have a couple of choices for exam preparation: the exercises here, Chapter 23, "Final Preparation," and the exam simulation questions in the Pearson Test Prep Software Online.

Review All Key Topics

Review the most important topics in this chapter, noted with the Key Topic icon in the left margin of the page. Table 3-3 lists these key topics and the page number on which each is found.

Table 3-3 Key Topics for Chapter 3

Key Topic Element	Description	Page Number
Section	Viewing SCSI Device Information	104
Section	The (Non-Linux) **fcstat** Command	108
Section	**fdisk**	108
Section	Partitioning with **parted**	112
Section	Creating and Inspecting a Software RAID	114
Paragraph	The pvs	117
Paragraph	The vgs	117
Paragraph	The lvs command	118
Section	Linux Unified Key Setup (LUKS)	123
Section	Using **du**	124
Section	Using **df**	125
Section	Tuning ext Filesystems	128
Table 3-2	Differences Between NAS and SAN Implementations	132
Paragraph	Samba vs. SMB and CIFS	133

Define Key Terms

Define the following key terms from this chapter and check your answers in the glossary:

disk partitioning, **fdisk, parted, partprobe, mdadm, /proc/mdstat, pvs, vgs, lvs, mount, /etc/fstab, systemd.mount,** Linux Unified Key Setup (LUKS), **du, df,** Btrfs, storage area network (SAN), network-attached storage (NAS), Common Internet File System (CIFS), Network File System (NFS), *Server Message Block (SMB)*

Review Questions

The answers to these review questions are in Appendix A.

1. You have finished partitioning your disk with the **fdisk** command and want to exit and save the configuration to disk. Which command will accomplish this?

   a. **wq**

   b. **q**

   c. **w**

   d. **c**

2. You want to configure a RAID setup for your server. Which of the following commands would you use to accomplish this?

   a. **rconfig**

   b. **raidadm**

   c. **mdadm**

   d. **raid-setup**

3. You have heard that resizing a filesystem is possible and have altered the space available on the LVM logical volume, but when you attempt the filesystem resize, you see messages that indicate you can only expand the filesystem. Why?

   a. The filesystem is mounted.

   b. The filesystem does not support resizing.

   c. The logical volume must be rebuilt.

   d. The volume group needs to be resized first.

4. When you restart your server, a particular filesystem you just added to the **/etc/fstab** file doesn't mount; it has to be manually mounted. What option can you add to that filesystem's line in **/etc/fstab** to cause the desired behavior?

   a. **mount**

   b. **auto**

   c. **onboot**

   d. **exec**

5. You initiated a copy of a directory tree from one disk to another, but it was taking so long that you canceled the operation; you didn't find any obvious errors. Before you retry the procedure, what command would you use to see how much disk space the directory tree and all its subfolders and files consist of?

   a. **df -h**

   b. **ls -lR**

   c. **tree -h**

   d. **du -sh**

6. You require your system to check a particular filesystem every 50 times the filesystem is mounted. Which command would you use to make this change?

   a. **debugfs**

   b. **dumpe2fs**

   c. **tune2fs**

   d. **setfs**

7. You have to explain to your direct supervisor why you are recommending the use of a network-attached storage device for your small law practice. Which of the following are key characteristics of a NAS? (Choose all that apply.)

   a. Relatively expensive

   b. Uses Ethernet/TCP/IP

   c. Shows the storage as a local device

   d. Requires special adapter cards and switches

   e. Mounts a filesystem across the network

This chapter covers the following topics:

- Managing Processes
- Sending Signals to Processes
- Job Control
- Managing Process Priorities
- systemd
- Scheduling Services
- Running ad hoc Jobs

The exam objective covered in this chapter is as follows:

- **Objective 1.4:** Given a scenario, configure and use the appropriate processes and services

## CHAPTER 4

Managing Processes and Services

Every system needs to run, to *operate*, and in order to do that, processes and services must be set up, configured, and used properly.

A process is code that has been executed and is now stored in memory. The code could come from an application, an executable file, a command, or any other sort of system code. System services are more of a backend set of processes, where you may run them, but they don't interact with the terminal, or the console; they provide, as their name indicates, services to either local requestors or, very often, remote requestors.

There are many processes that run on even the humblest of systems. Though processes come in different types—whether user-related processes, such as commands, or system-related processes, in the case of services—knowing how to manage them properly is critical to the role of anyone working with or managing a Linux system. For the Linux+ exam, you need to know how to start processes; run them at various priorities; query and display them; pause, stop, and outright kill them; and when to run them and as what user. You also need to know how to schedule them to run at various times or intervals.

The principles and practices presented in this chapter will help you immensely to manage your processes and the services that they make up, enabling you to provide the ability to run those processes and services consistently and reliably over time.

"Do I Know This Already?" Quiz

The "Do I Know This Already?" quiz enables you to assess whether you should read this entire chapter or simply jump to the "Exam Preparation Tasks" section for review. If you are in doubt, read the entire chapter. Table 4-1 outlines the major headings in this chapter and the corresponding "Do I Know This Already?" quiz questions. You can find the answers in Appendix A, "Answers to the 'Do I Know This Already?' Quizzes and Review Questions."

Table 4-1   "Do I Know This Already?" Foundation Topics Section-to-Question Mapping

Foundation Topics Section	Questions Covered in This Section
Managing Processes	1–3
System Services	4–5
Scheduling Services	6–7

CAUTION   The goal of self-assessment is to gauge your mastery of the topics in this chapter. If you do not know the answer to a question or are only partially sure of the answer, you should mark that question as wrong for purposes of the self-assessment. Giving yourself credit for an answer you correctly guess skews your self-assessment results and might provide you with a false sense of security.

1. You wish to terminate a process but don't want to cause unnecessary data loss or other problems. Which signal would be the most appropriate?

    a. SIGTERM

    b. SIGKILL

    c. SIGEXCUSEME

    d. SIGHUP

2. You have started a process normally but find through process management tools that it's consuming an inordinate amount of the CPU resources. What command would you use to change this process's priority to a more acceptable priority?

    a. sweeten

    b. renice

    c. like

    d. fg

3. When you run the **jobs** command, your output shows a + symbol next to one of the jobs in the list. What does the + symbol indicate?

    a. A process that is using more CPU than others

    b. A process that has been niced or reniced

    c. A process that is the most recently acted upon

    d. A process that has been run more than once recently

4. You are used to using the **service** command on your SysVinit system but have recently upgraded to a systemd-based system. Which of the following commands is the most direct replacement for the **service** command?

   a. **systemdcfg**

   b. **servicectrl**

   c. **controlsvc**

   d. **systemctl**

5. You are used to using the typical Linux process management commands, but require something that uses color to make differentiating between process states easy at a glance. Which command-line utility allows you to do this?

   a. **top**

   b. **pstop**

   c. **htop**

   d. **iftop**

6. What is true of the **at** command? (Choose two.)

   a. **at** can only schedule a single job instance.

   b. **at** cannot schedule scripts.

   c. **at** can run jobs periodically or on a frequency.

   d. **at** takes system load into account.

   e. **at** cannot schedule more than 24 hours in the future.

7. Consider the following cron entry and choose the correct statement:
   ```
   0/10 * * * 1 /usr/local/bin/ping.sh
   ```

   a. **ping.sh** will run every 10 minutes starting the minute it's run on Sunday.

   b. **ping.sh** will run once at 10 min after every hour on the first of the month.

   c. **ping.sh** will run every 10 min all day long on Mondays.

   d. **ping.sh** will run every 10 hours on the first Sunday of the month.

Foundation Topics

In this chapter we'll cover the concept and practice of managing Linux processes and services and how to schedule those services to maximum effect.

In order to be effective at managing processes and services, you have to be able to query and display process and service information, act on that information, and make the changes with the tools and utilities that will produce the effect you want.

I will take my usual liberties with the order of the subtopics in this exam objective so that they flow well and make sense.

Managing Processes

Managing programs and processes is essential to running a Linux machine. Various utilities can help you manage processes. Let's begin with viewing processes and then move on to removing processes. Finally, we cover process priorities.

Viewing Processes

When you need to see what's running on a machine, regardless of what GUI tools or programs are installed on the machine, you can use the **ps** command. The **ps** command is used to display process information and has switches to format the output.

For example, to show the processes started by a user and the user's shell, just type the **ps** command, like so:

```
# ps
 PID TTY TIME CMD
19856 pts/0 00:00:00 bash
20057 pts/0 00:00:00 ps
```

This is the simplest view of the system's processes, but it leaves out a lot of backgrounded or non-terminal-associated processes. The **-a** option shows essentially any process that the current user has started besides the BASH shell. Use the following to show progressively more information:

```
# ps -a
 PID TTY TIME CMD
 1497 tty1 00:00:00 startx
 1510 tty1 00:00:00 xinit
 1523 tty1 00:00:00 gnome-session
 1528 tty1 00:00:00 xinitrc <defunct>
15075 pts/1 00:00:00 ps
... output truncated for readability.
```

Obviously, you get more information here because a switch is used for showing all processes that are terminal bound. If another user is on the system, you can see her processes listed, too.

Now type the following:

```
ps -a | wc -l
 66
```

The important number is the one reported by the **wc** command: It's the number of lines in the output. Each one represents a running process. This machine has 66 processes found by the **ps** command.

More **ps** command switches to know are as follows:

- **a:** Shows all processes for all users
- **u:** Shows user information for processes
- **x:** Shows processes without a controlling tty

What's the Diff?

There's a lot of confusion among junior sysadmins about why you use **ps aux** sometimes and **ps -aux** at other times. The man page isn't very helpful, but it does tell you *why* the dash is used or not. Linux's version of the **ps** command is a latecomer. There are two main parents to this version, BSD and POSIX, offering different but similar ways of handling commands and options.

The BSD style of using options with the **ps** command is that you can group them (for example, **aux**) but without a preceding dash. The POSIX or Unix method is that you can group them, but they must be preceded with a dash (for example, **-aux**). In short, the two methods are similar, and Linux's version of **ps** allows for either method.

Use the **pstree** command to show the hierarchical nature of the processes on a system, as in the following example:

```
init-+-apmd
  |-atd
  |-bdflush
  |-bonobo-activati
  |-crond
  |-cupsd
  |-dhcpcd
  |-evolution-alarm
```

```
|-gconfd-2
|-gnome-cups-mana
|-gnome-name-serv
|-gnome-panel
|-gnome-settings-
|-gnome-smproxy
|-gnome-terminal-+-bash
|   `-mgt-pty-helper
```

> **NOTE**   The **ps** and **pstree** commands have many options. It's good to be aware of as many of them as possible for the Linux+ exam. Both commands have the capability of showing a system's running processes in a treelike, or hierarchical, fashion.

The Linux+ exam is likely to include questions that test how well you know the **ps** command, including what Linux uses as the equivalent of the command:

```
# ps -ef
```

Verify how similar **ps -ef** is to **ps aux** with the following:

```
# ps -ef > psef
# ps -aux > psaux
# vimdiff psef psaux
```

There are a number of similarities between the two output streams. The **ps aux** command is from Linux, whereas **ps -ef** originates from Unix.

The htop Command

The *htop* command is a utility that allows you to monitor your system's processes in a graphical manner, but it's much more friendly and visually pleasing than regular **top**.

For example, you can use a mouse with the **htop** command, it comes with color enabled by default, and depending on the options you use, you can do some other very useful things like sort by various columns and show either just the PID of the process or much more useful information such as the complete command line that was used to invoke the process. Another great feature of the **htop** command is its function key layout that makes using its features that much easier. Figure 4-1 shows what **htop** looks like when you run it.

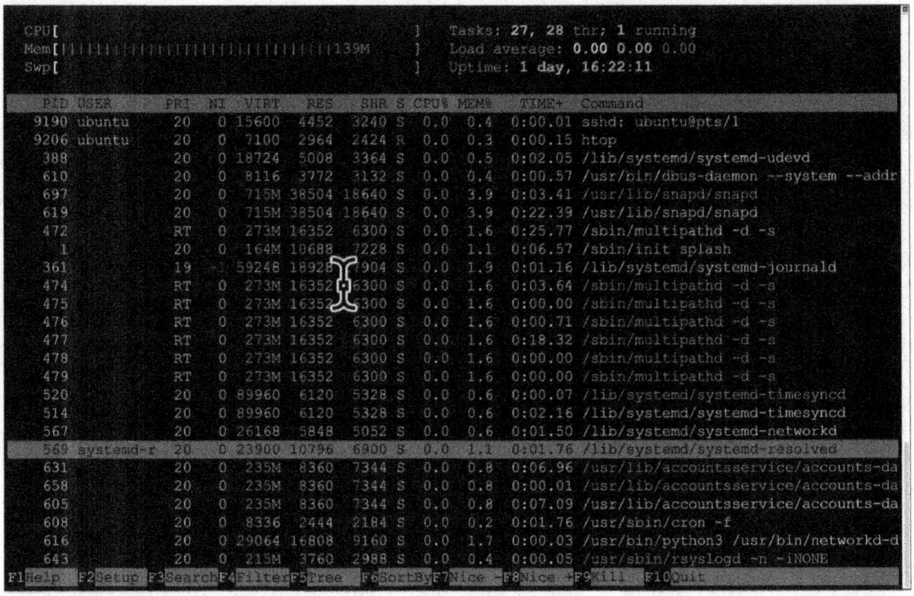

```
  CPU[                                    ]    Tasks: 27, 28 thr; 1 running
  Mem[||||||||||||||||||||||||||||||139M  ]    Load average: 0.00 0.00 0.00
  Swp[                                    ]    Uptime: 1 day, 16:22:11

    PID USER      PRI  NI  VIRT   RES   SHR S CPU% MEM%   TIME+  Command
   9190 ubuntu     20   0 15600  4452  3240 S  0.0  0.4  0:00.01 sshd: ubuntu@pts/1
   9206 ubuntu     20   0  7100  2964  2424 R  0.0  0.3  0:00.15 htop
    388            20   0 18724  5008  3364 S  0.0  0.5  0:02.05 /lib/systemd/systemd-udevd
    610            20   0  8116  3772  3132 S  0.0  0.4  0:00.57 /usr/bin/dbus-daemon --system --addr
    697            20   0  715M 38504 18640 S  0.0  3.9  0:03.41 /usr/lib/snapd/snapd
    619            20   0  715M 38504 18640 S  0.0  3.9  0:22.39 /usr/lib/snapd/snapd
    472            RT   0  273M 16352  6300 S  0.0  1.6  0:25.77 /sbin/multipathd -d -s
      1            20   0  164M 10688  7228 S  0.0  1.1  0:06.57 /sbin/init splash
    361            19  -1 59248 18928  7904 S  0.0  1.9  0:01.16 /lib/systemd/systemd-journald
    474            RT   0  273M 16352  6300 S  0.0  1.6  0:03.64 /sbin/multipathd -d -s
    475            RT   0  273M 16352  6300 S  0.0  1.6  0:00.00 /sbin/multipathd -d -s
    476            RT   0  273M 16352  6300 S  0.0  1.6  0:00.71 /sbin/multipathd -d -s
    477            RT   0  273M 16352  6300 S  0.0  1.6  0:18.32 /sbin/multipathd -d -s
    478            RT   0  273M 16352  6300 S  0.0  1.6  0:00.00 /sbin/multipathd -d -s
    479            RT   0  273M 16352  6300 S  0.0  1.6  0:00.00 /sbin/multipathd -d -s
    520            20   0 89960  6120  5328 S  0.0  0.6  0:00.07 /lib/systemd/systemd-timesyncd
    514            20   0 89960  6120  5328 S  0.0  0.6  0:02.16 /lib/systemd/systemd-timesyncd
    567            20   0 26168  5848  5052 S  0.0  0.6  0:01.50 /lib/systemd/systemd-networkd
    569 systemd-r  20   0 23900 10796  6900 S  0.0  1.1  0:01.76 /lib/systemd/systemd-resolved
    631            20   0  235M  8360  7344 S  0.0  0.8  0:06.96 /usr/lib/accountsservice/accounts-da
    658            20   0  235M  8360  7344 S  0.0  0.8  0:00.01 /usr/lib/accountsservice/accounts-da
    605            20   0  235M  8360  7344 S  0.0  0.8  0:07.09 /usr/lib/accountsservice/accounts-da
    608            20   0  8336  2444  2184 S  0.0  0.2  0:01.76 /usr/sbin/cron -f
    616            20   0 29064 16808  9160 S  0.0  1.7  0:00.03 /usr/bin/python3 /usr/bin/networkd-d
    643            20   0  213M  3760  2988 S  0.0  0.4  0:00.05 /usr/sbin/rsyslogd -n -iNONE
F1Help F2Setup F3Search F4Filter F5Tree  F6SortBy F7Nice - F8Nice + F9Kill  F10Quit
```

Figure 4-1 Viewing processes with the **htop** command

The free Command

The **free** command is used to determine the amount of free memory on a system, not just by displaying the amount of unused system RAM but also by giving you more detailed information about how much free and in-use physical memory you have, how much swap space or disk-based fake memory is in use, and how much of the used system RAM is being taken up by buffers and caches.

There is a moment in every class I teach when a student/attendee looks at the output of the **free** command and gets a quizzical look on her face because she can't reconcile the actual amount of RAM in use on the system with the current load. I always take the time to explain that system RAM on a lightly utilized system is like a bus that is only half full of passengers: Every passenger has room in the seat next to him or her for magazines, snacks, and drinks and ample room to stretch out a bit. I then make the correlation between the passenger and a running process. I point out that the room the passenger has allocated to her is similar to the working set (everything needed to run) for a process. The key here is that when lightly loaded, a system can allocate otherwise unused system RAM to handy and useful items such as cache and buffers, and the processes can stretch out a bit and have fully loaded working sets for efficient running of the processes.

Blocks and Buffers

Key to the running of processes and the speed of processing on a system are blocks and buffers. Block devices such as disks have an addressable unit called a block. This is typically (though not always) 512 bytes in size. System software also uses a construct called a block, but it's typically much larger than the physical size of a block on a hard disk or another block device.

When a disk block is read into system memory, it's stored in a buffer. A buffer is associated with one and only one block, and that buffer is used to address the data contained in that block while in memory.

Pages, Slabs, and Caches

The kernel uses *pages* to manage memory on a system. The processor can address very small units of memory (such as a "word" or "byte"), but the memory management unit uses pages and only addresses memory in page-sized chunks. The kernel addresses every single page of the memory in the struct_page table and includes in the table information that is critical to managing that page in each page's entry.

Pages are frequently populated with the same data, read from buffers and written back to caches for later reading. The system manages its own structure and marks pages as being used or free; the system can also use a number of other flags or parameters, but they are not important in this conversation.

Caches are made up of slabs; a slab is typically one page, though it can be multiple contiguous pages. To illustrate the relationship between a cache and a slab, we can say that a cache is like a city, a slab is like a neighborhood, and a page is like a block in that neighborhood.

To sum this all up, blocks are data locations on disk, blocks are read into buffers when a file or set of files is requested from disk, and then when those buffers are read into a page in memory, that page is a part of a slab or set of slabs that make up a cache.

To continue the bus and passenger analogy from earlier, remember that a lightly loaded system shows a large utilization of RAM but also a correspondingly hefty use of cache and buffers, while a heavily loaded system, with many processes running, shows a lot of RAM in use but relatively low cache and buffers. Effectively, as you load up the system with more processes, all the passengers/processes have to tighten up their working sets; put their magazines, snacks, extra luggage, and drinks in the overhead rack or under the seat; and be respectful of their fellow passengers/ processes.

Interpreting Displayed Information from free

free has a number of options, but before we look at execution examples, it's important to discuss and define the columns of output you see. The following definitions are from the **free** man page:

```
total Total installed memory (MemTotal and SwapTotal in /proc/
meminfo)used memory (calculated as total - free)
free Unused memory (MemFree and SwapFree in /proc/meminfo)
shared Memory used (mostly) by tmpfs (Shmem in /proc/meminfo,
available on kernels 2.6.32, displayed as zero if not available)
buffers Memory used by kernel buffers (Buffers in /proc/meminfo)
cached Memory used by the page cache (Cached in /proc/meminfo)
```

As you read this section, remember that all this information is available in raw formats in the **/proc/meminfo** directory in the various files mentioned. The **free** command simply reads that data and displays it in a more organized and configurable manner for your viewing pleasure.

Look at the **total** column in Figure 4-2. That's the total RAM on the virtual machine on which the **free** command is being run. The next two columns, **used** and **free**, tell exactly how much RAM is being used and how much remains not in use.

```
rbrunson@linux-ab2x:~> free -h
            total      used      free    shared   buffers    cached
Mem:         2.0G      1.2G      802M       20M      876K      744M
-/+ buffers/cache:     458M      1.5G
Swap:        2.0G        0B      2.0G
rbrunson@linux-ab2x:~> █
```

Figure 4-2 Running the **free** command with the **-h** option

The **buffers** and **cached** columns show the amounts of RAM currently being used to store the buffers and cache, and these numbers will likely change over time and with differing amounts of loads. If you want to see some of these items change, you can use commands. For example, to see changes in the **cached** column, execute the **find / -iname ".txt"** command to find every text file on the system that you have access to, and you see the **cached** column expand as it predictively loads a lot of files that the system now assumes you might read or use another utility upon. Then run the **free** command again to see the changes made to the numbers, particularly the **cached** column, as many files are found and predictively cached in case you might need to read them; that read would be from memory, not from disk.

In addition, you can use the **--lohi** long option to get a more detailed summary of the information. It's helpful to also include the **-h** option to get the summary information in kilobytes, megabytes, gigabytes, and so on (see Figure 4-3).

```
rbrunson@linux-ab2x:~> free --lohi -h
                total       used       free     shared    buffers     cached
Mem:            2.0G       1.2G       801M        20M       876K       745M
Low:            2.0G       1.2G       801M
High:             0B         0B         0B
-/+ buffers/cache:         458M       1.5G
Swap:           2.0G         0B       2.0G
rbrunson@linux-ab2x:~> ▮
```

Figure 4-3   Running the **free** command with the **--lohi** option

Sending Signals to Processes

Traditionally, when learning about *signals* and processes, you're introduced to a list of signals, with an explanation to the right of each signal, and then you're taught about the **kill** and **killall** commands. If you're lucky and your teacher likes to use *pgrep* or *pkill*, you learn a bit about those as well.

Table 4-2 shows the commonly used signal names, their numeric equivalents, and what each signal does to a process.

Table 4-2   Common Linux Signals

Signal Name	Numeric Code	Explanation of Action Taken
SIGHUP	1	Hang up or shut down and restart the process
SIGINT	2	Interrupt the process (used by **Ctrl+C**)
SIGKILL	9	Kill the process (cannot be ignored or caught elsewhere)
SIGTERM	15	Terminate the signal (can be ignored or caught)
SIGTSTP	20	Stop the terminal (used by **Ctrl+Z**)
SIGSTOP	23	Stop execution (cannot be caught or ignored)

The most common way to send a signal to a given process is by pressing **Ctrl+C** while the command or script is processing and not interrupting the process unnecessarily. If you wait a reasonable amount of time and nothing happens, or if the process seems locked up, by all means interrupt the process; just be aware that you might lose a small bit of data or suffer other unintended consequences.

> **NOTE**   Obviously, if you are running a data-generating command, interruption might have consequences, but merely interrupting a long file search or an output command is relatively risk free. At times a process is marked as "uninterruptible" or in a state of "uninterruptible sleep," and this typically means that the process is waiting on I/O from a disk or network. The presence of a **D** indicator in the eighth column of **egrep**, or in the **ps** output when using the **aux** switches or options, indicates the uninterruptible sleep state. More about this state can be found in the man page for the **ps** command, under the header "PROCESS STATE CODES."

Another common method of sending a signal to a running process is to press **Ctrl+Z** to send the process a SIGTSTP or 20 signal, effectively pausing the process, which is typically then put into the background by the *bg* command, as in job control. This is covered in the "Job Control" section, later in the chapter.

Killing Processes by PID

The normal method for stopping a process is to use either the **kill** or the **killall** utility to send a polite kill to it. When you encounter a process that can't be removed from memory because it's not receiving signals or perhaps due to sheer orneriness, you need to kill the process and remove it from memory.

Remember that the **kill** and **killall** commands simply send signals to the process; they don't actually remove the processes.

The default **kill** signal is number 15, with signal name SIGTERM. This signal politely requests the process to end and allows it to clean up its memory. If you type the **kill** command and the process ID (PID) of a program, the SIGTERM signal (15) is sent to that program.

The SIGHUP, HUP, or 1 signal is a special case. It's what we could call a bounce signal, where the process isn't just killed but instead is signaled to end and then restart itself. The most common reason to use a bounce signal is to have a process such as a server daemon stop, reread its configuration files, and then start up again. You can specify this signal by using either **-1** or **-HUP**, as shown here:

```
kill -1 PID or kill -HUP PID (bounces or restarts processes)
```

> **NOTE**   Many server admins have had to "bounce" a service on a server, either to reread a configuration file or to get the service working again after it mysteriously stopped working. You are likely to see bounce signals on the Linux+ exam; it's a commonly missed section of this topic.

The SIGKILL or 9 signal is the ultimate kill signal. Even if a process is a *zombie* (that is, can't be killed by any other means), a **kill -9 PID** command usually kills the process and removes it from memory:

```
$ kill -9 PID or kill -KILL PID (puts a bullet in the process, no
saves)
```

The process being killed with SIGKILL has no opportunity to save data or do anything else.

Using pgrep and pkill to Send Signals

Using the **ps** command to get PID information and then the **kill** command to send signals is fine, but there are times when it doesn't seem to be the most efficient way to interact with multiple processes.

When you need to send the same signal to many processes, such as worker threads for a web server, or Chrome helper agents, consider using the **pgrep** command to query those processes by name, and see what is returned.

The **pgrep** and **pkill** commands are like a good pair of criminal investigators: one does the questioning of the suspects, and the other is the enforcer. You will typically use the **pgrep** command to search for a string or regular expression, and then see if those PIDs are what you want to send signals to, and then use the **pkill** command to actually send those signals using that same exact string or regular expression.

For example, you might have run the **ps aux** command **| grep -i "Chrome Helper"** and gotten something similar to the following output:

```
$ ps aux | grep -i sshd
root          660  0.0  0.6  12212  6368 ?      Ss   Feb16   0:00
sshd: /usr/sbin/sshd -D
root          791  0.0  0.7  15464  7420 ?      Ss   Feb16   0:00
sshd: ubuntu [priv]
ubuntu        914  0.0  0.4  15600  4540 ?      S    Feb16   0:00
sshd: ubuntu@notty
root         7121  0.0  0.7  15464  7764 ?      Ss   18:10   0:00
sshd: ubuntu [priv]
ubuntu       7230  0.0  0.4  15600  4400 ?      S    18:10   0:00
sshd: ubuntu@pts/0
ubuntu       7251  0.0  0.0   7692   668 pts/0  S+   18:16   0:00
grep --color=auto sshd
```

You could laboriously and individually kill each of the PIDs you see here, or you can use the **pgrep** command to effectively do the same search and return the PIDs of the processes it matches:

```
$ pgrep -i sshd
660
```

```
791
914
7121
7230
```

As you can see, the PIDs that **pgrep** brings back match the ones that **ps aux** showed, but just the PIDs. If you want to, you can tell **pgrep** to show you some context of what it found:

```
$ pgrep -l sshd
660 sshd
791 sshd
914 sshd
7121 sshd
7230 sshd
```

Alternatively, or more explicitly, you can ask **pgrep** for *much* more information about the processes it returns, such as:

```
$ pgrep -ia sshd
660 sshd: /usr/sbin/sshd -D 0 of 10-100 startups
791 sshd: ubuntu [priv]
914 sshd: ubuntu@notty
7121 sshd: ubuntu [priv]
7230 sshd: ubuntu@pts/0
```

The **-a** option shows the full command line in addition to the PID, so you can ensure that you really are about to send a possibly process-terminating signal to the right processes!

NOTE Another option for querying the process table for a match between names of programs and their PID is the *pidof* command. Also known as the **killall5** command, **pidof** will work differently depending on what name you use to invoke it. Think of **pidof** as being similar in function to the **pgrep** command and **killall5** as being similar to the **pkill** command.

From this point, using **pkill** is really quite easy, now that you have determined that you have exactly the right processes to send the signal to. To change this just press the up arrow and then press the **HOME** button and change **pgrep** to **pkill** and then press **Enter** to execute a typical SIGTERM on the processes.

Should you wish to use **pkill** to send any other signals to the processes, just use the **--signal <*signal*>** option and parameter to send those processes that other signal:

```
$ pkill -i sshd --signal 9
```

> **NOTE**   We aren't done with the **pkill** command! The next section will show you how to use it with substitutions to make sending signals to many processes even easier.

Killing Processes Using Other Criteria

Sometimes you can't kill a process by the PID—because it's unavailable or you can't find it in the process table by using the **ps** command or for some other reason. Other times, there may be so many similarly named processes that you don't want to take the considerable time it would entail to kill them all by PID, or you don't really care which process it is; you want to clean house of that particular sort of named or similar process and reexecute the command.

The most common way to kill multiple similarly named processes is to use the **killall** command. I used to joke that the command was created by an insanely frustrated Netscape Communicator user who had programming skills, so he could clear off all the **netscape** processes on his machine and restart the browser, but this might not be completely true. (However, from my experience, it should be.) You might experience this problem with Google's **Chrome** browser, so if you prefer, use chrome in your **killall** commands.

Using **killall** is simple. You can run **ps aux** to find out the names of the processes you want to kill and then use the **killall** command followed by the name, such as

```
# killall process_name
```

On a more elegant or complex level, you can use the **pkill** or **process kill** command, which isn't just limited to the use of the process's command name but can find and send signals to processes based on numerous criteria, including

- Process name
- Process ID
- Username
- Session ID
- Terminal

Usage of **pkill** is not very complex, but if you use multiple criteria, such as username and controlling terminal, all the criteria must match, or the signal won't be sent. The **pkill** command has a companion app, **pgrep**, that is most often used to test a desired **pkill** command before figuratively pulling the trigger on it.

Another great and useful feature of **pgrep** is that you can use it to find processes and then feed them to another command, such as **renice**. For example, to find all running Chrome browser processes and change the *priority* level on them, you could use the following command:

```
# renice +5 'pgrep chrome'
```

This finds all the **chrome** named processes in the process table and executes the **renice +5** command on them, effectively dropping their priority from the default.

When using **pkill**, you typically use the same command and options used with **pgrep**, only **pkill** goes ahead and executes the signal pass on the process instead of sending the output to stdout or the *console*, as **pgrep** usually does.

NOTE   A quick warning about using **killall** or **pkill** as the root user: If you run either command as root, it kills *all* the processes on the system that match the criteria, regardless of the owner, which may not be what you wanted. It also introduces you to all your users, as they call to ask what happened on the server. The safest ways to run these commands are as a normal user or very carefully as the root user.

Finding What Is Using a Resource

Few things are as irritating to a system operator as having a process that is using a resource stop you from unmounting, performing disk checks, or otherwise interacting with a disk—all because some process is keeping it tied up.

Introducing lsof

For times when a process is keeping a resource tied up, there is the **lsof** command, which at its simplest lists the open files (as the name suggests), although it can be incredibly detailed in its use of parameters and options.

Before we look closely at **lsof**, it's important to be aware that open files come in many different flavors on Linux systems, as just about everything on the system is expressed as a file. Open files come in the following types:

- **Regular:** A regular file could be a text file, a graphic, a library, and so on.
- **Directory:** A directory file can contain links to other files or directory files.
- **Block:** Block files give access to devices that can be read and written to in blocks, such as disk devices.

- **Character:** Character files give access to character or raw devices such as scanners, keyboards, mice, and so on.

- **Library:** Library files include system libraries, such as **libc**, or any compiled collection of software routines that a program would call during its operation.

- **Socket:** A socket is an endpoint for communication. Examples include network sockets where data is sent through the socket to another system via network packets.

Using **lsof**

You can use *lsof* to list the open files on a system's root as demonstrated in Example 4-1.

Example 4-1   Listing the Open Files on System Root

```
# lsof /

COMMAND     PID  USER    FD    TYPE DEVICE SIZE/OFF    NODE NAME
systemd     893 rossb   cwd    DIR   8,1     4096       2 /
mate-sess   936 rossb   txt    REG   8,1   248144  918396 /usr/bin/
mate-session
mate-sess   936 rossb   rtd    DIR   8,1     4096       2 /
In the output above you see the following columns:
COMMAND - this is the program/executable/process name
PID - The Process ID (PID) of the command
USER - The user account the command belongs to
FD - File Descriptor (type of file), a full list is in the lsof man
page
TYPE - Short codes for the type of file, there are many, consult the
man page
DEVICE - The device numbers for files, or memory or kernel reference
SIZE/OFF - The size of the file, or the file's offset (distance from
the start of the file or a memory address)
NODE - The node number of local files, IP packets, streams or even an
IRQ of a device
NAME - The name of the mount point and file system where the file
lives
To find all the open files on a system that are in use by a user's
processes, you add the -u username option:
```

```
lsof -u rossb
COMMAND    PID  USER    FD    TYPE DEVICE SIZE/OFF    NODE NAME
systemd    893 rossb  cwd    DIR    8,1    4096        2 /
mate-sess  936 rossb  txt    REG    8,1  248144  918396 /usr/bin/
mate-session
mate-sess  936 rossb  rtd    DIR    8,1    4096        2 /
```
To find all the files that are NOT open for a particular user, such
as the root user, you can use the command:
```
lsof  -u^root
COMMAND    PID  TID       USER    FD    TYPE       DEVICE SIZE/OFF
NODE NAME
systemd-r  419    systemd-resolve  cwd    unknown
  /proc/419/cwd (readlink: Permission  denied)
systemd-r  419    systemd-resolve  rtd    unknown
  /proc/419/root (readlink: Permission denied)
systemd-r  419    systemd-resolve  txt    unknown
  /proc/419/exe (readlink: Permission  denied)
```

Job Control

Job control was invented when users had access to only a single terminal, and getting more work done usually required another terminal. Job control allows a user
to run multiple commands in a background mode while working in the foreground
application.

When using the shell, a program can be run, suspended, and then put into the background, or the command can be invoked and put into the background in one step.

NOTE   When you are putting commands into the background, you use the **&** character
at the end of the command line, separated by a space, such as **command1 -option &**.
This causes the command to be put into the background at execution time.

Job control involves the following steps:

Step 1.   Start a task such as an editor.

Step 2.   Suspend the program by pressing **Ctrl+Z**.

Step 3.   Execute the **jobs** command to see the status:

```
# jobs
[1]+ Stopped vim
```

Step 4.   Send job 1 to the background by typing bg and pressing **Enter**:

```
# bg
[1]+ vim &
```

Step 5.   Start another program, such as **top**, in the background:

```
# top &
```

Step 6.   Run the **jobs** command to see which jobs are there and how they are numbered:

```
# jobs
[1]- Stopped vim
[2]+ Stopped top
```

In the output of the *jobs* command, there are three designations a job can have:

- A plus sign (**+**) next to a job indicates the current job, and any commands such as **fg** or **bg** act on that job by default.
- A minus sign (**-**) next to a job indicates the previous job or the next-to-last job to be operated on.
- Lack of a character indicates a regular job, and no actions are taken on it unless specified by job number.

Step 7.   Put the default job into the foreground mode with the *fg* command. The top command comes to the foreground.

Step 8.   Quit the **top** command by pressing **Q**.

Step 9.   Run the **jobs** command again and notice that the vim job is now the current job again.

Step 10.   Kill the vim job by typing its ID with the **kill** command:

```
# kill %1
Vim: Caught deadly signal TERM
Vim: Finished.
```

Step 11.   Run the **jobs** command again. You see the results of your action as reported by the Job Control function. In this case, job 1 is terminated.

NOTE   Be prepared to answer a question on the Linux+ exam about what command or character sequences might put into the background or foreground a process listed in the **jobs** command output. You should also know what the **jobs** command **+** symbol indicates.

Managing Process Priorities

Linux uses a combination of priority and scheduling to run multiple processes in what appears to be multitasking on a single processor. On multiple processors, this makes for actual multitasking.

Strangely, the process priorities are backward, like a lot of other things, and they stretch from –20 as the highest to 19 as the lowest (see Figure 4-4).

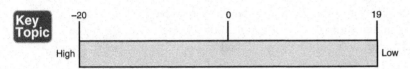

Figure 4-4   Linux process priorities

A process's default priority is normally 0 when started, unless the programmer needs to set the starting priority higher. Although users can start a process with a lower priority (from 0 to 19), only the root user can start a process with a higher priority (0 to –20).

Many sysadmins have discovered too late what it means to have multiple programs running at a priority that is too high. Having too many processes with high priorities can slow a machine drastically, cause it to become unresponsive, and even cause crashes.

There are two main times to specify or alter a process's priority: at program start and while the program is running.

To start a program with a lower priority (the default), use the **nice** command:

```
# nice kitty.sh
```

This causes the **kitty.sh** script to run at a priority of 10, which is the default when you don't specify a value. The *nice* utility makes programs play nicely with others, relieving some of the stress of running multiple processor- or I/O-intensive programs.

You can also specify a priority by using the **-n** option followed by the increment by which you want to alter the default, such as

```
# nice -n 10 kitty.sh
```

To change the priority of a process while it's running, you use the *renice* program, as shown here:

```
ps aux | grep mybigcompile
rbrunson 14729 19.2 0.6 1656 524/pts/0 R 01:30 mybigcompile
renice +5 14729
```

This command string causes the process mybigcompile (process ID 14729) to run at an altered priority of +5. When using the **renice** utility, there isn't a default priority; you must specify the priority.

NOTE A regular user can only change an existing process to a lower priority—that is, a higher number. Only the root user can change a process's priority to any value.

The other option for altering a running program's priority is a feature of the **top** command. The *top* command shows a refreshed screen of processes with the highest CPU usage, configurable to show only active processes or a specific number of processes (see Figure 4-5).

top reads its configuration from **/etc/toprc** or **.toprc**, where it can be restricted for use by users in order to make it less dangerous. **top** runs interactively by default, refreshing every 5 seconds.

You can make **top** do some fun things. Try these:

- **top d 1:** Runs and refreshes every 1 second.

- **top i:** Shows only active processes and may be toggled on and off.

```
top - 19:25:25 up 23:09,  1 user,  load average: 0.00, 0.00, 0.00
Tasks:  88 total,   1 running,  87 sleeping,   0 stopped,   0 zombie
%Cpu(s):  0.0 us,  0.3 sy,  0.0 ni, 99.3 id,  0.3 wa,  0.0 hi,  0.0 si,  0.0 st
MiB Mem :    970.0 total,    221.7 free,    136.5 used,    611.8 buff/cache
MiB Swap:      0.0 total,      0.0 free,      0.0 used.    750.1 avail Mem

    PID USER      PR  NI    VIRT    RES    SHR S  %CPU  %MEM     TIME+ COMMAND
      1 root      20   0  168328  10688   7228 S   0.0   1.1   0:02.43 systemd
      2 root      20   0       0      0      0 S   0.0   0.0   0:00.11 kthreadd
      3 root       0 -20       0      0      0 I   0.0   0.0   0:00.00 rcu_gp
      4 root       0 -20       0      0      0 I   0.0   0.0   0:00.00 rcu_par_gp
      6 root       0 -20       0      0      0 I   0.0   0.0   0:00.00 kworker/0:0H-kblockd
      8 root       0 -20       0      0      0 I   0.0   0.0   0:00.00 mm_percpu_wq
      9 root      20   0       0      0      0 S   0.0   0.0   0:01.85 ksoftirqd/0
     10 root      20   0       0      0      0 I   0.0   0.0   0:00.43 rcu_sched
     11 root      rt   0       0      0      0 S   0.0   0.0   0:01.10 migration/0
     12 root     -51   0       0      0      0 S   0.0   0.0   0:00.00 idle_inject/0
     14 root      20   0       0      0      0 S   0.0   0.0   0:00.00 cpuhp/0
     15 root      20   0       0      0      0 S   0.0   0.0   0:00.00 kdevtmpfs
     16 root       0 -20       0      0      0 I   0.0   0.0   0:00.00 netns
     17 root      20   0       0      0      0 S   0.0   0.0   0:00.00 rcu_tasks_kthre
     18 root      20   0       0      0      0 S   0.0   0.0   0:00.00 kauditd
     19 root      20   0       0      0      0 S   0.0   0.0   0:00.11 khungtaskd
     20 root      20   0       0      0      0 S   0.0   0.0   0:00.00 oom_reaper
     21 root       0 -20       0      0      0 I   0.0   0.0   0:00.00 writeback
     22 root      20   0       0      0      0 S   0.0   0.0   0:00.00 kcompactd0
     23 root      25   5       0      0      0 S   0.0   0.0   0:00.00 ksmd
     24 root      39  19       0      0      0 S   0.0   0.0   0:00.00 khugepaged
     70 root       0 -20       0      0      0 I   0.0   0.0   0:00.00 kintegrityd
     71 root       0 -20       0      0      0 I   0.0   0.0   0:00.00 kblockd
     72 root       0 -20       0      0      0 I   0.0   0.0   0:00.00 blkcg_punt_bio
     73 root       0 -20       0      0      0 I   0.0   0.0   0:00.00 tpm_dev_wq
```

Figure 4-5 The **top** command

You can also use some interactive options with **top**

- **space** Updates the display immediately.
- **h** Provides help for **top**.
- **k** Kills a process; a prompt appears for the PID.
- **i** Either displays or ignores zombie/idle processes.
- **n** Prompts for the number of processes to display.
- **r** Prompts for the PID to affect and then provides the new priority.

NOTE You can sort the output of the **top** command by pressing the **R** key to sort the PIDs from high to low (a reverse sort). You can also invoke **top** with the **-o** option and specify a sort field to show the results sorted on that field immediately.

Finally, you can use the **top** command as a "fire and forget" command to send the current **top** output to you via email by using the following command:

```
top -b -n 1 | mail root@yourserver.xxx -s "Top output from Server 1"
```

This command runs **top** in batch mode (**-b**) one iteration or time (**-n 1**) and sends the output not to the console but to the email address specified with the subject line (**-s**) specified. Try this on your local system, and then check system mail by running **mail**. You see the subject line for the email and can read the output.

systemd

systemd is both a new method of system initialization and a method that is vaguely familiar to those who have historically used SysVinit as their initialization method.

systemd was specifically written to replace the SysVinit system, while keeping some connection to the methodology of SysVinit as well as some command compatibility.

What's Different About systemd?

Although controversial at its introduction, often predicted to increase the likelihood of broken system dependencies, and just generally hated-upon because, well, it was new, systemd has nonetheless become the default system initialization method for most modern Linux distributions.

The hallmarks or major features of systemd are

- It's not SysVinit.

- It's considered more efficient than, and parallel in operation to, SysVinit.

- It's less dependency driven than other methods.

- It allows for more prioritization of what services start first and have precedence over system resources.

- It can dramatically reduce system startup times.

Similar to the init daemon from the SysVinit method, the systemd daemon is linked to by using a symlink from **/sbin/init**. More than 60 binaries are included in the entire systemd suite, with the following being its core components:

- **systemd:** The systems and services manager for the operating system

- *systemctl*: The systemd state inspection and state-controlling utility

- **systemd-analyze:** The utility that allows you to inspect performance statistics regarding system bootup as well as view trace and current state information

A number of additional daemons and libraries make up the core functionality of systemd, including

- **journald:** The default logging system for systemd, which uses binary files for logging. It can be replaced by more traditional logging mechanisms such as rsyslog and syslog-ng.

- **consoled:** A console daemon for use as a user console, which replaces the more traditional virtual terminal system with a potentially more system-friendly component.

- **networkd:** The daemon that provides networking support for systemd's network access.

- **logind:** A daemon designed to replace Consolekit, which supports X display managers, user logins, and so on.

Additional features of systemd that are useful to administrators include

- **Logging capabilities:** The system's *entire* set of log messages is stored securely in systemd's journal, reducing message loss and increasing the reliability of troubleshooting.

- **Service activation:** systemd's way of dealing with services frees them from a given runlevel and allows them to be more on-demand in nature, activated by a number of hardware and software events.

- **Component groups:** Cgroups are similar in structure and function to the historical SysVinit runlevels in that they have a hierarchy of what starts when and before or after what other service. Cgroups improve system memory space cleanliness dramatically by using a group tag for processes that allows the precise and total removal of groups of processes from memory.

- **System resource allocation:** Because you can determine exactly what Cgroup a service is associated with, it's possible to more precisely control what system resources a service or group of services can consume. Whereas before you could only control a runaway or hog process with **nice** or **renice**, systemd allows the exact setting of a limited set of resources per service. An example of this would be an Apache server that gets hit by an extreme number of visitors and would traditionally grow its processes to take over a majority of the system's resources. Now that service or group of services can be controlled exactly.

Units in systemd

When using systemd instead of SysVinit, you swap out the concept of "init scripts" for systemd "units." Effectively, a unit is a file that represents the configuration of a system service, much as the init scripts did in SysVinit.

> **NOTE** A *unit* is a capability of the system and is defined by a **.service** file, so you may find in the documentation, in conversation about systemd, and even in this book that *service* and *unit* are used interchangeably in discussing the units that are defined by a **.service** file.

systemd units come in a number of types. The name of the service is the prefix of the filename, followed by a . and then the type of service as the postfix of the filename, such as **blahwoof.service**.

Unit File Directory Locations

systemd units are typically located in the following directories and, in order of appearance, take precedence over each other:

- **/usr/lib/systemd/system/:** Units that have been installed with the distribution

- **/run/systemd/system:** Units that have been created at runtime; may have precedence over non-runtime or installed units

- **/etc/systemd/system:** Units that are controlled by the sysadmin and have ultimate precedence over all the other units

Table 4-3 lists the service types and the extension for each service, and it provides a description of each service.

Table 4-3   systemd Unit Types

Type of Service	Extension	Description
Service	**.service**	A given system service
Socket	**.socket**	An IPC (interprocess communication) socket
Target	**.target**	A grouping of units
Mount	**.mount**	A mount point on a filesystem
Automount	**.automount**	An automount point on a filesystem
Device	**.device**	A device file used by the kernel
Scope	**.scope**	A process created externally
Timer	**.timer**	A timer
Path	**.path**	A file or directory on a filesystem
Slice	**.slice**	A grouping of units in a hierarchy; used to manage system processes
Snapshot	**.snapshot**	A saved instance of the state of the systemd manager
Swap	**.swap**	A swap file or a swap device

systemd Environment Variables

systemd environment variables are set via the **EnvironmentFile=** directive in the [Service] section of the **foobar.service** file that defines that service.

For example, to make information from the **/etc/locale.conf** file available in the environment of the **display-manager.service** file, you would place the following line in the **/etc/systemd/system/display-manager.service** file:

```
EnvironmentFile=-/ec/locale.conf
```

NOTE   The **-** character is used before the file to disable the generation of any error messages in the event that this file is not found.

systemd Targets and Runlevels

In SysVinit systems, you had a defined but configurable set of runlevels numbered from 0 to 6. A *runlevel* is essentially a set of capabilities or running services that you can predefine and set the system to boot to so you have a predictable set of services.

In systemd, targets are the new runlevels. For example, the **default.target** file is typically a symbolic link to another target file, such as the **graphical.target** file. Targets correspond to the SysVinit runlevels. Table 4-4 shows the correlation between runlevels, targets, and the files, and describes what action occurs when each runlevel or target is initiated.

Table 4-4   What Happens When Runlevels and Targets Are Initiated

Runlevel	Target File	What It Does
0	**poweroff.target**	Shuts down and powers off the system
1	**rescue.target**	Configures a rescue shell session
2	**multi-user.target**	Sets the system to a nongraphical multiuser system, typically with no network services
3	**multi-user.target**	Sets up the system as a nongraphical multiuser system, with network services
4	**multi-user.target**	Sets up the system as a nongraphical multiuser system, with network services
5	**graphical.target**	Sets up the system as a graphical multiuser system with network services
6	**reboot.target**	Shuts down and boots the system again

NOTE   The targets also have another designation, for compatibility: **runlevel#.target**, where the # character would be 0 through 6.

Wants and Requires

The systemd procedure uses a set of options or requirements called "wants" and "requires" to indicate dependencies between units and groups of units.

For example, if you were to look at the typical contents of the **graphical.target** file, you might find the following lines:

```
Requires=multi-user.target
After=multi-user.target
Wants=display-manager.service
```

The **Requires** statement means that before **graphical.target** can be processed, all the items listed in **multi-user.target** must be started, which means that all the linked services in the **/usr/lib/systemd/multi-user.target** directory must be started. Only after that requirement is met will the **Wants** statement be processed (which again means the starting of linked services in the appropriate directory, this time the **/usr/lib/systemd/multi-user.target.want** directory), after which **graphical.target** will be used.

Booting with systemd

When booting a system that uses systemd, the same steps outlined previously occur. However, when the system starts **systemd/init** from GRUB, a structure reminiscent of SysVinit's init script structure is overlaid on the system.

The file that is read after the kernel and initramdisk is typically the **default.target** file, which is simply a link to the **multi-user.target** file. This is where it gets pretty strange because although the boot process might look simple, as shown in Example 4-2, it's not.

Example 4-2   Theoretical Hierarchy of the Boot Process

```
Kernel
 |
 V
multi-user.target
 |
 V
graphical.target
```

The reality of the situation is that **graphical.target** requires **multi-user.target**, which requires **basic.target**, which in turn requires **sysinit.target**. Each of these files must load its configured services successfully to move on to the next, and the real order of bootup is shown in Example 4-3.

Example 4-3   Actual Hierarchy of the Boot Process

```
local-fs-pre.target
 |
 V
sysinit.target -- wants local-fs.target and swap.target
 |
 V
basic.target -- wants
```

```
 |
 V
multi-user.target -- wants
 |
 V
graphical.target -- wants
```

It takes a while to bend your consciousness around the way systemd works, but in practice, it's not very different from SysVinit and its dozens of links in multiple directories.

Commands to Manage systemd

As briefly mentioned earlier, several commands are central to the systemd scenario. The goal of this section is to take you through the most common use of these commands, and in later sections we will expand on some of them for particular aspects of configuring and managing systemd devices.

The **systemctl** command is the main tool you will use to configure, modify, query, and manage unit files, services, targets, and just about anything else about systemd.

NOTE Typically you will need to use the **sudo** command as a prefix to any **systemctl** commands because of the nature of working with system-level services. You may be able to query status without elevated permissions, but you're unlikely on most systems to be able to make any changes.

The State of Services/Units

You can use **systemctl** to enable or disable unit/service files, essentially creating symlinks, the content of which is contained in the [Install] section of the unit file.

A systemd unit/service can be in a number of states, explained here:

- **enabled:** The service or unit has been configured to start on system boot.

- **disabled:** The service or unit has been configured to not start on system boot.

- **active:** The service or unit is running currently.

- **inactive:** The service or unit is not running currently, although if a connection request or similar function occurs, it may become active again.

- **stopped:** This means the service or unit will not respond until you either reboot (if it's configured to start on system boot) or manually restart.

Listing Services

Being able to list or find the services on a system is key to managing them properly. To list all of the services or units on your system, use the following command:

```
# systemctl list-units --type service
```

This command shows all the active units on the system. On my test system, it returned 69 units, all loaded and active, but some in an exited state, which can indicate an error or a service/unit that was run but isn't a daemon that continuously runs.

To show all the loaded units, including inactive ones on your system, use the following command:

```
# systemctl list-units --type service --all
```

This command shows all the active and inactive services/units on the system. My test system returned 151 units in its output from the command.

To list all the available services/units on a system, regardless of state or status, use the following command:

```
# systemctl list-unit-files
```

This command shows all the possible services/units on the system. My test system returned 403 services/units available, in various states.

Enabling and Disabling Services

To enable a given service, use the following command:

```
# systemctl enable servicename
```

This command reads the [Install] section of the unit file and creates an appropriate symlink in the **/etc/systemd/system** directory that points to the corresponding **/usr/lib/systemd/system/somename.service** file. The extension (**.service**) is not normally needed, however, as it's implied.

To disable a service, use the following command:

```
# systemctl disable servicename
```

This command removes the symlink to the **/usr/lib/systemd/system/somename.service** file from the **/etc/systemd/system** directory.

NOTE   The enabling or disabling of a unit is *not* the same as starting or stopping a unit; it simply creates the appropriate links so that it can be used properly or removes the links so that it's not restarted when that target is specified.

Reenabling a service involves disabling and then enabling the service in immediate succession, effectively removing and then creating the symlinks that are specified in the [Install] section of the service definition file.

To reenable a service, use the following command:

```
# systemctl reenable servicename
```

Service Start, Stop, Restart, and Status

One of the simplest or easiest things to do with a service is start it:

```
# systemctl start servicename
```

If the service is not already started, and you have permissions, the service will be started.

Starting and stopping services is fairly straightforward, but it is often wise to determine the service's *status command* first. To query a service's status, enter the **systemctl status** *servicename* command, as demonstrated in Example 4-4.

Example 4-4   Querying a Service's Status

```
# systemctl status tuned
tuned.service - Dynamic System Tuning Daemon
   Loaded: loaded (/usr/lib/systemd/system/tuned.service; enabled;
vendor preset: enabled)
   Active: active (running) since Sat 2019-01-05 18:29:04 EST;
2 weeks 2 days ago
     Docs: man:tuned(8)
           man:tuned.conf(5)
           man:tuned-adm(8)
 Main PID: 1170 (tuned)
    Tasks: 5
   CGroup: /system.slice/tuned.service
           |---1170 /usr/bin/python -Es /usr/sbin/tuned -l -P

Jan 05 18:29:01 localhost.localdomain systemd[1]: Starting Dynamic
System Tuning Daemon...
Jan 05 18:29:04 localhost.localdomain systemd[1]: Started Dynamic
System Tuning Daemon.
```

As you can see from the output in Example 4-4, the tuned service is loaded and active, and the vendor has specified that this service be enabled by default, so it will normally be running when the system has been booted.

To stop the tuned service and see what the output shows, use the following command:

```
# systemctl stop tuned
```

Now you can query the status with the same command as before, as demonstrated in Example 4-5.

Example 4-5   Getting the Status of a Tuned Service

```
# systemctl status tuned
tuned.service - Dynamic System Tuning Daemon
   Loaded: loaded (/usr/lib/systemd/system/tuned.service; enabled;
vendor preset: enabled)
   Active: inactive (dead) since Tue 2019-01-22 09:45:26 EST; 57s ago
     Docs: man:tuned(8)
           man:tuned.conf(5)
           man:tuned-adm(8)
  Process: 1170 ExecStart=/usr/sbin/tuned -l -P (code=exited,
status=0/SUCCESS)
 Main PID: 1170 (code=exited, status=0/SUCCESS)

Jan 05 18:29:01 localhost.localdomain systemd[1]: Starting Dynamic
System Tuning Daemon...
Jan 05 18:29:04 localhost.localdomain systemd[1]: Started Dynamic
System Tuning Daemon.
Jan 22 09:45:25 localhost.localdomain systemd[1]: Stopping Dynamic
System Tuning Daemon...
Jan 22 09:45:26 localhost.localdomain systemd[1]: Stopped Dynamic
System Tuning Daemon.
```

Notice from the output in Example 4-5 that the service is still loaded, but it's now inactive (dead) because it was stopped by the command.

It's easy at this point to either start the service again or, instead of stopping it and then starting it, you can issue a **restart** command:

```
# systemctl restart tuned
```

This has the same effect as stopping and starting the service. If for some reason you need to force a reloading of the service's configuration, you can use the **reload-or-restart** command:

```
# systemctl reload-or-restart tuned
```

This has the effect of causing the service to reload and read its configuration again.

Because of the way that systemd works, the concept of reloading a service or daemon is slightly more complex than with SysVinit. To reload a daemon running in the systemd world without causing it to be unavailable to user connections, the daemon is reloaded, the configuration files are reread, and the systemd dependency tree for the daemon is rebuilt. The **daemon-reload** command is very roughly similar to the concept of "hupping," or restarting a service without disrupting users, that occurs in SysVinit:

```
# systemctl daemon-reload
```

Masking Services

Starting and stopping services is fairly simple. At times a service starts a dependency that it thinks it wants or requires, and you really don't want that dependency to be used. Disabling the service does not guarantee that it won't be loaded; often it does get loaded by the upper-level service anyway. This is where *mask command* or masking comes in.

To mask a service, you use the **mask** command:

```
# systemctl mask servicename
```

This command creates a symlink that doesn't point to the normal location, which would be one of the service files in **/etc/systemd/system**, but instead the link is created to the bit bucket, **/dev/null**. Linking the dependency service to **/dev/null** guarantees that it will not load; even if it exists elsewhere on the system, that link takes precedence.

Once the service has been masked, unmasking it again (such as when you are done testing something that required it to be masked) is very easy. You just need to remove the symlink to **/dev/null**. To unmask a service, enter the following:

```
# systemctl unmask servicename
```

NOTE   Be careful not to mask critical system services, or your system will behave unreliably or will fail to function altogether.

Scheduling Services

cron is the main job scheduler in Linux. Named after the Greek word for time, *chronos*, cron runs a job for you on a fixed schedule. A job can be anything that can be run on the command line, including a job that calls another shell script.

People typically schedule intensive jobs at times when the system is expected to be underused, such as overnight. Separating interactive user sessions from heavy batch work leads to both classes experiencing better performance. Your Linux system almost certainly has a handful of jobs set to run overnight or at least on a daily basis.

cron has several moving parts. A daemon called **crond** runs in the background and executes tasks on behalf of all users. Jobs are configured through *crontab*, which is a utility that manipulates the individual user cron tables. Finally, a series of configuration files under **/etc** can contain jobs and control which users are allowed to add jobs using **crontab**.

Configuring crontabs

The cron system has evolved over time. The utilities themselves have improved to allow more configuration options. Distributions have also added more default settings to make common tasks easier. This chapter walks you through the various options available and makes it clear which are distribution configurations and which are cron options.

The term *crontab* is both an abbreviation for cron table, a table that stores a list of jobs for a user, and the **crontab** utility that you can use to manage the table.

Using the crontab Command

The simplest way to use **crontab** is to run it with the **-e** flag, which means you want to edit the current user's crontab. You are placed into an editor showing the current crontab. After you make changes and save, your input is checked to make sure the crontab is valid. If the validation check fails, you are given an option to go back and fix the problems so that you don't lose your changes.

> **NOTE**   The editor you use to make changes to the crontab is set through the **EDITOR** environment variable, and **vi** is the default. If you'd rather use **nano**, for instance, make sure that export **EDITOR=/bin/nano** is in your **.bash_profile** file.

If you are root, the **-u** option allows you to supply a username so that you can view or edit that user. To edit user bo's crontab, for example, run **crontab -e -u bo**.

You can use the **-l** flag to display the crontab rather than edit it:

```
# crontab -l -u bo
PATH=/usr/local/bin:/bin:/usr/bin:/usr/local/sbin:/usr/sbin:/sbin:/
home/bo/bin
MAILTO=bo@example.com
25 * * * * /usr/bin/php /home/bo/fof/update-quiet.php > /dev/null
2>&1
0 2 * * * /home/bo/bin/database_backup 2>&1
```

Matching Times

The crontab itself has undergone some improvements in formatting, and most crontabs are built around the idea that there are five columns to specify when a job is run and then the rest of the line contains the text to be executed.

The columns, in order, are

1. Minute (0–59)

2. Hour, in 24-hour time (0–23)

3. Day of month (1–31)

4. Month (1–12)

5. Day of week (0–7, with 0 and 7 being Sunday)

Each column must be filled in. If you want to match all values for a column, use an asterisk (*). The following examples illustrate how the schedules work:

- **0 12 * * *:** The minute is **0**, the hour is **12**, and the job is set to run on all months and days, at 12:00 noon every day.

- **0 0 1 1 *:** The minute and hour are both **0**, which means midnight. The day of the month and month are both **1**, which is January 1. This job runs at midnight on New Year's day.

- *** * * * *:** Runs every minute.

- **30 5 * * 1:** Runs at 5:30 a.m. every Monday.

All columns must match for the job to run. One interesting exception is that if you specify both the day of the month and the day of the week (columns 3 and 5), the job will run with either match. Otherwise, all columns must match up for the job to run. So **30 5 1 * 1** runs at 5:30 a.m. on the first of the month *and* every Monday.

Spelling Out Month and Day Names

The syntax shown previously uses a number for the month and day of the week (1 is January, 2 is February, and so forth).

You can spell out the month and day of the week names by using the first three letters. Not only is this easier to remember, but it helps make more sense of the columns.

0 0 * jan sun runs at midnight on every Sunday in January. The whole file doesn't have to be consistent, and you can use numbers or names at your convenience.

Making Multiple Matches

The syntax you've seen so far does not allow for the same job to run at multiple times. If you wanted to run the same job at midnight and noon, you would need two separate lines. Fortunately, cron's syntax has evolved to allow this.

The first way to specify multiple times is to separate the items with a comma. For example, use the following syntax to run a job at midnight and noon:

```
0 0,12 * * *
```

The first column is still **0** to indicate that the job runs when the minute is zero. The **hour** column is now **0,12**, which means the job will run when the hour is either 0 or 12 (that is, midnight or noon).

This also works when using the names of the months. A job can be run twice a day during June, July, and August with this:

```
0 0,12 * jun,jul,aug *
```

The second way to run a job at multiple times is to give a range of values. Rather than using **jun,jul,aug**, the previous example could be written as **jun-aug**. Or to run a job on the hour from 9:00 a.m. to 5:00 p.m., you could use this:

```
0 9-17 * * *
```

This setting runs the first job at 9:00 a.m. and the last job at 5:00 p.m.

These methods can also be combined (for example, **8-10,16-18**).

Step Values

The next optimization is to provide an easy way to run a job by stepping over certain periods, such as to run a job every two hours. You could do this with **0,2,4,6,8,10,12,14,16,18,20,22**, but that's messy!

Instead, you can run a job every two hours, on the hour, with

```
0 */2 * * *
```

Or you can run a job every 30 minutes:

```
*/30 * * * *
```

Or you can run a job on odd-numbered hours:

```
0 1-23/2 * * *
```

Think of the * operator as saying "skip this number."

Putting Together the crontab

So far we've looked at the first five columns of the crontab, which collectively describe the time that a job will run. Any remaining text on the line runs as a command at the appointed time. For example, this line runs the **/usr/local/bin/backup.sh** program every day at midnight:

```
0 0 * * * /usr/local/bin/backup.sh
```

The command you run can be any valid shell code. For example, the following code runs the backup script at midnight only if **/var/lock/maintenance** doesn't exist:

```
0 0 * * * if [[ ! -f /var/lock/maintenance ]]; then /usr/local/bin/
backup.sh; fi
```

Issues About PATH

Sometimes a script that works fine when run at the command line doesn't work when run from cron. The environment is different because cron doesn't run your **.bash_profile** and **.bashrc** scripts. Therefore, you can expect a minimal environment, including a basic PATH.

See it for yourself by adding a cron entry such as

```
* * * * * env > /tmp/env
```

This job runs every minute and dumps the environment to **/tmp/env**:

```
SHELL=/bin/sh
USER=rossb
PATH=/usr/bin:/bin
PWD=/home/bo
LANG=en_US.UTF-8
```

```
SHLVL=1
HOME=/home/rossb
LOGNAME=rossb
_=/usr/bin/env
```

The environment for a cron job is fairly sparse: The path has only **/usr/bin** and **/bin**. It is also missing any additions that you are used to at your own shell, such as in **.bash_profile**.

While the scripts run out of cron are free to set their own variables internally, cron lets you set environment variables in the usual format:

```
PATH=/usr/bin:/bin:/usr/local/bin:/home/rossb/bin
0 0 * * * /usr/local/bin/backup.sh
```

The backup script then is run with the extended path set on the first line.

You aren't limited to just setting the path. Any variable will work. Some variable names are special:

- **MAILTO:** Anything that a job prints to the screen is mailed to this address.

- **SHELL:** Run the job with a different shell. **/bin/bash** is used by default.

- **CRON_TZ:** Use an alternate time zone for the crontab; otherwise, use system time.

Dealing with Output

A script often prints something to the screen, either for debugging, for status updates, or to log an error. Anything that a job prints to the screen is sent in an email to the current user, and it can be overridden with the **MAILTO** variable inside the crontab. There are three ways of dealing with this:

- Just accept the emails. This often makes for a boring morning as you wade through all the night's emails.

- Write the scripts so that they generate output only when there's a legitimate error.

- Within the crontab, redirect output to **/dev/null**.

Each of these options has advantages and disadvantages. If a script failing to run is a problem, you should have some way of knowing about such a failure, either from an email with the output or an external monitoring system. Receiving too many emails usually means you end up ignoring them all. The option you choose depends on the job.

For a job that is chatty where the output doesn't matter, it's easy to redirect the output to the bit bucket:

```
25 * * * * /usr/bin/php /home/bo/fof/update-quiet.php > /dev/null
2>&1
```

At 25 minutes after the hour, a PHP script is executed. The output is redirected to **/dev/null**, and the error stream is redirected to the standard out stream with **2>&1**.

Recall every program has a standard output stream and an error stream, and normal redirects work only on the latter. The **2>&1** ensures that errors are redirected, too. Without this, the regular output would be redirected, but the errors would not, resulting in an email. This may be desirable in some cases.

Nicknames

Most distributions include a version of cron that includes the nicknames extension. This extension provides aliases to commonly used schedules:

- **@reboot:** Run once after reboot.
- **@yearly:** Run once a year at midnight on January 1.
- **@annually:** Same as **@yearly**—run once a year at midnight on January 1.
- **@monthly:** Run at midnight on the first of the month.
- **@weekly:** Run once a week on Sunday at midnight.
- **@daily:** Run once a day at midnight.
- **@hourly:** Run once an hour, on the hour.

Therefore, the following two crontabs are the same:

```
0 0 * * * /usr/local/bin/backup.sh
@daily /usr/local/bin/backup.sh
```

Other Files

As cron has grown over the years, the number of files that can be used to run jobs has increased.

The crontabs edited with the **crontab** command are stored in **/var/spool/cron**, which you can view by running this command:

```
# ls -l /var/spool/cron/
total 4
-rw------- 1 root root 0 Nov 17 19:54 root
-rw------- 1 bo   bo 559 Mar 29 12:16 bo
```

From this output you can see that there are two crontabs: one for root and one for bo. The root crontab is empty. The files are just text files.

Even though as the root user you can edit the files in **/var/spool/cron** yourself, you should always use the **crontab** command so that you have syntax checking. Regular users are prohibited from editing these files directly because they are not able to access the **/var/spool/cron** directory.

System crontabs

Some software packages need to bundle periodic tasks. For example, the **sysstat** package includes a valuable tool called the system activity reporter, or **sar**. A cron job fires every 10 minutes to collect some stats, and another job fires around midnight to archive the day's statistics.

If the utility were to manipulate root's crontab, it could accidentally get removed if the root user didn't understand why the entry was there. Removing the entry after the package is removed also becomes a problem.

Other crontabs are meant to be manipulated only by the root user. A shared file called **/etc/crontab** and a directory containing individual tables are available in **/etc/cron.d**. The file is usually used by the distribution itself to list any default jobs or for the administrator to list any manually entered jobs. The directory is most helpful for integration with package management when a software package needs its own cron file. When the package is removed or upgraded, the cron file can be removed or changed without accidentally affecting other cron entries.

These system crontabs have one important difference: They contain a sixth column that goes in between the schedule and the command to be run. This column indicates which user should be used to execute the job.

An example of a system crontab such as this looks as follows:

```
# Run system wide raid-check once a week on Sunday at 1am by default
0 1 * * Sun root /usr/sbin/raid-check
```

The first five columns schedule a job for Sunday at 1:00 a.m. Column 6 says the root user will run it. The command is **/usr/sbin/raid-check**.

Convenience crontabs

One problem with scheduling jobs by a specific time is that they all run at the same time. Often you don't care about the specific time a job runs but just want it to run on an hourly, daily, weekly, or monthly basis. cron is installed with a configuration that has a directory for each of these time periods, and it runs the jobs in each directory consecutively when the scheduled time comes up. The directories are as follows:

- **/etc/cron.hourly:** Jobs here are run once an hour.

- **/etc/cron.daily:** Jobs here are run once a day.

- **/etc/cron.weekly:** Jobs here are run once a week.

- **/etc/cron.monthly:** Jobs here are run once a month.

These convenience jobs don't necessarily run on a predictable schedule. (We look into the reasons later in this chapter.) For example, the system may guarantee that monthly jobs are run once every month, but you can't say for sure that it'll happen exactly on the first of the month at midnight.

The files that go in these directories are just scripts. You do not include any schedule columns or user columns as most of them are placed there by installation scripts. For example, the logrotate package needs to run daily to maintain system logs, so it places a script in **/etc/cron.daily** that runs the script. The periodic updating of the database that the **locate** command uses is also run from **cron.daily**.

Restricting Access

Sometimes you don't want everyone to be able to use cron jobs. Two files, **/etc/cron.allow** and **/etc/cron.deny**, implement a whitelist policy and a blacklist policy, respectively.

You should only have one of these files present; otherwise, the behavior is difficult to understand. cron's decision process for allowing a user access to edit her crontab is as follows:

Step 1.   If **/etc/cron.allow** exists, only users in this file and the root user can use **crontab**.

Step 2.   If **/etc/cron.allow** does not exist but **/etc/cron.deny** does, anyone in the latter file is denied access.

Step 3.   If neither file exists, only root can manage cron jobs.

Most systems ship with an empty **/etc/cron.deny** file so that anyone can access his or her crontab. It should be noted that any existing crontabs continue to run, and the root user can still manage a denied user's crontab. The **cron.allow** and **cron.deny** files only control who can edit his or her own crontab.

Running ad hoc Jobs

The final class of jobs that can be scheduled is ad hoc jobs. cron and anacron run jobs on a periodic basis—for example, to run your log rotation every night. There are times when you want to run a job once but not now. For such situations, you use the **at** command and its friend, **batch**.

The **at** Command

The *at* command is designed to run a task once at a specific time. The **at** command's tasks or jobs are queued up in the **/var/spool/at** directory, and a single file represents each job.

A typical **at** job is intended to take care of the one-off or very infrequent jobs that take place at odd times. For example, many sysadmins remind themselves of meetings or to perform some task with **at**:

```
$ at 2pm today
at> xmessage "take a break"
at> <EOT>
job 1 at 2004-04-02 14:00
```

You type the first line of the previous code block (**at 2pm today**) at the command line, causing the **at>** prompt to appear. Then you type the command you want to execute, press **Enter**, and press **Ctrl+D** to end the task. The <EOT> notice indicates the end of the task, and then a line echoes the job's scheduling information.

Alternatively, you can pass the job you want to run over the standard input:

```
$ echo '/usr/local/bin/backup.sh' | at 20:00 today
job 10 at Sun Mar 29 20:00:00 2015
```

The **at** command can be used with a variety of time specifiers, some complex and some simple:

- **midnight:** Runs the task at 00:00 on the current day.

- **noon:** Runs the task at 12:00 on the current day.

- **teatime:** Runs the task at 16:00. (The British roots of **at** are evident here.)

- **time-of-day:** Runs the task at a particular time, such as 2:00 p.m. or 5:00 a.m.

- **date:** Specifies a time on a specific day, such as **2pm jul 23** or **4am 121504**.

- **now + time:** Specifies any number of minutes, hours, days, and weeks from the current time, such as **now + 30 minutes**.

The **at** command just starts the jobs. A couple of commands can help you manage the **at** jobs on the system, including these:

- **atq:** This shows the summary of jobs in the **at** queue with the job number, date and time, and executing user. (You can also see this with **at -l**.) It does not show the contents of the job itself; for that, the root user needs to look at the file in **/var/spool/at**.

- **atrm:** This deletes **at** jobs by job number, which is determined by using the previous command and the syntax **atrm #** (where **#** is the job number). **at -d** is a synonym for this.

at has a pair of security files, **/etc/at.allow** and **/etc/at.deny**, which allow users to queue up **at** jobs or prevent them from doing so. These files behave the same way as the cron restrictions. If the **at.allow** file exists and contains usernames, only those users and the root user are allowed to use **at**. If the **at.deny** file exists and contains usernames, those users are denied, and all others are allowed. If neither file exists, only the root user is allowed to submit **at** jobs.

The **batch** Command

Using the **batch** command is relatively simple; it's somewhat of an extension of the **at** command and shares the same man page. The **batch** command is used to run tasks or jobs at no specific time but at a particular threshold of system utilization. As you can imagine, some systems are busy, and you need to determine which jobs might need to be run with another scheduling utility if they are time sensitive.

The metric used by **batch** and **at** to know whether the system has capacity to run a job is the *load average*. The load average of the system is seen in the three numbers that show up when you run the **w** (who) command:

```
$ w
 16:04:34 up 135 days, 17:40, 2 users, load average: 0.54, 0.60,
 0.51
```

These numbers—in this case, 0.54, 0.60, and 0.51—represent the average number of processes waiting to be run when sampled over the past 1 minute, past 5 minutes, and past 15 minutes, respectively. A load average of 0.60 over 5 minutes means that over the past 5 minutes, when sampled, there was a process waiting to be run 60% of the time.

You can expect that a system with two CPUs is busy when the load average is 2. By looking at the load average over the three different time intervals, you can tell whether the load is temporary, in which case the 1-minute measurement is high and the other two are low, or if it's sustained (in which case all three are high). Or, if the 15-minute measurement is high and the others are low, you know you had some high load but have recovered.

By default, **batch** runs jobs once at a future time when the system 1-minute load average is less than or equal to 0.8. This can be configured by specifying the desired utilization average with the **atrun** command, such as

```
$ atrun -l 1.6
```

This sets the threshold that **batch** will watch to 1.6, and if load average drops below that value, the **batch** job is run. A value of 1.8 would be good for a system with two processors. For a system with N processors, you want this value to be slightly less than N, such as 80% of N.

Submitting **batch** jobs is similar to using **at**, and it even involves the **at** prompt and interface. To submit a compile job that runs when the system threshold is reached, you would use the following:

```
$ echo bigcompile | batch
job 11 at Sun Mar 29 14:36:00 2015
```

You can create a job with **at** or **batch** and then **cat** the file by using a command such as

```
$ cat /var/spool/at/a000030112ea5c
```

at's spooled jobs are prefixed by the letter **a**, whereas **batch** jobs are prefixed by the letter **b**. When you view an **at** or **batch** file, notice all the environment settings stored in the job, including a line that exports the username used to submit the job. Only the root user can look at these files.

Remember that **at** and **batch** both export a lot of information when the jobs are run, and this information goes away after that shell is closed. An **at** or **batch** job runs in a replica of the environment that existed at the time the job was submitted, which means all variables, aliases, and functions in the shell are available to the job that was started in that shell.

Summary

In this chapter you learned a lot about how to view or display processes on your system, how to manage those processes using the various commands to send signals to them, and how to view and manage services, or processes, that run in the background.

Additionally, you learned how to schedule commands and services to run either at various regular intervals or one-off at a given time using the scheduling commands.

All of this information will serve you well: being able to properly manage your processes and services is a key skill for a system operator to have.

Exam Preparation Tasks

As mentioned in the section "Goals and Methods" in the Introduction, you have a couple of choices for exam preparation: the exercises here, Chapter 23, "Final Preparation," and the exam simulation questions in the Pearson Test Prep Software Online.

Review All Key Topics

Review the most important topics in this chapter, noted with the Key Topic icon in the outer margin of the page. Table 4-5 lists these key topics and the page number on which each is found.

Table 4-5 Key Topics for Chapter 4

Key Topic Element	Description	Page Number
Section	Viewing Processes	142
Section	The **htop** Command	144
Section	Pages, Slabs, and Caches	146
Table 4-2	Common Linux Signals	148
Paragraph	Purpose of the **pgrep** and **pkill** commands	150
Section	Introducing **lsof**	153
Figure 4-4	Linux process priorities	157
Table 4-3	systemd Unit Types	162
Table 4-4	What Happens When Runlevels and Targets Are Initiated	163
Section	Listing Services	166
Section	Masking Services	169
Section	System crontabs	176
Section	Restricting Access	177
Section	The **at** Command	178
Section	The **batch** Command	179

Define Key Terms

Define the following key terms from this chapter and check your answers in the glossary:

htop, pages, **pgrep**, **pkill**, SIGHUP, SIGKILL, SIGTERM, zombie, **bg**, **pidof**, **lsof**, **jobs**, **fg**, **nice**, **renice**, **top**, **systemctl**, **status**, **mask**, cron, **crontab**, **at**

Review Questions

The answers to these review questions are in Appendix A.

1. You want to run a task on the hour, every other hour, starting at 1:00 a.m., with no other restrictions. Which crontab entry accomplishes this?

   a. */120 * * *

   b. 1/2 * * * *

   c. 0 */2 * * *

   d. 0 1-23/2 * * *

2. You have configured a job to run with the **batch** command, but apparently system utilization never drops as low as the default value. Which of the following commands can you use to set a custom value for the **batch** command?

   a. **batchavg**

   b. **atconfig**

   c. **atrun**

   d. **crontab**

3. You are trying to set up a job to run every night, but the script keeps aborting with errors that the command was not found. Which of the following in your crontab might help?

   a. **PATH=/usr/local/bin:/sbin:/usr/sbin:/usr/bin:/bin**

   b. **SHELL=/bin/sh**

   c. **MAILTO=you@yourdomain.com**

   d. **ABORT_ON_ERROR=false**

4. Where are user crontabs stored?

   a. **/var/spool/cron**

   b. **$HOME/.cron**

   c. **/var/cron**

   d. **/usr/local/cron**

5. If both **cron.allow** and **cron.deny** exist, what occurs?

   a. Only deny users in **cron.deny** to use crontab.

   b. Only allow users in **cron.allow** to use crontab.

   c. Only allow the root user to use crontab.

   d. First check **cron.deny** and then check **cron.allow**.

6. Which of the following pauses a foreground job?

   a. **Ctrl+A**

   b. **Ctrl+C**

   c. **Ctrl+Z**

   d. **Ctrl+X**

This chapter covers the following topics:

- Interface Management
- Name Resolution
- Network Monitoring
- Remote Networking Tools

The exam objective covered in this chapter is as follows:

- **Objective 1.5:** Given a scenario, use the appropriate networking tools or configuration files

## CHAPTER 5

Using Network Tools and Configuration Files

Linux systems are great by themselves, but they really begin to shine when connected to a network and the Internet, primarily sharing data and providing services.

To begin, you'll need to know what networking is, how it is configured on a Linux system, and what your connectivity to other systems and networks requires. Sometimes it seems like there are a couple of dozen networking configuration files, and while it's not quite that bad, there are quite a few files, directories, and tools required to properly connect your system to other systems.

As usual, with a variety of options available, we'll start simple and then get more complex, ranging from pure command line and text editing to using some tools that are friendlier to newcomers.

Another key topic of this chapter will name resolution, which enables your system to convert between IP addresses and domain and hostnames. The entire Internet runs on name resolution. Every time you type a domain such as www. rossbrunson.com, the system queries and finds the destination network and addresses to go seek out. The mysterious and wonderful thing is that it works so well and at massive scale!

As with all things that are deemed important, there's the need to monitor and troubleshoot your networking configuration and operations with a variety of tools, all of which are covered to a more than adequate level in this chapter.

Lastly, because your systems are networked, there is the distinct possibility, the *inevitability*, that you'll need or want to send and receive information between your systems and remote systems, which we'll handle in the last section of this chapter.

The principles and practices in this chapter will help you immensely to manage your processes and the services that they make up, enabling you to run those processes and services consistently and reliably over time.

"Do I Know This Already?" Quiz

The "Do I Know This Already?" quiz enables you to assess whether you should read this entire chapter or simply jump to the "Exam Preparation Tasks" section for review. If you are in doubt, read the entire chapter. Table 5-1 outlines the major headings in this chapter and the corresponding "Do I Know This Already?" quiz questions. You can find the answers in Appendix A, "Answers to the 'Do I Know This Already?' Quizzes and Review Questions."

Table 5-1 "Do I Know This Already?" Foundation Topics Section-to-Question Mapping

Foundation Topics Section	Questions Covered in This Section
Interface Management	1–2
Name Resolution	3–4
Network Monitoring	5
Remote Networking Tools	6

CAUTION   The goal of self-assessment is to gauge your mastery of the topics in this chapter. If you do not know the answer to a question or are only partially sure of the answer, you should mark that question as wrong for purposes of the self-assessment. Giving yourself credit for an answer you correctly guess skews your self-assessment results and might provide you with a false sense of security.

1. Which command (with any needed options) will display the default gateway?

    a. **ifconfig**

    b. **route**

    c. **ifup**

    d. **ip**

2. The ARP table includes which of the following? (Choose all that apply.)

    a. Hostnames

    b. IP addresses

    c. MAC addresses

    d. Routers

3. Consider the following entry in the **/etc/nsswitch.conf** file:

```
hosts: files dns nis ldap
```

When the command **ping test.com** executes, which location will be searched first for hostname resolution?

   a. The DNS server

   b. The NIS server

   c. The LDAP server

   d. A local file

4. Which of the following is a valid entry for resolution methods on the **hosts:** line in the **/etc/nsswitch.conf** file? (Choose all that apply.)

   a. **files**

   b. **ylwpage**

   c. **dns**

   d. **nis**

5. Which of the following commands will display network traffic? (Choose all that apply.)

   a. **wireshark**

   b. **tcpdump**

   c. **tshark**

   d. **host**

6. Which SSH command is designed to function as a secure equivalent to the **cp** command?

   a. **rlogin**

   b. **sftp**

   c. **scp**

   d. **ssh**

Foundation Topics

In this chapter we'll cover the why and how of network *interface* management, as well as some methods of troubleshooting those interfaces.

I will take my usual liberties with the order of the subtopics in this exam objective so that things flow well and make sense.

Interface Management

Functional network addresses typically are automatically configured for you when you install the Linux system, as the installation and configuration routines usually set up the network device(s) properly.

However, like any default configuration that is automatic and "easy," deviating from that default configuration requires work, and to do that you need to use any of several commands, most notably the iproute2 suite of tools, as well as the more historical **net-tools** package's tools.

iproute2

One of two primary utilities in the *iproute2* toolset is the **ip** command and its functionality, which is designed to supersede the functionality of the **ifconfig** and **route** commands of the **net-tools** package.

NOTE   When you install your test lab systems, or spin up your VMs or images for testing, you'll find that most of the latest versions of distributions don't have the **net-tools** package installed by default, which means that **ifconfig** and **route** and other such tools will not be available by default. Those tools are very easy to install, and you'll need to do exactly that to prepare properly for those types of questions on the exam.

Wikipedia has a very informative table of what legacy commands are replaced by the iproute2 tools, such as **ip**, **ss**, and **bridge**. Figure 5-1 shows the replacement matrix (as of the time of writing; https://en.wikipedia.org/wiki/Iproute2).

Interface Management Commands

The two primary iproute2 [iproute2] tools for managing IP information are **ip** and **ss**. The most commonly used is the **ip** command, with most distributions moving to using this tool for managing interfaces.

Utilities obsoleted by iproute2

Legacy utility ⬥	Replacement command ⬥	Note ⬥
ifconfig	ip addr, ip link	Address and link configuration
route	ip route	Routing tables
arp	ip neigh	Neighbors
iptunnel	ip tunnel	Tunnels
nameif, ifrename	ip link set name	Rename network interfaces
ipmaddr	ip maddr	Multicast
netstat	ss, ip route	Show various networking statistics
brctl	bridge	Handle bridge addresses and devices

Figure 5-1 Utilities obsoleted by the iproute2 suite of tools (Table from Wikipedia.org)

The ip Command

As Figure 5-1 shows, the *ip* command is designed to replace or supersede many different commands. For example, the **ip** command can also display network configuration data, just like the **ifconfig** command. If you execute the **ip addr show** command, the output looks like that shown in Example 5-1.

Example 5-1 Example **ip addr show** Command Output

```
1: lo: <LOOPBACK,UP,LOWER_UP> mtu 16436 qdisc noqueue state UNKNOWN
   link/loopback 00:00:00:00:00:00 brd 00:00:00:00:00:00
   inet 127.0.0.1/8 scope host lo
   inet6 ::1/128 scope host
   valid_lft forever preferred_lft forever
2: eth0: <BROADCAST,MULTICAST,UP,LOWER_UP> mtu 1500 qdisc pfifo_fast
state UP qlen 1000
   link/ether 08:00:27:08:ea:ff brd ff:ff:ff:ff:ff:ff
   inet 192.168.1.22/24 brd 192.168.1.255 scope global eth0
   inet6 fe80::a00:27ff:fe08:eaff/64 scope link
   valid_lft forever preferred_lft forever
```

The **ip** command can also be used to accomplish such tasks as

- Managing system IP addressing
- Linking network devices together

- Managing network namespaces
- Handling routing tables
- Configuring IP tunneling
- Managing TCP metric info

One of the **ip** command's great features is its abbreviations. For example, the following spelled-out **ip** command shows the address information for the system:

```
# ip address show
```

To save time and keystrokes, you can get exactly the same information with the following shortened command:

```
# ip a s
```

Examples of the ip Command

You can use the **ip** command for such a wide variety of tasks that it's appropriate to show some of them in action here. You'll need to know how to perform these and more to properly answer the **ip**-related questions on the Linux+ exam.

We have just covered how to view IP address information for a system, so let's examine how to view the default gateway using the **ip** command:

```
# ip route show
default via 192.168.64.1 dev enp0s2 proto dhcp src 192.168.64.2
metric 100
192.168.64.0/24 dev enp0s2 proto kernel scope link src 192.168.64.2
192.168.64.1 dev enp0s2 proto dhcp scope link src 192.168.64.2 metric
100
```

You'll also want to know how to bring a configured interface from a status of down to up and back to down again:

```
# ip link set dev eth0 up
# ip link set dev eth0 down
```

The **arp** command has its own section later in the chapter, but you can use the **ip** command to show arp-related information as well:

```
# ip neigh show
192.168.64.1 dev enp0s2 lladdr 3e:22:fb:91:6a:64 DELAY
fe80::1c48:5e53:fc3f:ba66 dev enp0s2 lladdr 3e:22:fb:91:6a:64 router
STALE
```

NOTE   The move from **ifconfig** to **ip** and the use of the **ip** command for a plethora of tasks that used to require individual commands can be confusing, so get some solid experience with the **ip** command, its abbreviations, and how it works on a day-to-day basis before you tackle the exam!

The ss Command

The *ss* command is used to display socket information. Without any options, it lists all open sockets, as demonstrated in Example 5-2.

Example 5-2   Displaying Socket Information with **ss**

```
#  ss | wc -l
160
# ss | head
Netid   State   Recv-Q Send-Q   Local Address:Port    Peer Address:Port
u_str   ESTAB   0      0        /var/run/dovecot/anvil 23454966       *
23454965
u_str   ESTAB   0      0        /var/run/dovecot/anvil 23887673       *
23887672
u_str   ESTAB   0      0        /run/systemd/journal/stdout 13569     *
13568
u_str   ESTAB   0      0                            * 13893           *
13894
u_str   ESTAB   0      0                            * 13854           *
13855
u_str   ESTAB   0      0                            * 13850           *
13849
u_str   ESTAB   0      0                            * 68924           *
68925
u_str   ESTAB   0      0                            * 17996           *
17997
u_str   ESTAB   0      0        /var/run/dovecot/config 9163531       *
9163871
```

Table 5-2 describes some of the useful options for the **ss** command.

Table 5-2 **ss** Command Options

Option	Description
-lt	Lists open TCP sockets.
-lu	Lists open UCP sockets.
-lp	Lists the process IDs that own the sockets.
-n	Indicates not to resolve IP addresses to hostnames or port numbers to port names.
-a	Displays all information.
-s	Displays a summary.

NetworkManager

If you are working on a modern distribution of Linux, there is a good chance that your network is configured using NetworkManager. This utility's man page overview is helpful:

> The NetworkManager daemon attempts to make networking configuration and operation as painless and automatic as possible by managing the primary network connection and other network interfaces, like Ethernet, WiFi, and Mobile Broadband devices. NetworkManager will connect any network device when a connection for that device becomes available, unless that behavior is disabled. Information about networking is exported via a D-Bus interface to any interested application, providing a rich API with which to inspect and control network settings and operation.

Why on Earth would you want networking configuration and operation to be "as painless and automatic as possible"? Because more people are starting to use Linux on their own machines, and those machines are typically laptops, not servers. Laptops are mobile, so the networks they connect to are constantly changing. Network-Manager is designed to make life easier for mobile desktop users.

The nmtui Command

Several useful tools come with NetworkManager. For example, the **nmtui** command is an interactive tool for configuring a network device. See Figure 5-2 for an example of this tool.

The nmcli Command

The **nmcli** command is used for controlling the NetworkManager, including the status of interfaces, and is typically used in scripts and on systems that cannot run the graphical applets that control NetworkManager.

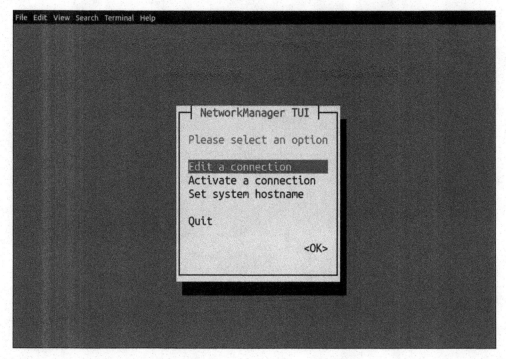

Figure 5-2 The **nmtui** command

It provides a command-line interface to NetworkManager, allowing you to view information about NetworkManager and change its behavior.

For example, you can see the current status of the components of NetworkManager by executing the following command:

```
# nmcli nm status
RUNNING   STATE       WIFI-HARDWARE   WIFI       WWAN-HARDWARE   WWAN
running   connected   enabled         enabled    enabled         enabled
```

You could also disable Wi-Fi by executing the following command:

```
# nmcli nm wifi off
```

Figure 5-3 shows an example of using **nmcli** to enumerate the networking details of a system.

```
ubuntu@primary:~$ nmcli device show
GENERAL.DEVICE:                            enp0s2
GENERAL.TYPE:                              ethernet
GENERAL.HWADDR:                            CA:3B:CC:0E:10:69
GENERAL.MTU:                               1500
GENERAL.STATE:                             10 (unmanaged)
GENERAL.CONNECTION:                        --
GENERAL.CON-PATH:                          --
WIRED-PROPERTIES.CARRIER:                  on
IP4.ADDRESS[1]:                            192.168.64.2/24
IP4.GATEWAY:                               192.168.64.1
IP4.ROUTE[1]:                              dst = 0.0.0.0/0, nh = 192.168.64.1, mt = 100
IP4.ROUTE[2]:                              dst = 192.168.64.0/24, nh = 0.0.0.0, mt = 0
IP4.ROUTE[3]:                              dst = 192.168.64.1/32, nh = 0.0.0.0, mt = 100
IP6.ADDRESS[1]:                            fd8e:a0cd:98f:8920:c83b:ccff:fe0e:1069/64
IP6.ADDRESS[2]:                            fe80::c83b:ccff:fe0e:1069/64
IP6.GATEWAY:                               fe80::1c48:5e53:fc3f:ba66
IP6.ROUTE[1]:                              dst = fd8e:a0cd:98f:8920::/64, nh = ::, mt = 100
IP6.ROUTE[2]:                              dst = fe80::/64, nh = ::, mt = 256
IP6.ROUTE[3]:                              dst = ::/0, nh = fe80::1c48:5e53:fc3f:ba66, mt = 100

GENERAL.DEVICE:                            lo
GENERAL.TYPE:                              loopback
GENERAL.HWADDR:                            00:00:00:00:00:00
GENERAL.MTU:                               65536
GENERAL.STATE:                             10 (unmanaged)
GENERAL.CONNECTION:                        --
GENERAL.CON-PATH:                          --
IP4.ADDRESS[1]:                            127.0.0.1/8
IP4.GATEWAY:                               --
IP6.ADDRESS[1]:                            ::1/128
IP6.GATEWAY:                               --
IP6.ROUTE[1]:                              dst = ::1/128, nh = ::, mt = 256
ubuntu@primary:~$
```

Figure 5-3 The **nmcli** command and output

The net-tools Suite

The **net-tools** collection of utilities has been around for some time, and has been deployed on many distributions. It has a long and useful history, but has recently been queued up for deprecation, starting in about 2009, by the former maintainers.

Regardless of the future of the **net-tools** suite, it's currently in heavy use, and the Linux+ exam requires you to know how to use the following net-tools commands:

- *ifconfig*: Used to set and display the host's IP address and network mask.

- *ifcfg*: The **ifcfg-*** files are used to configure an interface, such as **ifcfg-eth0** for the first Ethernet interface.

- *hostname*: Used to set or view the host's hostname; other name utilities can create name-related links to this file.

- *arp*: Used to view and/or make changes to the ARP table.

- *route*: Used to set and display the host's routing and gateway information.

There are other tools in the **net-tools** collection, but because they are being slowly deprecated and, most importantly, are not included in the Linux+ objectives, I will politely decline to cover them here.

The ifconfig Command

The **ifconfig** command is used primarily to view or set the IP addresses for a host. You can set everything except the default gateway with this command, including bringing up or activating the interface.

To set up the **eth0** interface to communicate on the 192.168.33.0 network with IP address 192.168.33.2 and network mask 255.255.255.0 and to activate the interface, use the following command:

```
# ifconfig eth0 192.168.33.2 netmask 255.255.255.0 up
```

The **ifconfig** command displays the working or activated interfaces for the system. If any are down or not activated, they can be shown with the **-a** switch:

```
# ifconfig -a
```

Configuring via ifcfg-* files and network-scripts

The location of the **ifcfg-lo**, **ifcfg-eth0**, and other **ifcfg-*** files differs depending on the type of distribution, as noted in the following sections, but they are similar in function. Any differences are noted in the correct distribution section below.

On a Red Hat machine, the **/etc/sysconfig/etc/sysconfig/network-scripts** directory contains the scripts used to configure and bring up and down the interfaces on the machine.

For example, if you have an **eth0** interface you need to configure with a static IP address and other configuration, you can modify the **/etc/sysconfig/network-scripts/ifcfg-eth0** file. This file can also be modified by a tool called **system-config-network**.

To display the **ifcfg-eth0** file, use the following command:

```
# cat /etc/sysconfig/network-scripts/ifcfg-eth0
```

With a static configuration for IPv4, you see output similar to the following:

```
DEVICE=eth0
ONBOOT=yes
BOOTPROTO=static
IPADDR=192.168.1.73
NETMASK=255.255.255.0
GATEWAY=192.168.1.1
```

With a static configuration for IPv6, you see output similar to the following (for autoconfiguration, just specify the first line):

```
IPV6INIT=yes
IPV6ADDR=3FFE:F200:0134:AB00:0143:1111:8901:0002
IPV6_DEFAULTGW=3FFE:F200:0134:AB00:0143:1111:8901:0001
```

If the interface is configured for DHCP, you see output similar to the following for IPv4:

```
DEVICE=eth0
ONBOOT=yes
BOOTPROTO=dhcp
```

If the interface is configured for DHCP, you see output similar to the following for IPv6:

```
IPV6INIT=yes
DHCPV6C=yes
```

The method you decide to use can be implemented by editing this file and setting the parameters you want. The parameters are self-explanatory, with the possible exception of the **BOOTPROTO** parameter. The **BOOTPROTO** parameter, when set to either **static** or **dhcp**, tells the network daemon how to configure this interface: either by reading the other parameters in the **ifcfg-eth0** file (if set to **static**) or by using DHCP to get the address (if set to **dhcp**).

After changing these settings, restart networking by executing **service network restart**. This restarts the networking and brings the interfaces down and back up again.

On Debian-based Systems

Debian uses a different style of configuring interfaces than Red Hat. Instead of having several smaller scripts or configuration files, Debian uses the **/etc/network/interfaces** file for all interfaces. Although Debian doesn't include the **system-config-networking** utility by default, the **netcardconfig** program is included in some Debian distributions and does roughly the same tasks.

To see the contents of this file, use the following command:

```
# cat /etc/network/interfaces
```

This produces output similar to that shown in Example 5-3.

Example 5-3 Example of Contents of the **/etc/network/interfaces** File

```
# /etc/network/interfaces -- configuration file for ifup(8), ifdown(8)
# The loopback interface
# automatically added when upgrading
auto lo eth0
iface lo inet loopback
iface eth0 inet static
 address 192.168.15.5
 netmask 255.255.255.0
 network 192.168.15.0
 broadcast 192.168.15.255
 gateway 192.168.15.2
```

Each interface defined in the interfaces file starts with the keyword **iface**, then the name of the interface, the type of address (**inet** for IP, **ipx** for IPX, and **inet6** for IPv6), and the method for the interface (either **static** or **dhcp**).

After configuring the interfaces file with the correct parameters, it's recommended to restart the network daemon with **/etc/init.d/networking restart**. This restarts the networking and brings the interfaces down and back up again.

Notice that the Debian interfaces file contains the gateway address but doesn't use uppercase letters, as Red Hat does. In addition, Debian does not use an equal sign (**=**) between the parameter and the value in the interfaces file. Debian also uses the scripts as an input or source file, whereas Red Hat actually executes its configuration scripts.

It's important to note that, although Debian does primarily use the previous method, an instance of the file **/etc/sysconfig/network-scripts/ifcfg-eth0** is often found on the Debian machine. You need to read the documentation for your distribution or method to determine what relationship exists between the two. You can safely assume that this won't be an issue on the Linux+ exam because the networking questions on the exam are distribution neutral.

The hostname Command

The **hostname** command is used to view and set the host and domain names for a system. The system's hostname can be set by using this command, or it can be set in the boot process by various scripts, depending on the distribution and version.

The **hostname** command is typically linked to the following commands:

- **domainname**
- **dnsdomainname**

- **nisdomainname**

- **ypdomainname**

You can also use options to the **hostname** command to get information, as in this example:

```
# hostname --fqdn
```

This returns output similar to the following:

```
localhost.localdomain
```

The arp Command

Most users and administrators use hostnames to communicate with remote systems. A hostname must be translated into an IP address because Internet Protocol (IP) uses IP addresses rather than hostnames. This function is provided by a resolver, such as a DNS server.

IP is part of a seven-layer networking model called the Open Systems Interconnection model (OSI model). At Layer 2 of this model, devices communicate using the network card's MAC address. In most cases, for two hosts to communicate, not only do they need to know each other's IP addresses, they also need to know each other's MAC addresses.

Initially, the local system does not know the MAC addresses of any other host. When a remote IP address is first used, a broadcast request sent on the network matches that IP address. The machine with the matching IP address responds to the original request, reporting to the original host what its MAC address is. The original system then stores this MAC address and corresponding IP address in a memory address called the *ARP table*.

The **arp** command is used to view the ARP table or make changes to it. When executed with no arguments, the **arp** command displays the ARP table, as shown here:

```
# arp
Address          HWtype  HWaddress          Flags Mask    Iface
192.168.1.11     ether   30:3a:64:44:a5:02    C             eth0
```

In the event that a remote system has its network card replaced, it may be necessary to delete an entry from the ARP table. This can be accomplished by using the **-d** option with the **arp** command:

```
# arp -i eth0 -d 192.169.1.11
```

When the address has been removed from the ARP table, there should be no need to add the new address manually. The next time the local system uses this IP address, it sends a broadcast request on the appropriate network to determine the new MAC address.

The route Command

The **route** command was featured earlier in this chapter for the purpose of viewing default gateways, but it can also be used in defending a system from an attack in progress.

When you have a host that is subject to a denial-of-service attack, or some sort of denial of service is being attempted, the quickest action you can take is to add a route that causes any responses to the attacker's IP address to be routed through the loopback address, effectively causing your system to misroute the traffic to that host.

To stop a particular host from attacking a server, open a shell on the server and enter the following command (where **10.1.1.69** is the attacker's IP address):

```
# route add 10.1.1.69 lo
```

Any of the traffic that your host would have sent in return to the attacking host is now sent to the loopback network, where it times out, causing the attacking host to time out and give up on your poor server.

Obviously, this is not a long-term solution, but try it on your local network: Use the **ping** command from a host and type the previous **route** command on the host being attacked. You see that the attacking or pinging host suffers a time-out very quickly.

> **NOTE** Although not directly related to the **route** command, if you need to turn on IP forwarding on a host, one of the ways is to echo a **1** into the **/proc/sys/net/ipv4/ip_forward** file:
>
> ```
> # echo 1 > /proc/sys/net/ipv4/ip_forward
> ```
>
> This effectively turns on the forwarding of traffic between the different interfaces on the machine.

Name Resolution

The resolving of names, including local hostnames, hostnames of other systems, and names of hosts and domains across the Internet, requires you to have a functional and flexible method of translating a human-friendly name into a numerical IP address of a target system or, in most cases, the nearest gateway that gets you on the path of additional routers until you get to that remote system.

Configuring Name Resolution

Local system name configuration is a mishmash of different files, the most notable of which are as follows:

- **/etc/hosts**
- **/etc/*resolv.conf***
- **/etc/*nsswitch.conf***

> **NOTE**   These files are distribution neutral and will definitely show up on the Linux+ exam!

These three files are used to configure how local (and remote) name resolution occurs. Figure 5-4 shows the relationship between these files and how they use each other to resolve the name for a host to which a client software application needs to connect.

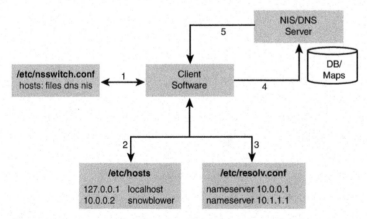

Figure 5-4   Name resolution diagram

The numbered steps in Figure 5-4 represent the steps that would be followed during a normal name resolution. The following examples show how different variations would work on a system with this configuration.

For the first example, say that you want to issue the **ping snowblower** command on a host with the sample configuration shown in Figure 5-4. When a name is used instead of an IP address, the client software asks the system to resolve that name to an IP address. The system follows these steps:

Step 1.   The system refers to the **/etc/nsswitch.conf** file and the **hosts:** line for the order in which it should look for the name's resolution. In Figure 5-4, the **hosts:** line is set to first look at the local files, then the DNS server, and then the NIS server:

```
hosts: files dns nis
```

Step 2.   The system looks in the file **/etc/hosts** for the resolution of the name **snowblower** to an IP address; in this case, it finds a matching entry with the IP address 10.0.0.2.

Step 3.   The system returns the IP address to the client, and the name resolution portion of the transaction is complete.

As a more complex example, let's see what happens if we issue the **ping shpdoinkle** command on a host that has the previous configuration. The system follows the same general set of steps, with an addition:

Step 1.   The system refers to the **/etc/nsswitch.conf** file and the **hosts:** line for the order of resolution.

Step 2.   The system inspects the **/etc/hosts** file for a matching entry.

Step 3.   When no match is found, the system reads the **/etc/nsswitch.conf** file and finds that the next option for resolution is DNS.

Step 4.   The system then reads the **/etc/resolv.conf** file for the name server entries, with an upper practical limit of three expected. The **/etc/resolv. conf** file defines the DNS servers used by this system.

Step 5.   The system queries the first found name server for the resolution of the name. If the name is resolved, resolution is halted. If the first name server doesn't reply in a reasonable amount of time, the system tries the next configured name server until no entries remain; if no resolution is found, it fails.

Step 6.   If the name is resolved, the system returns the IP address to the client, and the name resolution portion of the transaction is completed.

Step 7.   If all the DNS queries fail, then the NIS server is queried because the last entry on the **hosts:** line is **nis**. This assumes that an NIS server is configured for this system.

Other name resolution-related files can be used on a Linux system, but most are, by default, not on the Red Hat or Debian systems you see these days:

- **/etc/hostname:** Used to statically store the fully qualified domain name, such as snowblower.brunson.org.

- **/etc/networks:** Used to map a network name to an otherwise IP-related network; more often used in Solaris environments than Linux.

- **/etc/host.conf:** Similar in function to the **/etc/nsswitch.conf** file. It sets the order in which resolution sources are searched; this file is overridden by **/etc/nsswitch.conf**.

Controlling Resolution

A very useful tool for resolving and enumerating hostnames, domains, IP addresses is the *resolvectl* command. One of the new generation of tools that ends in "ctl," **resolvectl** interacts with the backend systemd-resolved service not only to resolve IP addresses to hostnames and domain names, but also the other way around, resolving hostnames and domain names to the routing and destination addresses for the target hosts.

Resolving a hostname locally is really easy; just use the **query** subcommand and give it the parameter of the hostname to resolve:

```
# resolvectl query localhost
localhost: 127.0.0.1                    -- link: lo
           ::1                          -- link: lo


-- Information acquired via protocol DNS in 1.2ms.
-- Data is authenticated: yes
```

Part of the real power of the **resolvectl** command shows itself when you query a remote domain and get authoritative information about that host:

```
# resolvectl query brunson.org
brunson.org: 3.33.152.147              -- link: enp0s2
             15.197.142.173            -- link: enp0s2


-- Information acquired via protocol DNS in 3.0ms.
-- Data is authenticated: no
```

You can also use **resolvectl** to mine a domain's configuration and records to find where a particular service is located, such as this query to find out which Mail Exchange (MX) service a domain is using:

```
# resolvectl -t MX query brunson.org
brunson.org IN MX 50 ASPMX3.GOOGLEMAIL.COM          -- link: enp0s2
```

```
brunson.org IN MX 40 ASPMX2.GOOGLEMAIL.COM          -- link: enp0s2
brunson.org IN MX 10 ASPMX.L.GOOGLE.COM             -- link: enp0s2
brunson.org IN MX 30 ALT2.ASPMX.L.GOOGLE.COM        -- link: enp0s2
brunson.org IN MX 20 ALT1.ASPMX.L.GOOGLE.COM        -- link: enp0s2
-- Information acquired via protocol DNS in 1.7ms.
-- Data is authenticated: no
```

As the output indicates, this domain uses the Google Workspace servers for its mail systems.

Another useful set of data can be obtained from the interfaces and protocols they transport by using the **statistics** option:

```
# resolvectl statistics
DNSSEC supported by current servers: no

Transactions
Current Transactions: 0
  Total Transactions: 217

Cache
  Current Cache Size: 0
          Cache Hits: 26
        Cache Misses: 426

DNSSEC Verdicts
              Secure: 0
            Insecure: 0
               Bogus: 0
       Indeterminate: 0
```

As you can see, the **resolvectl** command has a lot to offer in the realm of gathering useful information that can help you configure your system and aid in troubleshooting problems in reaching local and remote systems.

> **NOTE** On some distributions the **resolvconf** command is an alias to the **resolvectl** command, so when you take the Linux+ exam, keep an eye out for any question that is designed to show that you know the linkage or relationship between the two commands. You can read more about the limitations of using the **resolvconf** command in its man page that it shares with the **resolvectl** command.

Setting Hostnames on systemd Systems

In previous service management schemes, the simple editing of a file and a reboot could take care of setting the hostname on a system, or the hostname could be set by name resolution services.

The systemd method of managing the hostname is to use the *hostnamectl* command. And while some might not see the point of using a special command to set the hostname, it's important to understand the various hostnames at various levels to see why the use of a standardized command is recommended.

The **hostnamectl** command documentation explains that three different levels of hostnames are recognized by the tool:

- **pretty:** This high-level hostname can have special characters and is user-friendly (for example, **Ross's Knoppix Laptop**).

- **kernel or static:** This hostname is used to initialize the hostname used by the kernel at boot and is typically not seen or used elsewhere.

- **transient:** This hostname is typically the one set by DHCP or other IP management schemes.

The **hostnamectl** command shows the user what information it is aware of, and it pulls from **systemd-hostnamectl.service**, which is the gathering point for most of the hostname-related queries and information:

```
# hostnamectl
    Static hostname: n/a
Transient hostname: 217
         Icon name: computer-vm
           Chassis: vm
        Machine ID: b44977c3fc6d40acaa25893225235c11
           Boot ID: 18df362437c54d90b3f9b9eaf0e60dcd
    Virtualization: vmware
  Operating System: SUSE Linux Enterprise Server 15
       CPE OS Name: cpe:/o:suse:sles:15
            Kernel: Linux 4.12.14-23-default
      Architecture: x86-64
```

The host, dig, and nslookup Commands

The **host** and *dig* commands are two of the Bind-utils that are used for name lookups or troubleshooting of hostnames or fully qualified domain names.

The **host** command is simple and has little use other than to return the resolved IP address for a hostname. You run it with a hostname as shown here:

```
# host brunson.org
```

This returns output like the following:

```
brunson.org has address 192.168.1.1
```

> **NOTE**   You can use options with the **host** command to gather further information about the targeted host or domain, but these options are usually not tested on the Linux+ exam.

The **host** command is designed specifically to perform DNS lookups. This can pose problems when your system resolves hostnames from both DNS servers and the local host file (**/etc/hosts**).

The *nslookup* command is now deprecated. It's very old and has gone out of common usage, being replaced mostly by the **dig** command.

If you want to perform only DNS queries, the **dig** command is the correct tool. You can use the **dig** command in either command-line mode or batch mode for larger sets of target servers. The **dig** command uses this syntax:

```
dig server name type
```

In this case, *server* is the domain or server IP address you are querying for information. Typically, you use the *server* section only if you need to specify a particular one. *name* is the actual domain or host you are searching for, such as lpi.org. *type* enables you to specify whether you want to see MX, SIG, A, or ANY record types.

Using the **dig** command is relatively simple. To find just the MX (mail server) records for the brunson.org domain, use the command **dig brunson.org MX**, which returns the output shown in Example 5-4.

Example 5-4   Example **dig** Command Output

```
$ dig brunson.org MX
; <<>> DiG 9.2.4rc2 <<>> brunson.org MX
;; global options: printcmd
;; Got answer:
;; ->>HEADER<<- opcode: QUERY, status: NOERROR, id: 41375
;; flags: qr rd ra; QUERY: 1, ANSWER: 1, AUTHORITY: 2, ADDITIONAL: 3
```

```
;; QUESTION SECTION:
;brunson.org. IN MX
;; ANSWER SECTION:
brunson.org. 3598 IN MX 0 brunson.org.
;; AUTHORITY SECTION:
brunson.org. 1835 IN NS NS3.INDYSERV.NET.
brunson.org. 1835 IN NS NS4.INDYSERV.NET.
;; ADDITIONAL SECTION:
brunson.org. 1835 IN A 207.238.213.12
NS3.INDYSERV.NET. 167293 IN A 207.238.213.33
NS4.INDYSERV.NET. 167293 IN A 207.238.213.34
;; Query time: 65 msec
;; SERVER: 192.168.33.2#53(192.168.33.2)
;; WHEN: Wed May 12 11:31:16 2004
;; MSG SIZE rcvd: 141
```

The output for a **dig** query is structured and consists of the following:

- **HEADER:** This contains information about the **dig** environment and options.

- **QUESTION:** This section simply echoes back the query.

- **ANSWER:** This section is the reply to the query.

- **AUTHORITY:** This section shows the servers that are the authoritative name servers for the requested target.

- **ADDITIONAL:** This is a catch-all section, typically displaying the name servers for the target.

- **STATISTICS:** This section shows how much time it took, in milliseconds or seconds, to answer the query as well as the date and time of the query.

NOTE   Expect to see **host, dig,** and **nslookup** commands on the Linux+ exam. Especially be prepared to look for a particular type of host with the **dig** command. Note also that the **dig** command and the **resolvectl** command can query the same information about services on domains.

The whois Command

The *whois* command is useful for determining which company or person owns a domain. The whois command searches the WHOIS database, which is a database that stores domain information on the Internet. Often the output also contains information regarding how to contact this organization, but it might also be redacted for privacy reasons. The following is an example of using the **whois** command:

```
# whois brunson.org.com | head
Domain Name: BRUNSON.ORG
Registry Domain ID: D3115511-LROR
Registrar WHOIS Server: whois.godaddy.com
Registrar URL: http://www.whois.godaddy.com
Updated Date: 2022-01-14T13:22:06Z
Creation Date: 1999-01-19T05:00:00Z
Registry Expiry Date: 2027-01-19T05:00:00Z
Registrar Registration Expiration Date:
Registrar: GoDaddy.com, LLC
Registrar IANA ID: 146
Registrar Abuse Contact Email: abuse@godaddy.com
Registrar Abuse Contact Phone: +1.4806242505
```

Network Monitoring

Monitoring network traffic requires not only that you have the ability to run the cool and flashy tools like **wireshark** and **tcpdump**, but also that you understand how to determine if a host can be found and how to get there from where you are. We'll start with the basics and go upscale from there so things make sense and are in the proper order for your understanding.

Is the Remote Host Reachable?

At the foundational level, you must determine if you can even *reach* the other system, be it on the same network, a different network near you, or across the world somewhere.

Starting with the most basic tool, you can use the **ping** command to see if the host is reachable. If it is, then you can move up the stack slightly to the *traceroute* command, which, if ICMP isn't disabled, will show the set of routers that you traversed to get to the eventual remote system.

The **ping** Command

The *ping* command uses Internet Control Message Protocol (ICMP) ECHO_REQUEST and ECHO_RESPONSE packets to determine whether a host is functioning or is at least able to respond to a ping request. The **ping** command is used for many things, including finding whether a host is available, whether a network can be reached, and whether a gateway is functioning.

Using the **ping** command is the simplest and easiest way to determine whether a host is alive. If you need to determine the route taken by a set of packets, it's more useful and accurate to use the **traceroute** command, covered next.

To determine whether a host is functioning (or at least responding to an ICMP request), use this command:

```
# ping 192.168.1.1
```

This returns output similar to the following:

```
PING 192.168.1.1 (192.168.1.1) from 192.168.1.73 : 56(84) bytes of
data.
64 bytes from 192.168.1.1: icmp_seq=1 ttl=150 time=9.23 ms
64 bytes from 192.168.1.1: icmp_seq=2 ttl=150 time=0.774 ms
64 bytes from 192.168.1.1: icmp_seq=3 ttl=150 time=0.715 ms
64 bytes from 192.168.1.1: icmp_seq=4 ttl=150 time=11.3 ms
```

When using the **ping** command, watch the time it takes to return the ECHO_ RESPONSE. If you see anything higher than 1000ms, you might be experiencing some congestion between your host and the target. Some latency is to be expected. The best method is to periodically measure the response time; any large variation from the norm might indicate an issue.

When you use **ping**, **traceroute**, and similar utilities that typically accept either a hostname or an IP address as the target, it's important to remember that DNS might not be present or configured and that the speediest method is to use the **-n** option to indicate not to try to have DNS resolve the hostname.

The **traceroute** Command

When you send a network packet to a remote system, especially across the Internet, it often needs to go through several gateways before it reaches its destination. You can see the gateways that the packet passes through by executing the **traceroute** command, as shown in Example 5-5.

Example 5-5 Example **traceroute** Command

```
# traceroute brunson.org
traceroute to brunson.org (15.197.142.173), 30 hops max, 60 byte
packets
 1   10.0.2.2 (10.0.2.2)  0.606 ms  1.132 ms  1.087 ms
 2   b001649-3.jfk01.atlas.cogentco.com (38.104.71.201)   0.738 ms
0.918 ms  0.838 ms
 3   154.24.42.205 (154.24.42.205)   0.952 ms   0.790 ms 0.906 ms
 4   be2629.ccr41.jfk02.atlas.cogentco.com (154.54.27.66)   1.699 ms
1.643 ms 1.347 ms
```

```
 5   be2148.ccr41.dca01.atlas.cogentco.com (154.54.31.117)   8.053 ms
7.719 ms   7.639 ms
 6   be2113.ccr42.atl01.atlas.cogentco.com (154.54.24.222)   18.276 ms
18.418 ms 18.407 ms
 7   be2687.ccr21.iah01.atlas.cogentco.com (154.54.28.70)   32.861 ms
32.917 ms   32.719 ms
 8   be2291.ccr21.sat01.atlas.cogentco.com (154.54.2.190)   38.087 ms
38.025 ms   38.076 ms
 9   be2301.ccr21.elp01.atlas.cogentco.com (154.54.5.174)   48.811 ms
48.952 ms   49.151 ms
10   be2254.ccr21.phx02.atlas.cogentco.com (154.54.7.33)   57.332 ms
57.281 ms   56.896 ms
11   te2-1.mag02.phx02.atlas.cogentco.com (154.54.1.230)   56.666 ms
65.279 ms   56.520 ms
12   154.24.18.26 (154.24.18.26)   57.924 ms 58.058 ms   58.032 ms
13   15.197.142.178 (15.197.142.178)   79.306 ms 57.740 ms 57.491 ms
14   brunson.org (15.197.142.173)   58.112 57.884 ms 58.299 ms
```

This output might seem useful, but it is not going to help you solve networking issues as often as you would like. For example, suppose you try to connect to a remote system, such as **brunson.org**, and you are not able to get any response. You are confident that that system is up and connected to the Internet, so you execute the **traceroute** command to troubleshoot:

```
# traceroute brunson.org
traceroute to test.brunson.org (15.197.142.173), 30 hops max, 60 byte
packets
 1   10.0.2.2 (10.0.2.2)   0.606 ms   1.132 ms   1.087 ms
 2   b001649-3.jfk01.atlas.cogentco.com (38.104.71.201)   0.738 ms
0.918 ms   0.838 ms
 3   154.24.42.205 (154.24.42.205)   0.952 ms   0.790 ms 0.906 ms
 4   ***
 5   ***
#Output omitted
30   ***
```

Well, there is the problem: Gateway 4—whatever that is—doesn't seem to be responding! Well, not exactly. The **traceroute** command uses ICMP packets, and these packets can be (and often are) ignored by gateways. The *** that you see in this output could be a gateway functioning correctly but just not responding to ICMP packets.

Even if gateway 4 is the problem, you need to determine what to do next. The gateway listed at number 3 is most likely outside your scope of control. You could try to hunt down the person/company responsible for gateway 3, but by the time you find and contact that person or company, that gateway will likely already have adjusted to use a different gateway 4. Gateways are normally pretty smart, and the ones on the Internet are almost always configured to be able to switch to another gateway if the one they are communicating with becomes nonresponsive.

So, is the **traceroute** command completely worthless? Not for larger organizations that have many internal gateways. It is not uncommon in large organizations that a network packet travels through multiple gateways before heading out to the Internet. The **traceroute** command can be used to pinpoint errors due to nonresponsive internal gateways.

The mtr Command

If you want a really cool variation of the **traceroute** command, install the *mtr* command. This command performs a "**traceroute**-like" operation every second, updating the display with statistics, as demonstrated in Figure 5-5.

```
                            student@student-VirtualBox: ~               ● ● ⊗
 File  Edit  View  Search  Terminal  Help
                         My traceroute  [v0.92]
student-VirtualBox (10.0.2.15)                      2019-01-11T17:08:51-0800
Keys:  Help   Display mode   Restart statistics   Order of fields   quit
                              Packets              Pings
 Host                         Loss%   Snt   Last    Avg   Best  Wrst StDev
 1. _gateway                   0.0%    6    0.3    0.3    0.3    0.4   0.0
 2. 192.168.0.1                0.0%    6   19.6    6.6    2.9   19.6   6.4
 3. 10.159.0.1                 0.0%    6   11.4   11.8   11.1   12.5   0.5
 4. 68.6.14.98                 0.0%    6  103.1   27.7   12.3  103.1  37.0
 5. 100.120.108.14             0.0%    6   52.2   40.6   11.5  140.7  51.5
 6. ae56.bar1.SanDiego1.Level3.net  0.0%  6  73.1   39.0   13.5  102.8 -39.1
 7. 4.69.140.102              83.3%    6   37.2   37.2   37.2   37.2   0.0
 8. ???
 9. Cogent-level3-100G.LosAngeles1.L  0.0%  6  17.4  30.8   16.6   97.7  32.8
10. be3271.ccr41.lax01.atlas.cogentc  0.0%  6 116.0  39.9   18.3  116.0  38.9
11. be2931.ccr31.phx01.atlas.cogentc  0.0%  6  93.9  56.6   29.3  122.4  41.0
12. be2929.ccr21.elp01.atlas.cogentc  0.0%  6  43.2  66.0   36.7  200.1  65.8
13. be2927.ccr41.iah01.atlas.cogentc  0.0%  6  51.3  68.3   51.0  149.5  39.8
14. be2687.ccr41.atl01.atlas.cogentc  0.0%  6  67.7  84.0   66.7  162.0  38.3
15. be2112.ccr41.dca01.atlas.cogentc  0.0%  6 150.3  99.4   78.1  150.3  30.3
16. be2806.ccr41.jfk02.atlas.cogentc  0.0%  6 180.7 116.6   79.9  189.9  53.3
17. be2896.rcr23.jfk01.atlas.cogentc  0.0%  6 129.6  99.1   80.9  138.9  27.4
18. be2803.rcr21.b001362-2.jfk01.atl  0.0%  6  82.5 105.8   82.2  221.0  56.4
19. 38.104.71.202              0.0%    5  120.5  90.0   81.3  120.5  17.1
```

Figure 5-5   The **mtr** command output

NOTE   The **mtr** command also happens to make an excellent "boss screen"—a screen used to cover up messing around at work (not that I am condoning this!) when you are concerned your boss might pop into your office. A boss screen is a program that makes it look like you are doing something important. You just need to be ready to bring it to the forefront of your terminal when the boss arrives. To a typical manager, the **mtr** command looks impressive and makes it look like you are busy with something important!

For the Linux+ exam, you might also want to be aware of the ***tracepath command***, which is similar to the ***traceroute command***. In fact, the man page for the **tracepath** command does an excellent job of describing the differences: "It is similar to traceroute, only does not require superuser privileges and has no fancy options."

Is the Data Flowing Properly?

Now that we've established that a host exists and how to determine the possible path your data will be taking to get there, it's time to understand more about the bandwidth and speed of the links between you and the remote host. For that we'll be looking at the **netstat** command, **wireshark** and **tshark** (the text-mode version of **wireshark**), and, for analyzing traffic, both the ***shark** commands and the amazing **tcpdump** command.

Using **netstat**

The ***netstat*** command is useful for determining statistics for network interfaces, connections to and from the local machine, and a lot of other information.

Using **netstat** without any options outputs a list of the open sockets on the system, but the most useful output is produced when you use options or combine them for richer information and troubleshooting.

The **netstat** command has a lot of options, the most relevant of which include the following:

- **-t:** Shows TCP statistics.

- **-r:** Shows the routing table.

- **-a:** Shows all the sockets on all functioning interfaces.

- **-c:** Shows a refreshed (every 1 second) view of statistics for usage.

- **-p:** Shows the name and PID of the program related to each socket (which is very useful!).

To see all the interfaces' usage statistics, use the **netstat -s** command, which returns output similar to the following truncated example:

```
Ip:
 216167 total packets received
 0 forwarded
 0 incoming packets discarded
 216092 incoming packets delivered
 104652 requests sent out
 80 dropped because of missing route
```

The **netstat** command can also be used for viewing the routing table for the system:

```
# netstat -r
```

This returns output similar to the following:

```
Kernel IP routing table
Destination Gateway Genmask Flags MSS Window irtt Iface
192.168.1.0 * 255.255.255.0 U 40 0 0 eth0
127.0.0.0 * 255.0.0.0 U 40 0 0 lo
default 192.168.1.1 0.0.0.0 UG 40 0 0 eth0
```

The final and most exam-related use of the **netstat** command is for detection and troubleshooting of connections to and from your machine.

To see what connections your system has, use the following command (using the **head** command and line numbering to keep the output manageable):

```
# netstat -a | head -n 20
```

This command returns voluminous output. Example 5-6 shows a truncated version of this output to give you an idea of what you see on your system when you use this command.

Example 5-6   Example **netstat** Command Output

```
1 Active Internet connections (servers and established)
2 Proto Recv-Q Send-Q Local Address Foreign Address _____ State
3 tcp 0 0 *:pop3s *:* LISTEN
4 tcp 0 0 *:netbios-ssn *:* LISTEN
5 tcp 0 0 *:sunrpc *:* LISTEN
6 tcp 0 0 192.168.15.5:domain *:* LISTEN
7 tcp 0 0 *:ssh *:* LISTEN
8 tcp 0 0 *:smtp *:* LISTEN
9 tcp 0 0 *:7741 *:* LISTEN
10 tcp 0 1 192.168.15.5:36651 206.235.223.112:smtp SYN
11 tcp 0 48 192.168.15.5:ssh 192.168.15.1:4417 ESTABL
12 tcp 0 0 192.168.15.5:36619 www.certmag.com:www ESTABL
13 0 1 192.168.15.5:36657 206.235.223.112:pop3 SYN
14 tcp 0 1 192.168.15.5:36653 206.235.223.112:pop3 SYN
15 tcp 0 0 192.168.15.5:36594 moviesunlim:www ESTABL
16 tcp 0 0 192.168.15.5:36595 moviesunlim:www ESTABL
```

The output from the **netstat** command is divided up into a number of columns, including

- **Proto:** This is the protocol used, typically TCP or UDP.

- **Recv-Q:** This is the bytes not yet received by the service or client attached to the socket.

- **Send-Q:** This is the bytes not yet acknowledged by the remote host.

- **Local Address:** This is your machine, the address, and the port number or name of services.

- **Foreign Address:** This is the address and port number of the remote end of the connection, or the other user's machine.

- **State:** Typically this is set to ESTABLISHED if a connection is or has been recently active; otherwise, it might be TIME_WAIT when it's almost done processing packets and LISTEN when the socket is a service/daemon waiting for a connection.

The output in Example 5-6 includes the following key items:

- **Line 6: 192.168.15.5:domain** in the **Local Address** column and the state LISTEN represent a name server (typically Bind) listening for DNS queries on the local machine.

- **Line 10:** This is the beginning stage of connecting to the remote SMTP server from this machine with an email client (hence the SYN state).

- **Line 11: 192.168.15.5:ssh** in the **Local Address** column shows that this is the daemon side of an SSH connection, with the foreign address 192.168.15.1:4417 being the connecting client.

- **Line 12:** This is a web client on the local machine attaching and requesting data from a site on the remote machine (as are lines 15 and 16).

- **Lines 13 and 14:** These are POP3 connections from the local machine to the remote machine.

NOTE   Expect to see **netstat** output on the Linux+ exam and to be asked to pick the client and server sides of the right connections. This is important for real-life situations, too, because it's always a good idea to know who's connecting to the system you are responsible for!

Use **netstat -c** to show **netstat** output continuously; use **netstat** in cron jobs to keep track of what's happening to a host during off-hours.

Swimming with Wireshark

Wireshark is an amazing network sniffer tool. It is very useful in viewing network traffic and troubleshooting network issues. It is also a very robust tool, and entire books have been written on how to use it. The goal of this section is to cover the basics of Wireshark to prepare you for the Linux+ exam.

It is likely that Wireshark is not installed on your distribution by default. You will need to install Wireshark with the appropriate installation tool (**yum**, **apt**, and so on, discussed in Chapter 6, "Building and Installing Software").

NOTE   By default, sniffing a network requires root access. Run all Wireshark commands as the root user and keep this default (requiring the utility to run as root) on any production or Internet-facing system.

Wireshark provides both GUI-based and TUI-based tools. To start the GUI tool, execute the **wireshark** command. You should see the GUI shown in Figure 5-6.

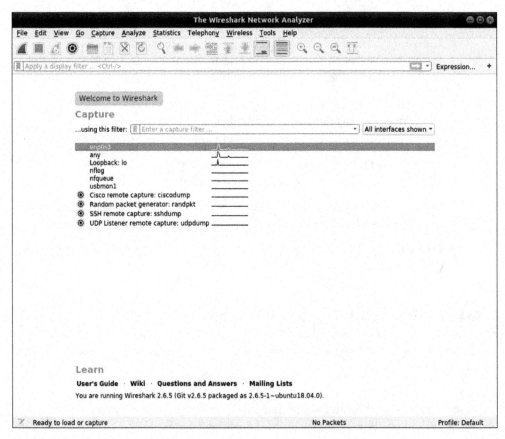

Figure 5-6   The Wireshark GUI

To view network traffic, you need to start a capture, which you do by clicking the **Capture** menu and then **Start**. You can also limit what is **captured** by setting filters and options (by clicking Capture and then **Options**). Figure 5-7 shows an example of captured packets.

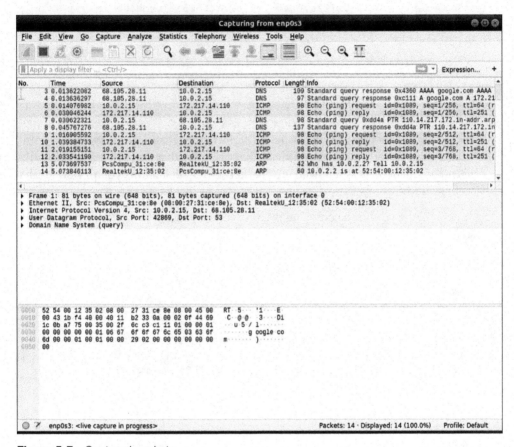

Figure 5-7   Captured packets

To use the TUI-based form of Wireshark, execute the **tstark** command as the root user:

```
# tshark
Capturing on 'enp0s3'
    1 0.000000000    10.0.2.15 →   68.105.28.11 DNS 81 Standard
query 0xeec4 A google.com OPT
    2 0.001031279    10.0.2.15 →   68.105.28.11 DNS 81 Standard
query 0x3469 AAAAgoogle.com OPT
    3 0.017196416 68.105.28.11 →   10.0.2.15    DNS 109 Standard
query response 0x3469 AAAA google.com AAAA 2607:f8b0:4007:800::200e
OPT
```

```
    4  0.017265061  68.105.28.11  →  10.0.2.15    DNS 97 Standard
query response 0xeec4 A google.com A 172.217.14.110 OPT
    5  0.018482388    10.0.2.15  →  172.217.14.110 ICMP 98 Echo
(ping) request   id=0x122c, seq=1/256, ttl=64
    6  0.036907577 172.217.14.110  →  10.0.2.15    ICMP 98 Echo
(ping) reply    id=0x122c, seq=1/256, ttl=251 (request in 5)
    7  1.021052811    10.0.2.15  →  172.217.14.110 ICMP 98 Echo
(ping) request  id=0x122c, seq=2/512, ttl=64
    8  1.039492225 172.217.14.110  →  10.0.2.15    ICMP 98 Echo
(ping) reply    id=0x122c, seq=2/512, ttl=251 (request in 7)
```

Key Topic

The **tcpdump** Command

When troubleshooting network issues or performing network security audits, it can be helpful to view the network traffic, including traffic that isn't related to the local machine. The *tcpdump* command is a "packet sniffer" that allows you to view local network traffic.

By default, the **tcpdump** command displays all network traffic to standard output until you terminate the command. This could result in a dizzying amount of data flying by on your screen. You can limit the output to a specific number of network packets by using the **-c** option, as shown here:

```
# tcpdump -c 5
tcpdump: verbose output suppressed, use -v or -vv for full protocol
decode
listening on eth0, link-type EN10MB (Ethernet), capture size 65535
bytes
11:32:59.630873 IP localhost.43066 > 192.168.1.1.domain: 16227+ A?
onecoursesource.com. (37)
11:32:59.631272 IP localhost.59247 > 192.168.1.1.domain: 2117+ PTR?
1.1.168.192.in-addr.arpa. (42)
11:32:59.631387 IP localhost.43066 > 192.168.1.1.domain: 19647+ AAAA?
onecoursesource.com. (37)
11:32:59.647932 IP 192.168.1.1.domain > localhost.59247: 2117
NXDomain* 0/1/0 (97)
11:32:59.717499 IP 192.168.1.1.domain > localhost.43066: 16227 1/0/0
A 38.89.136.109 (53)
5 packets captured
5 packets received by filter
0 packets dropped by kernel
```

You can also use this command to capture output based on some sort of criteria. For example, you can have the **tcpdump** command capture only packets that are available on a specific interface by using the **-i** option:

```
# tcpdump -i eth0
```

To limit packets to only a specific protocol, indicate the protocol name as an argument:

```
# tcpdump -i eth0 tcp
```

To display only packets associated with a specific port, use the **port** argument:

```
# tcpdump -i eth0 port 80
```

You can also limit the packets based on the source or destination IP address:

```
# tcpdump -i src 192.168.1.100
# tcpdump -i dst 192.168.1.100
```

In many cases, you will likely want to leave the **tcpdump** command running for a short period of time and view the data at some later time. In this case, it is best to use the **-c** option to limit the output and place the data into a file by using the **-w** option:

```
# tcpdump -c 5000 -w output-tcpdump
```

This file contains binary data. To read its contents, use the **-r** option to the **tcpdump** command:

```
# tcpdump -r output-tcpdump
```

NOTE You can expect to have to identify each of these netword monitoring commands, and some of their most common usages, on the Linux+ exam. Install each and every command, try the examples presented here, experiment some, and get experience—you'll need it on the exam!

Remote Networking Tools

Now we've established the basics of networking, how to resolve names, how to find your way to other hosts and networks, and how to troubleshoot and monitor them, let's talk about how to use remote networking tools to get your data from and to those other hosts.

SSH (Secure Shell)

Secure Shell (*SSH*) is a service that allows for secure communication between hosts. The securing features include symmetrical encryption, asymmetrical encryption, and hashing. SSH is used for the following:

- As a secure replacement for Telnet and other unsecure remote-connection services (such as rlogin). On the client side, the **ssh** command is used for this feature.

- As a secure replacement for file transfer methods, such as FTP or RCP. On the client side, the **sftp** command is used to replace **ftp**, and the **scp** command is used to replace **rcp**.

- As a secure replacement for remote execution methods, like **rsh**. On the client side, the **ssh** command is used for this feature.

NOTE   SSH is covered in detail in Chapter 11, "Using Remote Connectivity for System Management."

Using curl and wget

When you want to script the download of a package or file from a remote source as part of an update or script that will use that file, you can use the *wget* and *curl* commands.

For example, to get a file from a remote location without a need for further interaction, you use the following command:

```
# wget http://ftp.gnu.org/gnu/wget/wget-1.5.3.tar.gz
```

This command downloads the latest (at the time of publication) version of the source code for the **wget** command, as demonstrated in Figure 5-8.

Figure 5-8   Downloading software with the **wget** command

There is a lot of confusion about when to use **curl** instead of **wget** to download a file. While these two commands are very similar in function, **curl** is typically used to both download and execute a script file, such as in situations of automated installation of virtual machine or container environments.

Simply enough, the **wget** source code file previously downloaded can also be downloaded with the **curl** command, as demonstrated in Figure 5-9.

Figure 5-9 Downloading software with the **curl** command

The **curl** command needs to have either the **-O** option or the **--remote-name** option specified in order to download a file like **wget** does; otherwise, the file is sent to the standard output/console and is not created as a file on the disk.

The nc Command

The man page of the *nc* command (also referred to as the **netcat** command) provides an excellent summary of the **nc** command:

> The **nc** (or **netcat**) utility is used for just about anything under the sun involving TCP or UDP. It can open TCP connections, send UDP packets, listen on arbitrary TCP and UDP ports, do port scanning, and deal with both IPv4 and IPv6. Unlike **telnet(1)**, **nc** scripts nicely and separates error messages onto standard error instead of sending them to standard output, as **telnet(1)** does with some.

There are quite a few uses for the **nc** command. For example, suppose you want to know whether a specific port is being blocked by your company firewall before you bring online a service that makes use of this port. On the internal server, you can have the **nc** command listen for connections on that port:

```
# nc -l 3333
```

You should end up with a blank line below the **nc** command. Next, on a remote system outside your network, you could run the following **nc** command to connect (replacing *server* with the resolvable hostname or IP address of the local system):

```
# nc server 3333
```

If the connection is established, you see a blank line under the **nc** command line. If you type something on this blank line and press the **Enter** key, then what you typed appears below the **nc** command on the server. Actually, the communications work both ways: What you type on the server below the **nc** command appears on the client as well.

The following are some useful options to the **nc** command:

- **-w:** This option is used on the client side to close a connection automatically after a timeout value is reached. For example, **nc -w 30 server 333** closes the connection 30 seconds after it is established.

- **-6:** Use this option to enable IPv6 connections.

- **-k:** Use this option to keep the server process active, even after the client disconnects. The default behavior is to stop the server process when the client disconnects.

- **-u:** Use this option to use UDP connections rather than TCP connections (the default). This is important for correctly testing firewall configurations, as a TCP port might be blocked while the UDP port might not be blocked.

You can also use the **nc** command to display open ports, similar to the way you use the **netstat** command:

```
# nc -z localhost 1000-4000
Connection to localhost 3260 port [tcp/iscsi-target] succeeded!
Connection to localhost 3333 port [tcp/dec-notes] succeeded!
```

The **-z** option can also be used for port scanning on a remote host.

NOTE   There is one feature of the **nc** command that I don't expect you will see on the exam; however, it is a useful technique for transferring all sorts of data. Assuming that the transfer is from the client to the server, on the server, you use the following format:

```
nc -l 3333 | cmd
```

And on the client, you use this format:

```
cmd | nc server 3333
```

For example, you can transfer an entire **/home** directory structure from the client to the server, using the tar command, by first executing the following on the server:

```
nc -l 333 | tar xvf -
```

Then on the client, you execute the following command:

```
tar cvf - /home | nc server 333
```

The client merges the contents of the **/home** directory structure into a tarball. The - tells the **tar** command to send this output to standard output. The data is sent to the server via the client's **nc** command, and then the server's **nc** command sends this data to the **tar** command. As a result, the **/home** directory from the client is copied into the current directory of the server.

This is just one technique of many for using this powerful feature of the **nc** command.

Using rsync

This was covered in the *Everything and the Kitchen rsync* section of Chapter 2, "Managing Files and Directories."

Using scp

This was covered in the *Using the **scp** Command* section of Chapter 2.

Summary

In this chapter you learned a lot about how to configure and manage your network interfaces, how to configure and manage name resolution, including for local and remote hosts and domains, how to monitor and troubleshoot your network traffic, and how to use remote networking tools to transfer data from system to system, securely and with proper data integrity.

Exam Preparation Tasks

As mentioned in the section "Goals and Methods" in the Introduction, you have a couple of choices for exam preparation: the exercises here, Chapter 23, "Final Preparation," and the exam simulation questions in the Pearson Test Prep Software Online.

Review All Key Topics

Review the most important topics in this chapter, noted with the Key Topic icon in the outer margin of the page. Table 5-3 lists these key topics and the page number on which each is found.

Table 5-3   Key Topics for Chapter 5

Key Topic Element	Description	Page Number
Figure 5-1	Utilities obsoleted by the iproute2 suite of tools	189
Example 5-1	Example **ip addr show** Command Output	189
Table 5-2	**ss** Command Options	192
Paragraph	NetworkManager **nmcli** command	192
Paragraph	The **ifconfig** Command	195
Paragraph	Using the **arp** command to view or change the ARP table	198
List	Local system name configuration files	200
List	**hostnamectl** command hostname levels	204
Example 5-4	Example **dig** Command Output	205
Paragraph	Determining if a host is functioning	208
Paragraph	Using the **netstat** command to view the routing table	212
Section	The **tcpdump** Command	216
Section	Using curl and **wget**	218
Figure 5-8	Downloading software with the **wget** command	218

Define Key Terms

Define the following key terms from this chapter and check your answers in the glossary:

interface, iproute2, **ip**, **ss**, **nmcli**, **ifconfig**, **ifcfg**, **hostname**, **arp**, **route**, **network-scripts**, **resolv.conf**, **nsswitch.conf**, **resolvectl**, **hostnamectl**, **dig**, **nslookup**, **whois**, **traceroute**, **ping**, **mtr**, **netstat**, Wireshark, **tcpdump**, Secure Shell (SSH), **wget**, **curl**, **nc**, **rsync**, **scp**

Review Questions

The answers to these review questions are in Appendix A.

1. You wish to retrieve an RPM package file from a remote package repository, and you have the full URL of the required file. Which command do you use? (Choose two.)

   a. **wget**

   b. **dload**

   c. **getfile**

   d. **curl**

2. Which SSH command is designed to replace the **telnet** command?

   a. **rlogin**

   b. **sftp**

   c. **scp**

   d. **ssh**

3. Which SSH command is designed to function as a secure equivalent to the rcp command?

   a. **rlogin**

   b. **sftp**

   c. **scp**

   d. **ssh**

4. Which of the following commands display all of the routers that a packet travels through to get to the destination? (Choose all that apply.)

   a. **traceroute**

   b. **tracehop**

   c. **mtr**

This chapter covers the following topics:

- Package Management
- Sandboxed Applications
- System Updates

The exam objective covered in this chapter is as follows:

Objective 1.6: Given a scenario, build and install software

## CHAPTER 6

Building and Installing Software

Linux systems are made up of a lot of software, all organized packages, which are collections of software code, directories, files, supporting files, and often precompiled binaries of those applications.

Packages are the top-level manifestation of the software world. They are constructed to make distribution, installation, removal, updating, and other administrative tasks easier and less prone to errors and conflicts.

A Linux system is meant to be useful, such as serving as some kind of application server or allowing a user to read email or browse the Web. The Linux kernel is great, but by itself it doesn't do much; to make a Linux system useful, you need software.

A lot of software is available for Linux; you just need to install it. You can install software in a few ways, depending on your distribution and how the software was packaged.

At one point software was distributed in source format, which needed to be compiled into something that could run on a computer. Source format is still around, but as a community, we've moved on to distributing binary packages that are much easier to install. Binary packages avoid the compilation step (by being already compiled); in addition, dependencies, libraries, configuration, and documentation are automatically managed. There are a few different formats of these packages, but two are most prevalent: Debian style and Red Hat style. You are expected to know both of these main styles for the CompTIA Linux+ exam because many computing environments have both types of systems, and the package style used depends on the project and the services being provided by the systems.

Additionally, we'll look into the newer area of application sandboxing, or what is also called app containerization, via Snap, Flatpak, and AppImage.

Lastly, we will cover how to handle system updates, including both kernel updates and package updates.

"Do I Know This Already?" Quiz

The "Do I Know This Already?" quiz enables you to assess whether you should read this entire chapter or simply jump to the "Exam Preparation Tasks" section for review. If you are in doubt, read the entire chapter. Table 6-1 outlines the major headings in this chapter and the corresponding "Do I Know This Already?" quiz questions. You can find the answers in Appendix A, "Answers to the 'Do I Know This Already?' Quizzes and Review Questions."

Table 6-1 "Do I Know This Already?" Foundation Topics Section-to-Question Mapping

Foundation Topics Section	Questions Covered in This Section
Package Management	1–2
Sandboxed Applications	3–4
System Updates	5–6

CAUTION The goal of self-assessment is to gauge your mastery of the topics in this chapter. If you do not know the answer to a question or are only partially sure of the answer, you should mark that question as wrong for purposes of the self-assessment. Giving yourself credit for an answer you correctly guess skews your self-assessment results and might provide you with a false sense of security.

1. Which of the following is most likely a Debian/Ubuntu package file?

    a. packagename.tgz

    b. packagename.rpm

    c. packagename.deb

    d. packagename.sh

2. A type of package is described as being a derivative of a **cpio** archive with some added metadata. Which package type best describes this sort of package?

    a. RPM

    b. Slackware

    c. Debian

    d. Gentoo

3. Which of the following is *not* a desired feature of using sandboxed applications?

    a. Built for any and every distribution

    b. Full control over dependencies

    c. Requires permission to access host resources

    d. Application updates via the host distribution

4. Which of the following are common features among the three application sandboxing methods popular in Linux software (AppImage, Flatpak, and Snap)? Choose all that apply.

    a. Run without root access

    b. Must run from an uncompressed source

    c. Multiple running versions possible

    d. Can be updated independently from distro

    e. Has access to system-level resources

    f. Vendor-independent repositories

5. Which type of update is best suited for live kernel patching updates?

    a. Binary

    b. Security

    c. Feature

    d. Module

6. Which application sandboxing method has as a feature a "one file per app" specification?

    a. Snapd

    b. Flatpak

    c. AppImage

    d. AppArmor

Foundation Topics

Package Management

A *package* is a compressed archive file that contains all the necessary files that make up a given command, application, or set of applications. Packages come in several different formats, such as RPM, DEB, and a few others, but they are all similar in their function, if slightly different in format.

The Most Common Package Types

The most common package types are **.rpm** (Red Hat Package Manager) and **.deb** (Debian Package Format) files. Packages can come in several other formats, chief among them compressed files such as **.tar** (tar archive), **.tgz** (tar archives compressed with the **gzip** command), and **.gz** (a package that has been compressed with the **gzip** command).

A compressed (**.tar/.tgz/.gz**) file is not a package that can be installed by a package manager such as RPM or APT. Instead, it must be unarchived so the contained file or files can be either compiled from source or, if a binary, copied to the proper location for execution.

RPM package files are typically in the **cpio** archive format, with an **.rpm** extension (for example, **application.rpm**), and consist of the following:

- **Header:** The header is a separate structure that defines the file's format and tagged data that contains the package info, copyright and versions, build host, and a package integrity signature.

- **Archive:** An archive holds package files, including scripts to be run during installation, files to be copied, and links to be made.

Debian packages are usually in the **ar** archive format, have a **.deb** extension (for example, **application.deb**), and consist of the following:

- **data.tar.gz:** A hierarchically related set of files, man pages, links, and so on to be copied to the system during the install.

- **control.tar.gz:** All package information, including copyright, description, and so on. Also contains any scripts that should be run in the process of installation or removal of the package.

Package Managers

Package managers were invented to solve the problem of software version prolif-
eration and the cruft of extra or abandoned files that result from many upgrades or
installations.

A package manager keeps track of which files belong to which package, which packages depend on which other packages, and where the different types of files are
stored. All modern distributions of Linux use package managers in some fashion.

Debian Package Management

Debian and Debian-derived systems such as Ubuntu have a powerful package management system that provides a way for administrators to find, install, query, and
remove packages. The package tracks the parts of an application and helps you figure out which other packages (dependencies) are needed to install a given package
and whether any packages rely on other packages.

The basic unit of Debian package management is a file with a **.deb** extension (for
example, **application.deb**), as explained earlier.

You can install, remove, and query packages with the *dpkg* tool, typically in a single-
package mode. Installing multiple packages is possible but can quickly become cumbersome due to interlocking dependencies.

To install a package and all its dependencies and even get new packages from an
online and updated source, you need to employ a package management tool such as
the *APT* (Advanced Package Tool) suite.

Commonly known collectively as **apt-get**, the APT suite can make even many-part
package installs, updates, and entire system upgrades as simple as a couple of easily
remembered commands and options.

Graphical and text-based interfaces such as **aptitude** and **synaptic** are layered on
top of the APT tools. They give you an interface that's easier to use than having to
remember commands.

So, to recap: Local packages are **.deb** files and are installed with **dpkg**. APT handles
searching remote package repositories and downloading packages. Aptitude and the
like provide a graphical interface to APT. The graphical and APT tools use the **dpkg**
command as their underlying package interaction tool, supplying it with the needed
commands and options and arguments to effectively automate the process of installation, removal, and updating/upgrading large numbers of packages easily.

Managing Local Debian Packages

The **dpkg** tool manipulates packages on a system and can process the **.deb** packages you might download. If you have a package on a system, you can find out what's inside it by using the **--info** option, as shown in Example 6-1.

Example 6-1   Finding Out What's Inside a **.deb** File

```
# dpkg --info acct_6.5.5-1_amd64.deb
 new debian package, version 2.0.
 size 120424 bytes: control archive=1899 bytes.
 79 bytes, 4 lines conffiles
 746 bytes, 18 lines control
 1766 bytes, 27 lines md5sums
 507 bytes, 30 lines * postinst #!/bin/sh
 370 bytes, 26 lines * postrm #!/bin/sh
 163 bytes, 7 lines * prerm #!/bin/sh
 Package: acct
 Version: 6.5.5-1
 Architecture: amd64
 Maintainer: Mathieu Trudel-Lapierre <mathieu.tl@gmail.com>
 Installed-Size: 380
 Depends: dpkg (>= 1.15.4) | install-info, libc6 (>= 2.3)
 Section: admin
 Priority: optional
 Homepage: http://www.gnu.org/software/acct/
 Description: The GNU Accounting utilities for process and login
accounting
 ...
```

The information about the package is contained inside the **.deb** file; the **dpkg** command displays it nicely for you. The top section describes the control files that provide the metadata for **dpkg** to use. The file itself is 120,424 bytes, and inside it is an archive of control files totaling 1,899 bytes. Inside that archive are

- **conffiles:** A list of files used to configure the package after it's installed. These files are treated differently than other files in the package; for example, they are not removed when the package is removed.

- **control:** The file containing all the metadata about the packages, such as dependencies.

- **md5sums:** A list of files and a checksum so that you can verify that the file hasn't changed at any point.

- **postinst:** A shell script that is run after the installation.

- **postrm:** A shell script that is run after the removal of the package.

- **prerm:** A shell script that is run just before the package is removed.

After the control information you see various pieces of information about the package, such as the name, version, which hardware it is meant to go on, and the dependencies.

Installing Packages with dpkg

The most common way to install packages is by using one of the following commands at the command line from the current directory:

```
# dpkg --install gcc-4.7-base_4.7.2-5_amd64.deb
# dpkg -i gcc-4.7-base_4.7.2-5_amd64.deb
```

This returns output similar to the following:

```
Selecting previously unselected package gcc-4.7-base:amd64.
(Reading database ... 142987 files and directories currently
installed.)
Unpacking gcc-4.7-base:amd64 (from gcc-4.7-base_4.7.2-5_amd64.deb)
...
Setting up gcc-4.7-base:amd64 (4.7.2-5) ...
```

Sometimes you need to install dependencies for a package. You can either install the dependency first or specify all the necessary packages on the same command line. The command for the latter option looks like this:

```
# dpkg -i gcc-4.7-base_4.7.2-5_amd64.deb libgcc1_1%3a4.7.2-5_amd64.
deb
```

Removing Packages

When you need to remove a package with the **dpkg** command, you can use one of two methods: **remove** or **purge**. The **-r** or **--remove** option removes the package's files but leaves any configuration files intact on the disk. The other option for getting rid of packages is the **-P** or **--purge** option, which removes all the package's files, including any configuration files.

To remove a package but leave its configuration files in place, use one of the following:

```
# dpkg --remove package_name
# dpkg -r package_name
```

To purge a package, including its configuration files, use one of the following:

```
# dpkg --purge package_name
# dpkg -P package_name
```

When a package is installed, any configuration files are noted in the **conffiles** file. You can use this file to determine which files are left in place during a remove action and which files should also be purged in a purge action.

Dependency Issues

When you are working with packages, a desired package installation often finds entries in the package database that conflict with the files it is attempting to install. Also, sometimes during a removal, a package has a file it wants to remove that other packages depend on.

In keeping with the sturdy and less-than-verbose nature of Debian, using the package tools **--force** option can lead to some truly unpleasant circumstances for a machine. Take great care when removing packages that have dependencies, and read in detail the man page for **dpkg**'s **force** section. For the Linux+ exam, you need to know how to force an action, but you don't need to know all 20 or so forcing options.

To force the removal of a broken package marked in the database as requiring reinstallation, use the following:

```
# dpkg --force-reinstreq package_name
```

Use **--force-reinstreq** on packages marked as requiring reinstallation; it allows **dpkg** to remove those packages.

In addition, you can use the **--force-depends** option after **--install** to turn all those nasty error messages into dire warnings, but the tool then allows you to do whatever inadvisable action you're about to perform.

Here's an example:

```
# dpkg --install --force-depends package_name
```

Finally, you can use the **--force-remove-essential** option. Be warned, however, that overriding the dependency recommendations might leave your system in a broken state.

If you positively must (usually on direction from the vendor or a nearby Debian guru), you can force the installation of a package, regardless of the conflicts generated with the command and options, like so:

```
# dpkg --install new_pkg.deb --force-conflicts
```

If you have problems with the package or other packages after forcing past any conflicts, remember that you were warned.

Querying Packages

Keep in mind that when you are querying packages and not referring to a **.deb** file on the local disk or mounted filesystems, you are actually querying the package database—that is, the complete list of all the packages and their file locations that are currently installed to the system through **dpkg** or another package management tool.

Packages currently installed can be queried for a plethora of information. In particular, you can list the existence, version, name, and a description of a package by using the **-l** or **--list** option:

```
# dpkg --list krb*
# dpkg -l krb*
```

You can use either a singular package name, such as **krb5-user** for a Kerberos-related package, or the previous filename to see the listing shown in the following output:

```
# dpkg --list krb*
Desired=Unknown/Install/Remove/Purge/Hold
| Status=Not/Inst/Conf-files/Unpacked/halF-conf/Half-inst/trig-aWait/
Trig-pend
|/ Err?=(none)/Reinst-required (Status,Err: uppercase=bad)
||/ Name Version Architecture Description
+++-=================-================-================-
=============================
un krb5-doc <none> (no description available)
ii krb5-locales 1.10.1+dfsg-5+d all Internationalization support for
MIT Kerberos
un krb5-user <none> (no description available)
```

After some headers, the output shows that there are three packages starting with **krb5**. Two of them, with lines beginning with the string **un**, are uninstalled, while **krb5-locales** is installed as version 1.10.1. The Debian package system shows you packages previously installed on your system, which is different from other systems.

You can check the status of a particular package or packages by using the **-s** or **--status** option:

```
# dpkg --status krdc
```

The output returned is an abbreviated version of what you get with the **--info** option.

You can see the files that were installed by a package by using the **-L** or **--listfiles** option:

```
# dpkg --listfiles coreutils
```

This results in output similar to the following (which has been truncated to fit):

```
/.
/bin
/bin/cat
/bin/chgrp
/bin/chmod
/bin/chown
```

The use of either the **-S** or **--search** option lets you search the installed files on disk via the package database, such as

```
# dpkg -S apt.conf
```

The following output contains the various places an **apt.conf** file was found from the database entries:

```
apt: /etc/apt/apt.conf.d/01autoremove
unattended-upgrades: /etc/apt/apt.conf.d/50unattended-upgrades
apt: /usr/share/man/ja/man5/apt.conf.5.gz
apt: /usr/share/man/pt/man5/apt.conf.5.gz
apt: /usr/share/doc/apt/examples/apt.conf
apt-listchanges: /etc/apt/apt.conf.d/20listchanges
aptdaemon: /etc/apt/apt.conf.d/20dbus
aptdaemon: /etc/dbus-1/system.d/org.debian.apt.conf
```

The output lists all the packages that contain a file with **apt.conf** in the name. The package name is on the left, and the filename is on the right. Note that the search string can happen anywhere within the filename, even if it's a directory name.

Reconfiguring Packages

Some packages include a configuration tool that is executed when you install the package. This tool makes it easy to manage the initial setup of the software you are installing. If a package includes such a configuration tool, you can run that utility again with the **dpkg-reconfigure** command followed by the name of the package.

Figure 6-1 shows the output of running the Postfix mail server configuration with this command:

```
# dpkg-reconfigure postfix
```

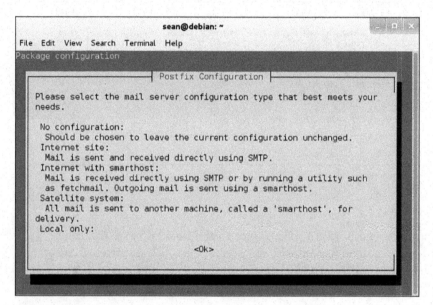

Figure 6-1 Reconfiguring Postfix with **dpkg-reconfigure**

Using Repositories

It is possible for a CD/DVD or an ISO image of a CD/DVD to hold only a limited amount of software (or packages). An ever-expanding amount of the available software for any distribution can be found online, either as a single source code set, as prebuilt packages for download, or in a combination of official, semi-official, and very unofficial locations collectively called *repositories*.

Repositories in Debian/Ubuntu can be confusing, as Ubuntu and Canonical have a close relationship, so when discussing repositories, it's impossible to avoid or not show the Main or official Canonical supported repository. To keep things easier, we'll discuss repositories from the standpoint of the Ubuntu distribution, and you can look up anything you might need to learn for standard Debian.

The APT tools work by maintaining a local cache of what packages are available on remote servers, including the dependencies. This means you can search your local cache much more quickly than if you had to query remote servers.

The list of remote package repositories is stored in **/etc/apt/sources.list** and in individual files under **/etc/apt/sources.list.d**. Each line represents one repository.

A **sources.list** file may look like Example 6-2.

Example 6-2   A Default Sources List File

```
deb http://cdn.debian.net/debian/ wheezy main
deb-src http://cdn.debian.net/debian/ wheezy main

deb http://security.debian.org/ wheezy/updates main
deb-src http://security.debian.org/ wheezy/updates main

# wheezy-updates, previously known as 'volatile'
deb http://cdn.debian.net/debian/ wheezy-updates main
deb-src http://cdn.debian.net/debian/ wheezy-updates main
```

What Is a Repository?

At its simplest, a repository is a collection or an archive of software that can be addressed by the system. Repositories can exist on local disk, on attached or mounted disk, or even across a local or wide area network on a server via a sharing protocol such as HTTP or FTP.

Ubuntu repositories come in various types, including

- **Main:** Canonical-supported free and open-source packages
- **Universe:** Community-maintained free and open-source packages
- **Restricted:** Proprietary driver packages for devices
- **Multiverse:** Software that has copyright or legal issues

Typically, the Ubuntu installation media contains packages that are drawn from the most recent version of the Main and Restricted repositories so that you can actually complete a proper install. In modern Linux, installation is just the start; in order to get updates and additional software, it's necessary to have the correct repositories configured.

Viewing Configured Repositories

During installation, the system configures a number of default repositories by placing the appropriate entries in the **/etc/apt/sources.list** file or, if you prefer, by having files that end with the **.list** extension in the **/etc/apt/sources.list.d** directory.

An example of a populated **sources.list file** is shown in Example 6-3.

Example 6-3   Contents of a **sources.list** File

```
# deb cdrom:[Ubuntu 18.04.1 LTS _Bionic Beaver_ - Release amd64
(20180725)]/ bionic main restricted
# See http://help.ubuntu.com/community/UpgradeNotes for how to upgrade
to
# newer versions of the distribution.
deb http://us.archive.ubuntu.com/ubuntu/ bionic main restricted
# deb-src http://us.archive.ubuntu.com/ubuntu/ bionic main restricted

## Major bug fix updates produced after the final release of the
## distribution.
deb http://us.archive.ubuntu.com/ubuntu/ bionic-updates main
restricted
# deb-src http://us.archive.ubuntu.com/ubuntu/ bionic-updates main
restricted
## N.B. software from this repository is ENTIRELY UNSUPPORTED by the
Ubuntu
## team. Also, please note that software in universe WILL NOT receive
any
## review or updates from the Ubuntu security team.
deb http://us.archive.ubuntu.com/ubuntu/ bionic universe
# deb-src http://us.archive.ubuntu.com/ubuntu/ bionic universe
deb http://us.archive.ubuntu.com/ubuntu/ bionic-updates universe
# deb-src http://us.archive.ubuntu.com/ubuntu/ bionic-updates universe
## N.B. software from this repository is ENTIRELY UNSUPPORTED by the
Ubuntu
## team, and may not be under a free licence. Please satisfy yourself
as to
## your rights to use the software. Also, please note that software
in
## multiverse WILL NOT receive any review or updates from the Ubuntu
## security team.
deb http://us.archive.ubuntu.com/ubuntu/ bionic multiverse
# deb-src http://us.archive.ubuntu.com/ubuntu/ bionic multiverse
deb http://us.archive.ubuntu.com/ubuntu/ bionic-updates multiverse
# deb-src http://us.archive.ubuntu.com/ubuntu/ bionic-updates
multiverse
```

In this example, several lines contain comments that are preceded with the **#** (hash or comment) character. Uncommented lines are actual repository configurations.

The repository lines break down as follows:

- **deb:** This denotes that the repository contains precompiled or binary packages; it is the most common repository type.

- **deb-src:** This means that the repository contains packages of source code that are put together for easy transport and "installation," or copying to the user's system.

- **URL:** In most cases (that is, the four main repository channels) the URL is http://us.archive.ubuntu.com/ubuntu/. Consult the official mirrors list on www.ubuntu.com for more options.

- **Bionic:** This is the release name or the version of the Ubuntu distribution and affects what software is being pulled from the repository.

- **Main:** This is the name of the component or section, in lowercase and separated by spaces. There can be several components or sections.

Adding Repositories

To manually add a repository from the command line, you can either edit the **/etc/apt/sources.list** file, add a file containing the appropriate line(s) to the **/etc/apt/sources.list.d** directory, or use the **add-apt-repository** command as shown in Example 6-4.

Example 6-4   Adding a Repository via the **add-apt-repository** Command

```
# sudo add-apt-repository "deb http://us.archive.ubuntu.com/ubuntu/
bionic universe"
Hit:1 http://us.archive.ubuntu.com/ubuntu bionic InRelease
Get:2 http://us.archive.ubuntu.com/ubuntu bionic-updates InRelease
[88.7 kB]
Get:3 http://security.ubuntu.com/ubuntu bionic-security InRelease
[83.2 kB]
Get:4 http://us.archive.ubuntu.com/ubuntu bionic-backports InRelease
[74.6 kB]
Get:5 http://us.archive.ubuntu.com/ubuntu bionic-updates/ main i386
Packages [389 kB]
Get:6 http://us.archive.ubuntu.com/ubuntu bionic-updates/ main amd64
Packages [437 kB]
Get:7 http://us.archive.ubuntu.com/ubuntu bionic-updates/ main
Translation-en [164 kB]
Get:8 http://security.ubuntu.com/ubuntu bionic-security/ main i386
Packages [164 kB]
```

```
Get:9 http://security.ubuntu.com/ubuntu bionic-security/ main amd64
Packages [206 kB]
Get:10 http://security.ubuntu.com/ubuntu bionic-security/ main
Translation-en [81.0 kB]
Fetched 1,687 kB in 1s (1,376 kB/s)
Reading package lists... Done
```

This process adds an appropriate repository line to the **/etc/apt/sources.list** file, making that software available to be queried, installed, and used.

While you can use the **apt-add-repository** command to do a lot of things, including add, remove, and auto-update on add, it's more traditional to use your favorite text editor and make the changes directly to the **/etc/apt/sources** tree of files and directories or even to use the graphical software tools, which are beyond the scope of this discussion.

Installing Remote Packages

Now that you know what repositories are and how to add them to your systems, you can use the **apt-get** utility for most remote software installation operations. Every **apt-get** invocation is followed by a command that indicates what to do. Use the **install** command to install a package, as shown in Example 6-5.

Example 6-5   Installing a Remote Package

```
# sudo apt-get install nginx-light
[sudo] password for tux:
Reading package lists... Done
Building dependency tree
Reading state information... Done
The following additional packages will be installed:
  libnginx-mod-http-echo nginx-common
Suggested packages:
  fcgiwrap nginx-doc
The following NEW packages will be installed:
  libnginx-mod-http-echo nginx-common nginx-light
0 upgraded, 3 newly installed, 0 to remove and 8 not upgraded.
Need to get 449 kB of archives.
After this operation, 1,503 kB of additional disk space will be used.
Do you want to continue? [Y/n] y
```

```
Get:1 http://us.archive.ubuntu.com/ubuntu bionic-updates/ main amd64
nginx-common all 1.14.0-0ubuntu1.2 [37.4 kB]
Get:2 http://security.ubuntu.com/ubuntu bionic-security/universe amd64
libnginx-mod-http-echo amd64 1.14.0-0ubuntu1.2 [21.3 kB]
Get:3 http://security.ubuntu.com/ubuntu bionic-security/universe amd64
nginx-light amd64 1.14.0-0ubuntu1.2 [390 kB]
Fetched 449 kB in 1s (448 kB/s)
Preconfiguring packages ...
Selecting previously unselected package nginx-common.
(Reading database ... 163823 files and directories currently
installed.)
Preparing to unpack .../nginx-common_1.14.0-0ubuntu1.2_all.deb ...
Unpacking nginx-common (1.14.0-0ubuntu1.2) ...
Selecting previously unselected package libnginx-mod-http-echo.
Preparing to unpack .../libnginx-mod-http-echo_1.14.0-0ubuntu1.2_
amd64.deb ...
Unpacking libnginx-mod-http-echo (1.14.0-0ubuntu1.2) ...
Selecting previously unselected package nginx-light.
Preparing to unpack .../nginx-light_1.14.0-0ubuntu1.2_amd64.deb ...
Unpacking nginx-light (1.14.0-0ubuntu1.2) ...
Processing triggers for ufw (0.35-5) ...
Processing triggers for ureadahead (0.100.0-20) ...
Setting up nginx-common (1.14.0-0ubuntu1.2) ...
Created symlink /etc/systemd/system/multi-user.target.wants/nginx.
service  /lib/systemd/system/nginx.service.
Processing triggers for systemd (237-3ubuntu10.6) ...
Processing triggers for man-db (2.8.3-2ubuntu0.1) ...
Setting up libnginx-mod-http-echo (1.14.0-0ubuntu1.2) ...
Setting up nginx-light (1.14.0-0ubuntu1.2) ...
Processing triggers for ureadahead (0.100.0-20) ...
Processing triggers for ufw (0.35-5) ...
```

Example 6-5 installs the **nginx-light** package through **apt-get install nginx-light**. The program determines that the **nginx-common** package is also required, so both packages are downloaded and installed. Any setup scripts, including **dpkg-reconfigure**, are run at this time as well.

Finally, pay attention to the differences between the **apt-get** and **dpkg** commands, especially with regard to the first option. **apt-get** commands do not have a leading dash or dashes, while **dpkg** commands do. For example, **dpkg -i** installs a local package, but **apt-get install** installs a remote package. Don't get tripped up on any Linux+ exam questions that try to conflate the two, such as with **apt-get --install pkgname**.

Working with the Cache

The APT tools work by maintaining a local cache of the packages available on remote servers, including the dependencies. You can search your local cache much more quickly than if you had to query remote servers.

You must update the package cache after modifying **sources.list** or to fetch any upstream changes. You do this by running **apt-get update**.

When the APT cache is up to date, you can investigate packages by using the **apt-cache** command:

- **apt-cache search** *term*: Searches for packages matching the term

- **apt-cache show package_name**: Shows information about a given package name, including a description and dependencies

- **apt-cache showpkg** *package_name*: Shows more technical details about a package, such as what depends on it, what it depends on, and what services it provides

Upgrading the System

A system has many packages installed—hundreds or even thousands of them. Each one of these packages might need updates at some point in time. Updates take the form of:

- Security updates that fix problems in a package that could lead to bad guys doing bad things on the machine

- Bug fixes to correct problems in software that cause it to perform incorrectly, crash, or even lose data

- Feature improvements that update to the latest version of some software

To update a specific package, you reinstall that package as shown here:

```
# apt-get install cpio
Reading package lists... Done
Building dependency tree
Reading state information... Done
Suggested packages:
 libarchive1
The following packages will be upgraded:
 cpio
```

The last two lines of the output show that **apt-get** upgrades the package rather than installing it fresh. If **cpio** weren't installed, it would be installed. If it's important that the package not be installed if it is missing, add the **--only-upgrade** long option.

Updating package by package is tedious. You can run **apt-get dist-upgrade** to upgrade all the packages on a system at once. If you are running a more conservative system, using **apt-get upgrade** is a safer choice. The difference between the two upgrade options is that **dist-upgrade** may remove some minor packages to handle dependency problems, while **upgrade** would rather fail than remove a package.

Removing Packages

A time will come when you want to get rid of a package entirely. The **apt-get** command has two options: **remove** and **purge**. The difference is that **remove** leaves behind configuration files, while **purge** gets rid of them entirely.

Graphical Managers

At times it's useful to view package management in an interface where you can look at packages graphically instead of working on a command line. Debian offers two graphical package managers: aptitude and synaptic. They are both front ends to the APT tools. Aptitude has a text mode interface, while Synaptic is fully graphical. Figure 6-2 shows the two next to each other, with Synaptic running on the left and Aptitude running inside a terminal window on the right.

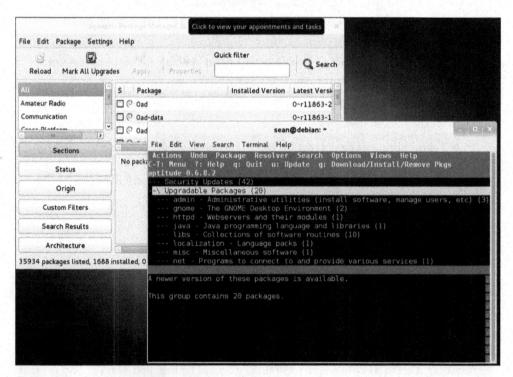

Figure 6-2   A look at graphical package managers

RPM and YUM Package Management

RPM refers not only to the package format but the **rpm** command and the RPM database. The components of the RPM package management style are as follows:

- **The RPM database:** A collection of files that manage the RPMs on a system

- **Package files:** The packages in RPM format that are distributed with the **.rpm** extension

- **The rpm command:** Used for all package installation, removal, and query tasks

Graphical package management tools such as gnorpm or the RPM-handling routines built in to various file managers (such as Nautilus and Konqueror) are typically just a front end to the text-mode **rpm** command and provide a friendly interface for installing packages.

> **NOTE**   Incidentally, RPM originally stood for Red Hat Package Manager before it became more widely used in other distributions. Referring to the system as RPM Package Manager will draw the ire of the graybeards in your office, almost as if you called an automated teller machine at your bank an "ATM machine."

The RPM Database

The RPM database is a collection of Oracle Berkeley DB files that together make up the database of packages and files installed by those packages on a system.

The RPM database is located in the **/var/lib/rpm** directory. That directory contains many files in a binary format that are used by the **rpm** command. Thankfully, you don't need to know all the files in the directory and their purposes, just that they are there and exist in an uncorrupted state.

Modifications to the RPM database are restricted to the root user. Unprivileged users can query and verify installed packages against this database.

The RPM database can become outdated or corrupted with heavy usage, and it might need to be rebuilt. To rebuild the database from the installed package's headers, you use the following command as the root user:

```
# rpm --rebuilddb
```

This command does not produce output unless errors are found, and even then the errors are purely informational and not of much use for fixing the problem.

Only one user can use the database at a time. This prevents corruption of the data and prevents two people from installing software on top of each other. If you accidentally try to run two **rpm** commands while one has the database locked, you see the following:

```
warning: waiting for transaction lock on /var/lib/rpm/.rpm.lock
```

This message simply indicates that the database is in use and cannot be locked for additional tasks at this time. This keeps multiple sysadmins from causing corruption by performing incompatible tasks simultaneously.

RPM Package Files

RPM packages come in two types: source and binary. A binary RPM file is a discrete package that, when installed, copies to specified locations the compiled binary files, other associated files such as documentation and configuration, and any other files needed to run that package.

A source RPM file is a collection of the source files needed for installing a package, plus some instructions for building the binary RPM from the source.

There is an important distinction between installed packages and uninstalled package files. Information about an installed package comes from the RPM database, whereas information about an uninstalled package comes from the RPM file itself. After an RPM file has been installed, the original RPM is no longer required.

An RPM package contains a set of files and configuration scripts that comprise a software program or application in most instances. Notable exceptions are packages strictly for placing text configuration files, such as files in the **/etc** directory.

An RPM package should contain at least the following:

- Compressed binary application files
- The name and version of the package's software
- The build date and host on which it was built
- A description of the package and its purpose
- The checksums and dependencies required

Package Name Conventions

An installed package is known by a short name, although some operations require that long names be used. Typically, long package names are needed for deletions when multiple packages whose short names match exist.

Here's an example of a short package name:

```
wireshark
```

Here's an example of a long package name:

```
wireshark-2.6.4-1.fc30
```

To find two packages installed with different versions of the same software, use the following:

```
# rpm -q kernel
5.19.0-39-generic.fcXX.x86_64
4.31.0-13-generic.fcXX.x86_64
```

Viewing a particular package's information can be difficult if you use the **-l** and **-i** options for file listings and info pages. Most of the time, you want to see information about only one of the packages, so to see just that package's details you must use the long name (**5.19.0-39-generic.fcXX**) in the query, which isolates that individual package for the query.

The rpm Command

The text-mode **rpm** package tool is used to perform all operations on packages on the system, either installed and in the RPM database or uninstalled and on disk.

Common operations that use the **rpm** command include

- Installing packages
- Upgrading packages
- Removing and uninstalling packages
- Querying the RPM database for information
- Verifying the package file
- Checking installed files

The **rpm** command keywords and options come in several formats. The common options are single letters (for example, **-i** for installation). There are almost always long options that match, and some options occur only in the long format.

> **NOTE** On the Linux+ exam, you might see long options in several locations, either right after a short option or on the end of the entire command. The important thing is to have tried the long options and to know that you can tack them on the end, as long as something else doesn't depend on that option's placement.

Validation of Packages

For purposes of security, it's important that you validate or check the signatures of packages that are downloaded from any source other than the distribution vendor's site; otherwise, you could end up installing malware. RPM uses two checks to ensure the integrity of a package: MD5 and PGP (or its open-source variant, GPG).

MD5 acts as a checksum to make sure that the package contents have not changed since the package was created. The PGP or GPG signature is tied to a particular person or organization and indicates that the person or organization created the package.

Validating a package typically takes place when the package is accessed or installed, although it can be triggered explicitly. To check the MD5 checksum and GPG signatures for the **R** statistics environment, you use the following command:

```
# rpm -K R-3.5.1-1.fcXX.x86_64.rpm
```

This returns the following output:

```
R-3.5.1-1.fcXX.x86_64.rpm: RSA sha1 ((MD5) PGP) md5 NOT OK (MISSING
KEYS: (MD5) PGP#8e1431d5)
```

The presence of **NOT OK** shows that the signatures could not be verified. Importing the key from the distribution site fixes the problem. For example, if you are working on a Fedora system, you can execute the following:

```
# rpm --import https://getfedora.org/static/8E1431D5.txt
# rpm -K R-3.5.1-1.fcXX.x86_64.rpm
R-3.1.2-1.fcXX.x86_64.rpm: rsa sha1 (md5) pgp md5 OK
```

Installation of Packages

Installing software via packages requires root access, the **rpm** command, and a package or packages. Prior to installation, the **rpm** command checks to ensure the following:

- Enough free disk space exists for the package.
- Existing files will not be overwritten.
- All dependencies listed in the package are met.

You install packages with at least the **-i** option (or **--install**), and you can often include other options that improve the experience. To install the **R** package and get a progress bar (consisting of hash marks printed onscreen) and verbose messages on the installation, use the following command:

```
# rpm -ivh R-3.5.1-1.fcXX.x86_64.rpm
Preparing... ################################# [100%]
```

```
Updating / installing...
 1: R-3.5.1-1.fcXX ################################# [100%]
```

These options work well for installing groups of packages, too. Instead of specifying a single package, as shown previously, specify a file glob instead:

```
# rpm -ivh *.rpm
```

Wildcards can be used for installing and upgrading but not removing packages because the glob operator, *, expands to match files in the current directory, not packages in the RPM database. For now, you just need to understand that ***.rpm** means "any file that ends in **.rpm**."

Additional Installation Options

Whenever you install RPM packages, keep in mind that there will be extenuating circumstances such as files that exist on the system that RPM doesn't know about but that will be overwritten by a package's contents. Sometimes this happens when someone installs software manually or if a previous package operation fails.

Such situations can be handled with the **--replacefiles** or **--force** options. (The **force** option overrides a variety of these safeguards, including **replacefiles**, which just overrides the duplicate file safeguard.) For example, if you try to install a package named **tarfoo-1.2-3.i386.rpm**, and it finds a file on the system that will be overwritten by a file in the package, you get an error message stating so, and the installation fails:

```
# rpm -ivh tarfoo-1.2-3.i386.rpm
tarfoo /etc/tarfoo.conf conflicts with file from foobar-1.1
```

The solution is to check the offending file and either remove it if it's unnecessary or use this command to force it:

```
# rpm -ivh --force tarfoo-1.2-3.i386.rpm
```

If the package won't install due to unresolved dependencies, you can (somewhat foolishly!) use the **--nodeps** option to have the **rpm** command ignore dependencies. Using **--nodeps** without a clear fix in mind or an understanding of where the dependencies will come from will almost certainly cause problems when you try to use the software that the package provides.

For example, if you try to install the **pebkac** package, and it has dependency issues, it might look like this:

```
# rpm -ivh pebkac.1-1.fcXX.x86_64.rpm
```

This returns output such as

```
error: Failed dependencies:
 id10t = 3.5.1-1.fcXX is needed by pebkac.5.1-1.fcXX.x86_64
 loosenut = 3.5.1-1.fcXX is needed by pebkac.5.1-1.fcXX.x86_64
 hubproblem = 3.5.1-1.fcXX is needed by pebkac.5.1-1.fcXX. x86_64
```

You face the possibility of seriously munging (messing up) your system if you use the **--nodeps** option outside a recommendation from the distribution vendor or a support professional. You might so severely damage the software that a full reinstall is the only option.

Verifying a Package's Integrity

There might be situations in which you need to verify that a package is working properly. For example, if users are complaining about problems with running the software that came with a package, or if you suspect that someone has been tampering with your computer, you might want to verify the package.

Verify an installed RPM with the **-V** option (or **--verify**) like so:

```
# rpm -V logrotate
S.5....T. c /etc/logrotate.conf
```

The status of the package is returned as a series of nine characters indicating the results of nine different tests:

- **S:** The file size differs.

- **M:** The mode differs (permissions or type of file).

- **5:** The MD5 sum differs; this is also seen with **--checksig**.

- **D:** The device's major/minor number doesn't match.

- **L:** A readLink(2) path problem exists.

- **U:** The user ownership was altered.

- **G:** The group ownership was altered.

- **T:** The modification time is different from the original.

- **P:** The capabilities set on the file differ.

Following the nine tests is an attribute marker that helps you understand whether the file should change as part of normal operations. The most common option is a configuration file, indicated by the letter **c**.

The output shown indicates that **/etc/logrotate.conf** is a configuration file that has changed in size, content, and modification time since the RPM was installed.

Change is not always a bad thing. Configuration files change often because the defaults provided by the distribution may not line up with current needs. Email configurations, log cleanup policies, and web server configurations are all things that get customized frequently and therefore show up as changes. If you expect them to change, you can ignore the output, which is why configuration files have the separate attribute marker. If you see a change to binaries, such as **/bin/ls**, you should be suspicious.

To verify the state of all the packages on the system, you add an **-a** instead of specifying a package name, as shown here:

```
# rpm -Va
```

> **NOTE**   If you choose to run the **rpm -Va** command, it will attempt to verify the nine points of status of *every* file installed by *every* package on your system, and this may/ will take a long time and use a lot of CPU.

If you want to log the state of your configuration files for comparison against a future date, you can check the condition of every configuration file on the system and write it to a file with this command:

```
# rpm -Vac > /root/somelog.txt
```

Freshening vs. Upgrading

The daily maintenance of a newly installed system is likely to involve updates and fixes downloaded as package updates. Properly applying these updates and fixes to the system takes some finesse, particularly with a system that must stay as stable as possible or not have new software added to it without strict testing.

The **-U** and **--upgrade** options are designed to install or upgrade versions of packages to the latest version. An interesting side effect of these options is the removal of all other versions of the targeted package, leaving just the latest version installed.

As an example, the following command upgrades the system to the latest version of the RPMs in a particular directory of patches and fixes downloaded from the distribution vendor:

```
# rpm -U *.rpm
```

The **-U** and **--upgrade** options upgrade packages that are already installed and install packages that aren't.

Freshening your system with the **-F** and **--Freshen** options is different in one important aspect: If a package isn't installed and you try to freshen it with a new RPM, the installation is skipped. If the package is installed already, freshening behaves the same as upgrading.

As an example, you use the following to apply a directory full of RPM files that contains security patches and fixes to a firewall or another security server:

```
# rpm -Fvh *.rpm
```

This feature is useful for local package cache updates, where you've downloaded the latest patches and fixes to a local network resource and want to run scripts on your machines to update them to the latest security releases.

One of the more fun analogies I have come up with for explaining this process is what happens when you finish a cocktail or drink in a pub: **-U** can get a completely different one or the same, as the glass is empty, whereas if you are half done with a drink and are asked if you want more, you'd of course simply **--Freshen** it with the same ingredients.

Removing Packages

Removing a package or set of packages consists of using the **-e** or **--erase** option and requires root access. Removal of packages can be even more fraught with dependency problems than installation because a package can be deeply buried in a tree of dependencies over time.

Removing a package without dependencies is easy. To remove the **tarfoo** package, you use the following command:

```
# rpm -e tarfoo
```

There's usually no output, the package is removed, and the system returns to the prompt.

The trouble begins when you have multiple packages that all have the same short name, such as a kernel. With two versions of the kernel package on a system, querying the database for the package as shown here returns both packages' long-format names:

```
# rpm -q kernel
5.19.0-39-generic.fcXX.x86_64
4.31.0-13-generic.fcXX.x86_64
```

If you attempt to remove the package by its short name, you get this error:

```
# rpm -e kernel
error: "kernel" specifies multiple packages:
 5.19.0-39-generic.fcXX.x86_64
 4.31.0-13-generic.fcXX.x86_64
```

Instead, use the long name of the package:

```
# rpm -e 5.19.0-39-generic.fcXX
```

You can remove both packages with one command, as shown here:

```
# rpm -e kernel --allmatches
```

No output is returned if all is successful; you just get returned to the prompt. If you don't want to remove both of the packages, the only choice is to specify the long package name of the package you want to remove.

Other Removal Options

At times you need to force the removal of a package or remove one regardless of the broken dependencies that will result. For example, you might fix a broken package by forcibly removing it and reinstalling it to refresh the files and links that were broken. (You should do this on the recommendation of support professionals, not some thread you found on a six-year-old forum!)

To remove a package that has other packages depending on it, use the following command:

```
# rpm -e foobar --nodeps
```

Be careful about removing packages you can't replace or when you don't have the original package file to reinstall from. You need to find the original package or rebuild it from source. If you remove a package that other packages depend on, those packages will not be able to run.

The process of removing packages can also leave behind altered or customized configuration files. For example, if you alter a package's main configuration file and then remove the package, the configuration file is saved with its original name suffixed with **.rpmsave**. This configuration file can be archived for future use or, if the package is to be upgraded with the **-U** option, a complex set of algorithms is used to ensure that the configuration is properly applied.

Querying Packages

Querying for package data is only one of the steps that take place when you manage packages, although it has arguably the most options of all the tasks RPM performs.

It's important that you understand the difference between packages installed on a system (that appear in the RPM database) and packages that exist simply as files on a disk or other resource. The chief difference in the **rpm** command's usage is the addition of the **-p** option to specify that the package being acted on is a file on disk.

The most basic of all queries is used to check whether a particular package is installed:

```
# rpm -q cogl
cogl-1.18.2-9.fc21.x86_64
```

Simply by adding a few modifier characters to this query, you can gather a lot of information about any package. For example, Example 6-6 shows how to get information on the package.

Example 6-6   Querying a Package for Information

```
# rpm -qi tree
Name            : tree
Version         :1.7.0
Release         :15.fcXX
Architecture: x86_64
Install Date: Wed 24 Oct 2018 08:01:29 PM EDT
Group           : Unspecified
Size            :114531
License         : GPLv2+
Signature       : RSA/SHA256, Sun 15 Jul 2018 07:08:52 PM EDT, Key ID
a20aa56b429476b4
Source RPM      : tree-1.7.0-15.fcXX.src.rpm
Build Date      : Sun 15 Jul 2018 10:27:43 AM EDT
Build Host      : buildvm-11.phx2.fedoraproject.org
Relocations : (not relocatable)
Packager        : Fedora Project
Vendor          : Fedora Project
URL             : http://mama.indstate.edu/users/ice/tree/
Bug URL         : https://bugz.fedoraproject.org/tree
Summary         : File system tree viewer
Description :
The tree utility recursively displays the contents of directories in
a tree-like format.  Tree is basically a UNIX port of the DOS tree
utility.
```

To get information about a package's files, use both the **-q** (query) option and the **-l** (file listing) option, as shown in the following output:

```
# rpm -ql tree
/usr/bin/tree
/usr/lib/.build-id
/usr/lib/.build-id/78
/usr/lib/.build-id/78/0d8723b45ad93065b6912439e4d2355d3c8e3e
/usr/share/doc/tree
/usr/share/doc/tree/LICENSE
/usr/share/doc/tree/README
/usr/share/man/man1/tree.1.gz
```

When you get Linux+ exam questions about listing package files or information, remember the difference between listing the contents of a package in the database and listing the contents of a package on disk:

- **rpm -qil** *package_name***:** Used for installed packages, with a short or long name specified

- **rpm -qilp** *package_name***.rpm:** Used for uninstalled packages, with a file specified

In addition, remember that you can specify these options in any order, as long as they are all there. In effect, **rpm -qipl**, **rpm -qlip**, and **rpm -pliq** all work.

To see a revision history or changelog for the package, use the following command:

```
# rpm -q --changelog tree
* Sat Jul 14 2018 Fedora Release Engineering
  <releng@fedoraproject.org> - 1.7.0-15
- Rebuilt for https://fedoraproject.org/wiki/Fedora_29_Mass_ Rebuild

* Fri Feb 23 2018 Florian Weimer <fweimer@redhat.com> - 1.7.0-14
- Use LDFLAGS from redhat-rpm-config
```

This output is similar to the release notes found in most software package source code repositories describing the history of package changes. Mixing the long and short options for the **rpm** command is a method exam writers love to use on the Linux+ exam. If you've never used RPM to this level, the questions will get the best of you. Don't forget that you must use the **-q** and **--changelog** options together; otherwise, you get a syntax error.

> **NOTE** Our usual example, the **tree** command, doesn't have config files, so we'll use something that does, such as the postfix suite.

To find all the configuration files for a package, you use the query and config options as shown in Example 6-7. This output shows only the files marked by the package as configuration files. If you want the whole list of files inside the package, you need to use **rpm -ql**.

Example 6-7   Finding a Package's Configuration Files

```
# rpm -qc postfix
/etc/pam.d/smtp.postfix
/etc/postfix/access
/etc/postfix/canonical
/etc/postfix/generic
/etc/postfix/header_checks
/etc/postfix/main.cf
/etc/postfix/master.cf
/etc/postfix/relocated
/etc/postfix/transport
/etc/postfix/virtual
/etc/sasl2/smtpd.conf
```

To see other capabilities or package dependencies, use the **--requires** or **-R** option (and remember that it's a package on disk, so use **-p**), as shown in Example 6-8.

Example 6-8   Querying the Dependencies of a Package File

```
# rpm -qRp tree-1.7.0-16.fcXX.x86_64.rpm
libc.so.6()(64bit)
libc.so.6(GLIBC_2.2.5)(64bit)
libc.so.6(GLIBC_2.3)(64bit)
libc.so.6(GLIBC_2.3.4)(64bit)
libc.so.6(GLIBC_2.4)(64bit)
rpmlib(CompressedFileNames) <= 3.0.4-1
rpmlib(FileDigests) <= 4.6.0-1
rpmlib(PayloadFilesHavePrefix) <= 4.0-1
rpmlib(PayloadIsXz) <= 5.2-1
rtld(GNU_HASH)
```

This method of finding the dependencies tells you which files or packages are needed without requiring you to install the package. You can track the dependencies back to a package, such as to find out which package provides the **libc.so.6** file required by **tree**, as shown here:

```
# rpm -qf /usr/lib64/libc.so.6
glibc-2.28-9.fcXX.x86_64
```

What about the problem of finding the package from which a particular file was installed? For example, if the **/etc/krb.conf** file were somehow damaged, you could find the package it came from with this command:

```
# rpm -qf /etc/krb5.conf
krb5-libs-1.16.1-21.fcXX.x86_64
```

Package Management with YUM

YUM, the Yellowdog Updater, Modified, is a front end to RPM. Just as the **apt-*** series of tools makes working with **dpkg** and remote repositories easier, YUM brings **rpm** and remote repositories together for you and packages them in an interface with far fewer options to remember.

Installing Packages

Install a package, such as the R statistical language, with **yum install**, as shown in Example 6-9.

Example 6-9 Installing a Package from a Remote Repository

```
# yum install R
Last metadata expiration check: 0:16:58 ago on Sun 25 Nov 2018
01:08:46 PM EST.
Dependencies resolved.
================================================================
 Package         Arch    Version                 Repository
Size
================================================================
Installing:
 R               x86_64 3.5.1-1.fcXX             fedora  11 k
Installing dependencies:
 java-1.8.0-openjdk    x86_64 1:1.8.0.191.b12-8.fcXX  updates 237 k
```

```
    java-1.8.0-openjdk-devel x86_64 1:1.8.0.191.b12-8.fcXX    updates 9.8 M
    java-1.8.0-openjdk-headless
                             x86_64 1:1.8.0.191.b12-8.fcXX    updates 32 M
    perl-XML-XPath           noarch 1.43-1.fcXX               updates 83 k
    perl-open                noarch 1.11-424.fcXX             updates 26 k
    R-core                   x86_64 3.5.1-1.fcXX              fedora  55 M
    R-core-devel             x86_64 3.5.1-1.fcXX              fedora  89 k
    R-devel                  x86_64 3.5.1-1.fcXX              fedora  10 k
    R-java                   x86_64 3.5.1-1.fcXX              fedora  11 k
    R-java-devel             x86_64 3.5.1-1.fcXX              fedora  11 k
    annobin                  x86_64 8.23-1.fcXX               fedora 122 k
    bzip2-devel              x86_64 1.0.6-28.fcXX             fedora 215 k
    dwz                      x86_64 0.12-9.fcXX               fedora 105 k
    efi-srpm-macros          noarch 3-3.fcXX                  fedora  21 k
    expat-devel              x86_64 2.2.6-1.fcXX              fedora  49 k
    fontconfig-devel         x86_64 2.13.1-1.fcXX            fedora 127 k
    fpc-srpm-macros          noarch 1.1-5.fcXX                fedora 7.5 k
    freetype-devel           x86_64 2.9.1-2.fcXX              fedora 441 k
    gcc-c++                  x86_64 8.2.1-2.fcXX              fedora  12 M
Transaction Summary
===============================================================================
Install  312 Packages

Total download size: 312 M
Installed size: 706 M
Is this ok [y/N]: Downloading Packages:
Installed:
  R-3.5.1-1.fcXX.x86_64
  perl-File-ShareDir-1.116-3.fcXX.noarch
  perl-List-MoreUtils-0.428-4.fcXX.noarch
  perl-Params-Util-1.07-25.fcXX.x86_64
  java-1.8.0-openjdk-1:1.8.0.191.b12-8.fcXX.x86_64
  java-1.8.0-openjdk-devel-1:1.8.0.191.b12-8.fcXX.x86_64
  java-1.8.0-openjdk-headless-1:1.8.0.191.b12-8.fcXX.x86_64
  perl-XML-XPath-1.43-1.fcXX.noarch
  perl-open-1.11-424.fcXX.noarch
Complete!
... output omitted ...
```

The output in Example 6-9 shows that **yum** calculates the dependencies, downloads all needed packages, and installs them.

NOTE   The output of the **yum** transactions in Example 6-9 was greatly condensed from its original almost 2,000 lines of returned text. If you are logging these upgrades/updates, keep in mind that the log files can become very large!

NOTE   **yum** commands typically do not use dashes or double dashes, whereas **rpm** commands do. However, next we explore some notable exceptions, such as the **-y** option, which effectively supplies the needed answer to an installation question so that automation can occur.

If you want to skip the step where you confirm the installation, simply add **-y**, as in this example:

```
# yum -y install foo
```

It is possible to just download the packages instead of installing them. There are several ways to accomplish this:

- At the **--y/d/N** prompt, answer **d** (download) instead of **y** (yes).
- Use **--yum install --downloadonly** instead of the plain **yum install**.
- Use **--yumdownloader** instead of **yum**.

The **--yumdownloader** command behaves similarly to **yum install** except that you have a few more options available to you:

- **source:** Downloads the source RPM instead of binary RPMs
- **urls:** Displays the URLs of the files instead of downloading them
- **resolve:** Modifies the command to also include any missing dependencies
- **destdir:** Specifies the location where the files will be stored

Fetching Updates

YUM knows where to get new packages and what's currently on a system, so it can also calculate which packages are out of date. Upgrading a package requires just **yum update** *package_name*, so **yum update tcpdump** updates the **tcpdump** package along with any dependencies.

You can check for any out-of-date packages with **yum check-update** and upgrade the whole system with **yum update** all by itself.

Finding Packages to Install

You can search remote repositories in different ways. If you know the name of the package, you can use **yum list**:

```
# yum list tomcat
Last metadata expiration check: 0:08:45 ago on Mon 26 Nov 2018
11:31:19 AM EST.
Available Packages
tomcat.noarch          1:9.0.10-1.fcXX                           fedora
```

Packages that can be split into separate components are usually distributed as separate packages sharing a common prefix. Suppose you want to see what components you could add to Tomcat. You could use a wildcard operator with the **yum list** command, as shown in Example 6-10.

Example 6-10   Listing Packages That Match a Wildcard

```
# yum list tomcat*
Last metadata expiration check: 0:09:01 ago on Mon 26 Nov 2018
11:31:19 AM EST.
Available Packages
tomcat.noarch                    1:9.0.10-1.fcXX          fedora
tomcat-admin-webapps.noarch      1:9.0.10-1.fcXX          fedora
tomcat-docs-webapp.noarch        1:9.0.10-1.fcXX          fedora
tomcat-el-3.0-api.noarch         1:9.0.10-1.fcXX          fedora
tomcat-javadoc.noarch            1:9.0.10-1.fcXX          fedora
tomcat-jsp-2.3-api.noarch        1:9.0.10-1.fcXX          fedora
tomcat-jsvc.noarch               1:9.0.10-1.fcXX          fedora
tomcat-lib.noarch                1:9.0.10-1.fcXX          fedora
tomcat-native.x86_64             1.2.17-2.fcXX            fedora
tomcat-servlet-4.0-api.noarch    1:9.0.10-1.fcXX          fedora
tomcat-taglibs-parent.noarch     3-8.fcXX                 fedora
tomcat-taglibs-standard.noarch   1.2.5-6.fcXX             fedora
tomcat-webapps.noarch            1:9.0.10-1.fcXX          fedora
tomcatjss.noarch                 7.3.5-1.fcXX             fedora
```

Finally, if you know you need a web server but aren't sure what to pick, you can use a general search, as shown in Example 6-11.

Example 6-11   Searching YUM Repositories for Packages That Match a Concept

```
# yum search "web server"
Loaded plugins: fastestmirror, langpacks
Loading mirror speeds from cached hostfile
 * base: repo.miserver.it.umich.edu
 * extras: repo.miserver.it.umich.edu
 * updates: repo.miserver.it.umich.edu
=========================== N/S matched: web server
===========================
libcurl.i686 : A library for getting files from web servers
libcurl.x86_64 : A library for getting files from web servers
pcp-pmda-weblog.x86_64 : Performance Co-Pilot (PCP) metrics from web
server logs
python-paste.noarch : Tools for using a Web Server Gateway Interface
stack
python-tornado.x86_64 : Scalable, non-blocking web server and tools
xbean.noarch : Java plugin based web server

  Name and summary matches only, use "search all" for everything.
```

Configuring YUM

The main configuration file for **yum** is **/etc/yum.conf**. In it are the global options for **yum** and some defaults for all the repositories. You will rarely have to edit this file, but it does contain helpful information if you're trying to figure out where files are kept. Example 6-12 shows a default Fedora configuration.

Example 6-12   A Default **yum.conf** Configuration for CentOS

```
[main]
cachedir=/var/cache/yum/$basearch/$releasever
keepcache=0
debuglevel=2
logfile=/var/log/yum.log
exactarch=1
obsoletes=1
gpgcheck=1
plugins=1
installonly_limit=5
```

```
bugtracker_url=http://bugs.centos.org/set_project.php?project_id=23&
ref=http://bugs.centos.org/bug_report_page.php?category=yum
distroverpkg=centos-release


#  This is the default, if you make this bigger yum won't see if the
metadata
# is newer on the remote and so you'll "gain" the bandwidth of not
having to
# download the new metadata and "pay" for it by yum not having
correct
# information.
#  It is esp. important, to have correct metadata, for distributions
like
# Fedora which don't keep old packages around. If you don't like this
checking
# interupting your command line usage, it's much better to have
something
# manually check the metadata once an hour (yum-updatesd will do
this).
# metadata_expire=90m


# PUT YOUR REPOS HERE OR IN separate files named file.repo
# in /etc/yum.repos.d
```

In Example 6-12 you can see that all the cached files are stored under **/var/cache/ yum**, and the log file is **/var/log/yum.log**. A full list of the options is in the man page for **yum.conf**.

The repository configuration files are stored in **/etc/yum.repos.d**. Each file may contain multiple repositories, but you will find that the repositories are grouped according to function. For example, the main distribution repository is in one file, along with the repository for the source packages and a repository for the debugging symbols. Another file contains the repositories for the updates, the source for the updates, and the debugging symbols for the updates.

A single repository configuration looks like Example 6-13.

Example 6-13 An Individual Repository's Configuration from CentOS

```
# CentOS-Base.repo
#
# The mirror system uses the connecting IP address of the client and
the
# update status of each mirror to pick mirrors that are updated to
and
```

```
# geographically close to the client.  You should use this for CentOS
updates
# unless you are manually picking other mirrors.
#
# If the mirrorlist= does not work for you, as a fall back you can
try the
# remarked out baseurl= line instead.
#
#


[base]
name=CentOS-$releasever - Base
mirrorlist=http://mirrorlist.centos.org/?release=$releasever&arch=$base
arch&repo=os&infra=$infra
#baseurl=http://mirror.centos.org/centos/$releasever/os/$basearch/
gpgcheck=1
gpgkey=file:///etc/pki/rpm-gpg/RPM-GPG-KEY-CentOS-7


#released updates
[updates]
name=CentOS-$releasever - Updates
mirrorlist=http://mirrorlist.centos.org/?release=$releasever&arch=$base
arch&repo=updates&infra=$infra
#baseurl=http://mirror.centos.org/centos/$releasever/updates/$basearch/
gpgcheck=1
gpgkey=file:///etc/pki/rpm-gpg/RPM-GPG-KEY-CentOS-7


#additional packages that may be useful
[extras]
name=CentOS-$releasever - Extras
mirrorlist=http://mirrorlist.centos.org/?release=$releasever&arch=$base
arch&repo=extras&infra=$infra
#baseurl=http://mirror.centos.org/centos/$releasever/extras/$basearch/
gpgcheck=1
gpgkey=file:///etc/pki/rpm-gpg/RPM-GPG-KEY-CentOS-7
```

In Example 6-13, note that several options start with a dollar sign (**$**). These are place-holders that are expanded when **yum** is invoked. **$releasever** becomes the distribution version, and **$basearch** becomes the hardware architecture, such as x86_64.

A repository either has a **baseurl**, which is a link to the repository, or a **metalink**, which returns a list of mirrors for the repository. (A mirror spreads the load across many different servers, hosted by different companies.)

An important directive in the configuration is **enabled**. When you **run** a yum command, only the enabled repositories are searched. You can enable a repository in a **yum** command by adding **--enablerepo reponame**.

Hiding repositories is helpful because it gives you access to a wider variety of packages without requiring you to configure the repository. You might, for example, hide the debugging symbol repository unless you actually need debugging symbols, such as when trying to track down crashes. You can also have access to bleeding-edge software when you need it but install more trusted software by default.

Dandified YUM

One of the recent additions to the package manager world is the *Dandified YUM (DNF)* tool, which debuted with Fedora 18 and is meant to be the next generation of the YUM package manager.

DNF is (mostly) compatible with YUM on the command line and options front, is considered to be a little easier to configure than traditional YUM, and uses fewer system resources in its operation, which can be very important with large updates or package management operations.

Overall, DNF is considered more reliable and consistent than YUM, is based on a later version of Python, and uses a more efficient algorithm than YUM. These reasons, along with concerns about documentation of the YUM API, have made DNF the choice for the future.

ZYpp

The name **zypper** is often used to refer to the *ZYpp* or libzypp package management engine, but *zypper* is the command-line interface to the engine, not the actual package manager. For the sake of clarity, when we talk about the ZYpp/libzypp package manager overall, we use ZYpp, and when referencing commands and the actual command-line tool, we use **zypper**.

ZYpp is used primarily on the openSUSE and SUSE Linux Enterprise product lines; several other distributions, such as Ark and Tizen, also make use of the ZYpp/libzypp package manager scheme.

The vast majority of a user's interactions with the ZYpp/libzypp scheme are through the **zypper** command, so let's go over a few very common commands with appropriate options for those.

The **zypper** command is functionally more capable than the **rpm** command, and it functions in many ways similarly to the Debian APT suite of package management tools. It can help you search for packages either in the package database or in repositories (as discussed later in this chapter), perform updates to existing software, and handle many other functions. It's a companion to graphical utilities such as the YaST software module on the SUSE system.

Installing Software Packages with **zypper**

To list the possible sources of software to install, use the **zypper** list repositories (**zypper lr**) command to produce output similar to that shown in Figure 6-3. This output shows the configured repositories from which you can install software.

```
217:~ # zypper lr
Repository priorities in effect:                              (See 'zypper lr -P' for details)
     99 (default priority) :  5 repositories
    100 (lowered priority) :  1 repository

# | Alias                             | Name                              | Enabled | GPG Check | Refresh
--+-----------------------------------+-----------------------------------+---------+-----------+--------
1 | Basesystem-Module_15-0            | sle-module-basesystem             | Yes     | (r ) Yes  | No
2 | Desktop-Applications-Module_15-0  | sle-module-desktop-applications   | Yes     | (r ) Yes  | No
3 | Development-Tools-Module_15-0     | sle-module-development-tools      | Yes     | (r ) Yes  | No
4 | SLES15-15-0                       | SLES15-15-0                       | Yes     | (r ) Yes  | No
5 | SLES15_15-0                       | SLES                              | Yes     | (r ) Yes  | No
6 | Server-Applications-Module_15-0   | sle-module-server-applications    | Yes     | (r ) Yes  | No
217:~ #
```

Figure 6-3 zypper lr command output

To refresh the metadata from your configured repositories (which is necessary to have the most updated repository information), use the **zypper ref** command. This command returns a list of metadata changes that will then be resident on your system to facilitate interactions with the repository and any installations or updates you choose to perform, as demonstrated in Figure 6-4.

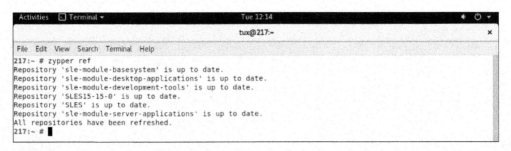

Figure 6-4 zypper ref command output

To initiate a search for a particular package in your repositories, use the **zypper se vim** command. The returned output will contain any matches on the character string **vim**, which will invariably include the gvim package, which you can see in the list in Figure 6-5.

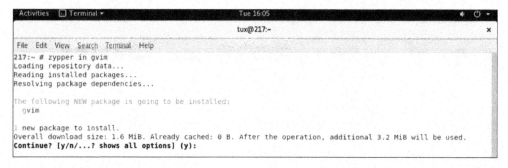

Figure 6-5   zypper se vim command output

NOTE   The **zypper** search output shows whether a package that is returned is installed or not; the lowercase **i** in the first column of the output indicates installed.

To install the gvim package on a system, use the **zypper in gvim** command, as demonstrated in Figure 6-6.

Figure 6-6   Installing the gvim package

The **zypper** command gets the desired package from the repository and lets the user know what will be happening. It usually requires the user to type **y** to agree to both download and install the package and any of its dependencies that **zypper** has identified. Once the user has answered this prompt, the package is downloaded and installed, and the console indicates that this has happened, as demonstrated in Figure 6-7.

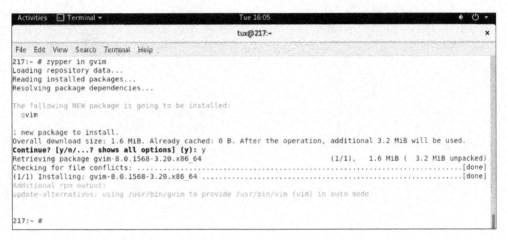

Figure 6-7 Confirming package download and installation

Removing a Package with **zypper**

Once a package is installed, it can easily be removed with the **zypper rm gvim** command.

Once again, a prompt requires a **y** answer to ensure that the package is really supposed to be removed or uninstalled from the system.

Managing Repositories

A software repository can take several forms, the most common of which is a network-reachable collection of software (typically RPM package files and accompanying metadata) that is configured as a repository on the machine(s) that wants to have access to its contents.

Repositories can be official and supported, such as the ones that are offered with a subscription of SUSE Linux Enterprise Server (SLES), official and unsupported, such as the ones that are configured and maintained as a part of the openSUSE project, and third party, such as the very fun and useful Packman repository. Packman is the largest and most diverse collection of additional software available for openSUSE and SLES distributions; it features multimedia applications, third-party drivers, and much more.

Listing the Repositories on a System

Listing the configured repositories on a system is very easy: Use the **zypper lr** command:

```
# zypper lr
```

Adding a Repository

To add a repository, you need to first list the repositories and then determine from a web search or another method the repository you want to add. To illustrate, this section shows how to add a non-oss repository to my test system; non-oss means the repository has packages that are not strictly open-source software, such as the browser Opera.

To add a repository to the configured set of repositories for a system, the command follows this format:

```
# zypper ar <uri> <alias>
```

The **zypper** command uses the **ar** directive to add a repository, and the network-reachable *<uri>* is basically a URL that the system uses for querying and download-ing packages and metadata. This is followed by *<alias>*, which is a friendly name for referring to this repository.

To add the non-oss repository for Leap 15.0 to the system, use this command:

```
# zypper ar http://download.opensuse.org/distribution/leap/15.0/
repo/non-oss/ Non-OSS
```

The repository is added to the system, and some useful information is shown about the repository, as demonstrated in Figure 6-8.

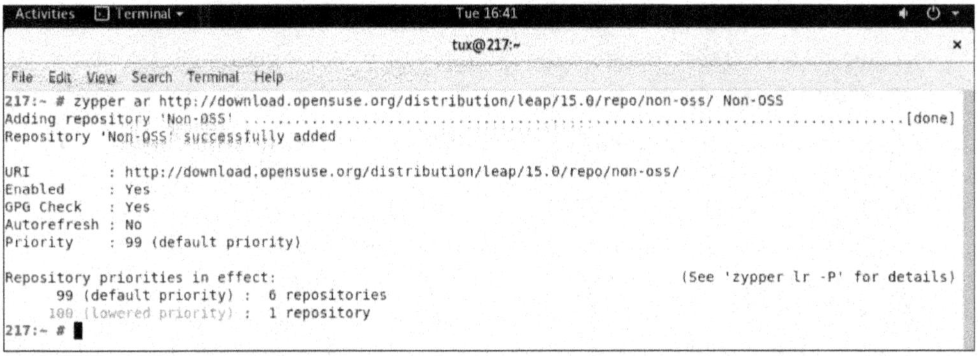

Figure 6-8 Adding a repository

Refreshing the Repository

To get the latest information about a repository (which you should do for all repositories before querying or installing from them), use the **zypper ref** command, as demonstrated in Figure 6-9.

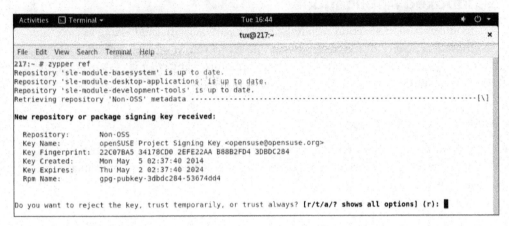

Figure 6-9   Refreshing the repository

New repositories must be accepted, and the package-signing key must be stored locally; **zypper** takes care of this when you answer **y** for "yes this once" or **a** for "always trust this repository." It is a good idea to choose **a**, as demonstrated in Figure 6-10.

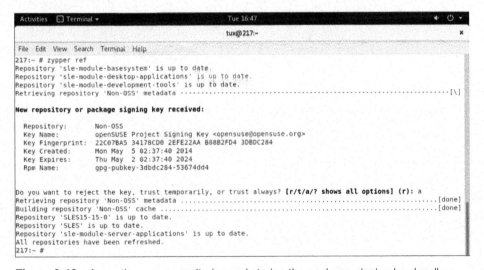

Figure 6-10   Accepting new repositories and storing the package-signing key locally

As shown in the output in Figure 6-10, the repository has been queried, its information has been downloaded, and it is ready to be used as an installation and update source.

Sandboxed Applications

To understand this section, you must first be familiar with sandboxing as a concept. To *sandbox* a piece of software is to execute it in a restricted space that is configurable by a developer or administrator and minimizes any chance of damage to the host operating system.

What Is a Sandboxed App?

A further step on this path is *application sandboxing*, packaging an application such that it can be distributed to users to run without needing backend system access, operating under very strict controls over what the application can read from or has access to on the host operating system.

Sandboxed applications typically do not require root access to download and run, have tuneable access to the hosting operating system, and typically include any dependencies for their operation.

There are a number of competing implementations of sandboxing, but they all share a similar set of characteristics or goals:

- To be distribution-neutral
- Easy to package up applications
- Ability to include dependencies
- Permit few or no modifications to the operating system
- Require no installation
- Include regular user permissions
- Simple to run and use
- Portable between distributions
- Ability to restrict access to resources

Depending on which of the application sandboxing schemes you choose, you will get more or less of the listed characteristics.

App Sandbox Applications

There are several sandboxing methods, but the Linux+ exam focuses on three in particular:

- Flatpak
- AppImage
- snapd

Let's discuss these in order, so you know what they do, what components are involved, and can identify them by characteristics or usage modality on the Linux+ exam.

Flatpak

Uniquely, *Flatpak* comes from the X Desktop Group (XDG) and so is inspired by different beginnings than the other two, but it has similar goals of enabling applications to be packaged up, distributed, and run by regular users with minimal fuss and minimal permission or access issues.

Flatpak uses a repository called Flathub, which lives at https://flathub.org and is the most likely place for a user to go to get an application, and so it is also the most popular destination for Flatpak developers to make their applications available to users.

Those using Flatpak applications will need to grant certain permissions so those applications can use the network and audio resources. Flatpak applications can even be updated independently of the distribution they are installed on.

AppImage

Initially named klik (as in mouse click?), *AppImage* came to prominence after it was renamed in 2013, and it aspires to being binarily compatible, independent of any one distribution and leaving the underlying host alone, and just being able to be run and used.

An AppImage-packed application is not installed per se, but rather is an image that is mounted using the FUSE (Filesystem in Userspace) software interface (introduced in Chapter 1) to make it available to be run.

AppImage applications are self-contained, including the libraries needed to have the application run. Running AppImage applications is simple and doesn't change the localhost. Shutting them down removes them from the process table and unmounts the ISO of the AppImage application.

Snapd

Unlike the other two methods, *Snapd* (or Snap, as it's commonly called) is from Canonical, the company closely associated with Ubuntu. Compared to Flatpak and AppImage, Snapd is more of an entire ecosystem, with a vendor backing it, and is intended to be a one-stop-shop for applications both for the regular user and for system purposes (though to a lesser degree).

Snap refers to the overall scheme, with *snaps* being what package applications are called and **snapd** being the utility that works to acquire them, run them, and perform some management of them.

Also of note is the Snap Store (https://snapcraft.io/store), where Canonical manages the snaps or applications that are submitted and does helpful tasks such as checking them for malware and viruses.

Snaps are also somewhat unique in that they can access resources from other snaps, as well as use a concept called "Portals" that allows snaps to have access to configured sets of host-based system resources.

System Updates

The concepts of updating or upgrading packages have been covered earlier in this chapter, so in this section we'll concentrate briefly on the more specific concept and practice of updating the Linux kernel.

Updating the Kernel

Why would you want to update your version of the kernel Among the variety of reasons, you should be familiar with the following for purposes of the Linux+ exam:

- Improvements to stability
- Security issues
- Advances in hardware drivers
- Efficiency
- New features

Regardless of the reason to update your kernel, there are a couple of ways it can happen, the choice of which depends on how critical the system is.

If the system is a desktop or a test system—not a production system!—updating it is much simpler because you're not interrupting a bunch of users or contributing to your organization's downtime; you're just rebooting a system after a package upgrade.

But what if your system is a production server, and rebooting this server after an update or upgrade will cause a lot of disruption? That very important question is addressed in the following discussion of both methods, which answers why you'd choose one method over the other depending on the scenario.

Choosing an Update Method

There are a couple of main ways to update the kernel:

- By replacing the kernel entirely (reboot mandatory)
- By patching a running kernel (no reboot involved)

We'll first cover the various ways to update with a reboot involved. We'll then cover the *live patch* option, also known as a *hot patch*, which leaves the kernel running and replaces portions of it without dropping the kernel or rebooting.

While the live patch method helps retain user connections and preserves system uptime, there are situations in which a live patch will *not* work and a reboot will be required anyway. The most likely reason to use a live patch is a security update that fixes a zero-day exploit or must be applied immediately to fix a known vulnerability.

Reboot Methods

There are three main ways to update the kernel that require a reboot: a simple manual package update, use of a package manager, and use of Linux kernel utilities.

Manual Update

The most rudimentary way to update the kernel is to perform the following steps:

Step 1.   Go to https://kernel.org and find the latest version of the stable kernel.

Step 2.   Download this package file to your system.

Step 3.   Unpack it and, depending on your packaging tool, simply run the install routine for the package.

Step 4.   Once the installation is complete, reboot the system and look for any errors.

Obviously, this is not the most highly recommended option, but it's doable and can result in an updated kernel for your system.

What is the likelihood that a manual kernel update will require you to download and install additional packages? It's nearly guaranteed, and this method is not a fun or efficient experience and is not recommended.

Update with Package Manager

The recommended and much less "adventurous" reboot method is to update your kernel using the package manager on your system, which has the following advantages over the manual method, including the following:

- You'll be following a path that is provided by the maintainer of your distribution.

- You'll be using a kernel that was packaged and may have customizations to it that ensure it is compatible with the rest of your distribution.

Using a package manager is actually a reasonable way to update your kernel, but people often accidentally update the *whole distribution* by using a command that is too generic or broad, as shown in the second example that follows.

To get the latest package information from your configured repositories, on an Ubuntu system, use the command:

```
# sudo apt-get update
```

This will refresh all your configured repositories with the latest information. Then you can upgrade your *entire* distribution, including the kernel, with the command

```
# sudo apt-get upgrade
```

However, if all you want to do is update your kernel, you can usually use just the command

```
# sudo apt-get upgrade linux-image-generic
```

Linux Kernel Utilities

The third reboot method is to use the Linux kernel utilities, a set of three scripts that you can use to update your kernel, compile it the way you want it, and remove old kernels as needed. The three scripts are

- **compile_linux_kernel.sh**
- **update_ubuntu_kernel.sh**
- **remove_old_kernels.sh**

Obviously, this particular set of script is for use on your Ubuntu system. There are multiple methods for many other distributions, but to anchor the concept, we'll focus on Ubuntu for this purpose.

You can retrieve a copy of the Linux kernel utilities from Mark Tompkins' GitHub page as follows:

Step 1.   Open a shell prompt.

Step 2.   Make a test directory with **mkdir ~/test**

Step 3.   Pull down the Linux kernel utilities with the command:

```
# git clone https://github.com/Tinram/Linux-Utilities.git
```

Step 4.   Change into the ~/test/linux-kernel-utilities directory and change the permissions with

```
# chmod 750 *.sh
```

Step 5.   Then do a git pull.

Step 6.   Run the compile script to list the available kernels.

Step 7.   Install the latest kernel with the command

```
# ./compile_linux_kernel.sh --latest
```

Step 8.   Install the updated kernel with the command

```
# ./update_ubuntu_kernel.sh
```

Step 9.   Reboot the system.

Alternatively, you can use the update script with the **--latest** option to get a precompiled version of the kernel from the Ubuntu kernel repository:

```
# ./update_ubuntu_kernel.sh --latest
```

Step 10.   Finally, you can remove old versions of the kernel with the remove script:

```
# ./remove_old_kernels.sh
```

This concludes the kernel update methods that you should be aware of that require a reboot. Of course, there are other methods that can be used, but it's probably a good idea to stick with whatever method your distribution vendor or maintainer recommends, and some of them have some pretty nice utilities, such as UKUU and UKtools, but those are not something you'll see on the Linux+ exam.

No Reboot Method

As previously discussed, it's important to understand when it's best to do a full kernel update and reboot (e.g., a desktop or a test system) and when it's best to live patch the kernel *now* (e.g., to protect a production server from an exploit) and keep the system rolling along, providing services.

Live Kernel Patching Overview

There are live kernel patching scenarios for most major distributions, and each one has its own take on what the process is and what tools work best, but let's focus on what a live patch involves before we get into the details.

When you patch a live or running kernel, the impetus almost always is to apply a security fix or update. System downtime can be costly not only in terms of lack of availability and lost productivity but also because it may cause compliance problems for your organization—for example, your organization may have service-level agreements (SLAs) with customers or it may be required by government or industry regulations to maintain a certain mix of uptime and service updates, both of which scenarios make long reboot cycles and service downtime windows detrimental.

Issues with Live Patching

As long as the fixes or updates are relatively minor, live patching makes very good sense. When patching a kernel's structure, the structure of data or the way processing is handled can cause live patching to be anything from a non-optimal choice, to outright impossible.

In other words, if the changes that need to be made to secure or protect the system are widespread or comprehensive, live patching may simply not be possible, and you are back to an update and reboot scenario.

The Live Patch Process

For purposes of demonstration, we'll concentrate on the Ubuntu/Canonical methodology for the live patch process. Canonical offers a Livepatch service (https://ubuntu.com/security/livepatch) that automatically updates the kernel of a system with any patches or fixes and doesn't reboot the system.

One of the caveats of this option is that you will need to schedule or remember to keep the system package information updated regularly with the following command:

```
# sudo apt-get update
```

You will have to notice when the kernel updates are available and initiate the patching with this command:

```
# sudo apt-get upgrade
```

You may be confused about the difference between the update option and the upgrade option. The update option is only updating the package index, which are the packages that are available to be updated. The upgrade command actually performs actions to apply the software changes.

SUSE has a service called KLP (Kernel Live Patching) that is similar in function to the Canonical Livepatch offering but is a bit more integrated. Both services require connecting the correct update repositories, and the SUSE version requires you to register the system with the SUSE Customer Center (you can also use the SUSE Manager system management product as the intermediary).

To check whether a Livepatch has been installed, use the following command:

```
# zypper se --details kernel-livepatch-*
```

The system will show you any installed Livepatch packages, and you can make your patching decision from there.

For SUSE KLP, you can determine patching status or installed patches with the following command:

```
# klp -v patches
```

As you can see, there are good reasons to consider live patching your kernel, but it's not for every situation. Live patching is like flying a glider: sooner or later you'll reach the ground and have to start over, just like sooner or later your system will need an update that will force a reboot.

Summary

In this chapter you learned a lot about software packages, package management, using sandboxed applications, and how to update your packages and your kernel.

These are great skills to have, but you'll need to do some solid studying of the options and additional command features and (especially in this area) do your lab work to master these skills. This will be very helpful not only in the real world but also for passing the Linux+ exam.

Exam Preparation Tasks

As mentioned in the section "Goals and Methods" in the Introduction, you have a couple of choices for exam preparation: the exercises here, Chapter 23, "Final Preparation," and the exam simulation questions in the Pearson Test Prep Software Online.

Review All Key Topics

Review the most important topics in this chapter, noted with the Key Topic icon in the left margin of the page. Table 6-2 lists these key topics and the page number on which each is found.

Table 6-2   Key Topics for Chapter 6

Key Topic Element	Description	Page Number
Section	The most common package types	228
Paragraph	The **dpkg** tool manipulates packages on a system	230
Paragraph	The information about the package is contained inside the **.deb** file	230
Paragraph	Example of the use of **--force-depends**	232
Paragraph	Using the **dpkg --status** command and option	234
Paragraph	The list of remote package repositories is stored in **/etc/apt/sources.list**	236
Paragraph	Definition of a simple repository	236
Paragraph	Differences between the **apt-get** and **dpkg** commands	240
Paragraph	RPM refers not only to the package format but the **rpm** command and the RPM database	243
Paragraph	The RPM database is located in the **/var/lib/rpm** directory	243
Paragraph	Two RPM package types: source and binary	244
List	What an RPM package should contain at minimum	244
Paragraph	The text-mode **rpm** package tool	245
Paragraph	Root access and **rpm** required to install software via packages	246
Paragraph	Verifying an installed RPM package with **-V**	248
Paragraph	Verifying the state of all packages on the system with **-Va**	249

Key Topic Element	Description	Page Number
Paragraph	Removing a package without dependencies	250
Paragraph	Removing a package that has dependent packages	251
Paragraph	Query to check whether a particular package is installed	252
Paragraph	Finding all the configuration files for a package	254
Paragraph	YUM package manager front end to RPM	255
Paragraph	DNF (Dandified YUM) tool, recent addition to the package manager world	262
Paragraph	Functionality of **zypper** compared to **rpm**	263
Section	What Is a Sandboxed App?	268
Paragraph	The three sandboxing methods	269

Define Key Terms

Define the following key terms from this chapter and check your answers in the glossary:

RPM, **dpkg**, APT, YUM, Dandified YUM (DNF), ZYpp, **zypper**, sandboxed, Flatpak, AppImage, Snapd

Review Questions

The answers to these review questions are in Appendix A.

1. You have downloaded what you thought were RPM binary packages, but when you install them, you don't get a binary. What have you likely downloaded inadvertently?

    a. Source RPMs

    b. Repositories

    c. Dependencies

    d. Libraries

2. After issuing the **install** command to install new software via packages, you encounter a lengthy preinstall process. Which of the following is the likely cause of the delay?

    a. Binary integrity checks

    b. Application dependency listings

    c. Software library amalgamation

    d. Downloading repository updates

3. When performing a verification of a package's integrity, how many fields are shown for each checked package?

   a. 5

   b. 7

   c. 9

   d. 11

4. When removing a package, you get an error because there are multiple versions of the same package and you want to remove all of them at once. Which option will do this?

   a. --allfiles

   b. --allmatches

   c. --allsets

   d. --allpackages

5. When running a sandboxed application, which of the following are you most likely to need permissions to access?

   a. Memory

   b. Network

   c. Display

   d. Keyboard

This chapter covers the following topics:

- Updating Configuration Files
- Configuring Kernel Options
- Configuring Common System Services
- Representing Locales

The exam objective covered in this chapter is as follows:

- **Objective 1.7:** Given a scenario, manage software configurations

## CHAPTER 7

Managing Software Configurations

In Chapter 6 you learned all about building and installing software. The logical next step is to learn how to manage software configurations, the focus of this chapter.

Installing packages with **dpkg** and **rpm** is one thing, but installing them from public repositories that are known, secure, and always updated with the latest software is another set of skills altogether.

In this chapter we'll look at how repositories are configured for the various package managers, how to deal with left-behind configurations. We will also see why trying to reload a package results in getting the same results, and why that happens.

We'll also talk about how to restart and reload services properly, without causing unnecessary interruptions of connected systems. We'll also discuss some of the tuneable kernel options and the commands and files that make up those options, how to apply them properly, and so forth.

Next we'll explore some very common system services and how to configure them at the basic level. We'll finish up with some localization options so that you know how to ensure your systems are in good synchronization, particularly with respect to synchronizing system time, a very important item for any set of systems to share.

"Do I Know This Already?" Quiz

The "Do I Know This Already?" quiz enables you to assess whether you should read this entire chapter or simply jump to the "Exam Preparation Tasks" section for review. If you are in doubt, read the entire chapter. Table 7-1 outlines the major headings in this chapter and the corresponding "Do I Know This Already?" quiz questions. You can find the answers in Appendix A, "Answers to the 'Do I Know This Already?' Quizzes and Review Questions."

Table 7-1 "Do I Know This Already?" Foundation Topics Section-to-Question Mapping

Foundation Topics Section	Questions Covered in This Section
Updating Configuration Files	1
Configuring Kernel Options	2
Configuring Common System Services	3
Representing Locales	4

CAUTION   The goal of self-assessment is to gauge your mastery of the topics in this chapter. If you do not know the answer to a question or are only partially sure of the answer, you should mark that question as wrong for purposes of the self-assessment. Giving yourself credit for an answer you correctly guess skews your self-assessment results and might provide you with a false sense of security.

1. Which term describes the updating of a service's configuration file without necessarily dropping connections or making the service unavailable?

   a. Restarting

   b. Rendering

   c. Reloading

   d. Revising

2. On a Linux system, which utility is often used to configure kernel options?

   a. **sysctl**

   b. **servicectl**

   c. **systemctl**

   d. **configctl**

3. Which files contain lists of SSH host public keys? (Choose two.)

   a. **/etc/ssh/ssh_known_hosts**

   b. **/etc/ssh_known_hosts**

   c. **/etc/known_hosts**

   d. **~/.ssh/known_hosts**

4. Which of the following commands cannot be used to set the system date? (Choose all that apply.)

   a. **dateconfig**

   b. **date**

   c. **timedatectl**

   d. **localectl**

Foundation Topics

Updating Configuration Files

This section could just as well be titled "How to Reload a Service with a New Configuration." Regardless, it's a very important topic, since the main reason we run servers, or systems, is to provide services to users as well as other systems, such as in the case of a backend processing system or database server that provides services to a web server, or many web servers. This makes it important to know how to modify services to meet the needs of the users, which may change over time.

Restart or Reload?

We discussed the mechanics of restarting and reloading services in Chapter 4, but let's take the discussion a bit further and examine *why* we would need to restart or reload a service.

Restarting a Service

To *restart* a service means to stop the service and then start the service again. As obvious as that sounds, it is important to think of it as two distinct states. Since we are restarting, not starting, the service, the following set of steps occurs:

1. The service is running with a specific process ID (PID).

2. The service is signaled to stop, usually with SIGTERM or the numerical equivalent value of 15.

3. The service is started by the system, using the next available PID, and the service reads its *configuration file* or files.

4. The service accepts connections or provides services as it is designed to.

You would typically restart a service if you were not sure whether it was running properly, or you wanted to drop all connections that it was currently servicing.

Reloading a Service

In nearly complete contrast to the process of restarting a service, reloading a running service primarily involves causing the service to reread its configuration file or files, all while not dropping or interrupting connections it is currently servicing.

A service *reload* will result in the service reloading its configuration file. The reload process consists of the following set of steps:

1. The service is running with a specific PID.

2. The service is signaled to stop, usually with SIGHUP or the numerical equivalent value of 1.

3. The service rereads its configuration file or files.

4. The service maintains the same PID.

Grace Under Pressure

Just how graceful or unexciting can a service reload actually be? It fully depends on the service. Some services just dump the process and restart a new process with the updated configuration, whereas others are designed to be as smooth as silk in how they handle a reload.

Services such as Apache, Postfix, and (in particular) NGINX will do a very smooth and almost uneventful reload of the new configuration with a SIGHUP or **reload** command.

NGINX uses a procedure where on the receipt of an **nginx -s reload** command, it fences off the old worker processes that are currently servicing connections and disallows new connections to them, while allowing the current connections to continue being serviced. Instead of allowing new connections to the worker processes servicing the old connections, NGINX brings up new worker processes using the *new* configuration, and handles all subsequent connections with those. As the old connections are serviced, and then timed out, the old worker processes are retired, eventually all being terminated.

NOTE   There are even situations and services where an **nginx -s reload** command being sent invokes a particular script that handles the very specific conditions of reloading that service.

Dealing with RPM Configurations

In Linux+ exam objective 1.7, CompTIA includes under the topic "Updating configuration files" both RPM package updates/removal and service handling, but they don't really belong in the same category. In a service reload or restart, the configuration file is reread and used, but the upgrades can result in overwriting configuration files. Because of the very real possibility of accidentally overwriting an existing configuration for a service with the updated default config, we'll discuss how that is currently handled, which is very gently and cautiously.

NOTE   This section applies to RPM-based distributions, such as Red Hat, Fedora, openSUSE, and SUSE Linux Enterprise, just to mention the enterprise support distributions.

Rage About Your Machine

When you are installing a package (rather than upgrading one), writing the default configuration to the disk is safe because you don't have to be concerned about an existing configuration. In this case, you have no reason to do anything other than just install the package, copying the files and directories as specified.

The real concern starts when you have an existing package and want to apply an update or upgrade. In that scenario, it's very important how you handle the configuration file, because wiping out a carefully crafted many-line masterpiece with a supposed package upgrade will cause a great deal of rage to be directed your way. Besides, it's just not graceful; it's considered heavy-handed.

Two Methods to retain the original configuration file

The real key here is the status of the existing configuration file in question when updating a package. If the file is marked with the **noreplace** attribute, then one of two methods will be used to ensure that the original configuration file is not lost.

The following methods are used to try to ensure that you don't have a tragic circumstance due to an overwritten configuration file during an upgrade:

- *.rpmsave*: Given the **noreplace** attribute is *not* set, if there are any differences between the existing file and the new file, the existing file is written to **configfile.rpmsave** and the new one is installed in its place.

- *.rpmnew*: Given the **noreplace** attribute is set, if there are any differences between the existing file and the new one in the upgrade package, the existing file is left in place and the new config file is written to **configfile.rpmnew**.

To recap simply, after the upgrade, if there is a **.rpmnew** file, your old config is in place and safe, and if there is a **.rpmsave** file, your old config was saved there and the new config was put in its place.

Handling .rpmsave and .rpmnew Files

If you are monitoring the status during an upgrade, you may see a message flash by about the creation of an **.rpmnew** or **.rpmsave** file, but the best way to determine whether one had been created is to look at your log files and see what has been installed recently. If the upgrade doesn't involve a service, there most likely will not be any need for any **.rpmnew** or **.rpmsave** files.

If you see a service has been upgraded, then inspect that service *very* carefully for clues as to what has occurred, and look for any **.rpmnew** or **.rpmsave** files.

When you have a need to search for the **.rpmsave** and **.rpmnew** files, you can use the **find** command with some command-line kung fu like that shown in Example 7-1.

Example 7-1 Finding **.rpmsave** and **.rpmnew** Files

```
# find / -iname "*.rpm[n,s]*" 2> /dev/null
/home/parallels/file1.rpmnew
/home/parallels/file2.rpmsave
/etc/containers/registries.conf.rpmnew
/etc/cups/cups-browsed.conf.rpmnew
```

The output of Example 7-1 shows that two **.rpmsave** files and two **.rpmnew** files were found, the most important being the last two listed, which are where the package manager found that the older configuration files were marked **noreplace** and so saved the new configuration file to an **.rpmnew** file.

Once you have found some of these files, you can use the **diff** command to view the old and new files, like the command shown in Figure 7-1.

```
$ diff /etc/cups/cups-browsed{.conf,.conf.rpmnew}
769,770c769,776
< UpdateCUPSQueuesMaxPerCall 20
< PauseBetweenCUPSQueueUpdates 5
---
>
> # NotifLeaseDuration defines how long the D-BUS subscription created by cups-browsed
> # in cupsd will last before cupsd cancels it. The default value is 1 day
> # in seconds - 86400. The subscription renewal is set to happen after half of
> # NotifLeaseDuration passed. The D-BUS notifications are used for watching over queues
> # and doing specific actions when a D-BUS notification comes.
>
> # NotifLeaseDuration 86400
```

Figure 7-1 Using **diff** to view configuration file differences

Another option for viewing differences between files is the **vimdiff** command, which is a module (i.e., utility) of the **vim** suite. To use **vimdiff**, you specify almost exactly the same command as shown in Figure 7-1, just using **vimdiff** instead of **diff**. The result is a colorful and easier-to-compare interface than the more simplistic **diff** command output, as shown in Figure 7-2.

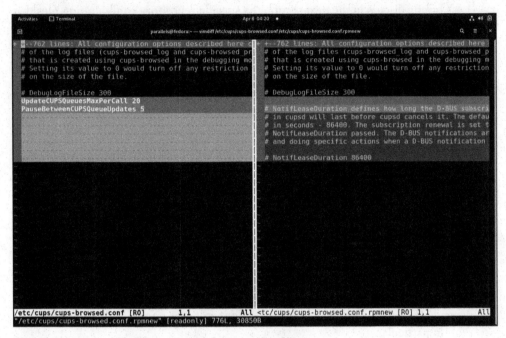

Figure 7-2   Using **vimdiff** to view configuration file differences

In summary, while you can just leave your **.rpmsave** and **.rpmnew** files lying around on your drive, there are times when you will need to find them, particularly the **.rpmsave** files, since the new configuration will have replaced your old, properly functioning configuration.

Repository Configuration Files

In the previous section, you learned how to update configuration files of all types. This section explores a specific type of configuration file, repository configuration files, which are integral to the process of obtaining packages from repositories.

A package *repository* is effectively a location, that can be either local, on your network or across the world, where your system can go and get new and updated software, patches, fixes, security updates, and, in some cases, even entire operating systems.

Configuring your repositories is also important, and the main configuration files for the package management scheme are typically used as the main configuration for all the dependent or subordinate utilities. For example, the **/etc/apt/*apt.conf*** file is the primary configuration source for all of the APT suite's tools, though some configuration can be made at a lower or tool-specific level, depending on the tool or need.

Let's briefly discuss in the next section the specific repository configuration files that are included in Linux+ exam objective 1.7.

Repository Configuration File Overview

The concept of package repositories came into being before they were used widely by Linux distributions, but they have become an essential part of installing, managing, and securing Linux software.

We'll cover the main configuration files for the various package managers, and then where actual repositories are configured and live on your systems.

The APT Configuration File

The **/etc/apt.conf** file is used by *all* the APT suite of tools, to make sure APT tools are predictable and behave in a consistent manner.

Configurations kept in **/etc/apt.conf** include what architecture the system is running on, what the APT cache size is, what packages are considered essential for dependencies, and sections that govern the **apt-get**, **apt-cache**, and **apt-cdrom** tools in particular.

APT uses three main sections that are located in the configuration file: the APT Group, the Acquire Group, and Directories. This configuration file also contains information about how the APT suite can call the RPM command to accomplish particular actions.

The YUM Configuration File

The **/etc/*yum.conf*** file is used by the Yellowdog Updater Modified (YUM) suite, which is both its own package management suite and the underlying suite that the DNF (Dandified YUM) suite is based on. Unlike the APT main configuration file, the YUM configuration file is like an **.ini** file that arranges things into sections, typically [main] and [repository], and that same configuration is in the format of **name=value**.

The DNF Configuration File

The **/etc/dnf/***dnf.conf* file is used for all DNF configuration by default. DNF also uses the **/etc/yum.repos.d/*.repo** files for repository management, which are discussed next.

Actual Repository Files

As opposed to the main configuration files and where they look for repository configuration files, now we can go down a step on the chain and talk about where the actual repository definitions are made.

The YUM Repo Files

Repositories can be configured in the **/etc/yum.conf** file, in the [repository] section of the file, and also via files in the **/etc/yum.repos.d** directory.

The **/etc/yum.repos.d** directory holds the individual **.repo** files configure the system to access the associated repositories. This is an include directory (the main clue is the **.d** suffix!), with the information for a repo or a set of related repos being contained in a single **<reponame>.repo** file.

The APT Repo Files

The APT repository scenario is similar to the YUM repository scenario, but with a small difference. Whereas YUM uses the main **.conf** file and an include directory where the individual files end in **.repo**, the APT setup has the **/etc/apt/sources.list** file as its main repository configuration location. Similarly to YUM, the APT repository include files directory (**/etc/apt/***sources.list.d*) contains individual **.list** repository configuration files.

Configuring Kernel Options

In the earlier days of Linux, compiling your own custom kernel was the thing to do, for a variety of reasons, ranging from "just because I can" to needing to control the kernel's performance and security. But there was one main drawback: if you custom-compiled the kernel, particularly with an enterprise distribution like Red Hat or SUSE, you were outside of the supported configuration, and on your own.

In this section you will learn about different kernel options and how modifying them can change the behavior of your system.

Viewing Kernel Parameters

Using **sysctl** to view kernel parameters in the running kernel is very easy—simply go to the shell and run the query as shown in Example 7-2.

Example 7-2 Viewing Kernel Parameters with **sysctl**

```
# sysctl -a
abi.vsyscall32 = 1
debug.exception-trace = 1
debug.kprobes-optimization = 1
dev.cdrom.autoclose = 1
dev.cdrom.autoeject = 0
dev.cdrom.check_media = 0
```

Of course, you can view all the parameters, but that's kind of messy and sometimes you just want to see a particular parameter and its value, in which case you can simply specify that parameter with **sysctl** to see the current value, as shown in Example 7-3.

Example 7-3 Viewing a Particular Kernel Parameter Value with **sysctl**

```
# sysctl kernel.osrelease
kernel.osrelease = 5.11.0-37-generic
```

Instead of looking at the value of a parameter through the **sysctl** interface, you can look at the actual file that contains that value. The key is to substitute the **/proc/sys** prefix and convert any dots (.) in the parameter name to a forward slash (/), such as you see in Example 7-4.

Example 7-4 Viewing a Particular Kernel Parameter in **/pro/sys**

```
# cat /proc/sys/kernel/osrelease
5.11.0-37-generic
```

Doing It the Manual Way

Of course, there are several ways to do everything in Linux, sometimes many more than just several!

Since all the kernel parameters are stored in **/proc/sys** and its subdirectories and files, you can simply view them with the **cat** command. You set them by having the right permissions and using the **echo** command to send the value you want to the right file. This technique is a temporary change.

To make persistent changes requires modifying parameters that are located in the **/etc/sysctl.conf** file. The system uses the parameters of this file when the system is rebooted to set the values.

Getting Used to Using **sysctl**

Nowadays, there are many tunable parameters, most of which don't require a custom compilation, and those parameters and their settings are located in the **/etc/sysctl.conf** file or in the include directory, **/etc/sysctl.d**.

The **/etc/sysctl.conf** file contains a large number of parameters that can be viewed and set with the *sysctl* command, either via the default **/etc/sysctl.conf** file or by specifying a **.conf** file to read parameters and values from.

Ways to Set Kernel Parameters

Various ways exist to set the kernel parameters, but this section focuses on the ways that you need to know for the Linux+ exam (and in a real production environment).

Using the **sysctl.conf** File

The primary method of making a persistent (across reboots!) change to a kernel parameter is by changing the **/etc/*sysctl.conf*** file and reloading the kernel, typically with a reboot of the system. This can be disruptive, to say the least, so let's discuss other ways.

Using the **sysctl** Command Directly

A more immediate way to modify kernel parameters is to use the **sysctl** command and set them from the command line.

To set kernel parameters from the command line, you use the **sysctl** command and the **-w** option, plus the **parameter=value** you want to set, as shown in Example 7-5.

Example 7-5 Setting a Particular Kernel Parameter via **sysctl**

```
# sysctl -w net.ipv4.ip_forward=1
net.ipv4.ip_forward = 1
```

The value that set is reflected for confirmation. You can also run the **sysctl** command against this parameter, or go view the **/proc/sys/net/ipv4/ip_forward** file to see the value.

> **NOTE** If you get an error stating permission to make the change is denied, make sure you are either using the root account to make the change or, much more reasonably, using the **sudo** command to preface your **sysctl** write command.

Using /etc/sysctl.conf

The final way to set kernel parameters is actually a very old way, and while a bit mechanical and manual, it's a tried and true way to do the task!

Echoing a value to a file is a great way to make a temporary change to a writeable file in the **/proc/sys** structure, but it is not persistent—upon the next reboot, the value will revert either to the default value or to whatever value is set in the **/etc/sysctl.conf** file.

To make a nonpersistent change to a value, use the **echo** command like you see in the following.

```
# echo 1 > /proc/sys/net/ipv4/ip_forward
```

If you use this method, you'll want to use the **cat** command (for example) to check that the value was properly entered into the file.

Again, the main problem with making a change this way is that it is not persistent. To make sure that the value is persistent across system reboots, you can either edit the **/etc/sysctl.conf** file and put the parameter and value there or, if you want to make sure you have it set for the future, you can set the value both manually and in the file, like you see in the following.

```
# sysctl -w net.ipv4.ip_forward=1 >> /etc/sysctl.conf
```

Using the sysctl Command to Load Parameters

Loading up other configurations from the **/etc/sysctl.d** directory happens automatically, with those files being read first, and then the **/etc/sysctl.conf** is read, or you can cause one of those files to be read manually using the **sysctl** command, as shown in Example 7-6.

Example 7-6   Using **sysctl.d** Include Files to Set Parameter Values

```
# sysctl -p /etc/sysctl.d/10-someparameter.conf
```

The name of those files is used to set the order in which they are processed, so if you have a couple of parameters that depend one on the other, make them numerically load one before the other by prefixing the one that will be depended on with the lower numerals, such as 10, and then the one that will be depending on the first with 20, and so forth.

When you are done viewing, setting, and making persistent all those kernel parameters and values, you might make sure to run the **service procps reload** command or the equivalent on a non-RPM-based system. This **service** command will make the changes in this file effective now. If you don't use this method, you need to reboot the system to have the changes take effect.

Understanding Kernel Modules

Kernels traditionally fall into two categories: monolithic and micro (also called modular). A monolithic kernel includes all of the kernel code in a single executable program. This poses issues on modern systems because a monolithic kernel includes a lot of code that isn't needed for all systems.

To understand this better, consider that the kernel includes code that is able to perform tasks like the following (though this list is not complete):

- Access hardware devices, such as USB devices, network interfaces, Bluetooth devices, and terminal interfaces

- Communicate to different filesystem types, including CIFS, Ext4, and FAT

- Perform various cryptography tasks, such as encrypting drives

- Secure the network with firewall rules

Consider a situation in which you have installed a server that doesn't have any Bluetooth hardware and only uses Ext4 filesystems (no Microsoft-based FAT devices and no SAMBA mounts for CIFS filesystems). If Linux were a monolithic kernel, then all of these features would be included in the kernel, which would result in wasted time (because during boot the kernel is loaded into memory) and wasted memory (to store the unnecessary kernel featured).

Because the Linux kernel is a micro kernel, only the components (called kernel modules) that are needed should be loaded. The phrase "should be" is used here because it is possible that unnecessary kernel modules are loaded. Kernel modules are loaded in one of two different ways:

- **Loaded by default as a result of how the kernel was compiled:** The process of compiling a kernel includes specifying what modules are part of the kernel by default. Standard kernels are "minimal" in that they include very few modules by default. However, custom kernels can be built that may include kernel modules that aren't necessary for specific systems. Further discussion on this topic is beyond the scope of this book and the Linux+ exam.

- **Loaded as needed or manually:** For example, if you connect an external drive that has a FAT filesystem and then mount that resource, the kernel will load the FAT kernel module into memory automatically in order to be able to communicate with that device. Using this technique yields a *loadable kernel module*.

With loadable kernel modules, the boot process is quicker as the kernel is smaller overall than a monolithic kernel. In addition, less space is needed in memory because the micro kernel is smaller. It is also possible to remove a kernel module from memory, which may be useful if it is causing conflicts or issues to the system.

Managing Kernel Modules

To display all of the kernel modules that are currently loaded into memory, execute the *lsmod* command, as shown in Example 7-7. (In this example, the output is limited by the **head** command because typically **lsmod** yields 50 to 75 lines of output.)

Example 7-7 The **lsmod** Command

```
[root@OCS ~]# lsmod | head
Module             Size     Used by
tcp_diag           12591    0
udp_diag           12801    0
inet_diag          18222    2 tcp_diag,udp_diag
unix_diag          12601    0
binfmt_misc        18035    1
ip6t_REJECT        12625    1
nf_reject_ipv6     13301    1 ip6t_REJECT
nf_log_ipv6        12726    6
ip6table_filter    12815    1
```

Each line of output of the **lsmod** command describes one module. There are three fields of information, as described in Table 7-2 (where examples are taken from the fourth line of output from Example 7-7).

Table 7-2   Fields of the **lsmod** Command Output

Field	Description	Example
Module	The name of the module.	**inet_diag**
Size	The size of the module, in bytes.	**18222**
Used by	The number (and perhaps names) of the things that use this module, such as other modules (listed by name) or other system components. Without this dependency module loaded into memory, these things would not be able to function.	**2 tcp_diag,udp_diag**

While the **lsmod** command displays which modules are currently loaded into memory, the **dmesg** command can display the module being loaded by the kernel. For example, the following **dmesg** command shows that the kernel recognized a USB device and then loaded the **usbhid** module into memory (the **lsmod** command is also provided to verify that the module is still loaded into memory):

```
[root@OCS ~]# dmesg | grep usbhid
usbcore: registered new interface driver usbhid
usbhid: USB HID core driver
[root@OCS ~]# lsmod | grep usb
usbhid                  49152  0
hid                    118784  2 hid_generic,usbhid
```

Note that while the module was loaded into memory when a USB device was attached to the system, that device no longer appears to be attached. If it were still attached, then the last value of the **usbhid** line in the **lsmod** command's output would not be **0**. This value indicates that nothing is currently using this module, which means the USB device is no longer attached.

The size of the buffer that stores the **dmesg** command's information is limited. Don't expect to be able to determine what loaded into memory months ago. Use this command to troubleshoot current issues, not as a means of discovering what went wrong six months ago.

Loading and Unloading Modules Manually

In most cases, modules are loaded automatically as needed. Once they are loaded into memory, they stay in memory until the next time the system is booted or until unloaded manually.

In the event that you want to remove a module from memory, you can use the *rmmod* command:

```
# lsmod | grep usb
usbhid                    49152      0
hid                       118784     2 hid_generic,usbhid
[root@OCS ~]# rmmod usbhid
[root@OCS ~]# lsmod | grep usb
[root@OCS ~]# lsmod | grep hid
mac_hid                   16384      0
hid_generic               16384      0
hid                       118784     1 hid_generic
```

Consider the following important notes regarding removing modules from memory:

- Removing modules from memory is a rare task. Even if a module isn't being used, there aren't many reasons to remove it from memory. Modules take up very little memory and have little to no impact on the system when they are not in use. You may remove a module that is causing a problem, but this is rarely done on production systems (and is more likely to be done in testing and development).

- Note that the **hid** module, which the **usbhid** module depended on, was not removed from memory. The **rmmod** command does not remove dependency modules, even if all modules that rely on the module are removed. That is why in the previous example the **hid** module, which the **usbhid** module depends on, was not removed from memory.

- If the **usbhid** module had anything that depended on it, the **rmmod** command would fail because the system will not allow the removal of a module if it is being used by another module. See the section "The **modprobe** Command," later in this chapter, for more details.

Inserting modules to memory can be accomplished by using the *insmod* command. For example, the following command inserts the **fat** module into memory:

```
# lsmod | grep fat
# pwd
/usr/lib/modules/5.19.8-100.fc35.x86_64/kernel/fs/fat
# ls
```

```
fat.ko   msdos.ko   vfat.ko
# insmod fat.ko
# lsmod | grep fat
fat                     65107   0
```

Consider the following important notes regarding inserting modules into memory:

- You must specify exactly where the module is located. In the previous example, the module is located in the current directory. If it was not, a path to the file location must be provided, not just the filename.

- On most systems, modules are located under the **/usr/lib/modules/***kernel_version***/kernel** directory structure. You will find that the **/usr/lib/modules** directory probably has a few kernel names. For example:

```
[root@OCS fat]# ls /usr/lib/modules
```

```
5.17.8-200.fc35.x86_64   5.18.7-100.fc35.x86_64 5.19.8-100.fc35.
x86_64
```

This means the system has three kernels, and you need to use the uname command to determine which kernel you are using in order to know what directory to descend into:

```
# uname -r
```

```
5.19.8-100.fc35.x86_64
```

- The **insmod** command will fail if a module dependency isn't already loaded.

Note how the **insmod** command fails when attempting to load a module that requires another module that isn't currently loaded:

```
# rmmod fat
# ls
fat.ko   msdos.ko   vfat.ko
# insmod vfat.ko
insmod: ERROR: could not insert module vfat.ko: Unknown symbol in
module
```

This issue could be solved by loading the dependency module, but if you look at the error message, it is difficult to tell what this dependency module is. As a result, most administrators use a different command to insert a module into memory (and remove modules from memory): the **modprobe** command.

The modprobe Command

Because of the drawbacks of the **rmmod** and **insmod** commands, it is important to know how to use the *modprobe* command. For example, when using the **modprobe** command, you don't need to know where a module is located:

```
# pwd
/root
# modprobe fat
# lsmod | grep fat
fat                         65107   0
```

You also don't need to worry about dependency modules, as they are loaded automatically. For example, note how the **fat** module is automatically loaded when using the **modprobe** command to load the **vfat** module:

```
# rmmod fat
# lsmod | grep fat
# modprobe vfat
# lsmod | grep fat
vfat                        17411   0
fat                         65107   1 vfat
```

How does the **modprobe** command know where the modules are located and what the dependency modules are? It makes use of a database file called **modules.dep**:

```
# ls /usr/lib/modules/5.19.8-100.fc35.x86_64
build                   modules.dep          modules.softdep
kernel                  modules.dep.bin      modules.symbols
modules.alias           modules.devname      modules.symbols.bin
modules.alias.bin       modules.drm          source
modules.block           modules.modesetting  updates
modules.builtin         modules.networking   vdso
modules.builtin.bin     modules.order
# grep vfat /usr/lib/modules/5.19.8-100.fc35.x86_64/  modules.dep
kernel/fs/fat/vfat.ko: kernel/fs/fat/fat.ko
```

In this output, the location to the **vfat** module is listed first, and then after the colon character, the dependency is listed.

The database file **modules.dep** is not a file that you need to manage in most cases. This database can be updated by running the **depmod** command; however, this is rarely a task that is performed manually. If you install software that includes kernel modules, the software should be configured to run the **depmod** command as part of the installation process. If you download a kernel module manually, you should run the **depmod** command after placing the kernel module in the correct directory (somewhere under the **/usr/lib/modules/*kernel_version*/kernel** directory structure, where ***kernel_version*** is the version number of the kernel).

The **modprobe** command can also remove modules and their dependencies. Just use the **-r** option to the command:

```
# lsmod | grep fat
vfat                    17411   0
fat                     65107   1 vfat
# modprobe -r vfat
# lsmod | grep fat
#
```

The **modprobe** command can also be configured by modifying either the **/etc/modprobe.conf** file or the files located in the **/etc/modprobe.d** directory. The **/etc/modprobe.conf** file is the primary configuration file, and it doesn't exist on all Linux distributions. The files in the **/etc/modprobe.d** directory are additional configuration files. The format of all of these files is the same. The purpose of the **/etc/modprobe.d** directory files is to provide a place where developers can place files without having to modify the primary configuration file. It is also now the standard place for administrators to create custom configuration files.

Several settings can be used in a **modprobe** command configuration file:

- **alias:** Makes a nickname for a module (for example, **alias eth0 ipw2200**)

- **install:** Used to specify commands to execute when a module is loaded (for example, **install scsi_hostadapter /sbin/modprobe ahci; /bin/true**)

- **remote:** Used to specify commands to execute when a module is removed (for example, **remove snd-hda-intel /sbin/modprobe -r snd-pcm-oss;**)

- **options:** Used to specify which options to pass to a module when it is loaded (for example, **options e1000 debug=1**)

The options are based on features supported by a specific module. To see these features, display the module's parameters by using the ***modinfo*** command, as shown in Example 7-8.

Example 7-8   The **modinfo** Command

```
# modinfo e1000 | grep parm
parm:    TxDescriptors:Number of transmit descriptors (array of int)
parm:    RxDescriptors:Number of receive descriptors (array of int)
parm:    Speed:Speed setting (array of int)
parm:    Duplex:Duplex setting (array of int)
parm:    AutoNeg:Advertised auto-negotiation setting (array of int)
parm:    FlowControl:Flow Control setting (array of int)
parm:    XsumRX:Disable or enable Receive Checksum offload (array of
int)
parm:    TxIntDelay:Transmit Interrupt Delay (array of int)
parm:    TxAbsIntDelay:Transmit Absolute Interrupt Delay (array of int)
parm:    RxIntDelay:Receive Interrupt Delay (array of int)
parm:    RxAbsIntDelay:Receive Absolute Interrupt Delay (array of int)
parm:    InterruptThrottleRate:Interrupt Throttling Rate (array of int)
parm:    SmartPowerDownEnable:Enable PHY smart power down (array of
int)
parm:    copybreak:Maximum size of packet that is copied to a new
buffer on receive (uint)
parm:    debug:Debug level (0=none,...,16=all) (int)
```

In the output of the command displayed in Example 7-2, you can see that the **debug** option assumed an integer value between 0 and 16. This could be set to be automatically used by placing the following in a **modprobe** command configuration file:

```
options e1000  debug=1
```

It could also be manually set when running the **modprobe** command (which would override the configuration file):

```
# modprobe e1000 debug=1
```

Configuring Common System Services

This section covers some common services that you will see on just about any server (and on the Linux+ exam):

- Secure Shell (SSH)
- Network Time Protocol (NTP), including chrony
- Syslog

What's so special about these services? They not only are extremely likely to be on most servers that run in your enterprise, in some fashion, but also might be critical services for your enterprise.

Because of the way the objectives for the Linux+ are designed, some commands, suites of tools, and so forth are listed in multiple places, which is the case for SSH. Chapter 5 covers SSH in depth, so the following section serves only as a quick refresher. That is followed by deeper coverage of NTP and chrony, localization, and Syslog.

Secure Shell (SSH)

NOTE If you have already read Chapter 5 and feel confident in your understanding of SSH, feel free to skip this section, which is a simple refresher.

Secure Shell (SSH) is a service that allows for secure communication between hosts. The securing features include symmetrical encryption, asymmetrical encryption, and hashing. SSH is used for the following:

- As a secure replacement for Telnet and other unsecure remote-connection services (such as rlogin). On the client side, the **ssh** command is used for this feature.

- As a secure replacement for file transfer methods, such as FTP or RCP. On the client side, the **sftp** command is used to replace **ftp**, and the **scp** command is used to replace **rcp**.

- As a secure replacement for remote execution methods, like **rsh**. On the client side, the **ssh** command is used for this feature.

Network Time Protocol (NTP)

The *Network Time Protocol (NTP)* is designed to resolve issues regarding the system time of server and client systems. Having an accurate system time is important for several reasons, including:

- **Log files:** These files have timestamps embedded within log entries. These timestamps are often critical in determining exactly when an error or a security breach occurred. Inaccurate system times result in inaccurate timestamps, which can lead to problems in determining the causes of problems and also present potential legal issues, as log files are sometimes used in legal cases but can be disregarded by the court system if the timestamps are not accurate.

- **Client/server interactions:** Some services require the client and server systems to be in sync regarding system time. If these systems are not in sync, the service may fail completely.

- **Searches for file by timestamp:** Users and administrators often search for lost or missing files using timestamps. If the system time isn't accurate, then the file timestamps won't be accurate, making it difficult to find files.

- **Transaction log timestamps:** Many transaction operations include timestamps. For example, each email that is sent or received has a timestamp of these actions. Another example is banking and credit card transactions. It is critical to ensure that these timestamps are as accurate as possible for both security and reliability of the transactions.

The purpose of NTP is to ensure accurate system times. A system is configured as an NTP client, which sets the system time based on data received from one or more NTP servers. Typically three or more NTP servers are used to best ensure the most accurate time.

Organizations may deploy their own NTP servers, but there are also publicly available servers on **pool.ntp.org**. Servers are categorized by how accurate they are. Their accuracy is determined by assigning a "stratum" value to each server—a numeric value from 0 to 15; the lower this value, the more accurate the clock is considered to be.

A clock that advertises itself as a stratum-0 likely gets its timestamps from an atomic clock and has very little delay in responding to NTP requests. A clock that advertises itself as a stratum-1 gets its timestamps from stratum-0 servers.

NTP Expressed Through Chrony

Nowadays, the most common implementation of Network Time Protocol is through the *chronyd* service, driven and configured by the *chronyc* command.

I first encountered *chrony* through a SUSE Linux Certified Engineer course I wrote for a customer, and I found it to be a very faithful and easy to understand and use method of implementing NTP.

The primary way you'll typically interact with chrony is through the **chronyd.service** systemD unit file, and the **chronyc** (c for command?) command that is used in place of the **ntp*** commands.

For example, to get a listing of the NTP servers your chronyd daemon is configured to use, you'd issue the **chronyd sources** command, shown in Figure 7-3. This command also is available with **-a** for all sources and **-v** for extra verbosity of the output.

```
$ chronyc sources
210 Number of sources = 8
MS Name/IP address          Stratum Poll Reach LastRx Last sample
===============================================================================
^+ golem.canonical.com           2   6   377     42  -6115us[-6115us] +/-   122ms
^+ pugot.canonical.com           2   6   377     45   +18ms[  +18ms] +/-   173ms
^+ chilipepper.canonical.com     2   6   257     44  -2303us[-2303us] +/-   128ms
^+ golem.canonical.com           2   6   377     44   +18ms[  +18ms] +/-   117ms
^+ 66.85.78.80                   2   6   377     48   +11ms[  +12ms] +/-    88ms
^+ mx2.dutt.ch                   2   6   377    108  +6681us[+7534us] +/-   147ms
^* startkeylogger.hungrycat>     2   6   377     47  +3760us[+4745us] +/-    58ms
^+ clock.xmission.com            1   6   377     46   -14ms[  -14ms] +/-    55ms
$
```

Figure 7-3 The **chronyc** command being used to view NTP sources

In addition to **sources**, the **chronyc** command has a whole host of subcommands you can invoke. The following are some of the more notable ones:

- **sourcestats:** As you would expect, this command shows statistics for the sources and can be used to monitor drift and other important stats for each of the sources. It is compatible with **-a** and **-v** for more information.

- **activity:** This command shows online and offline status of sources, which is useful when interruptions to the network occur.

- **ntpdata:** If you have ever wanted a way to show just about every possible piece of data regarding your NTP service, this is the command for you. It is comprehensive to a fault.

As you can see, the **chronyc** command is very useful for helping you manage your NTP services.

The timedatectl Command

For the Linux+ exam, you should be aware of the relatively new command *timedatectl*, which can be used to view and change both the date and the time zone on the system. Example 7-9 shows an example of displaying date and time zone information.

Example 7-9 Displaying the Date and Time Zone

```
# timedatectl status
      Local time: Mon 2018-10-01 18:23:23 PDT
  Universal time: Tue 2018-10-02 01:23:23 UTC
        RTC time: Mon 2018-10-01 13:32:48
        Timezone: America/Los_Angeles (PDT, -0700)
```

```
        NTP enabled: yes
   NTP synchronized: yes
   RTC in local TZ: no
         DST active: yes
   Last DST change: DST began at
                          Sun 2018-03-11 01:59:59 PST
                          Sun 2018-03-11 03:00:00 PDT
   Next DST change: DST ends (the clock jumps one hour backwards) at
                          Sun 2018-11-04 01:59:59 PDT
                          Sun 2018-11-04 01:00:00 PST
```

The **timedatectl** command can also be used to modify the system clock, the RTC (real-time clock, or hardware clock), and the time zone setting.

System Logging with Syslog

Logs tell you what was happening while you weren't looking. The kernel and running applications emit logs when events happen. These logs might be informational, such as a web request, or they might be errors, such as the ntpd daemon exiting because the time difference was too large.

Most applications in Linux conduct logging in some form or another. Linux provides a centralized logging facility that applications can use. This means that an application can use a standard interface to log and doesn't have to configure file locations. It also means that administrators can split up logs according to function or ignore unimportant logs and have errors emailed directly to themselves.

Some applications, such as web servers, can do their own logging. Usually this is needed to get the performance or customization that the application needs, or sometimes it's because the application was designed to work on many different systems, some of which don't have syslog. As a systems administrator, you will have to deal with all kinds of logs.

Representing Locales

Each locale is represented in terms of two or three variables:

- Language code (ISO 639)
- Country code (ISO 3166)
- Encoding (optional)

It might seem odd to have both a language and a country, but consider that multiple languages may be spoken in a country and that two countries sharing a common language may speak different dialects. Just ask anyone from France what they think about how French is spoken in Quebec, Canada!

Thus, the language and country are different. ISO 639 describes language names, such as **en** for English, **de** for German, and **es** for Spanish. ISO 3166 is for the country. While Germany happens to be **DE** for country and **de** for language, a country doesn't necessarily have the same designation for both. The United States and Canada, which both have English as an official language (**en**), are **US** and **CA**, respectively.

The encoding further describes how the characters are stored in the locale file. A particular locale file may use the old ISO 8859 encoding or the more robust Unicode, and even within Unicode there are multiple variants, such as UTF-8, UTF-16, and UTF-32.

American English is in the **en_US.UTF-8** locale, and Spanish is in **es_ES.utf8**. See what locales are installed on your system with the **locale -a** command, as shown in Example 7-10.

Example 7-10   Using the **locale -a** Command to See the Locales Installed on a System

```
# locale -a
C
C.UTF-8
en_AG
en_AG.utf8
en_AU.utf8
en_BW.utf8
en_CA.utf8
en_DK.utf8
en_GB.utf8
... output omitted ...
es_ES.utf8
es_GT.utf8
es_HN.utf8
es_MX.utf8
es_NI.utf8
POSIX
```

Fallback Locales

Sometimes you don't want to deal with locales, especially if you're writing a script that deals with output of other programs, which could change based on the user's locale. In such a case, you can temporarily use the **C** locale. **C**, which can also be called **POSIX**, is a generic 8-bit ASCII locale.

Contents of a Locale

Each locale file contains instructions on how to display or translate a variety of items:

- **Addresses:** Ordering of various parts in ZIP code format
- **Collation:** How to sort, such as the ordering of accented characters or whether capitalized words are grouped together or separately from lowercase
- **Measurement:** Display of various units
- **Messages:** Translations for system messages and errors
- **Monetary:** How currency symbols are displayed and named
- **Names:** Conventions for displaying people's names
- **Numeric:** How to display numbers such as the thousands and decimal separators
- **Paper:** Paper sizes used in the country
- **Telephone:** How telephone numbers are displayed
- **Time:** Date and time formats, such as the ordering of year, month, and date, or 24-hour clock versus using a.m. and p.m.

These locale files are usually distributed with the operating system as separate packages to save on space. If you don't need the translations, you can generate the rest of the items without installing packages by using **locale-gen** on systems that support it (see Example 7-11).

Example 7-11   Using **locale-gen**

```
# locale-gen fr_FR.UTF-8
Generating locales...
 fr_FR.UTF-8... done
Generation complete.
# locale -a | grep FR
fr_FR.utf8
```

The localectl Command

Some Linux distributions include a command that changes not only the locale but also the keyboard layout. When provided with the **status** option, the **localectl** command displays these values, as shown in Example 7-12.

Example 7-12   Using **localectl**

```
# localectl status
   System Locale: LANG=en_US.utf8
       VC Keymap: us
     X11 Layout: us
      X11 Model: pc105+inet
    X11 Options: terminate:ctrl_alt_bksp
```

You can set the locale and keyboard by using a command like the following:

```
# localectl set-locale "LANG=de_DE.utf8" set-keymap "de"
```

The advantage of the **localectl** command over the **locale** command is that when you change a locale setting, you typically want to change the keyboard layout to match the local region, and **localectl** lets you do this.

How Linux Uses the Locale

Internationalization in Linux is handled with the GNU **gettext** library. If programmers write their applications with that library and annotate their messages correctly, the user can change the behavior with environment variables.

Multiple things can be localized, such as numbers and messages, and **gettext** has a series of environment variables that it checks to see which locale is appropriate. In order, these are

- **LANGUAGE**
- **LC_ALL**
- **LC_XXX**
- **LANG**

The **LANGUAGE** variable is consulted only when printing messages. It is ignored for formatting. Also, the colon (:) gives the system a list of locales to try in order when trying to display a system message. You can use **LC_ALL** to force the locale even if some of the other variables are set.

LC_XXX gives the administrator the power to override a locale for a particular element. For example, if **LANG** were set to **en_US.UTF-8**, the user could override currency display by setting **LC_MONETARY**. The **locale** command displays the current settings, as shown in Example 7-13.

Example 7-13 Using **locale**

```
# locale
LANG=en_CA.UTF-8
LANGUAGE=en_CA:en
LC_CTYPE="en_CA.UTF-8"
LC_NUMERIC="en_CA.UTF-8"
LC_TIME="en_CA.UTF-8"
LC_COLLATE="en_CA.UTF-8"
LC_MONETARY="en_CA.UTF-8"
LC_MESSAGES="en_CA.UTF-8"
LC_PAPER="en_CA.UTF-8"
LC_NAME="en_CA.UTF-8"
LC_ADDRESS="en_CA.UTF-8"
LC_TELEPHONE="en_CA.UTF-8"
LC_MEASUREMENT="en_CA.UTF-8"
LC_IDENTIFICATION="en_CA.UTF-8"
LC_ALL=
This example is from a typical English system. You can override just
parts of it:
# LC_TIME=fr_FR.UTF8 date
samedi 7 mars 2015, 23:11:23 (UTC-0600)
# LC_MESSAGES=fr_FR.UTF8 man
What manual page do you want?
# LANGUAGE='' LC_MESSAGES=fr_FR.UTF8 man
Quelle page de manuel voulez-vous ?
```

In Example 7-13, the time setting is switched to the French locale, and the date is displayed in French. The second command sets the messages setting to French, but the English variant is used because the higher-priority **LANGUAGE** is set. A French error message is used when **LANGUAGE** is set to nothing.

systemd and syslog

Linux has two different logging systems: syslog and systemd's journal. *syslog* is a standardized system that can receive messages from local applications or remote servers and write them to disk or send them to another server. It is ubiquitous in that many network-enabled appliances generate syslog messages. The systemd journal is a newer form of logging for distributions that have moved to systemd. Fortunately, it is backward compatible so that applications that can log to syslog can also log to systemd, and it can also forward messages to a syslog server for centralized logging.

Applications that use systemd's version of logging can also log the additional metadata tracked by the journal. For example, the name of the method and the line number are logged alongside the message, which allows for additional statistics to be gathered.

syslog

syslog is a simple protocol that has been adopted across many different systems and applications.

A message can be logged in several ways:

- From within an application by using the **syslog** library call
- From the command line by using the **logger** command
- Remotely by connecting to and sending log entries to a syslog server over the network

A message is logged with a severity and a facility, and the syslog daemon takes care of processing the message.

Each log is tied to a facility (category or channel of messages) that describes what generated the log. The combination of facility and level of severity gives you control over what is stored. You may choose, for example, to log the email system at the informational level; in this case, you get reports of each email that goes through the system, but then you can limit syslog so that it begins logging the **cron** facility starting at the **warning** level of severity, so you only hear about things that go wrong.

Table 7-3 lists the available facilities.

Table 7-3 Log Facilities

Facility	Type of Messages
kern	Kernel messages
user	Random user-level messages
mail	Email server messages
daemon	Other system daemons
auth	Security logs that can be public

Facility	Type of Messages
syslog	Internal messages for syslog
lpr	Printing messages
cron	Scheduled jobs such as **cron** and **at**
authpriv	Security logs that need to be private
local0-7	Eight different user-definable facilities

Table 7-4 lists the syslog severity levels.

Table 7-4   Syslog Severities

Level	Severity	Meaning
0	**emerg**	Emergency: The system is unusable.
1	**alert**	Alert: Immediate action is needed to prevent a failure.
2	**crit**	Critical: The system has reached a critical level, such as disk space almost running out.
3	**err**	Error: Some part of the system encountered an error.
4	**warn** **warning**	Warning: Something happened that may have been processed incorrectly.
5	**notice**	Notice: Not an error condition, but special handling may be needed.
6	**info**	Informational: This is a normal log entry about a routine event that happened successfully.
7	**debug**	Debug: This is a message about an internal state that is for debugging problems.

When you log at a particular level, you're indicating that you want to capture the logs only at that level, or with a lower priority level, and want to throw away anything else. For example, most systems log at the **informational** level (6). Such a system would ignore **debug** logs (7) and capture anything else. You might decide to log at the **warning** level (4) to ignore reports of normal operation at levels 5, 6, and 7 and only concern yourself with level 4 warnings and more severe items at levels 1, 2, and 3.

For the Linux+ exam, it is important to know the eight log levels and their order, as well as which one doesn't get logged by default if you specify all (that is, **debug**).

The syslog daemon is responsible for the collection and distribution of log messages. You can think of it as a pipeline that takes messages from various sources and directs them to the appropriate destination. Figure 7-4 shows a typical syslog configuration in graphical form.

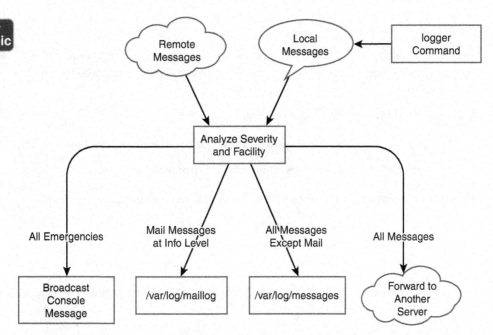

Figure 7-4 The flow of logging information

In Figure 7-4 the logs come in from one of two places: remotely, over the network, or from the local system. Locally, the **logger** command acts as an application and takes messages from the command and turns them into local syslog messages.

The box at the center of Figure 7-4 represents the point at which syslog analyzes the messages and, based on the severity and facility, decides where to send them. Starting from the left, anything with an **emergency** severity is displayed to the system console. This is partially done to capture the attention of anyone who happens to be watching the console, but it also ensures that a trace is left. If the log entry is truly about an emergency, it's possible that it's related to the disks or that the system is in the process of crashing. Next, all mail messages logged with a severity of at least **info** are stored in **/var/log/maillog**. All messages except for mail messages go to **/var/log/messages**. Finally, all messages are sent to a remote syslog server.

A single message may be sent to multiple outputs or to none. An emergency mail message would go to the console, **/var/log/maillog**, and the remote syslog server. A mail-related debugging message would only go to the remote server.

Keep in mind that Figure 7-4 shows an example. Your needs might be different and call for a different configuration.

The logger Command

The **logger** command is helpful for both testing your logging configuration and for logging within scripts. The easiest way to use it is just to pass the log message on the command line:

```
$ logger Starting script processing
```

If you look in a log, such as **/var/log/messages**, you see something like this:

```
Apr 20 19:55:02 bob sean: Starting script processing
```

The log entry contains both the hostname (bob) and the user (sean).

For additional information, you can pass the process ID with the **-i** flag:

```
$ logger -i Starting script processing
Apr 20 19:55:57 bob sean[8969]: Starting script processing
```

The default destination of the message is the **user** facility at the **notice** level, which can be overridden with the **-p** flag:

```
$ logger -i -p mail.info Checking user quotas
Apr 20 19:57:28 bob sean[9054]: Checking user quotas
```

Configuring syslogd

Linux has several syslog daemons that can be used, but the simplest one is part of the **sysklogd** package. The name is an amalgamation of *syslog* and **klogd**. **syslogd** is the component that handles the logging of messages, as described earlier (refer to Figure 7-1). **klogd** listens specifically for kernel logs and forwards them to **syslogd**. **klogd** can also do processing on a message before sending it along, such as to translate memory addresses into names that would be helpful to kernel developers.

klogd has very little to configure, and the interesting parts are found in **syslogd**.

syslogd's configuration file is in **/etc/syslog.conf**. This file defines a set of rules, one per line. Each rule is evaluated, and if the log matches that rule, the log is sent to the destination specified in the rule.

Example 7-14 shows a simple **syslog.conf** file.

Example 7-14   A Simple **/etc/syslog.conf** File

```
# This is a comment
authpriv.* /var/log/secure
*.info;mail.none;authpriv.none;cron.none /var/log/messages
mail.* -/var/log/maillog
cron.* /var/log/cron
*.emerg *
local7.* /var/log/boot.log
local4.* /var/log/slapd.log
```

syslogd ignores comments, which start with a hash sign. The rules in Example 7-14 are split into a selector and a destination, separated by whitespace. Each selector is made up of one or more patterns, and each pattern is a facility and a severity separated by a period (.).

For most of the patterns in Example 7-14, there is a single facility and the selector *, which means any severity will match. (This could also be written with the severity **debug**, as that is the lowest severity possible.) Thus, **authpriv.*** matches all the private authentication messages. If the destination part of the rule is a filename, the logs go to that file.

The line associated with the **mail** facility has a dash (-) in front of the destination. This tells **syslogd** that it shouldn't commit each log entry to disk as it's logged but should let the kernel write to disk when it has time, because the **mail** facility can log heavily; this delay in writing improves performance at a cost of potential data loss after a crash.

The second selector has more than one pattern, and the patterns are separated by semicolons (;). The first pattern matches any facility at **info** level or greater, and the remaining three use the special **none** severity to ignore any log coming from **mail**, **authpriv**, or **cron**. Those logs have their own files, so this selector is in place to eliminate duplication.

The ***.emerg** selector matches any log at the emergency level and sends it to a special destination; the * causes a message to be sent to the console of anyone logged in to the system.

Key File Locations

While individuals are free to place logs wherever they want, several conventions have emerged to make logs easier to find when moving from system to system (see Table 7-5).

Table 7-5   Common Logs and Their Locations

Log File	Purpose
/var/log/messages	General-purpose log messages that aren't in one of the other files
/var/log/secure	Security logs, such as records of connection attempts and failures
/var/log/maillog	All logs related to email
/var/log/cron	Logs of scheduled job activity
/var/log/xferlog	Logs of local File Transfer Protocol (FTP) server activity
/var/log/kern.log	The log file that **dmesg** uses to display the boot messages from the most recent system bootup

Splitting log files so that each major application has its own makes it easier to find what you want; when the records of multiple logs are mingled, it can be difficult to review the logs. A common pattern is to watch a log in real time—or "follow the log." To follow a log, run **tail -f** *logfile* (for example, **tail -f /var/log/secure**) to watch for people logging in.

When you have more than a few servers, especially if more than one of them do the same role, you'll get tired of accessing different servers to read logs. One solution is to have the various **syslogd**s on your servers forward all their messages to a single server. You can then read all your logs on a single server.

Centralizing your syslogging requires two things. First, the centralized syslog server must be started with the **-r** flag, which tells it that it can receive remote messages.

Second, you need a rule that forwards the desirable messages to the remote server by supplying a destination hostname prefixed with an **@**. For example, the following line sends all **info** messages and above to **logserver.example.com** for central analysis:

```
*.info @logserver.example.com
```

Other syslog Implementations

The **syslogd** package isn't the only syslog implementation available for Linux systems. There are two prominent alternatives: **rsyslogd** and **syslog-ng**.

rsyslogd is meant to be a "rocket-fast" implementation of a syslog daemon with support for plugins, alternative storage mechanisms, and more flexible rules processing. With **rsyslogd** you can store your logs in a database, filter the logs based on keywords, and keep statistics. One advantage of **rsyslogd** is that the basic **ksyslogd** configuration is also a valid **rsyslogd** configuration, which gives you an easy transition mechanism. The **rsyslogd** daemon uses the **/etc/rsyslog.conf** configuration file, which is similar in form and function to **syslogd**.

NOTE   rsyslog is similar in function and format to **syslogd**; the main differences are the enhancements just mentioned and the different configuration files. You need to be aware of **rsyslog** for the Linux+ exam, but mainly you need to understand **syslogd**.

syslog-ng is a next-generation syslog server offered in both open-source and commercial versions. It has many of the same features as **rsyslogd**, but the configuration syntax has been reworked so that complicated filters are easier to write with **syslog-ng** than with **rsyslogd**.

Summary

In this chapter you learned more about managing software. This included learning about procedures and methods related to package configuration files and how repository configuration files are managed.

You also learned about how kernel parameters are used to modify the behavior of the system. During that section you learned how to set kernel paraments, both temporarily and persistently. You also were introduced to kernel modules, which are small bits of code that provide more functionality to the kernel.

The later part of this chapter explored configuring command services, like SSH and NTP.

Exam Preparation Tasks

As mentioned in the section "Goals and Methods" in the Introduction, you have a couple of choices for exam preparation: the exercises here, Chapter 23, "Final Preparation," and the exam simulation questions in the Pearson Test Prep Software Online.

Review All Key Topics

Review the most important topics in this chapter, noted with the Key Topic icon in the left margin of the page. Table 7-6 lists these key topics and the page number on which each is found.

Table 7-6   Key Topics for Chapter 7

Key Topic Element	Description	Page Number
Paragraph	The steps of a service reload	284
Section	Handling **.rpmsave** and **.rpmnew** Files	286
Paragraph	**/etc/apt.conf** file used by all the APT suite of tools	288
Paragraph	**/etc/sysctl.conf** file contains a large number of parameters	291
Paragraph	Kernel categories	293
Table 7-2	Fields of the **lsmod** Command Output	295
Section	The **modprobe** Command	298
Figure 7-3	The **chronyc** command being used to view NTP sources	303
List	Examples of locale variables	304
Paragraph	Applications using systemd logging can also log additional metadata	309
Table 7-3	Log Facilities	309
Table 7-4	Syslog Severities	310
Figure 7-4	The flow of logging information	311
Table 7-5	Common Logs and Their Locations	314

Define Key Terms

Define the following key terms from this chapter and check your answers in the glossary:

restart, configuration file, reload, .rpmsave, .rpmnew, repository, apt.conf, yum.conf, dnf.conf, yum.repos.d, sources.list.d, sysctl, sysctl.conf, lsmod, rmmod, insmod, modprobe, modinfo, Secure Shell (SSH), Network Time Protocol (NTP), syslog, chronyd, chronyc, chrony, timedatectl

Review Questions

The answers to these review questions are in Appendix A.

1. If you have updated a service and afterward the existing configuration file is apparently missing and a default configuration file is in place, what **filename. extension** would your old configuration possibly have been stored in?

   a. **configfile.conf.rpmsave**

   b. **/var/save/configfile.conf.bak**

   c. **/Lost+Found/configfile.conf.bkz**

   d. **~/upgraded/configfile.conf.tmp**

2. Which two RPM-based package management schemes are very closely related and use the same files and directories for storing their repository configuration? (Choose two.)

   a. DNF

   b. RPM

   c. APT

   d. YUM

3. When configuring a kernel parameter, which file in the **/etc** directory would be the right one in which to put that parameter and any associated value?

   a. **kernel.conf**

   b. **tuning.conf**

   c. **sysctl.conf**

   d. **skel.conf**

4. The Linux+ objectives list an incorrect command in the section regarding modules for the kernel. Which of the following is that incorrect command?

   a. **lsmod**

   b. **imsmod**

   c. **rmmod**

   d. **devmod**

5. You have installed the latest distribution of your favorite enterprise Linux and want to change the NTP time servers for your system. Which of the following commands will give you information about your current time servers?

   a. **ntpinfo**

   b. **chronyc**

   c. **timedatectl**

   d. **date**

6. You are configuring your syslog logging levels and want to ensure that you get all information about a particular category of logging. Which of the following is the most verbose level of logging?

   a. **info**

   b. **crit**

   c. **debug**

   d. **emerg**

This chapter covers the following topics:

- Managing Public Key Infrastructure Certificates
- Certificate Use Cases
- Authentication
- Linux Hardening

The exam objective covered in this chapter is as follows:

- **Objective 2.1:** Summarize the purpose and use of security best practices in a Linux environment

## CHAPTER 8

Understanding Linux Security Best Practices

Breaking into the realm of security can be daunting for the newcomer, and Linux security is no easy topic to grasp quickly, unless you have a security background and are just picking up Linux skills. This is a very important set of topics for those who are charged with protecting everything from a single Linux web server or file server all the way to huge infrastructures serving millions of customers!

There is a lot to cover in this chapter, starting with the concepts involved in public key infrastructure (PKI) and how certificates are used. Next is the topic of authentication, which covers tokens, pluggable authentication modules (PAMs) and the System Security Services Daemon (SSSD), Lightweight Access Directory Protocol (LDAP), and single sign-on (SSO).

Finally, we'll hit the fascinating subject of hardening a Linux system, which I sum up for my classes with my own version of a quote from Coco Chanel, "Before you leave the house, look in the mirror and take one thing off." As I like to advise students, "Before you leave the server secured, turn off any service you can live without."

"Do I Know This Already?" Quiz

The "Do I Know This Already?" quiz enables you to assess whether you should read this entire chapter or simply jump to the "Exam Preparation Tasks" section for review. If you are in doubt, read the entire chapter. Table 8-1 outlines the major headings in this chapter and the corresponding "Do I Know This Already?" quiz questions. You can find the answers in Appendix A, "Answers to the 'Do I Know This Already?' Quizzes and Review Questions."

Table 8-1 "Do I Know This Already?" Foundation Topics Section-to-Question Mapping

Foundation Topics Section	Questions Covered in This Section
Managing Public Key Infrastructure Certificates	1
Certificate Use Cases	2
Authentication	3
Linux Hardening	4

CAUTION   The goal of self-assessment is to gauge your mastery of the topics in this chapter. If you do not know the answer to a question or are only partially sure of the answer, you should mark that question as wrong for purposes of the self-assessment. Giving yourself credit for an answer you correctly guess skews your self-assessment results and might provide you with a false sense of security.

1. You run a whistleblowers' website for reporting fraud and abuse in a particular industry and you are unable to get a central authority to issue you a certificate. Which of the following best describes your certificate authority status?

    a. Rogue

    b. Self-signed

    c. Protected

    d. Resigned

2. Your intern asks you what the difference is between SSL and TLS. Which of the following is a true response?

    a. SSL is part of TLS

    b. SSL was obsoleted by TLS

    c. SSL and TLS are competing standards

    d. TLS is much older than SSL

3. You have enabled a service definition rule as a file in the PAM configuration directory and suddenly notice that other authentication service rules are not working or are clearly missing. What is the issue?

    a. You need to restart the PAM daemon.

    b. You have obviated the **/etc/pam.conf** file.

    c. You need to rename the service file so that it ends in **.conf**.

    d. None of these answers are correct.

4. You are ordered to disallow access to the Telnet service on your server for the host snuffypc and to use the TCP wrappers files and utilities to accomplish this. In which file would you add this entry to accomplish this task?

    a. **/etc/hosts.deny**

    b. **/etc/hosts.block**

    c. **/etc/hosts.disallow**

    d. **/etc/hosts.stop**

Foundation Topics

Public Key Infrastructure

Public key infrastructure (PKI) is a complex range of roles, procedures, and methods to provide public key encryption/decryption services, ranging from an email sent between two parties to bank-to-bank transactions to the entirety of all e-commerce activity on the Web.

Purpose of Certificates

The main purpose of a PKI setup is to ensure that a given certificate (used to sign and identify an entity) belongs to and identifies who it says it does.

Certificate Authentication

To understand PKI, let's use the open Web as an example. If you are going to be doing commerce, accepting payments and handling people's personal and (hopefully) private information, you can try to convince everyone how trustworthy you are purely through marketing, or you can take the time and trouble necessary to get a certificate from a managing authority and then use that to identify your services as being properly managed and secured. A central certificate management scheme requires you to interact with and trust the centralized authority—something that not every organization will do.

Self-Signed Certificates

One of the other methods of using PKI is to be self-signing and develop a web of trust among and with other self-signers and to slowly build a reputation for being trustworthy. This is effectively the PKI version of word-of-mouth marketing or compliance. There are advantages to both scenarios—and downsides as well.

Certificate Authorities

A distinct upside of being verified as trustworthy by a central *certificate authority* is that the verified site, service, or company can then very quickly be verified by even individual users as being trustable. This is an example of self-signed certificates, as your certificate authority is the authority for these.

A distinct downside of a central authority is that if you provide a good or service, or have customers that the central authority does not approve of, it might be impossible to secure a certificate and participate in being approved as trustworthy. Then the entity will have to go unsigned or work to create a circle of trust with other like entities.

Private Keys

Private keys are always paired with public keys in the PKI process. Everyone has a pair of public and private keys, generated by their favorite tool, and while everyone can and should make their public key accessible to all they wish to communicate with, a private key should remain utterly inaccessible to anyone but the owner.

Public Keys

The role of *public keys* in this whole experience is that when someone wants to send you a message that is verifiably from her only, she will use your public key and her private key to sign or encrypt that message; then she will deliver it to you.

You can then use the other user's public key and your private key to decrypt the message, and if you have verified that the other user's public key is truly hers (such as by looking at a certificate authority or finding it publicly posted on her website), then you can be certain the message is from her and not from a third party.

It kind of goes like this:

Say that Rebecca has her public and private keys and wants to encrypt a file to send to Robert. She uses her private key and Robert's public key to encrypt the file and then sends it to Robert.

Robert either has verified Rebecca's public key or does so and then uses his private key and her public key to decrypt the message.

It's the combination of the encrypter's private and the decrypter's public key that creates the encrypted file, and only the decrypter's private key can decrypt the file that was encrypted with the public key.

This is somewhat simplistic, but it is more than is needed for the scope of this book and the Linux+ exam.

Encryption and Hashing

The concept and practice of *encryption* just described is a two-way process. There is another method of encrypting something, involving *hashing* or using *message digests*, which enables you to effectively run math functions on an object to derive a hash sum. Then, anyone else who runs that same math or hash calculation on the object gets the same number.

Vendors use this method in practice when they post publicly available RPM and DPKG package files that they want users to download and use to patch their systems. If there were no method of verifying that these packages are authentic and have not been altered, applying them would be unwise. The vendor hash sums the packages and posts the sums, and when the user downloads the package, he runs the same hash calculation, and if he gets the same sum as the vendor, he knows the file is unaltered. If he gets a different sum, he should not trust the package and should report the issue to the vendor and re-obtain the package file from the vendor's source and do the calculation again.

Digital Signatures

Another example of the PKI concept is for *digital signatures*. PKI can be used to authoritatively sign a document, such as an employment contract or contract for services, while never having the document exist as paper or be physically signed.

A prime example of a digital signatures service is DocuSign, which allows you to upload a document and then invite someone to review and sign that document, entirely electronically, and have complete trust that the signed document will stand up in a court of law as the equivalent of a physically signed document.

Certificate Use Cases

The Linux+ exam objectives list three certificate use cases, two of which are covered in the previous section, certificate authentication and encryption. This section covers the third use case, SSL/TLS, by describing the differences between SSL and TLS and why the changeover is important to the security of the public and private Internet.

Secure Sockets Layer (*SSL*) and *Transport Layer Security* (*TLS*) are the technologies behind Hypertext Transfer Protocol Secure (HTTPS). HTTPS allows web clients and servers to connect in a secure manner. On a web server in which sensitive data is accessed, such as a banking site or an online shopping site, enabling these technologies is critical. Information-only websites to which users may log in also should have these technologies enabled to secure user account data. These technologies are also used to ensure that the web client is accessing the correct web server rather than some rogue web server masquerading as the real website.

SSL used to be alone in the field of securing web transactions, but TLS now encompasses SSL. Originally developed as a security protocol to allow browsers and servers to securely pass information to and from each other, this security layer is now considered essential for proper network citizens on the public Internet. One of the hallmarks of SSL encryption in a browser session is the telltale padlock icon to the left of the URL in the address, which appears when a session is properly established.

Authentication

Linux has come far from the days of just using the local **/etc/passwd** or user database file, and a key reason for this is the concept of pluggable or swappable authentication choices, many of which we will cover here, particularly those listed in the Linux+ exam objectives.

Multifactor Authentication

With *multifactor authentication* (*MFA*), a user must provide multiple bits of evidence to prove her identity. One common multifactor authentication method is called two-factor authentication, or 2FA. For this method, the user is required to provide two forms of identification, which could include the following:

- Something the user knows
- Something the user has
- Something that the user is

Another common multifactor method is two-step authentication. This requires the user to perform a primary authentication, such as providing a username and password, and then provide additional information from another source, such as an authentication token.

This section covers various topics related to multifactor authentication.

Tokens

A *token* is a unique value (typically either a number or an alphanumeric value) that is generated by either a hardware device or a software program. Tokens are typically automatically generated on an ongoing basis and normally are valid for only short periods of time, such as 30 seconds.

Hardware Tokens

A hardware token is a token that is generated by a hardware device. Typically it is a very small device, such as a key fob. A hardware token may have additional authentication methods, such as a fingerprint scanner, but this tends to be somewhat rare.

Software Tokens

A software token is a token that is generated by a program. A common example is an app on a mobile device.

OTP

One-time password (OTP) is an authentication technique that is often incorporated in two-factor authentication. It is also a technique that can be used in the event that a user has lost or forgotten his password.

Biometrics

Biometrics takes advantage of the "something that the person is" component of multifactor authentication. Fingerprint scanning, iris scanning, and identification based on other biological data can be used to verify a user's identity.

LDAP

Lightweight Directory Access Protocol (LDAP) is a protocol that provides directory services information. LDAP can be used to provide user account information, but it does not provide the full AAA functionality that RADIUS and TACACS+ provide. LDAP is also often used to store other information not directly related to user accounts, such as hostnames.

LDAP can be used to authenticate users, but when considering a security policy, you should realize that RADIUS and TACACS+ provide more robust solutions. For example, LDAP does not provide the accounting part of AAA that protocols like RADIUS and TACACS+ provide.

Pluggable Authentication Modules (PAMs)

Linux has come far from the days of just using the local **/etc/passwd** or user database file, and a key reason for this is the concept of *pluggable authentication modules (PAMs)*.

PAMs, which are used by a large superset of Unix/Linux systems for authentication, ensure that an overall common scheme or method is used by any number of applications, services, and so on. The alternative would be for every application or service to have its own method of authenticating.

PAMs are pluggable, meaning that the sysadmin or even the developer of a distribution can decide which methods are used and when, and that person can add mechanisms without necessarily replacing all authentication backend services for existing services and applications.

PAM doesn't work alone; it takes PAM-aware applications and services to work properly, and thanks to the very well-designed and implemented application programming interface (API), application programmers can insert minimal code into their applications to take advantage of the services of PAMs on a system.

Password Policies

By default, Linux requires a minimum password length of six characters, which is laughably simple in today's world of high computing power and compute clusters. It could take many years to brute-force crack a six-character password manually, but with a reasonable bot group or a supercomputer, it would take about four or five hours.

The password and other authentication-specific files that affect (and, well, effect!) authentication policy are the **/etc/pam.conf** file and the **/etc/pam.d** directory. This section focuses on DPKG/Debian system examples, which can be easily translated to RPM systems with a quick Google search.

PAM uses the **/etc/pam.conf** configuration file by default, and the configuration of services is laid out in lines or rules that follow this format:

```
service   type   control   module-path   module-arguments
```

The PAM configuration rules fields are as follows:

- *service*: The name of the application or service being affected, such as **su** or **login**.

- *type*: Made up of **account**, **auth**, **password**, and **session** options, the types separate and control the different types of requirements for the user to access a service. For example, the **auth** type establishes that the user is who she appears to be with a password prompt and handles group and other privileges being granted.

- *control*: This item governs what happens if a module can't successfully establish authentication. Configuration happens in **key:value** sets in brackets. Options include **required**, which denies access if authentication fails; **requisite**, which defers access back to the overall application; **sufficient**, which can fail while allowing authentication to still occur; and **optional**, which doesn't negatively affect authentication if it fails.

PAMs can additionally use service configuration files located in the **/etc/pam.d** directory, with each file being the configuration for a given service. In this case, the service name is the (all-lowercase) name of the file.

Password Length

An example of a PAM rule would be a rule that governs password length. Setting a ten-character password length requirement on a Linux system is as easy as editing the **/etc/pam.d/common-password** file and editing the following line:

```
password [success=2 default=ignore] pam_unix.so obscure sha512
```

so that it reads:

```
password [success=2 default=ignore] pam_unix.so obscure sha512
minlen=10
```

Pay special attention to the spacing and make sure to duplicate this line exactly, or it may error out.

LDAP Integration

In order to set up LDAP integration with PAM, there must be an LDAP server configured and available, and the **pam_user_map** module must be installed and available in the authentication server's PAM configuration.

The upshot of the integration is that you will be configuring LDAP authentication and then making a choice of whether to allow authentication for users on this system to occur solely via LDAP sources or to allow *either* local or LDAP authentication.

This is a complex subject, and while it's a worthwhile field of endeavor to pursue, it is beyond the scope of this book and the Linux+ exam.

User Lockouts

Another important feature of PAM is the ability to configure user or password lockout policy, essentially being able to stop brute-force password guessing by making the system stop allowing subsequent password tries until a timeout period has been met.

An example of setting a 10-minute timeout would entail editing the **/etc/pam.d/ system-auth** file by adding the following text to the **auth** line:

```
auth required pam_tally2.so deny=3 unlock_time=600
```

This requires a 10-minute timeout to occur after three unsuccessful password attempts by the same user. Such a measure will significantly slow down any brute-force system cracking attempts.

The /etc/pam.d Directory

For simpler systems, the **/etc/pam.conf** file should be sufficient for the configuration of PAM, but on more complex systems with many different services and more complex configurations, the **/etc/pam.d** directory is another choice.

Use of the **/etc/pam.d** directory or the presence of service files in that directory will cause a PAM to skip the use of the **/etc/pam.conf** file, so be very aware that even a *single* service file in **/etc/pam.d** will obviate any configuration in the **pam.conf** file.

The **/etc/pam.d** directory contains files that follow the general format of the lines in the **/etc/pam.conf** file, also called *rules*. The main difference is that whereas the **/etc/pam.conf** file has a line that begins with **service**, in the **/etc/pam.d** directory the name of the service rule file is the name of the service, and each of the files configures just that service.

Another great feature of a PAM is that it allows for the stacking or layering of configuration rules, and the failure of any of the stacked rules causes the authentication to fail, which safeguards the system.

pam_tally2 and faillock

One of the workhorses of a PAM system is the **pam_tally2** module, which comes as a separate module or a shared object (**.so**) and is designed to ensure that brute-force attacks fail so the system remains secure. This module is designed to count the number of attempts to gain access, refer to any timeouts configured, ensure that those timeouts are followed, and upon successful access, reset any failed attempt counters.

An important note about lockouts is that the root user is typically not configured to access the system through remote means, such as SSH, so in the default lockout configuration, the root user is *not* affected, as this would mean a root user who fumbles the login too many times would effectively be locked out of the system from the console—not a good thing!

The companion utility to this process is the **faillock** command, which allows the system operator to query, display, and make needed changes to the failed attempts that the **pam_faillock.so** module keeps in per-user listings in the tally directory structure.

For example, you might query a user named snuffyg's record of failed logging attempts with this command:

```
$ faillock -user snuffyg
```

If the user has too many failed login attempts and is currently in timeout, you can reset the user's failed login attempts back to zero and give the user a new start with the following:

```
$ faillock -user snuffyg --reset
```

System Security Services Daemon

The *System Security Services Daemon* (*SSSD*) is a PAM extension that allows and provides access to multiple possible authentication sources in a concentrated and purposeful manner.

SSSD is often used to allow a user to access one resource via a given authentication method, and access another resource using a different authentication method. In other words, the user takes on a "dual personality."

An example of this might be the local usage of authentication for a user of the system, while using a configured Active Directory remote authentication source for those systems or resources that require that authentication source.

SSSD is effectively a broker or one-stop shop that, when configured for multiple sources, will allow for relatively seamless authentication and access to the various resources.

Attributes that SSSD is well-known for (and you might have to identify on the exam!) include

- **Single source for authentication stores:** SSSD helps decrease performance issues from multiple authentication sources while increasing the possible available sources through a common framework.

- **Online and offline authentication options:** The option to locally cache an authentication token or proof while offline and then use that token or information to negotiate an updated token is a seriously helpful option for those with a lot of remote users.

- **Smoother Kerberos and SSO:** Those using Kerberos for single sign-on will have an easier time through the use of the offline caching configuration option.

Figure 8-1 shows how SSSD works conceptually.

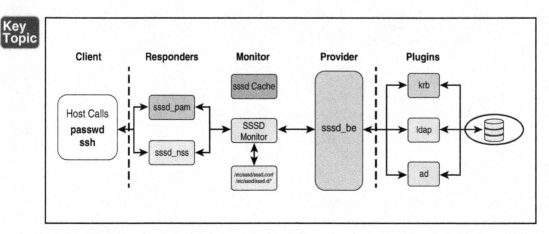

Figure 8-1   SSSD overview

In Figure 8-1, the requesters or client processes such as **ssh** and **passwd** will be configured to make their respective requests to a responder, one for each method. Those responders will interact with the SSSD monitor, configured by **/etc/sssd/sssd.conf** and its associated include directory and backed up by the SSSD cache, which will help with authentication via Kerberos and SSO when the system is offline from the backend authentication providers. Those backend authentication providers are serviced in turn by the appropriate plugin via the **sssd_be** or backend provider, which in turn takes the authentication request and matches it up with the appropriate source and brokers the request and response.

In short, the client process makes its usual request, and the SSSD process and its helpers make it happen, online or offline, in most cases.

Single Sign-On (SSO)

Single sign-on (SSO) is an authentication mechanism that permits a user to sign-in or authenticate into not just a single system or service, but rather to an environment of multiple connected and possibly synchronized data services.

At its simplest, SSO works by having an agent in an application that will request and store the user's authentication details, and act on that user's behalf as they work their way to various configured services in the environment.

There are multiple possible SSO providers, with more coming on the market all the time. Some of those providers are

- Microsoft

- OAuth

- OpenID

- MiniOrange

- Auth0

- Okta

- Ping

Single sign-on is essential for today's Software as a Service (SaaS) environments, which provide not just one service, but a combination or amalgamation of several to many services to give an integrated and comprehensive overall service to the users.

Linux Hardening

Hardening a Linux system is a multilayered scenario, with no one single thing that you can do to completely secure a Linux system from attack other than unplug it or remove the battery and make it impossible to power on.

One of the activities you can undertake is to harden our Linux system is to scan it for vulnerabilities, using tools such as the **nmap** or **nc** command.

The nmap Command

The **nmap** command is used to probe a remote system to determine which network ports are reachable from the local system. This is useful for many reasons, including

- Determining what services are available on the remote system

- Testing security features on the remote system, such as TCP wrappers

- Verifying the effectiveness of the network's firewall by executing **nmap** from a remote network

NOTE The **nmap** command is considered a port scanning tool. Scanning ports on systems that you don't have written authorization to scan can land you in trouble, as port scanning can be considered a hacking technique.

To use the **nmap** command, provide either the IP address or hostname of the system that you want to scan. For example, Example 8-1 shows the output of a scan performed on a router.

Example 8-1   The **nmap** Command

```
# nmap 192.168.1.1
Starting Nmap 7.8 ( http://nmap.org ) at 2022-1-31 23:22 PDT
Nmap scan report for 192.168.1.1
Host is up (2.9s latency).
Not shown: 987 closed ports
PORT       STATE SERVICE
23/tcp     open  telnet
25/tcp     open  smtp
53/tcp     open  domain
80/tcp     open  http
110/tcp    open  pop3
119/tcp    open  nntp
143/tcp    open  imap
465/tcp    open  smtps
563/tcp    open  snews
587/tcp    open  submission
993/tcp    open  imaps
995/tcp    open  pop3s
5000/tcp open   upnp
Nmap done: 1 IP address (1 host up) scanned in 4.89 seconds
```

The lines that describe the open ports start with the port number/protocol (for example, **23/tcp**) and end with the corresponding service (for example, **telnet**).

By default, only Transmission Control Protocol (TCP) ports are scanned. To scan User Datagram Protocol (UDP) ports, use the **-sU** option combination, as demonstrated in Example 8-2.

Example 8-2   Scanning UDP Ports

```
# nmap -sU 192.168.1.1
Starting Nmap 5.51 ( http://nmap.org ) at 2022-1-31 23:36 PDT
Nmap scan report for 192.168.1.1
Host is up (0.0011s latency).
Not shown: 999 open|filtered ports
PORT    STATE SERVICE
53/udp open   domain
Nmap done: 1 IP address (1 host up) scanned in 4.09 seconds
```

By default, only certain common ports (about 2,000 of them) are scanned. To scan all ports, use the command shown in Example 8-3 (and then take a coffee break because it could take a while to run).

Example 8-3   Scanning All Ports

```
# nmap -p 1-65535 192.168.1.1
Starting Nmap 5.51 ( http://nmap.org ) at 2022-1-01 00:26 PDT
Nmap scan report for 192.168.1.1
Host is up (1.0s latency).
Not shown: 65521 closed ports
PORT       STATE SERVICE
23/tcp     open  telnet
25/tcp     open  smtp
53/tcp     open  domain
80/tcp     open  http
110/tcp    open  pop3
119/tcp    open  nntp
143/tcp    open  imap
465/tcp    open  smtps
563/tcp    open  snews
587/tcp    open  submission
993/tcp    open  imaps
995/tcp    open  pop3s
1780/tcp   open  unknown
5000/tcp   open  upnp
Nmap done: 1 IP address (1 host up) scanned in 5731.44 seconds
```

Typically a port has an associated local service. The **nmap** command can also probe these services to determine what version of the service is available. This feature isn't available for all services, but for those that it is available for, it can provide useful information. Use the **-sV** option combination to see service version information, as shown in Example 8-4.

Example 8-4   Scanning Service Version Information

```
# nmap -sV 192.168.1.1
Starting Nmap 7.8( http://nmap.org ) at 2022-1-01 09:41 PST
Nmap scan report for 192.168.1.1
Host is up (1.0s latency).
Not shown: 987 closed ports
PORT       STATE SERVICE       VERSION
23/tcp     open  telnet?
25/tcp     open  smtp?
53/tcp     open  domain        dnsmasq 2.15-OpenDNS-1
###Remaining output omitted
```

Say that you discover a machine with IP address 192.168.1.11 on your network, but you don't even know what sort of system it is. One of the benefits of the **nmap** command is that it might provide a clue as to what sort of system this is by probing it. For example, executing the **nmap** command on that IP address can provide you with an idea of what sort of system a machine is, as demonstrated in Example 8-5.

Example 8-5   Probing a Machine

```
# nmap -sU 192.168.1.11
Starting Nmap 7.8 ( http://nmap.org ) at 2022-1-31 23:38 PDT
Nmap scan report for 192.168.1.11
Host is up (0.00045s latency).
Not shown: 992 filtered ports
PORT        STATE           SERVICE
67/udp    open|filtered dhcps
137/udp   open            netbios-ns
138/udp   open|filtered netbios-dgm
443/udp   open|filtered https
1900/udp  open|filtered upnp
4500/udp  open|filtered nat-t-ike
5353/udp  open|filtered zeroconf
5355/udp  open|filtered llmnr
Nmap done: 1 IP address (1 host up) scanned in 52.23 seconds
```

Given that **netbios-ns** and some of the other services listed in this output are Microsoft Windows-based services, it is likely that Windows is the operating system of this unknown system.

In some cases, you might be able to use the **-O** option to determine the operating system type, but it isn't always successful, as demonstrated in Example 8-6.

Example 8-6   Attempting to Determine the Operating System Type

```
# nmap -O 192.168.1.11
###Output omitted
Aggressive OS guesses: QEMU user mode network gateway (91%),
  Bay Networks BayStack 450 switch (software version 3.1.0.22) (85%),
  Bay Networks BayStack 450 switch (software version 4.2.0.16) (85%),
  Cabletron ELS100-24TXM Switch or Icom IC-7800 radio transceiver
(85%),
  Cisco Catalyst 1900 switch or RAD IPMUX-1 TDM-over-IP
```

```
     multiplexer (85%), Sanyo PLC-XU88 digital video projector (85%),
     3Com SuperStack 3 Switch 4300, Dell PowerEdge 2650 remote access
     controller, Samsung ML-2571N or 6555N printer, or Xerox Phaser 3125N
     printer (85%), Dell 1815dn printer (85%)
No exact OS matches for host (test conditions non-ideal).
OS detection performed. Please report any incorrect results at
http://nmap.org/submit/ .
Nmap done: 1 IP address (1 host up) scanned in 15.37 seconds
```

So, how did you discover that 192.168.1.11 machine in the first place? Another useful feature of the **nmap** command is its capability to scan an entire network to determine which IP addresses are in use. To perform this operation, use the **-sP** option combination, as demonstrated in Example 8-7.

Example 8-7   Probing a Network

```
# nmap -sP 192.168.1.0/24
Starting Nmap 7.8 ( http://nmap.org ) at 2022-1-31 23:51 PDT
Nmap scan report for 192.168.1.0
Host is up (0.00043s latency).
Nmap scan report for 192.168.1.1
Host is up (0.0026s latency).
Nmap scan report for 192.168.1.2
Host is up (0.70s latency).
Nmap scan report for 192.168.1.3
Host is up (0.045s latency).
Nmap scan report for 192.168.1.4
Host is up (0.043s latency).
Nmap scan report for 192.168.1.7
Host is up (0.00011s latency).
Nmap scan report for 192.168.1.11
Host is up (0.0020s latency).
Nmap scan report for 192.168.1.12
Host is up (0.00013s latency).
Nmap scan report for 192.168.1.14
Host is up (3.7s latency).
Nmap scan report for 192.168.1.16
Host is up (0.00088s latency).
```

You can even see information about your own system, including a list of network interfaces and the routing table, by using the **--iflist** option, as shown in Example 8-8.

Example 8-8   Listing Network Interfaces

```
# nmap --iflist

Starting Nmap 7.8 ( http://nmap.org ) at 2022-1-01 09:39 PST
************************INTERFACES************************
DEV   (SHORT) IP/MASK        TYPE      UP MTU   MAC
lo    (lo)    127.0.0.1/8    loopback  up 65536
eth0  (eth0)  10.0.2.15/24   ethernet  up 1500  08:00:27:E0:E2:DE


*************************ROUTES**************************
DST/MASK      DEV  GATEWAY
10.0.2.0/24 eth0
0.0.0.0/0   eth0 10.0.2.2
```

The nc Command

The man page of the **nc** command (also referred to as the **netcat** command) provides an excellent summary of the **nc** command:

> The **nc** (or **netcat**) utility is used for just about anything under the sun involving TCP or UDP. It can open TCP connections, send UDP packets, listen on arbitrary TCP and UDP ports, do port scanning, and deal with both IPv4 and IPv6. Unlike **telnet(1)**, **nc** scripts nicely and separates error messages onto standard error instead of sending them to standard output, as **telnet(1)** does with some.

There are quite a few uses for the **nc** command. For example, suppose you want to know whether a specific port is being blocked by your company firewall before you bring online a service that makes use of this port. On the internal server, you can have the **nc** command listen for connections on that port:

```
# nc -l 3333
```

You should end up with a blank line below the **nc** command. Next, on a remote system outside your network, you could run the following **nc** command to connect (replacing *server* with the resolvable hostname or IP address of the local system):

```
# nc server 3333
```

If the connection is established, you see a blank line under the **nc** command line. If you type something on this blank line and press the **Enter** key, then what you typed appears below the **nc** command on the server. Actually, the communications works both ways: What you type on the server below the **nc** command appears on the client as well.

The following are some useful options to the **nc** command:

- **-w:** This option is used on the client side to close a connection automatically after a timeout value is reached. For example, **nc -w 30 server 333** closes the connection 30 seconds after it is established.

- **-6:** Use this option to enable IPv6 connections.

- **-k:** Use this option to keep the server process active, even after the client disconnects. The default behavior is to stop the server process when the client disconnects.

- **-u:** Use this option to use UDP connections rather than TCP connections (the default). This is important for correctly testing firewall configurations, as a TCP port might be blocked while the UDP port might not be blocked.

You can also use the **nc** command to display open ports, similar to the way you use the **netstat** command:

```
# nc -z localhost 1000-4000
Connection to localhost 3260 port [tcp/iscsi-target] succeeded!
Connection to localhost 3333 port [tcp/dec-notes] succeeded!
```

The **-z** option can also be used for port scanning on a remote host.

NOTE There is one feature of the **nc** command that I don't expect you will see on the exam; however, it is a useful technique for transferring all sorts of data. Assuming that the transfer is from the client to the server, on the server, you use the following format:

```
nc -l 3333 | cmd
```

And on the client, you use this format:

```
cmd | nc server 3333
```

For example, you can transfer an entire **/home** directory structure from the client to the server, using the **tar** command, by first executing the following on the server:

```
nc -l 333 | tar xvf -
```

Then on the client, you execute the following command:

```
tar cvf - /home | nc server 333
```

The client merges the contents of the **/home** directory structure into a tarball. The - tells the **tar** command to send this output to standard output. The data is sent to the server via the client's **nc** command, and then the server's **nc** command sends this data to the **tar** command. As a result, the **/home** directory from the client is copied into the current directory of the server.

This is just one technique of many for using this powerful feature of the **nc** command.

Secure Boot and UEFI

Please see Chapter 1, "Understanding Linux Fundamentals," section "Booting with UEFI."

System Logging Configurations

Please refer to Chapter 7, "Managing Software Configurations," for coverage of the system logging scenario in the section "System Logging with Syslog."

Using umask

If your system is a typical Linux system, a value is set in either the **/etc/bashrc** file or the **~/.bashrc** file that governs the default permissions of any created object. This value is known as the *umask*, and this single value is used to determine default permissions for both directories and files. The umask applies only when you create a new file or directory.

The maximum default permissions for directories and files are different, which means the umask value results in different default permissions for files than it does for directories. The default permissions with no umask value set are

- **For files:** rw-rw-rw- (or 666)

- **For directories:** rwxrwxrwx (or 777)

View the umask for your current shell by executing the following command:

```
# umask
0022
```

This just means that of the four possible positions to mask out (special permissions, user owner permissions, group owner permissions, and other permissions), the last two have the write permission masked out or not used. Note that the first position never has any effect because the special permissions are never set by default. As a result, the umask value of 0022 is really the same as 022.

If you create a file when the umask is set to 022, the file's permissions are as follows:

```
-rw-r--r-- 1 root root 881 Feb 17 09:11 file1
```

If you create a directory with the same umask set, the directory's permissions are as follows:

```
drwxr-xr-x 2 root root 4096 Feb 17 14:47 dir1
```

To understand why these permission sets are different, think about the process of how the umask is applied. To begin with, recall the default permissions:

	For Files	For Directories
Maximum	rw-rw-rw-	rwxrwxrwx

Now, consider a umask value of 022. This means you are "masking out," or removing, the write permissions for the group owner and others (represented by the M values here):

	For Files	For Directories
Maximum	rw-rw-rw-	rwxrwxrwx
MASK	----M--M-	----M--M-

When those permissions are masked out, you end up getting the following permissions on new files and directories:

	For Files	For Directories
Maximum	rw-rw-rw-	rwxrwxrwx
MASK	----M--M-	----M--M-
Result	rw-r--r--	rw-r--r--

As you can see, the umask value changes the default permissions of a created object based on the following formula:

```
Maximum default value - umask value = create value
```

You can change the umask value to a more restrictive one with the **umask 027** command.

Now, you can create another file, and the permissions should be

```
-rw-r----- 1 root root 881 Feb 17 09:22 file2
```

Create another directory with the umask value 027, and the permissions should be

```
drwxr-x--- 2 root root 4096 Feb 17 14:48 dir2
```

Notice in the previous example that the umask has a value greater than the default value of the file being created. The umask values go from 000 to 777 because a directory object has a maximum default value of 777; however, a file has a maximum default value of 666. The umask value must encompass both sets of possible values, so if you have a 7 in a umask value, it affects the file default permission as if it were a 6. In other words, in this case 6 – 7 = 0.

Expect to see the umask value on the Linux+ exam. For example, you might see a question that provides a file permission listing and asks you to provide the umask value that resulted in those permissions. To become familiar with how umask values work, try different scenarios to determine what the result would be. Use the following chart and plug in different values for your umask value for practice:

	For Files	For Directories
Default	rw-rw-rw-	rwxrwxrwx
MASK		
Result		

Finally, it is important to note that while all of your shells initially have the same umask value, you can change this value in one shell without affecting the umask values in other shells. Recall that this value is initially set via an initialization file (typically either **/etc/bashrc** or **~/.bashrc**).

Disabling/Removing Insecure Services

We have covered how to disable, mask, and remove services in Chapter 4, "Managing Processes and Services."

A quick note about unsecure services: there are some obvious ones, such as Telnet and FTP, that are *not* secure, and have been replaced by the SSH suite of commands. Conduct your own research in your test or production environment to determine which services are unsecure, and use the knowledge you gain here to manage them.

Enforcing Password Strength

Password strength is another of those simple phrases that has some complexity underlying it. Passwords are how we control who has access to what on the system, and there are ways that we can make sure that passwords are not only strong but also a moving target for those who might want to try to brute-force attack a system by guessing passwords.

There are three main things I recommend to system managers to ensure their passwords are strong and solid:

- Set initial password options
- Routinely age passwords
- Never use group passwords

Setting Password Parameters

Probably the most important file for establishing and maintaining password strength is **/etc/login.defs**. It's the configuration file for the Shadow Suite, which is the piece of a Linux system that manages the actual password or **/etc/shadow** file and contains the settings or rules that must be followed by anything that works with passwords.

The **/etc/login.defs** file has a lot of very important parameters, and it's where you set the ground rules for the type, length, encryption, and many other parameters for your system's passwords. It is a text file, easily read and parsed, and editable with the proper account and permissions.

Important settings in **/etc/login.defs** include

- **ENCRYPT_METHOD:** This sets the encryption algorithm for the group passwords. Possible values are DES, MD5, SHA256, and SHA512. The PAM (covered earlier in this chapter) governs user account passwords.
- **FAIL_DELAY:** This very important setting determines how long you have to wait before you can attempt another login after a password fails.
- **LOG_OK_LOGINS:** Normally only failed logins are recorded, but this setting allows for logging of *all* logins, successes and failures.
- **LOGIN_RETRIES:** This sets the maximum number of retries if a bad password is detected, usually three, but this is also normally governed by PAM.

Aging Your Passwords

Users' passwords need to be changed frequently enough that attackers don't have sufficient time to guess them. Most users just want to get their work done; system security is of much lower importance to them than convenience, and they consider having to change their passwords an inconvenience, so forcing them to do so is necessary.

To age passwords properly, use the **chage** command. The syntax for the **chage** command is

```
chage -option value username
```

This command acts on fields in the **/etc/shadow** file and has the following options:

- **-m:** Changes the minimum value, or how long after a password is changed that the user must wait until it can be changed again.

- **-M:** Changes the maximum value, which is the maximum number of days that can go by before the user must change the password.

- **-d:** Changes the last change value, which is the number of days since January 1, 1970, that the password was last changed. This is rarely modified directly; when a password is changed with the **passwd** command, this value is automatically updated.

- **-E:** Changes the expiration value, which is the number of days since January 1, 1970, that represents the day the user's account will be disabled. The format used is *YYYY-MM-DD*.

- **-I:** Changes the inactive value, or the number of days of inactivity (no logins) after the account has reached the maximum limit before the user account is locked, at which point root attention will be required to reenable the account. Setting this to **0** disables the feature.

- **-W:** Changes the warning value, or the number of days before the user must change her password. This warning is provided only when the user logs in to the system.

Thankfully, you don't have to memorize these values except to know them for potential Linux+ exam questions. Just execute the **chage username** command as the root user, and the system prompts you interactively for each value that can be configured for the specified user.

Users can use the **-l** option to view their own information, or the root user can view another user's information with this option:

```
# chage -l snuffy
```

This produces the following output:

```
Minimum: 0
Maximum: 99999
Warning: 7
Inactive: -1
Last Change: Mar 19, 2022
Password Expires: Never
Password Inactive: Never
Account Expires: Never
```

The **passwd** utility includes some of the previous options, such as these:

- **-d:** Disables a user account by removing its password.

- **-n:** Sets the minimum password lifetime, in days.

- **-x:** Sets the maximum password lifetime, in days.

- **-w:** Sets the warning number of days before the password expires.

- **-i:** Sets the number of days an account with an expired password can be inactive before it's locked.

- **-S:** Shows the user password information, such as what encryption is used and whether a password is set.

No Wire Hangers (Group Passwords)

Passwords are usually the domain of individual accounts, but in some cases you might want to have a group password, to allow users to change groups and possibly allow users to change their primary group.

Group passwords are a big security risk, and although they might be useful in certain atypical circumstances, they often cause security audits to flag their presence and should normally be avoided.

Removing Unused Packages

Having packages installed that are not necessary to the functioning of your system during its normal operations is a simple but common issue.

If you are not sure whether you need a particular package, there are ways to find out when the package was last installed or updated, but those methods are like mining for a needle in a haystack. It's best to run a listing of all your installed packages, and if you don't know what something is, run a package info command on it. The exact command to run depends on the Linux distribution, but as an example, on a RPM system you could use the command and options shown in Example 8-9.

Example 8-9   View Package Details

```
# rpm -qi vim-enhanced

Name          : vim-enhanced
Epoch         : 2
Version       : 8.2.4485
Release       : 1.fc34
Architecture  : x86_64
Install Date  : Thu 07 Apr 2022 10:19:16 PM MDT
Group         : Unspecified
Size          : 4438331
License       : Vim and MIT
Signature     : RSA/SHA256, Tue 01 Mar 2022 05:13:56 AM MST, Key ID
                1161ae6945719a39
Source RPM    : vim-8.2.4485-1.fc34.src.rpm
Build Date    : Tue 01 Mar 2022 05:00:15 AM MST
Build Host    : buildhw-x86-07.iad2.fedoraproject.org
Packager      : Fedora Project
Vendor        : Fedora Project
URL           : http://www.vim.org/
Bug URL       : https://bugz.fedoraproject.org/vim
Summary       : A version of the VIM editor which includes recent
enhancements
Description   :
VIM (VIsual editor iMproved) is an updated and improved version of the
vi editor.  Vi was the first real screen-based editor for UNIX, and
is still very popular.  VIM improves on vi by adding new features:
multiple windows, multi-level undo, block highlighting and more.  The
vim-enhanced package contains a version of VIM with extra, recently
introduced features like Python and Perl interpreters.
```

As you can see, there is a great deal of information shown about the package, such as when it was built, installed, and so on.

You can also look at the various logs that package managers such as YUM, ZYpp, RPM, APT use to store the information about what is installed. Those logs vary by package manager, so look at the man pages for the particular command and search for keywords such as "installed" and so forth.

Tuning Kernel Parameters

Please refer to Chapter 7 for coverage of how to set and tune the kernel's parameters, in the section "Configuring Kernel Options."

Securing Service Accounts

A service account is similar to a user account except that a service account is not configured to have someone log in as that account. A service account is used solely for a service to have an account owner for security, and it should never show up as having been logged in.

The **lastlog** command shows information formatted with the following headers:

```
Username    Port    From    Latest
```

The command shows you an entry for every user account or service account that exists in the **/etc/passwd** file. Most of these accounts will have not logged in or should never log in, as they are service account for managing and owning processes, not user accounts. This is problematic in that you have to sort through a lot of output where the last field, **Latest**, shows the text **"Never logged in"** and only down at the bottom do you see actual users' data.

Probably my favorite use of the **grep** command (other than to search for swear words in the kernel source code, that is) is to use the **-v** (inverse) option, which shows you everything that does *not* match what you just searched for.

For example, you can use **-v** on the **lastlog** command output to mask out any line of output that contains the string **"Never logged in"**, thereby showing only the users that have logged in:

```
# lastlog | grep -v "Never logged in"
Username    Port    From              Latest
ross        pts/1   192.168.33.144    Wed, Feb 22, 08:20 -0700 2022
ulogin      pts/2   192.168.33.88     Wed, Feb 22, 07:10 -0700 2022
shaggy      pts/3   192.168.33.76     Wed, Feb 22, 05:50 -0700 2022
```

Note that if you run this command and see that a service account, such as **ntp**, **systemd-network**, or **kernoops**, has logged in, you should immediately start investigating why. Service-related accounts are not supposed to be used to log in, so such a login indicates some sort of system hack.

Configuring the Host Firewall

You can see the entire set of information about configuring firewalls in Chapter 10, "Implementing and Configuring Firewalls."

Summary

In this chapter you learned about how to apply Linux security best practices to your systems to protect your communications and data, through such technologies as PKI, certificates, SSL/TLS, authentication options such as tokens, PAM, SSSD, and SSO.

You also learned how to harden or more tightly secure a Linux system by applying best practices that remove vulnerabilities, remove unused packages, tighten up password policies, and ensure you can find issues that need to be fixed.

Exam Preparation Tasks

As mentioned in the section "Goals and Methods" in the Introduction, you have a couple of choices for exam preparation: the exercises here, Chapter 23, "Final Preparation," and the exam simulation questions in the Pearson Test Prep Software Online.

Review All Key Topics

Review the most important topics in this chapter, noted with the Key Topic icon in the left margin of the page. Table 8-2 lists these key topics and the page number on which each is found.

Table 8-2   Key Topics for Chapter 8

Key Topic Element	Description	Page Number
Paragraph	To understand PKI, let's use the open Web as an example	321
Paragraph	One of the other methods of using PKI...	321
Paragraph	The concept and practice of encryption...	322
Paragraph	SSL and TLS are the technologies...	323
Paragraph	With multifactor authentication, a user must...	324
Paragraph	LDAP provides directory services information	325
Paragraph	PAM uses the **/etc/pam.conf** configuration file by default	326
Paragraph	Use of the **/etc/pam.d** directory or the presence of service files...	328
Figure 8-1	SSSD overview	330
Paragraph	Single sign-on is how you permit a user to sign on or authenticate...	330
Paragraph	Viewing the umask for your current shell	338
Paragraph	Probably the most important file for establishing and maintaining password strength is...	341
Paragraph	Using the **chage** command to age passwords properly	342
Paragraph	I like to show people how to use the **lastlog** command...	345

Define Key Terms

Define the following key terms from this chapter and check your answers in the glossary:

certificate authentication, self-signed certificate, certificate authority, private key, public key, encryption, hashing, digital signature, Secure Sockets Layer (SSL), Transport Layer Security (TLS), multifactor authentication (MFA), token, Lightweight Directory Access Protocol (LDAP), pluggable authentication modules (PAMs), System Security Services Daemon (SSSD), single sign-on (SSO)

Review Questions

The answers to these review questions are in Appendix A.

1. Secure Sockets Layer is now encompassed within what suite of security protocols?

    a. Polynomial Security Services

    b. Security Services Protocols

    c. Multifactor Token Authentication

    d. Transport Layer Security

2. In public key infrastructure, what does a client or host need from the other system in order to properly encrypt or decrypt data?

    a. Hashed key

    b. Public key

    c. Secure key

    d. Private key

3. Which command is used to set the effective permissions mask for files and folders on a Linux system?

    a. fmask

    b. chgmask

    c. setmask

    d. umask

4. Besides being controlled by local authorities, what advantage does using self-signed certificates offer your organization?

    a. Ease of configuration

    b. Support options

    c. Standards compliance

    d. Lesser costs

5. To enforce the use of SSL/TLS on a web server means which of the following protocols should be used?

    a. SSH

    b. SSH

    c. HTTPS

    d. gopher

6. Which of the following are valid control values for use in the pluggable authentication modules configuration files? (Choose all that apply.)

    a. **requisite**

    b. **supposed**

    c. **efficient**

    d. **optional**

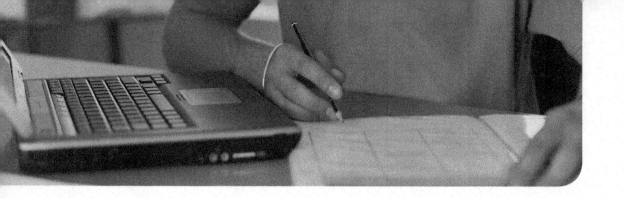

This chapter covers the following topics:

- Account Creation and Deletion
- Account Management

The exam objective covered in this chapter is as follows:

- **Objective 2.2:** Given a scenario, implement identity management

## CHAPTER 9

Implementing Identity Management

Accounts and identity are at the heart of a Linux system. No processes can be executed outside of the kernel without being associated or "owned" by an account, be it a service account or a user account.

Along with accounts come groups, passwords, all the associated *configuration files* that define accounts and groups, templates for user home directories, user and group management commands, and commands that affect the overall environment.

Many of the commands are designed to be used by a root user, but some are also dual-use, where different sets of privileges are available depending on the user running the command.

"Do I Know This Already?" Quiz

The "Do I Know This Already?" quiz enables you to assess whether you should read this entire chapter or simply jump to the "Exam Preparation Tasks" section for review. If you are in doubt, read the entire chapter. Table 9-1 outlines the major headings in this chapter and the corresponding "Do I Know This Already?" quiz questions. You can find the answers in Appendix A, "Answers to the 'Do I Know This Already?' Quizzes and Review Questions."

Table 9-1 "Do I Know This Already?" Foundation Topics Section-to-Question Mapping

Foundation Topics Section	Questions Covered in This Section
Account Creation and Deletion	1–2
Account Management	3–4

CAUTION The goal of self-assessment is to gauge your mastery of the topics in this chapter. If you do not know the answer to a question or are only partially sure of the answer, you should mark that question as wrong for purposes of the self-assessment. Giving yourself credit for an answer you correctly guess skews your self-assessment results and might provide you with a false sense of security.

1. Which **useradd** option can you use to specify the user's login shell?

   a. -m

   b. -d

   c. -k

   d. -s

2. Which command enables you to change password aging for a user account?

   a. **usermod**

   b. **chage**

   c. **passwd**

   d. **gpass**

3. You are about to add dozens of users to a given test system and want them all to have a particular set of files in their home directory upon login. Where would you stage these files so that they are included in a new user's home directory when the user is created?

   a. **/home/newusers**

   b. **/etc/default/useradd**

   c. **/etc/skel**

   d. **/usr/baredir**

4. On modern Linux systems, which file stores the user account passwords?

   a. **/etc/passwd**

   b. **/etc/security**

   c. **/etc/shausers**

   d. **/etc/shadow**

Foundation Topics

Account Creation and Deletion

> **NOTE** I've been working on describing and demonstrating this set of information for about 30 years now, and regardless of what the order of the items is in the Linux+ objectives, I will be presenting this in my own flow and order, which I have found works very well and is very understandable that way. I hope you enjoy my way of presenting the topics.
>
> In this chapter you will explore the topic of identity management. You will learn how to create and manage user and group accounts. This will include exploring a variety of account-based commands and account-based configuration files.

User Account Fundamentals

User and group accounts are not known to the kernel by the names humans use and see but by the *user ID* (*UID*) and *group ID* (*GID*) associated with the name. Early versions of the kernel supported two tables of static numbers representing up to 65,536 users and 65,536 groups. Then, the 2.6 kernel made available 4,294,967,296 possible users and groups.

The only associations between the username and the UID are entries in the */etc/passwd* file that defines users. The only associations between the group name and the GID are entries in the */etc/group* file that defines groups.

A user must have a username entry in the **/etc/passwd** file to log in to the system. Users cannot log in using their UID; only the username is accepted.

What Accounts Are What?

The **/etc/passwd** file contains a number of system accounts, all of which are assigned UIDs that range from 0 to 499. Some of the most interesting accounts (which are also most likely to be on the Linux+ exam) are shown here:

- **0:** The root user on the system.
- **1:** The bin user, which is responsible for some system binaries and non-login accounts.
- **48:** The apache user; the HTTPD daemon runs as apache.
- **99:** The nobody account, which is used for many things. It is mainly used for anonymous access on FTP and HTTP servers, but it also maps to root accounts that attempt NFS access to shares that have been configured to deny access to the root user.

> **NOTE**   I normally assign to my junior sysadmin and server operator accounts UIDs in the 500–1000 range, just to differentiate them from the other users and to make keeping track of them easier. Users with UIDs in the 500–1000 range don't automatically gain special privileges. However, these are the accounts that I set up to have extra access by using the **sudo** command.

Regular User Accounts

We never say "normal" users, the joke being no user is normal! With that in mind, typical users are assigned UIDs ranging from 500 to 65,000. This is fine for a single system, but it can cause problems in larger environments.

If you have the need to allow for both local user accounts and network accounts (for using NFS and NIS), it is a good idea to assign to network accounts UIDs that start at the five-digit UID mark—in other words, with UIDs from 10,000 to 65,000—and assign to local user accounts UIDs from 500 to 9,999. Such a scheme provides more structure in your UID numbering system.

> **NOTE**   If you can, force the use of a standardized UID and GID structure across all your enterprise systems. If you have more than 100 users, consider using LDAP for managing how users log on to their systems. The now deprecated NIS and the newer LDAP methods are beyond the scope of this discussion and not on the Linux+ exam objectives, but they provide great ways to centralize account and password management across all machines in an environment.

If you are working on a system that has both network and local accounts, displaying user account information can be tricky. Local user account data is stored in local files, such as the **/etc/passwd** and **/etc/shadow** files. Network account information is stored in databases located on a server. One command, **getent**, can be used as follows to search both local and network sources for account information:

```
# getent passwd ross
```

This command searches both local and network sources in an order determined by the **/etc/nsswitch.conf** file:

```
passwd: files nis
shadow: files nis
```

files nis means "search local files first and then search the database for the specified value."

User Entries in /etc/passwd

A user's entry in the **/etc/passwd** file consists of the following:

```
ross:x:500:100:Ross Brunson:/home/ross:/bin/bash
```

The entries in the **/etc/passwd** file are as follows:

- **ross:** The username; this must be eight or fewer characters and should be lowercase.

- **x:** Passwords used to be stored in this file. The **x** value tells the system that the password for this account is now stored in the **/etc/shadow** file. For security reasons, the password should never be in the **/etc/passwd** file on modern Linux systems.

- **500:** The user's UID.

- **100:** The user's *primary group*. This group is used as the group owner of all the file objects created by this user account, except in situations where ownership inheritance has been set.

- **Ross Brunson:** This field is a description field (also known as the *GE Common Operating System*, or *GECOS*, for historical purposes). It can be blank or can have a comment or a full name in it.

- **/home/ross:** The home directory field is used to define the complete path to the user's home directory.

- **/bin/bash:** This field defines the login shell for the user.

> **NOTE** The GECOS field is normally just used for simple comments. However, historically it was used to specify more complex data, including useful information like the user's name, office location, and phone number. This information (and other user information) could be displayed with the **finger** command.

Special Login Files

Several files affect the user's login experience and define when a user can log in and from where. These files are as follows:

- **/bin/false:** If the user's shell is set to **/bin/false**, the user cannot log in. This is best used for system accounts that should never be logged in to.

- **/sbin/nologin:** When used as a login shell for a user's account, this program displays a message that the account is unavailable and exits with a nonzero exit code. If the **/etc/nologin.txt** file exists, the contents of that file are shown instead of the standard message.

- **/etc/motd:** After a successful login, the **/etc/motd** file contents are displayed, right before the user's shell is executed. This is a great place for warning and legal messages to be displayed.

- **.hushlogin:** This file, if created in the user's home directory, changes the login process so it does not perform a mail check and does not display the last login information or the message of the day to the user.

- **/etc/login.defs:** This file defines the defaults for when users are created using the **useradd** command. These defaults include entries for mail, password complexity and limitations, UID and GID minimum and maximum values, and whether the user's home directory is created by default.

- **/etc/securetty:** This file specifies from where the root user is allowed to log in. If it does not exist, root can log in from any location.

- **/etc/usertty:** This file is used to set the parameters for login locations, days, times, and systems the user can connect from. The **/etc/usertty** file is used only on systems that don't have *PAMs* (*pluggable authentication modules*).

pam_tally2 and faillock

The **pam_tally2** module and **faillock** command are covered in Chapter 8, "Understanding Linux Security Best Practices," as part of the discussion of pluggable authentication modules.

Group Accounts

A group is a grouping of users. No nesting of groups is possible in Linux or Unix. Users are associated with groups using two methods:

- **Primary:** A GID appears in the **/etc/passwd** file entry in the fourth field; this group is made the group owner of all created objects (files, directories, and so on) for this user. The primary group for a user is special; if a user is assigned a primary group in the **/etc/passwd** file, she does not have to be listed as a member in the **/etc/group** file because the GID in the **/etc/passwd** entry complements the secondary group membership defined in the **/etc/group** file.

- **Secondary:** If a user's name appears in the **/etc/group** entry for a group, the user is a member of that group, and she gets access to the objects of which that group is the group owner. The last field of each entry of the **/etc/group** file stores the secondary member list.

Groups are assigned GIDs, just as user accounts are assigned UIDs. The following are a few important GIDs:

- **0:** The root group. Anyone who is a member of this group has access to resources restricted to the root account.

- **1:** The bin group, which is similar to the bin user account.

- **100:** The users group, where you can place regular users and then give them access to resources by assigning that group ownership of things that all users should have access to.

NOTE On BSD-related systems (recall that BSD is a Unix flavor), a user cannot use the **su** command unless her account is a member of the wheel group, even if she knows the root password. This wheel group feature is not implemented by default on Linux systems, but the group is there for compatibility. Many administrators use the wheel group on Linux to create a sort of "administrator group" and provide special access to commands via the **sudo** command.

A special situation exists primarily on Red Hat-based systems when a user account is created without a specific primary group assigned. In this case, the system creates and assigns a group whose GID should match the number of the user's UID (although if that GID is not available, the next incremented number available would be used) and whose group name should be the same as the user account name. This type of group is called a *user private group* (*UPG*).

A UPG is a security feature. If you have created a user and haven't assigned her to a primary group, the system might assign her to the users group as a primary group. This is a security risk because this user might be a contractor or an auditor who should not, by default, have access to the users group's resources.

However, a UPG can also cause security issues. If a user is the only member of this private group, it is difficult for the user to share file objects with others. Users are forced to share their files with everyone (the others permission set) to be able to share files with one other person.

Debian-based systems don't use UPGs but rather assign new accounts to the users (100) group by default.

In reality, both of these systems pose security issues. The best solution is to create groups for people who need to share files and place the appropriate users in the correct groups. This approach requires more work for the administrator but leads to better security.

Group Entries in **/etc/group**

The entries in the **/etc/group** file are much simpler and shorter than the ones in the **/etc/passwd** file. A group file consists of the following fields:

```
users:x:100:ross,snuffy
```

The entries in a group file are

- **users:** The name of the group, which should be eight or fewer characters and lowercase.

- **x:** Like user passwords, group passwords are kept in a separate file. The group passwords are in **/etc/gshadow**. (Note that while understanding this file can be useful, it is not a Linux+ exam objective and is not covered further in this book.)

- **GID:** This is the system's number for this group and is resolved (translated) to the group name for user viewing convenience.

- **ross,snuffy:** Users in the group are listed one after the other, separated with commas (,); no spaces should occur. This list defines secondary group membership.

Group Passwords

A user can have only a single primary group; a user who needs to create an object that has to be assigned to another group can use the **chgrp** command. For a single file, this is easy, but if the user wants to create a bunch of files owned by a different group, this technique can be tedious.

Another option is for a user to temporarily change his or her primary group with the **newgrp** command. For example:

```
# newgrp users
```

The **newgrp** command doesn't alter the **/etc/passwd** file or the **/etc/group** file; it opens a new shell with a different primary group. By default, a user can use the **newgrp** command to temporarily change her primary group to any group she is a member of. After creating the necessary files, the user can return to the shell that has the default primary group by executing the **exit** command. Keep in mind that users can change only to groups of which they are secondary members.

A password can be assigned to a group with the **gpasswd** command, but there is only one password, and you have to give it to every user who needs to use this functionality. Once a group is assigned a password, users need to use the password to execute the **newgrp** command, even if the user is a member of that group.

Adding Users and Groups

Although you can edit the **/etc/passwd** and **/etc/group** files directly, doing so can lead to serious problems if you make errors in these files. It is much safer to use the commands described in the following sections.

Adding Users with **useradd**

The *useradd* command is used to create new user accounts. To add a user with the default values (default primary GID, default home directory, and so on), execute the following command:

```
# useradd snuffy
```

Currently, on a Red Hat machine, this command performs several operations, including the following:

- It creates the user snuffy with the next available UID (typically the next available UID above 500).

- It creates a group with the same group name and GID as the username and UID.

- It sets the user's primary GID to the newly created group.

- It creates a home directory for the user under the **/home** directory and with the same name as the username (**/home/snuffy** in this case).

- It copies the contents of the **/etc/skel** directory into the new user's home directory and gives the new user ownership of the copied files and directories.

Currently, on a Debian machine, the command **useradd snuffy** creates the user snuffy with the next available UID and the GID set to the users group (100); no home directory is created.

To set up the user on a Debian system with a specified home directory, you have to specify the **-m** and **-d** options. To copy the contents of the **/etc/skel** directory into the user's home directory, use the **-k** option. To specify the primary group, use the **-g** option. The **-u** option can be used to specify the UID for the new user. Note that all these options can also be used on a Red Hat system, but often they are omitted in favor of default values. For example:

```
# useradd -m -d /home/snuffy -k /etc/skel -g 100 -u 1025 snuffy
```

This creates the user with all the specified information. On a Red Hat machine, the **/bin/bash** shell is auto-supplied, whereas on a Debian machine, the shell is blank by default, causing the system to assume the **/bin/sh** shell (which is a symbolic link to **/bin/bash**). On both systems, this value can be defined with the **-s** option.

Other important **useradd** options are as follows:

- **-D:** Executing the **useradd** command with this option displays the defaults defined in the **/etc/default/useradd** file. This option can also be used to modify the defaults.

- **-e:** This option sets an expiration date on the account; after that date, the account is disabled.

- **-G:** This option sets secondary group membership at account creation, which is often done after creating the account by using the **usermod** command.

- **-f:** This is the number of days after the password has reached its maximum life that the user can still log in (if the user changes his password during the login process). Setting the maximum and minimum password values is discussed later in this chapter.

- **-o:** This allows the creation of a user with a nonunique UID. This option is very dangerous and not recommended.

- **-s:** The full path and filename of the user's login shell must follow the **-s** option.

useradd Defaults

On Red Hat-based systems, the **useradd** defaults are defined in the **/etc/default/useradd** file and can be altered with the use of the **-D** option for the **useradd** command.

The Default Shell

For example, to change the *default shell* from **/bin/bash** to **/bin/tcsh**, execute the following command:

```
# useradd -D -s /bin/tcsh
```

Debian-based systems also use this file. For example, executing the **useradd -D -g 10** command sets the default group to be the wheel group (with GID 10) when you add a user on Debian.

skel Templates

When you use the **useradd** command and the **-m** and **-d** options, a home directory is created for the user. By default, the new home directory is a copy of the **/etc/skel** directory and its contents.

For example, **useradd -m -d /home/snuffy snuffy** creates the home directory
/home/snuffy. This home directory is copied by default from the **/etc/skel** directory, and the ownership is changed to match the new user (as demonstrated in
Example 9-1).

Example 9-1   Using **/etc/skel**

```
[root@server1 ~]# ls -la /etc/skel
total 24
drwxr-xr-x. 3 root root 74 May 9 18:15 .
drwxr-xr-x. 154 root root 8192 May 28 20:18 ..
-rw-r--r--. 1 root root 18 Mar 5 14:06 .bash_logout
-rw-r--r--. 1 root root 193 Mar 5 14:06 .bash_profile
-rw-r--r--. 1 root root 231 Mar 5 14:06 .bashrc
drwxr-xr-x. 4 root root 37 May 9 18:15 .mozilla
[root@server1 ~]# useradd snuffy
[root@server1 ~]# ls -la /home/snuffy
total 12
drwx------. 3 snuffy snuffy 74 May 28 21:25 .
drwxr-xr-x. 4 root root 30 May 28 21:25 ..
-rw-r--r--. 1 snuffy snuffy 18 Mar 5 14:06 .bash_logout
-rw-r--r--. 1 snuffy snuffy 193 Mar 5 14:06 .bash_profile
-rw-r--r--. 1 snuffy snuffy 231 Mar 5 14:06 .bashrc
drwxr-xr-x. 4 snuffy snuffy 37 May 9 18:15 .mozilla
```

You can put just about anything in a new user's home directory by placing files or
directories in the **/etc/skel** directory. It's even more elegant to create a set of **/etc/
skel_XXX** directories to make creating certain groups of users easier. For example,
to have a special home directory structure for users in the payroll department, you
might use the following steps:

Step 1.   Copy the **/etc/skel** directory to a new directory named **/etc/
skel_payroll_staff**.

Step 2.   Populate **/etc/skel_payroll_staff** with the files and directories that you
want users who are in the payroll department to have.

Step 3.   The next time you create a user from the payroll department, use the
following syntax to specify the correct **skel** *template* directory:

```
# useradd -k /etc/skel_payroll_staff bob
```

Adding Groups with **groupadd**

The *groupadd* command is much simpler than the **useradd** command, with fewer options and shorter command lines. To add a group named somegroup with the defaults for new groups, type the following:

```
# groupadd somegroup
```

This command creates a group with a GID determined by using the "next available" number above 500. The result should be an entry like the following in the **/etc/ group** file:

```
somegroup:x:516:
```

Note that no users are added to the group; the last field is empty. The **usermod** command, discussed in the next section, is used to add users to existing groups.

To add a group with a particular GID, execute a command like the following:

```
# groupadd -g 1492 somegroup
```

Modifying Users and Groups

Creating users and groups is one thing, but being able to make them fit a changing system environment is another. Typically, you add and remove users from secondary groups, locking and unlocking accounts, and even changing a password expiration now and then.

Modifying User Accounts with **usermod**

To modify a user account with the *usermod* command, you need to decide which of the following options is needed:

- **-c:** Describes the user; this modifies the GECOS field in the **/etc/passwd** file.

- **-d:** Changes the user's new home directory. If there are files in this new home directory, you need to also change the user ownership of these files.

- **-e:** Changes the date the user account expires and is disabled.

- **-f:** Changes the number of inactive days. When a user account is locked out because the maximum password time frame has been exceeded, the user can have a grace period in which she can still log in as long as she changes her password during the login process. (This is discussed further later in this chapter, in the section "Aging Passwords.")

- **-g:** Changes the primary group for the user; either GID or group name can be specified. Warning: This changes which file objects the user has access to.

- **-G:** Changes the user's secondary groups. This is a single value or a list of comma-separated values of groups of which the user is to be a secondary member. Important note: Be sure to include all groups, including groups to which the user already belongs as a secondary member. This command replaces all secondary group memberships with the argument provided to the **-G** option.

- **-s:** Changes the path to the user's login shell.

- **-u:** Changes the user's UID. Warning: While this changes the UID ownership of files in the user's home directory to match the new UID, other files on the system will not automatically be changed!

- **-L:** This locks a user's account by altering the **/etc/shadow** file and prefixing the current encrypted password with an exclamation point (!).

- **-U:** This removes the lock on the user's account by removing the ! from the front of the encrypted password in the **/etc/shadow** file.

NOTE Another way to lock and unlock a user's account is to use the **passwd** command and its **-l** and **-u** options to accomplish the locking and unlocking.

Modifying Groups with **groupmod**

The *groupmod* command has fewer options than the **usermod** command, and there are only a few reasons to use this command. It's primarily for altering a group's name and GID. To modify a group's GID, execute the following command:

```
# groupmod -g 101 users
```

Think twice before altering the GID of a group because you could orphan a lot of important files if you do. Remember: Files and directories are not owned by usernames and group names but rather by UIDs and GIDs. If you modify a group's GID, a file previously owned by that GID now no longer has a group name associated with the file, as demonstrated in Example 9-2.

Example 9-2 *Changing GID*

```
[root@server1 tmp]# ls -l sample
-rw-r--r--. 1 root test 0 May 28 20:17 sample
[root@server1 tmp]# grep test /etc/group
test:x:1001:
[root@server1 tmp]# groupmod -g 2000 test
[root@server1 tmp]# grep test /etc/group
test:x:2000:
[root@server1 tmp]# ls -l sample
-rw-r--r--. 1 root 1001 0 May 28 20:17 sample
```

You should also look in the **/etc/passwd** file to see which users' primary groups will be affected when you change a group. Do not attempt to change the GID of a group that has a user member currently logged in. Finally, be aware that on some systems, if you remove or orphan the primary group of a user, the user defaults to being a member of the staff (GID 50) group.

Removing Users and Groups

Removing users and groups isn't difficult, but several options need attention. Removing accounts from the system isn't like on a Windows machine, which uses SIDs (security IDs) that are numerically unique and cannot be re-created easily. Linux accounts can be re-created easily (unless you delete the user's home directory, which could only be recovered from a backup). Remember that Linux uses tables of static UIDs and GIDs, not SIDs.

Removing Users

If a user leaves the company, you are faced with either deleting the user account and leaving the user's home directory on the system (perhaps for his replacement) or purging the system of the user by removing his account and home directory in one step.

Removing a user without affecting his home directory is accomplished by executing the *userdel* command:

```
# userdel snuffy
```

To remove the user along with his home directory (the one configured in the **/etc/passwd** entry), you execute the following command:

```
# userdel -r snuffy
```

> **NOTE**   Keep in mind that the **userdel -r** command also deletes the user's mail file. However, other files on the system owned by this user will not be deleted. Those files will be owned by just the UID, not the name, of this user. In addition, if you create a new user with the same UID as the old user, the new user would be the owner of these files.

You cannot delete a currently logged-in user, so you must find out why he is still logged on. On some Linux systems, if the user is logged in and you attempt to delete that account, you receive an error message like the following:

```
# userdel: user snuffy is currently used by process 17098
```

If you don't receive this sort of message, you can execute the **ps** command to determine the login shell's PID. Before you kill this user's login shell, use the **usermod -L** command to lock the account; then use **kill -9 PID** to log the user off the system. For example, to log off the snuffy user and delete the account, execute the following commands:

```
# usermod -L snuffy
# kill -9 17098
# userdel -r
```

One reason you shouldn't just remove a user's home directory is that usually either important files or important evidence (perhaps of wrongdoing on the user's part) exists in that directory. If you are planning to replace the user, consider keeping the directory and just deleting the user account. This leaves the home directory and its contents with only a UID where the username was:

```
drwxr-sr-x 2 1002 staff 4096 Mar 18 07:17 snuffy
```

This is actually not a bad thing to see because it is a visual clue to you that the user who owned this home directory was deleted. However, because the home directory still belongs to the UID 1002 and the old user's login name was set as the directory name, you have everything you need to re-create the user or set up a new user. For example, the following uses snuffy's old home directory for the new sarah account:

```
# mv /home/sarah /home/snuffy
# useradd -u 1002 -d /home/snuffy snuffy
```

Removing Groups

Before you delete a group, consider checking the following:

- Confirm that the group has no secondary members.

- Confirm that the group isn't a primary group for a user account.

- Use the **find** command to find all files owned by the group. After you find them all, change the group ownership of all these files to another group.

To delete a group, execute the *groupdel* command:

```
# groupdel grpname
```

NOTE   The majority of the identify management questions on the Linux+ exam focus on the **useradd**, **usermod**, and **userdel** commands. There isn't much to ask about the group commands, but there might be a couple of questions about them in the fill-in-the-blank questions just to see whether you're paying attention.

The Shadow Suite

An important piece of a Linux machine with regard to security is the *Shadow Suite*. The Shadow Suite is a set of authentication tools and utilities that insinuates itself into the mix of the **/etc/passwd** file and user accounts. Without the use of the shadow tools, your encrypted passwords would be exposed to anyone who wants to see them because they would be in the world-readable **/etc/passwd** file in field 2. The Shadow Suite also provides password aging properties that don't exist without this suite. All this is accomplished by storing this data in another file: the **/etc/shadow** file.

Encrypted Passwords and Shadow Fields

The following is an example of an entry from the **/etc/passwd** file on a system that doesn't use the Shadow Suite:

```
snuffy:$1$vEEOvj1b$GlzLuD9F..DjlQr/WXcJv1:501:10::/home/snuffy:/bin/sh
```

As you can see, an encrypted string appears in the second field. Unfortunately, all users can view this file, making this a potential security risk. In the next example, the **/etc/passwd** entry is shown on a system with the Shadow Suite enabled; note that the encrypted string is replaced with an **x**:

```
snuffy:x:501:10::/home/snuffy:/bin/sh
```

When the Shadow Suite is installed, the system stores encrypted passwords in the **/etc/shadow** file for user accounts and in the **/etc/gshadow** file for group accounts. The fields in the **/etc/shadow** file contain the user's account password and password aging information. The following is an example of a **/etc/shadow** file entry:

```
snuffy:$1$vEEOvj1b$GlzLuD9F..DjlQr/WXcJv1:16263:0:99999:7:30:17000:
```

The fields in the **/etc/shadow** file are

- **snuffy:** Login name: The user's login name.

- **1vEEOvj1b$GlzLuD9F..DjlQr/WXcJv1:** Password: The user's encrypted password.

- **16263:** Last change: The days since January 1, 1970, that have elapsed since the password was last changed.

- **0:** Minimum: The days that must elapse before the password can be changed. (**0** effectively always allows immediate changes.)

- **99999:** Maximum: The days before the password must be changed. (**99999** effectively disables the need to change the password because this is over 273 years.)

- **7:** Warning: The number of days before the password expires due to the Maximum field when the user will be warned.

- **30:** Inactive: The number of days after the account expires due to the Maximum field in which the user could still log in if the password is changed during login.

- **17000:** Expiration date: The number of days from January 1, 1970, and the day the account will expire.

NOTE   The last field in the file is reserved for future use and is not tested or much talked about.

Some of the fields of the **/etc/shadow** file are tricky. Consider the following:

```
julia:$1$vEEOvj1b$GlzLuD9F..DjlQr/WXcJv1:16263:5:90:7:30::
```

The julia account does not have an expiration date (the Expiration field is empty); however, this user is required to change her password every **90** days (the Maximum field is 90). Seven days before the 90-day time frame is up, the user will receive a warning when she logs in (the Warning field is **7**). If she does not heed this warning, her account will be locked out on day 91. She can still log in for up to 30 days after her account is locked (the Inactive field is **30**), provided that she creates a new password during the login process. Finally, after changing her password, she cannot change her password again for at least 5 days (the Minimum field is **5**); this is meant to prevent her from just switching back to her original password.

NOTE   The password aging provided by the Shadow Suite is far from perfect. Pluggable authentication modules (PAMs) provide much richer and more powerful password aging features.

/etc/shadow File Permissions

The permissions on the **/etc/shadow** file are important to be aware of. Because the **/etc/shadow** file isn't world readable and only the system updates it, your passwords are much safer than without Shadow Suite installed.

The **/etc/shadow** file permissions are prominently featured on the Linux+ exam, as are the permissions for the **/etc/passwd** file. Here is a listing of the files and permissions on both Red Hat and Debian:

```
/etc/passwd"
Red Hat = -rw-r--r-- (644)
```

```
Debian = -rw-r--r-- (644)
/etc/shadow"
Red Hat = -r-------- (400)
Debian = rw-r----- (640)
```

> **NOTE** Take note of the security permissions on the shadow files of your various test systems. You'll find small but important variations. Some systems use ------- and some use r------; make sure to note what each system uses. The **/etc/passwd** file is essentially open and readable by anyone, even those not on the system. The important and private encrypted passwords are in the **/etc/shadow** file. The **/etc/gshadow** file mentioned previously is also part of the Shadow Suite. However, this file is not listed in the Linux+ exam objectives.

Changing Passwords

Users' passwords are typically initially set to some value that is easily remembered by the root user when the account is created, and then the user is told to change her password immediately.

To change the root password, execute the following command when you are logged in as the root user:

```
# passwd
```

You are prompted to enter a password twice for verification. If you are executing this command as a normal user, the user's current password is required before the new password will be accepted. This measure is meant to prevent a situation where you walk away from the system and someone quickly tries to change the password.

If you're changing another user's password, like the password of the snuffy user, you execute the following when you are logged in as the root user:

```
# passwd snuffy
```

> **NOTE** It's important to remember who you are logged in as and what you type on the command line when changing a password. I've seen many a sysadmin change her own password instead of a user's because she was in a big hurry!

Aging Passwords

See Chapter 8, "Understanding Linux Security Best Practices," section "Aging Passwords."

A Login Shell Session

A *login shell* is a shell that is executed when logging in to the system. In other words, a login shell executes when either the user approaches the physical system and logs in normally as a user or logs in across the network and gets the full benefit of the contents of the files that make up the user's environment.

The */etc/profile* script is the global configuration file that affects all users' environments if they use the BASH shell. It's sourced (read) every time a user performs a login shell. This file is a script and is executed right before the user's profile script. After this, any files inside **/etc/profile.d** are sourced.

The user's **~/.bash_profile** script, if it exists, is the next script sourced. This file contains variables, code, and settings that directly affect that user's—and only that user's—environment. If **.bash_profile** doesn't exist, the shell looks for **.bash_login** or **.profile** and stops when it has found a match.

The **.bash_profile** script—or an alternative script if found—sources *.bashrc*. Note that this isn't behavior in the shell; it's a convention that makes everything easier later.

When the user logs out, the shell sources the **.bash_logout** file. This file is used to issue the **clear** command, so text from any previous command is not left on the user's screen after the user logs out. It can also clean up anything that may have been launched as part of the session.

Be careful with questions on the Linux+ exam about login shell sessions. A lot of test takers do not pick the **.bash_logout** file as part of the user's login session. It's definitely one of the more commonly missed elements in the shell section of the exam.

The following is an example of a user's login session:

Step 1.   The user logs in with a username and password.

Step 2.   The **/etc/profile** is sourced.

Step 3.   Files under **/etc/profile.d** are sourced.

Step 4.   The user's **~/.bash_profile** is sourced.

Step 5.   The user's **~/.bashrc** is sourced from within **~/.bash_profile**.

Step 6.   The user conducts her business.

Step 7.   The user initiates a logout with the **logout** or **exit** command or by pressing **Ctrl+D**.

Step 8.   The user's **.bash_logout** script is sourced.

A Non-Login Shell Session

Non-login shell sessions are typically the root user using the **su** command to temporarily become another user or a sysadmin using **su** to become the root user without loading the entire environment of the root or other user. Non-login shells are also started by opening new terminals from within a graphical session.

> **NOTE** The **su** command creates a non-login shell. If you need a login shell, place a dash after the **su** command (for example, **su - sean**).

When a user executes a non-login session, the only file sourced is the target account's **~/.bashrc** file. (On Red Hat machines, the first action in the **~/.bashrc** file is to source the **/etc/bashrc** file if it exists. Other distributions run different files.)

Upon exiting that shell, no logout files or scripts are sourced; in addition, the source account's scripts are not run again.

User Identity Query Options

An interesting problem that occurs often on a Linux system is losing track of which user account you might be logged in as, or what effective rights and privileges you currently have, since you can easily transition over into the root user or other users with the **su** command and effectively act as a semi-root user with the **sudo** command's help.

IDing Who You Are

The *id* command is a very useful tool in determining which user account you are logged in as and what your current UID and GID are. It can also be used in scripts to ensure that the user is in the right security context.

Running the **id** command produces the following output:

```
# id
uid=1000(rossb) gid=1000(rossb) groups=1000(rossb),4(adm), 24(cdrom),
27(sudo),30(dip),46(plugdev),115(lpadmin), 128(sambashare)
```

As you can see, the output shows the UID, primary GID, and other groups this user belongs to.

Who Am I?

Two commands begin with the characters *who*, and they have different reasons for existing.

The *who* command tells you more than just who you are; as shown in the following example, it tells you who else is on the system, either locally on a console or on a pseudo terminal (aka ssh'ed in from elsewhere), and it includes not only the user's name but the port the user is signed in on/from as well as when he signed in:

```
# who
rossb      tty7           2022-03-17 06:02 (:0)
rossb      pts/4          2022-03-30 07:33 (127.0.0.1)
```

In this output, you can see that the user ross is signed in locally on tty7, which indicates either a shell session from the console after pressing **Ctrl+F7** and signing in or, much more likely, a terminal application within the Linux Desktop GUI (which is the case here).

The second line of output is the same user ssh'ed in from another system, as indicated by the **pts/X** pseudo-terminal connection type. Another indication of where the user is coming from is the notation in parentheses, where the first line of output shows **:0**, or the graphical display **0**, and **127.0.0.1** in the second line of output shows that the user is connected in from the localhost.

The w command

Contrast the very simple and clean **whoami** command with the more complex *w* command, whose output shows several useful bits of information:

```
$ w
09:33:07 up 1 day, 18:10, 2 users,     load average:  0.00, 0.00,
0.00
USER      TTY    FROM            LOGIN@  IDLE    JCPU    PCPU WHAT
rossb     tty7   :0              17Mar19 15days  1:16    0.59s
mate-session
rossb     pts/5  127.0.0.1       09:32   19.00s  0.03s   0.03s -bash
```

The **w** command shows you the current time, the uptime in days and hours, the number of logged-in users, and the system loads for the last 1, 5, and 15 minutes.

Most importantly, the **w** command also shows you the command or applications that various users are running. While this isn't very helpful if users are using an X terminal or a graphical application, you can see exactly what they are running on the command line. For example, the user in the following example is clearly looking for all spreadsheet files on the entire system—something that is at the very least slightly questionable and at worst an attempt to find pricing or salary information:

```
# watch -n 15 w
Every 15.0s: w              brunsonix: Mon Apr  1 09:42:20 2022

 09:42:20 up 1 day,18:19,2 users,   load average: 0.06, 0.06, 0.02
```

```
USER     TTY     FROM        LOGIN@    IDLE    JCPU    PCPU WHAT
rossb    tty7    :0          17Mar19 15days   1:21     0.59s mate-session
rossb    pts/5   127.0.0.1 09:32    20.00s   0.03s   0.03s find / -iname
"*.xls"
```

Therefore, if you want to keep an eye on who is logged in to your system with console access and monitor what they are running, execute the **watch** command with a reasonable time period, such as 30 seconds, and have it run the **w** command in a console that you can easily refer to.

Summary

In this chapter you learned about accounts, both user and group accounts, as well as the concept of what a service account is and does. You also know now how to add, delete, and modify users and group accounts, how to identify which user is logged in, and how to determine other details about the user.

You also learned how to monitor your system using tools that report the logged-in and connected users, how to configure the user's environment for the best effect, and how to station files and directories you want in all new user account home directories.

Exam Preparation Tasks

As mentioned in the section "Goals and Methods" in the Introduction, you have a couple of choices for exam preparation: the exercises here, Chapter 23, "Final Preparation," and the exam simulation questions in the Pearson Test Prep Software Online.

Review All Key Topics

Review the most important topics in this chapter, noted with the Key Topic icon in the left margin of the page. Table 9-2 lists these key topics and the page number on which each is found.

Table 9-2   Key Topics for Chapter 9

Key Topic Element	Description	Page Number
List	Important Linux account UID meanings	355
Paragraph	The meaning of the fields in a user's **/etc/passwd** entry	357
List	The difference between the two types of groups on Linux systems	358
Paragraph	Removing a user and their home directory with the **userdel -r** *username* command	366
List	Fields in the **/etc/shadow** file and their meanings	368
Paragraph	What a login shell session consists of	371
Paragraph	What a non-login shell session consists of	372
Paragraph	Contrasting the **whoami** command with the more detailed and useful **w** command	373

Define Key Terms

Define the following key terms from this chapter and check your answers in the glossary:

configuration files, **/etc/passwd**, **/etc/group**, **/etc/shadow**, **useradd**, **/etc/skel**, default shell, **groupadd**, **usermod**, **groupmod**, **userdel**, **groupdel**, **/etc/profile**, **.bash_profile**, **.bashrc**, **id**, **who**, **w**

Review Questions

The answers to these review questions are in Appendix A.

1. Which field in the **/etc/shadow** file sets the number of warning days before the user's password expires? Fill in just the numeral of this field in the following blank:

   _____

2. What does the following output of the **ls -l** command indicate?

   ```
   drwxr-sr-x 2 1002 staff 4096 Mar 18 07:17 snuffy
   ```

   a. The account was deleted, but the user's home directory was not.

   b. The file is not owned by any account.

   c. The **/etc/passwd** file is corrupt.

   d. The user's group is incorrect.

3. If you created ten accounts beginning with UID 501 and then deleted 501 and 504, what would be the UID of the next user you create, by default? Write your answer in the following blank:

   _____

4. By default, which directory is copied to a newly created user's home directory when the **-m** and **-d** options are used with the **useradd** command? Fill in the full path and name of the directory in the following blank:

   _____

5. Which command is used to set the password expiration, warning, and other **/etc/shadow** file field information interactively?

   a. **passwd**

   b. **chpass**

   c. **vipw**

   d. **chage**

6. Which command allows a user to open a shell with a different primary group? Fill in the blank below with just the command:

   _____

This chapter covers the following topics:

- Common Firewall Technologies
- Understanding iptables
- Additional Firewall Technologies

The exam objective covered in this chapter is as follows:

- **Objective 2.3:** Given a scenario, implement and configure firewalls

## CHAPTER 10

Implementing and Configuring Firewalls

Linux is relatively secure right at the outset, unlike a lot of other options in the operating system world. This doesn't mean that you don't need to take steps to further secure your Linux systems and services—you definitely do, and one of the firewall offerings such as **iptables** or **firewalld** is perfect for that purpose.

It used to be that **iptables** was the standard command used to manage firewall rules, but there was nothing simple or easy about **iptables**, particularly for those without a security background.

Today you can use the venerable and dependable **iptables**, or you can also choose to use the easier-to-configure **firewalld**, which isn't a complete replacement for **iptables**, but more of a front-end configuration tool for the **iptables** rules that are the underlying basis of its functionality, embedded into the kernel.

We'll start off with an exploration of the majority player, **iptables**. Then we'll look at how **firewalld**, with its closer relationship with systemd and its ability to be configured and implemented without a restart/reboot, makes our lives that much easier.

We'll also cover the key firewall features along the way, and talk about common firewall use cases as and where appropriate.

"Do I Know This Already?" Quiz

The "Do I Know This Already?" quiz enables you to assess whether you should read this entire chapter or simply jump to the "Exam Preparation Tasks" section for review. If you are in doubt, read the entire chapter. Table 10-1 outlines the major headings in this chapter and the corresponding "Do I Know This Already?" quiz questions. You can find the answers in Appendix A, "Answers to the 'Do I Know This Already?' Quizzes and Review Questions."

Table 10-1   "Do I Know This Already?" Foundation Topics Section-to-Question Mapping

Foundation Topics Section	Questions Covered in This Section
Common Firewall Technologies	1–2
Understanding **iptables**	3–4
Additional Firewall Technologies	5–6

CAUTION   The goal of self-assessment is to gauge your mastery of the topics in this chapter. If you do not know the answer to a question or are only partially sure of the answer, you should mark that question as wrong for purposes of the self-assessment. Giving yourself credit for an answer you correctly guess skews your self-assessment results and might provide you with a false sense of security.

1. A user who normally works in a corporate office goes on a road trip, and in order to protect her machine from intrusions and attacks, she chooses to run which technology to best protect her system?

    a. Virtual private network

    b. Web application firewall

    c. TOR client

    d. Firewall

2. You have a small business office and have experienced what appears to be hacking attempts on your computers through your Internet router. You grab a handy Linux server and use which package to provide protection by running it and having that server be in between the outside router and your local network?

    a. **checkpoint**

    b. **firewalld**

    c. **iptables**

    d. **apparmord**

3. The process of receiving incoming packets, doing a stateful inspection of them, and forwarding only certain ones that meet a particular criteria is commonly known as packet _____. (Choose the best answer.)

    a. inspecting

    b. monitoring

    c. filtering

    d. transitioning

4. Your firewall finds that a certain packet or set of packets does not meet the requirements to be forwarded to the destination host and informs the sender of the situation. What best describes this activity?

   a. Flogging

   b. Dropping

   c. Responding

   d. Rejecting

5. On your Red Hat/Fedora system, you are using a command to configure your **iptables** rules via the **firewalld** technology. What is the name of that command?

   a. **ufw**

   b. **rhiptables**

   c. **apparmorctl**

   d. **firewall-cmd**

Foundation Topics

A *firewall* is a hardware or software device that is designed to either allow or block network traffic. Firewalls can be implemented on a variety of devices, including routers, network servers, and users' systems.

A large variety of firewall software is available within the IT industry. Any organization that creates router devices will have some form of firewall software available. This includes wireless access devices such as your home wireless router.

Even within Linux, there are several choices when it comes to firewall software. Dozens of open-source and commercial software packages are available. Having so many choices can complicate matters, both in terms of the content in this book and real-world implementation of firewalls.

For the purposes of learning about firewalls, this chapter focuses on **iptables**, a firewall that is available by default on most Linux distributions. In a real-world scenario, **iptables** is a good solution and is commonly used. However, you should also consider exploring other firewall software, as the requirements for your environment may necessitate a different solution.

NOTE   The Linux+ exam objectives are not in a useful order for explaining what you need to understand about implementing and configuring firewalls; it's not the logical order in which the discussion would follow in a book or in a class. So, I'm going to present most of the objectives and subobjectives where they make sense, and not in the order you see in the three sections of objective 2.3. Here's how the sections are handled:

- **Firewall use cases:** This section is handled throughout the discussion, mostly in the "Understanding **iptables**" section, where the topic traditionally belongs and is in perfect context.

- **Common firewall technologies:** This is a great section that follows this list directly, and describes which tools are available for configuring firewalls.

- **Key firewall features:** This is also laid out as it's needed and where it makes the most sense in the various areas, all of it's covered, but it's best in context, like the Use Cases section is.

Common Firewall Technologies

The firewall landscape has changed a lot since the previous version of this book was published, with several new entrants to the field, most notably the **firewalld** and **nftables** packages.

There are several firewall technologies that can be used with Linux, but what most people typically think are the actual firewalls are the programs used to configure the actual firewalls, most often using **iptables** on the back end.

The venerable (read: old and reliable but hard to work with) **iptables** package is still very much a part of the Linux firewall world, but it's recently been superseded by **nftables** in several Linux distributions, making the market share even more fractured.

To help alleviate any stress that you may have about all the firewall choices that you need to be familiar with for the Linux+ exam, this section provides a basic overview of what's currently happening in terms of firewall technologies, what tools work with other tools, and how everything fits together.

iptables: Old and Reliable, but Complicated

The *iptables* package has been around for a very long time and has been a mainstay for protecting Linux systems since, well, 1998! The **iptables** command runs in user-space and configures the IP packet filtering rules in the Linux kernel firewall, which is based on the Netfilter modules.

nftables: Newer, Tighter, More Dynamic

The *nftables* package is a new implementation of how the kernel classifies packets and is intended to replace the older **iptables** structure, while still supporting it, because the process of transitioning firewall technologies can be a bit complex to do in a short time frame.

Available since the 3.13 version of the kernel, **nftables** has a new command structure, tighter implementation, and less vulnerabilities because it is designed specifically to address problems in **iptables**.

Using **nftables** will help reduce duplication of code. It also will decrease issues resulting from inconsistent application of rulesets. It's simply faster, due to streamlining of how it maps packets. Additionally it's easier to manage both IPv4 and IPv6 stacks, as well as having support for more dynamic updates to the rules.

One of the really cool features that **nftables** offers is the ability to take an **iptables** command to configure a ruleset, and get the **nftables** exact match using one of the **iptables-translate** options tools.

In the following command, the **iptables-translate** command is being fed an **iptables** command, which it will convert into a compatible **nftables** command:

```
# iptables-translate -A INPUT -p tcp --dport 22 -m conntrack
--ctstate NEW -j ACCEPT
nft add rule ip filter INPUT tcp dport 22 ct state new counter
accept
```

As you can see, the translation is done immediately and you can use that to configure your **nftables** ruleset.

> **NOTE** The **nftables** package is complex and has a large number of configuration options, all of which are beyond the scope of the Linux+ exam. You'll primarily encounter questions seeking to establish that you know what **nftables** is, how to identify its characteristics, and what the command (and possibly simple output) looks like. Be sure to look up more information about this package, because it's on track to be the majority player in the Linux firewall market.

firewalld: Newer, Flexible, Easier to Use

On most RPM- and Red Hat-based distributions, it is common to use a utility called *firewalld* to configure **iptables** rules. However, in the most recent release of Red Hat, **firewalld** now configures **nftable** rules. Rules are configured into categories called *zones*, and the rules are managed by using the **firewall-cmd** command.

For example, you can execute the command **firewall-cmd --get-zones** to display all available zones:

```
# firewall-cmd --get-zones
block dmz drop external home internal public trusted work
```

You can set different rules on different zones and assign zone rule sets to different interfaces. For example, if your **eth0** interface connects to your internal network, you may apply to it the **trusted** or **internal** zones, which should have less restrictive rules. If your **eth1** interface connects to the Internet, you may use the **dmz** or **external** zones with it.

> **NOTE** Rules created on the command line using the **firewall-cmd** command affect the active firewall on the system. This is referred to as the *runtime firewall*. If the system is rebooted or the firewall service is restarted, these rules would be lost.

> **NOTE** The **firewalld** utility is a large topic, and complete coverage is beyond the scope of the Linux+ exam. To prepare for the exam, be sure you understand zones.

UFW: Uncomplicated Indeed

On Debian-based distributions, you will likely have the ability to use **ufw** (uncomplicated firewall). Like **firewalld**, *ufw* acts as a front-end interface to create **iptables** rules. For example, the following command creates a rule to allow for both inbound and outbound SSH connections:

```
root@localhost:~# ufw allow ssh
```

NOTE The rules that are created are stored in the following locations:

- The **/etc/default/ufw** file
- The **/etc/ufw** directory

NOTE The **ufw** utility is a large topic, and complete coverage is beyond the scope of the Linux+ exam. To prepare for the exam, be sure you understand where the configuration data for UFW is stored.

Understanding iptables

To create *firewall rules* on a system, you can use the **iptables** command. This command allows you to create rules to do one or more of the following functions:

- Block network packets. For example, you may have a use case in which you want to close network ports (ports are typically left open by default).
- Forward network packets to another system. In this case, the local system would act as both a firewall for another network and a router.
- Perform network address translation (NAT) operations. NAT offers a method to provide hosts within a private network access to the Internet.
- Mangle (modify) network packets. Although this can be a useful function, it is beyond the scope of this book and the Linux+ exam.

Overview of Filtering Packets

Before you start creating rules with the **iptables** command, you should understand how the firewall service works. Figure 10-1 shows how packets that are sent to the system are filtered.

In Figure 10-1, the process starts in the upper-left corner, with the packet being sent to the system. The **iptables** service uses sets of rules to determine what to do with this packet. The first set of rules takes place on the PREROUTING filtering point. These rules can be used either to allow the packet to continue to the next step or to block the packet.

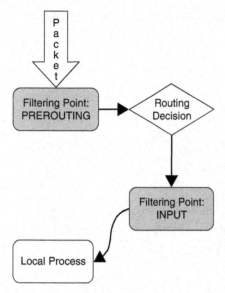

Figure 10-1   Packet filtering—incoming packets

If the packet is allowed to continue past the PREROUTING filtering point, the kernel determines whether the packet is designed to be sent to the local system or whether it should be passed to another network (in other words, routed to another network). Figure 10-1 does not include what happens to the packet if it is routed to another network; refer to Figure 10-2 for that scenario.

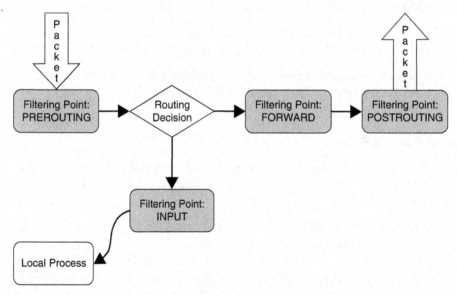

Figure 10-2   Packet filtering—routed packets

For packets destined for the local system, another filtering point is used to determine whether the packets are allowed or blocked. The INPUT filtering point rules are applied to these packets.

You might be wondering why there are two sets of rules so far (there will be more). Consider this: There might be some packets you want to entirely block, regardless of whether they are destined for the local system or will be routed to a different network. You can place rules to block these packets on the PREROUTING filtering point. If you want to block only some packets that will be sent to the local system, however, you can place rules on the INPUT filtering point.

Figure 10-2 demonstrates what happens with a packet that's routed to another network.

Packets that are routed to another network first must pass through a set of rules on the FORWARD filtering point. This allows you to create a set of rules that will apply only to packets that are routed to another network.

Note that after the FORWARD filtering point, the packets are sent to another filtering point (POSTROUTING). It might seem strange to have two filtering points with two separate sets of rules, but the reason for this is shown in Figure 10-3.

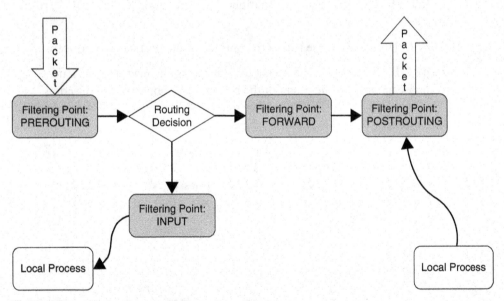

Figure 10-3 Packet filtering—outbound packets

Packets are subject to filtering not only when they are sent to a host but also when they are sent from the host. Rules can be applied on the OUTPUT filtering point for any packet that originates from a process that is running on the local system.

If you want to have a rule that applies to all outbound packets (both routed packets and packets that originate from the local system), you should place rules on the POSTROUTING filtering point.

Important Terms

In the previous section, you were introduced to the term *filtering point*. Types of rules, referred to as a *table*, can be placed on a filtering point. A filtering point can have one or more sets of rules because **iptables** performs multiple functions: Either filter (block or allow) the data, perform a NAT operation on the packet, or mangle the packet. The filtering point and the table (filter, NAT, or mangle) are combined into a single set of rules called a *chain*. Consider a chain to be a set of rules that determines what actions to take on a specific packet. For example, a rule on the **filter INPUT** chain could block an incoming packet based on the source *IP address*. Another rule could be used to allow packets destined for a specific network port.

The order of rules is important. Once a matching rule is found, an action (called a target) takes place, and additional rules are ignored (with one exception, as noted next). Here are the different types of targets:

- **ACCEPT:** Allow the packet to continue to the next step (filtering point, routing decision, and so on).

- **DROP:** Do not allow the packet to continue to the next step; just discard it.

- **REJECT:** Do not allow the packet to continue to the next step but send a response message to the origin of the packet, informing it of the rejection. This is different from DROP because with DROP, the origin of the packet is never informed of what happens with the packet.

- **LOG:** Create a log entry. Note that the target ACCEPT, DROP, or REJECT results in no further rules being evaluated, but LOG results in the creation of a log entry and then evaluation of additional rules. So, you can create a rule to log a connection attempt and then drop or reject the attempt with another rule.

NOTE Typically DROP is considered a more secure method than REJECT because hackers use REJECT responses as a means to probe a system or network. Even a negative response provides a hacker with useful information. For example, a REJECT could indicate that the destination machine might be worth hacking into (why secure an unimportant system?), or it could indicate that some ports are blocked but others are allowed.

Each chain also has a default chain policy. If you have not edited a chain, this policy should be set to ACCEPT. This means that if a packet does not match any DROP or REJECT rules in the chain, the default policy ACCEPT will allow it to continue to the next step.

On systems where security is paramount, you might want to change this default rule to DROP, which means that the only packets that are allowed to move to the next step in the process are those that match an ACCEPT rule in the chain.

Terms such as filtering point, table, chain, rule, and default chain policy will become clearer as examples are provided throughout this chapter. So, if some of these terms are a bit fuzzy now, they should make more sense as you explore using the **iptables** command to implement firewall rules.

A firewall created by **iptables** can be very complex, well beyond the scope of this book. For example, besides filter, NAT, and mangle tables, there is a table called "raw" that is not covered in this book. Also, filter points can have multiple rules (for example, a set of rules for OUTPUT-filter, one for OUTPUT-nat, and one for OUTPUT-mangle). However, not every table can be used to create rules (for example, you cannot have a PREROUTING filter rule). These complex situations would be covered in a book that focuses purely on firewalls; the discussion in this book includes specific scenarios of firewalls.

Using iptables to Filter Incoming Packets

A common firewall task involves configuring a system to either allow or block incoming packets. Such a task could be applied to a single host or an entire network (if the current system also acts as a router). To perform this task, you place rules on the INPUT-filter chain.

It is fairly common with modern Linux distributions to include some default firewall rules. You can see the current rules by executing the following command:

```
root@localhost:~# iptables -t filter -L INPUT
Chain INPUT (policy ACCEPT)
target          prot opt source                  destination
ACCEPT          udp  --  anywhere          anywhere    udp dpt:domain
ACCEPT          tcp  --  anywhere          anywhere    tcp dpt:domain
ACCEPT          udp  --  anywhere          anywhere    udp dpt:bootps
ACCEPT          tcp  --  anywhere          anywhere    tcp dpt:bootps
```

At this point, we are not going to worry about what these rules do; they are described later. To take these rules out of the chain, you could delete them individually. For example, the following command deletes the first rule in the INPUT-filter chain:

```
root@localhost:~# iptables -D INPUT 1
root@localhost:~# iptables -L INPUT
Chain INPUT (policy ACCEPT)
target        prot opt source                destination
ACCEPT        tcp  --  anywhere              anywhere     tcp dpt:domain
ACCEPT        udp  --  anywhere              anywhere     udp dpt:bootps
ACCEPT        tcp  --  anywhere              anywhere     tcp dpt:bootps
```

Here you do not need to include **-t filter** because **filter** is the default table.

You can also remove all rules in a chain by using the **-F** option (where **F** stands for *flush*):

```
root@localhost:~# iptables -F INPUT
root@localhost:~# iptables -L INPUT
Chain INPUT (policy ACCEPT)
target        prot opt source                destination
```

To block all network packets that originate from a specific host, use the following commands:

```
root@localhost:~# iptables -A INPUT -s 192.168.10.100 -j DROP
root@localhost:~# iptables -L INPUT
Chain INPUT (policy ACCEPT)
target        prot opt source                destination
DROP          all  --  192.168.10.100        anywhere
```

The **-s** option stands for "source." This value can be either an IP address or a network:

```
root@localhost:~# iptables -A INPUT -s 192.168.20.0/24 -j DROP
root@localhost:~# iptables -L INPUT
Chain INPUT (policy ACCEPT)
target        prot opt source                destination
DROP          all  --  192.168.10.100        anywhere
DROP          all  --  192.168.20.0/24       anywhere
```

You can use the **-A** option to place the new rule at the end of the chain. Recall that this is important because the rules are evaluated in order. Suppose you want to allow one machine in the 192.168.20.0/24 network access to this system. Use the **-I** option to insert a new rule above the rule that blocks that network (for example, **-I INPUT 2** states "insert this rule as rule 2 and move all remaining rules down by one"):

```
root@localhost:~# iptables -I INPUT 2 -s 192.168.20.125 -j ACCEPT
root@localhost:~# iptables -L INPUT
Chain INPUT (policy ACCEPT)
```

```
target          prot opt source              destination
DROP            all  --  192.168.10.100      anywhere
ACCEPT          all  --  192.168.20.125      anywhere
DROP            all  --  192.168.20.0/24     anywhere
```

Filtering by Protocol

It is common to filter packets by protocol. This could either be a ***protocol*** like
ICMP, TCP, or UDP, or a protocol associated with a specific port (like Telnet, which
uses port 23). To block a protocol like ICMP, use a command like the following
(where the first command flushes previous rules so we can focus on the rule being
discussed):

```
root@localhost:~# iptables -F INPUT
root@localhost:~# iptables -A INPUT -p icmp -j DROP
root@localhost:~# iptables -L INPUT
Chain INPUT (policy ACCEPT)
target          prot opt source              destination
DROP            icmp --  anywhere            anywhere
```

See the **/etc/protocols** file for a list of protocols that can be used in conjunction
with the **-p** option.

To block a specific port, you need to provide the **-m** option and either **--sport**
(source port) or **--dport** (destination port). For incoming packets, you typically use
the **--dport** option because you are concerned about connections established on a
specific port on the local system:

```
root@localhost:~# iptables -A INPUT -m tcp -p tcp --dport 23 -j DROP
root@localhost:~# iptables -L INPUT
Chain INPUT (policy ACCEPT)
target          prot opt source              destination
DROP            icmp --  anywhere            anywhere
DROP            tcp  --  anywhere            anywhere   tcp dpt:telnet
```

The **-m** option is required for **iptables** to make use of an extension module, which
is an optional add-on feature for **iptables**. In the previous example, the TCP match
extension module was used.

NOTE   You can also specify a range of ports as follows: **--dport 1:1024**

The output of the **iptables -L** command automatically converts port numbers into
names (for example, 23 is converted to Telnet). It also converts IP addresses into
hostnames if it can perform a DNS lookup. To avoid these conversions, use the **-n**
option:

```
root@localhost:~# iptables -L INPUT -n
Chain INPUT (policy ACCEPT)
target        prot opt source                destination
DROP          icmp --  anywhere              anywhere
DROP          tcp  --  anywhere              anywhere   tcp dpt:23
```

Remember that you can also look up port numbers in the **/etc/services** file. Recall that ports 1 through 1023 are considered privileged ports.

Multiple Criteria

You can combine multiple criteria to create a more complex rule. For the rule to match, all the criteria must match. For example, suppose you want to create a rule that matches both a protocol and a source IP address. The following rule would perform this task:

```
root@localhost:~# iptables -A INPUT -p icmp -s 192.168.125.125 -j
DROP
root@localhost:~# iptables -L INPUT
Chain INPUT (policy ACCEPT)
target        prot opt source                destination
DROP          icmp --  anywhere              anywhere
DROP          tcp  --  anywhere              anywhere   tcp dpt:telnet
DROP          icmp --  192.168.125.125       anywhere
```

The rule added in this example states "drop any ICMP packet that originates from the 192.168.125.125 host."

Filtering Based on Destination

If you look at the output of the **iptables -L INPUT** command, you will see that there is a **destination** column:

```
root@localhost:~# iptables -L INPUT
Chain INPUT (policy ACCEPT)
target        prot opt source                destination
DROP          icmp --  anywhere              anywhere
DROP          tcp  --  anywhere              anywhere   tcp dpt:telnet
DROP          icmp --  192.168.125.125       anywhere
```

In situations where you have multiple network cards or multiple IP addresses for a network card, you may want to create different rules for different network interfaces. In a situation where each network card has a single IP address, you can create different rules for each network interface:

```
root@localhost:~# iptables -F INPUT
```

```
root@localhost:~# iptables -A INPUT -i eth0 -s 192.168.100.0/24 -j
DROP
root@localhost:~# iptables -A INPUT -i eth1 -s 192.168.200.0/24 -j
DROP
root@localhost:~# iptables -L INPUT
Chain INPUT (policy ACCEPT)
target     prot opt source              destination
DROP       all  --  192.168.100.0/24    anywhere
DROP       all  --  192.168.200.0/24    anywhere
```

The output of the previous **iptables -L INPUT** command does not display the different network ports. To see them, you have to use the **-v** option (for "verbose"):

```
root@localhost:~# iptables -L INPUT -v
Chain INPUT (policy ACCEPT 2 packets, 144 bytes)
 pkts bytes target prot opt in      out  source           destination
    0     0 DROP   all  --  eth0    any  192.168.100.0/24  anywhere
    0     0 DROP   all  --  eth1    any  192.168.200.0/24  anywhere
```

The **-v** option provides more information, including how many network packets have matched the specified rule. This information can be useful while testing the firewall rules.

In a situation where an interface is assigned multiple IP addresses, use the **-d** option to indicate that the rule applies to a destination address:

```
root@localhost:~# iptables -F INPUT
root@localhost:~# iptables -A INPUT -d 192.168.50.1 -s
192.168.200.0/24 -j DROP
root@localhost:~# iptables -L INPUT
Chain INPUT (policy ACCEPT)
target     prot opt source              destination
DROP       all  --  192.168.200.0/24    192.168.50.1
```

Changing the Default Policy

A common use of a firewall is to allow specific packets and deny all others by default. This can be accomplished by changing the default *policy*. For example, suppose the current system is on an internal network, and you want to make sure only a handful of systems can access it. The following rules would perform that task:

```
root@localhost:~# iptables -F INPUT
root@localhost:~# iptables -A INPUT -s 10.0.2.0/24 -j ACCEPT
root@localhost:~# iptables -P INPUT DROP
root@localhost:~# iptables -L INPUT
Chain INPUT (policy DROP)
```

```
target         prot opt source            destination
ACCEPT         all  --   10.0.2.0/24       anywhere
```

Be very careful when setting the default policy to DROP. If you are remotely logged in to the system and you did not create a rule that allows your login session's packets to get through, your new default policy could end up blocking your access to the system.

Revisiting the Original Rules

Now that you have learned some of the basics of creating firewall rules, recall from earlier in this chapter that the system has some rules in place by default:

```
root@localhost:~# iptables -t filter -L INPUT
Chain INPUT (policy ACCEPT)
target         prot opt source            destination
ACCEPT         udp  --   anywhere          anywhere   udp dpt:domain
ACCEPT         tcp  --   anywhere          anywhere   tcp dpt:domain
ACCEPT         udp  --   anywhere          anywhere   udp dpt:bootps
ACCEPT         tcp  --   anywhere          anywhere   tcp dpt:bootps
```

Part of understanding firewalls is not just writing rules but also knowing how the rules apply. For example, if you review the rules from this output, you will see that several ports (**domain**, which is port 53, and **bootps**, which is port 67) are allowed to pass through the INPUT filtering point because the target is ACCEPT. This really has no impact on the firewall because the default policy for the chain is also ACCEPT. If the policy were changed to DROP, the rules would have an impact on which packets are allowed and which are blocked.

Saving the Rules

Up until now, all changes that have been made have affected only the currently running firewall. If the system were rebooted, all changes made using the **iptables** command would be lost, and the rules would revert back to the defaults (the persistent rules).

You can save the rules into a file by using the **iptables-save** command. Normally the output of this command is sent to the screen, but you can redirect the output to a file:

```
root@localhost:~# iptables-save > /etc/iptables.rules
```

Where exactly you should save the rules and how they are loaded automatically is dependent on your distribution. Some distributions make use of front-end utilities, such as **firewalld** on Red Hat Enterprise Linux or **ufw** (uncomplicated firewall) on

Ubuntu. These utilities are not only used to configure firewall rules (running **iptables** commands on your behalf), they also save rules. The rules are also automatically restored during a system reboot.

> **NOTE** Because there are so many of these "**iptables** helper" utilities (including GUI-based utilities), we cover the **iptables** command. You can always use this command to implement a firewall, and you are welcome to explore the "**iptables** helper" utilities for the distribution you are working on by consulting the documentation.

If you are not using one of these utilities, there may be another solution enabled on your system. If not, you can just create a shell script that restores the rules from the saved file by using the following command:

```
root@localhost:~# iptables-restore> /etc/iptables.rules
```

Using iptables to Filter Outgoing Packets

You might wonder why you would want to block outgoing packets. Consider that in many organizations, one of the biggest security concerns is users who visit Internet sites that could result in compromising security. For example, suppose there is a file-sharing site that your organization does not permit users to access because it lacks the proper security restrictions. To prevent this access, you can create a firewall rule on the OUTPUT-filter chain:

```
root@localhost:~# iptables -F OUTPUT
root@localhost:~# iptables -A OUTPUT -m tcp -p tcp -d 10.10.10.10
--dport 80 -j DROP
root@localhost:~# iptables -L OUTPUT
Chain OUTPUT (policy ACCEPT)
target      prot opt source         destination
DROP        tcp  --  anywhere       10.10.10.10 tcp dpt:http
```

If you are going to disallow access to a remote system, it might be considered more user friendly to use the REJECT target rather than the DROP target. Recall that with DROP, no response is returned to the origin of the packet. Therefore, if a user goes to a website and the DROP target is used, it appears that the website is just hanging. However, a REJECT target would respond with an error message, so the web browser would display an error message to the user.

Perhaps you want to allow this access but create a log entry so you can determine what systems are attempting to access the remote system:

```
root@localhost:~# iptables -F OUTPUT
root@localhost:~# iptables -A OUTPUT -m tcp -p tcp -d 10.10.10.10
```

```
--dport 80 -j LOG
root@localhost:~# iptables -L OUTPUT
Chain OUTPUT (policy ACCEPT)
target     prot opt source              destination
LOG        tcp  --  anywhere            10.10.10.10
tcp dpt:http LOG level warning
```

Stateful Rules

All of the rules provided so far in this chapter have been stateless rules. In firewall terminology, a *stateless rule* is one that doesn't depend on any established connection (or "state"). This can pose a problem when you have a firewall that uses rules like the following:

- Allow most outbound connections, including connections to websites, SSH access, FTP sites, and so on

- Block most inbound connections, so outside users can't connect to services you may have running

The problem with this scenario is that when you connect to a remote system, both outbound and inbound rules apply. The outbound rules apply when you establish a connection, and the inbound rules apply when the remote server responds. If you have a rule that blocks most inbound connections, you may never receive the response from that website you are trying to visit.

You can overcome this situation by creating *stateful rules*, which essentially mean "if a network packet is responding to a request that the local machine initiated, let it pass through the firewall." Here is an example of a stateful rule that allows responses to web servers (at least port 80) to pass through the firewall:

```
iptables -A INPUT -p tcp --dport 80 -m state --state NEW,ESTABLISHED
-j ACCEPT
```

Logging Rules

Suppose you want to drop inbound packets, but you want to keep a log of these packets. You can make a LOG rule like the following:

```
iptables -A INPUT -i eth0 -s 192.168.100.0/24 -j LOG
```

This is a pretty straightforward rule. Any package inbound on the **eth0** network device and from the 192.168.100.0/24 network should be logged. However, recall that there will also have to be a rule to drop the packets:

```
iptables -A INPUT -i eth0 -s 192.168.100.0/24 -j DROP
```

To both log and drop the packet, the LOG rule must come first. Once the DROP target is chosen, no further rules in the chain will apply. If a LOG target is chosen, **iptables** will continue to look for more rules in the chain.

Implementing NAT

There are several different forms of NAT:

- **Destination NAT (DNAT):** Use when you want to place servers behind a firewall and still provide access from an external network. DNAT rules are placed on the PREROUTING filtering point. Further discussion of this topic is beyond the scope of this book.

- **Source NAT (SNAT):** Use when you have an internal network with *statically* assigned private IP addresses. Using SNAT, you can funnel access to the Internet via a single machine that has a live IP address (an address that is routable on the Internet). This system is configured with SNAT, which is used to map internal addresses with external communication. SNAT rules are placed on the POSTROUTING filtering point. Further discussion of this topic is beyond the scope of this book.

- **MASQUERADE:** Use when you have an internal network with *dynamically assigned* private IP addresses (for example, using DHCP). Using MASQUER-ADE, you can funnel access to the Internet via a single machine that has a live IP address (an address that is routable on the Internet). This system is configured with MASQUERADE, which is used to map internal addresses with external communication. MASQUERADE rules are placed on the POSTROUTING filtering point.

Because most internal networks use DHCP to assign IP addresses, MASQUERADE is more common than SNAT. It is also easier to configure because SNAT requires you to create rules for each internal system. With MASQUERADE, a single command handles all the internal systems:

```
root@localhost:~# iptables -t nat -A POSTROUTING -j MASQUERADE
```

Note that NAT by itself isn't enough. You also have to implement the IP forwarding feature in the kernel. This is simply a matter of setting the value of each of the following files to **1**:

- **/proc/sys/net/ipv4/ip_forward**
- **/proc/sys/net/ipv6/ip_forward**

See Chapter 7, "Managing Software Configurations," to see how to make these changes permanently by modifying the **/etc/sysctl.conf** file.

> **NOTE**   The component of the kernel that performs NAT and IP forwarding is called Netfilter.

Additional Firewall Technologies

The **iptables** utility is a very popular firewall technology. There are several tools that work with the **iptables** utility, as well as different firewall solutions. This section explores these topics.

Not all rules are created by hand. Several utilities can dynamically create firewall rules. The goal of these utilities is to recognize when a system is under attack and create rules to block the hacking attempt.

The fail2ban Service

The *fail2ban* daemon scans specific log files, searching for IP addresses of systems that attempt to breach the system with repeated connection attempts. It isn't typically installed by default on most distributions, so you need to install it with either the **yum** or the **get-apt** command.

After installing the utility, you have a new configuration directory: **/etc/fail2ban**. The primary configuration file is the **/etc/fail2ban/jail.conf** file. However, if you look at this file, you will likely see the following message:

```
# HOW TO ACTIVATE JAILS:
#
# YOU SHOULD NOT MODIFY THIS FILE.
#
# It will probably be overwritten or improved in a distribution
update.
#
# Provide customizations in a jail.local file or a jail.d/
customisation.local.
# For example to change the default bantime for all jails and to
enable the
# ssh-iptables jail the following (uncommented) would appear in the
.local file.
# See man 5 jail.conf for details.
```

The problem that you run into in modifying this file directly is that updates to the **fail2ban** software package could result in overriding this file. As the warning in this file recommends, you can create **.local** files with customizations.

The file is called **jail.conf** because remote hosts are placed in a "jail" due to suspicious activity. As with a real jail, the intent is to let the host out of jail after a specific period of time.

Table 10-2 describes some key settings in this file.

Table 10-2   Key **fail2ban** Configuration Settings

Setting	Description
bantime	Allows you to set the amount of time, in seconds, a host is banned.
maxretry	Allows you to set the number of failures in connecting within the **findtime** before a host is banned.
findtime	Allows you to set the period of time, in seconds, that the **maxretry** entry uses. For example, say that the following settings are applied: **bantime = 600** **findtime = 600** **maxretry = 5** In this case, five failures within 600 seconds would result in a ban for 600 seconds.
enabled	If set to **true**, the jail is enabled. This is a very important setting because the default value for this setting in the **jail.conf** file is **false**. Only specific sections (the ones you want to use) should be enabled.
ignoreip	Allows you to create whitelists of IP addresses to never ban.

In addition to the global settings described in Table 10-2, there are sections for different jails. For example, you can have a section that relates to SSH connections, like the following:

```
[sshd]
enabled = true
maxretry = 3
```

This is a very simple example, and there are many other possible features you can use in the section. For example, you could create a custom action rule, including sending someone an email in the event that a rule is used to block an IP address:

```
[sshd]
enabled = true
maxretry = 3
action   = iptables[name=SSH, port=ssh, protocol=tcp]
             sendmail-whois[name=SSH, dest=root, sender=fail2ban@
example.com]
```

The **action** setting tells the **fail2ban** daemon what actions to take. The actions are normally defined in the **/etc/fail2ban/action.d/iptables.conf** file, which you can review to determine more about what these actions are designed to do.

DenyHosts

The **DenyHosts** utility is similar to **fail2ban**, but it is designed specially to protect SSH servers, and it doesn't create **iptables** rules but rather TCP wrapper rules. If it appears that a remote system is attempting a brute-force attack (using a dictionary of possible passwords as a means of guessing a user's password), **DenyHosts** will create a rule in the **/etc/hosts.deny** file to block the remote system.

IPset

The **IPset** utility is designed to create sets of IP addresses and then use those sets to apply rules to a collection of systems. For example, the following command creates a set:

```
root@localhost:~# ipset create test hash:net
```

The next set of rules adds IP addresses to the **test** set:

```
root@localhost:~#  ipset add test 192.168.100.0/24
root@localhost:~#  ipset add test 192.168.110.0/24
root@localhost:~#  ipset add test 192.168.120.0/24
```

The next command applies a rule to this set:

```
root@localhost:~# iptables -I INPUT -m set --match-set test src -j
LOG
```

Summary

The focus of this chapter is firewalls, not just **iptables**, which has dominated the landscape for decades. You learned how to secure a system or network from hackers by creating rules on the INPUT-filter chain. You also learned how to block access to external hosts by creating rules on the OUTPUT-filter chain and how to configure NAT to allow internal private systems access to the Internet.

You also explored some utilities that are designed to be helpers in creating firewalls, such as **nftables**, **firewalld**, **ufw**, and **fail2ban**.

Exam Preparation Tasks

As mentioned in the section "Goals and Methods" in the Introduction, you have a couple of choices for exam preparation: the exercises here, Chapter 23, "Final Preparation," and the exam simulation questions in the Pearson Test Prep Software Online.

Review All Key Topics

Review the most important topics in this chapter, noted with the Key Topic icon in the left margin of the page. Table 10-3 lists these key topics and the page number on which each is found.

Table 10-3 Key Topics for Chapter 10

Key Topic Element	Description	Page Number
Paragraph	The **nftables** command description	383
Note	Warning about the runtime firewall versus saving the configuration for future use	384
List	The different types of targets that make up an **iptables** rule	388
Paragraph	Saving rules using the **iptables-save** command	394
Paragraph	Making a logging rule to document dropped packets	396
List	The different forms of NAT	397
Paragraph	Defining the **fail2ban** command	398
Paragraph	The **jail.conf** file and its use	398

Define Key Terms

Define the following key terms from this chapter and check your answers in the glossary:

firewall, **iptables**, **nftables**, **firewalld**, ufw, firewall rules, table, chain, IP address, accept, drop, reject, protocol, policy, fail2ban

Review Questions

The answers to these review questions are in Appendix A.

1. Which of the following options need to be used to create a rule that will filter based on a destination port when using the **iptables** command? (Choose all that apply.)

   a. -p

   b. --dport

   c. -d

   d. -m

2. For netstat and other networking utilities, to view port numbers and IP addresses instead of names, which option should you use?

   _____

3. Which of the following describes a use of DNAT?

   a. To block network packets from entering a network

   b. To log network packets

   c. To redirect network packets to another host

   d. None of the above

4. Fill in the blank to configure NAT for all client systems connecting to the **eth0** network interface:

   iptables -t nat -A POSTROUTING -o eth0 -j _____

5. Which of the following files can be used to configure a Linux system to be an IPv6 router?

   a. **/proc/sys/net/ipv6/conf/all/ip_forwarding**

   b. **/proc/sys/net/ipv6/ip_forwarding**

   c. **/proc/sys/net/ipv6/forwarding**

   d. **/proc/sys/net/ipv6/conf/all/forwarding**

6. Which of the following are built-in targets? (Choose all that apply.)

   a. DROP

   b. LOG

   c. ACCEPT

   d. REJECT

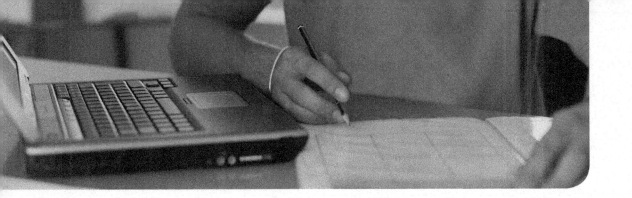

This chapter covers the following topics:

- SSH (Secure Shell)

- Executing Commands as Another User

The exam objective covered in this chapter is as follows:

- **Objective 2.4:** Given a scenario, configure and execute remote connectivity for system management

## CHAPTER 11

Using Remote Connectivity for System Management

Used to be that you could just move your chair and work on a server system, way back in the day, but so very quickly that changed to having all the servers in the server room somewhere else, and not wanting to walk there, or even being in the location or even city or country as the servers!

Having grown up in the era of computing when using Telnet (an unsecure remote connectivity option that preceded SSH) and clear-text FTP was commonplace, I've witnessed the evolution of the world of remote networking from a much kinder and gentler place in which hacking was not very common to the current situation in which hacking is a persistent threat and secure terminal access to connect to remote systems safely and reliably to do work, mainly administering them, is an absolute requirement.

Today, you must have SSH installed and configured to be the most secure you can make it, as described in this chapter. You also need to know the importance of using passphrase authentication instead of password authentication to connect to a remote server or group of servers.

Another topic of great importance discussed in this chapter is the concept of privilege elevation or, as the Linux+ exam objectives state, "executing commands as another user." This requires you to have an understanding of several different tools, both for the exam and as a responsible systems administrator.

The elevation of privilege is even more appropriate in conjunction with SSH because typically you should never allow the root user to sign in over SSH. Gaining access to root-restricted resources means you need to elevate yourself to having root access or equivalent when you get *to* the other system.

"Do I Know This Already?" Quiz

The "Do I Know This Already?" quiz enables you to assess whether you should read this entire chapter or simply jump to the "Exam Preparation Tasks" section for review. If you are in doubt, read the entire chapter. Table 11-1 outlines the major headings in this chapter and the corresponding "Do I Know This Already?" quiz questions. You can find the answers in Appendix A, "Answers to the 'Do I Know This Already?' Quizzes and Review Questions."

Table 11-1   "Do I Know This Already?" Foundation Topics Section-to-Question Mapping

Foundation Topics Section	Questions Covered in This Section
SSH (Secure Shell)	1–3
Executing Commands as Another User	4–6

> **CAUTION**   The goal of self-assessment is to gauge your mastery of the topics in this chapter. If you do not know the answer to a question or are only partially sure of the answer, you should mark that question as wrong for purposes of the self-assessment. Giving yourself credit for an answer you correctly guess skews your self-assessment results and might provide you with a false sense of security.

1. You want to use a more secure tool than rpc to remotely copy data across the network. Which of the following tools would you use?

   a. ssh-add

   b. sftp

   c. ssh-agent

   d. scp

2. You want to disable Secure Shell logins for all users except the root user. Which of the following files would you create to make this happen?

   a. **/etc/nossh**

   b. **/etc/nologin**

   c. **/etc/disablessh**

   d. **/etc/sshrootonly**

3. The process of allowing remote-running GUI-based applications to display locally when connected to the remote system via SSH is called _____.

   a. Remote Display

   b. SSH GUI Mode

   c. X11 Forwarding

   d. Tunnel Mode

4. Which command allows you to execute commands as another user, but only if you know the other user's password?

   a. **runas**

   b. **pkexec**

   c. **sudo**

   d. **su**

5. Which option to the su command allows you to fully take on the user's account settings, including settings that are applied during the login process?

   a. **-a**

   b. **-u**

   c. **-l**

   d. **-r**

6. Which file is used to configure sudo access?

   a. **/etc/config/sudo.config**

   b. **/etc/default/sudoers**

   c. **/etc/sudo**

   d. **/etc/sudoers**

Foundation Topics

SSH (Secure Shell)

As mentioned at the beginning of the chapter, the Telnet protocol sends passwords and data in clear text and shouldn't be trusted for important sessions and tasks. The *Secure Shell (SSH)* suite includes a protocol, a daemon, and client utilities that make your host-to-host shell sessions much more secure—about as secure as being at the physical console.

One of the features that makes SSH desirable as a remote protocol is its end-to-end encryption, which encrypts not only the username and password but also all communications.

The SSH suite replaces **telnet**, as well as **rsh**, **rexec**, **rcp**, and other unsecure utilities. You can use SSH to connect for a shell session, or you can use the **scp** command to remotely transfer files through the secure pipe that SSH builds between the hosts.

SSH Components

SSH includes a number of programs and files:

- *ssh*: Used for remote shell sessions on another host, it replaces the **telnet**, **rsh**, and **rexec** commands.

- **scp**: Used for remote copying operations, it replaces the **rcp** command.

- **sshd**: The SSH daemon.

- **ssh-agent**: Runs as a wrapper to the user's session and provides authentication when requested.

- *ssh-add*: Loads the user's key(s) into the agent.

The SSH package configuration files are somewhat scattered. SSH daemon and global configuration files are kept in the **/etc/ssh** directory, and local or user-specific configuration files are kept in the **~/.ssh** directory for each user.

The global configuration files include

- */etc/ssh/sshd_config*: This is the main configuration for the **sshd** daemon.

- **/etc/ssh/ssh_host_[dr]sa_key**: These files, the **ssh_host_dsa_key** file and the **ssh_host_rsa_key** file, are in the same directory and are the private parts of the host's key structure and should be protected from public view. The permissions for these files are 600 or rw for the root user and no permissions for anyone else.

■ **/etc/ssh/ssh_host_[dr]sa_key.pub:** These files, the **ssh_host_dsa_key.pub** file and the **ssh_host_rsa_key.pub** file, are in the same directory and are the public parts of the host's key structure. These must be world-readable and write-only by the root user or set to 644.

■ **/etc/nologin:** This isn't a part of SSH. However, if it's present, no one can log in via SSH except the root user. Non-root users see the contents of the **/etc/ nologin** file and then are denied access to the system.

A couple of special file pairs affect how SSH works, particularly the **/etc/ssh/ssh_ known_hosts** and **~/.ssh/*known_hosts*** files. The global file (**/etc/ssh/ssh_known_ hosts**) is used to check the public key of a host attempting to attach via SSH. The local file (**~/.ssh/known_hosts**) is the file from which the client gets the public key of the remote server. If a new connection is begun to a previously unknown host, the user sees a message saying that the host is unknown and asking whether the user wants to store the host's key in his known hosts file. If the user answers in the affirmative, the host's public key is added to the **~/.ssh/known_hosts** file.

The **/etc/ssh/ssh_known_hosts** file should be world-readable and root-writable. The **~/.ssh/known_hosts** file must be owned by and writable for the user.

A file of interest, the **~/.ssh/authorized_keys** file, affects only a particular user's environment. This file is used to store the public keys that can be used for logging in as this user. These keys are matched with the keys presented by an **ssh** or **scp** client upon login request.

The SSH client utilities are versatile, with a number of options available to customize the experience. You just need to know the basics for the Linux+ exam, but this section includes a few fun options.

The SSH client command is used to replace the RSH and Telnet programs specifically. Its syntax is as follows:

```
# ssh -l username remotehost
```

If you don't specify a username with the **-l** option, the **ssh** command assumes that you want to use the name of the account with which you are locally logged in. For example, if you are logged in as the user ross and you execute the **ssh** command without the **-l** option, the command attempts to log you in as ross on the remote system.

For example, I could attach to the host mp3server as the user snuffy with this command:

```
# ssh -l snuffy mp3server
```

If I have not connected to this server before, I get a message similar to what's shown here:

```
The authenticity of host 'mp3server (192.168.33.44)' can't be
established.
RSA key fingerprint is 73:4f:fa:b0:42:a4:3a:a8:64:2c:ad:26:1
d:b1: 21:e0.
Are you sure you want to continue connecting (yes/no)?
```

If I answer **yes**, the host's public key is added to my **~/.ssh/known_hosts** file and looks something like this:

```
192.168.3.44 ssh-rsa
AAAAB3NzaC1yc2EAAAABIwAAAIEA1gFIB9VQpFKWAZUzNM+ac/U81Tk9R8OCFfUkegVJXw
j6nqCISPyV2iJwaukcVVaVAQ+JR3EhvOvh4PhoSg4yzBSUkJ8aUBYoRSGj7PCD+vyWyi19
22HGxWbWooMBAO/Was8I7N0zQ6jxDO9qNOHcrIFeU7qbOCrKjQDM08HQjk0=
```

Rather than work with RCP or FTP for file transfer work, I tend to use SCP. The **scp** command uses the SSH protocol and encrypts the files sent from one host to another host. For example, if I wanted to transfer **file1** from my root user's home directory on my machine to the same location on a host named remotehost, I could use the following command:

```
# scp /root/file1 root@remotehost:/root/file1
```

The system would prompt me with the RSA key question (as shown in the previous **ssh** example) if I have not connected to this system previously from this account. I would be prompted for the password, and then the system would transfer the files. The output from a file transfer looks like this:

```
# root@192.168.1.73's password:
mypubkey.txt 100% |********************| 1379 00:00
```

You can copy files from your host to another host, as shown previously, or copy files from a remote host to your system by reversing the source and target specifications.

You can even copy files from one remote system to another remote system. For example, the following command recursively copies the **/data** directory and all its contents from the remote1 host to the remote2 host after prompting you for the password for both hosts:

```
# scp -r root@remote1:/data root@remote2:/data
```

Another use of the SSH protocol is to log in to a host and use SSH to forward the output from an X client back to your display. This feature, which can be specifically invoked with the **-x** option, is referred to as an *X11 tunnel*.

SSH allows for skipping the password prompt when signing on between computers, which can be convenient if you use the **ssh** or **scp** command frequently and don't mind the possibility that someone could sit down at your accidentally unlocked station and have her way with your network!

NOTE   There has been a lot of talk about why it's important to delete **.rhosts** files from user directories. Basically, if you have a user who has a hostname in her **.rhosts** file and that host also has the user's hostname in its **/etc/hosts_equiv** file, that user can log in without a password by using the **rlogin** command. This would be a security risk, so my advice is to delete these files with the following command:

```
# find /home -iname .rhosts -exec rm -f {} \;
```

This deletes all **.rhosts** files it finds in users' home directories and does not prompt you for each deletion.

NOTE   The system-wide configuration for the SSH client is kept in the **/etc/ssh/ ssh_config** file, while each user's individual configuration file for the SSH client is kept in the user's **~/.ssh/config** file.

The following example shows the steps required to enable SSH use without a password. In this example I have two machines, fattyre and murphy, both of which are Linux workstations with the necessary SSH software loaded, as per the defaults. This demonstration assumes that fattyre and murphy are both in each other's **/etc/hosts** files or resolvable via DNS.

Here's how you can enable SSH use without passwords:

Step 1.   Log in to fattyre as the root user.

Step 2.   For this example, create a new user named user1:

```
useradd -m user1
```

Step 3.   Set user1's password with the **passwd** command to whatever you want:

```
passwd user1
```

Step 4.   Switch to the user1 user account:

```
su - user1
```

Step 5. Create and set the permissions for the **.ssh** directory:

```
mkdir .ssh ; chmod 700 .ssh
```

Step 6. Generate an RSA key by using the *ssh-keygen* command:

```
ssh-keygen -b 1024 -t rsa
```

Step 7. When prompted for the location for the file, press **Enter** to accept the default.

Step 8. When prompted for a passphrase, enter

```
seatec astronomy
```

Step 9. Reenter the passphrase when prompted.

Step 10. Change to the **.ssh** directory and set the permissions on the **id_rsa.pub** file:

```
cd .ssh ; chmod 644 id_rsa.pub
```

Step 11. Copy the **id_rsa.pub** file to a new file called **authorized_keys**:

```
cp id_rsa.pub authorized_keys
```

NOTE The next steps take place on the host murphy.

Step 12. From the host murphy, ensure that you can contact the host fattyre with a ping:

```
ping fattyre
```

Step 13. Sign on to the host murphy as the root user.

Step 14. Add a user named user2:

```
useradd -m user2
```

Step 15. Set the password for user2:

```
passwd user2
```

Step 16. Enter the password twice to confirm it.

Step 17. Switch to the user2 account:

```
su - user2
```

Step 18. Make a directory and set its permissions with the following command:

```
mkdir .ssh ; chmod 700 .ssh
```

NOTE The next steps take place on the host fattyre.

Step 19. From the host **fattyre**, connect to the murphy host as user2:

```
ssh -l user2 murphy
```

Step 20. When prompted about the RSA key, answer **yes** and then enter user2's password.

Step 21. While logged in as user2 on the host murphy via SSH, copy the **authorized_keys** file from the fattyre host with the following command:

```
scp user1@fattyre:~/.ssh/authorized_keys ~/.ssh
```

The output of the **scp** program should look similar to this:

```
authorized_keys 100% |***********************| 236 00:00
```

Step 22. Exit user2 on the host murphy and return to being user1 on fattyre.

Step 23. On fattyre as user1, invoke the **ssh-agent** as a wrapper to your shell:

```
ssh-agent $SHELL
```

Step 24. Add your key to the agent:

```
ssh-add
```

Step 25. When prompted for the passphrase, enter the following:

```
no more tears
```

You then see output similar to this:

```
Identity added: /home/ssha/.ssh/id_rsa (/home/ssha/.ssh/
id_rsa)
```

Step 26. Try to log in as user2 on murphy and watch what happens:

```
ssh -l user Murphy
```

You shouldn't see any password prompt; you should see only the confirmation of where you last logged in from:

```
Last login: Wed May 26 13:46:55 from fattyre
```

Step 27. If you do see a prompt for the passphrase, enter **no more tears** as you did before.

This is all it takes to get two accounts and machines set up to use SSH utilities without having to enter anything but the **ssh-agent** command along with the passphrase. Remember that **ssh-agent** resides in memory and wraps a security blanket around your shell session, answering any SSH-related security requests for you. The **ssh-add** utility is for adding key information into the agent and doesn't have to be run again as long as your key information remains the same.

> **NOTE**   The *ssh-copy-id* command is also a possible choice for sending a user's autho-
> rized key to another server. For example, to have the user zakkw's authorized key exist
> on the Eternal server, you could use the command
>
> ```
> # ssh-copy -id -i ~/zakkw/.ssh/keyfile zakkw@eternal
> ```
>
> This will copy the user zakkw's file to the remote server and install it into the
> **authorized_keys** file, prompting for a password to authenticate the process.
>
> Ideally, this would be performed by the root user for both systems and assumes that
> you are on a remote system from the Eternal server.

Tunneling

One of the greatest features of SSH is that it can *tunnel*—provide a conduit from
inside one network, and even behind a firewall, through to another network. In
many cases, using *tunneling* can enable you to do things that either your network
administrator doesn't want you to do or you need to do because of an overly restrictive policy, such as at a coffee shop or Internet cafe.

Let's talk about some of the various scenarios where tunneling can come in handy.

X11 Forwarding

X is complex and hard to set up sometimes, and it might seem that tunneling X from
another machine to show on yours would be hard too, but *X11 forwarding* is fairly
straightforward due to the magical properties of ssh tunneling.

Let's say you have a Linux system named cygnusx1 on which you want to run an
application in the GUI environment, but you want that application that runs on the
remote host to display on your local system.

Here's a possible set of steps you might take:

Step 1.   On a Mac, download and install XQuartz (https:/www.xquartz.org).

Step 2.   Run the command **ssh -X ursulak@cygnusx1**.

Step 3.   After a shell opens in the terminal on the remote host (cygnusx1), run the
app.

Step 4.   In a second or two, the remote application, running as a process on the
remote host, will display on your system as if it were being run locally.

This is just an example of how forwarding X11 applications from the host they are
running on to your local system would work. All sorts of things could go wrong, but

that topic is beyond the scope of the Linux+ exam. The main thing is to understand the concept of X11 forwarding, which we have more than adequately covered.

Port Forwarding

Port forwarding is typically used in scenarios in which there is a need to get around some overly strict or controlling network or firewall. Keep in mind, though, that often there are *very* good reasons for those restrictions and rules being in place, so be responsible and don't willingly cause issues using port forwarding.

Using SSH to forward ports takes several paths, but the main concept is the same: you are using the ssh client on one system to tunnel out to the ssh server on another system and cause services that are represented by a port on the latter system to be mapped, or to appear to be connected, to the other system.

In general, port forwarding occurs in three main ways:

- **Local port forwarding:** This enables you to cause a remote port to be mapped to, and to appear as if it were on, your local system. Kind of like mounting an NFS share locally, mapping a port from a remote system to yours locally effectively makes your local system appear as if it is providing that service.

- **Remote port forwarding:** Flip the scenario around and allow your local system resources to be used by a remote machine. For example, I might map a remote system's port 8080 to my local 5500 port, and anyone connecting to that remote server on the 8080 port will get transported to my local port and service.

- **Dynamic port forwarding:** The term *dynamic port forwarding*, also known as dynamic SOCKS proxying, is a method used to securely tunnel network traffic through a remote server or proxy. Sometimes you don't want to explicitly assign ports and just want the SOCKS proxy on your system to use dynamically assigned local ports and handle all the details. Think of a situation where you need to access ports and protocols that are not allowed through a convention center's network setup. You can use what is effectively a VPN/ proxy to drill through the local restrictive network stack and connect to and communicate freely with your desired target hosts, services, and ports.

NOTE   The beauty of using SSH tunneling for these purposes is that you don't have to worry that by doing so you are exposing the local network or system unnecessarily; you're using the very secure SSH protocols and stack to do all of this!

Executing Commands as Another User

There are times when you need to execute a command as a different user account. For example, if you log in to the system as a non-root user, but need to execute a command with root privileges.

This section describes methods of running commands as different user accounts, including the **sudo** command, the **su** command and the **pkexec** command.

The sudo Command

The problem with the *su* command is that to provide a user with elevated privileges, you need to provide the user with the root password, which would give that user full administrative access to the system.

Often you want to allow a regular user to execute some commands, but not all commands, as the root user. For example, if a network error occurs on a user's workstation, you might want that user to be allowed to restart the networking service. On some systems, this can be accomplished by executing the following command:

```
# /etc/rc.d/init.d/network restart
```

To execute this command successfully, the user needs to have root privileges. This is where you either give the user the root password (which is not recommended) or you give limited root access the correct and reasonable way, via the *sudo* command and its partner tools.

Instead of providing the user with the root password, you can set up the **sudo** command to allow the user to run just the necessary command. To do this, you need to log in as the root user and then execute the *visudo* command.

```
# visudo
```

This command allows you to edit the */etc/sudoers* file, the file that allows you to provide root access for specific commands to specific users. The **visudo** command automatically assumes that you want to use the **vi** editor to edit this file. To use a different editor, such as the **nano** editor, execute a command like the following:

```
# export EDITOR=nano
```

NOTE Why use the **visudo** command instead of editing the **/etc/sudoers** file directly? The **visudo** command performs some error checking when you exit the editor to make sure you didn't make formatting mistakes.

The sudoedit Command

One of the conundrums of granting a user access to edit a configuration file is that if you are using **vi/vim**, you are essentially giving the user the ability to run *any* command as root.

To prevent a user from gaining shell access with a simple set of keystrokes from **vi/vim** while running it as root, there exists the *sudoedit* command, which is really just a symbolic link to a function contained in the **sudo** command.

The **sudoedit** command lets you allow a user to use any editor, not just **vi/vim**. It also enables the user to edit the using sudo access, rather than having to log in to the root user account.

When a user edits a file by using the **sudoedit** functionality, a temporary copy of the file(s) is made, and it is owned by the user in question. Since the user is now the owner of the temporary file(s), he can successfully edit the file(s) without having root access. Upon saving the file(s), the temporary copy owned by the user is copied back to the original file location, and the original ownership is restored; the now unnecessary temporary copy is discarded.

To configure **sudoedit**, add the following line to the **/etc/sudoers** file:

```
%newsudo ALL = sudoedit /some/path/to/a/file
```

Configure the newsudo group in **/etc/sudoers** to have the users you want to use **sudoedit**, and then all they need to do is run the command:

```
sudoedit /path/to/that/file
```

The **/etc/sudoers** file has many options. For the Linux+ certification exam, you just need to know how to provide a user with the ability to execute commands as the root user. For example, if you want a user account with the name ross to be able to run all commands as the root user, add the following line:

```
ross ALL=(ALL) ALL
```

To limit a user to a specific command, such as the **/etc/rc.d/init.d/network** command, add the following line:

```
ross ALL=(ALL) /etc/rc.d/init.d/network
```

For a user to execute a command as root, she needs to use the **sudo** command. The syntax is as follows:

```
# sudo /etc/rc.d/init.d/network restart
```

The user is then prompted for her own password (not the root password). If the correct password is given and the access is permitted based on an entry in the **/etc/sudoers** file, the command is executed as the root user. If the user attempts to execute a command that she is not authorized to execute, an error message appears on the screen, and the attempt is logged.

User Privilege Escalation

Users on a Linux system come in the following types, and it is important to know all three types, which type you are logged in, and how to escalate or deescalate your privileges at will by switching from one type to another:

- **Root:** This is the root user, who is the super user and the most privileged user on the system. There should be only one of them, characterized by the name root and the UID (user ID) 0.

- **Standard:** Otherwise known as "regular" or "normal" users, these are the rank-and-file users on the system; they have no special privileges and typically have UIDs that range from 1000 and higher.

- **Service:** These are the accounts that have to exist to ensure that every service or daemon on the system is running as a user, since every process must have a user attached. These accounts are never signed into; they exist in the **/etc/passwd** file and may even have **/bin/nologin** as the specified shell.

The best security practice is to avoid logging in as the root user unless you need to perform specific administration commands. In most cases, you should not log in as the root user directly but rather should gain root access by executing either the **su** command or the **sudo** command.

> **NOTE** The wheel group is an odd thing on the Linux system these days. Traditionally used on Unix systems to allow users to gain root access, the wheel group is often now tied directly to having **sudo** access.

If the wheel group is configured to have privileged access via **sudo** and the **/etc/sudoers** file, then adding a user to the wheel group gives the user those privileges. For example, in our openSUSE system, the wheel group is set up to be able to allow members of that group to execute any command, just as the root would be able to:

```
%wheel  ALL=(ALL) ALL
```

This entry is normally commented out, but it would be very easy to remove the single # comment in front of it in the default file to enable the wheel group (and its members) to have full administrative access to the system.

The su Command

To gain access to another user account with the **su** command, use the following syntax:

```
su account_name
```

For example, to switch to the root account, execute the following command:

```
# su root
```

This provides you with a non-login shell for the root user. Typically you want a login shell because it provides you with the full user environment (environment variables, shell customizations, and so on). This can be accomplished by using the **-l** option or just a **-** option:

```
# su - root
# su -l root
```

To gain access to a regular user account, you must provide the account name. However, if you don't provide an account name, the **su** command assumes that you want to switch to the root account. As a result, the following commands are all the same:

- **su - root**
- **su -l root**
- **su -**
- **su -l**

When switching from the root account to a regular user account, no password is required. This means the root user can switch to a regular user account to test that account's features (or troubleshoot problems for the user) without having to change that user's password.

To switch from a regular user account to any other account, you must know the password of the account you are switching to.

NOTE Some distributions' versions of the **su** command allow for the use of X and remote X; simply use the **sux** command instead of the **su** command. This is most notably present on the openSUSE and SUSE Linux Enterprise distributions.

PolicyKit

PolicyKit, also known as polkit, is a system service in Linux that provides a framework for controlling system-wide privileges and permissions.

PolicyKit exists to provide application-level definition and handling of unprivileged access to privileged processes. For example, you might use PolicyKit to provide a user the ability (and the rights) to perform a task by executing a command with elevated privileges. If you think that sounds like the **sudo** command, it's understandable, because they both have fairly similar goals.

One difference is that PolicyKit is a little easier to use, and certainly less tedious, because you don't have to preface almost everything you do with the **sudo** command.

> **NOTE**   The name PolicyKit is used in this book to match the Linux+ exam objectives, but the current package has been renamed Polkit. One of the main positives of PolicyKit is that it's a central place for defining and accessing policies that allow unprivileged users to perform what would normally be privileged actions.
>
> The PolicyKit local configuration is kept in **/etc/polkit-1/localauthority** and uses the common method of include files that contain PolicyKit configuration and end either in **.conf** or, for the more specialized files, **.pkla**.
>
> The following are examples of the types of actions PolicyKit can be configured for:
>
> - Allow the user to configure wireless connections
> - Make it possible to mount and unmount USB and other detached media devices
> - Let the user manage shutdown, reboot, and hibernate events
> - Make devices accessible that are traditionally difficult to access, such as system audio

The pkexec Command

With the previous discussion of the PolicyKit package, **pkexec** makes a lot more sense, as it's the most common way to utilize the PolicyKit rules.

The *pkexec* command, when used to run another command, will execute that command as the targeted user. The user can be specified, but if it is not, **pkexec** attempts to execute the target command as the root user.

For example, to execute the **lemmy.sh** script as the root user, you would type

```
# pkexec lemmy.sh
```

Since a user is not specified, the default for **pkexec** is to attempt to run the subsequent command, script, or executable as the root user.

Summary

This chapter focused on how to remotely and securely connect with systems for the purposes of administering them, using the SSH suite of technologies and the various **ssh**-prefaced commands you learned about in this chapter.

You also learned about the methods for privilege elevation, or running commands or acting as another user, such as **su**, **sudo**, and **pkexec**.

Exam Preparation Tasks

As mentioned in the section "Goals and Methods" in the Introduction, you have a couple of choices for exam preparation: the exercises here, Chapter 23, "Final Preparation," and the exam simulation questions in the Pearson Test Prep Software Online.

Review All Key Topics

Review the most important topics in this chapter, noted with the Key Topic icon in the left margin of the page. Table 11-2 lists these key topics and the page number on which each is found.

Table 11-2   Key Topics for Chapter 11

Key Topic Element	Description	Page Number
List	Programs and files that SSH includes	408
List	SSH global configuration files	408
Paragraph	Description of the **~/.ssh/authorized_keys** file	409
Paragraph	Example syntax for connecting to a remote system via the **ssh** command	409
Note	Example of deleting all the **.rhosts** files on a given system	411
Step list	Enabling SSH use without passwords	411
Section	Tunneling	414
Note	Reason to use the **visudo** command instead of editing **/etc/sudoers** directly	416
Paragraph	Using the **sudoedit** command to allow a user to use any editor	417
Paragraph	Switching to the root account using the **su** command	419
Paragraph	Example of using the **pkexec** command to run a script as an different user	420

Define Key Terms

Define the following key terms from this chapter and check your answers in the glossary:

ssh, ssh-add, /etc/ssh/sshd_config, known_hosts, ssh_config, ssh-keygen, ssh-copy-id, tunneling, X11 forwarding, port forwarding, dynamic forwarding, privilege escalation, **su, sudo, visudo, /etc/sudoers, sudoedit**, PolicyKit, **pkexec**

Review Questions

The answers to these review questions are in Appendix A.

1. After configuring the PolicyKit rules for your system, what command would you use to use those rules when executing a target command that your current user doesn't have rights to execute alone?

   a. sudo

   b. pkexec

   c. suexec

   d. execit

2. When configuring the **sudo** command, what is the full path and filename of its primary configuration file?

   _____

3. You are able to access a remote system using just a passphrase for authentication. What must you have copied from your system to the remote system in order for this to happen?

   a. Your personal public key

   b. The system's public key

   c. The wheel group's public key

   d. The remote user's private key

4. When configuring your system to allow or deny certain groups or users to sign in via SSH, what is the full path and filename of the configuration file where these settings are kept?

   _____

5. If you invoke the **ssh** command with the **-X** option, what are you likely to be doing after you sign on to the remote system?

   a. Just standard commands

   b. Running xeyes locally and displaying remotely

   c. Running X11 on the remote system and displaying locally

   d. Running remote X apps that display locally

6. Which of the following commands is specifically designed to make it more secure to edit files when using **sudo** to elevate your privileges?

   a. **sudovim**

   b. **visudo**

   c. **sudoedit**

   d. **nanobot**

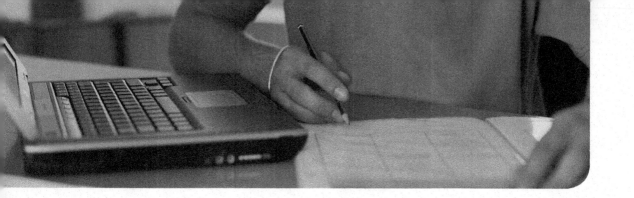

This chapter covers the following topics:

- File Permissions
- File and Directory Ownership
- Understanding and Using umask
- Permission Granularity Issues
- Finding Files by Permission
- Access Control Lists
- Context-Based Access

The exam objective covered in this chapter is as follows:

- **Objective 2.5:** Given a scenario, apply the appropriate access controls

## CHAPTER 12

Understanding and Applying Access Controls

Setting, maintaining, and verifying access to system resources is a key part of being a valid systems administrator. In this chapter, we'll be looking at the world of straightforward access controls, and then taking the complexity and intensity of the tools up a level by exploring the two competing Linux security systems, SELinux and AppArmor.

"Do I Know This Already?" Quiz

The "Do I Know This Already?" quiz enables you to assess whether you should read this entire chapter or simply jump to the "Exam Preparation Tasks" section for review. If you are in doubt, read the entire chapter. Table 12-1 outlines the major headings in this chapter and the corresponding "Do I Know This Already?" quiz questions. You can find the answers in Appendix A, "Answers to the 'Do I Know This Already?' Quizzes and Review Questions."

Table 12-1 "Do I Know This Already?" Foundation Topics Section-to-Question Mapping

Foundation Topics Section	Questions Covered in This Section
File Permissions	1–2
File and Directory Ownership	3–4
Understanding and Using umask	5–6
File permissions	1,2
Security-enhanced Linux (SELinux)	4
AppArmor	3
Command-line utilities	5,6

CAUTION The goal of self-assessment is to gauge your mastery of the topics in this chapter. If you do not know the answer to a question or are only partially sure of the answer, you should mark that question as wrong for purposes of the self-assessment. Giving yourself credit for an answer you correctly guess skews your self-assessment results and might provide you with a false sense of security.

1. As a sysadmin, you need to set up a shared directory with multiple users. What special permission can you set to cause the inheritance of group ownership?

   a. 0

   b. 1

   c. 2

   d. 4

2. You want to change the group owner of a file or directory. Which of the following commands can accomplish this? (Choose two.)

   a. **chuser**

   b. **chgrp**

   c. **chown**

   d. **chmod**

3. Which of the following is considered a MAC security system?

   a. SecureMAC

   b. AppArmor

   c. Lockdown

   d. AppSecure

4. Which of the following is a valid SELinux mode? (Choose all that apply.)

   a. Disabled

   b. Enforcing

   c. Defensive

   d. Permissive

   e. Progressive

5. Which command is used to display security context on processes?

   a. **show**

   b. **list**

   c. **ps**

   d. **ls**

6. Which command is used to display security context on files?

   a. **show**

   b. **list**

   c. **ps**

   d. **ls**

Foundation Topics

As a sysadmin, having proper control over access to system resources is very important. Linux traditionally, prior to the point of the addition of *access control lists (ACLs)*, did not support allowing different permission sets for multiple user or accounts. ACLs now provide that functionality.

Additionally, using SELinux or AppArmor is another way to secure your systems and maintain control over system resources.

NOTE As in previous chapters, the order in which the Linux objectives are presented doesn't align well with what I consider the best order of presentation, so I'll address them in the latter order. In particular, where Linux+ objective 2.5 lists a large lump of command-line utilities at the end, I will present them in their proper context throughout the discussion of the various topics as we go along.

File Permissions

Permissions determine how users can access resources on a system. System security is configured by the user's UID (user ID), GIDs (group IDs—both primary and secondary), and the permissions on the object the user is attempting to access.

Every object on a system must belong to at least a user owner and group owner. This is a security feature, and it helps establish who has rights to do what to objects on the filesystem, as discussed in the following sections.

Permission Trio Bits

Figure 12-1 shows the ten positions (one type bit and three trios of permission bits) that make up the permissions section of a file.

T y p e	User			Group			Other		
	r	w	x	r	w	x	r	w	x
	4	2	1	4	2	1	4	2	1

Figure 12-1 Permission trios

The first of the 10 bits is the type of the object:

- **.:** Indicates that this is a normal file.

- **l:** Indicates that this is a symlink (symbolic link), which is a file that points to another object.

- **b:** Indicates that this is a block device file.

- **c:** Indicates that this is a character device file.

- **d:** Indicates that this is a directory.

The next 9 bits are the *permission trios*. Each of the trios affects a certain set of users (user owner, group owner, or other). To determine which permissions a user has to a given object, begin from the left, and as soon as a match is made, that trio alone is the permissions in effect for that user and object. Here are the three trios:

- *User owner:* If the user is the user owner, this permission trio is in effect.

- *Group owner:* If the user is not the user owner and the user's primary or secondary groups are this group, this permission trio is in effect.

- *Other:* If the user is neither the user owner nor a member of the group owner, this permission trio is in effect.

NOTE On some modern Linux systems, you see another character right after the permission set. This could either be a . character, which is related to SELinux, or a + character, which is related to ACLs. Do not mix up the Windows environment and Linux in your mind. Linux filesystem permissions (non-ACL permissions) do not have "effective permissions"; you must use an ACL to have more than a single user owner or more than a single group owner.

Each of the trios is made up of 3 bits (which can have the values 4, 2, 1). The bits work like light switches: If a bit is on, then the value counts; if it is off, the value doesn't count. That value is used with the **chmod** command as well as with other commands.

The bit values equate to the following permissions for files:

- **4:** Read, which is the ability to view the file's contents.

- **2:** Write, which is the ability to change the file's contents.

- **1:** Execute, which means the file can be executed. (The read permission is also needed for a script, but a binary can execute with only the execute permission.)

These permissions have similar, but slightly different, meanings for directories:

- **4:** Read, which is the ability to view the directory's contents (using the **ls** command). However, to see file attributes (such as with the **-l** option to the **ls** command), execute permission on the directory is also required.

- **2:** Write, which is the ability to add and delete files in the directory. This is a powerful permission for directories because a user can delete every file in a directory, even files that he doesn't own, if he has the write permission on the directory. Caveat: For write permission to be valid, the user also must have execute permission.

- **1:** Execute; the user can use the **cd** command to get into the directory or use the directory in a pathname. For example, if the user attempts to execute **cd /home/bob**, she needs execute permission on the **/** directory, the **home** directory, and the **bob** directory.

To better understand directory permissions, think of a directory as a room. If you want to see what is in the room, you need a window. Think of the read permission as the window. If this permission is set, you can see into the directory (room). If you want to get into the room, you need a door. Think of the execute permission as the door. This concept helps the caveat for the write permission make more sense: To remove something from a room, you first need to be able to get into the room!

If you execute the **ls -l** command on an object, and its permission trios are 666 (or rw-rw-rw-), the only way that number could be arrived at with the possible bit values is for the 4 and 2 bits to be on—or rw- (read and write, but not execute). If you see a file that is set to 666, that equates to all three trios having the same permissions—read and write but not execute.

NOTE Watch for Linux+ exam questions that try to trick you with a user who is both the user owner and a member of the group owner, but the correct permissions for executing or changing the file aren't in a single trio. You can't mix the trios, even if your user account encompasses several of the trios.

For example, say that a user named fred is the user owner of the file object **/home/fred/22AcaciaAvenue.mp3** and is a member of the group owner of that object. The file's listing has the following permissions set:

```
-rw-r-xr-x 2 fred users 0 Jan 26 13:08 22 AcaciaAvenue.mp3
```

The fred user's permissions might seem to span the various trios, but because fred is the user owner, he matches the first trio and stops there. In other words, the user fred has read and write permission, but not execute, even though fred is a member of the users group, and members of that group do have execute permission on this file.

Manipulating Permissions

The *chmod* command is used when modifying or altering an object's permission trio bits. Only the root and the object's owner can alter permissions.

The two modes of manipulating the permissions for an object are octal and symbolic. Both modes have their place, but it's hard to say which is used more to set permissions these days.

The general rule is that if you want to set permissions (that is, wipe out the current permissions and set them to a given permission), you use the octal method, which looks like this: (644, 777, and so on). If you want to alter permissions, you use the symbolic or letters method: (g+rx, o=a). Many times I have needed to clean up after someone who has accidentally set an entire directory structure's permissions and caused havoc. You should be familiar with and skilled at both methods, but remember that the symbolic method is more exacting and precise.

Octal Mode

The octal notation method uses the same bits to describe what you want your permissions to be (4 = read, 2 = write, 1 = execute). For example, if you are told that the current permissions for an object are 644 and you are asked to ensure that all users have read and write access to that object, execute the following command:

```
# chmod 666 file1
```

The **chmod** command works great on groups of files, too:

```
# chmod 644 /home/lukec/*.txt
```

It even works on directories and their contents. For example, say that the user bertrandr has a directory on which he wants to set all the files to the permission 640 to make the files more secure. He could use the following command:

```
# chmod -R 640 /home/bertrandr/data/*
```

Take a moment to understand why this command works the way it does. The **chmod** command has an **-R** option that affects the object named and all its child objects. The user bertrandr doesn't want to change the permission of the data directory itself; he just wants to change the permission on the contents, which is why the slash and asterisk characters are on the end of the target. This command acts on the entire contents of the **/home/bertandr/data** directory but doesn't modify the directory's permissions. However, if there were any directories within the **/home/bertandr/data** directory, all those directories would have the permissions changed (along with all files and directories beneath them)!

The **chmod** command has a few useful options:

- **-c:** Reports only which files were changed.

- **-v:** Reports all files.

- **-h:** Changes symbolic links, not the original file.

- **-f:** Suppresses error messages.

- **-R:** Operates recursively through directories.

The **chmod** command's recursive option is an uppercase R, not a lowercase r, as with some other commands. If you are familiar with the cases of the various command options, you will be fine on the Linux+ exam.

NOTE   When using the octal notation method, you should always specify three values: owner, group, and others. If you specify only one value, the system uses that value for the others permission set and assumes a value of 0 for the owner and group permissions. This is never a good idea!

Symbolic Mode

When using the **chmod** command with symbolic values, keep in mind that you can change all the permissions, as in the numeric mode, but you need to use a much longer command. The primary reason to use *symbolic mode* is to affect, or alter, smaller sets of permissions rather than to overwrite them all.

With symbolic mode, you use a letter to identify each trio:

- User owner = u, group owner = g, other = o, and all = a

- A qualifier: + to add, - to remove, or = to assign

- The permissions being set: r = read, w = write, and x = execute

To use the symbolic values to set permissions, you can change them all at once, as the following command demonstrates:

```
# chmod a=rwx file
```

This produces permission trios that are set to -rwxrwxrwx.

Or you can use each one of the identifiers, with its qualifier and permissions separated by commas:

```
# chmod u=rw,g=rx,a= file
```

This produces a file that has its permissions set to -rw-r-x---.

> **NOTE** This method of using the symbolic mode is unwieldy and somewhat inelegant for constant use. Use symbolic mode when you want to fine-tune permissions, not when you want to set all the permissions.

To change just the user owner's permissions to rwx, use the following command:

```
# chmod u=rwx mystuff
```

To change the group owner's permissions to r-x, use the following command:

```
# chmod g=rx mystuff
```

To change the other or everyone else's permissions to r, use this command:

```
# chmod o=r mystuff
```

Keep in mind when using symbolic mode that the permissions you are not specifying stay as they were before you executed the **chmod** command.

You can use several methods to set a file to be executable without knowing its other permissions. For example, if you know a file exists but don't know the permissions and you are told to make sure it's executable by all permission trios, use the following command:

```
# chmod a+x file1
```

Alternatively, you can leave off the a and get all the trios by default:

```
# chmod +x file1
```

Remember: When changing permissions, you can always use either the numeric method or the symbolic method. The numeric method is normally easier when changing all the permissions, while the symbolic method is normally easier when changing one or just a few permissions.

File and Directory Ownership

Ownership is critical to any Linux/Unix system—everything must be owned by at least a user owner and a group owner, not to be confused with additional groups.

You can use the **ls** command to view the ownership of any object that you have access to, but be sure to use the **-l** option so that the permissions and ownership show up properly.

Changing File Ownership

The *chown* command is used to set the user owner, group owner, or a combination of the two with one command. The format for the **chown** command is

```
# chown -options user:group object
```

The **chown** command accepts both of the following commands as valid (where the owner/group separator can be either a : or a . character):

```
# chown snuffy:users file1
# chown snuffy.users file1
```

In addition, you can use the following syntax with **chown**:

- **owner:** Changes only the user owner.

- **owner:group:** Changes both the user owner and the group owner.

- **owner::** Changes the user owner and sets the group owner to the primary group of the current user.

- **:group:** Changes only the group owner and leaves the user owner unaffected.

Let's say that the user snuffy's primary group is called users, and the account is a secondary group member of the accounting group. By default, every object snuffy creates on the system has snuffy as the user owner and users as the group owner. This can cause problems in shared directories. For example, if snuffy visits a shared directory whose group ownership is set to the accounting group and creates a file named **snuffysexpenses.txt**, that file is inaccessible to any of the other users who share that directory unless they are also members of the group users.

Say the user martha does expenses and needs to have ownership of the **snuffysexpenses.txt** file, and you, as the administrator, want to change the group ownership of this file to the accounting group. To accomplish this task, use this command:

```
# chown martha:accounting snuffysexpenses.txt
```

Let's say that now the file needs to be owned by another user who cuts the checks, fluchre; you can change just the user owner without having to bother with the group owner:

```
# chown fluchre snuffysexpenses.txt
```

If for some reason you decide that an entire directory tree of files needs to have ownership changed, you can change them all with the following command:

```
# chown -R root:accounting /accounting
```

> **NOTE** The only user on the system who can change the user ownership of an object is the root user. Even the owner of a file can't "give ownership" to another user. However, a regular user can change the group ownership of an object as long as the user is a member of the group whose ownership she is changing.

Changing Group Ownership

When just the group owner needs to be changed, the simplest method is to use the *chgrp* command. The syntax of the command is straightforward:

```
# chgrp staff file1
```

Changing a large set of files to another group owner requires the use of the **-R** (recursive) option:

```
# chgrp -R staff /data/*
```

This command changes the contents of the **/data** directory (and all its subdirectories) to the group owner staff but leaves the user owner alone.

Options for the **chgrp** command include the following:

- **-c:** Shows a line of output only for changed objects.
- **-h:** Changes symbolic links, not the original file.
- **-R:** Recursively affects the target and all children.
- **-v:** Shows a line of output for every object, regardless of the actions performed on the object.

> **NOTE** Although it is not a Linux+ exam objective, the **newgrp** command can be handy when it comes to group ownership. A regular user can execute the command **newgrp** *groupname* if he is a member of *groupname*. This opens a new shell in which the primary group is *groupname*, which is useful when creating a bunch of files that need to be group owned by a secondary group. To close this new shell, simply execute the **exit** command.

Understanding and Using umask

The umask command is used to specify default permissions for when a new file or directory is created. This command was covered in detail in Chapter 8, "Understanding Linux Security Best Practices."

Permission Granularity Issues

Several aspects of how the Linux and Unix filesystems are constructed can cause problems for administrators. For example, if you are not using ACLs, only a single group can be the group owner for a given object. Whoever wants access to that object needs to be a member of the group that owns the file (unless you, as the owner of the file, want to give permission to all others). For example, consider the following **ls -l** output:

```
-rw-r----- 1 bob staff 0 Jan 26 13:08 22 data.txt
```

To be able to see the contents of this file, you need to be either the bob user or a member of the staff group.

Configuring many groups and users to have access to the right files can be difficult. Every user has a primary group and could be a member of additional groups (secondary groups). This poses problems when sharing files between members who are in shared secondary groups. For example, say that the bob user (primary group staff, secondary group project), the sue user (primary group payroll, secondary group project), and the steve user (primary group acct, secondary group project) are working on a joint project and sharing files in the **/home/project** directory. The bob user creates a file that ends up looking like the following when listed with the **ls -l** command:

```
-rw-r----- 1 bob staff 0 Jan 26 13:08 22

data_for_sue_and_steve.txt
```

Unfortunately, even though all users are in the same group (the project group), the sue and steve users can't view the contents of this file. They are not members of the staff group, so their permission set is others for this file.

As described later, the bob user can change the group ownership of the file to the project group, but then users must perform this action every time they create a file. It is unreasonable to assume that all users will remember to do this all of the time (and, as an administrator, you don't want to have to teach all the users to perform this action on their files).

There's a way out of this situation: You can set an additional or special bit on the shared directory, which causes all users who have access to inherit the group owner of the directory on all objects they create in that directory. This permission set, called *SGID*, is covered in detail in this chapter.

NOTE   Historically, only a few Linux distributions featured ACLs, and sysadmins often were relegated to using the special bit permissions to try to allow multiple sets of users access to resources. Now many distributions feature ACLs, so special bits are used less often.

Special Bit Permissions

The following special bits are available for Linux filesystem use:

- **SUID:** The *set user ID (SUID)* permission allows a user to run a program as if he or she were the user owner of the program; in most cases, the user owner is the root user. The numeric value of this permission set is 4*XXX* (where *XXX* is replaced by the numeric values for the trio sets mentioned previously).

- **SGID:** When set on a directory, the *set group ID (SGID)* permission automatically gives group ownership of all new files created in the directory to the group owner of the directory (numeric = 2*XXX*). When set on a file, the SGID allows a user to run a program as if he or she were the group owner of the file.

- **Sticky bit:** This permission set is used to keep "nonowners" from deleting files in a common directory (numeric = 1*XXX*). In a *sticky bit* directory, only the owner of the file or the owner of the directory can delete the file. (Root can always delete files as well.)

Remember that these special permissions are used only when necessary, which isn't often; the SUID and SGID permission sets on an executable file pose a security risk, even when properly used. Avoid providing write permission to SUID and SGID executables. This permission enables a regular user to replace the code within the file and opens a security hole on the system.

Special permissions can be set using either the numeric method or the symbolic method, just as other permissions can be set using both methods with the **chmod** command.

NOTE   The use of the characters *XXX* in the following examples indicates that permissions exist and need to be included but removes the focus from the permissions. In other words, these are the regular permissions discussed previously, and I have substituted the *XXX* characters in these examples to focus on the special bits instead.

The first way to set these special permissions is to use the numeric mode when executing the **chmod** command. All permissions must be overwritten when using the numeric mode; the following sets the SUID permission on the file:

```
chmod 4XXX /some/program
```

Several bits can be changed or set simultaneously. The following command, for example, sets both the SUID and SGID bits for the program (which is somewhat rare but permitted):

```
chmod 6XXX /some/program
```

The second way to set special permissions is to use the symbolic mode. For example, to add SUID on a file:

```
chmod u+s /some/program
```

Again, you can set several special bits at once even with the symbolic mode, although the syntax is a bit more complex:

```
chmod u+s,g+s /some/program
```

Setting the SUID Bit on Files

A command related to the SUID bit is **chsh**. The **chsh** command allows a regular user to change her login shell. Note the current permissions for this command:

```
-rws--x-- 1 root root 15432 Apr 29 2013 /usr/bin/chsh
```

The **s** in place of the user owner's execute permission indicates that this is an SUID command. When this command executes, it modifies the contents of the **/etc/passwd** file. The **/etc/passwd** file is not normally something that can be modified by non-root users; as you can see, normally only the root user has this ability:

```
-rw-r--r-- 1 root root 2036 Mar 8 18:39 /etc/passwd
```

However, with the SUID permission set, the **chsh** program is able to access files as either the person who runs the command or as the owner of the **chsh** program (which, in this case, is root).

What if you, as the administrator, do not want users to change their login shells? Just execute the following command as root:

```
# chmod u-s /usr/bin/chsh
```

Example 12-1 shows a live example.

Example 12-1 Demonstration of SUID

```
[root@localhost ~]# ls -l /usr/bin/chsh
-rws--x--x. 1 root root 15432 Apr 29 2013 /usr/bin/chsh
[root@localhost ~]# su - student
[student@localhost ~]$ chsh
Changing shell for student.
Password:
New shell [/bin/bash]: /bin/csh
Shell changed.
[student@localhost ~]$ exit
logout
[root@localhost ~]# chmod u-s /usr/bin/chsh
[root@localhost ~]# su - student
[student@localhost ~]$ chsh
Changing shell for student.
Password:
New shell [/bin/csh]: /bin/bash
setpwnam: Permission denied
Shell *NOT* changed. Try again later.
```

NOTE While the user can "try again later," as the last line of output in Example 12-1 suggests, until the root user resets the SUID permission set, no regular user will be able to change his login shell.

Setting the SGID Bit on Files

The SGID permission is rarely set on files. Consider the following program with the SGID bit set:

```
-r-xr-sr-x 1 root tty 10996 Jul 19 2011 /usr/bin/wall
```

The **s** in place of the group owner's execute permission indicates that this is an SGID command. The **wall** command allows users to send messages to the terminal windows of all users who are logged in. Normally this would be a security issue; you don't want a user to interfere with another user's terminal window. Having a message pop up in a terminal where a user is working can be distracting.

Users can use the **wall** command in this way because it is an SGID program. When this program executes, it accesses files as if the person executing the command were

a member of the tty group. This, in turn, allows the **wall** program to have write
access to the terminal device files group owned by the tty group:

```
# ls -l /dev/tty1
crw--w---- 1 root tty 4, 1 Jun 2 17:13 /dev/tty1
```

If you are having problems with users abusing the **wall** command, simply take away
the SGID access:

```
# chmod 0555 /usr/bin/wall
```

NOTE The **wall** program can be used to communicate with other users, but because
maturity levels vary among humans and definitely among computer users, you
may have users harassing others or inappropriately sending broadcast messages. By
restricting access to this command, you improve the productivity of all system users.

Setting the SGID Bit on Directories

Consider the earlier scenario in which the bob user (primary group staff, secondary
group project), the sue user (primary group payroll, secondary group project), and
the steve user (primary group acct, secondary group project) are working on a joint
project and sharing files in the **/home/project** directory. The bob user creates a file
that ends up looking like the following when listed with the **ls -l** command:

```
-rw-r----- 1 bob staff 0 Jan 26 13:08 22 data_for_sue_and_steve.txt
```

Recall that this results in a problem: Even though bob, sue, and steve all have a common group, sue and steve can't access this file. If bob were to change the group ownership to the project group, then sue and steve would be able to view the contents
of this file. However, expecting users to do this every time they create a file isn't
reasonable.

The solution is to add SGID permission to the **/home/project** directory:

```
# chmod g+s /home/project
```

This command changes the group ownership to be the projects group, which means
all new files created in the **/home/project** directory are automatically group owned
by the group owner of the directory (which would have to be set to the project
group, of course). Note that this doesn't solve the problem of the existing file; it
affects only new files.

Setting the Sticky Bit

The sticky bit is used mostly for ensuring that users in a shared directory can't delete anyone else's files. A good example of this is the **/tmp** directory:

```
drwxrwxrwt 29 root 4096 Jun 2 17:27 /tmp
```

The t in place of the others execute permission indicates that this is a sticky bit directory. The **/tmp** directory is a location where all users must be able to create files. Unfortunately, the permission that allows users to create files also allows them to delete files—all files—in that directory.

When you add the sticky bit permission, the meaning of the write permission for directories changes. Instead of meaning "add and delete all files in the directory," it means the only users who can now delete files in this directory are as follows:

- The owner of the file

or

- The owner of the directory (which is normally the root user)

or

- The root user

Anyone can still add a file to this directory, as long as it doesn't result in overwriting another user's file.

Viewing and Changing File Attributes

In addition to permissions, there are file *attributes*, which you can think of as "advanced settings" for each file or directory on the filesystem.

Handling file attributes from the command line is accomplished by the following dynamic duo of commands:

- *lsattr*: This command displays the attribute set for a given set of files and/or directories.

- *chattr*: This command is used to set attributes of a file or directory, with some notable exceptions, which are out of scope for the Linux+ exam.

Displaying File Attributes

The primary way to view a file's attributes is by using the **lsattr** command, which displays a line of attribute notations, typically a bunch of minus symbols punctuated by a letter, such as:

```
# lsattr file1
--------------e----- file1
```

The command displays that only the **e** (or extent) format attribute is set, which in this case means that the file is using something called extents to map blocks on the disk. This happens to be one of the very few attributes that isn't easily changed by the **chattr** command.

Key File Attributes

Far from being just an oddity, there are some very important attributes that affect files on a filesystem. The following are some of the more notable attributes:

- **a:** The a attribute being set means the file can only be appended to, not overwritten.

- **A:** The A attribute is used very often for read-only data sets that are accessed frequently, such as busy static portions of a website; it means the access time-stamp (atime) record is not updated.

- **C:** The C attribute is used to change the file's copy-on-write attribute and how it's handled on filesystems that support C-O-W.

- **i:** The i attribute is a very powerful one that prevents the file from being modified, deleted, or renamed, along with many other restrictions.

There are a number of other attributes, which you absolutely should look up in the man page for the **chattr** command; it's good information but the preceding lists covers the attributes most likely to appear on the Linux+ exam.

Setting File Attributes

Setting an attribute on a file couldn't be simpler:

```
#   chattr +A file1
```

Now if you were to display the file's attributes again, you'd see

```
#   lsattr file1
--------A-----e----- file1
```

If you were to display the file contents, or read the file with a program, the file's atime record would not be updated.

Removing File Attributes

Removing an attribute on a file is as easy as setting the attribute:

```
#   chattr -A file1
```

Now if you were to display the file's attributes again, you'd see

```
#   lsattr file1
--------------e----- file1
```

This removes or unsets the A attribute, which means that the atime record will be updated as usual when this file is accessed.

> **NOTE** Please note that there are many options that have restrictions or don't work on a particular filesystem, or even don't work on *any* but a couple of filesystems. Consult the **chattr** and **lsattr** man pages for a lot of good information. Additionally, use test files and directories to gain skills with **chattr** and **lsattr** (*don't* use important password or system files or you'll end up having to troubleshoot and maybe fix some issues).

Finding Files by Permission

> **NOTE** You won't find this topic in the Linux+ objectives, but I have always gone beyond the objectives to make sure you have the information you'll need when you get into the production environment, so enjoy this little bonus section!

Attackers who breach a system often attempt to set certain files to have the SUID or SGID bit set in order to allow their otherwise normal accounts to perform all sorts of unauthorized tasks.

The **find** command has an operator that makes it easy to find vulnerable files. The **-perm** operator is usually followed by a three- or four-digit set of permissions, as shown in this example:

```
# find /usr/bin -perm 777
```

This example searches for any object in the **/usr/bin** directory, and all subdirectories, that has the exact permissions rwxrwxrwx. This is fine, but it doesn't help you find security risks caused by the SUID and SGID bits. This next command does, however:

```
# find / -perm -4000
```

At first glance, this might look as if it's a search for all files that have the SUID bits and then blank permissions from that point on. In fact, it searches the entire system for all files that have the SUID bit set, regardless of the other permissions.

You should install the system and then run a **find** command that reports any file that has an SUID bit set, like so:

```
# find / -perm -4000 -ls
```

Redirect this output to a file and keep that file on a disk or in some safe place off the system (such as on a USB drive). Every so often (especially after installing new software or when you think your system has been exploited), you should run the same **find** command and then compare the results to the original with the **diff** command, like this:

```
# diff /root/latestfindperm /mnt/usb/findperm.orig
```

Investigate any differences!

Access Control Lists

Anyone who spends any amount of time using Unix/Linux standard permissions will either cultivate a habit of swearing bitterly at their restrictions or choose to learn more about ACLs.

Not Enough Granularity

Why would you need more than the regular Unix/Linux permissions? In a number of instances, the limitations of having only one user owner or only one group owner are debilitating or overly restrictive. Yes, it's true that you can add people to the group that owns an object, but you can have only one group that is the owner, with a single set of permissions, and there will be times when you need another group of people to have fewer or more permissions—and then what do you do? For example, you might have a set of pricing spreadsheets that are maintained by the purchasing department, which must have read and write access to the contents of the pricing subdirectory. Also, you might have a group of sales associates who depend on being able to have read access to those spreadsheets so they can refer to them when giving pricing quotes to customers.

In the standard Unix/Linux permissions scheme, there can be only one group owner, and if you put both the sales associates and the purchasing people into a single group, one of these groups will not have adequate or appropriate access to the shared files.

ACLs to the Rescue

An ACL enables you to attach multiple user owners, multiple group owners, and even multiple other owners to a filesystem object or group of objects. In the pricing spreadsheets example, you can assign a secondary set of group ownership with different permissions to the pricing spreadsheets, using a command that sets the ACL to allow that group to have different capabilities on the directory and, by default, its contents.

Viewing ACLs

Before you assign any alternative or additive permissions to a directory or file, you should view its permissions by using the **getfacl** command. This keeps you from accidentally setting conflicting or overriding permissions if someone else has already set an ACL on the object.

To view the full permissions of a file named **test**, you would issue the following command:

```
$ getfacl test
# file: test
# owner: ross
# group: users
user::rwx
group::rwx
other::rwx
```

The first line of the output confirms that you are viewing the file **test** and its access control list settings, which at this time are blank, though they can be set. The next two lines confirm who the user owner and the primary group owner are. The next three lines after that are the blank permissions that you can now set.

Setting an ACL

Using the **setfacl** command is fairly easy, though things can get complex if you are trying to set multiple groups to access an object with different permissions.

When setting the permissions on an object, you use three sections for those permissions. The following example sets user permissions (u) for the user snuffy and adds the permissions to read and write but not execute for this object. The **-m** option enables you to modify the permissions:

```
# setfacl -m u:snuffy:rw test
```

This results in the user snuffy being given rw access as a user owner, not disturbing or displacing the original (and current owner) ross. You can confirm this by using the **getfacl** command:

```
$ getfacl test
# file: test
```

```
# owner: ross
# group: users
user::rwx
user:snuffy:rw-
group::rwx
mask::rwx
other::rwx
```

Notice in the output of the **getfacl** command that under the default permission set, which is the original user owner's permissions, there is now a line that details what permissions the user snuffy has on this file.

Setting an ACL for a group owner is just about as easy: You simply change the **u** in the command to **g** and replace the user snuffy with the proper group and alter the permissions to reflect the permissions you want this now secondary group owner to have on the object:

```
# setfacl -m g:itcrowd:r-x
```

Now retrieve the permissions again with

```
$ getfacl test
# file: test
# owner: ross
# group: users
user::rwx
user:snuffy:rw-
group::rwx
group:itcrowd:r--
mask::rwx
other::rwx
```

As you can see, the group itcrowd has now been added to the ACL for the file test. Effectively, this means that users who are not the owner of the file who belong to the users group will have full rwx access to this file, but users who are not the user owner and are a member of the itcrowd group will have only r access to the file.

We All Wear Masks

The final facet of ACLs that we need to cover is the concept of masks. Masking for an ACL involves restricting permissions for all configured users and groups in the ACL. It's an easy way to ensure that people can read scripts in a directory but not execute them or to ensure that users and groups can view files but not change them.

To set a mask that restricts all ACL users and groups from reading an object, enter the following:

```
# setfacl -m m::rx test
```

You can run the **getfacl** command on the file to see that the mask has been altered from its default full permissions to be restrictive to r and x:

```
$ getfacl test
# file: test
# owner: ross
# group: users
user::rwx
user:snuffy:rw-                         #effective: r--
group::rwx                              #effective:r-x
group:itcrowd:r--
mask::rwx
other::rwx
```

You can see additional text next to any additional user owners and group owners that tells you what their effective rights are now. If the displayed rights are not acceptable, then don't use the mask but instead restrict the permissions by the groups and users.

Context-Based Access

Files and directories may be compromised by users who either do not understand permissions or who are accidently provided with more access than intended. There's an old sysadmin saying: "If we didn't have users, nothing would break, and the system would be more secure." Of course, the response to this saying is, "Without users, we wouldn't have a job!" Users' mistakes often do provide unintended access to the data that is stored in files.

Context-based access can be configured to deal with compromised permissions by providing an additional level of security when processes are used to access files. The control of file and directory access is not in the hands of the user but rather is handled by the administer.

It isn't just user files and directories that are a concern. Imagine a situation in which a remote hacker is able to utilize an exploit to gain control of your web server process (the **httpd** process). Without context-based controls, this hacker could direct the **httpd** process to read critical system files (such as the **/etc/passwd** file) and get information that could lead to further intrusions on the system or the network.

Traditional Linux permissions (read, write, and execute on files and directories) make use of discretionary access control (DAC), while context-based permissions utilize mandatory access control (MAC). However, when a context-based solution is enabled, DAC still applies (both MAC and DAC are enforced). Typically, the MAC controls are first evaluated and, if the access is granted, then the file's permissions are checked.

This section covers two commonly used context-based methods: SELinux and AppArmor.

Security-Enhanced Linux (SELinux)

SELinux, which stands for Security-Enhanced Linux, is a security framework implemented in the Linux kernel and various Linux distributions. It provides an additional layer of access control and security policies beyond the traditional discretionary access controls (DAC) and mandatory access controls (MAC) present in standard Linux distributions.

The main purpose of SELinux is to enforce fine-grained access control policies to limit the actions that processes and users can perform on a system. It goes beyond traditional Linux permissions by assigning labels to processes, files, and other system resources. These labels define the context and type of each resource, and access decisions are based on them.

An *SELinux* security policy can require processes to be a part of an SELinux security context (think "security group") in order to be able to access files and directories. Regular permissions are still used to further define access, but for accessing the file/directory, this SELinux policy would be applied first.

A bigger concern, and one that most SELinux policies are designed to address, is how daemon (or system) processes present a security risk. Consider a situation in which you have many active processes that provide a variety of services. For example, one of these processes might be a web server, as shown in the following example:

```
# ps -fe | grep httpd
root        1109       1  0  2022 ?       00:51:56 /usr/sbin/httpd
apache      1412  1109  0 Dec24 ?        00:00:09 /usr/sbin/httpd
apache      4085  1109  0 05:40 ?        00:00:12 /usr/sbin/httpd
apache      8868  1109  0 08:41 ?        00:00:06 /usr/sbin/httpd
apache      9263  1109  0 08:57 ?        00:00:04 /usr/sbin/httpd
apache     12388  1109  0 Dec26 ?        00:00:47 /usr/sbin/httpd
apache     18707  1109  0 14:41 ?        00:00:00 /usr/sbin/httpd
apache     18708  1109  0 14:41 ?        00:00:00 /usr/sbin/httpd
```

```
apache   19769  1109  0 Dec27 ?           00:00:15 /usr/sbin/httpd
apache   29802  1109  0 01:43 ?           00:00:17 /usr/sbin/httpd
apache   29811  1109  0 01:43 ?           00:00:11 /usr/sbin/httpd
apache   29898  1109  0 01:44 ?           00:00:10 /usr/sbin/httpd
```

In this output, each line describes one Apache web server process (**/usr/sbin/httpd**) that is running on the system. The first part of the line is the user who initiated the process. The process that runs as root is used only to spawn additional **/usr/sbin/httpd** processes. The others, however, respond to incoming web page requests from client utilities (web browsers).

Imagine for a moment that a security flaw is discovered in the software for the Apache web server; this flaw allows a client utility to gain control of one of the **/usr/sbin/httpd** processes and issue custom commands or operations to that process. One of those operations could be to view the content of the **/etc/passwd** file, which would be successful because of the permissions placed on this file:

```
# ls -l /etc/passwd
-rw-r--r-- 1 root root 2690 Dec 11  2022 /etc/passwd
```

As you can see from the output of this command, all users have the ability to view the contents of the **/etc/passwd** file, based on the fact that all users have read permission. Do you want some random hacker to have the ability to view the contents of the file that stores user account data?

With an SELinux policy, the **/usr/sbin/httpd** processes can be "locked down" so that each one can access only a certain set of files. This is what most administrators use SELinux for: to secure processes that may be compromised by hackers making use of known (or, perhaps, unknown) exploits.

SELinux Mode

There are three *SELinux modes*:

- **Disabled:** When in disabled mode, SELinux is not functional at all. No checks are performed when users attempt to access files or directories.

- **Enforcing:** When in enforcing mode, SELinux performs checks and blocks access to files or directories, if necessary.

- **Permissive:** When in permissive mode, SELinux performs checks but never blocks access to a file or directory. This mode is designed for troubleshooting problems, as log messages are created when in this mode.

Use the **getenforce** command to determine the current SELinux mode:

```
# getenforce
Enforcing
```

The result Enforcing means SELinux is installed, and the security policy is currently active.

You can change the mode (which is useful when testing a new policy or trouble-shooting SELinux problems) by issuing the **setenforce** command:

```
# setenforce 0
# getenforce
Permissive
```

While in permissive mode, SELinux does not block access to files and directories, but warnings are issued and viewable in the system log files.

You can switch between enforcing and permissive modes, but disabling SELinux requires changing a configuration file and then rebooting the system. For example, on a RHEL (Red Hat Enterprise Linux) system, you would change the SELINUX setting in the **/etc/selinux/config** file as follows:

```
# cat /etc/selinux/config
# This file controls the state of SELinux on the system.
# SELINUX= can take one of these three values:
#         enforcing - SELinux security policy is enforced.
#         permissive - SELinux prints warnings instead of enforcing.
#         disabled - No SELinux policy is loaded.
SELINUX=disabled
# SELINUXTYPE= can take one of these two values:
#         targeted - Targeted processes are protected,
#         mls - Multi Level Security protection.
SELINUXTYPE=targeted
```

Conversely, if the current SELinux mode is *disabled*, you can change the SELINUX setting to either *enforcing* or *permissive* in the **/etc/selinux/config** file and reboot the system. It is always a good policy to verify that a change has taken place by running the **getenforce** command after the reboot is complete.

SELinux Policy

An *SELinux policy* is a collection of rules that determine what restrictions are imposed by the policy. The policy itself is often very complex, and details are beyond the scope of the Linux+ exam. It is, however, important to know that the policy sets the restrictions based on rules.

You should also know that one of the most commonly used policies is the targeted policy. This policy normally exists by default on systems that have SELinux installed, and it is typically the default policy that is enabled when SELinux is first enabled.

A targeted policy contains rules that are designed to protect the system from services rather than regular users. Each service is assigned one or more security contexts, boolean values, and additional rules that limit the service's ability to access files and directories.

The minimum policy type or module in SELinux is typically called the "base" or "default" policy. This base policy includes the fundamental rules and settings necessary for SELinux to function and provide basic access control. It ensures that the system can operate securely even without any additional policy modules.

The **sestatus** command provides overall status information about SELinux, including the current policy:

```
# sestatus
SELinux status:                 enabled
SELinuxfs mount:                /sys/fs/selinux
SELinux root directory:         /etc/selinux
Loaded policy name:             targeted
Current mode:                   enforcing
Mode from config file:          enforcing
Policy MLS status:              enabled
Policy deny_unknown status:     allowed
Max kernel policy version:      28
```

SELinux Booleans

What exactly a policy consists of and how to create a policy are beyond the scope of the Linux+ exam and, as a result, this book. However, you can modify the behavior of a policy by using booleans. A *boolean* is a true/false value that changes how SELinux performs MAC.

An SELinux policy typically has dozens of different booleans. To determine what a boolean is used for, use the **semanage** command:

```
# semanage boolean -l | head
SELinux boolean          State   Default Description

privoxy_connect_any      (on   ,   on)   Allow privoxy to connect any
smartmon_3ware           (off  ,   off)  Allow smartmon to 3ware
mpd_enable_homedirs      (off  ,   off)  Allow mpd to enable homedirs
xdm_sysadm_login         (off  ,   off)  Allow xdm to sysadm login
xen_use_nfs              (off  ,   off)  Allow xen to use nfs
mozilla_read_content     (off  ,   off)  Allow mozilla to read content
ssh_chroot_rw_homedirs   (off  ,   off)  Allow ssh to chroot rw
homedirs
mount_anyfile            (on   ,   on)   Allow mount to anyfile
```

For example, in this output, there is a boolean named xdm_sysadm_login. XDM is a display manager, which means it is a tool that enables a user to log in to the system by using a GUI. This boolean is used to determine whether the XDM software will allow the root user to log in. The state (off , off) shows the default value and the current value for this boolean. In this case, off means the root user is not able to log in using the GUI because the description for this boolean is "Allow xdm to sysadm login."

You can also use the **getsebool** command to display just the current value of a boolean:

```
# getsebool -a | head
xdm_sysadm_login --> off
abrt_handle_event --> off
abrt_upload_watch_anon_write --> on
antivirus_can_scan_system --> off
antivirus_use_jit --> off
auditadm_exec_content --> on
authlogin_nsswitch_use_ldap --> off
authlogin_radius --> off
authlogin_yubikey --> off
awstats_purge_apache_log_files --> off
```

When a boolean is provided as an argument, the **getsebool** command gives only that boolean's current value:

```
# getsebool xdm_sysadm_login
xdm_sysadm_login --> off
```

To set an SELinux boolean as either on or off, use the **setsebool** command:

```
# getsebool xdm_sysadm_login
xdm_sysadm_login --> off
# setsebool xdm_sysadm_login 1
# getsebool xdm_sysadm_login
xdm_sysadm_login --> on
```

Provide the argument **0** to turn off a boolean and **1** to turn on a boolean.

Note that, by default, the **setsebool** command modifies only the current state of a boolean. A reboot causes all booleans to return to their previous status unless the **-P** (for *persistent*) option is used with the **setsebool** command:

```
# setsebool -P xdm_sysadm_login 1
```

The boolean values are typically a bit lengthy and a pain to type. Commands like **setsebool** and **getsebool** provide a unique tab completion feature. For example, note the behavior of the following when the **Tab key** is pressed:

```
# setsebool samba_<tab>
samba_create_home_dirs          samba_portmapper
samba_domain_controller         samba_run_unconfined
samba_enable_home_dirs          samba_share_fusefs
samba_export_all_ro             samba_share_nfs
samba_export_all_rw
```

SELinux Contexts

SELinux protects files (and directories) from unauthorized use by using *SELinux contexts*.

Each file can have a context applied that will affect the ability of a process to access the file. Processes themselves have an SELinux context applied, and this context essentially places the processes in a security group.

An SELinux label, also known as a security context label, is a fundamental concept in SELinux that is used to uniquely identify and categorize various system resources, such as files, processes, sockets, and more. Each process runs with a security context. To see this, use the **-Z** option to the **ps** command as shown here (where the **head** command is used simply to limit the output of the command):

```
# ps -eZ | grep httpd | head -2
system_u:system_r:httpd_t:s0 root          1109      1   0  2022 ?
   00:51:56 /usr/sbin/httpd
system_u:system_r:httpd_t:s0 apache        1412   1109   0 Dec24 ?
   00:00:09 /usr/sbin/httpd
```

The security context (**system_u:system_r:httpd_t:s0**) is complicated, but for understanding the basics of SELinux, the important part is **httpd_t**, which is like a security group or domain. As part of this security domain, the **/usr/sbin/httpd** process can only access files that are allowed by the security policy for **httpd_t**. This policy is typically written by someone who is an SELinux expert, and that expert should have proven experience regarding which processes should be able to access specific files and directories on the system.

Files and directories also have an SELinux security context that is defined by the policy. To see a security context for a specific file, use the **-Z** option to the **ls** command:

```
# ls -Z /var/www/html/index.html
unconfined_u:object_r:httpd_sys_content_t:s0 /var/www/html/index.html
```

Note here that the SELinux context contains so much data that the filename cannot fit on the same line. As you might conclude, a process running with the security context **system_u:system_r:httpd_t:s0** is able to access files that have been labeled with the **u:object_r:httpd_sys_content_t:s0** context. It isn't always so simple, as SELinux booleans can have a major impact on how contexts are applied, but this is essentially the idea. Remember that you don't need to be an SELinux expert for the Linux+ exam (which is a good thing because it is a very large topic).

How did the context of **u:object_r:httpd_sys_content_t:s0** get applied to the **/var/www/html/index.html** file? Typically, SELinux security contexts are applied automatically, depending on where the file is placed. So, a new file placed in the **/var/www/html** directory would also be labeled with the context **u:object_r:httpd_sys_content_t:s0**.

In some cases, you might need to apply this context manually. For example, if you were to move a file from another location, it might retain its original security context. In such cases, use the **chcon** command to change the context of a file or directory:

```
# chcon -t user_home_t /var/www/html/index.html
```

You can also take advantage of the SELinux rules that define the default security contexts for a majority of the system files. The **restorecon** command is used to reset the default security context on a file or directory based on its current location and these SELinux rules. Here is an example:

```
# restorecon /var/www/html/index.html
```

A commonly used option to the **restorecon** command is the **-R** option, which performs the changes recursively on a directory structure.

The "autorelabel" process in SELinux refers to an operation where the security context labels of all files, directories, and other system resources are automatically reconfigured or relabeled to match the specifications defined in the SELinux policy. This process is typically used during system initialization or after significant changes to the SELinux policy, security contexts, or filesystem structure.

The audit2allow Command

The **audit2allow** command enables you to parse the log files for events where the system has disallowed an access or permission for some action and then very handily to create a little snippet of policy rule that specifically allows that particular action or access.

You still have to load the snippet into the current policy and ensure it's active, but this is a *huge* timesaver for SELinux administrators who are facing some tiny but important access issue.

NOTE   As noted in the documentation, you should be very careful when you use the snippets **audit2allow** produces—they are not to be implemented lightly—and make sure you are not accidentally enabling some sort of security risk with these possible additions to the policy.

AppArmor

AppArmor is a MAC system that plays a role similar to SELinux in that it provides a context-based permission model. This section describes the key components of AppArmor that might be tested on the Linux+ exam.

NOTE   This chapter provides less information on AppArmor than on SELinux. There are a few reasons for this:

- As a MAC system, AppArmor's concepts are similar to those of SELinux.

- SELinux tends to be used much more often than AppArmor. While there are a few Linux distributions that use AppArmor as the default MAC, it is primarily SUSE that uses AppArmor.

- SELinux is emphasized more strongly in the Linux+ exam objectives than AppArmor.

aa-disable Command

An *AppArmor profile* is a rule set that describes how AppArmor should restrict a process. It is possible to disable a profile for a specific profile by using the **aa-disable** command. Another technique that is commonly used is shown in the following example:

```
# ln -s /etc/apparmor.d/usr.sbin.mysqld /etc/ apparmor.d/disable
#  apparmor_parser -R /etc/apparmor.d/usr.sbin.mysqld
```

NOTE   To view the status of a profile, use the **aa-status** command. To enable a profile again, use the following commands:

```
# rm /etc/apparmor.d/disable/usr.sbin.mysqld
# apparmor_parser -r /etc/apparmor.d/usr.sbin.mysqld
```

aa-complain Command

If you need to troubleshoot an AppArmor profile, it is best to put it into complain mode. In this mode, no restrictions are enforced, but any problems will be reported.

Use the **aa-complain** command to put a profile into complain mode:

```
#   aa-complain /usr/sbin/mysqld
Setting /usr/sbin/mysqld to complain mode.
```

To put the profile back into enforcing mode, use the following command:

```
#   sudo aa-enforce /usr/sbin/mysqld
Setting /usr/sbin/mysqld to enforce mode
```

aa-unconfined Command

Use the **aa-unconfined** command to list processes that are not restricted by the AppArmor profiles.

/etc/apparmor.d/ Directory

The **/etc/apparmor.d** directory is the location of the definitions of the AppArmor profiles. Knowing how to create or read these files is beyond the scope of the Linux+ exam, but it is important to know the locations of these profiles in order to determine which profiles are available and to use the AppArmor commands, such as the **aa-disable** command.

/etc/apparmor.d/tunables Directory

The **/etc/apparmor.d/tunables** directory holds files that can be used to fine-tune the behavior of AppArmor. Knowing how to create or read these files is beyond the scope of the Linux+ exam.

Command-Line Utilities

Linux+ objective 2.5 presents a long list of command-line utilities without any context other than that they are related to the objective topic of access controls. As I explained at the beginning of this chapter, I incorporated all the commands into the normal flow of the discussion of the topics, so I won't rehash them here.

Summary

The focus of this chapter was on how to further secure your system resources using special permissions, context-based access controls like SELinux and AppArmor, and all the different utilities that support these actions.

Exam Preparation Tasks

As mentioned in the section "Goals and Methods" in the Introduction, you have a couple of choices for exam preparation: the exercises here, Chapter 23, "Final Preparation," and the exam simulation questions in the Pearson Test Prep Software Online.

Review All Key Topics

Review the most important topics in this chapter, noted with the Key Topic icon in the outer margin of the page. Table 12-2 lists these key topics and the page number on which each is found.

Table 12-2   Key Topics for Chapter 12

Key Topic Element	Description	Page Number
Figure 12-1	Permission trios	429
List	The bit values for the permissions for files	430
Section	Octal Mode	432
Section	Symbolic Mode	433
List	The special bits for Linux filesystems	438
Paragraph	Setting several special bits at once	439
Paragraph	Adding the SGID special permission to a directory	441
List	The SELinux modes	450
Paragraph	The **sestatus** command	452
Paragraph	Defining the **/etc/apparmor.d** directory	457

Define Key Terms

Define the following key terms from this chapter and check your answers in the glossary:

access control lists (ACLs), permissions, user owner, group owner, **chmod**, symbolic mode, **chown**, **chgrp**, umask, special permissions, attributes, **lsattr**, **chattr**, SELinux, SELinux modes, SELinux policy, SELinux contexts, AppArmor, AppArmor profile

Review Questions

The answers to these review questions are in Appendix A.

1. What type of access does the execute permission for directories provide?

   a. The ability to list filenames in a directory

   b. The ability to add files to a directory

   c. The ability to remove files from a directory

   d. The ability to change into a directory

2. Consider the following output of the **ls -l** command:

   ```
   -rw-rwxr-x 2 ross users 0 Jan 26 13:08 22 test.mp3
   ```

   Which of the following statements is true?

   a. The user ross has only read permission on **test.mp3**.

   b. The user ross has only read and write permission on **test.mp3**.

   c. The user ross has read, write, and execute permission on **test.mp3**.

   d. The user ross has no permission on **test.mp3**.

3. Which of the following are SELinux contexts applied to? (Choose all that apply.)

   a. Files

   b. Users

   c. Processes

   d. All of these answers are correct.

4. In which mode is SELinux not functional at all?

   a. Permissive

   b. Disabled

   c. Inactive

   d. Null

5. Which of the following commands can be used to set or alter the filesystem attributes that are attached to a file or directory?

   a. **auditdisplay**

   b. **SEperms**

   c. **cfgobject**

   d. **chattr**

6. As a systems administrator, you have discovered a file on disk that won't allow you to delete it, change its permissions, read its contents, or just about anything else you try. Which of the following commands will allow you to view the special settings for this file?

a. **displayattr**

b. **vimattr**

c. **lsattr**

d. **cfgattr**

This chapter covers the following topics:

- Shell Script Elements
- Common Script Utilities
- Environment Variables
- Relative and Absolute Paths

The exam objective covered in this chapter is as follows:

- **Objective 3.1:** Given a scenario, create simple shell scripts to automate common tasks

## CHAPTER 13

Automating Tasks via Shell Scripting

Scripting is the art of noticing that you have done a series of tasks multiple times in roughly the same way and then automating the process by putting those tasks into a script file and executing that script instead of doing all those tasks manually each time.

Even scripting a string of simple commands can save you a lot of time in the long run. However, if you pursue learning how to script in more depth, you'll discover a whole world of things that you can do to make your scripts much more useful, flexible, and, well, complicated but useful!

"Do I Know This Already?" Quiz

The "Do I Know This Already?" quiz enables you to assess whether you should read this entire chapter or simply jump to the "Exam Preparation Tasks" section for review. If you are in doubt, read the entire chapter. Table 13-1 outlines the major headings in this chapter and the corresponding "Do I Know This Already?" quiz questions. You can find the answers in Appendix A, "Answers to the 'Do I Know This Already?' Quizzes and Review Questions."

Table 13-1 "Do I Know This Already?" Foundation Topics Section-to-Question Mapping

Foundation Topics Section	Questions Covered in This Section
Shell Script Elements	1–3
Common Script Utilities	4–5
Environment Variables	6
Relative and Absolute Paths	7

CAUTION The goal of self-assessment is to gauge your mastery of the topics in this chapter. If you do not know the answer to a question or are only partially sure of the answer, you should mark that question as wrong for purposes of the self-assessment. Giving yourself credit for an answer you correctly guess skews your self-assessment results and might provide you with a false sense of security.

1. A BASH comment starts with which character?

   a. "

   b. !

   c. #

   d. --

2. When reviewing a shell script you have found, you see this:

   ```
   if [[ -x /etc/zoid ]]; then
   . /etc/zoid
   elif [[ -x $HOME/.zoid ]]; then
   . $HOME/.zoid
   fi
   ```

   Which of the following is true?

   a. **/usr/bin/elif** needs to be present for this to work.

   b. The script will run **/etc/zoid** and **$HOME/.zoid** if they exist.

   c. If **/etc/zoid** is marked as executable, it will be executed.

   d. **$HOME/.zoid** takes priority over **/etc/zoid**.

3. During a script's execution, what is stored in **$1**?

   a. The first argument to the script

   b. The shell that called the script

   c. The name of the script

   d. The process ID of the script

4. Consider the following transcript:

   ```
   $ ./report.pl
   $ echo $?
   1
   ```

   What can be said about what just happened?

   a. The command completed successfully.

   b. One argument was passed to **report.pl** through the environment.

   c. The script ran for 1 second.

   d. An error occurred during the script.

5. You are using the scripting statement **case** in a script and keep getting a message such as the following:

```
script1: line 10: syntax error: unexpected end of file
```

What is the likely cause of the error?

   a. You didn't have a default condition set.

   b. You forgot to close the **case** with **esac**.

   c. You were using the old [ ] BASH style instead of [[ ]].

   d. You were comparing an integer when you should have been comparing a string.

6. You want to work with the text streams on your system. Which of the following properly matches the text stream names and file descriptors?

   a. **0=stdin, 1=stdout, 2=stderr**

   b. **0=stdout, 1=stderr, 2=stdin**

   c. **0=stderr, 1=stdir, 2=stdout**

   d. None of the answers are correct.

7. Which of the following is an absolute path?

   a. **/etc/passwd**

   b. **../usr/local**

   c. **usr/local**

   d. **/home**

Foundation Topics

> **NOTE**   As I have done in many of the previous chapters, I will use my own order of presentation and highlight the most important items in my own preferred way, never mind the order or grouping that the Linux+ objectives put them in. I'll more than cover everything, but it'll be a conversation, not a listing.

Shell Script Elements

Shell scripting is about writing your own tools to automate some of your routine work. Do you commonly use a procedure that involves a handful of commands? A shell script can turn it into one command. The time you invest in learning to script will pay for itself many times over with the time you save.

You don't have to be a programmer to be a good scripter. You already know how to work with the Linux command line, and all scripting starts there.

A shell script is just a text file that contains some commands. The following is a typical script used to deploy new software:

```
#!/bin/bash
# Deploy the application. Run as deploy foo-1.2.war
cp $1 /usr/local/tomcat/webapps/application.war
service tomcat restart
echo "Deployed $1" | mail group@example.com
```

Line by line, this script works as follows:

- **Line 1:** Known as the *shebang* line after the hash or sharp (#) and bang (!) that starts it, this line tells the kernel that the script should be interpreted by the **/bin/bash** command. It's also known as a *hashspling*.

- **Line 2:** Comments, which begin with a #, are used to help humans understand the program. Computers just ignore the # and everything after it on that line.

- **Line 3: $1** is the first argument passed to the script on the command line. This line copies the specified file to the destination directory.

- **Line 4:** Runs another script to restart the service.

- **Line 5:** Sends an email.

Other than the **$1** variable, the shebang line, and the comment, this script is identical to what you would do at the command line. With only three commands in this sample script, you might wonder what the value of putting these commands into a shell script would be. Consider these issues:

- Even if it takes a minute to run this process manually, it's a distraction because it consumes your attention for the whole procedure.

- You may make mistakes.

- It may be three commands today, but it's likely to grow over time.

- You can't take a vacation without writing down this procedure and training your coworkers on how to run it.

All these problems can be solved with scripting. A script is predictable and not as vulnerable to human error as running commands manually. You can add commands to the script over time. Instead of complicated documentation and training, you just need to teach people how to run your script.

Globbing

A *glob* is a wildcard operator that matches some number of files based on a pattern. For example, **/etc/*** matches all files in the **/etc** directory, such as **/etc/foo** and **/etc/bar**; however, it does not match **/etc/foo/bar** because this means **bar** is a file in a subdirectory named **foo**.

One thing that's distinct about Linux (and all Unixes) is that the shell is responsible for expanding the glob to the list of files it matches. If you type **ls /tmp/thing*** and there are two files that start with **thing**, such as **thing1** and **thing2**, it's the same as if you typed **ls /tmp/thing1 /tmp/thing2**:

```
$ ls thing*
thing1 thing2
```

This *globbing* feature makes renaming a group of files more difficult. In Windows you could type **ren *.foo *.bar**, and any file with the extension **foo** would then have the extension **bar**. In Linux, typing **mv *.foo *.bar** would expand the globs to the list of files matched: ***.foo** would match the files you want to rename, and ***.bar** would match nothing. This is different from what you might expect! The following output shows this problem:

```
$ ls *.foo *.bar
ls: *.bar: No such file or directory
file1.foo file2.foo
$ echo mv *.foo *.bar
```

```
mv file1.foo file2.foo *.bar
$ mv *.foo *.bar
mv: target '*.bar' is not a directory
```

In the output, the first command shows that there are three files with the extension **foo** but none with the extension **bar**. The **echo** command displays the output that follows it, such that it shows what would be executed if you ran the **mv** command by itself. The ***.bar** glob shows up because there are no files that match it. The error happens because there is not a directory called ***.bar**.

There are other glob operators. Example 13-1 shows some uses of file globs.

Example 13-1 Examples of Using Globs

```
$ ls
file file1 file10 file11 file2
$ ls file*
file file1 file10 file11 file2
$ ls file?
file1 file2
$ ls *1
file1 file11
$ ls file[123]
file1 file2
```

Example 13-1 starts by listing all the files in the directory. The same list of files is also available with **file***, which matches the word **file** followed by anything or nothing at all. Note that it includes the bare name **file**. Next, the **file?** glob matches anything starting with the word **file** and followed by one character. Both **file** and the files with two-digit numbers in their names are excluded.

NOTE A glob doesn't have to appear at the end of a filename. For example, ***1** matches anything ending in the number 1.

Finally, **file[123]** uses the square bracket (or *brace expansion*) operator that means "any one character from the set." It matches **file1** and **file2**.

NOTE You'll see the Linux+ objectives refer to the square bracket [] characters as "brace expansion," which is just plain weird and misleading, but it's their way of referring to square brackets. You'll see more of the square brackets, or "*braces*," and their expansion in the section "Using grep and Friends."

Environment Variables and Settings

Variables are used to store information for the shell or program that is running. Each process has its own set of variables. In the BASH shell there are two different types of variables:

- **Local variables:** These variables are only available to the current BASH shell. When new programs or commands are executed in the BASH shell (or BASH script), these variables are not provided to the new process.

- **Environment (also called global) variables:** These variables store values just like local variables and can be used by the current BASH shell. However, when another process is started from the BASH shell, these variables are passed into the new process. The benefit is that variables can be created in the shell and then used to modify the behavior of another process.

To create a local variable, use a command such as the following:

```
$ a=25
```

You can display the contents of a variable by using the **echo** command. Note that you use a **$** character before the variable name when retrieving its value (but not when assigning the variable):

```
$ echo $a
25
```

Typically you see quotation marks used around the string that the **echo** command is supposed to print:

```
$ echo "It was the best of times, it was the worst of times."
It was the best of times, it was the worst of times.
```

This is often not necessary, but if there are metacharacters (characters special to the BASH shell), you should consider using quotation marks to escape the special meaning. For example, the following command prints **this | that** on the screen:

```
$ echo "this | that"
this | that
```

Remove the quotes, and the | character is treated as a redirection character. If you enter the following command, you run **echo** and attempt to send the output to a command named **that**:

```
$ echo this | that
-bash: that: command not found
```

Double quotation marks disable the special meaning of redirection characters (<, >, and |) and globbing characters (*, ?, [, and]). Within double quotation marks, variable and command substitution still occurs:

```
$ echo "Current directory is `pwd`.  Home directory is $HOME."
Current directory is /home/sarah.  Home directory is /etc.
```

Use single quotation marks to disable all metacharacters, including those for redirection, globbing, command substitution, and variable substitution:

```
$ echo 'this | that'
this | that
$ echo 'Current directory is `pwd`.  Home directory is $HOME.'
Current directory is 'pwd'.  Home directory is $HOME.
```

You can also place a \ (backslash) character before any metacharacter to make it a plain character for the BASH shell:

```
$ echo this \| that
this | that
$ echo Current directory is \`pwd\`.  Home directory is \$HOME.
Current directory is 'pwd'.  Home directory is $HOME.
```

To display all shell variables, including both environment and local variables, use the **set** command. This command provides a large amount of output, so you can use the head command to limit the output. The **head** command will display the specified number of lines, as shown in the following example:

```
$ set | head -5
BASH=/bin/bash
BASHOPTS=checkwinsize:cmdhist:expand_aliases:extquote:force_fignore:hi
stappend:hostcomplete:interactive_comments:login_shell:progcomp:prompt
vars:sourcepath
BASH_ALIASES=()
BASH_ARGC=()
BASH_ARGV=()
```

Environment variables are typically created using one of two methods. The first method is to create the variable as a local variable and then use the **export** command to convert it to an environment variable:

```
$ b=50
$ export b
```

The second method is to set the variable directly with the **export** command:

```
$ export c=75
```

Both methods result in the variable being set as an environment variable. After the variable has been set, it behaves just like a local shell variable except when another process is executed within the shell. As a demonstration, the following script is used in this section:

```
$!/bin/bash
#display.sh
echo "This is a: $a"
echo "This is b: $b"
```

Consider the following commands and their output:

```
$ a=25
$ export b=50
$ ./display.sh
This is a:
This is b: 50
```

As you can see from this output, the environment variable (**$b**) was passed into the **display.sh** shell program. The local variable (**$a**) was not passed into the **display.sh** program, so no value was printed for this variable.

To display all the environment variables, use either the **env** command or the **print-env** command. The **env** command provides a large amount of output, and the following example is limited to five lines of output:

```
$ env | head -5
XDG_SESSION_ID=8447
HOSTNAME=mail.onecoursesource.com
TERM=xterm
SHELL=/bin/bash
HISTSIZE=1000
```

The **PATH** Variable

You can always refer to an executable in your current directory with one of two methods:

- **Absolute pathname: /home/sarah/command**
- **Relative pathname: ./command**

These methods are cumbersome because they require you to either memorize the location of each command or move to the directory where the command resides. Instead of using these methods, consider using the *PATH* variable, which contains a colon-separated list of directories that are used to find the location of a command.

For example, if you tried to execute a command without using an absolute pathname or using the ./ relative pathname method, the directories listed in the **PATH** variable would be searched as follows (in order from left to right):

```
$ echo $PATH
/usr/local/bin:/usr/bin:/usr/local/sbin:/usr/sbin:/home/sarah/.local/
bin:/home/sarah/bin
```

The **PATH** variable can be modified to have the shell look in different directories. It is usually set for all users by the administrator in the **/etc/profile** file. Each user can modify his own **~/.bash_profile** file to customize his **PATH** variable. It's easy to alter the current path and add a directory without disrupting the previous path definitions:

Step 1.   Edit the **~/.bash_profile** file.

Step 2.   Navigate to the bottom of the file.

Step 3.   Add the following line, replacing **yournewpath** with the path that's correct for your system:

```
export PATH=$PATH:yournewpath
```

The SHELL Variable

Another useful variable that often follows up on **PATH** is the *SHELL* variable, which contains the full path and filename of the user's current shell.

For example, if you were to echo the **SHELL** variable to the display, it would typically show the user's default shell, in this case the BASH shell:

```
$ echo $SHELL
/bin/bash
```

> **NOTE**   Be aware, if you have changed the shell or have used a privilege elevation command such as **su** or **sudo**, your own shell may be obscured in which case the target user's shell will be shown.

Variable Expansion

What happens when you try to display a variable that hasn't been set? By default, a null string ("") value is returned:

```
$ echo "Hello, $name"
Hello,
```

With the variable expansion BASH feature, you can return a different value. For example, the following returns **Bob** if the **$name** variable isn't set:

```
$ echo "Hello, ${name:-Bob}"
Hello, Bob$
echo "Hello, $name"
Hello,
```

Note that using this command doesn't set the variable but rather uses the provided value for this one situation. To return a value and set the variable, use the following command:

```
$ echo "Hello, ${name:=Bob}"
Hello, Bob
$ echo "Hello, $name"
Hello, Bob
```

There are other variable expansion features. For example, the following syntax returns only the first 24 characters of the variable, resulting in a more uplifting statement:

```
$ times="It was the best of times, it was the worst of times."
$ echo ${times: 0:24}
It was the best of times
```

Note that in this example, **0** represents the first character to return, and **24** represents the total number of characters to return (starting with character 0).

Running a Script

There are three ways to run a script. The first is the same as if it were a binary application:

```
$ ./test.sh
Hello, world
```

It is important to note that for the first method to work, the script must have the execute permissions set. For example, after creating the **test.sh** file, the file can be made executable for everyone with the following command:

```
$ chmod a+x test.sh
```

The second way is to pass the script as an argument to a new shell:

```
$ bash test.sh
Hello, world
```

The second method has the advantage during testing because you can pass arguments to the **bash** command. For example, the **-x** option for the **bash** command provides some debugging information as the script is being executed.

A third way of running a script is called *sourcing*. With this method, the script isn't executed as a separate process but rather as if the commands were run within the current shell. The BASH shell provides two different ways to source a program (both of which yield the same result), either to use the **source** command or to use the **.** character in place of where you normally type the command:

```
source script_name
. script_name
```

The sourcing method is useful when there are settings placed within a script that you want to implement within your current shell or within a shell script that you are writing. For example, suppose you had a bunch of variables set in the **set-var.sh** script and you wanted these same variables to be created in the **my-prog.sh** script. The **my-prog.sh** script could include the following:

```
$!/bin/bash
#my-prog.sh
source set-var.sh
#rest of the code goes here
```

Good Script Design

Before you start writing shell scripts, you should think about what makes a good shell script. At a high level, you're not writing a script for yourself; instead, you're writing it for your coworker, who might have to use it at 2 a.m. To create a good script, ensure that it

- Does one thing and does it well.

- Prints descriptive error and success messages.

- Is written in a simple manner and uses comments to make steps obvious to someone looking at the source.

- Has a name that communicates its intent. **deploy_website.sh** is good. The name of your favorite football team is not, nor are cryptic 2-letter script names, unless you're trying to obfuscate your work.

- Has a file extension that indicates how it's to be run, such as **.sh**. Keep in mind that extensions are not required for Linux, but they are helpful to others because they can indicate the contents of files.

Follow these guidelines, and your scripts will be maintainable long after you write them. Also, you won't have to explain things to coworkers over and over.

Working with Input/Output Streams

Linux supports having separate streams to handle data on the shell command line. These streams, called *file descriptors*, are used primarily to send data to and from programs and files and to handle errors.

Table 13-2 lists the three file descriptors and their associated files.

Table 13-2 Linux File Descriptors

Name	File Descriptor Number	Associated File
/dev/stdin	0	/proc/self/fd/0
/dev/stdout	1	/proc/self/fd/1
/dev/stderr	2	/proc/self/fd/2

Standard In

Standard in, or *stdin*, is what all programs accept or what they are assumed to accept. Most programs accept stdin either from a redirected file argument or using the file as an argument to the program:

```
program < file
```

or

```
program file
```

NOTE   Often, the stdin of a program is the stdout of another program, and the stdin and stdout are connected by a pipe symbol.

Standard Out

Standard out, or *stdout*, is the text or data that's produced by a command and shows up on the screen or console. By default, all text-mode commands produce stdout and send it to the console unless it's redirected. To understand this, run the following command:

```
$ cat /etc/fstab
```

The text shown onscreen is a perfect example of the stdout stream. It's considered elegant to run commands first to see what they produce before redirecting the output to a file, particularly because you might get errors.

Standard Error

Standard error, or *stderr*, is a parallel stream to the stdout, and by default it shows up mixed into the stdout stream as the errors occur.

> **NOTE** To visualize this, think of two pitchers of water. One is stdout and the other stderr. If you pour them out and mix the streams of water together, they might be different, but they both go to the same place.

Find Errors on Demand

It's hard to produce errors on purpose; however, you can always use the *find* command to produce some access denied or permission errors to experiment with.

As a normal user, run the following command:

```
# find / -iname "*.txt"
```

Right away, you see errors indicating that the user can't access certain directory trees to find certain items. Notice that useful output (stdout) is mixed directly with error messages (stderr), making it potentially difficult to separate the streams and use the good data for anything constructive.

> **NOTE** The life of a sysadmin is defined by the search for producing good data and properly discarding or storing the errors produced. Good data can be sent on to another program, while errors are usually dumped at the earliest possible moment to use the processor and resources to produce good data more efficiently.

To clean up good data and get rid of bad data, you need to use redirection operators. To see this work, use the Up arrow and rerun the previous command, as shown here:

```
# find / -iname *.txt 2> /dev/null | more
```

This produces output similar to

```
./.kde/share/apps/kdeprint/printerdb_cups.txt
./1.txt
./2.txt
./3.txt
```

Notice that you get only good data (stdout) after using a 2> redirection symbol to dump the bad data (stderr) to the system's black hole, or garbage disposal—in other words, a pseudo-device designed to be a place to discard data securely.

You'll learn more about this in the "Redirecting Standard Error" section, later in this chapter.

NOTE   There is an entire section about the **find** command at the end of this chapter, but you'll get a great idea of its power through use of it in a lot of upcoming examples where we need to produce lots of output—and, of course, errors!

Here Documents

Because we have been talking about the concept of streams, we need to address a particular aspect of the stdin or standard input stream, called a *here document*, or *heredoc*.

You use a here document when you need to have a point in the execution of a program—typically a script—where you are allowed to enter text from the console. Once a specific string is entered (DONE in the following example), the text is sent to the command as input. The following simple command line element is an example of this:

```
# cat << DONE
> this is input
> this is more input
> DONE
this is input
this is more input
#
```

In this example, the string limiter is the text DONE. When you press the **Enter** key after the text DONE, the shell recognizes that you are done with the text entry, removes the two instances of the string limiter DONE from the text entered, and outputs that text to the console with the **cat** command.

Here documents were effectively created so that you can type an amount of text that might contain quoting and variables and not have to use escaping (prefacing a character with a \). Quoting and variables work as expected in the body of a here document. It's good to note that the string limiter can also be used inside the here document text; it's only when it's on its own line that it's interpreted as a string limiter.

Redirection of Streams

In the quest for good data, being able to redirect or change the destination of stdout and stderr—and to some degree stdin—is essential to your tasks.

Redirection symbols include

- See Here Documents earlier in this chapter.

- **<:** Redirects a file's contents into a command's stdin stream. The file descriptor for the < input redirection symbol is 0, so it's possible to see <0 used.

- **>:** Redirects the stdout stream to the file target to the right of the symbol. The file descriptor for the > output redirection character is 1, which is implied except in certain instances.

- **>>:** Redirects stdout to a file, appending the current stream to the end of the file rather than overwriting the file contents. This is a modifier of the > output redirection descriptor.

- **2>:** Redirects stderr to a file, appending the current stream to the end of the file rather than overwriting the file contents. This is a modifier of the > or 2> output redirection descriptor.

NOTE If you use the > redirection symbol to write to a file, that file is overwritten unless the **noclobber** BASH shell option is set. With this option set, you cannot overwrite the file; it produces an error and file. The only way to get data into that file is to use the >> redirection append symbols. This can be configured by running the **Set -o noclobber** command.

Redirecting Standard Input

Redirecting stdin involves sending a file's contents to a program's stdin stream. An example of this is **sort < file1**. This command is essentially the same as the **cat file1 | sort** command.

NOTE As we discussed previously, input redirection is usually seen as being the same thing as specifying something as a parameter but as you'll see later in the chapter, the **tr** command requires the use of input redirection to function properly.

Redirecting Standard Output

Redirecting stdout involves using either a single redirection symbol (>) or two of them (>>) for appending. The main difference is that the use of a single redirection descriptor overwrites a file, whereas using double redirection descriptors appends to the end of a file. For example, the following command overwrites the contents of **file2** or, if it doesn't exist, creates it:

```
# cat file1 > file2
```

The following command appends the data from **file1** to **file2** or, if it doesn't exist, creates **file2**:

```
# cat file1 >> file2
```

As an alternative example, say you run the **find** command and it produces errors and prints found files to the screen. You can capture the good data to a file and let the errors show on the console with the following command:

```
# find / -iname *.txt > foundfiles
```

When you are redirecting stdout, the numeral or file descriptor 1 doesn't need to be used in most cases. (In other words, you can just use > rather than 1> because the 1 is implied and not necessary.) Redirection of stdout is so common that a single > symbol suffices.

Redirecting Standard Error

Redirecting stderr involves understanding that, by default, stderr shows up on the same target as stdout, mixed right in but separable.

To continue the previous example but capture the stderr and let the good data show on the default target (console), you would change the command to

```
# find / -iname *.txt 2> errors
```

The **2> errors** section of the command redirects the stderr and puts it into the file **errors**, leaving the stdout stream free to show on the default target (console) or even get written to another file.

The key to understanding what happens when using stdout and stderr is to visualize them, as shown in Figure 13-1.

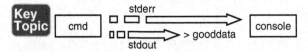

Figure 13-1 Path of data streams

As you can see, the > character grabs the stdout stream and puts that data into the file **gooddata**, whereas the stderr stream is unaffected and is sent to the console for display.

Grabbing both streams and putting them into different files is as simple as adding a redirection symbol preceded by the stderr numeral. This example grabs both streams and puts them into their proper files, with nothing displayed to the console:

```
# find / -iname *.txt > gooddata 2> baddata
```

Redirection Redux

Sometimes all the possible output from a particular command must be trapped because it will cause problems, such as when a command is run as a background job, and you're using **vi** or some other console-based program. Having stderr show up onscreen during an editing session is disconcerting at the least, and if you're configuring important files, it's downright dangerous.

To trap all output from a command and send it to the **/dev/null** or black hole of the system, you use the following:

```
# find / -iname *.txt > /dev/null 2>&1
```

You will see items like this example on the Linux+ exam, and it's important that you've run such commands yourself—multiple times if possible. Take a few minutes to experiment with the examples shown in this text. Getting the symbols right in a fill-in-the-blank question is difficult if you haven't typed them a number of times.

NOTE   Don't be confused by the use of the **/dev/null** device; its sole purpose is to be a catch-all fake device that you can use to discard output of any kind.

Understanding /dev/tty

There will be times when you want to use one of the other special files on a system, such as **/dev/tty**. The purpose of **/dev/tty** is to give you a device that will always be connected to the controlling terminal or, to be clearer, the terminal that is being used to launch a given program.

For example, if you want to ensure that output *always* displays on the terminal that a command is executed on, any references to output can be redirected to **/dev/tty**, and regardless of whether you are on a local console (for example, **/dev/ttyXX**) or a remote console (for example, **/dev/pts/XX**), the output will be sent to the same console that executed the program.

To determine the type and number of the console you are currently on, use the **tty** command:

```
# tty
/dev/pts/0
```

This output shows the user currently in a terminal application on a GUI, not on a text console in a non-graphical environment.

Pipes

A *pipe* (|) is used for chaining together two or more programs' output, typically filtering and changing the output with each successive program the data is sent through.

Quite possibly the simplest use of a pipe is to take the output of a particular command and use a pipe to send the output to one of the pagers, such as **more** or **less**. Pagers are so named because, especially with the **more** command, you are shown the output not in a running stream down the console but as if it had been cut up into pages that fit your screen. For example, in Figure 13-2 the **ls** command's standard output is sent to the **less** command as that command's standard input:

```
# ls -l | less
```

```
Activities    GNOME Terminal                                Fri 10:19                                        • ○
                                        root@linux-8zG4:/etc                                                      ×
File  Edit  View  Search  Terminal  Help
total 2332
-rw-------  1 root root        0 Oct 26  2014 .pwd.lock
drwxr-xr-x  1 root root       26 Oct 26  2014 ConsoleKit
-rw-r--r--  1 root root     2875 Sep 11  2014 DIR_COLORS
lrwxrwxrwx  1 root root        8 Oct 26  2014 HOSTNAME -> hostname
drwxr-xr-x  1 root root      388 Apr  9 19:44 ImageMagick-6_Q16-2
drwxr-xr-x  1 root root      104 Oct 26  2014 NetworkManager
drwxr-xr-x  1 root root       70 Oct 26  2014 PackageKit
-rw-r--r--  1 root root       24 Oct 25  2014 SUSE-brand
-rw-r--r--  1 root root      156 Oct 22  2014 SUSE-release
drwxr-xr-x  1 root root       22 Oct 26  2014 UPower
drwxr-xr-x  1 root root      150 Apr  9 23:00 X11
drwxr-xr-x  1 root root       94 Apr  9 19:45 YaST2
-rw-r--r--  1 root root       16 Apr  9 23:00 adjtime
-rw-r--r--  1 root root     2579 Oct 14  2014 aliases
drwxr-xr-x  1 root root        0 Sep 25  2014 aliases.d
-rw-r--r--  1 root root    12288 Apr  9 23:01 aliases.db
-rw-r--r--  1 root root      279 Sep 25  2014 alsa-pulse.conf
drwxr-xr-x  1 root root     1988 Apr  9 19:45 alternatives
drwxr-xr-x  1 root root      198 Oct 26  2014 apparmor
drwxr-xr-x  1 root root     1454 Oct 26  2014 apparmor.d
-rw-r--r--  1 root root      263 Sep 25  2014 asound-pulse.conf
drwxr-xr-x  1 root root       36 Oct 26  2014 at-spi2
-rw-r-----  1 root root       62 Oct 14  2014 at.deny
drwxr-x---  1 root root       42 Oct 26  2014 audisp
drwxr-x---  1 root root       58 Oct 26  2014 audit
-rw-r--r--  1 root root      798 Sep 25  2014 auto.master
drwxr-xr-x  1 root root        0 Sep 25  2014 auto.master.d
-rw-r--r--  1 root root      524 Sep 25  2014 auto.misc
-rwxr-xr-x  1 root root     1268 Sep 25  2014 auto.net
-rwxr-xr-x  1 root root     2191 Sep 25  2014 auto.smb
-rw-r--r--  1 root root    12156 Sep 25  2014 autofs.conf
-rw-------  1 root root      232 Sep 25  2014 autofs_ldap_auth.conf
drwxr-xr-x  1 root root      142 Oct 26  2014 avahi
-rw-r--r--  1 root root     8996 Sep 11  2014 bash.bashrc
-rw-r--r--  1 root root     1336 Oct  8  2014 bash_command_not_found
drwxr-xr-x  1 root root      280 Apr  9 19:44 bash_completion.d
-rw-r--r--  1 root root     2389 Oct  6  2014 bind.keys
-rw-r--r--  1 root root      415 Oct  6  2014 bindresvport.blacklist
drwxr-xr-x  1 root root        0 Oct 14  2014 binfmt.d
-rw-r--r--  1 root root      135 Oct  8  2014 blkid.conf
-rw-r--r--  1 root root     7439 Sep 25  2014 bogofilter.cf
drwxr-xr-x  1 root root       12 Oct 25  2014 bootsplash
-rw-r--r--  1 root root       37 Oct  8  2014 boto.cfg
-rw-r-----  1 root brlapi      33 Oct 26  2014 brlapi.key
drwxr-xr-x  1 root root     7964 Oct 26  2014 brltty
lines 1-46
```

Figure 13-2   The output of a command being piped to **less**

The **less** command offers a lot of great functionality for viewing output. You can search forward for something by entering the / character followed by the string you want to find, as in this example:

```
/somestring
```

Also while in **less**, you can use most of the typical navigation commands used in other programs, such as **vi** or **vim** (covered in earlier chapters). The command **1G** goes to the first character of the first line of the file, and **G** goes to the end of the file. The **Page Up** and **Page Down** keys work as well as the traditional cursor movement (**hjkl**) and **arrow** keys to navigate around the file.

Pipes can also be used to chain together several commands that each add to the output of the first command to produce something useful.

NOTE It is important to remember that commands pipe output to other commands until the output is finally sent to the screen/console or is committed to a file with an output redirect, such as the > or >> characters. Standard error is *not* being redirected or trapped unless the 2> designator sends it to a file location or the **/dev/null** device.

For example, to print a code sample with numbered lines (**nl**) and printer formatting (**pr**), you use the following command string:

```
# cat codesamp.c | nl | pr | lpr
```

It's essential that you know the difference between a redirection symbol and a pipe. Say that you see a command like this:

```
# cat file1 | nl > pr
```

This command produces a file in the current directory, named **pr**, not output that has been filtered through both **nl** and **pr**.

NOTE Remember that redirection always comes from or goes to a file, whereas piping always comes from or goes to a program.

The following is a good example of using a pipe to produce usable data:

```
# sort < names | nl
```

This command sorts and then numbers the file **names**.

> **NOTE**   Remember that you usually don't have to include the < or input redirect when specifying a file argument to a program such as **sort**, but we include it here because you may see this on the Linux+ exam.

Another example is

```
# who | wc -l
```

This counts the users attached to the system and shows just the total number.

Here's one more example:

```
# lsof /mnt/cdrom | mail root -s"CD-ROM Users"
```

This command is designed to show you who is currently accessing or has opened files on the CD-ROM of the server, so you know who to tell to log off when needed.

Executing Multiple Commands

There are several methods for executing multiple commands with a single press of the **Enter** key. You can use special characters to just have the system execute multiple commands, or you can get fancy with if/then types of multiple-command execution.

Multiple Command Operators

When compiling software, scheduling backup jobs, or doing any other task that requires a particular program's exit status to be a particular value, you need to use these operators:

> **NOTE**   It's important to remember that each of these commands has its own set of stdin, stdout, and stderr descriptors. They flow into and out of each of the commands in between the operators.

- **;:** The semicolon causes all listed commands to be executed independently of each other. The following example echoes back when a long compile is done:

  ```
  make modules ; echo DO MAKE MODULES_INSTALL NEXT
  ```

  The commands are independently executed, and neither command fails or succeeds based on the other's exit status.

  - **&&:** The double ampersand causes the second command to be executed if the first command has an exit status of 0 (success). If an exit status of nonzero (failure) is returned, the second command is not attempted. If you're a sysadmin and want to have a second program do something if the first succeeds, use the double ampersand like this:

```
longcompile && mail root -s "compile complete"
```

This set of commands starts a long compile; if it succeeds, you get an email stating "compile complete" in the subject line.

- **||:** The double pipe causes the second command to not be attempted if the first command has an exit status of 0 (success). If the first command has an exit status of nonzero (failure), the second command is attempted. What if you want to have a second command let you know whether a particular process failed without having to dig through the log files every morning? You could use the following:

```
tar -czvf /dev/st0 / || mail root -s "doh, backup failed"
```

As you can probably guess, this command set attempts a full system backup to a SCSI tape device. Only if it fails does the root user get an email with the subject line indicating it failed.

Command Substitution

In some instances, you need to take the output of a command and place it into a variable, usually for scripting purposes. Substituting the output of a command for the command itself is accomplished by bracketing the command with the backtick (`) (which is typed using the same key as the tilde [~] character, but without the **Shift** key), like so:

```
# `somecmd`
```

For example, you could insert the output of the **date** command into a variable, possibly for use in a script, as in this example:

```
# export DATETIME=`date`
# echo $DATETIME
Tue Jan 13 17:18:35 PST 2004
```

The **export** command is used to create a variable named **DATETIME** that is being populated by the `date` command. When this is executed, the backticks around the **date** command cause the output for that command to be inserted into the **DATETIME** variable as a value.

Another facet of substituting commands is to enclose a command in parentheses and declare it as a variable, as in this example:

```
# file $(grep -irl crud /usr/src/linux-2.4)
```

The main reason to use a command substitution like this is that it allows you to nest commands within commands. Rather than having to use wildcards, you just use the right substitution.

Another fun example of using command substitution is looking at a given binary and seeing what libraries it requires without knowing where that binary is actually located. Here is an example:

```
# ldd `which ls`
 linux-gate.so.1 => (0xb778c000)
 libselinux.so.1 => /lib/i386-linux-gnu/libselinux.so.1 (0xb774e000)
 libacl.so.1 => /lib/i386-linux-gnu/libacl.so.1 (0xb7745000)
 libc.so.6 => /lib/i386-linux-gnu/libc.so.6 (0xb7595000)
 libpcre.so.3 => /lib/i386-linux-gnu/libpcre.so.3 (0xb7557000)
 libdl.so.2 => /lib/i386-linux-gnu/libdl.so.2 (0xb7552000)
 /lib/ld-linux.so.2 (0xb778d000)
 libattr.so.1 => /lib/i386-linux-gnu/libattr.so.1 (0xb754c000)
```

Splitting Streams with the tee Command

The *tee* command is designed to accept a single stdin stream and simultaneously send one set of identical output to a specified file and use the other set as stdin to another program by using a pipe.

You might use **tee** when you are running a program that must produce output to a file and you want to monitor its progress onscreen at the same time, such as by using the **find** command. To redirect one stream of output to a single file and see the same output on the screen, use

```
# find / -iname *.txt | tee findit.out
```

This command is designed to log the standard output of a stream to a file and pass another complete stream out to the console. Financial institutions that have to log and simultaneously process data find **tee** useful.

Processing Output with the xargs Command

The *xargs* command is another useful command. It takes a list of returned results from another program (such as the output of the **locate** or **find** commands, essentially a series of path/filenames) and parses them one by one for use by a simpler or less-capable command.

As an example, say that you want to have all readme files on the entire system in one large file called **mongofile.txt** in your home directory. This would enable you to search the documentation with a single command:

```
# less mongofile.txt
```

To do this, you use the **find** command to find the full path and filename of the readme files on your system; then you use the **cat** command to redirect the results to the target file:

```
# find / -iname readme | cat > mongofile.txt
```

It would appear from the apparent lack of critical errors that you are able to get the results you want here: All lines from each file are output to **mongofile.txt**, one after the other. This turns out not to be the case, however.

To see what went wrong, issue the **less mongofile.txt** command, which reveals that you didn't get the output you wanted: The **cat** command isn't smart enough to determine that the output from the **find** command is actually discrete lines that can be used individually as if they were arguments. It just echoes the output as it was given it, in one big text blob, and it doesn't treat the individual lines as lines of usable output for the **cat** command.

NOTE   Perhaps an easier way to see what happened is to use the **wc -l** command against **mongofile.txt**. It comes back with a discrete number of lines in the file for your initial reference. (For reference, I got 679 lines of output when I ran the command.)

Run the command again with the **xargs** command acting as a buffer for the **cat** command. It reads all the output and individually feeds **cat** a single line as an argument until there are no more lines to feed to **cat**, like so:

```
# find / -iname readme | xargs cat > mongofile.txt
```

Now use the **less mongofile.txt** command to verify that it worked as you originally intended. You now see that all the files have been enumerated and appended to each other to make one large file.

NOTE   Again, the **wc -l** command shows the resulting number of output lines, and after you use **xargs**, that will be significantly larger, as the final **mongofile.txt** file is a concatenation of all the output of the files, not just the output of the file listing, as in the first command. (For reference, I got 76,097 lines of output when I ran the command.)

Shell Script Elements

Any command from the command line can be used within a script. The shell itself provides some built-in commands that make shell scripting more powerful.

Using the Output of Another Command

You will frequently need to run a command and capture the output in a variable for later use. For example, you can find the process IDs of your web server:

```
$ ps -ef | grep nginx
root 4846 1 0 Mar11 ? 00:00:00 nginx: master process /usr/sbin/nginx
-c /etc/nginx/nginx.conf
nginx 6732 4846 0 Mar11 ? 00:00:12 nginx: worker process
nginx 19617 2655 0 18:54 ? 00:00:01 php-fpm: pool www
nginx 19807 2655 0 19:01 ? 00:00:00 php-fpm: pool www
nginx 19823 2655 0 19:03 ? 00:00:00 php-fpm: pool www
sarah 20007 19931 0 19:07 pts/0 00:00:00 grep nginx
```

From here you can pick out just the master process by fine-tuning your **grep** statement:

```
$ ps -ef | grep "nginx: master process"
root 4846 1 0 Mar11 ? 00:00:00 nginx: master process /usr/sbin/nginx
-c /etc/nginx/nginx.conf
sarah 20038 19931 0 19:09 pts/0 00:00:00 grep nginx: master process
```

You can weed out the **grep** line, which is the **grep** you ran to find the process, by using a regular expression that matches the **nginx** process but not the **grep** command line:

```
$ ps -ef | grep "[n]ginx: master process"
root 4846 1 0 Mar11 ? 00:00:00 nginx: master process /usr/sbin/nginx
-c /etc/nginx/nginx.conf
```

Finally, you can extract column 2, which is the process ID:

```
$ ps -ef | grep "[n]ginx: master process" | awk '{ print $2 }'
4846
```

Enclosing the last command in backticks within your script gets you the output in a variable, which is known as *command substitution*:

```
$ PID=`ps -ef | grep "[n]ginx: master process" | awk '{ print $2 }'`
$ echo nginx is running at $PID
4846
```

Another way you might see this written is in the **$()** style:

```
$ PID=$(ps -ef | grep "[n]ginx: master process" | awk "{ print $2
}")
$ echo nginx is running at $PID
4846
```

The two methods do the same thing. Parentheses are easier to match up when debugging problems, which makes the second method better to use.

You can then use the PID variable to kill the process or restart it:

```
$ echo Telling nginx to reopen logs using pid $PID
$ kill -USR1 $PID
```

Conditionals

Scripts don't have to run from start to finish and always do the same thing. Scripts can use *conditionals* to test for certain cases and do different things depending on the output of the test. For example, the following code executes the **echo** command if the outcome of the statement after **if** returns true:

```
if ps -ef | grep -q [n]agios; then
 echo Nagios is running
fi
```

The **if** statement executes some statements, and if the condition is true, the code between the **then** and the **fi** is run. In the previous example, the code is **ps -ef | grep -q [n]agios**, which looks for **nagios** in the process listing, using the regular expression to exclude the **grep** command. The **-q** argument tells **grep** not to print anything (that is, to be quiet) because all you care about is the return value, which is stored in the **$?** Environment variable.

In the following example, **$?** holds the return code of the last command executed, which is the **grep** command from the previous examples:

```
$ ps -ef | grep -q [n]agios
$ echo $?
0
$ ps -ef | grep -q [d]oesNotExist
$ echo $?
1
```

The return code is 0 when the string is matched and 1 when it isn't. Anything greater than 1 indicates some kind of error, so it's generally better to test for either 0 for success or any positive integer for failure.

> **NOTE**   In most computer situations, 1 is true and 0 is false. With BASH programming, however, it's the opposite.

If you want to test for the absence of a condition, you can negate the outcome of a statement with an exclamation point:

```
if ! ps -ef | grep -q [n]agios; then
 echo Nagios is NOT running
fi
```

Often you want to do one thing if the condition holds true and another thing when it's false, which is where **else** comes in:

```
if ps -ef | grep -q [n]agios; then
 echo Nagios is running
else
 echo Nagios is not running. Starting
 service nagios start
fi
```

In this example, if the **grep** condition is true, the script just prints a statement to the screen. If it is false, it prints a statement and starts the service.

If three possibilities are available, you need **elif**, which is short for "else if":

```
if ps -ef | grep -q [h]ttpd; then
 echo Apache is running
elif ps -ef | grep -q [n]ginx; then
 echo Nginx is running
else
 echo No web servers are running
fi
```

> **NOTE**   Linux is very picky about syntax related to conditionals. Don't forget the ; character after **if** and **elif** statements (but not after an **else** statement). Also, note that the **then** statement is required after **if** and **elif** statements but is not used after an **else** statement. If the ; character bothers you, you could place the **then** statement on a separate line—just be consistent with which style you choose.

Testing Files

In a range of common cases, writing a shell command to test for a condition would be awkward, so the **test** command was introduced. With **test** you can perform a series of checks on files, strings, and numbers. For example, the following code returns a value of **true** (or success) if the **/etc/passwd** file exists as a plan file:

```
if test -f /etc/passwd; then
  echo "password file exists"
fi
```

The **test** command reads a series of options up until the semicolon or the end of the line and returns a value that depends on the results of the test. There are many other file test operations. Some accept one filename and others test only one file:

- **FILE1 -ef FILE2: FILE1** and **FILE2** have the same device and inode numbers.

- **FILE1 -nt FILE2: FILE1** is newer (based on the modification date) than **FILE2**.

- **FILE1 -ot FILE2: FILE1** is older than **FILE2**.

- **-d FILE: FILE** exists and is a directory.

- **-e FILE: FILE** exists.

- **-f FILE: FILE** exists and is a regular file.

- **-h FILE: FILE** exists and is a symbolic link.

- **-r FILE: FILE** exists and the user can read it.

- **-s FILE: FILE** exists and has a size greater than zero.

- **-w FILE: FILE** exists and the user can write to it.

- **-x FILE: FILE** exists and the user has the execute bit set.

There are even more options than these; for details, see the **test** man page.

An Easier Test Syntax

The **test** command is used so much that BASH has the [ ] (square *brackets*) shortcut, which is used as follows:

```
if [ test_statement ]; then
```

Anything between the square brackets is considered a **test** statement. For example, a test to see whether **/usr/bin/nginx** is executable could be performed this way:

```
if [ -x /usr/bin/nginx ]; then
  echo nginx is executable
fi
```

Newer versions of BASH can also use two sets of square brackets:

```
if [[ -x /usr/bin/nginx ]]; then
  echo nginx is executable
fi
```

The new style of double square brackets is more forgiving of errors, such as using a variable that's unset. An unset variable has not been assigned a value and therefore contains nothing when you try to reference its contents. If you're dealing entirely with Linux systems, double square brackets is the safer option to use.

> **NOTE**   Linux is very picky about syntax related to the [ ] characters. Make sure you include space characters on the inside of the brackets (for example, [test], not [test]).

Testing Strings

Words, also known as *strings*, can be easily tested, as shown here:

```
echo -n "Say something: "
read STRING
if [[ -z $STRING ]]; then
  echo "You didn't say anything"
else
  echo Thanks for that
fi
```

The first line prints a prompt to the screen; the **-n** option eliminates the newline character that is normally printed at the end of the **echo** string. The **read** command stores the data gathered from stdin (typically data typed by the user) and places the input into the variable called **$STRING**.

The test uses **-z** to check for a zero-length string. If the user didn't enter anything, the result of **-z $STRING** is true. If the user provides any input, **-z $STRING** returns false.

The opposite of **-z** is **-n**, which tests for a nonzero-length string.

You can test string equality with a single equals sign:

```
if [[ 'hostname' = 'bob.ertw.com' ]]; then
 echo You are on your home machine
else
 echo You must be somewhere else
fi
```

The conditional expression does not have to include a variable. In the preceding example, the output of the **hostname** command (using command substitution) is compared to a string.

The opposite of **=** is **!=**.

Testing Integers

Strings and integers are treated differently, and they therefore need different operators for testing. Integers are tested by using arithmetic operators. There are six integer operators:

- **X -eq Y:** Tests whether X is equal to Y.

- **X -ne Y:** Tests whether X is not equal to Y.

- **X -gt Y:** Tests whether X is greater than Y.

- **X -ge Y:** Tests whether X is greater than or equal to Y.

- **X -lt Y:** Tests whether X is less than Y.

- **X -le Y:** Tests whether X is less than or equal to Y.

You might want to count processes, files, numbers of users, or elapsed time. For example, the following script looks for a file with the name **lastrun** and reads the contents into memory. It also reads the current timestamp, in seconds, since epoch and then calculates the difference into a third variable:

```
LASTRUN=$(cat lastrun)
NOW=$(date +%s)
ELAPSED=$((NOW - LASTRUN))

if [[ $ELAPSED -ge 60 ]]; then
 echo A minute or more has passed since the last time you ran this
script
 echo $NOW > lastrun
fi
```

The script can then check to see whether a minute or more has elapsed, take an action, and then reset the last run timestamp.

Combining Multiple Tests

All the previous examples address the need to run a single test. More complicated tests can consider multiple options. This is the realm of boolean logic:

- **A AND B:** True if both A and B are true.

- **A OR B:** True if either A or B is true.

With **test** and **[condition]**, AND and OR are handled with **-a** and **-o**, respectively. Inside **[[condition]]** blocks, use **&&** and **| |**, as shown here:

```
if [ -f /etc/passwd -a -x||/usr/sbin/adduser ]
if [[ -f /etc/passwd && -x /usr/sbin/adduser ]]
```

boolean logic assigns a higher precedence to AND than it does to OR. It's like BED-MAS in arithmetic: Brackets happen before exponents, then division and multiplication, then addition and subtraction. In boolean logic, the order is

1. Brackets

2. AND

3. OR

Therefore, **[[A | | B && C]]** is evaluated as **[[A | | (B && C)]]**. This shows that you can take steps to make your code clearer for the people reading it. If you can write your tests so that there's no way to be confused by the order of operations, then do it!

case Statements

if/elif/else statements get bulky if you have more than three possibilities. For such situations you can use **case**, as shown in Example 13-2.

Example 13-2   Using **case** Instead of **if/elif/else**

```
case $1 in
 start)
 echo "Starting the process"
 ;;
 stop)
 echo "Stopping the process"
 ;;
 *)
 echo "I need to hear start or stop"
esac
```

A **case** statement starts with a description of the value to be tested, in the form **case** *$variable* **in**. Then each condition is listed in a specific format:

1. First comes the string to be matched, which is terminated with a closing parenthesis. The * matches anything, which makes it a default. You can use globbing characters for matching.

2. Zero or more statements are run if this case is matched.

3. The list of statements is terminated by two semicolons (;;).

4. Finally, the whole statement is closed with **esac** (which is the word *case* spelled backward).

Processing stops after the first match, so if multiple conditions are possible, only the first one is run.

The string to be matched can also be matched as if it were a file glob, which is helpful for accepting a range of input, as shown in Example 13-3.

Example 13-3   A String Matched as if It Were a File Glob

```
DISKSPACE=$(df -P / | tail -1 | awk '{print $5}' | tr -d '%')
case $DISKSPACE in
 100)
 echo "The disk is full"
 echo "Emergency! Disk is full!" | mail -s "Disk emergency" root@
example.com
 ;;
 [1-7]*|[0-9])
 echo "Lots of space left"
 ;;
 [8-9]*)
 echo "I'm at least 80% full"
 ;;
 *)
 echo "Hmmm. I expected some kind of percentage"
esac
```

In this example, the **DISKSPACE** variable contains the percentage of disk space used, which was obtained by command substitution as follows:

Step 1.   Take the output of **df -P /**, which shows just the disk used for the root filesystem in a single line.

Step 2. Pipe it through **tail -1**, which only prints the last line so that the header is removed.

Step 3. Print the fifth column, which is the percentage of the disk that's free, by piping through **awk**.

Step 4. Remove the % character with the translate (**tr**) command.

If the disk usage is 100%, a message indicates that the disk is full, and the script even sends an email to root with an appropriate subject line (using **-s**). The second test looks for something that begins with the numbers 1 through 7 and, optionally, anything after, or just a single digit. This corresponds to anything under 80% full. The third test is anything beginning with 8 or 9. The first-match-wins rule ensures that a disk that is 9% full is caught by the second rule and doesn't pass through to the third. Finally, a default value is caught just in case bad input is passed.

switch Statements

A switch statement is used in place of having multiple if checks, which can get cumbersome after one or two. Think of a switch statement as a way to have a case statement menu, with a default you can set if nothing is specified and a choice [on the "menu"] of multiple case statements to evaluate given an entered parameter.

An example of a simple but featureful switch statement is shown in Example 13-4.

Example 13-4   Using a Switch Statement

```
let a = 3 + 3;
switch (a) {
  case 5:
    alert( 'Not Enough );
    break;
  case 6:
    alert( 'Just Right!' );
    break;
  case 7:
    alert( 'Too Many' );
    break;
  default:
    alert( "Enter a valid value" );
}
```

The Linux+ exam might expect you to know what a switch statement is, but you're unlikely to have to know much more about how switch statements work.

Loops

Loops are the real workhorses of shell scripting. A *loop* lets you run the same procedure over and over.

BASH offers three types of loops. A **for** loop iterates over a fixed collection. A **while** loop keeps running until a given condition is met. A **unitl** loop keeps running as long as a given condition is met.

For Loops

The **for** loop's basic syntax is

```
for variable in collection; do
  # Do something on $variable
done
```

The collection can be fixed:

```
$ for name in Ross Sarah Mary-Beth; do
> echo $name
> done
Ross
Sarah
Mary-Beth
```

Here the collection is a list of three names, which starts after the **in** keyword and goes up to the semicolon or the end of the line. Note that this isn't stored in a shell script; anything that you can do in a shell script can be done directly on the command line. Loops are powerful tools that can save work both inside shell scripts and in ad hoc commands.

Each time around the loop, the variable called **name** holds the current value. For this example, the loop executes three times.

Note that the declaration of the variable is just the name of the variable, and using the variable's value requires the dollar sign prefix.

The collection can also be a file glob:

```
for file in *.txt; do newname='echo $file | sed 's/txt$/doc/''; mv
$file $newname; done
```

This example, all on one line, renames every file in the current directory that ends in **.txt** to **.doc**. It does this by iterating over the ***.txt** wildcard and each time setting the variable **file** to the current file. It assigns a temporary variable, **newname**, to the output of a **sed** command that replaces the extension with the new one. Finally, it moves the old name to the new name before moving on to the next file.

Sequences

Loops are just as happy iterating over the output of another command as they are iterating over a static list of names or a file glob. The **seq** command is particularly suited to this task. It counts from a starting point to an ending point for you:

```
$ seq 1 5
1
2
3
4
5
```

Or it counts by twos when the arguments are start, skip, and end:

```
$ seq 1 2 5
1
3
5
```

Or it pads the output with leading zeros if the number of digits changes (using the **-w** flag):

```
$ seq -w 8 10
08
09
10
```

With all this in mind, iterating over something ten times becomes straightforward:

```
for i in $(seq -w 1 10); do
  curl -O http://example.com/downloads/file$i.html
done
```

Here the loop counter is meant to do more than just count the number of iterations. The counter, **i**, forms part of a URL on a remote web server. Also note that the **seq** command includes **-w** so that all the numbers are two digits, which is common in remote web files. Ultimately, this script downloads ten files with a predictable name from a remote website using the **curl** command.

while and until Loops

Some kinds of loops have to run for an unpredictable amount of time. What if you had a script that couldn't run at the same time as another program, and it had to wait until the other program finished? If the program created a "lock file," you could test for the existence of this file repeatedly by using the following code:

```
while [[ -f /var/lock/script1 ]] ; do
 echo waiting
 sleep 10
done
```

The command on the **while** line looks for the presence of the lock file and pauses for 10 seconds if it's found. The file is checked each time through the loop, and the loop ends only when the file is removed.

The opposite of **while** is **until**, which behaves as if the loop condition were written with an exclamation point in front of it. In other words, the loop continues while the expression is false and ends the loop when the condition is true. You could use this if you're waiting for another script to drop a file in a certain location:

```
until [ -f /var/tmp/report.done ]; do

 # Waiting until the report is done
 sleep 10

done

rm /var/tmp/report.done
```

This program waits until a file is present, such as from a report job that is run. It then cleans up the state file (by removing the **/var/tmp/report.done** file) and continues on.

Interacting with Other Programs

A shell script is expected to run other programs in order to do its job. If you use **cp**, **awk**, **sed**, **grep**, or any other Unix utility, you are running another program.

Programs you run might produce output that you want to ignore. You already saw that command substitution lets you capture the output, but if you don't want to see the output, you need to use redirection.

The *grep* command can produce warnings if it reads a binary file or can't read a file because of missing permissions. If you're fine with these errors happening, you can eliminate them by redirecting the output to **/dev/null** and redirecting the error stream to the regular output stream:

```
grep -r foo /etc > /dev/null 2>&1
```

You can still test the return status of this command by looking at **$?** or the usual **if/while/test** commands. The only difference is that the output has been thrown away.

Returning an Error Code

You've seen how testing the return value of another program can let you branch and do different things based on the output. It's possible to make your own scripts return success or error conditions to whomever is calling them.

You can use the **exit** keyword anywhere within a program. By itself it returns 0, the success value. If you write **exit 42**, it returns 42. The caller sees this number in the **$?** variable.

Be careful to return something that makes sense. The shell expects that successful execution returns exit code 0. If you are going to return anything other than the typical 0 for success and 1 for error, you should describe that in comments at the top of the code.

Note that if a program exits with a nonzero value, you should probably also print an error message to stderr (standard error). This can be accomplished by using the following code:

```
echo "error message" 1>&2
```

Accepting Arguments

You can run a script with arguments, as shown in this example:

```
./deploy foo.war production
```

Each of the arguments is stored in **$1**, **$2**, **$3**, and so forth. **$0** is the name of the script itself.

The special BASH variable **$#** contains the number of arguments passed to a script. You can use it to provide some basic error checking of the input:

```
if [[ $# -lt 2 ]]; then
  echo Usage: $0 deployable environment
  exit 1 # return an error to the caller
fi
```

Perhaps you're dealing with an unknown number of arguments. The **shift** keyword removes the current **$1** value and moves **$2** to **$1**, **$3** to **$2**, and so forth. Shifting at the end of the loop means that **$1** is a new value for the next iteration of the loop, as shown in Example 13-5.

Example 13-5   Using the **shift** Keyword

```
while [[ $# -gt 0 ]]; do
 echo Processing $1
 shift
 echo There are $# to go
done
$ ./test.sh one two three
Processing one
There are 2 to go
Processing two
There are 1 to go
Processing three
There are 0 to go
```

Using **shift** is helpful when you are processing an unknown list of options, such as filenames.

Feeling a Bit (awk)ward

The *awk* command, whose name comes from the three originators of the command (Aho, Weinberger, and Kernigan) is another amazingly useful and somewhat terrifyingly powerful text processing command.

The design goals of **awk** are to allow you to process text files to select some lines of text and drop the rest, find bits of text and act on them (leaving the rest untouched), perform data validation, and generate meaningful reports from large amounts of text.

Much of **awk**'s functionality is well beyond the scope of the Linux+ exam and objectives, but a few useful examples will serve to drive home the usefulness and functionality of **awk** for nearly all system administrators.

At its very simplest, an **awk** command uses this syntax:

```
awk pattern { action }
```

Another way to look at the **awk** command line structure is

```
awk options program file
```

The **grep** and **awk** commands can be used almost identically in a simple search. For example, both of the following commands find and print or display to stdout the lines the search string is on:

```
# grep vagrant README.md
'''vagrant up'''
'''vagrant halt'''
```

```
# awk /vagrant/ README.md
'''vagrant up'''
'''vagrant halt'''
```

Another (sort of) easy-to-understand example would be to use **awk** to reorder the fields in the **/etc/passwd** file, such as

```
# awk -F: '{print $1"\t""ID #"$3"\t""In the role of""\t"$5}' /etc/
passwd
gnats      ID #41     In the role of Gnats Bug-Reporting System (admin)
nobody     ID #6553   In the role of nobody
kernoops   ID #106    In the role of Kernel Oops Tracking Daemon,,,
lightdm    ID #110    In the role of Light Display Manager
speech     ID #117    In the role of Speech Dispatcher,,,
ross       ID #900    In the role of Ross,,,
```

Here, the **/etc/passwd** file is a colon-delimited file, so you use **-F:** to tell **awk** that the fields are separated by that character. Then you rearrange the file columns in between the curly brackets ({ }) by using the **print** statement.

Here is what each element of the preceding example does:

- **awk:** This is, obviously, the command.

- **-F::** This is the previously mentioned option that tells the **awk** command the field delimiter character—in this case the colon (:) character.

- **'{:** This starts the transformation section.

- **print:** This is the action taken; it prints everything that follows.

- **$1:** This is the first field of the **/etc/passwd** file, the username.

- **"\t":** This denotes an inserted tab between the **$1** and the next element.

- **"ID #":** This is a string of text.

- **$3:** This is the third field of the **/etc/passwd** file, the UID.

- **"\t":** This is another inserted tab between elements.

- **"In the role of":** This is another descriptive string of text.

- **"\t":** Represents a tab character.

- **$5:** This is the fifth field of the **/etc/passwd** file, the description.

- **}':** This ends the transformation section.

This is a relatively simple example of how you can use **awk** not just to transform a file but to use the file's fields and information to produce a report that is more informative than just a listing out of an **/etc/passwd** file.

Translating Files

The *tr* command is for changing characters in files or streams. However, it does not change whole words or phrases; that's the job of the **sed** command, discussed in the section after the next one.

For example, if you have a file that contains a lot of commands from a sample in a book, but some of the commands are dysfunctional because the editor capitalized the first characters of the lines, you can translate the file's uppercase letters to lowercase with the following command:

```
# tr 'A-Z 'a-z' < commands.txt
```

The **tr** command isn't capable of feeding itself or accepting a file as an argument. It's unfair, but we often say that the **tr** command is less intelligent than **cat**, since **cat** *can* feed itself. The **<** operator is therefore mandatory when using **tr**; without it, the command won't work.

The following command can be used to accomplish the same results:

```
# tr [:upper:] [:lower:] < commands.txt
```

NOTE   Remember that **tr** is incapable of feeding itself or accepting a file as an argument, so the **<** redirection symbol is needed to send the input file to the command. Anything else is a broken command and produces a syntax error.

Cutting Columns

In many cases, you will need to take a file that contains columns of data, regardless of the delimiter or separator, and either extract information on a column-by-column basis or perhaps even reorder the columns to make it more usable. For example, you can use the *cut* command as shown here to display only from column 20 to column 40 of **file1**, excluding all other data on each line:

```
# cut -c 20-40 /etc/passwd | tail -n 5
ar/spool/postfix:/bin
hare/pvm3:/bin/bash
ross brunson:/home/rb
home/snuffy:/bin/bash
:/home/quotaboy:/bin/
```

The **cut** command can also grab certain fields from a file, such as from the **/etc/passwd** file. To grab the username, description, and home directory fields for each user, use the following command:

```
# cut -d: -f 1,5,6 /etc/passwd | tail -n 5
postfix::/var/spool/postfix
```

```
pvm::/usr/share/pvm3
rbrunson:ross brunson:/home/rbrunson
snuffy::/home/snuffy
quotaboy::/home/quotaboy
```

The **-d** option sets the delimiter, which in this case is the : character. By default, **cut** uses tabs as delimiters.

He sed, She sed

The *sed*, or stream editor, command is used to process and perform actions on streams of text, such as the lines found in a text file. **sed** is amazingly powerful, which is a way of saying it can be difficult to use.

A good illustration of the way **sed** works is to imagine that a text file is a long string that stretches from one side of the room to the other. On that string, you can put special transforming beads and slide them down the string, having the program perform each particular transformation as it slides along the string or the lines of the file. The neat thing about **sed** is that you can stack the beads or send them one behind the other and make what can appear to be an almost magical transformation of a text file occur with a single command or set of commands.

A former colleague used **sed** in a really impressive way: He regularly pulled a financial feed from a vendor and used a single execution of a complex **sed** script to transform that information into a dynamic web page that was refreshed all day long from subsequent transformations.

sed is very often used for searching and replacing text, including words and complete phrases. Whereas **tr** works only on characters/numerals as individuals, **sed** is capable of complex functions, including multiple operations per line.

sed uses the following syntax:

sed -*option* *action/regexp/replacement/flag filename*

Rather than struggle through an explanation of what happens when certain options are entered, let's look at what **sed** does when you use those options. Using **sed** properly includes being able to, ahem, "reuse" **sed** commands from other sysadmins.

To replace the first instance of **bob** with **BOB** on each line in a given file, use this command:

```
# sed s/bob/BOB/ file1
```

To replace all instances of **bob** with **BOB** on each line in a given file, use this command:

```
# sed s/bob/BOB/g file1
```

sed allows for multiple operations on a given stream's lines, each of which is performed before moving on to the next line.

To search for and replace **bob** with **BOB** and then search for **BOB** and replace it with **snuffy** for every line and every instance for a given file, use this command:

```
# sed 's/bob/BOB/g ; s/BOB/snuffy/g' file1
```

Here the semicolon character is similar to BASH's capability to run several commands independently of each other. However, this whole operation, from the first single quotation mark (') to the last single quotation mark, is all performed inside **sed**, not as part of BASH.

When **sed** is used for multiple commands, you can either use a semicolon to separate the commands or use multiple instances of **-e** to execute the multiple commands:

```
# sed -e s/bob/BOB/g -e s/BOB/snuffy/g file1
```

On the Linux+ exam, and whenever you might use **sed** with spaces in your patterns, bracket the whole pattern/procedure in single quotation marks, such as

```
# sed 's/is not/is too/g' file1
```

This keeps you from getting syntax errors due to the spaces in the strings.

Sooner or later, you'll get tired of typing the same operations for **sed** and will want to use a script or some method of automating a recurring task. **sed** has the capability to use a simple script file that contains a set of procedures. An example of the previous set of procedures in a **sed** script file is shown here:

```
s/bob/BOB/g
s/BOB/snuffy/g
```

This script file is used in the following manner:

```
sed -f scriptfile targetfile
```

Multiple procedures can be performed on a single stream, and the whole set of procedures can be performed on each successive line.

Obviously, doing a large number of procedures on a given text stream can take time, but it is usually worthwhile because you only need to verify that it worked correctly when it's done. It sure beats doing it all by hand in **vi**!

Another feature of **sed** is its capability to suppress or not display any line that doesn't have changes made to it. For example, if you want to replace **machine** with **MACHINE** on all lines in a given file but display only the changed lines, use the following command with the **-n** option to have the command suppress normal output:

```
# sed -n 's/machine/MACHINE/pg' watchdog.txt
```

The **pg** string at the end prints the matched or changed lines and globally replaces for all instances per line rather than just the first instance per line.

To do a search and replace on a range of lines, prefix the **s/** string with either a line number or a range separated by a comma, such as

```
# sed -n '1,5s/server/SERVER/pg' sedfile
```

```
The X SERVER uses this directory to store the compiled version of
the current keymap and/or any scratch keymaps used by clients. The X
SERVER time. The default keymap for any SERVER is usually stored in:
```

On the Linux+ exam, the **sed** questions are all about what will find and replace strings, with particular attention on global versus single replaces.

Using grep and Friends

Being able to find files is one thing, but being able to find the text within them is a very useful skill. Remember, almost everything in Linux is text, including the contents of files and the output from commands, so all of this information is searchable!

Getting a grep

The grep is used for searching plain-text data for lines that match a regular expression (a text pattern). It is a very powerful tool that can be used to find specific text in a large amount of data. One of the more fun text-processing commands is **grep** (global regular expression print). Properly used, it can find almost any string or phrase in a single file, a stream of text via stdin, or an entire directory of files (such as the kernel source hierarchy).

grep uses the following syntax for its commands:

```
grep -options pattern file
```

The **grep** command has many useful options, including

- **-c:** This option shows only a numeric count of the matches found and not any output of filenames or matches.

- **-C #:** This option surrounds the matched string with a specified (#) number of lines of context.

- **-H:** This option prints the filename for each match; it's useful when you want to then edit that file, and it is the default option when multiple files are searched.

- **-h:** This option suppresses the filename display for each file and is the default when a single file is searched.

- **-i:** This option searches for the pattern with no case sensitivity; all matches are shown.

- **-l:** This option shows only the filename of the matching file; no lines of matching output are shown.

- **-L:** This option displays the filenames of files that don't have matches for the string.

- **-w:** This option selects only lines that have the string as a whole word, not part of another word.

- **-r:** This option reads and processes all the directories specified, along with all the files in them.

- **-x:** This option causes only exact line matches to be returned; every character on the line must match.

- **-v:** This option shows all the lines in a file that don't match the string; this is exactly the opposite of the default behavior.

Examples of Using **grep**

grep can either use files and directories as target arguments or be fed **stdout** for parsing. An example of using **grep** to parse output follows:

```
# who | grep ross
```

This command parses the **who** command's **stdout** for the name **ross** and prints that line, if found.

The following more complex example of **grep** combines **grep** with the command **find**:

```
# find / -name readme -exec grep -iw kernel {} \;
```

This command finds all the files on the system named **readme** and then executes the **grep** command on each file, searching for any instance of the whole word **kernel**, regardless of case. A whole word search finds the string *kernel* but not *kernels*.

An innovative use of the **grep** command's options for finding strings is to have it show you lines that don't match a string. For example, you might want to check **/etc/passwd** periodically for a user who doesn't have a shadowed password:

```
# grep -v :x: /etc/passwd
snuffy:$1$3O238jrk15uHEgxdtFTlxkK1:501:501::/home/snuffy:/bin/bash
```

It looks like **snuffy** has an encrypted password in the **/etc/passwd** file. You should therefore run the **pwconv** command to fix this and make **snuffy** change his password immediately.

NOTE This section shows how to use **grep** to search for certain terms, and I've been careful to choose tame examples. For the Linux+ exam, you need to be able to use **grep** and its options.

NOTE The **tail** command and its options are used in the following examples to limit the number of items of output so that the output fits on a typical screen.

To search for the word *fool* in the additional documentation directories, use the following command (see Figure 13-3):

```
# grep -ir fool /usr/share/doc | tail -n 15
```

```
linux-ab2x:/usr/share/doc # grep -ir fool /usr/share/doc | tail -n 15
/usr/share/doc/packages/libpng12-devel/README:fact that it's the first release fool you.  The libpng library ha
s been in
/usr/share/doc/packages/docbook_3/html/ref/refpages/inte1.htm:&lt;INTERFACEDEFINITION&gt;PixFool API&lt;/INTERF
ACEDEFINITION&gt;.
/usr/share/doc/packages/kipi-plugins/ChangeLog: be after $(LIBKIPI_CFLAGS) since that one is local (nice way to
 fool
/usr/share/doc/packages/kipi-plugins/ChangeLog: be after $(LIBKIPI_CFLAGS) since that one is local (nice way to
 fool
/usr/share/doc/packages/amarok/ChangeLog:      not to fool users.
/usr/share/doc/packages/xine/faq.html:      for example). When you decided to dig out the url by hand don't get
 fooled
/usr/share/doc/packages/xine/faq.txt:dig out the url by hand don't get fooled by the many redirectors that are
often
/usr/share/doc/packages/libbonoboui/ChangeLog:  remove bogus remote faking, we need to fool Gdk too.
/usr/share/doc/packages/digikam/ChangeLog:      being fooled by the empty string, which sometimes comes from th
e
/usr/share/doc/packages/digikam/ChangeLog:      5012.  Now snapZoom() is fooled when the current zoom is 5012 a
nd
/usr/share/doc/packages/digikam/ChangeLog:      Carsten Lohrke to fix .desktop file to foolow last change from
/usr/share/doc/packages/digikam/ChangeLog:      bad, as user can fool around with the imageeditor without risk
of
/usr/share/doc/packages/glib2-devel/ChangeLog:   to fix it is to declare GLIB_COMPILATION around it and fool t
he single
/usr/share/doc/kde/HTML/en/kcontrol/useragent/index.docbook:necessary to fool the web site by having &konqueror
; report itself to be
Binary file /usr/share/doc/kde/HTML/en/digikam/superimposepreview.png matches
linux-ab2x:/usr/share/doc # █
```

Figure 13-3 Output of the **grep** command search for *fool*

Notice that you get matches with the pattern *fool* as a whole word and as part of things like *fooled* or *foolish*. If you press the **up arrow** key and change the word *fool* to *foolish* and execute the command again, you get the results shown in Figure 13-4.

```
linux-ab2x:/usr/share/doc # grep -ir foolish /usr/share/doc | tail -n 15
/usr/share/doc/packages/gstreamer/ChangeLog:        gst/gstvalue.c: If someone is foolish enough to compare 2 fra
ctions with denominator = 0, return UNORDERED rather tha...
/usr/share/doc/packages/gstreamer/ChangeLog:        If someone is foolish enough to compare 2 fractions with deno
minator =
/usr/share/doc/packages/man-pages/Changes.old:      "A foolish consistency is the hobgoblin of little minds, ador
ed by
/usr/share/doc/packages/man-pages/Changes.old:      "A foolish consistency is the hobgoblin of little minds, ador
ed by
/usr/share/doc/packages/graphviz/FAQ.html:<A HREF="http://msdn.microsoft.com/library/default.asp?url=/library/e
n-us/dnhfact/html/hfactor8_5.asp">How To Avoid Foolish Consistency</A>
/usr/share/doc/packages/grub/ChangeLog: Add BIOS drive remapping support for chain-loading some foolish
/usr/share/doc/packages/grub/NEWS: chain-load some foolish operating systems (such as DOS) even if such
/usr/share/doc/packages/gstreamer-0_10/ChangeLog:        gst/gstvalue.c: If someone is foolish enough to compa
re 2 fractions with denominator = 0, return UNORDERED rather tha...
/usr/share/doc/packages/gstreamer-0_10/ChangeLog:        If someone is foolish enough to compare 2 fractions w
ith denominator =
/usr/share/doc/packages/gnome-vfs2/ChangeLog:   Fix foolish crasher
linux-ab2x:/usr/share/doc # ▮
```

Figure 13-4 Output of the **grep** command search for *foolish*

Now say that you want to just do a search for the exact word *fool* and not any variation of it. To see lines that contain only the whole word, add the **-w** option (see
Figure 13-5):

```
# grep -irw fool /usr/share/doc | tail -n 15
```

```
linux-ab2x:/usr/share/doc # grep -irw fool /usr/share/doc | tail -n 15
/usr/share/doc/packages/librsvg-2-2/ChangeLog:        * acinclude.m4: Change comment so that we won't fool
/usr/share/doc/packages/ncurses/NEWS:   + the panel_window() function was not fool-proof.
/usr/share/doc/packages/libmjpegutils-2_0-0/README.lavpipe:fool proof at the moment. So if you feed matteblend.
flt the wrong number
/usr/share/doc/packages/sane-backends/ChangeLog:        Use MDL string instead of DES as it is mre fool proof
when matching
/usr/share/doc/packages/sane-backends/NEWS:    to scanning to fool the memory management and scanned a full pag
e
/usr/share/doc/packages/libpng16-devel/README:fact that it's the first release fool you.  The libpng library ha
s been in
/usr/share/doc/packages/libpng12-devel/README:fact that it's the first release fool you.  The libpng library ha
s been in
/usr/share/doc/packages/kipi-plugins/ChangeLog: be after $(LIBKIPI_CFLAGS) since that one is local (nice way to
 fool
/usr/share/doc/packages/kipi-plugins/ChangeLog: be after $(LIBKIPI_CFLAGS) since that one is local (nice way to
 fool
/usr/share/doc/packages/amarok/ChangeLog:     not to fool users.
/usr/share/doc/packages/libbonoboui/ChangeLog: remove bogus remote faking, we need to fool Gdk too.
/usr/share/doc/packages/digikam/ChangeLog:    bad, as user can fool around with the imageeditor without risk
of
/usr/share/doc/packages/glib2-devel/ChangeLog:    to fix it is to declare GLIB_COMPILATION around it and fool t
he single
/usr/share/doc/kde/HTML/en/kcontrol/useragent/index.docbook:necessary to fool the web site by having &konqueror
; report itself to be
Binary file /usr/share/doc/kde/HTML/en/digikam/superimposepreview.png matches
linux-ab2x:/usr/share/doc # ▮
```

Figure 13-5 Output of the **grep** command search for *fool* as a whole word

Finally, let's look at a useful option to the **grep** command (**grep -l**) that allows you to see not the normal output of lines that match the item you are searching for but a listing of the files that match the search. This is useful when you want to send the output to an editor, a stream editor, or another file transformation command (see Figure 13-6).

```
linux-ab2x:/usr/share/doc # grep -irwl fool /usr/share/doc | tail -n 15
/usr/share/doc/packages/gnutls/NEWS
/usr/share/doc/packages/librsvg-2-2/ChangeLog
/usr/share/doc/packages/ncurses/NEWS
/usr/share/doc/packages/libmjpegutils-2_0-0/README.lavpipe
/usr/share/doc/packages/sane-backends/ChangeLog
/usr/share/doc/packages/sane-backends/NEWS
/usr/share/doc/packages/libpng16-devel/README
/usr/share/doc/packages/libpng12-devel/README
/usr/share/doc/packages/kipi-plugins/ChangeLog
/usr/share/doc/packages/amarok/ChangeLog
/usr/share/doc/packages/libbonoboui/ChangeLog
/usr/share/doc/packages/digikam/ChangeLog
/usr/share/doc/packages/glib2-devel/ChangeLog
/usr/share/doc/kde/HTML/en/kcontrol/useragent/index.docbook
/usr/share/doc/kde/HTML/en/digikam/superimposepreview.png
linux-ab2x:/usr/share/doc #
```

Figure 13-6   Output of the **grep** command search with options to show only the path/files

The **grep** command is versatile. You can discover more of its useful options by reading the man page or other documentation. The discussion in this section is more than enough to be useful and covers the items typically included on the Linux+ exam.

> **NOTE** As a final recommendation, try adding the **-n** option to show the line numbers of found items within a file.

One additional expansion of the use of **grep** is to show the inverse or opposite of what you know exists, such as the output of the **lastlog** command. By default, the **lastlog** command shows the following columns:

```
Username     Port     From     Latest
```

By default, this command shows you an entry for every user or service account that exists in the **/etc/passwd** file, most of which will have not logged in or should never log in, as they are service accounts for managing and owning processes, not user accounts. This is problematic in that you have to sort through a lot of output where the last field, **Latest**, shows the text **"Never logged in"**, and only down at the bottom do you see actual users' data.

Probably my favorite way to use **grep** (other than to search for swear words in the kernel source code, that is) is to use the **-v** (inverse) option, which shows you everything that does *not* match what you just searched for.

For example, you can use **-v** on the **lastlog** command output to mask out any line of output that contains the string **"Never logged in"**, thereby showing only the users that have logged in:

```
# lastlog | grep -v "Never logged in"
Username     Port     From                 Latest
ross         pts/1    192.168.33.144       Wed, Feb 22, 08:20 -0700 2019
ulogin       pts/2    192.168.33.88        Wed, Feb 22, 07:10 -0700 2019
shaggy       pts/3    192.168.33.76        Wed, Feb 22, 05:50 -0700 2019
```

Note that if you run this command and see that a service account, such as **ntp**, **systemd-network**, or **kernoops**, has logged in, you should immediately start investigating why. Again, service-related accounts are not supposed to be used to log in, so such a login indicates some sort of system hack.

Expanding **grep** with **egrep** and **fgrep**

The most important thing to know about **egrep** and **fgrep** is that they exist as commands primarily so you do not have to use **grep -E** and **grep -F**. Historically, there have been separate binaries, and indeed there are separate binaries on both the RPM-based distribution and the DPKG-based distributions we typically use.

The *egrep* command has many uses, but the main one to focus on is using **egrep** or **grep -E** to process search terms that feature operators, such as **OR**. For example, say that you want to find lines in a very large **/etc/passwd** file that start with the letter **r** and have either **p** or **t** as the next letter, followed by any other letters. You can try the following:

```
# egrep '^r(p|t) /etc/passwd
```

This search finds the following lines, if they exist on your learning system:

```
rpc:x:490:65534:user for rpcbind:/var/lib/empty:/sbin/nologin
rtkit:x:492:490:RealtimeKit:/proc:/bin/false
```

You can also search using **egrep** or **grep -E** for any line in the **/etc/passwd** file that contains **false** or **nologin** with this command:

```
# egrep '(false|nologin)' /etc/passwd
```

This command should return a number of output lines, all of which have either **false** or **nologin** somewhere in the line.

The **fgrep** command is similar in execution to **egrep**, but it essentially allows you to use a file that contains a set of terms to be searched for, instead of requiring you to specify them all, separated by pipes. First, create a file named **filetosearch.txt** and make it match the following output:

```
one
two
three
four
five
six
seven
eight
nine
ten
```

Then create a file named **searchterms.txt** and make it match the following output:

```
one
three
eight
```

Then run the following commands, which should produce the same output:

```
# egrep '(one|three|eight)' filetosearch.txt
# fgrep -f searchterms.txt foobartar.fu
```

It's easy to use **fgrep** to refer to a file for the discrete search terms you want to use; this is a much more elegant method than packing an **egrep** command line with a dozen or so search terms.

Don't forget that you can use [ ] ranges, globs (*) of text, and several other special characters to display what you want when using the **egrep** and **fgrep** commands.

Using Regular Expressions and grep

Using **grep** to find particular words and phrases can be difficult unless you use *regular expressions*. A regular expression has the capability to search for something that you don't know exactly, either through partial strings or using the following special characters:

- **.:** A period matches any single character and enforces that the character must exist (for example, **a.v** is a three-letter regular expression).

- **?:** A question mark matches an optional item and is matched only once.

- ***:** An asterisk matches from zero to many characters (for example, **a*v** finds av, a2v, andv, and so on).

- **+:** A plus sign means that the item must be matched once and can be matched many times.

- **{*n*}:** A curly bracketed number means that the item is matched *n* times.

- **{*n*,}:** A curly bracketed number followed by a comma means the item is matched *n* or more times.

- **{*n,m*}:** A curly bracketed pair of numbers separated by a comma matches from *n* to *m* times.

What's the use for all of this? Try finding just the word *Kernel* in the source tree with the following command:

```
# grep -rl Kernel /usr/share/doc | wc -l
  138
```

> **NOTE** The **wc** command shows a count for any combination of lines, words, and characters and is used extensively for the very situation shown here: showing lines of output as a number instead of showing the actual lines of output.

The command finds 138 files that each contain at least one match for *Kernel*. Now try finding just the word *Kernel* as a whole word with this command:

```
# grep -rlw Kernel /usr/share/doc | wc -l
  131
```

Now try the same command again but modify it so that the word *Kernel* is searched for, but only followed by a period:

```
# grep -rwl Kernel\. /usr/share/doc | wc -l
  27
```

Now search for the word *silly* as the search pattern:

```
# grep -rwl silly /usr/share/doc | wc -l
  93
```

Run the command again with the context number set to two lines to get more information about what is being commented on:

```
# grep -rwn -C2 silly /usr/share/doc
```

The output varies on different systems, but essentially you see consecutive lines preceded with the same filename and the number of the lines shown, so you see that there are two lines of context being shown above and below each found search term. This can be useful when trying to find a particular instance of a search term based on the lines around it.

> **NOTE** For the Linux+ exam, you need to be familiar with how to use regular expressions, particularly how to find strings that start and end with a particular letter or letters but contain other text in between.

Another example of regular expressions in action is searching for a particular phrase or word but not another that is similar. The following file, **watch.txt**, contains the following lines:

```
01 The first sentence contains broad
02 The second contains bring
03 The third contains brush
04 The fourth has BRIDGE as the last word: bridge broad
05 The fifth begins with BROAD
06 The sixth contains none of the four
07 This contains bringing, broadened, brushed
```

To find all the words that begin with *br* but exclude any that have *i* as the third letter, use the following command:

```
# grep "\<br[^i]" watch.txt
01 The first sentence contains broad
03 The third contains brush broad
05 The fifth begins with BROAD
```

The **\<** string just means that the word begins with those letters. You use **[^i]** to find all but the letter in that position. If you use a **^** in front of a search term inside a program such as **vi**, it searches at the front of a line, but using the **^** symbol inside a set of square brackets excludes that character from being found.

To find a set of words that ends with a certain set, use this command:

```
# grep "ad\>" watch.txt
01 The first sentence contains broad broad
05 The fifth begins with BROAD
```

As with the previous example, the **\>** characters on the end of a search cause **grep** to look for words that end in that string.

grep allows a number of search strings:

- **broad:** Searches for exactly *broad* but as part of other words (such as *broadway* or *broadening*) unless you use **-w** to cause *broad* to be searched for as a stand-alone word.

- **^broad:** Searches for the word *broad* at the beginning of any line.

- **broad$:** Searches for the word *broad* at the end of the line.

- **[bB]road:** Searches for the words *broad* and *Broad*.

- **br[iou]ng:** Searches for *bring*, *brong*, and *brung*.

- **br[^i]ng:** Searches for and returns all but *bring*.

- **^......$:** Searches for any line that contains exactly six characters.

- **[bB][rR]in[gG]:** Searches for *Bring*, *BRing*, *BRinG*, or any combination thereof.

Pasting and Joining

Two commands that are similar in function are **paste** and **join**. **paste** doesn't remove any data from the output, but **join** removes redundant key fields from the data.

For example, say you have the following files:

file1:
```
Line one of file1
Line two of file1
```

file2:
```
Line one of file2
Line two of file2
```

Using **paste** on these two files produces this output:
```
Line one of file1 Line one of file2
Line two of file1 Line two of file2
```

Notice that nothing is lost from the files. All the data is there. This can be redundant in the extreme if you want to produce a joint file from two or more files.

Rather than just pasting one file's contents after the other on the same line, catenation style, the **join** command is more of a database join style. It takes a file as the first argument and, by default, treats the first field of that file as a key field. The second and subsequent files are treated in the same fashion. It outputs each matching line of the files, in order, minus the redundant key fields from any but the first file.

For example, say that you have the following files, **users** and **location**:

users:

```
rbrunson:500:
snuffy:501:
quotaboy:502:
```

location:

```
rbrunson 123 anystreet anytown ID 83858
snuffy 123 circle loop chicago IL 88888
quotaboy 123 some lane anyburg MT 59023
```

As you can see, the output of using **join** on these files includes only the unique information from each file and leaves out the location key field:

```
# join users location
rbrunson:500: 123 anystreet anytown ID 83858
snuffy:501: 123 circle loop chicago IL 88888
quotaboy:502: 123 some lane anyburg MT 59023
```

Finding Files

The **find** command is the most accurate but time-consuming method for searching a system for file objects because it crawls the list of files in real time as opposed to the way **locate** searches the indexed database. The command consists of several (sometimes confusing) sections. But, if it's learned properly, it can be a powerhouse for a busy sysadmin.

The syntax of a **find** command is

```
find startpath -options arguments
```

To make sense of this syntax, let's take a look at a useful **find** command example:

```
# find /home -iname *.mp3
/home/snuffy/g3 - red house.mp3
```

This command sets the start path to the **/home** directory and then looks for any instance of the string **mp3** as a file extension or after the last **.** in the filename. It finds a file in the user **snuffy**'s home directory and returns the full path for that file.

Options for **find** include

- **group:** Searches for files belonging to the specified group.

- **newer:** Searches for files newer than the specified file.

- **name:** Searches for files with names matching a case-sensitive string.

- **iname:** Searches for files with names matching a non-case-sensitive string.

- **user:** Searches for files belonging to the specified user.

- **mtime:** Searches for the modify time; used for finding files a specified number of days old.

- **atime:** Searches for the number of days since last accessed.

- **ctime:** Searches for the number of days since the directory entry was last changed.

A useful feature of the **find** command is its capability to execute another command or script on each and every entry normally returned to standard output.

For example, to find all MP3 files in the user's home directories and archive a copy into the root user's home directory, you could use this command:

```
# find /home -iname *.mp3 -exec cp -f {} .\;
```

This command uses the **-exec** option, which accepts every line returned to standard output, one by one, and inserts the full path and filename between the curly brackets (**{}**). When each line of output is parsed and the command is executed, it reaches the **\;** at the end of the line and goes back to standard input for the next line. The last line of output is the last one with a command executed on it; it doesn't just keep going and error out.

Running multiple operators in a single command is possible, too. Just be sure not to get the values for one operator mixed up in the next. You could look for all MP3 files owned by a given user with the following command:

```
# find /home -iname *.mp3 -user snuffy
/home/snuffy/bls - all for you.mp3
```

The **find** command is complex, and rather than bore you with more possible options, this section provides a number of examples of how to use **find**.

To find a file and execute **cat** on it, use

```
# find /etc -iname fstab -exec cat {} \;
```

To delete all **core** files older than seven days, use the following:

```
# find /home -mtime +7 -iname core -exec rm -f {} \;
```

To find all files on the system owned by **bob** and change the ownership to **root**, use

```
# find / -user bob -exec chown root {} \;
```

To find all files by user **tjordan** and change his group, use this command:

```
# find /data -user tjordan -exec chGRP users {} \;
```

For safety, you can use **-ok** instead of **-exec** to be prompted for confirmation each time the command runs:

```
# find /data -user tjordan -ok chgrp users {} \;
```

To find all inodes related to a hard link, use the command

```
$ find / -inum 123456
```

The Linux+ exam covers the **find** command's operators and the capability to execute commands on the search results. Practice all the examples you see here and get inventive with the possibilities. Particularly watch out for the use of **-mtime** and its cousins, **-atime** and **-ctime**.

Summary

In this chapter you learned all about the concept and practice of scripting, from simply placing multiple commands into a script and executing it, to how to make those scripts much more useful using loops, conditionals, testing, redirection and handling of streams, and much more.

Start simply and gradually work your way into the more advanced uses of scripting as they make sense or you find that you need that functionality—it'll all fall into place for you like it did me, and probably faster!

Exam Preparation Tasks

As mentioned in the section "Goals and Methods" in the Introduction, you have a couple of choices for exam preparation: the exercises here, Chapter 23, "Final Preparation," and the exam simulation questions in the Pearson Test Prep Software Online.

Review All Key Topics

Review the most important topics in this chapter, noted with the Key Topic icon in the outer margin of the page. Table 13-3 lists these key topics and the page number on which each is found.

Table 13-3   Key Topics for Chapter 13

Key Topic Element	Description	Page Number
List	Line-by-line description of how a script works	466
Paragraph	How to echo the **PATH** variable	472
Paragraph	Defining an absolute path	473
Section	Running a Script	474
Table 13-2	Linux File Descriptors	475
Paragraph	When to use a here document (heredoc)	477
List	The redirection symbols	478
Figure 13-1	Path of data streams	479
Paragraph	Defining what a pipe (|) is used for	481
List	Multiple command operators	483
Paragraph	Testing for a file's existence	483
Paragraph	Defining a **case** statement	494
Example 13-4	Using a Switch Statement	495
Paragraph	Using **sed** to replace the first instance of a phrase with another instance	503
Paragraph	Using the **grep -v** inversion option to show what is not found	506
Paragraph	The most important thing to know about **egrep** and **fgrep**	510
Paragraph	Finding a set of files in a particular directory tree with the **find** command	515

Define Key Terms

Define the following key terms from this chapter and check your answers in the glossary:

globbing, braces, variables, **PATH**, **SHELL**, source, stdin, stdout, stderr, **find**, here document, redirection, **tee**, **xargs**, conditionals, brackets, boolean, loop, **grep**, **awk**, **tr**, **cut**, **sed**, **egrep**, regular expressions

Review Questions

The answers to these review questions are in Appendix A.

1. Which of the following is the file descriptor that matches stdout?

   a. **/proc/self/fd/0**

   b. **/proc/self/fd/1**

   c. **/proc/self/fd/2**

   d. **/proc/self/fd/3**

2. What is the result of the following command?

   ```
   $ find / -iname "*.txt | file > sort
   ```

   a. A file named **file** in the current directory

   b. An error message indicating that the files could not be found

   c. A file named **sort** in the current directory

   d. An endless loop on the system

   e. None of the above

3. On a Linux system installed with the default BASH shell, you need to execute a shell script that contains variables, aliases, and functions by simply entering its name on the command line. What should be the first line of the script?

   a. A comment

   b. **#/bin/csh**

   c. **#!/bin/bash**

   d. **exec=/bin/bash**

4. You are writing a shell script that calls another program, called **/bin/foo**. If the program does not return successfully, you should print an error to the screen. Which of the following can you use to test for an error condition?

   a. if [-e /bin/foo]

    b. if [$? -gt 0]

    c. if [$? -eq 0]

    d. until [/bin/foo]

5. If you had an operation you wanted to perform on every process currently running, what would be the most appropriate loop construct?

    a. seq

    b. while

    c. for

    d. until

6. When writing a BASH script, you find yourself needing to exit early because of an error condition. Which of the following commands should you use?

    a. die

    b. exit 1

    c. raise

    d. exit

This chapter covers the following topics:

- Container Management
- Container Image Operations

The exam objective covered in this chapter is as follows:

- **Objective 3.2:** Given a scenario, perform basic container operations

## CHAPTER 14

Perform Basic Container Operations

In this chapter we'll not only cover the basic container operations specified in objective 3.2, but also work our way through a typical testing environment setup, pulling and running images, configuring them, querying for more information about them, and running instances.

"Do I Know This Already?" Quiz

The "Do I Know This Already?" quiz enables you to assess whether you should read this entire chapter or simply jump to the "Exam Preparation Tasks" section for review. If you are in doubt, read the entire chapter. Table 14-1 outlines the major headings in this chapter and the corresponding "Do I Know This Already?" quiz questions. You can find the answers in Appendix A, "Answers to the 'Do I Know This Already?' Quizzes and Review Questions."

Table 14-1 "Do I Know This Already?" Foundation Topics Section-to-Question Mapping

Foundation Topics Section	Questions Covered in This Section
Container Management	1–4
Container Image Operations	5–6

CAUTION The goal of self-assessment is to gauge your mastery of the topics in this chapter. If you do not know the answer to a question or are only partially sure of the answer, you should mark that question as wrong for purposes of the self-assessment. Giving yourself credit for an answer you correctly guess skews your self-assessment results and might provide you with a false sense of security.

1. A container is based on a(n) _____? (Choose the best answer.)

   a. Repository

   b. Pod

   c. Image

   d. Scope

2. What must you do with a container image before you can list it?

   a. Inspect it

   b. Scope it

   c. Download it

   d. Build it

3. Which keystroke combination disconnects from a running container? (Choose all that apply.)

   a. **Ctrl+q**

   b. **Ctrl+c**

   c. **Ctrl+z**

   d. **Ctrl+s**

   e. **Ctrl+p**

4. To see the latest log entries from the most recently executed container, which command would you use?

   a. **podman logs -T**

   b. **podman logs**

   c. **podman logs -a**

   d. **podman logs -l**

5. Which of the following can you push a container image to? (Choose all that apply.)

   a. Public repository

   b. Private repository

   c. Portal repository

   d. Primary repository

6. If you have multiple identically named images in your local storage, which option to the **podman rmi** command would allow you to remove those identically named images?

   a. **-f**

   b. **-x**

   c. **-z**

   d. None of the answers are correct.

Container Management

A *container* is a lightweight, standalone, executable package of software that includes everything needed to run an application: code, runtime, system tools, system libraries, and settings.

Containers are similar to virtual machines (VMs) in that they provide a way to isolate an application from its environment. However, containers are much more lightweight than VMs, which means that they can be started and stopped much faster. This makes containers ideal for deploying and managing applications in cloud environments.

Managing **containers** is more important now that we can run local root-less container scenarios, making it much easier for developers and system engineers to test changes without having to port everything off to a cloud instance somewhere. A root-less container is a container that is run by an unprivileged user, without root privileges. This means that the container cannot access the host machine's root filesystem or perform certain privileged operations.

Installing and Verifying the Container Tools

The first thing you need to know is how to install the container tools that you will need to manage containers. This package provides the software needed to manage containers.

Installing the Container-Tools Package and Dependencies

You can start with a simple clean install, say of Red Hat Enterprise Linux, and then install the container-tools package as follows:

```
# sudo yum module install container-tools
```

The install process will ask you if you'd like to install the container-tools package and a fair amount of dependencies, so enter **y** to answer yes and allow the install to finish. Figure 14-1 shows the ending of this process and the query to which you'd answer yes.

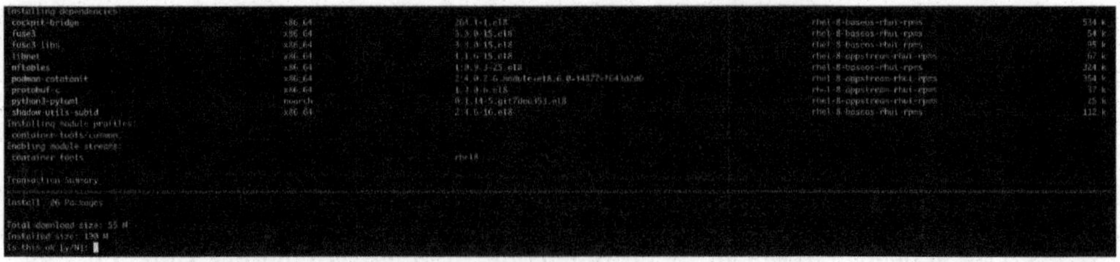

Figure 14-1   Installing the container-tools packages

Verifying the Podman and Skopeo Tool Installation

Podman is a daemonless container engine for developing, managing, and running containers on your Linux® systems. Skopeo is a tool for inspecting, copying, and transferring container images and image repositories. You can verify that the *Podman* and Skopeo tools are installed by inspecting the output, which should be similar to what you see in Figure 14-2.

Figure 14-2   Verifying the installation of the container-tools packages

However, a far easier method of verifying their installation than reading through all that output is to see if they are found in the path by entering the following command:

```
# which podman skopeo
/usr/bin/podman
/usr/bin/skopeo
```

Finding and Pulling a Container Image

A *container image* is the software that is used to launch containers. Everything in containers comes from images, so we'll have to find some to work with first. Once we find the correct image, we use a process called a "pull" to grab the container image from a remote repository.

Finding a Suitable Image

We'll look for an image that will work for our purposes, which can be a little difficult, given the amount of possible images in the repository. Different images provide different features. For example, one container may provide access to a database software while another may be used to host a web server.

Search for the Universal Basic Images (UBI) for RHEL 8 with the following command:

```
# podman search registry.access.redhat.com/ubi8 | wc -l
26
```

The output indicates 26 UBI images are available in RHEL 8. Instead of boring you with a listing of all 26 of the images, using the **wc** command just counts them and reports the tally. Since 26 is still a *lot* of images to select from, let's make it easier and further focus our output to the latest image with the following command:

```
# podman search registry.access.redhat.com | grep -i latest
```

This displays the listing of available "latest release" images, which may also include previous and later versions such as RHEL 7 and RHEL 9, similar to what is shown in Figure 14-3.

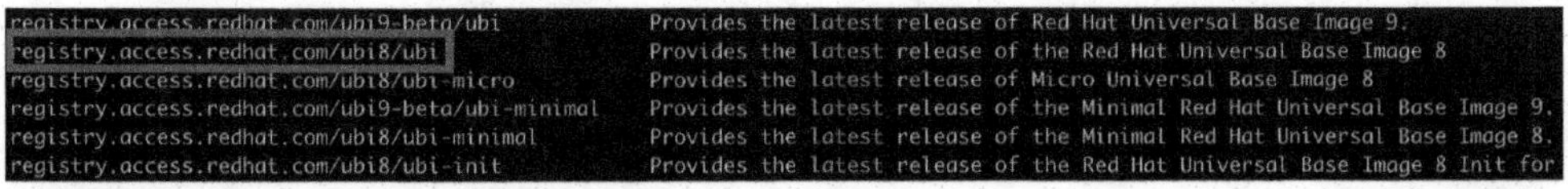

Figure 14-3 Finding the latest UBI images

You can see that the latest generic image is simply notated as **/ubi**, and we'll use that one in our demonstration.

To see more information about the **/ubi** image, use the **skopeo** command. A container image, *er*, contains a lot of information, so we'll pipe the output from **skopeo** to the **grep** command as follows, using the context parameter (**-A 1**) to just show the description line. Figure 14-4 shows the results.

```
# skopeo inspect docker://registry.access.redhat.com/ubi8/ubi | grep
-i -A 1 \"description\"
```

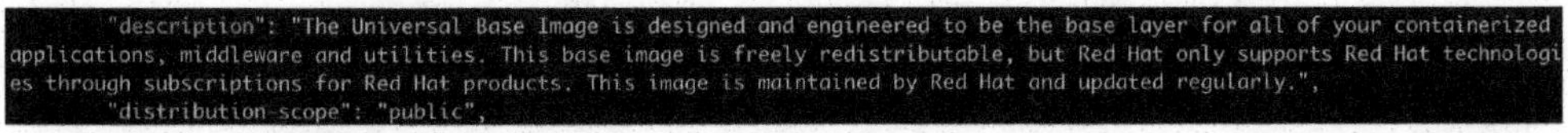

Figure 14-4 Displaying the container image description

Pulling an Image

Key Topic

Next we'll pull the image from the repository by using the **podman pull** command:

```
# podman pull registry.access.redhat.com/ubi8/ubi:latest
Trying to pull registry.access.redhat.com/ubi8/ubi:latest...
Getting image source signatures
```

```
Checking if image destination supports signatures
Copying blob 0c673eb68f88 done
Copying blob 028bdc977650 done
Copying config 2fd9e14788 done
Writing manifest to image destination
Storing signatures
2fd9e1478809c0c53820517b998e1b2a044207515e5d61eccb6295276bbbaffc
```

As you can see, the image was pulled from the repository, and the extremely long signature of the image is now stored locally.

NOTE   The **IMAGE ID** column shows the Image ID, which is what we'll use to control the image as we start it or otherwise interact with it as an image. You'll see the similar length Container ID numbers shortly, which we'll use to control and manage running containers. You'll want to keep these two ID types firmly in mind when answering image- and container-related questions on the Linux+ exam.

Viewing and Inspecting Images

After pulling an image, you need to view and inspect it to ensure that it includes the correct code.

Viewing Local Images

Once an image has been pulled, you can inspect it in several ways, the first being to see if it's listed on your host by running

```
# podman images
```

```
REPOSITORY                     TAG     IMAGE ID   CREATED    SIZE
registry.access.redhat.com/ubi8/ubi latest 2fd9e1478809  3 week
225MB
```

The Image ID is much shorter in this listing because it's being truncated to the first 12 characters of the much longer ID.

NOTE   The Image ID will stay the same over time as you work with it—it's the one that identifies this image overall, and shouldn't change unless the registered image on the repository changes. However, the running Container ID should be different each time you run it, and definitely different between running container instances. Watch for this difference on the Linux+ exam.

Inspecting a Local Image

You can find out much more about the image now by using the **podman inspect** command with the shortened Image ID as a parameter:

```
# podman inspect 2fd9e1478809
```

There's no need to show the output of this command, because it's essentially the same as what you saw displayed with the **skopeo** command output fed to the **grep** command a bit earlier. This proves it's the same image we queried previously, while it was still in the repository.

This section shows you how to properly connect and detach from containers, leaving them running and functional.

Running an Image as a Container

Now we'll run the image by specifying the **-i** (interactive) and **-t** (attach pty to the terminal) parameters, which allows us to immediately access and use the command line inside the now-running container.

Let's start the instance with the following command:

```
# podman run -i -t 2fd9e1478809
```

The only visual indication that something is different is that the prompt will change to a shell prompt identifying the host you are now on, such as:

```
[root@ 35c54f588bbc /]#
```

You can verify that you are on a different host either by running an **ls** command and looking at the files in the home directory or, as shown next, by checking the host release information with the **cat** command:

```
[root@ 35c54f588bbc /]# cat /etc/redhat-release
Red Hat Enterprise Linux release 8.6 (Ootpa)
```

Assigning a Container-Friendly Name

You can associate a friendly name with a Container ID by specifying the friendly name you want at the time of instance creation:

```
# podman run -it --name OpenContainer 2fd9e1478809
[root@ 35c54f588bbc /]#
```

You can also rename a container very easily; just use the **rename** command instead of the **name** command:

```
# podman run rename OpenContainer ClosedContainer
```

Detaching from and Attaching to Containers

If you have run a container with the **-it** options to give you immediate access to it on the shell prompt, you might be surprised when you type the **exit** command to get out of the container and it also *quits* the container!

In order to detach from a running container that you are attached to, execute the following key combinations in close succession:

```
Ctrl+p Ctrl+q
```

This will detach you from the container and leave it running. You can verify it's still running with the **podman images** command:

```
# podman images
CONTAINER ID   IMAGE       COMMAND    CREATED      STATUS
PORTS          NAMES
35c54f588bbc   registry.access.redhat.com/ubi8/ubi:latest
/bin/bash    About 5 minutes ago   Up 5 minutes ago
compassionate_chatelet
```

> **NOTE** Unfortunately, due to the width limitations of the physical book page, there's no way to display on one line all the columns of the **podman images** and **ps -a** command output. The output will be much easier to read when you execute the commands on your own virtual machine.

Exiting and Ending Execution of a Container

To exit from an interactive session and also terminate the execution of the container, at the command prompt, type

```
# exit
```

You can then make sure the container has exited by inspecting the status of the container processes with

```
# podman ps -a
CONTAINER ID   IMAGE       COMMAND    CREATED      STATUS      PORTS
NAMES
35c54f588bbc   redhat.com/ubi8/ubi:latest   /bin/bash    About a minute
ago   Exited (0) 6 seconds ago      infallible_khayyam
```

> **NOTE** Remember that the Container ID in the **CONTAINER ID** column is how you interact with a running or exited container, not by using the Image ID.

Removing a Container

Keeping in mind that a container image becomes a container when it's run or executed, use the Container ID to remove the container from the host's table of existing containers with the following command:

```
# podman rm 35c54f588bbc
35c54f588bbcb8acddbda95dfe91f02c553f211421fd7149a01729e0639c6379
```

The display of the full Container ID confirms the removal of the container from the host's list.

Verify that the container was removed with the following command:

```
# podman ps -a
CONTAINER ID   IMAGE   COMMAND   CREATED   STATUS   PORTS   NAMES
```

Now that the container has been removed, you can either use the container image to start another running container or, as shown next, remove that container image from your system with the **podman rmi** command followed by the Image ID:

```
# podman rmi 2fd9e1478809
Untagged:registry.access.redhat.com/ubi8/ubi:latest
Deleted:2fd9e1478809c0c53820517b998e1b2a044207515e5d61eccb6295276bbba
ffc
```

Your host should now not show that container image if you use the **podman rmi** command again:

```
# podman rmi 2fd9e1478809
REPOSITORY   TAG          IMAGE ID   CREATED      SIZE
```

Viewing Container Logs

You work with container logs by using the **podman logs** command followed by the Container ID:

```
# podman logs 35c54f588bbc
This was a logger test entry
```

The command accepts the Container ID of the container you want to query the main log entries for. If you are just looking to see what the latest log entries are for your most recently started container, use the following command (**-l** is the lowercase letter *l*, not the number 1):

```
# podman logs -l
This was a logger test entry
```

> **NOTE** You may also wish to investigate the **podman events** command, and compare and contrast it with the **podman logs** command.

Exposing and Mapping Ports

Ports are not automatically available to the host from a container; you have to expose them first, typically at the inception of the container, which makes them available for contacting. For example, the following command exposes port 80 on an NGINX container shown in the following that we have exposed port 80 on, with the command:

```
# podman run --expose=80 --publish-all registry.access.redhat.com/
rhscl/nginx-16-rhel7 &
```

This will run the image indicated (an NGINX 1.7 image) as a container and expose port 80, then publish all of its exposed ports to the host. The **&** suffix sets the process to execute in the background.

We can also map a container port, such as the 8080 port on this NGINX container, to a specific port on the host by using the following command:

```
# podman run -d -p 8080:80 registry.access.redhat.com/rhscl/
nginx-16-rhel7
```

We can then view the exposed ports using either of two methods, the first of which is to run a **podman** subcommand named **port**, as shown here:

```
# podman port -a
52ee615ae4b7        80/tcp -> 0.0.0.0:8080
ae054514e8f6        80/tcp -> 0.0.0.0:36319
ae054514e8f6        443/tcp -> 0.0.0.0:44783
```

Notice that the container starting with "ae" has an entry per port, showing the numbers and where they mapped to on the host.

The other method of viewing the exposed ports produces a slightly longer, more explicit set of information:

```
# podman ps -a
CONTAINER ID   IMAGE
COMMAND                 CREATED           STATUS                PORTS
                                          NAMES
ae054514e8f6   registry.access.redhat.com/rhscl/nginx-16-rhel7:latest
nginx -g daemon o...   32 seconds ago   Up 31 seconds ago
0.0.0.0:36319->80/tcp, 0.0.0.0:44783->443/tcp   optimistic_archimedes
52ee615ae4b7   registry.access.redhat.com/rhscl/nginx-16-
rhel7:latest   nginx -g daemon o...   6 seconds ago    Up 6 seconds ago
0.0.0.0:8080->80/tcp                            infallible_easley
```

Using either method, you can see that the ports are exposed in the case of the ae054514e8f6 container and mapped in the case of the 52ee615ae4b7 container.

Container Image Operations

Now that you are familiar with the basic container operations involved in container management, this section presents the commands for conducting container operations that you are expected to know for the Linux+ exam.

build Command

Building a container with Docker typically requires root-level access, but now Podman and *Buildah* (a tool Podman uses) allow even regular users to build an image without additional access.

Building a container involves a lot of complex details, but for purposes of the Linux+ exam, you simply need to know conceptually what happens when you build a container image, not all the gory details. For in-depth information, I highly recommend the excellent Red Hat documentation "Building, running, and managing containers," available via the Red Hat Customer Portal (search for the title in quote marks).

Building from a Dockerfile is the same conceptually as using Buildah with a Containerfile. When you issue the **podman build** command, the command that is being used under the covers is the **buildah** command. Here's how it works:

Step 1.   Create a Containerfile.

Step 2.   Create a script to run as a test.

Step 3.   Set the permissions of the script.

Step 4.   Build the image with the **buildah** command.

Step 5.   Verify the image with the **buildah images** command.

Step 6.   Run the image with the **podman run** command.

push Command

Pushing an image is the process of sending it from your local storage either to a public repository or to a private repository you maintain or use.

Pushing to a private registry is not hard. You can create a private registry on your system by using the **podman** command with its **registry** subcommand and some parameters.

Once the repository is created, you can use the **buildah push** command to send the image to the registry, including the source signatures and manifest that causes it to be listed as part of the repository.

You can then verify that the registry properly contains the image with the **curl** command, which will display the listing showing that the image exists.

pull Command

Pulling an image is the process of retrieving an image from a public or private repository, which is very easy if the repository is open, and only slightly less easy if you have to obtain the proper authentication for the repository. Pulling images was covered in the demonstration in the first part of this chapter.

list Command

Listing an image or images requires you to have already pulled an image or have local storage for the images. Use the **podman images** command to list the local images your system knows about.

rmi Command

The **podman rmi** command is how you remove an image (or images) from your system's local storage, but first you must stop the image by issuing the **podman stop** command, which stops the running container and allows the image that underlies it to be removed.

Additionally, you can remove all the images from your local storage using the **podman rmi -a** command.

If you have multiple images with the same name, or wish to use what amounts to a "force" option, you can use the **podman rmi -a -f** command.

Summary

In this chapter, I first led you through a hands-on demonstration of how to perform the basic container operations necessary to manage containers. The demo also showed you how to perform basic container image operations, which were summarized in the latter part of the chapter.

You know now how to install the container-tools package and use those tools to pull container images, list them, start and stop them, connect to and disconnect from them, view their logs, and expose and map their ports.

Exam Preparation Tasks

As mentioned in the section "Goals and Methods" in the Introduction, you have a couple of choices for exam preparation: the exercises here, Chapter 23, "Final Preparation," and the exam simulation questions in the Pearson Test Prep Software Online.

Review All Key Topics

Review the most important topics in this chapter, noted with the Key Topic icon in the outer margin of the page. Table 14-2 lists these key topics and the page number on which each is found.

Table 14-2   Key Topics for Chapter 14

Key Topic Element	Description	Page Number
Paragraph	Pulling an image with the **podman pull** command	527
Paragraph	Viewing local images with the **podman images** command	528
Paragraph	Starting a Podman instance with the **podman run** command	529
Paragraph	Detaching from a running container with **Ctrl+p Ctrl+q**	530
Paragraph	Viewing container logs with the **podman logs** command	531
Paragraph	Definition of pulling an image	534
Paragraph	Removing an image with the **rmi** command	534

Define Key Terms

Define the following key terms from this chapter and check your answers in the glossary:

container, container image, Podman, Buildah

Review Questions

The answers to these review questions are in Appendix A.

1. While executing or starting a container from an image, you want to immediately execute commands from the shell prompt as if you had ssh'ed to the container. Which option/options should you specify at the start of the container to allow this?

    a. -in

    b. -it

    c. -if

    d. -ssh

2. Which **podman** subcommand enables you to connect to a container that you started without use of the interactive or tty options?

    a. connect

    b. ssh

    c. attach

    d. pipe

3. When listing images, containers, and processes, you have noticed that the ID of one of them stays consistent throughout all operations while the others seems to change each time. Which one of the IDs stays consistent?

    a. Container ID

    b. Process ID

    c. Image ID

    d. None of the above

4. To inspect the logs for a given container, which **podman** subcommand would you use?

    a. event

    b. logs

    c. logger

    d. syslog

5. When building a container, which components are the most likely to be used to create that new container? (Choose two.)

   a. **buildah**

   b. **skopeo**

   c. **Containerfile**

   d. **Histsize**

   e. **Manifest**

6. Your organization has ceased its use of Docker and instituted another set of tools to manage root-less containers for its developer staff. Which of the following is the most likely set of tools your organization has implemented?

   a. Walkabout

   b. Podman

   c. ContainerCrew

   d. Virtualtool

This chapter covers the following topics:

- Version Control Concepts
- Using Git for Version Control

The exam objective covered in this chapter is as follows:

- **Objective 3.3:** Given a scenario, perform basic version control using Git

## CHAPTER 15

Performing Basic Version Control Using Git

Version control is an important technology and practice—it's essential to having full control of your code or materials. Proper code management requires the ability to track changes, merge changes, revert to previous versions, and develop using multiple branches of the same original code.

There are multiple source control methods and tools, but Git is the most popular and the one you need to know how to use for the Linux+ exam. Git is also one of the tools that fuels the use of infrastructure as code, web development, containerized applications, and much more.

"Do I Know This Already?" Quiz

The "Do I Know This Already?" quiz enables you to assess whether you should read this entire chapter or simply jump to the "Exam Preparation Tasks" section for review. If you are in doubt, read the entire chapter. Table 15-1 outlines the major headings in this chapter and the corresponding "Do I Know This Already?" quiz questions. You can find the answers in Appendix A, "Answers to the 'Do I Know This Already?' Quizzes and Review Questions."

Table 15-1 "Do I Know This Already?" Foundation Topics Section-to-Question Mapping

Foundation Topics Section	Questions Covered in This Section
Version Control Concepts	1
Using Git for Version Control	2–5

CAUTION The goal of self-assessment is to gauge your mastery of the topics in this chapter. If you do not know the answer to a question or are only partially sure of the answer, you should mark that question as wrong for purposes of the self-assessment. Giving yourself credit for an answer you correctly guess skews your self-assessment results and might provide you with a false sense of security.

1. Distributed version control systems represent which generation of version control systems?

   a. First

   b. Second

   c. Third

   d. Fourth

2. Which commands can you use to create a repository in the current directory? (Choose all that apply.)

   a. **git config**

   b. **git init**

   c. **git create**

   d. **git clone**

3. To create a Git development environment that won't affect the main development area, what should you create?

   a. A section

   b. A hub

   c. A repo

   d. A branch

4. To compare the staged version of a file to the committed version, which option should you use with the **git diff** command?

   a. **--staged**

   b. **--committed**

   c. **--diffboth**

   d. **--diffall**

5. Which of the following commands would change your current branch to the test branch?

   a. **git set -b test**

   b. **git commit -b test**

   c. **git branch -b test**

   d. **git checkout -b test**

Foundation Topics

Version Control Concepts

To understand *Git* and the concept of version control, it is helpful to look at version control from a historical perspective. There have been three generations of version control software.

The First Generation

The first generation of version control software was very simple. Developers worked on the same physical system and "checked out" one file at a time.

This generation of version control software made use of a technique called *file locking*. When a developer checked out a file, it was locked, and no other developer could edit the file while it remained locked. Figure 15-1 illustrates this type of version control.

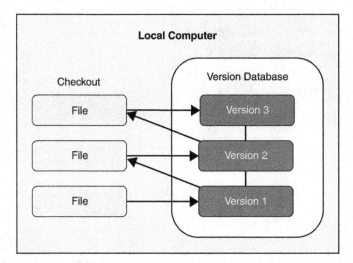

Figure 15-1 First-generation version control software

Examples of first-generation version control software include Revision Control System (RCS) and Source Code Control System (SCCS).

First-generation version control involves two big problems:

- Only one developer can work on a file at a time. This results in a bottleneck in the development process.

■ Developers have to directly log in to the system that contains the version control software.

These problems were solved by the second generation of version control software.

The Second Generation

In second-generation version control, files are stored on a centralized server in a *repository* (sometimes called a *repo*). Developers can *check out* separate copies of a file. When a developer completes work on a file, the developer *checks in* the file to the repository. Figure 15-2 shows the concept of this type of version control.

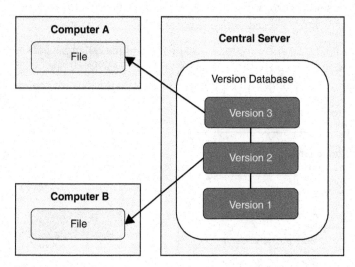

Figure 15-2   Second-generation version control software

With second-generation version control, if two developers check out the same version of a file, there is a potential for issues. This is addressed by a process called a *merge*.

What Is a Merge?

Suppose two developers, Bob and Sue, check out version 5 of a file named **abc.txt**. After Bob completes his work, he checks the file back in. Typically, this results in a new version of the file, version 6.

Sometime later, Sue checks in her file. This new file must incorporate her changes and Bob's changes. This is accomplished through the process of a merge.

Depending on the version control software that you use, there could be different ways to handle a merge. In some cases, such as when Bob and Sue have worked on completely different parts of the file, the merge process is very simple. However, in cases in which Sue and Bob worked on the same lines of code in the file, the merge process can be more complex. In those cases, Sue will have to make decisions, such as whether Bob's code or her code will be in the new version of the file.

After the merge process has been completed, the process of committing the file to the repository takes place. *Committing* a file essentially means creating a new version in the repository—in this example, version 7 of the file.

Examples of second-generation version control software include Concurrent Versions System (CVS) and Subversion.

The Third Generation

The third generation of version control software is referred to a ***distributed version control systems (DVCS)***. As with the second generation, there is a central repository server that contains all of the files for a project. However, developers don't check out individual files from the repository. Instead, a developer checks out an entire project and can work on the complete set of files rather than just individual files. Figure 15-3 illustrates this type of version control.

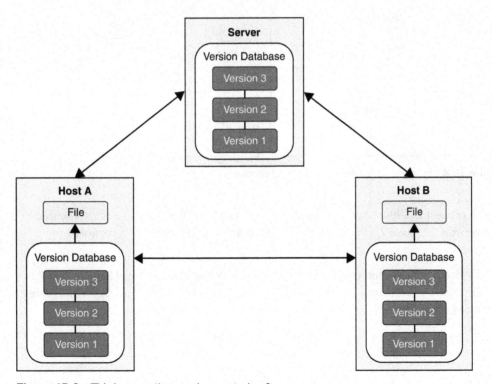

Figure 15-3   Third-generation version control software

Another (very big) difference between the second and third generations of version control software has to do with how the merge and commit process works. As previously mentioned, in the second generation, a merge is performed, and then the new version is committed to the repository.

With third-generation version control software, files are checked in, and then they are merged. To understand the difference between these two techniques, first look at Figure 15-4.

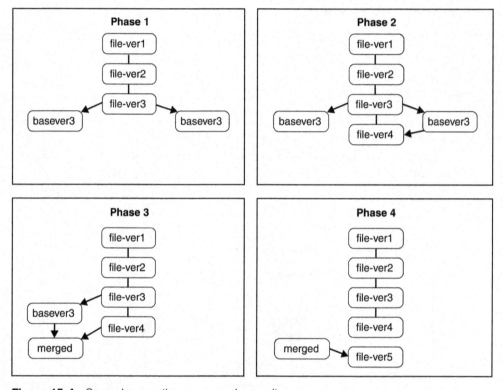

Figure 15-4 Second-generation merge and commit

In phase 1 in Figure 15-4, two developers check out a file that is based on the third version. In phase 2, one developer checks that file in, resulting in a version 4 of the file.

In phase 3 the second developer must first merge the changes from his checked-out copy with the changes of version 4 (and, potentially, other versions). After the merge is complete, the new version can be committed to the repository as version 5.

If you focus on what is in the repository (the center part of each phase), you see that there is a very straight line of development (ver1, ver2, ver3, ver4, ver5, and so on).

This is a very simple approach to software development that poses some potential problems:

- Requiring a developer to merge before committing often results in developers not wanting to commit their changes on a regular basis. The merge process can be a hassle, and developers might decide to wait until later and do one merge rather than a bunch of regular merges. Suddenly adding huge chunks of code to a file has a negative impact on software development. In addition, it is a good idea for developers to regularly commit changes to the repository, just as it is a good idea for someone who is writing a document to save on a regular basis.

- Importantly, version 5 in this example is not necessarily the work the developer originally completed. During the merging process, the developer might discard some of his work in order to complete the merge process. This isn't ideal as it results in the loss of potentially good code.

A better—although arguably more complex—technique can be employed. This third-generation process is called *Directed Acyclic Graph (DAG)*, and you can see an example of how it works in Figure 15-5.

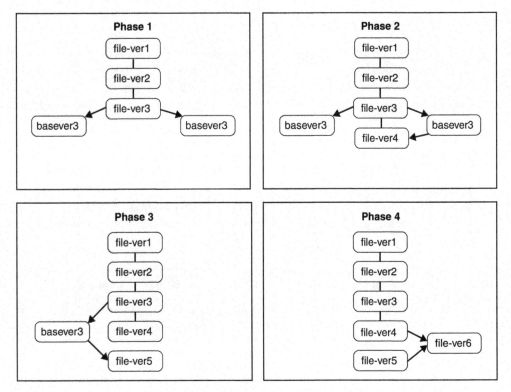

Figure 15-5   Third-generation commit and merge

Phases 1 and 2 in Figure 15-5 are the same as phases 1 and 2 in Figure 15-4. However, note that in phase 3, the second check-in process results in a version 5 file that is not based on version 4 but rather is independent of version 4. In phase 4 of the process, versions 4 and 5 of the file have been merged to create a version 6.

While this process is more complex—and potentially much more complex with a large number of developers—it does provide some advantages over "single line" development:

- Developers can commit their changes on a regular basis without having to worry about merging until a later time.

- The merging process can be delegated to a specific developer who has a better idea of the entire project or code than the other developers have.

- At any time, the project manager can go back and see exactly the work of each individual developer.

There certainly are arguments for both methods. However, this book focuses on Git, which uses the Directed Acyclic Graph method of third-generation version control systems.

Using Git for Version Control

Now that you have learned some of the basic concepts of Git, it is time for you to install Git on your Linux distribution and learn how to use Git commands. In this section you will learn key Git commands, including the clone, push, pull, add, and commit commands. You will also learn how to perform more advanced Git operations, like branching and merging.

Installing Git

You might already have Git on your system because it is sometimes installed by default (or another administrator may have installed it). If you have access to the system as a regular user, you can execute the following command to determine if you have Git installed:

> **NOTE**   Git with a capital *G* refers to the software project; **git** with a lowercase *g* refers to the command.

```
$ which git
/usr/bin/git
```

If Git is installed, then the path to the **git** command is provided, as shown in the previous output. If it isn't installed, then you either get no output or get an error like the following:

```
# which git
/usr/bin/which: no git in (/usr/lib64/qt-3.3/bin:/usr/local/bin:/usr/
local/sbin:/usr/bin:/usr/sbin:/bin:/sbin:/root/bin)
```

As an administrator on a Debian-based system, you could use the **dpkg** command to determine whether the Git package has been installed:

```
# dpkg -l git
Desired=Unknown/Install/Remove/Purge/Hold
| Status=Not/Inst/Conf-files/Unpacked/halF-conf/Half-inst/trig-aWait/
Trig-pend
|/ Err?=(none)/Reinst-required (Status,Err: uppercase=bad)
||/ Name       Version        Architecture  Description
+++-=========-=============-=============-===========================
ii  git       1:1.9.1-1ubun amd64                fast, scalable, distributed
revision con
```

As an administrator on a Red Hat-based system, you could use the **rpm** command to determine if the Git package has been installed:

```
# rpm -q git
git-1.8.3.1-6.el7_2.1.x86_64
```

If Git isn't installed on your system, you need to either log in as the root user or use **sudo** or **su** to install the software. If you are logged in as the root user on a Debian-based system, you can use the following command to install Git:

```
# apt-get install git
```

If you are logged in as the root user on a Red Hat-based system, you can use the following command to install Git:

```
# yum install git
```

NOTE Consider installing the software package **git-all**. This package includes some additional dependency packages that bring more power to Git.

Git Concepts and Features

One of the challenges with using Git is just understanding the concepts behind it. If you don't understand the concepts, then all of the commands can seem like some sort of black magic. This section focuses on critical Git concepts and introduces some of the basic commands.

Git Stages

It is very important to remember that you "check out" (although with Git, the process is really called *cloning*) an entire project and that most of the work you do is local to the system that you are working on. The files that are checked out are placed in a directory under your home directory.

To get a copy of a project from a Git repository, you use a process called *cloning*. Cloning doesn't just mean creating a copy of all the files from the repository; it actually involves three primary functions:

- Creating a local repository of the project under the ***project_name/*.git** directory in your home directory. The files of the project in this location are considered to be "checked out" from the central repository.

- Creating a directory where you can directly see the files. This is called the "working area." Changes made in the working area are not immediately version controlled.

- Creating a staging area. The staging area is designed to store changes to files before you commit them to the local repository.

If you were to clone a project called Jacumba, the entire project would be stored in the **Jacumba/.git** directory under your home directory. You should not attempt to modify the files in **Jacumba/.git** directly. Instead, look directly in the **~/Jacumba** directory, and you see the files from the project. These are the files that you should change.

Suppose you have made a change to a file, but you have to work on some other files before you are ready to commit changes to the local repository. In that case, you would *stage* the file that you have finished working on to prepare it to be committed to the local repository.

After you have made all changes and have staged all files, you commit the changes to the local repository. Figure 15-6 provides a visual demonstration of this process.

It is important to realize that when you commit the staged files, you only send them to the local repository, which means that only you have access to the changes that have been made. The process of checking in the new versions to the central repository is called a *push*.

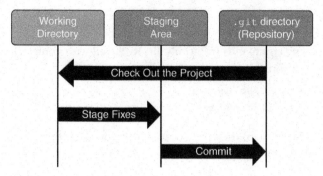

Figure 15-6   Git stages

Each of the steps briefly described here will be explained in greater detail later in the chapter. The concepts you have learned in this section will help you understand the process better when the Git commands are introduced.

Choosing Your Git Repository Host

First, the good news: Many organizations provide Git hosting; in fact, there are more than two dozen choices at this writing. This means you have many options to choose from. But this good news is also the bad news. It is bad news because it means you really need to spend some time researching the pros and cons of the different hosting organizations. For example, most don't charge for basic hosting but do charge for large-scale projects. Some provide only public repositories (so that anyone can see your repository), while others enable you to create private repositories. There are many other features to consider.

One of the features that might be high on your list is a web interface. While just about all repository operations can be accomplished locally on your system, it can be very useful to be able to perform some operations via a web interface. Explore the interface that is provided before making a choice about Git hosting.

NOTE   For the purposes of practicing with the examples in this chapter, consider using Bitbucket (https://bitbucket.org). The examples in this chapter use this site, but you can choose a different option to fit your specific needs.

Configuring Git

This section assumes the following:

- You have installed the **git** or **git-all** software package on your system.
- You have created an account on a Git hosting service.

At this point, you need to perform some basic setup. Whenever you perform a commit operation, your name and email address are included in the metadata. To set this information, execute the following commands (replacing Bo Rothwell with your name and bo@OneCourseSource.com with your email address):

```
$ git config --global user.name "Bo Rothwell"
$ git config --global user.email "bo@onecoursesource.com"
```

Next, you need to clone your project from the Git hosting service by using the **git clone** command. Note that before cloning, there is only one file in the user's home directory:

```
$ ls
first.sh
```

The following command clones a project named ocs:

```
$ git clone https://gitlab.com/borothwell/ocs.git
Cloning into 'ocs'...
Username for 'https://gitlab.com': borothwell
Password for 'https://borothwell@gitlab.com':
remote: Counting objects: 3, done.
remote: Total 3 (delta 0), reused 0 (delta 0)
Unpacking objects: 100% (3/3), done.
Checking connectivity... done.
```

NOTE   You typically want a Git repository to be initially stored on a central server, from which multiple people can clone. However, if you want your own private repository, you can use the **git init** command to create one on your local system.

After successful execution, you see a new directory in the user's home directory:

```
$ ls
first.sh   ocs
```

If you switch to the new directory, you can see what was cloned from the repository (which in this case is only one file so far):

```
$ cd ocs
~/ocs$ ls
README.md
```

Next, you can create a new file in the repository directory by either creating one from scratch or copying a file from another location:

```
~/ocs$ cp ../first.sh .
```

Remember that anything placed in this directory is not version controlled, as this is the working directory.

To put a file in the local repository, you first have to add it to the staging area, and then you need to commit it to the repository:

```
~/ocs$ git add first.sh
~/ocs$ git commit -m "added first.sh"
[main 3b36054] added first.sh
 1 file changed, 5 insertions(+)
 create mode 100644 first.sh
```

The **git add** command places the file in the staging area. The **git commit** command commits all the new files in the staging area to the local repository. The **-m** option is used to add a message (in this case, the reason for the commit).

It is important to note that no changes have been made to the repository on the server. The **git commit** command only updates the local repository. Figure 15-7 shows that the server repository has not been modified; it shows a screenshot of the current project in the web-based interface. Notice that the original file, **README. md**, was pushed to the server several days ago, but the new file, **first.sh**, does not have an entry.

Figure 15-7 The server repository is unchanged after **git commit**

Most likely you would make additional changes to your local project and then push the changes to the server's repository by using the **git push** command:

```
~/ocs$ git push -u origin main
Username for 'https://gitlab.com': borothwell
Password for 'https://borothwell@gitlab.com':
Counting objects: 4, done.
```

```
Compressing objects: 100% (3/3), done.
Writing objects: 100% (3/3), 370 bytes | 0 bytes/s, done.
Total 3 (delta 0), reused 0 (delta 0)
To https://gitlab.com/borothwell/ocs.git
   12424f5..3b36054  main -> main
Branch main set up to track remote branch main from origin.
```

Figure 15-8 shows that the push was successful.

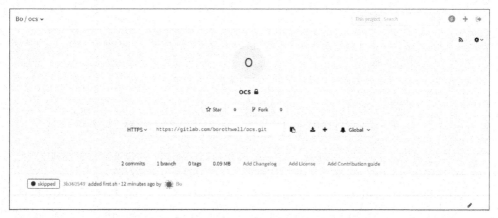

Figure 15-8   The server repository is changed after **git push**

At this point, all changes to the files from the staging area have been updated to the local repository and the central server repository.

NOTE   If changes have been made to files on the remote repository, use the **git pull** command to download the changed files into your local repository. This may require you to perform a merge operation, as discussed in more detail later in this chapter.

Using git tag

In Git, a tag is a reference to a specific commit. Tags are often used to mark important points in the history of a project, such as releases or milestones. Tags can also be used to bookmark commits for personal use.

There are two types of tags in Git: annotated tags and lightweight tags. Annotated tags are more complex than lightweight tags, but they provide more information. Annotated tags include the following:

- The tagger name and email address
- The date and time the tag was created

- A tagging message

- A GPG signature (optional)

Lightweight tags are simply pointers to a commit. They do not contain any additional information.

To create a tag in Git, you use the git tag command. The syntax for the git tag command is as follows:

```
git tag <tag_name> [<commit_hash>]
```

The <tag_name> is the name of the tag. The <commit_hash> is the hash of the commit that you want to tag. If you do not specify a commit hash, Git will tag the HEAD commit.

For example, the following command will create a tag named v1.2.3 that points to the commit with the hash 111111111aaaaaa:

```
$ git tag v1.2.3 111111111aaaaaa
```

To view a list of all tags in your repository, you use the **git tag** command without any arguments. For example, the following command will list all of the tags in the current repository:

```
$ git tag
```

To view the details of a specific tag, you use the **git show** command with the tag name as an argument. For example, the following command will show the details of the tag v1.2.3:

```
$ git show v1.2.3
```

To delete a tag, you use the **git tag -d** command. For example, the following command will delete the tag v1.2.3:

```
$ git tag -d v1.0.0
```

Getting the Status of Files

Imagine that you are working on some files one Friday afternoon, and you just can't wait for the weekend to start. You leave work without paying a lot of attention to your files. On the following Monday, you arrive at work and realize that you have no idea where you left your files. Were some or all of them added to the staging area? Did you commit any of them to the local repository? In such a situation, you can run the **git status** command:

```
~/ocs$ git status
On branch main
Your branch is up-to-date with 'origin/main'.

nothing to commit, working directory clean
```

If you make changes to a file and don't add it to the staging area, the output of the **git status** command looks as follows:

```
~/ocs$ git status
On branch main
Your branch is up-to-date with 'origin/main'.

Changes not staged for commit:
  (use "git add <file>..." to update what will be committed)
  (use "git checkout -- <file>..." to discard changes in working
directory)

        modified:   first.sh

no changes added to commit (use "git add" and/or "git commit -a")
```

Notice the **Changes not staged for commit** section in this output. The output in this section is helpful in showing you how you can stage the file with the **git add** command or stage and commit the file with the **git commit -a** command.

If a file has been added to the staging area but not committed to the local repository, the output of the **git status** command looks as follows:

```
~/ocs$ git add first.sh
~/ocs$ git status
On branch main
Your branch is up-to-date with 'origin/main'.

Changes to be committed:
  (use "git reset HEAD <file>..." to unstage)

        modified:   first.sh
```

In this output, **Changes to be committed** means the modified file is in the staging area but not in the local repository. If a file has been committed to the local repository but not committed to the central repository server, the output of the **git status** command looks like this:

```
~/ocs$ git commit -m "demonstrating status"
[main 9eb721e] demonstrating status
1 file changed, 2 insertions(+), 1 deletion(-)
~/ocs$ git status
On branch main
Your branch is ahead of 'origin/main' by 1 commit.
  (use "git push" to publish your local commits)

nothing to commit, working directory clean
```

In this output, **nothing to commit, working directory clean** means the staging area no longer contains files, and the working directory reflects the current contents of the local repository. In addition, the message **Your branch is ahead of 'origin/ main' by 1 commit** makes it clear that you need to execute **git push** to push the contents of the local repository to the central repository server.

The .git Directory

Local repository data is stored in the **.git** directory under which the Git repository was created. For example, consider the following command:

```
$ git init test
Initialized empty Git repository in /tmp/test/.git/
```

This command was executed in the **/tmp** directory and created the local repository directory **/tmp/test**. The repository data is actually stored in the **/tmp/test/.git** directory:

```
$ ls /tmp/test/.git
branches   config   description   HEAD   hooks   info   objects   refs
```

The **.git** directory should not be modified directly. This directory contains a collection of databases that contain all of the files and versions for the Git repository.

Telling Git to Ignore a File

In some cases, you might want a file in the working directory but have the file staged or placed in the repository. For example, maybe you want to keep track of some notes about the project but only for your own purposes. Of course, you could simply not add this file to the staging area, but that would mean **git status** would never return **nothing to commit, working directory clean.**

To have **git** commands ignore a file, you can create a file named **.gitignore** in the working directory and place the filename to ignore inside of this file:

```
~/ocs$ touch notes
~/ocs$ git status -s
?? notes
~/ocs$ vi .gitignore        #added notes as shown below:
~/ocs$ cat .gitignore
notes
~/ocs$ git status -s
?? .gitignore
```

Notice that the **.gitignore** file itself must also be placed in the **.gitignore** file:

```
~/ocs$ git status -s
```

```
?? .gitignore
~/ocs$ vi .gitignore        #added .gitignore as shown below:
~/ocs$ cat .gitignore
notes
.gitignore
~/ocs$ git status -s
```

NOTE   You can also use wildcard characters (*, ?, and [*range*]) in the **.gitignore** file to match a collection of files.

Handling Branches

Say that you decide that you want to test some new features of a project that you are working on, but you don't want your testing to impact the current development process. This is an ideal time to create a branch.

When you first create a project, the code is associated with a branch called main. If you want to create a new branch, execute the **git branch** command:

```
~/ocs$ git branch test
```

This doesn't mean you are suddenly working in the new branch. As you can see from the output of the **git status** command, the **git branch** command doesn't change your current branch:

```
~/ocs$ git status
On branch main
Your branch is ahead of 'origin/main' by 2 commits.
  (use "git push" to publish your local commits)

nothing to commit, working directory clean
```

The first line of this output, **On branch main**, denotes that you are still working in the main branch. To switch to the new branch, execute the **git checkout** command:

```
~/ocs$ git checkout test
Switched to branch 'test'
```

NOTE   You can create a branch and switch to it by using the **-b** option to the **git checkout** command:

```
~/ocs$ git checkout -b test
```

Switching actually does two things:

- Makes it so any future commits occur on the test branch.

- Causes the working directory to reflect the test branch.

To understand how switching causes the working directory to reflect the test branch, observe the following commands, which will end up with a new version of the **hidden.sh** file being placed in the test branch repository:

```
~/ocs$ git add hidden.sh
~/ocs$ git commit -m "changed hidden.sh"
[test ef2d7d5] changed hidden.sh
 1 file changed, 1 insertion(+)
```

Note what the file looks like in the current working directory:

```
~/ocs$ more hidden.sh
#!/bin/bash
#hidden.sh


echo "Listing only hidden files:"
ls -ld .* $1
```

If the project was switched back to the main branch, the **hidden.sh** file in the working directory would be different (note the missing **echo** line, which was added for the test branch only):

```
~/ocs$ git checkout main
Switched to branch 'main'
Your branch is ahead of 'origin/main' by 2 commits.
  (use "git push" to publish your local commits)
~/ocs$ more hidden.sh
#!/bin/bash
#hidden.sh


ls -ld .* $1
```

You can see the changes that are made on different branches, along with the comments you provided for each change, by using the **git log** command:

```
~/ocs$ git log --oneline --decorate --all
ef2d7d5 (test) changed hidden.sh
2b44792 (HEAD, main) deleting test.sh file
19198d7 update 27
07bb91c (origin/main, origin/HEAD) adding showmine.sh and hidden.sh
75d717b added first.sh
```

```
9eb721e demostrating status
3b36054 added first.sh
12424f5 add README
```

The **--oneline** option has the **git log** command provide a one-line summary of each change. The **--decorate** option requests additional information such as the branch name. The **--all** option asks to see the log for all branches, not just the current branch.

Executing Diffs

Say that you arrive at work Monday morning, ready to start on your project. It's always a good habit to execute the **git status** command when you haven't been working on the project for a while, so you execute this command and discover that you have a file in the working area that hasn't been staged:

```
~/ocs$ git status
On branch main
Your branch is up-to-date with 'origin/main'.

Changes not staged for commit:
  (use "git add <file>..." to update what will be committed)
  (use "git checkout -- <file>..." to discard changes in working
directory)

        modified:   hidden.sh

no changes added to commit (use "git add" and/or "git commit -a")
```

You could just stage and commit the file, but you wonder what changes were made to this file. If you didn't finish making the changes last Friday, this might pose problems, so you want to compare the version of the file in the working directory with the version that has most recently been committed to the local repository. You can do this by executing the **git diff** command:

```
~/ocs$ git diff hidden.sh | cat -n
     1  diff --git a/hidden.sh b/hidden.sh
     2  index 05151ce..714482b 100644
     3  --- a/hidden.sh
     4  +++ b/hidden.sh
     5  @@ -1,4 +1,5 @@
     6   #!/bin/bash
     7   #hidden.sh
     8
```

```
 9   +echo "Hidden files:"
10    ls -ld .* $1
```

> **NOTE** If you run this on your own system and don't pipe the output to the **cat** command, you should see some color highlights that help you to understand the data.

The output of this command requires a bit of explanation. Ignore the first two lines of output, as they aren't important at this point.

Lines 3 and 4 refer to the two versions of the file. Each version is assigned a letter (a or b) to distinguish between the two. Line 3 refers to the version that has been committed, and line 4 refers to the version in the working directory.

Line 5 gives directions on how to make the two files look the same. In this case, it is simply saying "at line 4 of the *a* file, add line 5 of the *b* file." Following these directions would make the files look the same by making the committed version look like the version in the working directory.

Lines 6 through 10 visually show what changes would have to take place in the committed version in order to make it look like the version in the working directory. A **+** at the beginning of a line means "add this," and a **–** at the beginning of a line means "remove this."

It is important that you understand that this comparison is performed on a line-by-line basis. A single change on one line would make the lines completely different to the **git diff** command. For example, in Example 15-1, notice that the only difference between lines 9 and 11 is a single character and that one has + and one has –.

Example 15-1 A Single Difference

```
~/ocs$ git diff hidden.sh | cat -n
     1    diff --git a/hidden.sh b/hidden.sh
     2    index 05151ce..6de92ae 100644
     3    --- a/hidden.sh
     4    +++ b/hidden.sh
     5    @@ -1,4 +1,5 @@
     6     #!/bin/bash
     7     #hidden.sh
     8
     9    -ls -ld .* $1
    10    +echo "Hidden files:"
    11    +ls -ldh .* $1
```

Comparing Versions

By default, the **git diff** command compares versions in two situations:

- If the working directory version is different from the committed version but the working version hasn't been staged

- If the working directory version is different from the staged version

That means if you stage a file, the **git diff** command won't compare the staged version to the committed version—at least not by default. As you can see, there is no output for the following **git diff** command:

```
~/ocs$ git add hidden.sh
~/ocs$ git diff | cat -n
```

To compare a staged version to a committed version, use the **--staged** option, as shown in Example 15-2.

Example 15-2   Staged vs. Committed Differences

```
~/ocs$ git diff --staged hidden.sh | cat -n
     1    diff --git a/hidden.sh b/hidden.sh
     2    index 05151ce..6de92ae 100644
     3    --- a/hidden.sh
     4    +++ b/hidden.sh
     5    @@ -1,4 +1,5 @@
     6     #!/bin/bash
     7     #hidden.sh
     8
     9    -ls -ld .* $1
    10    +echo "Hidden files:"
    11    +ls -ldh .* $1
```

Dealing with Whitespace

A useful option to the **git diff** command is **--check**, which looks for whitespace. To understand the importance of this, first look at the output of Example 15-3.

Example 15-3   Whitespace Mystery

```
~/ocs$ git diff --staged  hidden.sh | cat -n
     1    diff --git a/hidden.sh b/hidden.sh
     2    index 6de92ae..519eb3c 100644
```

```
 3    --- a/hidden.sh
 4    +++ b/hidden.sh
 5    @@ -1,5 +1,5 @@
 6     #!/bin/bash
 7    -#hidden.sh
 8    +#hidden.sh
 9
10     echo "Hidden files:"
11     ls -ldh .* $1
```

In Example 15-3, you can see that lines 7 and 8 of the output are different from each other, even though they look the same aside from the – and +. You can see why they are different by using the **--check** option:

```
~/ocs$ git diff --staged --check | cat -n
 1    hidden.sh:2: trailing whitespace.
 2    +#hidden.sh
```

The message **trailing whitespace** means there are some sort of whitespace characters (such as spaces or tabs) at the end of the line.

Comparing Branches

You can use the **git diff** command to compare files in different branches. For example, to see a list of files that are different between two branches, use the following command:

```
~/ocs$ git diff --name-status main..test
M        hidden.sh
```

In the previous **git diff** command, the **--name-status** option provides a summary of the files that are different in the two branches. The two branches, main and test, are listed separated by **..** characters.

To see the differences between the versions in the two branches, use the syntax shown in Example 15-4.

Example 15-4   git diff Between Branches

```
~/ocs$ git diff main:hidden.sh test:hidden.sh
diff --git a/main:hidden.sh b/test:hidden.sh
index 519eb3c..804fcf7 100644
--- a/main:hidden.sh
```

```
+++ b/test:hidden.sh
@@ -1,5 +1,5 @@
 #!/bin/bash
-#hidden.sh
+#hidden.sh

-echo "Hidden files:"
-ls -ldh .* $1
+echo "Listing only hidden files:"
+ls -ld .* $1
```

If you find the output of the **git diff** command to be confusing, consider using the **git difftool** command (which requires having the **git-all** package installed):

```
~/ocs$ git difftool hidden.sh
```

```
This message is displayed because 'diff.tool' is not configured.
See 'git difftool --tool-help' or 'git help config' for more details.
'git difftool' will now attempt to use one of the following tools:
opendiff kdiff3 tkdiff xxdiff meld kompare gvimdiff diffuse diffmerge
ecmerge p4merge araxis bc3 codecompare emerge vimdiff

Viewing (1/1): 'hidden.sh'
Launch 'vimdiff' [Y/n]: y
2 files to edit
```

Note that this output prompts you for the tool to use to display the differences. It also lists the tools that could be available. (Most likely not all of these tools are installed on your system.) If you want to use a different tool than the one that the **git difftool** command chooses, execute the following command:

```
git difftool --tool=<tool> file
```

The output of **git difftool** is provided in a more readable format. For example, Figure 15-9 shows the output of **git difftool** when the **vimdiff** command is used as the display tool.

Merging Files

Suppose you create a new branch to add a new feature to a file, as demonstrated in Example 15-5.

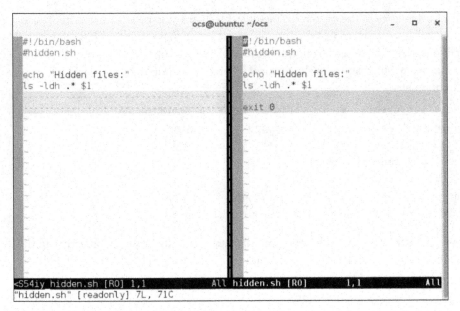

Figure 15-9 **git difftool** using **vimdiff**

Example 15-5 Features Branch

```
~/ocs$ more showmine.sh
#!/bin/bash
#showmine.sh

echo "Your processes:"
ps -fe | grep $USER | more
~/ocs$ git checkout -b feature127
Switched to a new branch 'feature127'
~/ocs$ vi showmine.sh
~/ocs$ more showmine.sh
#!/bin/bash
#showmine.sh

echo -n "Enter name username or press enter: "
read person

echo "${person:-$USER} processes:"
ps -fe | grep "^${person:-$USER}" | more
```

The last two lines of the output in Example 15-5 show the new feature. After testing this new feature, you are ready to implement it in the main branch. To do this, you need to merge the content from the feature127 branch into the main branch. Start by committing all changes in the feature127 branch and then switch back to the main branch:

```
~/ocs$ git commit -a -m "feature added to showmine.sh"
[feature127 2e5defa] feature added to showmine.sh
 1 file changed, 5 insertions(+), 2 deletions(-)
~/ocs$ git checkout main
Switched to branch 'main'
Your branch is ahead of 'origin/main' by 3 commits.
  (use "git push" to publish your local commits)
```

You must be in the branch that you want to merge into in order to correctly run the **git merge** command. The following command merges the changes from the feature127 branch into the main branch:

```
~/ocs$ git merge feature127
Updating 4810ca8..2e5defa
Fast-forward
 showmine.sh | 7 +++++--
 1 file changed, 5 insertions(+), 2 deletions(-)
```

This merge process can be more complex. For example, say that there is a separate branch named test that was branched off an earlier version of the main branch. In the test branch, the most recent **showmine.sh** script looks as follows:

```
~/ocs$ git checkout test
~/ocs$ more showmine.sh
#!/bin/bash
#showmine.sh

echo "Your programs:"
ps -fe | grep $USER | more

echo -n "Enter a PID to stop: "
read proc
kill $proc
```

The current version of **showmine.sh** that has been committed to the main branch looks as follows:

```
~/ocs$ git checkout main
Switched to branch 'main'
Your branch is ahead of 'origin/main' by 4 commits.
```

```
  (use "git push" to publish your local commits)
ocs@ubuntu:~/ocs$ more showmine.sh
#!/bin/bash
#showmine.sh

echo -n "Enter name username or press enter: "
read person

echo "${person:-$USER} processes:"
ps -fe | grep "^${person:-$USER}" | more
```

Should you merge the changes from the main branch into the test branch? Or should you merge the changes from the test branch into the main branch? Typically, if you have more work to do in the test branch, you should merge the changes from the main branch into the test branch. Otherwise, merge the changes from the test branch into the main branch.

The following example shows the changes from the main branch being merged into the test branch:

```
~/ocs$ git checkout test
Switched to branch 'test'
Your branch is ahead of 'origin/test' by 1 commit.
  (use "git push" to publish your local commits)
~/ocs$ git merge main
Auto-merging showmine.sh
CONFLICT (content): Merge conflict in showmine.sh
Auto-merging hidden.sh
CONFLICT (content): Merge conflict in hidden.sh
Automatic merge failed; fix conflicts and then commit the result.
```

You can see that the merge was not completed because the automated merge process ran into some conflicts. You can see these conflicts by executing the **git status** command:

```
~/ocs$ git status
On branch test
Your branch is ahead of 'origin/test' by 1 commit.
  (use "git push" to publish your local commits)

You have unmerged paths.
  (fix conflicts and run "git commit")

Unmerged paths:
  (use "git add <file>..." to mark resolution)
```

```
        both modified:        hidden.sh
        both modified:        showmine.sh
```

```
no changes added to commit (use "git add" and/or "git commit -a")
```

This output makes it clearer that two files have conflicts (rather than just one). If you look at the new **showmine.sh** file in the working directory, it looks something like Example 15-6.

Example 15-6 Merged File

```
~/ocs$ cat -n showmine.sh
     1    #!/bin/bash
     2    #showmine.sh
     3
     4    <<<<<<< HEAD
     5    echo "Your programs:"
     6    ps -fe | grep $USER | more
     7
     8    echo -n "Enter a PID to stop: "
     9    read proc
    10    kill $proc
    11
    12    =======
    13    echo -n "Enter name username or press enter: "
    14    read person
    15
    16    echo "${person:-$USER} processes:"
    17    ps -fe | grep "^${person:-$USER}" | more
    18    >>>>>>> main
```

Essentially, the file contains the contents of each file. Rather than try to edit this file directly, one way to handle these conflicts is to use the **git mergetool** command (which requires that the **git-all** package be installed):

```
~/ocs$ git mergetool showmine.sh
```

```
This message is displayed because 'merge.tool' is not configured.
See 'git mergetool --tool-help' or 'git help config' for more
details.
'git mergetool' will now attempt to use one of the following tools:
opendiff kdiff3 tkdiff xxdiff meld tortoisemerge gvimdiff diffuse
diffmerge ecmerge p4merge araxis bc3 codecompare emerge vimdiff
```

```
Merging:
showmine.sh

Normal merge conflict for 'showmine.sh':
  {local}:  modified file
  {remote}: modified file
Hit return to start merge resolution tool (vimdiff):
```

The **git mergetool** command displays the files using one of the diff tools. For example, the **vimdiff** tool looks as shown in Figure 15-10.

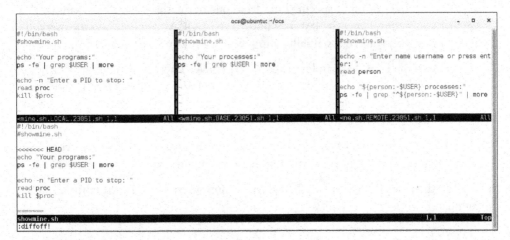

Figure 15-10   **git mergetool** using **vimdiff**

> **NOTE** The **vimdiff** utility highlights differences using colors that are sure to give you a headache if you look at them too long. Execute the : "the **vim** command **:diffoff!** immediately to avoid visual problems and dizziness. But keep in mind that when you want to make changes to the file, you need to turn this feature back on by executing the : the **vim** command **:windo diffthis**.

The first time you see this output, you might be a bit overwhelmed. It isn't as bad as you might think, though. Figure 15-11 helps explain how it works.

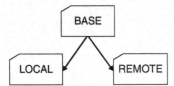

Figure 15-11   Understanding **vimdiff**

BASE is what the file looked like when the two branches were last in sync. LOCAL represents how the file looks in the current branch (the test branch in this example). REMOTE represents how the file looks in the branch that is being merged into this branch (the main branch in this example). The file at the bottom is the file that you are creating/merging.

The first three lines of all versions of the file shown in Figure 15-10 are identical. If you go to the first line that differs between the LOCAL and REMOTE files, you can execute the **:diffget RE** command to grab the code from the REMOTE file. It would grab the **echo**, **read**, **echo**, and **ps** commands in this example.

Suppose you want to input specific lines from one of the three files. For example, say that you want to copy the last four lines of the LOCAL version into the merged area. In this case, you are essentially going to do a copy and paste operation.

To switch to the **LOCAL** window, press **Ctrl+W+W**. Then copy the four lines by going to the first line you want to copy and typing **4yy**. Again press **Ctrl+W+W** to move forward until the cursor returns to the merged copy. Then move to where you want to make the change and press the **P** key.

Once you have made all of your changes, you need to save and quit all four versions. The easiest way to do this is by using the **vim** command **:wqa**.

You can then merge all files and then stage/commit them with the **git commit -a** command.

Summary

In this chapter you first explored the key concepts of Git, including the different generations of version control and how Git uses a working directory, a staging area, and a repository to manage versions of files.

You also learned how to perform Git operations, like cloning projects from Git repositories. You learned how to create a new file and place it in a repository, how to place new versions of the file in the repository, and how to handle issues when you merge two versions of a file into a new version.

Exam Preparation Tasks

As mentioned in the section "Goals and Methods" in the Introduction, you have a couple of choices for exam preparation: the exercises here, Chapter 23, "Final Preparation," and the exam simulation questions in the Pearson Test Prep Software Online.

Review All Key Topics

Review the most important topics in this chapter, noted with the Key Topic icon in the margin of the page. Table 15-2 lists these key topics and the page number on which each is found.

Table 15-2 Key Topics for Chapter 15

Key Topic Element	Description	Page Number
Paragraph	Cloning	546
Paragraph	The **git clone** command	550
Note	The **git init** command	550
Paragraph	The **git add** and **git commit** commands	560
Paragraph	The **git push** command	560
Note	The **git pull** command	552
Section	The **.git** directory	552
Paragraph	The **.gitignore** file	555
Paragraph	The **git branch** command	555
Paragraph	The **git log** command	556
Paragraph	The **git merge** command	557

Define Key Terms

Define the following key terms from this chapter and check your answers in the glossary:

Git, repository (repo), check out, check in, merge, distributed version control system (DVCS), Directed Acyclic Graph (DAG), Git, tag

Review Questions

The answers to these review questions are in Appendix A.

1. You have created a new file named **test.sh** in a Git directory but have not yet committed the changes to the local repository. Which command should you execute?

   a. **git add test.sh**

   b. **git commit test.sh**

   c. **git config test.sh**

   d. **git push test.sh**

2. Which command do you use to provide initial values to Git, such as your username and email address?

   a. **git init**

   b. **git config**

   c. **git setup**

   d. **git set**

3. Fill in the blank with the correct option: **git commit _____ "new file"**

   a. **-c**

   b. **-m**

   c. **-a**

   d. **-s**

4. Which of the following **git** commands sends changes from the local repository test branch to the remote repository?

   a. **git push -l test main**

   b. **git push -a main test**

   c. **git push -u origin test**

   d. **git push -p origin test**

5. Which command can be used to determine whether any file's changes are in the working area and need to be committed?

   a. **git working**

   b. **git update**

   c. **git changed**

   d. **git status**

6. You need to ensure that Git does not include a file in the repo. Which file can you modify to make this happen?

   a. .gitignore

   b. .gitskip

   c. .gitavoid

   d. .gitnull

This chapter covers the following topics:

- File Formats
- Utilities
- Continuous Integration/Continuous Deployment
- Advanced Git Topics

The exam objective covered in this chapter is as follows:

- **Objective 3.4:** Summarize common infrastructure as code technologies

## CHAPTER 16

Understanding Infrastructure as Code

This chapter is all about how today's infrastructure is mostly expressed and configured in code, be it YAML or JSON; how you can use the available infrastructure automation options to build, test, and deploy your applications and projects; how continuous integration and continuous deployment and their components can help you to do that without undue manual effort; and how to use a couple of the more advanced Git options such as **merge**, **rebase**, and pull requests.

"Do I Know This Already?" Quiz

The "Do I Know This Already?" quiz enables you to assess whether you should read this entire chapter or simply jump to the "Exam Preparation Tasks" section for review. If you are in doubt, read the entire chapter. Table 16-1 outlines the major headings in this chapter and the corresponding "Do I Know This Already?" quiz questions. You can find the answers in Appendix A, "Answers to the 'Do I Know This Already?' Quizzes and Review Questions."

Table 16-1 "Do I Know This Already?" Foundation Topics Section-to-Question Mapping

Foundation Topics Section	Questions Covered in This Section
File Formats	1–2
Utilities	3–4
Continuous Integration/Continuous Deployment	5–6
Advanced Git Topics	7

CAUTION The goal of self-assessment is to gauge your mastery of the topics in this chapter. If you do not know the answer to a question or are only partially sure of the answer, you should mark that question as wrong for purposes of the self-assessment. Giving yourself credit for an answer you correctly guess skews your self-assessment results and might provide you with a false sense of security.

1. Which of the following is *not* a characteristic of the JSON data definition?

   a. Hyphens

   b. Spaces

   c. Comments

   d. Periods

2. Which of the following is *not* a characteristic of the YAML data definition?

   a. Tabs

   b. Spaces

   c. Hyphens

   d. Periods

3. When working with Ansible, you create lists of tasks that will be executed on a set of hosts. What are these lists commonly called in the Ansible world?

   a. Recipes

   b. Taskers

   c. Formats

   d. Playbooks

4. You are using an infrastructure as code tool that causes you to work in three main stages: Code, Plan, and Apply. Which IaC tool are you almost certainly using?

   a. Terraform

   b. Puppet

   c. Chef

   d. Ansible

5. Which of the following are reasonable use cases for a continuous integration/ continuous deployment scenario? (Choose all that apply.)

   a. Gaming application

   b. Financial services

   c. Asynchronous Transfer Mode

   d. Social media site

6. What are the two possible terms for the CD portion of the CI/CD initialism? (Choose two.)

   a. Continuous development

   b. Continuous deployment

   c. Continuous defense

   d. Continuous delivery

Foundation Topics

File Formats

Understanding commonly used file formats will be important as we cover the topics of this chapter. The two file formats that you need to understand are YAML and JSON. These will be covered in this section of the book

YAML

YAML Ain't Markup Language, commonly known by the recursive acronym *YAML*, is a data serialization language that is used to store a text-based representation of objects, or *object state*. YAML is mainly used for configuration files with a stanza-based format of hierarchical items and is eminently human friendly and readable.

YAML also allows for a larger feature set, as well as the ability to include comments for documentation and clarity. A set of information in YAML is known as a *stream*, and there can be multiple streams in a given YAML file.

Key Characteristics of YAML

YAML has a certain set of identifying characteristics that distinguish it from other data-serialization languages or scenarios:

- Typically begin with the use of three hyphens (---).

- Typically end, or show end of stream, with three periods (...).

- Uses whitespace indentation for structure—spaces only; *no* tabs.

- Comments start with a # character and continue to the end of the line (EOL), except inside of a string, where they are literal.

- Lists (regular) are denoted by a preceding single hyphen (-) and are one entry per line. A list can also be shown inline as [*item1,item2,item3*].

YAML Stream Examples

You can display items in a list in YAML in a couple of ways. The first way is the regular method for listing items and is more obviously a list, but it takes a lot of vertical space to render:

--- # *Favorite Bands*

- The Psychedelic Furs

- Accept

- Dokken

- Marty Friedman

- Motorhead

The second, more-condensed way to represent a list is inline fashion:

--- # *Favorite Bands*

[The Psychedelic Furs, Accept, Dokken, Marty Friedman, Motorhead]

NOTE   A good friend and fellow instructional designer likes to wear a T-shirt at the office that proclaims

```
Yaml:
- Y: Yelling
  - A: At
  - M: My
  - L: Laptop
```

Just a little humor, but also a good visual aid for remembering how YAML lists are formatted.

JSON

JavaScript Object Notation (JSON) is used as a way to serialize data. JSON is simpler in format than YAML and can be used to conduct data exchange and transfer between APIs and their requesting applications or services.

JSON is a subset of YAML, and it can be parsed with a YAML interpreter or parser, so you can use YAML and JSON together for your templating needs.

JSON is also primarily recognizable by the fact that all the keys and values in JSON are enclosed in "double quotes." (I spent a couple of years working with AWS CloudFormation templates that were mostly expressed in JSON, and I don't miss it much, with all those quotes all over the data—just one unmatched double quote and *nothing works!*)

Key Characteristics of JSON

JSON also has a certain set of identifying characteristics that distinguish it from other data-serialization languages or scenarios:

- Stanzas begin with the left curly bracket, {, and end with the right curly bracket, }.

- Typically the JSON statement begins with the top and leftmost { and end with the bottom and leftmost }.

- JSON allows the use of tabs and spaces, carriage returns, and linefeeds as structural tools.

- No comments are allowed.

- Lists are defined by a string in double quotes followed directly by a colon character, then a space left square bracket, data which is separated by commas, and finally finished off with a right square bracket on a new line. For example: "colors": ["red", "green", "blue"].

JSON Examples

JSON often is used to define different types of objects, such as the object used to describe a particular band defined in Example 16-1. Example 16-1 also creates an array named "Albums", and the items in the array are the album names.

Example 16-1 Example of JSON Formatted Data

```
{
   "Favorite Band": {
      "name": "The Psychedelic Furs",
      "Begun": 1977,
      "First Album": "The Psychedelic Furs",
      "Soundtrack Credits": "Pretty in Pink, 1986",
      "photo": " https://en.wikipedia.org/wiki/File:Psychedelic_Furs.
jpg",
      "Albums": [
            "The Psychedelic Furs",
            "Talk Talk Talk",
            "Forever Now",
            "Mirror Moves",
```

```
        "Midnight to Midnight",
        "Book of Days",
        "World Outside",
        "Made of Rain"
    }
}
```

NOTE   I am certain that the explanations, definitions, and examples of YAML and JSON presented in this section are sufficient for you to ace related questions on the Linux+ exam. You just need to know a reasonable amount about these file formats or rather, file definitions to fulfill the objectives.

The real reason you need to know about YAML and JSON is that you'll encounter them infinitely in the infrastructure as code world, for all kinds of configuration and data storage uses.

Infrastructure as Code Concepts

Infrastructure as code (IaC) can be defined as the process of visualizing, designing, testing, revising, implementing, running, troubleshooting, and managing your project or companies infrastructure through the medium of code.

NOTE   The word "code" in *infrastructure as code* refers not to coding languages such as C, C++, C#, assembly, Java, etc., but rather to the code instructions and settings in the text files that you use to make a default service perform as you want it to.

Of course, not all the infrastructure is code—the code (actually text in a particular format) feeds the software configuration, settings, and modifications from the default behaviors.

In the remainder of this section, we will explore more details about IaC.

Just Making a Config Change

As an example, you can run the NGINX web server with its default configuration and make changes to it by editing the configuration files and restarting the service, but that's not IaC in practice, it's just making a configuration change.

Even the simplest configuration change, given enough scale (or systems to make the change to), will cause you to move to a more manageable method, which IaC is perfect for.

Using Source Control

To really be using the IaC concepts, you'd have your configuration files for NGINX as a part of a Git repository (or other source control) so that you can spool up your service or application, note how it works, make any changes to the IaC files, and then redeploy it, this time with the changes implemented.

Getting Started with IaC

First, do an inventory of everything you want to run with IaC, be it your current (and future desired) applications, back-end services, what configuration is needed for each of those items and every single application's settings, configuration and any of the other files that might make it not work well across multiple systems.

Next, with your completed inventory in hand, consider the following steps:

- Always try to use version control for everything. It makes fixing mistakes as simple as a couple of quick commands and a restart.

- Automate absolutely everything. Don't do anything manually except make everything automated.

- Verify absolute consistency in implementing your IaC. Run it 50 times and you should get an identical result every single time.

- Try to make your IaC as modular as possible, so that a change to one section doesn't affect many others just because it's not modular. (But don't get ridiculous with the modularization; some things belong together.)

- Do a hundred dry runs—heck, do a thousand, it should all be automated!

- Develop a quick but thorough manner with which to test functionality.

Next up we'll talk about the tools that you can use to make these tasks more automated and actually cause a given state to be not only created but also maintained in some instances.

Utilities: Infrastructure as Code

IaC utilities are not quite a dime a dozen these days, but there are an increasing number of them out there, which is both a good thing, because you can shop around and find the tool that suits the needs of you and your organization, and a bad thing, because the variety of tools and approaches that go along with them can be confusing.

The following are the two main approaches that IaC tools offer:

- **Functional:** Also known as the declarative approach, the functional approach focuses on what the actual configuration of the targeted unit should be. This is not a complete list of exactly how to achieve the finished state, but more of a declaration of intent to achieve it.

- **Procedural:** Also known as the imperative approach, the procedural approach is a set of steps and commands that need to be run or executed so that you get to the results you are looking for.

IaC Utility Choices

The IaC utilities listed in objective 3.4 are all great, so I'll present them in the order in which they are listed, giving particular attention to the unique characteristics of each.

NOTE   Linux+ objective 3.4 doesn't list all the IaC utility choices available, of course, so I will focus only on those that you will encounter on the exam.

Ansible

Ansible is an open-source IT automation tool that automates tasks such as configuration management, application deployment, intraservice orchestration, and provisioning. It is designed to be simple to use and easy to learn, even for users with no prior programming experience.

Ansible works by using playbooks, which are YAML files that describe the tasks that you want to automate. Playbooks are divided into tasks, which are the smallest unit of automation in Ansible. Tasks can be chained together to create complex workflows.

The Ansible documentation is excellent. To demonstrate, I've included an example of an Ansible playbook in Example 16-2.

Example 16-2   Example Ansible Playbook

```
---
- name: Update web servers
  hosts: webservers
  remote_user: root

  tasks:
  - name: Ensure apache is at the latest version
    ansible.builtin.yum:
      name: httpd
      state: latest
  - name: Write the apache config file
    ansible.builtin.template:
      src: /srv/httpd.j2
      dest: /etc/httpd.conf

- name: Update db servers
  hosts: databases
  remote_user: root

  tasks:
  - name: Ensure postgresql is at the latest version
    ansible.builtin.yum:
      name: postgresql
      state: latest
  - name: Ensure that postgresql is started
    ansible.builtin.service:
      name: postgresql
      state: started
```

In Example 16-2, you can see the simplicity of an Ansible playbook, where the purpose of each line is about as obvious as it can be.

The playbook in this example includes two *plays*, "Update web servers" and "Update db servers," identified by the two **– name:** fields listed leftmost in the hierarchy. In the first play, the **hosts:** field identifies the target hosts to be updated as "webservers" and the **remote_user** field identifies the user to execute the update, "root." The second play is similar but identifies "databases" as the target hosts to be updated.

Once the hosts and user have been defined, the **tasks:** section specifies the instructions that the play will execute. For example, the "Update web servers" play has two sets of instructions: the first set makes sure that Apache (httpd) is updated to the latest version and then the next set of instructions uses Ansible's ability to complete file actions by copying the source file from **/srv/httpd.j2** to the desired destination of **/etc/httpd.conf**.

The rest of the playbook follows the same simplistic and very readable format that is characteristic of Ansible.

Puppet and Chef

It's not really possible to talk about Puppet without talking about Chef as well. They are possibly the oldest of the IaC utilities, or *configuration managers*, as they were called before the fancy buzzword, infrastructure as code, became popular.

Puppet

Puppet is a declarative (or functional) utility. As mentioned earlier in this chapter, you use a declarative tool to describe the final state that you want your system to be in, and the IaC tool performs the actual steps to achieve that state. Puppet's configuration is constructed in JSON or YAML, contained in simple text files.

Puppet users should be comfortable with JSON and YAML and editing configuration files, but not to the depth that would be considered programming, which isn't necessary to work competently with Puppet.

Chef

Chef, on the other hand, is a great example of an imperative utility, which enables you to specify exactly what actions will be taken and what you want the eventual state to be. Chef uses the Ruby Domain Specific Language (DSL), so you have everything available to you that the Ruby language can do.

Chef aggressively uses culinary terms, with *recipes* and cookbooks and the concept of a staging area referred to as a Test Kitchen. A Chef recipe is a Ruby file that defines the steps that Chef will take to configure a system or application. A Chef cookbook is a collection of Chef recipes that are used to configure and manage a specific type of system or application. Chef cookbooks are written in Ruby and they are stored in a Git repository (the Test Kitchen).

Chef users, which tend primarily to be developers, should be comfortable with Ruby DSL and have at least moderate programming skills.

SaltStack

SaltStack is a very featureful and capable IaC utility. It has been used as the basis for other products such as versions of the SUSE Manager configuration manager and, most recently, the VMware vRealize Automation Suite. SaltStack is declarative.

> **NOTE**   SaltStack as a company was bought by VMware in late 2020, and the Salt-Stack team is now internal to VMware. The Salt Open offering (the SaltStack Open Source project) is now called the Salt Project, but there are no real differences other than the name change.

Salt Architecture

SaltStack is made up of a master/minion pairing. The Salt master (this phrase is used by the project and not a term that I created) is the server that manages the minion systems, essentially the clients.

Salt masters communicate with the Salt minions via ports 4505/4506, and the ZeroMQ messaging library manages all of this for Salt.

Salt Master Options

SaltStack can run in several manners, depending on your needs:

- **Single Salt master:** One Salt Master, with no backups or failovers, communicating with its configured Salt Minions.

- **Salt master failover:** Two Salt Master Servers, one configured as the live or hot Salt Master, the other as a failover in case the live one fails.

- **Salt master of masters:** For those who have a more enterprise-friendly or scalable set of Salt masters, you can have a master of masters, which has subordinate Salt masters, each of which governs a set of minions. (This might be for business divisions, or roles within an organization.)

Additionally, you can use SaltStack in a masterless manner, where you just load up the Salt minion on a system and then use that for development and testing of your Salt states and routines—this usually should not be used for production systems.

Salt masters are fed by what is known as *Salt states*, which are text files that end in the **.sls** extension and contain the configuration that is used by SaltStack to push the Salt state instructions to the Salt minions where the Salt modules will perform the needed functions.

Salt Configuration Locations

Salt configuration files are typically in the **/etc/salt/** directory, initially in the **/etc/salt/master** and **/etc/salt/minion** locations. Additionally, the usual **.d** include directory feature (such as **/etc/salt/conf.d**) exists, so any additional configuration put there will be read in after the main configuration is parsed.

Salt State Files

The Salt file root is normally located at **/srv/salt**, and that is where you put **.sls** State files.

A *State file* is effectively a set of instructions that is designed to produce a particular "state" to be achieved on the minion when the minion gets the state instructions from the master and runs it through the Remote Execution Modules.

Remote Execution Modules, of which there are *many*, are usually small instruction execution programs that do things like add users to the system, install requested packages, copy files from the Salt master to the Salt minion, and many other functions.

An example of how to install and keep NGINX (the best web server!) running is shown in the example state file **nginx_inst.xls** in Example 16-3.

Example 16-3   Example of an NGINX State File

```
nginx:
  pkg:
    - installed
  service:
    - running
    - watch:
      - pkg: nginx
      - file: /etc/nginx/nginx.conf
```

What's happening in this state file is relatively simple, as explained here line by line:

- **nginx:** is the name of the package or service you want to affect.

- **pkg:** indicates to the Salt system this is a package, not just a file.

- **- installed** indicates to Salt that this package should be installed.

- **service:** indicates to Salt that this is a system service.

- ■ **- running** causes Salt to keep the service running.

- ■ **- watch:** notifies Salt to watch or monitor what follows.

- ■ **- pkg: nginx** instructs Salt to restart the NGINX service if the NGINX package is updated.

- ■ **- file: /etc/nginx/nginx.conf** instructs Salt to restart the NGINX service if the **nginx.conf** file is changed.

This is more than enough information to enable you to easily answer any SaltStack-related questions you may encounter on the Linux+ exam.

I recommend perusing the SaltStack documentation or looking at the excellent SaltStack courses that A Cloud Guru (Pluralsight) has on their site; the main SaltStack DevOps instructor there is an excellent teacher; she really breaks things down for you.

Terraform

Terraform is arguably the newer and more difficult of the many IaC options listed in the Linux+ objectives. There are many people who can tell you how to *do* Terraform, but there are very few who can tell you *why* to choose Terraform over the other more "mentally accessible" IaC options. Let's see if we can get there.

Terraform is the epitome of the declarative manner of using IaC, in that you just tell it what you want the result to be and let the tool take care of how it gets done. This allows you to focus on architecting your infrastructure, while not getting down in the weeds with every single step or command that needs to be run to accomplish it.

There are three main phases of using Terraform:

1. Code(ing)

2. Plan(ning)

3. Apply(ing)

Coding

When you are in the Coding phase, you are creating the actual **.tf** file that contains what you want to have happen. Figure 16-1 shows declaring a final state or environment of three elements: a couple of virtual machines, each containing an NGINX server, and a Kubernetes cluster, networked together.

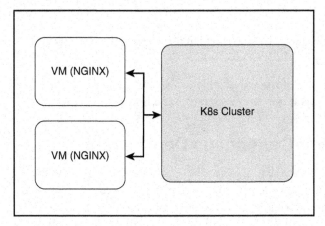

Figure 16-1 Three-element environment for use in the Coding phase

Assume for purposes of this example that the file is named **myenvironment.tf**. This file contains the relatively simple instructions that Terraform uses in the next phase to create the plan.

NOTE   The environment file to create the outcome shown in Figure 16-1 is too long to reasonably list here, and goes way beyond the scope of what the Linux+ objectives require you to know. There are many examples of valid and useful Terraform **.tf** files available online, including from Terraform itself.

Planning

The plan generated by Terraform enables you to review the actual changes that will be made to your infrastructure if you apply the plan. Taking the opportunity to review the plan is very important, because there's nothing like thinking you've got a good environment setup only to find out that something has gone horribly awry and you've created 1024 VMs by accident.

When you enter the Plan phase of Terraform, the tool takes the **myenvironment. tf** file (code), runs through it, and generates an actual plan file that shows the actions the plan contains. You execute the **terraform plan** command to launch this process. To do this, you'll run the **terraform** command with the subcommand **plan**, which will do the run-through and generate an actual plan file as well as let you know with the output what the Plan contains.

Applying

In this phase, you instruct Terraform to take the plan it has generated for you and apply it to your infrastructure.

There is a whole lot more to Terraform, all of which is beyond the scope of the Linux+ objectives, but at least you now know what it is and how it works overall.

Continuous Integration/Continuous Deployment

Continuous integration/continuous deployment, almost always shortened to CI/CD, is the process of having a continuous development, fix, test, and release process that keeps your code updated and the latest fixed and tested code in production.

Software and environments have gotten so multivalued and multilayered, with dozens to hundreds of different resources in some cases, that an essential skill of Linux sysadmins is the ability to automate as much of this infrastructure as possible.

How Can It Be Solved?

Instead of running around doing manual development, building, testing, and deployment of all the different applications (think of these as published services such as a web application that uses multiple resources to provide that service as an "application service"), a better solution is to find a way to automate all of these processes.

CI/CD is often visualized as a three-step process, as shown in Figure 16-2.

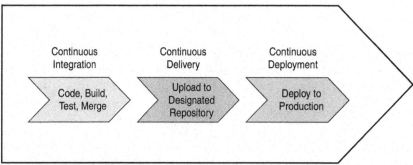

Figure 16-2   CI/CD three-step process

Continuous Integration

When you are properly using *continuous integration (CI)*, you have reached a state where multiple developers are working at the same time on different portions, aspects, or modules of your infrastructure or app and their work is all being integrated on a consistent basis into the main branch or set of code.

At this same time, automated (hopefully!) testing and building procedures check to ensure that what's been checked in, or submitted, works with the other portions (sometimes many) that make up what will be the next update of the application.

Continuous Delivery

The abbreviation CD actually represents two slightly different processes:

- *Continuous delivery*, which means that after the developers check in their code, it's tested and merged into the main app code, and then it's delivered automatically to a repository (grouping of code or packages, typically). If all has gone well in the continuous integration area, then continuous delivery just makes sure that code is available for use in the next step of making your application as up to date as possible in an automated way.

- *Continuous deployment*, which means that after the code is delivered to the repository, it's then included as part of an update or release of the application to go into production. This could mean there are mere minutes between a check-in of code, its automated testing and building, and its being deployed on the production systems. Continuous delivery is a great way to get almost instantaneous feedback on the true state of your application's most recent release, which can be either exhilarating or horrifying (or both, depending on the range of feedback).

The continuous nature of the CI/CD methodology depicted in Figure 16-2 enables teams and organizations to build, text, fix, and deploy their software much faster and often more reliably than is possible with manual methods.

CI/CD Use Cases

The number of possible CI/CD use cases for handling application environments and workflows is in the thousands, yet objective 3.4 lists "use cases" under CI/CD. Don't fret; you are expected to know only general categories of CI/CD use cases for the Linux+ exam.

At this point, most any shop or project that is starting a new project should consider using Continuous Integration, but many current and even legacy projects are using a form of CI/CD these days.

Some of the general categories of CI/CD uses cases that you might encounter on the Linux+ exam include the following:

- Web applications
- Financial services

- Shopping sites
- Gaming applications
- Social media applications

Any project that has development, test, and production phases, can benefit from the use of the CI/CD methodology, so a listing of use cases could literally include, for example, a majority of the projects hosted on GitHub!

Advanced Git Topics

If you haven't read Chapter 15, with its discussion of all things Git, please do so; it'll make the more advanced topics for Git at the end of this chapter make a lot more sense. This brief section explains a couple of objective-driven commands that are part of the Git world, merge, rebase, and pull requests.

merge

Git uses the *merge* command as a way to reunite forked history. When you've created independent lines of developing, also known as *branches*, you can then reunite those branches to create a single united branch. The **merge** command allows you to combine branches in a manner that moves a project forward.

rebase

Git uses the *rebase* command slightly differently than the **merge** command, which moves a project forward, where **rebase** can allow you to create a new base commit.

Effectively, a **rebase** operation allows you to change the base of a branch so that it seems as if the new branch is from a completely different commit.

As another way to visualize this, consider a Microsoft Word document that has been developed by several authors and has hundreds of embedded Track Changes entries showing the revisions of the various authors. You might want to take that base document, save it as a new version, strip out all those Track Changes entries, and start with a clean base document.

This is very similar to what the **rebase** command enables you to do: declare an existing branch as a new branch, unencumbered with possibly hundreds of commit history items.

Pull Requests

A *pull request (PR)* is the mechanism whereby a contributor notifies the maintainer of a Git repo that they would like to submit new code or code changes for the maintainer to review and possibly incorporate for review.

Issuing a pull request from a contributor standpoint tells the server that there are some local unreviewed commits that you are presenting for the maintainer to review and possibly integrate into this repository.

A pull request is a great way for someone who is interested in the contents of a repository to get commits made, without having to be the maintainer, or have authorization via an SSH key to the repository.

Summary

In this chapter we worked hard to help you understand the concepts and some of the higher-level functions of the of the continuous integration/continuous delivery process, and the final step, continuous deployment. We explored core CI/CD concepts and IaC tools, such as Ansible, Puppet, and Chef.

You also learned about the very important data definition languages or formats, YAML and JSON. You are now even more aware of Git's higher-end features such as **merge**, **rebase**, and the ever-popular pull requests.

Exam Preparation Tasks

As mentioned in the section "Goals and Methods" in the Introduction, you have a couple of choices for exam preparation: the exercises here, Chapter 23, "Final Preparation," and the exam simulation questions in the Pearson Test Prep Software Online.

Review All Key Topics

Review the most important topics in this chapter, noted with the Key Topic icon in the margin of the page. Table 16-2 lists these key topics and the page number on which each is found.

Table 16-2   Key Topics for Chapter 16

Key Topic Element	Description	Page Number
List	The key characteristics of YAML	576
List	The key characteristics of JSON	578
Paragraph	Ansible playbooks	571
Paragraph	Puppet is a declarative utility	583
Paragraph	Chef is an imperative utility	583
Paragraph	Salt masters communicate with Salt minions via ports 4505/4506	584
List	Three main phases of using Terraform	586
Figure 16-2	Continuous integration process	588
Paragraph	Git uses the **merge** command to reunite forked history	590
Paragraph	Git uses the **rebase** command to allow the creation of a new base commit	590
Paragraph	A pull request is how a contributor notifies the maintainer of code of a change to review and possibly merge	591

Define Key Terms

Define the following key terms from this chapter and check your answers in the glossary:

infrastructure as code (IaC), Ansible, playbooks, Puppet, Chef, recipes, SaltStack, State file, Terraform, continuous integration (CI), continuous delivery, continuous deployment, **merge**, **rebase**, pull request (PR)

Review Questions

The answers to these review questions are in Appendix A.

1. You have created a text file that contains instructions about creating and deploying infrastructure as code, and that file ends with the **.tf** extension. That file is used with the **terraform** command to generate the _____ file.

   a. code

   b. test

   c. plan

   d. analyze

2. You have been researching methods of deploying and managing your infrastructure through the medium of text or code. Which main data definition formats have you found in your research? (Choose all that apply.)

   a. EBCDIC

   b. YAML

   c. ASCII

   d. JSON

   d. XML

3. You're a Red Hat Enterprise Linux user and want to choose the most direct and closely associated infrastructure-as-code option to create, deploy, and manage your infrastructure. Which of the available methods is most closely associated with Red Hat?

   a. Puppet

   b. Chef

   c. Ansible

   d. RPM

4. You are putting instructions into a file that will cause a particular set of actions to happen in the SaltStack IaC utility. What is the generic name of such a file?

   a. State file

   b. Salt file

   c. Salt book

   d. Minion file

5. Which Git command enables you to take a branch with previous commits and effectively allow it to become a new branch with no previous commit history?

   a. **git emerge**

   b. **git asnew**

   c. **git nocommit**

   d. **git rebase**

6. You are used to working with one of the main data definition formats and accidentally include a comment as you would normally do in your preferred format, but it causes an error. Which of the data definition formats does not allow the use of comments?

   a. EBCDIC

   b. YAML

   c. ASCII

   d. JSON

   e. XML

This chapter covers the following topics:

- Kubernetes Benefits and Application Use Cases
- Single-Node, Multicontainer Use Cases
- Container Persistent Storage
- Container Networks
- Service Mesh
- Bootstrapping
- Container Registries

The exam objective covered in this chapter is as follows:

- **Objective 3.5:** Summarize container, cloud, and orchestration concepts

## CHAPTER 17

Understanding Containers, Cloud, and Orchestration

When the CompTIA Linux+ team created this objective, apparently they designed it to be a catch-all for container and mesh concepts. From the number of included subtopics, you'd think this chapter would be the size of a whole book! Obviously, that isn't the case. Focus on the words "summarize" and "concepts" in objective 3.5 and you'll realize that you don't need to know every detail of these topics for the Linux+ exam; rather, you have to demonstrate some familiarity with the technologies and how they work together overall.

You are meant to study these concepts, understand when they are meant to be used, or are to your advantage to study further and consider implementing, and there are some great technologies and options here!

"Do I Know This Already?" Quiz

The "Do I Know This Already?" quiz enables you to assess whether you should read this entire chapter or simply jump to the "Exam Preparation Tasks" section for review. If you are in doubt, read the entire chapter. Table 17-1 outlines the major headings in this chapter and the corresponding "Do I Know This Already?" quiz questions. You can find the answers in Appendix A, "Answers to the 'Do I Know This Already?' Quizzes and Review Questions."

Table 17-1 "Do I Know This Already?" Foundation Topics Section-to-Question Mapping

Foundation Topics Section	Questions Covered in This Section
Kubernetes Benefits and Application Use Cases	1
Single-Node, Multicontainer Use Cases	2
Container Persistent Storage	3
Container Networks	4
Service Mesh	5
Bootstrapping	6
Container Registries	7

CAUTION   The goal of self-assessment is to gauge your mastery of the topics in this chapter. If you do not know the answer to a question or are only partially sure of the answer, you should mark that question as wrong for purposes of the self-assessment. Giving yourself credit for an answer you correctly guess skews your self-assessment results and might provide you with a false sense of security.

1. Which organization is the originator of the Kubernetes technology?

   a. Kube Foundation

   b. Linux Professional Institute

   c. Google

   d. F5

2. Why would you use a multicontainer node or pod in Kubernetes?

   a. Network isolation for all containers

   b. CPU isolation for all containers

   c. Process isolation for all containers

   d. Ingress isolation for all containers

3. When using stateful applications in containers, what type of storage resources are most appropriate?

   a. Resistant

   b. Consistent

   c. Insistent

   d. Persistent

4. What is a main advantage of implementing container networking over traditional pod networking?

   a. IP address per container

   b. Security at the container level

   c. Process isolation at the pod level

   d. The ability to bridge containers

5. What technology takes the logic that controls service-to-service communication and implements it as a layer of infrastructure?

   a. API gateway

   b. Reverse proxy

    c. Control plane

    d. Service mesh

6. When bootstrapping a container instance in AWS, which of the following are types of passable data you can use to execute configuration on the instance? (Choose two.)

    a. .ec2 files

    b. Cloud boot-init

    c. Bootstrap container scripts

    d. cloud-init directives

7. What is a primary purpose for having a container registry?

    a. Make package management easier

    b. Monitor the services installed on your system

    c. Scale workloads more easily

    d. Store and access container images

Foundation Topics

Kubernetes Benefits and Application Use Cases

Not long ago, the question "What is Kubernetes and what can you use it for?" would have been rather hard to answer, but it's been a long road since its announcement in 2014 by Google to today where it's a very large part of the cloud computing landscape and still growing its market share.

Kubernetes, often abbreviated K8s, was the first seed project of the Cloud Native Computing Foundation, the creation of Google and the Linux Foundation.

Within the space of three or so years, Kubernetes had won over most of the large cloud providers, including the "Big 3," Google Cloud Services (or GCS), Microsoft Azure, and Amazon Web Services (AWS), all of which offer support for Kubernetes.

Kubernetes has become such a large part of the cloud computing environment that it's important to ensure you understand what Kubernetes is and at least the broad strokes of how it functions.

What Is Kubernetes, Really?

Kubernetes is an open-source system for automating deployment, scaling, and management of containerized applications. It is a portable, extensible, and scalable platform that can be used to deploy applications on a variety of infrastructure, including on-premises, public cloud, and hybrid cloud.

In other terms, Kubernetes is an orchestration manager for containers and the applications that run in or on them. *Orchestration* in this context means using software to automate actions that would otherwise have to be done manually, such as configuring, coordinating, managing, and monitoring large-scale applications that run on your computing architecture.

> **NOTE**   Following up on the Chapter 16, "Understanding Infrastructure as Code," discussion of the distinction between functional/declarative tools and procedural/imperative tools, Kubernetes is definitely on the declarative side of things. For example, you do not tell Kubernetes *how* to do something but rather what you *want* to happen, or you set a parameter such as CPU utilization that will then cause Kubernetes to increase or decrease resources.

The High-Level Structure of Kubernetes

Kubernetes is made up of a lot of different components, including control plane, nodes, services running that you mostly don't see, so let's demystify it a bit.

- **Kubernetes control plane:** Consists of multiple components that have the duty to manage the whole cluster. These components are sometimes called Kubernetes masters or controllers.

- **Kubernetes node:** A machine on which the containers that make up a Kubernetes cluster run. While a Kubernetes cluster can have any number of nodes, you can run a Kubernetes cluster on a single machine easily.

- **Kubernetes *Pod*:** The smallest item in the Kubernetes world and, when deployed, consists of one or more containers. Containers in a Pod are linked together and have the same lifecycle, as well as other characteristics of note.

The previous list is a very high-level overview of Kubernetes clusters; let's explore which components are located where next.

Kubernetes Control Plane Structure

The Kubernetes control plane contains the following components that manage the Kubernetes nodes:

- **kube-controller-manager:** The process/component that manages all the control loops for Kubernetes.

- **kube-scheduler:** The component that takes Pods that have no containers yet and assigns the containers to the Pods based on the requirements that are the default or configured for the Kubernetes environment.

- **cloud-controller-manager:** The component that works with cloud providers via their APIs to handle specific tasks like name resolution and how to scale up and down across hardware resources.

- **kube-apiserver:** The component that performs the front-end operations for the Kubernetes API process.

- **etcd:** A key-value store that performs in a highly available manner to store all the database information for Kubernetes, keeping great log records of all that occurs and making sure the databases and logs are available across its nodes and other components.

NOTE   In a default Kubernetes deployment, components are not in a highly available state, meaning multiple replicas of components do not exist. However, Kubernetes can be deployed in a highly available state in which certain components are replicated for redundancy and an order of leader election is established. This is far beyond the scope of the Linux+ objectives, but good for you to know.

Kubernetes Node Structure

Kubernetes nodes are the systems/servers that run the applications that make up your Kubernetes environment. Nodes can contain various processes, but they at least contain the following:

- **kubelet:** The process that gets the orders for what a given Pod's desired or target state is and then makes sure that Pod gets deployed properly and is healthy.

- **kube-proxy:** The process that handles all the UDP, TCP, and SCTP proxy tasks of all the nodes and helps provide the load-balanced services.

- **Pods:** Pods are the smallest unit of deployment in Kubernetes. A pod is a group of one or more containers that are scheduled together on the same node. Pods share the same network and filesystem, which makes them easy to manage.

- **Containers:** The *only* piece of Kubernetes that is not actually a part of or native to Kubernetes. Kubernetes supports multiple container standards, but it doesn't have its own container scheme.

Container Runtime Interface

Kubernetes and Docker both run containers, but Docker can access the containerd runtime directly, whereas Kubernetes uses an access API called Container Runtime Interface (CRI).

From there either CRI-O or containerd is used, which both use the Open Container Initiative's OCI specification to cause runC to create and run the actual container-ized processes. CRI-O is a lightweight container runtime that is compatible with the Kubernetes Container Runtime Interface (CRI). CRI-O is an alternative to Docker that is designed to be more efficient and scalable. runC is a lightweight container runtime that is used by Kubernetes and other container orchestration systems.

Specialized Container Types

Along with regular application containers, introduced earlier in the chapter, there are a couple of specialized container types you need to know about:

- **Sidecar:** A *sidecar* container is one that rides along with the main application container, or containers, and shares the same storage and network resources as the other containers. A sidecar can be thought of as an executive assistant, available to perform functions for all the various application containers in a Pod, such as traffic routing, high availability support, aggregated logging, and certificate distribution, to name a few functions.

- **Ambassador:** An *ambassador container* typically sits between a web server and its backend microservice so that in the event the microservice has to be moved, no changes need to be made to the website—the web server communicates exactly as it did before the microservice was moved, and the ambassador container receives the communication and routes the traffic to the new location or new backend microservice. NGINX users will recognize this as a form of reverse proxy, which handles client requests for backend resources so that clients don't need to know or care where the backend resources are located.

Benefits of Using Kubernetes

Many organizations use Kubernetes, but some of the largest organizations are its biggest fans due to the large amount of automation necessary within large organizations. Some of the benefits of running Kubernetes include

- Improved resource utilization

- Shorter software development timelines

- Easing of application upgrades and associated maintenance

- Ability to containerize older and monolithic applications

- Reduction in the use of public cloud service provider services and their associated costs

- Flexibility of operations

- Developer efficiency gains

- Operator efficiency

These and the many other benefits of running Kubernetes have resulted in it becoming integral to the cloud computing landscape, and certainly it's a huge part of the public cloud and, increasingly, the private cloud.

> **NOTE** This section has given you a good overview of Kubernetes and its main components, as well as how they interact together. As a further avenue of understanding Kubernetes, as the Linux+ is not where you'll get the fullest level of understanding of it, I recommend the fine set of resources on the Kubernetes site hosted by the Cloud Native Computing Foundation (CNCF), https://kubernetes.io/.

Single-Node Multicontainer Use Cases

Once again, the Linux+ objectives cryptically specify that we should know about a topic and then don't really tell us what aspect or even what about that topic we really need to know.

The fact that they gave us a tiny clue with the single word "Compose" for this topic does lead us down a set of related use cases for creating a development environment that roughly mimics a production environment.

Similar to the objective 3.4 cryptic reference to CI/CD use cases, discussed in Chapter 16, objective 3.5 refers to single-node multicontainer use cases, with "Compose" given as the only clue. I interpret that clue to mean *Docker Compose*, which you can use to create a single-node multicontainer development environment that roughly mimics a production environment.

There are a few ways you could roll with this scenario, the simplest of which would be to set up a couple of containers on the same node, in the same Pod, and have them work together to make a larger set of capabilities. Two examples of this *single-node multicontainer* use case are provided next, followed by a more-complex use case with three container nodes.

Two-Container Node Example A

One example of configuring multiple containers on a single node would be to set up a relatively simple development environment in which your node has an NGINX reverse proxy container that protects a backend Elasticsearch container.

Putting the NGINX reverse proxy and the Elasticsearch containers in the same Pod would enable you to address both containers with the same IP address, just on different ports.

You can use Elasticsearch for a number of things, none of which actually matter to our example, but it excels at enabling application, website, and enterprise-wide searching of data, analytics, and monitoring, and a lot more.

Two-Container Node Example B

Another example of configuring multiple containers on a single node would be to have a node in which an NGINX web server and a backend database such as MariaDB are configured such that the database container can be accessed solely by the web server container. The web server container would be configured to be publicly accessible through the Pod's networking configuration, and the database container would work solely behind the scenes with the web server to provide content.

Three-Container Node Example

A more complex scenario regarding single-node multicontainer use cases would be to use a traditional pairing such as in the preceding example but then incorporate a service mesh into your environment.

This would add a sidecar proxy, which would help protect and enhance the capabilities of the main container, which might be doing something very specific, such as providing web services via NGINX.

NOTE The standard Kubernetes cluster explanations typically say there should be one service per container, and that's true, the reason being that it's good to keep your Pod as simple as possible, effectively tied together, and are affected by common networking settings, restart cycles, etc.

Container Persistent Storage

Container persistent storage is not as complex as it might seem, as containers themselves have nothing persistent—they have to depend on other tools to keep and store anything that is needed across container instances. Container persistent storage is a way to store data that is persistent across container restarts. This data can be used to store things like logs, databases, or configuration files. In this section we will explore different options for implementing container persistent storage.

Docker Volumes

Since objective 3.5 doesn't specifically list Kubernetes as the container persistent storage tool, let's start with a simpler tool, Docker volumes, which involves using the **docker volume create** *<dockervol>* command to create a volume on the local system that runs Docker, such as the following command:

```
$ docker volume create mydatavol
```

From there, you can mount the volume to a new container using the following command:

```
$ docker -d -p 5000:5000 -v mydatavol:/mydatavol mydatavol
```

Now you can open a BASH shell in the container and see that the **/mydatavol** storage location is present.

Advantages of Using Docker Volumes

A Docker volume can be created, attached and interacted with from the container or containers that have it attached, and when those containers are stopped and go away, the data volume remains and can be used again and again.

Obviously, this allows you to store configuration and other data on that locally resident volume and have containers access it either in read-write mode or read-only mode, depending on what the container needs and what you want to have happen.

In short, the main advantages of using Docker volumes are that it's faster, it is not tied to the container's lifecycle, and it is designed for multicontainer usage.

Disadvantages of Using Docker Volumes

Frankly, there are not many significant challenges to using Docker volumes, except, of course, if you are *not* using Docker. If you are using Docker, always remember that Docker volumes are destroyed when the last container using that volume is stopped or killed.

There are some indications that the best way to keep your data, even across the removal of the last *other* container, is to have a container that is dedicated to collecting and storing that data from more transient containers and then commit that data either to the image you are using for standing up containers or to more permanent filesystem storage.

Bind Mounts

In contrast to Docker volumes, bind mounts have existed almost since the very beginning of Docker.

A *bind mount* binds a file or directory on the host system's storage to the container's filesystem. Bind mounts are always referred to in an absolute path/file way.

If you are familiar with the concept of using a file on disk to add additional swap space to a Linux system, then using a bind mount will make sense.

Advantages of Using Bind Mounts

A bind mount also allows you to have persistent storage for containers, and can be high-performing, depending of course on the state and busyness of the filesystem that is being mounted.

Bind mounts are very easy to use, and because they have been around for a long time, a lot of code has been built around creating, managing, and removing them.

Disadvantages of Using Bind Mounts

Although bind mounts are easy to use, like a lot of things that are easy, using bind mounts has the potential to introduce significant issues to your environment.

Most significantly, a bind mount actually directly accesses a file on the host's filesystem, which is a security risk, to say the least. It would be a very simple hack to create a very large file or set of files through a bind mount of a directory that would fill up the host filesystem, or even to access other files, processes, and so forth on the host, particularly if you had bind mounts in the **/tmp** or **/var/run** locations.

Kubernetes Persistent Volumes

No discussion on data persistence for containers is complete without discussing how Kubernetes handles persistent storage for containers.

Kubernetes has a very large number of volume types, everything from AWS-specific volume types to vSphere-specific volume types, but that functionality is far beyond what you need to know for the Linux+ exam.

The Kubernetes PersistentVolume Subsystem

The Kubernetes PersistentVolume subsystem handles how storage is consumed. There are two API resources or calls that govern this:

- **PersistentVolume (PV):** This is a resource in the cluster that has been either manually or automatically provisioned for use. A PV is at the same level as a node in the cluster, and, unlike a volume where the lifecycle is tied to a container, a PV has its own persistence and lifecycle, and is independent of any Pod (or one of its containers) that requests storage from it.

- **PersistentVolumeClaim (PVC):** This is a request from a user or process for storage resources (AKA, the PV). PVCs occur at the Pod level and can take many forms, depending on what the requesting user/process needs the storage for.

The PV and PVC Lifecycles

Remember that a PV exists independently in the Kubernetes cluster, and has its own lifecycle, and that PVCs are very ephemeral and are created and destroyed, or reclaimed, depending on whether the user/process is done with the Claim, and the PV receives instructions to reclaim, retain, or delete that resource.

NOTE   The Linux+ exam will test you on your overall knowledge of volumes, persistence of storage, and how Docker and Kubernetes deal with storage persistence. I've gone beyond that scope, but it's important to give you full context so that you understand how this all fits together and are not left piecing together phrases.

Container Networks

A container network is a way to connect containers together so that they can communicate with each other. *Container networking* can be a complex topic, so it's best to start with defining what an overlay network is, and why overlay networks exist.

What's an Overlay Network?

As the name indicates, an *overlay network* is a network construct or schema that is put on *top* of an existing network infrastructure. In some cases, the concept of having subnets is having an overlay that resides over the actual physical hardware that provides the networking infrastructure.

In containers, an overlay network enables you to have a distributed network that allows multiple containers (through their Pods) to access each other via a network scheme.

The type of communications supported by an overlay network is different, where the containers within a Kubernetes Pod can communicate safely between each other without using any outer resources.

Overlay networks are also useful and necessary when you have several host systems that have resident containers that need to communicate not only between containers on the same host but also between containers located on separate hosts.

Docker Swarm

Docker has a concept called a *Swarm* that supports encrypted communication between containers, and the Swarm is an overlay of the networking configuration of the actual Docker hosts.

A couple of networks are created when you create an overlay network with Docker:

- **ingress:** This network handles the Swarm-related data and traffic, and Swarm services automatically connect to this network unless directed to connect to user-created overlays.

- **docker_gwbridge:** This network interconnects the Docker daemons to each other, those that are joined to the swarm.

Kubernetes Overlay Networks

Not surprisingly, whereas Docker's overlays and Swarms are relatively easy to understand and implement, Kubernetes is more complex because it has many choices for overlaying network structures, including but not limited to the following:

- **Flannel:** The Flannel agent (flanneld) resides on each host and, once the IP and subnet information is assigned, uses the Kubernetes API to store the host's networking configuration information.

- **Calico:** Continuing the fabric (get it?) theme, Calico is more complex and full-featured and provides a robust networking stack that includes the presence of a virtual router that uses BGP (Boundary Gateway Protocol) to advertise the presence of services to the rest of the environment.

- **Cillium:** At the top end, the Cillium solution is the most full-featured and complete network solution for Kubernetes at present. It can do everything from assignment, to filtering and policy enforcement, to even replacing the actual kube-proxy agents with its own.

NOTE The Linux+ exam will test you on the general concept of overlay networks, but I've provided more details than what you need to know to answer overlay network-related questions because in the real world you really do need to know how overlays are used, both in Docker and Kubernetes.

Bridging Networks

In this example, we'll use Docker and examine how it uses a bridge to connect resources. A *bridging* network is a type of network that connects containers on the same host together. A bridge is the default network setup for allowing containers to communicate with each other in the Docker world. Any container connected to the bridge network can contact and communicate with the other containers connected to the same bridge.

However, a bridge network is only for communications between containers on the same host, so an overlay network would be necessary to have inter-host communications or to have containers on separate hosts communicate with each other. (See the earlier Note in the "What's an Overlay Network?" section about overlay networks and inter-host communications.)

By default, on startup, Docker creates a bridge network named, rather unimaginatively, bridge, and any containers started after its creation are automatically connected to the same default bridge network.

If the default bridge network is not to your satisfaction, it's easy to create user-defined bridges with custom settings.

Swotting a NAT

The concept of a NAT setup is something that most people use every single day on their work or home router. *Network address translation (NAT)* is a type of overlay networking in which the network router has a public IP address that is capable of communication in every sense with the outside networks, or Internet. A private IP address scheme is used (either 10.0.0.0, 172.16.0.0 or 192.168.0.0), and all hosts inside the NAT can communicate with each other on the same subnet scheme, or with the host or router, but they are *not* publicly addressable through the router. The network address translation function allows multiple devices to share a single public IP address.

When a host system has a NAT setup running, that external interface is the egress or jumping-off point for all NAT-generated traffic from the virtual machines or containers that are on the private address schemes behind the NAT.

This has a big advantage for use in containers, because there is no need for any external address other than the one assigned to the host system, and all traffic that is sent outside of that host to the public networks or Internet is from the external address, with no outer indication it's from a NAT source.

However, NAT knows that traffic was sent from internal sources and, upon receiving a response to any sent request, it routes that response back to the source internal virtual machine or container, all without exposing the virtual machine or container to the dangerous outside networks or Internet.

NAT is especially useful when external IP addresses are expensive or difficult to obtain; it enables an organization to spend less on IP management and more on getting actual work done.

Host Networking

The *host networking* mode is where a container can share, or piggyback on, the host system's networking stack. In this case, the container does not have its own IP address, but instead shares the host IP address, and traffic is separated by the network driver to get to the host destination or to the container destination.

Think of host networking as a "party line," such as back when a telephone line was shared by several rural households or locations, all of whom had equal access to the line.

Service Mesh

The topic of service meshes is complex and multilayered, almost always involving Kubernetes or another clustering setup, a need for security and observability, and some patience, as service meshes are sometimes difficult to install, operate, and get the right value from.

Also, the need for a service mesh often exists only in organizations that provision services to customers by using a combination of containers, Kubernetes, the CI/CD pipeline, and IaC.

What Is a Service Mesh?

A service mesh is a dedicated infrastructure layer for managing communication between services in a microservices architecture. The world of using modern applications to provide services to clients is mostly constructed of micro-services, collected into groups of services that provide a particular function. The knitting together of a modern application, such as an Amazon or Alibaba shopping site, can involve dozens to hundreds of separate but critical micro-services, all of which need to be managed, secured, observed for faults, monitored for performance, and so on.

This need for an overlay of management and security, combined with the need for the component services to communicate not only with the cluster or application but also with each other, poses a unique challenge: how to manage all of this without so burdening the application/microservices with that management that it affects performance.

Example Service Mesh

The most recognizable service mesh provider is Istio. The Istio product is open source, it overlays and injects itself into your Kubernetes (for example) cluster, and it inserts its components into sidecars in each Pod, effectively becoming a sidecar proxy, but with much more functionality than just a simple proxy.

To quote the Istio website (https://istio.io/latest/about/service-mesh/), the project offers the following features when the service mesh is deployed and used:

- Secure service-to-service communication in a cluster with TLS encryption, strong identity-based authentication and authorization

- Automatic load balancing for HTTP, gRPC, WebSocket, and TCP traffic

- Fine-grained control of traffic behavior with rich routing rules, retries, failovers, and fault injection

- A pluggable policy layer and configuration API supporting access controls, rate limits, and quotas

- Automatic metrics, logs, and traces for all traffic within a cluster, including cluster ingress and egress

Istio Components

Istio is made up of the same general style of components as Kubernetes, a control plane and a data plane, but it's designed to fit over and into Kubernetes like snapping on an exoskeleton to a soldier to make them stronger, have more control, and have extra capabilities. In computer networking, the control plane and data plane are two distinct functional layers that make up a network. The control plane is responsible for managing the network, while the data plane is responsible for forwarding traffic.

Commercial Istio Distributions

There may be others, but the prime example of using an Istio distribution as the basis of a commercially viable product is the Aspen Service Mesh, recently acquired by F5, Inc.

Aspen Service Mesh is based on the Istio open-source project code, and adds some key features, support and training, and all the usual enhancements that come with a commercially available distribution of an open-source project.

Non-Istio Service Meshes

The NGINX Service Mesh product is a very interesting adjunct to the Istio Service Mesh, in that it's meant to do very much the same sort of tasks as Istio, but it's based on the NGINX Plus, NGINX Ingress Controller, and NGINX-specific sidecar proxies that are inserted in between service containers and the rest of the cluster, very similar in concept to the Istio model.

Bootstrapping

Bootstrapping is the process of starting a system from a minimal state. This is often done by loading a small amount of code into memory and then using that code to load the rest of the system. Just about every way you can manage your infrastructure requires you to first install a tool, and with several instances, that's manageable, but what if you need to bring up and configure dozens, hundreds, or even thousands of instances of multiple configurations?

A handy little tool named cloud-init is the solution. It is included on a large subset of current Linux images, ready to take your orders and make your cloud images usable upon bootup or shortly after.

You can think of *cloud-init* as a script interpreter, which effectively it is. The cloud-init script data is usually delivered from what is commonly called "userdata". This data is used to complete the cloud-init script, which is used to perform the actions and configuration contained in that set of instructions.

You write cloud-init scripts in YAML, which makes them very easy to read and troubleshoot.

A cloud-init script can do an impressive number of tasks, such as:

- Pass user data on to the system
- Set up users and groups
- Set the locale and timezone information
- Install, update, and remove packages (and more)
- Add, change, or update repositories
- Configure encryption, such as SSH and CA certificates
- Configure any client OS setting you can type a command for
- Boot, reboot, and shut down systems
- Install management frameworks

Container Registries

A *container registry* is a repository for container images. Imagine a scenario in which a team of a dozen developers all have their own local folder(s) full of experimental, in-development, and production container images. Compare this to a central repository that you post your images to, that maintains them like a source code version control system would. This would mean that you can always find a particular image when you want it, as well as all its versions and revisions.

Additionally, having a repository helps you to maintain container image security, fix any security issues that occur, and post the secure updated version, all without multiple spreadsheets, sticky notes on monitors, and crippling confusion.

What Is a Container Registry?

There are two main types of container registries, public and private.

Public container registries are accessible to anyone. Private container registries are only accessible to authorized users.

What About Bigger Teams?

Container registries can scale along with your needs. Replicating a single central registry to back up your registry is one application, but another is to have a local and synchronized container registry copy in each of your global regions, which can be a huge time and bandwidth saver as well.

What Are My Container Registry Options?

You know now *why* you'd choose to have a private registry, so the question is *how* do you choose among the many options that are available, both for free or for pay. To help you narrow down the options, the following are the top-rated container registries:

- Amazon Elastic Container Registry (ECR): https://aws.amazon.com/ecr/

- Microsoft Azure Container Registry: https://azure.microsoft.com/en-us/services/container-registry

- Docker Hub: https://hub.docker.com/

- GitHub Package Registry: https://github.blog/2020-09-01-introducing-github-container-registry/

- Google Cloud Artifact Registry: https://cloud.google.com/artifact-registry/

- Red Hat Quay: https://quay.io/

All of the above will give you a great idea of what your container registry options are, and where to get all the information you need to make a solid choice that will serve your needs, large or small, public or private.

Summary

This chapter helped you to understand the concepts and some of the higher-level functions of containers, cloud, and orchestration.

Between Chapter 16, which discussed infrastructure as code, and this chapter, which delved deeper into the cloud and its components, you should now have a clearer and exam-friendly view of the current state of cloud computing and its components as they pertain to the needs of you and your organization.

Exam Preparation Tasks

As mentioned in the section "Goals and Methods" in the Introduction, you have a couple of choices for exam preparation: the exercises here, Chapter 23, "Final Preparation," and the exam simulation questions in the Pearson Test Prep Software Online.

Review All Key Topics

Review the most important topics in this chapter, noted with the Key Topic icon in the margin of the page. Table 17-2 lists these key topics and the page number on which each is found.

Table 17-2 Key Topics for Chapter 17

Key Topic Element	Description	Page Number
List	Kubernetes high-level components	601
List	Kubernetes control plane components	601
List	Kubernetes node components	602
List	Definitions of sidecar containers and ambassador containers	603
Paragraph	Definition of a bind mount	606
List	The two API resources that govern how storage in Kubernetes is handled	607
Paragraph	Definition of an overlay network	608
Paragraph	Why an overlay network is used instead of a bridge	610
Paragraph	When NAT is especially useful	610
Paragraph	Definition of a service mesh, using Istio as an example	611
Paragraph	cloud-init configurations expressed configurations are expressed in	613
Paragraph	Two main types of container registries, public and private	614

Define Key Terms

Define the following key terms from this chapter and check your answers in the glossary:

Kubernetes, Pod, sidecar, ambassador container, Docker Compose, single-node multicontainer, container persistent storage, container networking, overlay network, bridging, network address translation (NAT), host networking, service mesh, bootstrapping, cloud-init, container registries

Review Questions

The answers to these review questions are in Appendix A.

1. What deployed component of Kubernetes is made up of at least one container? (Choose the best answer.)

   a. Node

   b. Sidecar

   c. Pod

   d. Cluster

2. Which of the following types of networks are typically in use when virtual machines or containers are resident and running on a host system? (Choose all that apply.)

   a. Overlier

   b. Host

   c. Switch

   d. Bridge

   e. Token

3. You have an application container inside a Pod on a node and decide to place another container in that Pod to serve as a proxy to the outside. What is the proper term to describe this proxy container?

   a. Helper

   b. Utility

   c. Sidecar

   d. Ingress

4. You have a need for storing data that does not go away when a container is removed, so you create and use which type of storage in Docker or Kubernetes?

    a. Persistent volume

    b. Solid state

    c. Consistent storage

    d. Mount point

5. You have a fairly large Kubernetes cluster providing several micro-services and you need to have between-application encryption and better visibility of application states and stats. What is the likely tool or system that you will now add to your cluster?

    a. Sidecar proxy

    b. Helm

    c. Cloud registry

    d. Service mesh

6. Your cloud development team is going crazy trying to find, retain, and catalog all their development, testing, preproduction, and production container images. What might you consider using to bring some sanity to all this madness?

    a. Mount point

    b. Service mesh

    c. Cloud broker

    d. Container registry

This chapter covers the following topics:

- High Latency Issues

- Low Throughput Issues

- Input/Output Operations per Second Scenarios

- Capacity Issues

- Filesystem Issues

- I/O Scheduler Issues

- Device Issues

- LVM Issues

- Mount Option Issues

The exam objective covered in this chapter is as follows:

- **Objective 4.1:** Given a scenario, analyze and troubleshoot storage issues

## CHAPTER 18

Analyzing and Troubleshooting Storage Issues

In this first chapter of five covering the "Troubleshooting" domain of the Linux+ objectives, you'll notice that we are covering a good bit of ground. The exam objectives in this domain are wide and not very deep, and we'll move briskly through them.

Troubleshooting storage issues is an important skill because just about everything in computing either is being read from or written to storage, all the time, including every block of disk, every page of RAM, and all application data and settings, including logging and user data.

Sometimes storage can cause issues in other parts of the computing cycle (network, CPU, memory, display), such as when storage can't respond fast enough to either reads or writes and therefore slows most everything down, since those other components of the computing cycle are dependent on reading and writing from and to storage.

"Do I Know This Already?" Quiz

The "Do I Know This Already?" quiz enables you to assess whether you should read this entire chapter or simply jump to the "Exam Preparation Tasks" section for review. If you are in doubt, read the entire chapter. Table 18-1 outlines the major headings in this chapter and the corresponding "Do I Know This Already?" quiz questions. You can find the answers in Appendix A, "Answers to the 'Do I Know This Already?' Quizzes and Review Questions."

Table 18-1 "Do I Know This Already?" Foundation Topics Section-to-Question Mapping

Foundation Topics Section	Questions Covered in This Section
High Latency Issues	1
Low Throughput Issues	2
Input/Output Operations per Second Scenarios	3
Capacity Issues	4

Foundation Topics Section	Questions Covered in This Section
Filesystem Issues	5
I/O Scheduler Issues	6
Device Issues	7
LVM Issues	8
Mount Option Issues	9

CAUTION The goal of self-assessment is to gauge your mastery of the topics in this chapter. If you do not know the answer to a question or are only partially sure of the answer, you should mark that question as wrong for purposes of the self-assessment. Giving yourself credit for an answer you correctly guess skews your self-assessment results and might provide you with a false sense of security.

1. Which of the following is a known cause of I/O wait time on a Linux system?

    a. Light volume of read and write requests

    b. Slow RAM speeds

    c. Slow disk access times

    d. High-end RAID array usage

2. Which of the following is typically *not* a cause of low network throughput on a Linux system?

    a. Gigabit Ethernet cards

    b. Maximum use of bandwidth

    c. High number of router hops

    d. Frame losses

3. When you switch from spinning-disk storage arrays to flash-memory storage options, which integer-based measurement becomes mostly irrelevant in measuring transfer rates?

    a. System firmware revision

    b. RAM page count

    c. Disk block size

    d. Input/output operations

4. What is the main cause of a Linux filesystem that seemingly has enough space but cannot create any more files?

   a. Inode exhaustion

   b. Superblock exhaustion

   c. Filehandle exhaustion

   d. Disk block exhaustion

5. When running the **fsck** command to check a filesystem for corruption, what must be true about the state of the filesystem?

   a. It must be mounted.

   b. It must be mounted read-only.

   c. It must be ejected.

   d. It must be unmounted.

6. What is true about changing your I/O scheduler settings on a Linux system? (Choose two.)

   a. All mounted devices are affected.

   b. Changes are per device.

   c. No testing is necessary because it's automatic.

   d. Scheduler changes are immediate.

   e. The system must be rebooted.

7. What is the term for when you mark an SSD device's data blocks for erasure?

   a. CLIP

   b. ERASE

   c. AVAIL

   d. TRIM

8. Which LVM command will display your LVM setup?

   a. **lvmlist**

   b. **lvmdisplay**

   c. **lvmdump**

   d. **lvmconfig**

9. If you get a message on your NFS client that "Server *xxx* is not responding, still trying," what is a likely cause of the problem?

   a. The client is overloaded.

   b. The server IP address was changed.

   c. The DNS server has failed.

   d. The NFS server is overloaded.

Foundation Topics

High Latency Issues

There is often confusion about which terminology to use to describe the various situations or conditions that cause computing to take longer than normal. *High latency* is such a term, and in this section we'll examine what it is and what you can do about it.

High Latency Overview

High latency typically results from what's called I/O wait time. In effect, ***input/output (I/O) wait*** time is how we measure the amount of time a CPU waits for disk I/O operations to complete their full function.

High input/output wait times clearly indicate that a lack of throughput from I/O devices or locations is starving the CPU, or making it idle.

A CPU that is not being fed the instructions that it can handle is not a failure but a symptom of bottlenecks on the rest of the system.

Causes and Symptoms of High Latency

The numerous possible causes of I/O wait time include the following:

- Storage system bottlenecks
- RAM shortage
- Higher use of swap
- Sustained heavy-duty read and write access to devices, particularly off-system sources
- RAID array (I/O) errors, regeneration processing, and low RAID system RAM

Symptoms of high latency commonly include the following:

- Sluggish application performance
- Slow responses to network requests
- High disk access without corresponding performance gains

Diagnosing and Fixing High Latency

The following three utilities will give you a good view of the I/O wait times on your system:

- **top:** The **top** command shows you an overview of what's going on with your system processes, priorities, and wait times.

- **vmstat:** The **vmstat** command gets you closer to the actual issues by showing statistics about the system since its last reboot.

- **iotop:** The **iotop** command reads the I/O usage information from the kernel and produces a table that shows the current and updated I/O figures for processes and/or threads on your system.

Diagnosing with the **top** Command

The **top** command output shows you many details about the system, but the important piece of information for diagnosing high latency is contained to the right of the **wa** (wait time) text, in the **%Cpu(s)** line, as highlighted in the example shown in Figure 18-1. A wa value of 10% or less is generally considered to be normal. A wa value of 20% or more may indicate that the system is experiencing I/O bottlenecks. A wa value of 30% or more may indicate that the system is severely I/O bound.

Executing the **top** command couldn't be simpler; just type the command name and it'll start displaying information. Don't let that apparent simplicity fool you, because the **top** command can show you a great deal of useful information about your system and its health, or lack thereof.

```
top - 21:42:48 up 1 min,  1 user,  load average: 1.26, 0.62, 0.23
Tasks: 119 total,   1 running, 118 sleeping,   0 stopped,   0 zombie
%Cpu(s):  0.0 us,  0.3 sy,  0.0 ni, 99.7 id,  0.0 wa,  0.0 hi,  0.0 si,  0.0 st
MiB Mem :   976.9 total,    422.2 free,    143.5 used,    411.2 buff/cache
MiB Swap:     0.0 total,     0.0 free,     0.0 used.    685.7 avail Mem

   PID USER      PR  NI    VIRT    RES    SHR S  %CPU  %MEM     TIME+ COMMAND
   721 root      20   0       0      0      0 I   0.3   0.0   0:00.04 kworker/0:5-mm_percpu_wq
     1 root      20   0  101900  11544   8504 S   0.0   1.2   0:02.78 systemd
     2 root      20   0       0      0      0 S   0.0   0.0   0:00.00 kthreadd
     3 root       0 -20       0      0      0 I   0.0   0.0   0:00.00 rcu_gp
     4 root       0 -20       0      0      0 I   0.0   0.0   0:00.00 rcu_par_gp
     5 root      20   0       0      0      0 I   0.0   0.0   0:00.02 kworker/0:0-cgroup_destroy
     6 root       0 -20       0      0      0 I   0.0   0.0   0:00.00 kworker/0:0H-kblockd
```

Figure 18-1   Example **top** command output showing the **wa** (wait time) value

NOTE   Although I'd like to show you **top** command output displaying a system with this condition, I/O wait time is hard to cause on purpose. I've seen numbers as high as 80% before on a very distressed server, but that doesn't happen often.

Diagnosing with the **vmstat** Command

The **vmstat** command is another tool available for monitoring your system, and while it's named and described as providing statistics for virtual memory, it does more than that, including statistics for processes, memory, paging, I/O, traps, disks, and CPUs.

The **vmstat** command is similar to the **top** command in that it gives you information in a columnar table, albeit not for every process like **top** does. It also can either display a single output of a moment in time or display updated output over time.

You can invoke **vmstat** either by itself or with options. Just running **vmstat** will display system statistics in a static display of output that is a snapshot of a moment of your system's time. Figure 18-2 shows an example of the output of the **vmstat** command when executed without any options.

```
ubuntu@primary:~$ vmstat
procs -----------memory---------- ---swap-- -----io---- -system-- ------cpu-----
 r  b   swpd   free   buff  cache   si   so    bi    bo   in   cs us sy id wa st
 0  0      0 351944  53748 450136    0    0   119    24  114   78  1  1 99  0  0
```

Figure 18-2   Example output of the **vmstat** command without options

Alternatively, you can control the **vmstat** command by specifying options and a delay amount to cause it to add to its output on a given interval. This is different entirely than the **top** command, which refreshes its entire display in place, every 2 seconds by default.

To use **vmstat** to display a running list of outputs that scrolls down the screen and continues indefinitely unless you specify otherwise, use a delay value, such as the value **2** shown in Figure 18-3.

```
ubuntu@primary:~$ vmstat 2
procs -----------memory---------- ---swap-- -----io---- -system-- ------cpu-----
 r  b   swpd   free   buff  cache   si   so    bi    bo   in   cs us sy id wa st
 0  0      0 351968  53788 450160    0    0    87    18  103   63  0  0 99  0  0
 0  0      0 351960  53788 450160    0    0     0     0   79   23  0  0 100  0  0
 0  0      0 351960  53788 450160    0    0     0     0   93   24  0  0 100  0  0
 0  0      0 351960  53788 450160    0    0     0     0   86   24  0  0 100  0  0
 0  0      0 351960  53788 450160    0    0     0     0   75   21  0  0 100  0  0
 0  0      0 351960  53788 450160    0    0     0     0   88   22  0  0 100  0  0
```

Figure 18-3   Example output of the **vmstat** command using a delay value of **2**

You can quit the continual display by pressing **Ctrl+c**, or if you want to display the output only a specified number of times, with a 2-second delay, you could use the following command:

```
# vmstat 2 10
```

This would run the **vmstat** command with no options at 2-second intervals for a total of ten times and then exit.

You can also use the **watch** command to cause **vmstat** to run at an interval but *not* scroll down the page:

```
# watch vmstat
```

This works because **watch** runs the **vmstat** command every 2 seconds by default, but it replaces the output that is displayed, never taking up more room on the screen, which eliminates the historical perspective of the **vmstat** information as it scrolls down, adding lines of output. That is, using **watch**, you can't scroll down to view more output.

> **NOTE**   It is important to remember that **vmstat** only shows you the information that exists since the last reboot or system startup.

Fixing the Problem

Fixing the problem of high latency requires you to identify which process (or processes) is causing the problem. One of the better ways to do that is to use the **iotop** command, which works similarly to the **top** command but, as its name suggests, shows you the top generators of I/O, ranked from highest to lowest on a screen that refreshes every 1 second by default.

You can just run the **iotop** command by itself, but you might get more helpful results by using one of the more focused subcommands. Figure 18-4 shows an example of the output of the **iotop** command when executed without any options.

```
Total DISK READ:         0.00 B/s | Total DISK WRITE:         3.78 K/s
Current DISK READ:       0.00 B/s | Current DISK WRITE:      11.33 K/s
    TID  PRIO  USER      DISK READ  DISK WRITE  SWAPIN      IO>    COMMAND
    272 be/3 root         0.00 B/s    3.78 K/s  0.00 %   6.84 % [jbd2/vda1-8]
      1 be/4 root         0.00 B/s    0.00 B/s  0.00 %   0.00 % init
      2 be/4 root         0.00 B/s    0.00 B/s  0.00 %   0.00 % [kthreadd]
      3 be/0 root         0.00 B/s    0.00 B/s  0.00 %   0.00 % [rcu_gp]
      4 be/0 root         0.00 B/s    0.00 B/s  0.00 %   0.00 % [rcu_par_gp]
      6 be/0 root         0.00 B/s    0.00 B/s  0.00 %   0.00 % [kworker/0:0H-kblockd]
```

Figure 18-4   Example output of the **iotop** command without any options

One of the most useful **iotop** options is **--only,** which specifies that only the processes that are generating or conducting I/O be shown. You can either run **iotop --only** directly or press the **o** key while **iotop** is already running to toggle on and off the option.

Figure 18-5 shows example output of the **iotop --only** command.

```
Total DISK READ:          0.00 B/s | Total DISK WRITE:          0.00 B/s
Current DISK READ:        0.00 B/s | Current DISK WRITE:       11.15 K/s
    TID  PRIO  USER      DISK READ  DISK WRITE  SWAPIN      IO>    COMMAND
    272 be/3 root         0.00 B/s    0.00 B/s  0.00 %   0.13 % [jbd2/vda1-8]
  22240 be/4 ubuntu       0.00 B/s    0.00 B/s  0.00 %   0.02 % watch find / -iname findtext.out
```

Figure 18-5 Example output of the **iotop --only** command

> **NOTE**   Due to the nature of the information that **iotop** is reading and displaying, you need to either be the root user when you execute it or use the **sudo** command as a prefix; otherwise you'll get a message regarding a Netlink error and an operation not being permitted.

Low Throughput Issues

Low throughput issues is one those overly generally exam objectives that tend to irritate book and courseware authors. Fortunately, this one doesn't faze me, because I know all about issues related to system storage low throughput.

Low Throughput Overview

Many system operators do not clearly understand what throughput is. Practically speaking, *throughput* is how much data can be read or transferred across various system devices and the system bus to other devices, sustainably, over periods of time.

From a throughput perspective, storage issues occur either when hardware fails or when the amount of seeks, reads, and writes exceeds the hardware's capacity to keep up.

Low throughput to and from storage resources will affect all portions of a system, because the lack of throughput starves the CPU for instructions, limits swap in its ability to read and write caches and blocks, and starves the RAM because caches, blocks, swap, and RAM are inextricably linked.

And, of course, if the system is not able to keep up with requests from internal or external users, and applications cannot get a reply to their requests for a service, they will be affected as well.

Causes and Symptoms of Low Throughput

The numerous possible causes of low throughput for storage include the following:

- Failed disk, spinning or solid state
- Malfunctioning storage controller

- RAID disk failure, impending failure, or regeneration

- Too many requests from clients to the system's resources or applications

- Memory issues, causing rereads and lost pages

Symptoms of low throughput might include

- Slow data access

- Excessive disk chattering (spinning devices)

- Read or write (I/O) errors (spinning and solid-state devices)

- Abnormally long load or response times for new modules or functionality for a program or application

- External client requests timing out with no network issues

Diagnosing and Fixing Low Throughput

The following utilities will give you a good view of the throughput on your system:

- **df:** The **df** command can show you how much disk space you have used and is free, both in terms of absolute value and percentages to total disk space.

- **vmstat:** The **vmstat** command shows statistics about the system since its last reboot. See the earlier section "Diagnosing with the **vmstat** Command" for details of the **vmstat** command.

- **iostat:** The **iostat** command shows input and output statistics of various measurements and types for the system.

Diagnosing with the **df** Command

The **df** (or **disk free**) command is used to view the statistics regarding your mounted filesystems, spinning platters, solid-state, or virtual filesystems like swap space.

Often, when you are wondering what is wrong with a system, a good first step for diagnosing potential issues is to check whether disk space is full or nearly full, in which case it is a quick and easy fix. You might be surprised how often lack of free disk space is the cause, given the sparse disk sizes typically in use in virtual machines and, especially, containerized instances of applications.

Figure 18-6 shows an example of the output of the **df** command with **-hT** options to show the disk utilization in % format and display the **Type** column (highlighted) for more information.

```
ubuntu@primary:~$ df -hT
Filesystem      Type        Size  Used Avail Use% Mounted on
udev            devtmpfs    472M     0  472M   0% /dev
tmpfs           tmpfs        98M  932K   97M   1% /run
/dev/vda1       ext4        4.7G  2.8G  2.0G  59% /
tmpfs           tmpfs       489M     0  489M   0% /dev/shm
tmpfs           tmpfs       5.0M     0  5.0M   0% /run/lock
tmpfs           tmpfs       489M     0  489M   0% /sys/fs/cgroup
/dev/loop1      squashfs     47M   47M     0 100% /snap/snapd/16292
/dev/loop2      squashfs     62M   62M     0 100% /snap/core20/1587
/dev/loop3      squashfs    1.2M  1.2M     0 100% /snap/multipass-sshfs/145
/dev/loop4      squashfs     68M   68M     0 100% /snap/lxd/22526
/dev/loop0      squashfs     68M   68M     0 100% /snap/lxd/22753
/dev/loop5      squashfs    128K  128K     0 100% /snap/bare/5
/dev/vda15      vfat        105M  5.2M  100M   5% /boot/efi
tmpfs           tmpfs        98M     0   98M   0% /run/user/1000
:/Users/rossb   fuse.sshfs 1000G     0 1000G   0% /home/ubuntu/Home
/dev/loop8      squashfs     64M   64M     0 100% /snap/core20/1695
/dev/loop7      squashfs     50M   50M     0 100% /snap/snapd/17576
```

Figure 18-6   Example output of the **df -hT** command

The beauty of the **df** command is that it shows you all in one spot the most useful information about all your mounted filesystems. Pay special attention to the **Used** and **Avail** columns, or just look at the **Use%** column to see if there are any current or upcoming issues.

Diagnosing with the **iostat** Command

The **iostat** command shows input and output statistics for the system. The output that you see is gathered from the system's information in the **/proc** and/or **/sys** directories and presented to you by the command.

One of the things **iostat** does is establish a correlation between the length of time the device has been active and the amount of data transferred, on average, during that time.

For example, if you wanted to just see the raw **iostat** output for your mounted filesystems, you'd run the command by itself, as shown in Figure 18-7.

```
ubuntu@primary:~$ iostat
Linux 5.4.0-99-generic (primary)          11/18/22       _x86_64_        (1 CPU)

avg-cpu:  %user   %nice %system %iowait  %steal   %idle
           0.58    0.43    0.53    0.06    0.00   98.40

Device            tps    kB_read/s    kB_wrtn/s    kB_dscd/s    kB_read    kB_wrtn    kB_dscd
loop0            0.00         0.02         0.00         0.00       2423          0          0
loop1            0.17         0.17         0.00         0.00      27151          0          0
loop2            0.01         0.02         0.00         0.00       2515          0          0
loop3            0.01         0.01         0.00         0.00       1062          0          0
loop4            0.00         0.02         0.00         0.00       2422          0          0
loop5            0.00         0.00         0.00         0.00          7          0          0
loop6            0.00         0.01         0.00         0.00        958          0          0
loop7            0.12         0.13         0.00         0.00      19884          0          0
loop8            0.00         0.00         0.00         0.00        477          0          0
loop9            0.00         0.00         0.00         0.00          4          0          0
scd0             0.00         0.00         0.00         0.00        266          0          0
vda              1.01         9.29        26.62        13.86    1467172    4204409    2188453
```

Figure 18-7   Example output of the **iostat** command without any options

The **iostat** command can show an incredible amount of data, much too much to fit on any reasonably sized screen at once, so familiarize yourself with the options that will show the data you want and perhaps think of making groupings of those options to show you certain types of transactions. Because **iostat** can show so much output, and because you want to be able to read your output without a lot of hassles and scrolling, you can combine some helpful options like the following, which help make the output easier to read on a regular-sized terminal:

- **-h:** This option shows your output in a more human-readable format, such as 1M for 1024 kilobytes.

- **-m:** This option simply forces the use of displaying data in megabytes, instead of the kilobytes that human-readable format causes.

- **-z:** This option causes no output to be displayed for devices that have not had any activity during the measurement period.

With those options added to **iostat**, you can see in Figure 18-8 that the amount of data displayed fits nicely on the screen, but also it shows only those devices that have had activity since the last reboot, and in human-readable and megabyte formats.

```
ubuntu@primary:~$ iostat -hmz
Linux 5.4.0-99-generic (primary)          11/18/22          _x86_64_          (1 CPU)

avg-cpu:  %user   %nice %system %iowait  %steal   %idle
           0.6%    0.4%    0.5%    0.1%    0.0%   98.4%

        tps    MB_read/s    MB_wrtn/s    MB_dscd/s     MB_read    MB_wrtn    MB_dscd Device
       0.00         0.0k         0.0k         0.0k        2.4M       0.0k       0.0k loop0
       0.17         0.2k         0.0k         0.0k       26.5M       0.0k       0.0k loop1
       0.01         0.0k         0.0k         0.0k        2.5M       0.0k       0.0k loop2
       0.01         0.0k         0.0k         0.0k        1.0M       0.0k       0.0k loop3
       0.00         0.0k         0.0k         0.0k        2.4M       0.0k       0.0k loop4
       0.00         0.0k         0.0k         0.0k        7.0k       0.0k       0.0k loop5
       0.00         0.0k         0.0k         0.0k      958.0k       0.0k       0.0k loop6
       0.12         0.1k         0.0k         0.0k       19.4M       0.0k       0.0k loop7
       0.00         0.0k         0.0k         0.0k      477.0k       0.0k       0.0k loop8
       0.00         0.0k         0.0k         0.0k        4.0k       0.0k       0.0k loop9
       0.00         0.0k         0.0k         0.0k      266.0k       0.0k       0.0k scd0
       1.01         9.3k        26.7k        13.9k        1.4G       4.0G       2.1G vda
```

Figure 18-8   Example output of the **iostat** command with helpful format options

NOTE   As previously mentioned, the **iostat** command has lots of options to display a wide variety of data sets. They are too numerous to cover here, and beyond the scope of the Linux+ example, but to gain practical experience, you'll want to spend some time experimenting to see what data display options will get you the information you want and need.

Input/Output Operations per Second Scenarios

NOTE   Please note that low throughput is linked with the other topics in the first part of this objective. Low throughput, high latency and *low IOPS* all contribute to how sluggish, unresponsive, or overburdened a system "feels" to you the operator, or to the clients it is responding to.

IOPS stands for Input/Output Operations per Second. It is a performance measurement used to characterize computer storage devices like hard disk drives (HDD), solid state drives (SSD), and storage area networks (SAN).

IOPS measures the number of read and write operations that a storage device can perform in a second. A higher IOPS value indicates that the storage device is faster and can handle more data requests. A lower IOPS value indicates there will be performance issues with the storage device.

IOPS Overview

Important: IOPS are much less important now that a lot of "disk" is flash or memory storage! IOPS were critical to measure when there were spinning platters with read/write heads that needed to find the data, position themselves, and complete a read/write transaction. This is completely irrelevant when flash memory storage is used, because there is no "seek time"—there is just the accessing of a particular memory address.

With the flash memory scenario discussed previously, let's turn to what happens to your number of IOPS when different workload scenarios are played out.

Scenario 1: Transferring Ten 500MB Files

In this scenario, you have the need to read ten files from a disk, each of the individual files is 1MB in size. This set of reads would take 10 IOPS, with the typical spinning disk able to handle 20 times that number of IOPS easily. This would give you 5GB of data being transferred with an effective throughput of 50MB/s.

> **NOTE**   Remember that IOPS is *not* the actual transfer rate. The IOPS are made to the controller and disk and then cause the transfers to happen.

This number of IOPS is well within a range that should not cause a bottleneck, even if the disk is servicing other requests.

Scenario 2: Transferring 5,000 1MB Files

In this scenario, you have the need to read 5,000 files from a disk, each of which files is 1MB in size. This set of reads would take 5,000 IOPS and, for a spinning disk, you'd get probably 200 IOPS, so it would take some time longer than the example in scenario 1 for the controller and disk to handle the sheer number of IOPS.

Though the files are relatively small, you can't crowd all those IOPS into the queue at once, so the transfer time might take measurably longer.

Why IOPS Are Effectively Irrelevant

First, as previously stated, IOPS are important only for spinning disks. They are essentially meaningless to those operating from a flash-based disk, as there is no seek time to position the read/write heads, just reads/writes from a particular memory register.

Secondly, as the two previous scenarios show, counting IOPS as a measure of transfer rate is also meaningless. It's like saying that your car can achieve 14,000 RPM but not mentioning which gear you are in when revving it up that high. 14,000 RPM in first gear is a guarantee of slower speeds, and a ruined engine in most vehicles, but 14,000 RPM in fifth or sixth gear while already at speed on the highway means some serious velocity!

NOTE In summary, think of IOPS, high latency, and throughput as being linked—you can't have issues with one and not have issues with the others.

Capacity Issues

Capacity issues come from several effects, at least one of which will be completely foreign or incomprehensible to those joining the Linux world from Windows.

Causes and Symptoms of Capacity Issues

The numerous possible causes of *capacity issues* for Linux include the following:

- Disk controller/RAID controller failure
- Hard disk or SSD failure
- RAID software failure
- Disk corruption
- Filesystem corruption
- Disk quota issues
- Low disk space
- Inode exhaustion

Symptoms of capacity issues might include any of the following:

- Error messages that indicate there is "No space left on device."
- Error messages that indicate there is a "Read-only file system."
- You see free disk space, but can't create files.
- Your drive is making noises, or there are mysterious delays with I/O.
- Your system is running hot or the environment in the server location is too hot.

- Files and directories are mislabeled, they contain incorrect entries, and so forth.

- You get a message about a drive failing, or see logged messages regarding RAID volumes and disks.

Diagnosing and Fixing Capacity Issues

Since there are so many potential capacity issues and the Linux+ objectives list only *low disk space* and *inode exhaustion*, we'll focus on those in this section. To see all the known filesystems and their limits, consult the Wikipedia page titled "Comparison of file systems" and click the **Limits** link in the Contents pane on the left. While inodes are only mentioned once or twice, the **Max number of files** column is where you can see appropriate information for the filesystems. Just look for the ones that Linux uses.

The following utilities will help you diagnose capacity issues on your system:

- **df:** The **df** command was introduced earlier in the context of diagnosing low throughput, and it's also pertinent in this section because of its ability to show information about the number and percentages of inodes being used and remaining on the filesystems.

- **du:** Similar to the **dir /s** command in DOS or Windows, the **du** command is very useful for showing the space utilization of a file, directory, or even an entire tree of files and directories. Its **-s** (summarization) parameter is the most useful, I find.

- **find:** The **find** command is most helpful with inode exhaustion problems, as it's able to find files and show the number of inodes in use in any given directory or set of directories. The **find** command also is great for finding files that are larger than a given size.

Diagnosing with the df Command

The **df** (**disk free**) command in this scenario is used to display disk usage statistics, along with the number of inodes overall, those in use, and those free. It also can display these statistics in human-readable format (KB, MB, and GB) and in percentages.

As an example of how **df** can be used to diagnose capacity-related issues, Figure 18-9 shows the output of the **df -hT** command, where **-T** shows the optional column denoting filesystem type and **-h** displays human-readable output so that we can easily see the stats we need.

```
ubuntu@primary:~$ df -hT
Filesystem      Type        Size  Used Avail Use% Mounted on
udev            devtmpfs    472M     0  472M   0% /dev
tmpfs           tmpfs        98M  908K   97M   1% /run
/dev/vda1       ext4        4.7G  2.8G  2.0G  59% /
tmpfs           tmpfs       489M     0  489M   0% /dev/shm
tmpfs           tmpfs       5.0M     0  5.0M   0% /run/lock
tmpfs           tmpfs       489M     0  489M   0% /sys/fs/cgroup
/dev/loop0      squashfs    128K  128K     0 100% /snap/bare/5
/dev/loop2      squashfs     68M   68M     0 100% /snap/lxd/22753
/dev/loop3      squashfs     68M   68M     0 100% /snap/lxd/22526
/dev/loop1      squashfs     62M   62M     0 100% /snap/core20/1587
/dev/loop4      squashfs    1.2M  1.2M     0 100% /snap/multipass-sshfs/145
/dev/loop5      squashfs     50M   50M     0 100% /snap/snapd/17576
/dev/loop6      squashfs     64M   64M     0 100% /snap/core20/1695
/dev/loop7      squashfs     47M   47M     0 100% /snap/snapd/16292
/dev/vda15      vfat        105M  5.2M  100M   5% /boot/efi
tmpfs           tmpfs        98M     0   98M   0% /run/user/1000
:/Users/rossb   fuse.sshfs 1000G     0 1000G   0% /home/ubuntu/Home
```

Figure 18-9   Example output of the **df -hT** command

The highlighted line in Figure 18-9 shows the **/dev/vda1** filesystem, which is of the type ext4. The important statistics here are the values in the **Size**, **Used**, **Avail**, and **Use%** columns, which indicate no serious disk capacity issues currently exist.

Additionally, for the purposes of checking to see how many inodes you may be using for each of your filesystems, use the **df -ih** command, the output of which is shown in Figure 18-10.

```
ubuntu@primary:~$ df -ih
Filesystem      Inodes IUsed IFree IUse% Mounted on
udev              118K   401  118K    1% /dev
tmpfs             123K   622  122K    1% /run
/dev/vda1         630K  134K  497K   22% /
tmpfs             123K     1  123K    1% /dev/shm
tmpfs             123K     3  123K    1% /run/lock
tmpfs             123K    18  123K    1% /sys/fs/cgroup
/dev/loop0          29    29     0  100% /snap/bare/5
/dev/loop2         802   802     0  100% /snap/lxd/22753
/dev/loop1         12K   12K     0  100% /snap/core20/1587
/dev/loop4          41    41     0  100% /snap/multipass-sshfs/145
/dev/loop6         12K   12K     0  100% /snap/core20/1695
/dev/vda15           0     0     0    - /boot/efi
tmpfs             123K    26  123K    1% /run/user/1000
:/Users/rossb     954M     0  954M    0% /home/ubuntu/Home
/dev/loop8         491   491     0  100% /snap/snapd/17883
/dev/loop7         815   815     0  100% /snap/lxd/23991
```

Figure 18-10   Example output of the **df -ih** command

Once again, noting the highlighted line, you see that the total number of inodes is shown in the **Inodes** column, the amount in use in the **Iused** column, the amount remaining in the **Ifree** column, and the amount in use as a percentage in the **Iuse%** column.

> **NOTE**   If you are tired of looking for your load-bearing actual memory or spinning disks in the **df** command or other command output, you can use the **grep** command to filter out everything but what you're looking for.

Diagnosing with the **du** Command

The **du** command in this scenario is used to list the number of inodes in use by a file, set of files, or a directory and its contents, all the way down its tree structure, and even provide a summary of these numbers.

Figure 18-11 shows several commands being run against the **/etc/ssh** directory, including the **du --inodes** command, all of which are explained in the following paragraphs.

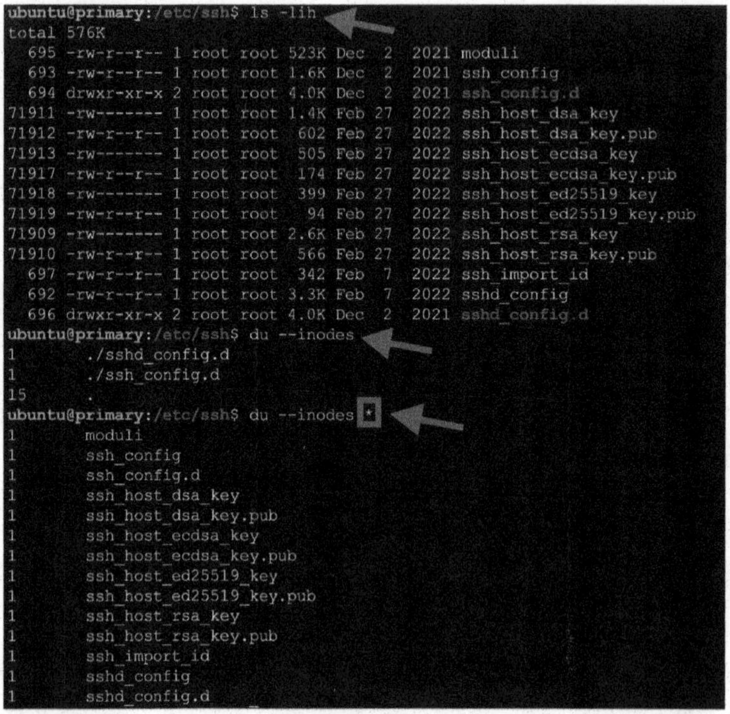

Figure 18-11   Example output of the **ls -lih** and **du --inodes** commands

The top superimposed arrow in Figure 18-11 points to the **ls -lih** command, the output of which displays the contents of the **/etc/ssh** directory, its space utilization in human-readable output, and the inode numbers as the first column of the output. Those inode numbers are very useful, but for purposes of diagnosing capacity issues, what we really want to see is the number of inodes in use by the directory contents, not what those inode numbers are.

The middle arrow in Figure 18-11 points to the useful **du --inodes** command, which shows that 15 inodes are in use. If you total up the inodes listed in the **ls -lih** output, you come up one short, which is solved by knowing that the current directory (.) is counted as an inode too.

The bottom arrow points to the addition of the * character, which causes the **du --inodes** command to individually list the individual items in the directory and how many inodes they use.

NOTE   Don't be confused if you see references to "extents," which are used to save metadata space for large and, therefore, multiblock files. When a multiblock file is contiguous, or takes up sequential space on the filesystem, you will see filesystems such as Ext4 using a starting and ending address called extents, basically to say "this file goes from here to there." This saves space for metadata, which may not seem like much, but if you have multiple millions of files on disk, it all adds up!

Diagnosing with the **find** Command

The **find** command in this scenario is used to seek out and list for your further use all files that are above a given size, from whatever starting location you wish.

In Figure 18-12 you see the **find** command being used to locate files that are above 16KB in size, starting with the **/etc** directory and going all the way through all of its contents.

```
ubuntu@primary:/etc$ find /etc -size +16k -exec du -h {} \; 2> /dev/null
28K     /etc/apparmor.d/usr.lib.snapd.snap-confine.real
64K     /etc/udev/rules.d/70-snap.snapd.rules
28K     /etc/wpa_supplicant/functions.sh
192K    /etc/ssl/certs/ca-certificates.crt
28K     /etc/ld.so.cache
100K    /etc/lvm/lvm.conf
44K     /etc/grub.d/10_linux_zfs
20K     /etc/grub.d/10_linux
24K     /etc/mime.types
524K    /etc/ssh/moduli
88K     /etc/vmware-tools/vgauth/schemas/XMLSchema.xsd
```

Figure 18-12   Example output of the **find -size** command

The command used is slightly longer than usual, but here is a breakdown of what is happening:

- **find /etc:** This executes the **find** command against the starting point of the **/etc** directory, and all of its contents.

- **-size +16K:** This sets a parameter that says if the filesystem object is larger than 16KB, it's a match.

- **-exec du -h {}:** This executes the **du -h** command against each of the full path and filename output items, and instead of displaying just them, it shows the **du -h** output on subsequent lines as if it had been executed manually on each item, the **{}** being where the output is grabbed and used.

- **\;:** This causes the **find** command to run the **-exec** portion multiple times, until all the output is processed.

- **2> /dev/null:** This sends all standard error (stderr) output to the black hole of the system, effectively discarding it and not displaying those input/output errors.

I'm sure you recognize the usefulness of a command that can be easily altered to show objects on your filesystems of essentially any size or larger! The examples shown use the K or kilobyte notation, but M for megabyte and G for gigabyte are also options, as well a number of other more technical options.

Read the **find** manual (**man find**) page for a whole lot more information. The **find** command is an immense and very useful command, one of the very best in the entire world of Unix and Linux.

NOTE *Inode exhaustion* occurs when you run out of file notations, or the ability to have additional files on the filesystem, even though there may be plenty of space left. Some filesystems do not have set or static inode tables or amounts, but instead generate more inodes as they are needed.

Filesystem Issues

Linux+ objective 4.1 specifically lists filesystem corruption and mismatch as filesystem issues, so the focus of this section is directly on those topics.

Filesystem Corruption Overview

Linux is very robust, but it can suffer from corruption of its filesystems. *Filesystem corruption* usually results from a terminated write operation, and can be relatively mild to extremely severe, depending on what was happening at the time the write (or, in most cases, many writes) was taking place.

The worst cases are where you find a system that has been rebooted and is showing error messages that state that the filesystem is corrupted and that you should consider running the **fsck** command.

Causes and Symptoms of Filesystem Corruption

There are a number of possible causes of filesystem corruption, including the following:

- A failure of hardware (or virtual hardware in case of a virtual machine)

- An ungraceful (forceful) dismount of a filesystem (USB most often)

- Actual bad blocks on a spinning disk, or flash memory errors on an SSD (relatively rare)

- Software issues in packages that are designed to directly interact with a low-level disk (rare)

- Power failures or "accidental" ungraceful or abrupt shutdowns (often)

Symptoms of filesystem corruption might include any of the following:

- Corrupted or incomplete data files

- Odd characters inserted into data files or directory entries that appear to be garbled or non-typical

- Nonbootable system drives with filesystem check errors

- Unmountable filesystems, particularly ones that are typically auto-mounted or are part of the system normally

- Entries for files and directories that contain no data, or when inspected are not linked to any data blocks

- System shuts down and won't reboot

- A normally writeable filesystem is suddenly read-only

Diagnosing and Fixing Filesystem Corruption

There is one main utility to diagnose filesystem corruption issues on your system:

- **fsck:** The **fsck** command is used to inspect and repair corrupted filesystems. There are a number of filesystem-specific **fsck** versions that can be used directly, such as **fsck.ext4**, **fsck.btrfs**, and so on.

There are other utilities that can be used to diagnose and repair Logical Volume Manager (LVM) and RAID subsystems, but those are described in the respective sections later in the chapter.

Diagnosing and Fixing Filesystem Corruption with the fsck Command

The **fsck** command is really a suite of tools, used either by specifying a filesystem type as a parameter to the main **fsck** command or by using one of the **fsck** filesystem-specific helper utilities (such as **fsck.ext4**) directly.

Either way, the helper utility code is what is actually used to do the diagnosing and repairing of the filesystem.

> **NOTE**   This methodology is also used in the creation of filesystems, as the **mkfs** command uses a similar helper utility structure.

Regardless of what the actual error is, you'll need to eventually use the **fsck** command suite to diagnose and repair the filesystem that was corrupted, so we'll focus on using the utility as it will likely occur in real life.

> **CAUTION**   *Do not* run the **fsck** command on a mounted filesystem! Doing so can cause severe and lasting damage. You should run **fsck** *only* on a read-only filesystem, and typically **fsck** is run on all filesystems as a part of the booting process, or as a part of the early service initialization process.

Figure 18-13 shows the dire warning message you would receive if you were to attempt to run **fsck** against a write-enabled filesystem (don't do it!).

```
ubuntu@primary:~$ fsck
fsck from util-linux 2.34
e2fsck 1.45.5 (07-Jan-2020)
/dev/vda1 is mounted.



WARNING!!! The filesystem is mounted.   If you continue you ***WILL***
cause ***SEVERE*** filesystem damage.

Do you really want to continue<n>?
```

Figure 18-13   Example output of the **fsck** command on a mounted filesystem

The one thing you *can* do while a filesystem is mounted as writeable is to do a dry-run on it using the **-N** parameter, which essentially looks at what *would* be done if it were a real **fsck** session, and reports back to you the results, such as you see in Figure 18-14.

```
ubuntu@primary:~$ sudo fsck -N
fsck from util-linux 2.34
[/usr/sbin/fsck.ext4 (1) -- /] fsck.ext4 /dev/vda1
[/usr/sbin/fsck.vfat (1) -- /boot/efi] fsck.vfat /dev/vda15
```

Figure 18-14 Example output of the **fsck -N** command on a mounted filesystem

All the filesystems on a Linux computing device can be unmounted and checked, except the root filesystem, which *technically* can be remounted as read-only, but it's a very tricky operation to perform on a running system.

You're much better off taking the system to the equivalent of Runlevel 1, which on a systemd device would be the **rescue.target**. To get to the **rescue.target**, as root issue the command:

```
systemctl isolate rescue.target
```

This will take the system to a point of having very little running, and allow you to use the **fsck** command on the root filesystem safely.

Alternatively, on a Ubuntu system you can reboot the device, press the **Shift** key while it's rebooting, and then enter the Advanced Options for Ubuntu menu shown in Figure 18-15.

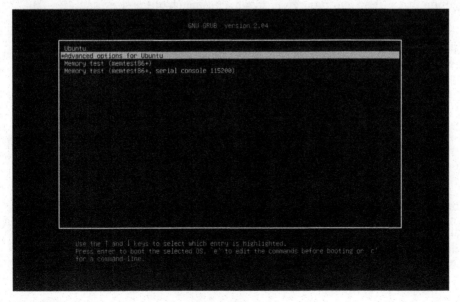

Figure 18-15 The Advanced Options for Ubuntu menu on boot

From there you can follow the prompts to run **fsck** on your root and all other file-systems. Then, after the system is done, you will be prompted to reboot normally if all has been fixed.

Summary

The **fsck** command is implemented across Linux distributions in different ways, but the main concept is that it is used when something really bad has happened and your filesystem(s) has been corrupted, in whatever way that manifests, and it's time to fix it and hopefully get the system back up and running.

Filesystem Mismatch Overview

Filesystem mismatch is an issue that occurs when you have tried to shrink a partition underlying a filesystem to be smaller than the filesystem itself. Imagine that you have a bed that is just long enough for the person lying on it and suddenly you shorten the bed significantly. This is similar to shrinking the underlying partition and leaving the filesystem's "feet" or "head" hanging off the end of it, only with likely or certain data loss from this mismatch of partition and filesystem.

Causes and Symptoms of File Mismatch

The main cause of this issue is that you have inaccurately resized the underlying partition that a filesystem is on, resulting in a mismatch of the sizes.

A likely symptom of this problem is that data cannot be written (as it's trying to write to a filesystem that is not backed by the partition, so doesn't really exist) or inexplicable *input/output errors* occur while applications are trying to save items to disk.

Diagnosing and Fixing File Mismatch

Mismatch issues can be particularly vexing, as they are not very obvious, but I'll show you how to troubleshoot them properly.

Diagnosing a Mismatch Issue

The main utility that will show you what the problem is, is the **e2fsck** program, which will report back something similar to the following output:

```
$ e2fsck /dev/sda1
e2fsck 1.45.5 (20-Mar-2020)
The filesystem size (according to the superblock) is 19345678
blocks
```

```
The physical size of the device is 178945672 blocks
Either the superblock or the partition table is likely to be
corrupt!
Abort<y>?
```

The big question is, did you just resize the underlying partition or did you also use that extra "free space" to create and format an additional partition? If you did create and format another partition, you may have done irretrievable damage to your filesystem, but fortunately you have backups of the data or another copy somewhere, right?

Fixing a Mismatch Issue

The fix for this issue is to use the **parted** tool to increase the partition back up to *at least* the size of the filesystem. Hopefully you didn't already do something else with that "free space," because if you did, there is only a chance that your data is still there.

The first thing you'll want to do is resize that partition back up to match or exceed slightly the size of the filesystem, using the **parted** command (or another way of your choosing). Since you probably got into this mess with **parted**, it's a great way to get back out of it! Just retrace your steps.

NOTE A very important tip is to always resize your filesystem first, and pay very close attention to the filesystem's block size, because you may be looking at a size that is *not* similar to the typical ext2/3/4 block size of 4K. This would be similar to getting an estimate for work to be done in British pounds and then trying to pay the same numeric amount with U.S. dollars—there is a definite gap there!

I/O Scheduler Issues

I/O schedulers are an interesting and sometimes anachronistic (that is, kind of old-fashioned) part of how Linux systems get data to and from the right places at the most efficient and effective speeds.

NOTE The structure of this section differs from that of the other sections in the chapter because the only real "issue" with a given I/O scheduler is that it just is not as efficient as another scheduler more suited to grouping your requests.

I/O Scheduler Overview

Linux has a number of options for attempting to order how I/O requests (either reads or writes) are performed. For example, Linux will try to group together requests that are for similarly located data addresses to make handling requests for things more efficient.

This technique would be similar to cooking a big meal and finding yourself making a dozen trips to each part of the kitchen—pantry, refrigerator, cupboards, drawers—whereas if you had looked at the plan for the meal prior to preparing it and identified which ingredients and utensils you need from each location, you could have made a few trips to retrieve all the ingredients and utensils located near each other all at once, saving a lot of time and energy.

You can let Linux choose the most likely I/O scheduler option, or you can fiddle with the options yourself and find the best one by trial and error.

Types of I/O Schedulers

There are two types of I/O schedulers: the older version, which has been in place for many years, and the newer (multiqueue) versions introduced a few versions ago. In the case of Ubuntu, the newer schedulers are the only ones included and are used by default.

NOTE *Multiqueue*, as it pertains to storage devices, refers to the ability to achieve many IOPS by queuing up requests through an API and having newer, faster, and more capable storage devices accept those I/O requests simultaneously and process them very quickly.

Older I/O schedulers include

- **deadline:** The deadline scheduler is used to fix some starvation (lack of throughput) issues in other schedulers. This scheduler prefers read requests over write requests, making it great for most read operations such as informational websites.

- **cfq:** cfq stands for completely fair queuing and, as the name indicates, the cfq scheduler gives precisely the same amount of preference for reads and writes, which may result in wasted or idle time if a read or write takes less time than allocated.

- **noop:** The noop scheduler is great for grouping requests, but not for sorting them, which works really well for random or flash/SSD devices because the traditional seek times are not an issue—there are no heads or platters, so seeks are just to a memory address.

Newer I/O schedulers are all multiqueue-specific and include

- **bfq:** The bfq (budget fair queuing) scheduler is a complex beastie, and can be advantageous to desktop or large application codebase operations. It features fair sharing based on the sector counts requested and doesn't use time slices. It is not recommended for slow devices or CPUs.

- **kyber:** The kyber scheduler is a simple and very fast scheduler that is tuned to limit the number of requests per dispatch, and thus ensures that there isn't a long wait time due to a large number of grouped requests. The kyber scheduler keeps things moving!

- **mq-deadline:** The mq-deadline scheduler is very similar to the older deadline scheduler but is tuned for moderate all-around performance and doesn't task the CPU(s) unduly.

- **none:** The none scheduler is a plain-vanilla scheduler that doesn't do any request ordering or grouping, has the least overhead of the schedulers, and is a very good choice for NVMe, flash, and SSD devices.

Viewing and Setting I/O Schedulers

With something as important as I/O scheduling, you'd think there would be a fancy interface or something more eventful than echo'ing text to a file in the **/sys** directory, but that's exactly how you query and then change your I/O scheduler!

NOTE Remember that I/O schedulers can be specified on a per-block-device basis. This can be confusing, and most settings of this level or type are set on a system-wide basis.

Viewing the Current I/O Scheduler

The I/O scheduler you currently have in use is viewable, again, on a per-block-device basis, so you'll be spending a lot of time looking at files in that directory.

To view the current scheduler for any of your block devices, use the following formula:

```
$ cat /sys/block/<devicename>/queue/scheduler
[mq-deadline] none
```

In this output, the active scheduler is listed in square brackets, [mq-deadline], and the other scheduler that is available (and there may be several!) is listed after that with no brackets.

Setting the Current I/O Scheduler

Setting an I/O scheduler is just a matter of putting the right text in the right files, or profile in the case of Red Hat and TuneD, which is definitely out of scope for our discussion here.

The first and simplest way to change an I/O scheduler is to echo the scheduler string you want to make active into the proper file in the **/sys** directory tree. For example, running the following command as root sets the mq-deadline scheduler for the **/dev/sda** block device:

```
$ sudo echo none > /sys/block/sda/queue/scheduler
```

Verify that this took effect with

```
$ cat /sys/block/sda/queue/scheduler
[none] mq-deadline
```

As you can see, it simply made the other scheduler that's available, none, the active one.

> **NOTE**   Be aware that if you make this sort of change, it is not persistent! The next section describes how to make a scheduler change persistent.

Making the I/O Scheduler Change Persistent

While setting an I/O scheduler is just a matter of putting the right text in the right files. Rebooting or unmounting will cause the scheduler to revert to the default.

The different distributions may have differing methods for making the I/O scheduler change persistent, but a very simple way to make the scheduler change persistent is to add it as a configuration line in the **/etc/udev/rules.d/60-schedulers.rules** file (if it doesn't exist, simply use **vim** as root and make the file).

You'll want to add a configuration line per block device that you want to make scheduler changes to, such as the **/dev/vda** device configuration line shown here:

```
ACTION=="add|change", KERNEL=="vda", ATTR{queue/scheduler}="none"
```

Reboot the system, and when it comes back up, verify that the change is in place with the command

```
$ cat /sys/block/sda/queue/scheduler
[none] mq-deadline
```

As you can see, the change has been made. There are other ways to effect a persistent I/O scheduler change, including using the GRUB configuration, but the method demonstrated here is the simplest and most direct.

> **NOTE**   For purposes of the Linux+ exam, probably the most important takeaways from this section are that you know what an I/O scheduler is and does, that I/O schedulers are per block device, and that changing the I/O scheduler is not persistent unless you explicitly make it persistent.

Device Issues

Identifying *device issues* is an important part of troubleshooting system issues, in that a physical device that fails is a real blocker, whereas software failures are often fixable just by replacing or reloading the software, or applying a patch to it.

All of the device issues covered in this section are similar in that they involve physical problems in devices that hold or transport or store data. Also, they are the specific storage device issues listed in objective 4.1, so you need to know how to diagnose and fix them for the Linux+ exam.

NVMe Issues Overview

Non-volatile memory express, or *NVMe*, is a newer protocol for managing flash or SSD storage that has some significant advantages, and a few shortcomings.

> **NOTE**   The official name is NVM Express (NVMe), but the Linux+ exam objectives list this as "Non-volatile memory express".

NVMe differs some from other flash storage management protocols, but varies greatly from traditional SATA and SCSI drive management protocols, primarily since those are tuned mostly for spinning drives with platters and read/write heads and suffer from seek times, or the amount of time it takes the drive controller to position the heads over the right set of blocks on the right platter.

Causes and Symptoms of NVMe Issues

The following are possible causes of NVMe issues:

- Mismatch of other components with NVMe
- NVMe not fully implemented on a device or controller

- Using NVMe devices on older systems in an attempt to improve performance
- Stranding NVMe SSDs on their own instead of using them as cache for larger devices or arrays
- Using NVMe devices improperly, such as for caching workloads with a very high amount of randomized write requests

Symptoms of NVMe issues might include any of the following:

- Less-than-expected performance gains
- Too-fast NVMe disk access clogging other, slower components with through-put that is too high
- NVMe devices overheating and failing even under modest workload requirements

Diagnosing and Fixing NVMe Issues

These two utilities will help you to diagnose and fix NVMe issues on your system:

- **hddtemp:** The **hddtemp** command reads your drive's information from the command line and displays a temperature reading, if there is one. This may not work on virtual machine drives.

- **nvme:** This set of tools (contained in the nvme-cli package) provides access to, management of, and information about NVMe devices on Linux. With at least 100 utilities, the **nvme-cli** package is the best source for keeping your NVMe devices healthy.

The world of NVMe devices is still growing, and although there are various man-agement schemes, they are not as fully implemented as they eventually will be. These management schemes are very much out of scope for this objective.

Using the **nvme** Command-Line Tool

As mentioned, the nvme-cli package contains around 100 tools that can be used to manage your NVMe devices, including the ability to connect those devices to the NVMe management frameworks, allow you to get and set information, and do much more to your NVMe devices.

To get a listing of your NVMe devices, use the following command:

```
$: sudo nvme list
Node              SN              Model
Namespace Usage                   Format        FW Rev
```

```
----------------  --------------------  ----------------------------
--------------  ---------  -------------------------  ------------
----  --------
/dev/nvme0n1      SN1234567890123456878  Parallels Virtual NVMe
Disk              1               34.36  GB /  34.36  GB       512
B +   0 B
```

As you can see, the display of the output requires a much longer set of characters than is available here (or any standard terminal window). There is a lot of room for improvement in these utilities and how they are used and display information.

Another command sequence you can use to get more information about the NVMe devices on your system is shown in Figure 18-16.

```
~ $: sudo nvme list-subsys
nvme-subsys0 - NQN=nqn.2014.08.org.nvmexpress:lab80000SN123456789012345678Parallels Virtual NVMe Disk
\
+- nvme0 pcie 0000:00:1f.7 live
```

Figure 18-16   The **nvme** command with **list-subsys** subcommand

For purposes of the Linux+ exam, the main takeaway about troubleshooting NVMe is to know why it's in use and how to best take advantage of it, while keeping an eye on how it could be misused and cause you problems in the ways described in this section.

Solid-State Drive Issues Overview

Whereas NVMe is more of a drive management protocol, solid-state drives, or *SSD*s, are flash-based drives that are, basically, just big chunks of RAM.

Unlike spinning disk drives, which suffer issues related to moving parts, SSDs suffer issues related to transient voltages, software errors, wearing out, and so forth.

Causes and Symptoms of SSD Issues

There are several possible causes of SSD issues, including

- New devices conflicting with the drive
- A cable being unplugged (if applicable; many SSDs are soldered into the motherboard)
- Application or software issues
- Module or driver issues
- Bad blocks or sectors

- Filesystem corruption

Symptoms of SSD issues might include any of the following:

- Extreme seek times, general system slowness
- Frequent system crashes without any other known issues
- Periodic failure to boot
- Error messages about no disk being found
- Suddenly finding your drive is mounted read-only

Diagnosing and Fixing SSD Issues

Unlike spinning disk drives, SSDs and flash memory-based drives often don't have an activity light, so you can't just look at a light and see a lack of activity. If you note one or more of the symptoms previously listed and suspect that an SSD drive may be failing, you can take the following steps to address the possible issues:

Step 1. Check all physical connections. You cannot imagine how many times a physical cable has come loose and simply needed to be connected.

Step 2. Boot the system and inspect the BIOS or setup utility to see if the drive is listed and whether there are any utilities that would allow you to trouble-shoot the device at this level. If there are, run the utility. Try this at least twice before giving up on this method.

Step 3. Use the emergency mode on your distribution to run the **fsck** command on the device (as described earlier in this chapter).

Step 4. Visit the website of the drive manufacturer or system manufacturer and see if there is an update to the firmware for the controller or device. If so, download and install the update. I have fixed several issues this way over the years.

Step 5. Inspect the Legacy Support BIOS settings, especially if the device has been moved from an older device to a newer one.

Step 6. View the BIOS settings to see if that has gotten changed or if a power outage has reset it.

NOTE   There aren't any utilities that will help with an SSD failure. Most of the issues described here are that of the drive not being accessible, or recognized, whereas it's impossible to run a utility from a drive that isn't able to be read.

SSD Trim

Many sysadmins have no idea what *SSD TRIM* is, and generally that's not a problem, but you need to know what it is since it's listed in the Linux+ objectives. Understanding it will also help you to be a better administrator of your devices, particularly SSD devices.

When you first install an SSD disk that has never been written to (or just tested once), keep in mind that it will survive a finite number of writes before its end of life, as every write action causes a minute but important amount of damage to the layer of oxide that surrounds each data cell.

The very common NAND-based SSDs have a read and write unit of one page, and those pages are often arranged in 128-page data blocks.

A key difference here from other devices is that the controller reads and writes data at a *page* level but erases at a *data block* level.

NOTE Data blocks and pages can come in many sizes. Very common data block sizes range from 64 to 256 pages per block, depending on configuration. Page sizes typically range from 4K to 16K, also depending on configuration parameters.

Imagine an array of 128 Post-it Note stacks that represent the pages located in a data block.

If you write on a note, you can't write on it again, but must pull it off and discard it (aka garbage collection, covered in the next section) so that you can write on the one below it. Eventually, you'll run out of fresh ones to write on, and that stack location is unusable. This analogy is somewhat similar to how an SSD device degrades.

NOTE SSDs use a program/erase (P/E) cycle to write data to an SSD drive. If you think about it, a write is a program action, and so is an erase.

When the SSD disk is read from or written to, it happens at the page level, which is fairly exact and very efficient. When files are erased, it happens at the data block level, so an entire data block that contains some invalid or deleted pages will have to be moved to another data block so that the original data block can be erased.

Garbage Collection

Periodically, a process called *garbage collection* runs that helps manage your storage and handles in particular the differences that happen if the system needs to harvest or get rid of the deleted pages in a data block.

Continuing the Post-it Note analogy, imagine that you now have to run between the Post-it Note stacks, identify which notes are old and invalid, and then copy all of the valid notes or pages to another array of fresh Post-it Note stacks. You would then remove all of the top-level notes from the original array of stacks and throw them away.

This would be the equivalent of a data block program/erase function, and would make that array of notes, or data block, ready for a new set of writes and reads.

If this seems inefficient, it's because it is, but it occurs at speeds that we cannot quite imagine, and so we don't think about it much.

The real issue is that since there is a finite number of writes that can occur to an SSD device before the oxide is too thin to work, we need to make this process more efficient and prolong the life of our devices.

The **TRIM** Helper

SSD Trim is a feature of the OS that serves as a helper to the garbage collection routine by notifying the SSD which data pages are available for garbage collection in a block, enabling the garbage collection routine to *note* they are invalid but to *ignore* them in favor of accomplishing reads and writes.

TRIM greatly reduces the amount of copying of data during a garbage collection cycle and lowers the instance of P/E cycles, both of which can prolong the drive's life and increase the write performance of the drive.

Think of TRIM as a more intelligent form of deferring P/E operations until they can be done at scale and at times when the system is being used less or under lighter loads.

RAID Issues

RAID, or Redundant Array of Independent (or Inexpensive) Disks, is covered extensively elsewhere in this book, particularly in Chapter 1, "Understanding Linux Fundamentals," and Chapter 3, "Configuring and Managing Storage," so the focus of this section is on troubleshooting RAID issues.

> **NOTE**   A good friend once told me the best fix for anything RAID-related is to have multiple extra similar disks ready to go on the shelf, something I make sure I have at all times!

Causes and Symptoms of RAID Failures

There are a number of possible causes of RAID failures, including

- RAID controller suffers from a power surge
- Rebuild operations fail, causing catastrophic data loss
- Striping operations fail, causing data loss
- Multiple disk failures cause complete data loss
- Software RAID errors occur

Symptoms of RAID failure might include any of the following:

- Loss of data on the filesystems on the RAID array
- Inability to access the RAID array entirely
- Extreme slowness due to failing disks in the array
- Data errors due to being written to a failing device

Diagnosing and Fixing RAID Failures

RAID is made up of at least two disks, of course, and where you have multiple disks, eventually one or more of them will fail. The simplest and most straightforward way to monitor the health of your RAID devices is to use a couple of commands and some intuition to monitor either the individual devices or, more commonly, the entire array.

Overview of Tools

The following utilities will give you a good view into the health of your RAID devices:

- **mdadm:** The **mdadm** command is used to do most operations for software-based RAID on Linux systems. It has a number of options for creating, managing, and querying your RAID arrays.
- **smartctl:** A part of the smartmontools package, the **smartctl** command makes it easy to monitor your devices using the SMART (Self-Monitoring, Analysis and Reporting Technology) monitoring capability built into most drive controllers.
- **smartd:** Also part of the smartmontools package, the **smartd** daemon periodically monitors configured devices for SMART parameters and information and uses logging functions to report them.

Monitoring and Alerting with smartd

The smartd daemon runs and uses system logging to let you know if anything is wrong with the RAID device, making it very important to keep an eye on your log files, but you can also have **smartd** send an email to you if it notices any conditions that are abnormal.

The smartd daemon man page has examples of what you can do with **smartd**, as does the actual **/etc/smartd.conf** file, and its man page is particularly helpful in showing what can be done with the daemon.

Checking Device Health with smartctl

The **smartctl** command can report on most devices, but if you are using virtual machines and software-based drives, it will typically not be able to read much about them. Figure 18-17 shows what happened when I ran **smartctl** against **/dev/sda** attached to a VM on my test server.

```
~ $: sudo smartctl -a /dev/sda -T verypermissive
smartctl 7.1 2019-12-30 r5022 [x86_64-linux-5.15.0-56-generic] (local build)
Copyright (C) 2002-19, Bruce Allen, Christian Franke, www.smartmontools.org

=== START OF INFORMATION SECTION ===
Device Model:     Ubuntu Linux 20.04-0 SSD
Serial Number:    77K2QZSVM2GM58JB40DD
Firmware Version: F.TZBJ28
User Capacity:    68,719,476,736 bytes [68.7 GB]
Sector Sizes:     512 bytes logical, 4096 bytes physical
Rotation Rate:    Solid State Device
Device is:        Not in smartctl database [for details use: -P showall]
ATA Version is:   ATA8-ACS, ATA/ATAPI-5 T13/1321D revision 1
SATA Version is:  SATA 2.6, 3.0 Gb/s
Local Time is:    Sat Dec  3 20:23:36 2022 MST
SMART support is: Unavailable - device lacks SMART capability.
```

Figure 18-17 The **smartctl** command being run against a SCSI VM disk device

Although **smartctl** can't read all of the device's information, since it's not a real hardware SCSI device, it does output a fair bit of information.

Think of **smartctl** as the ad hoc "Hmm, I wonder how things are going?" kind of tool, whereas smartd is the "I want to have this monitoring my device health on a regular basis and notifying me" kind of option.

Monitoring RAID Array Health

There are several ways to get information about your RAID array. We'll start with the simplest and go up from there.

A quick and easy way to monitor your RAID, whatever level the array is set up to operate at, is to use the **cat** command to see the contents of the **/proc/mdstat** file:

```
$ cat /proc/mdstat
Personalities : [linear] [multipath] [raid0] [raid1] [raid6]
[raid5] [raid4]
md0 : active raid0 nvme0n2[1] nvme0n1[0]
        67041280 blocks super 1.2 512k chunks
unused devices: <none>
```

> **NOTE** You can continuously run the **cat /proc/mdstat** command by using the **watch** command in front of it, so that it displays the **mdstat** contents every 2 seconds by default, which is configurable.

You can additionally use a graphical tool like GParted, which when you click to get information on the array will display output like the example shown in Figure 18-18.

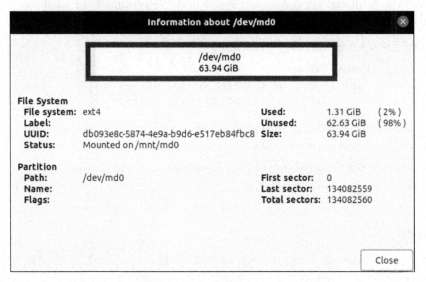

Figure 18-18 Example output of the GParted tool for an array

This will give you good information, but it's not the most useful level of monitoring, which is covered next.

Monitoring RAID Array Health with **mdadm**

When we discuss RAID arrays and **mdadm** together, it means software-based RAID arrays, because most hardware-based RAID will have its own set of utilities that act on and monitor that hardware and the arrays it holds.

The **mdadm** command has its own way of notifying you of changes to RAID arrays that it manages, either in the command output, covered previously, or by sending an email to you.

The **mdadm** command will notify you if any of the following events occur:

- Fail
- FailSpare
- DegradedArray
- TestMessage

You can invoke this capability from the command line by "daemonizing" the command:

```
mdadm --monitor --scan --daemonize --mail=jdoe@somemail.com
```

This should also be placed as a configuration line in the **/etc/init.d/boot.local** file or otherwise invoked at system startup so that it's always running.

You can check to see if it's running by executing

```
$ ps aux  | grep mdadm
root       13136  0.0  0.0   3188   128 ?          Ss   18:13
0:00 mdadm --monitor --scan --daemonize --mail=root@localhost
```

You can also alter the line in the **/etc/mdadm.conf** file that tells the system where to send alerts; its default is the root user, but you can make it your own address:

```
# instruct the monitoring daemon where to send mail alerts
(c)MAILADDR root@example.com
```

LVM Issues

LVM, or Logical Volume Manager, is covered extensively in Chapter 3. In this chapter, you will learn about some LVM troubleshooting techniques.

LVM Troubleshooting Overview

Recall from Chapter 3 that the structure of LVM comprises a stack that includes physical volumes (PVs) that are grouped into a volume group (VG), which then is carved into logical volumes (LVs) that can be used to partition and make filesystems upon.

That's a lot of components to monitor and to have possible failures with, so this section covers some good ways to monitor and troubleshoot your LVM setups.

Causes and Symptoms of LVM Issues

The numerous possible causes of LVM issues include the following:

- Disk failures

- LVM software failure

- Power failure for external LVM

Symptoms of LVM issues might include any of the following:

- Filesystem errors

- Disk access errors

- System slowness due to disk access errors

- RAID rebuild issues when RAID is used with LVM

Diagnosing and Fixing LVM Issues

There are three sets of utilities that you can use to gain information about LVM, listed here starting at the bottom of the technology stack:

- **Physical volumes:** The three utilities that give you information about PVs are **pvs**, **pvdisplay**, and **pvscan**.

- **Volume groups:** The three utilities that give you information about VGs are **vgs**, **vgdisplay**, and **vgscan**.

- **Logical volumes:** The three utilities that give you information about LVs are **lvs**, **lvdisplay**, and **lvscan**.

If you suspect anything is wrong, investigate immediately using the listed utilities, looking for any instance of an error message or missing components.

Diagnosing LVM Issues

The first thing you'll want to do after running the three sets of basic commands that are mentioned in the previous section is to use what I jokingly call the "Flying Vs" for those commands.

For example, running the **lvs** command gives you information, but you can add a **-v** to that command to increase the information displayed. You can do this up to four times, by adding up to **-vvvv** to get the very most information from any of the **pv***, **vg***, or **lv*** commands.

Among the other diagnostic commands you can pursue, the first should probably be the **lvmconfig** command, which will display the configuration information for your LVM setup. Running **lvmconfig** against my LVM volume **lvm-vol1** produced the following output:

```
sudo lvdisplay lvm-vol1
  --- Logical volume ---
  LV Path                /dev/lvm-vol1/logicalvol
  LV Name                logicalvol
  VG Name                volgrp1
  LV UUID                br549-plex-mbr2-jmbo-spn8
  LV Write Access        read/write
  LV Creation host, time … -0400
  LV Status              available
  # open                 0
  LV Size                2.00 GiB
  Current LE             514
  Segments               1
  Allocation             inherit
  Read ahead sectors     auto
  - currently set to     256
  Block device           273:3
```

Next is the **lvmdump** command, which offers the ability to gather a large amount of useful data and put it into a **tar.gz** or **.tgz** archive for sending to your vendor, or archiving until needed. Just running **lvmdump** produces output similar to the following:

```
# lvmdump
Creating dump directory: /root/lvmdump-zakkhost.in-209456
Gathering LVM & device-mapper version info...
Gathering dmsetup info...
Gathering process info...
Gathering console messages...
Gathering /etc/lvm info...
Gathering /dev listing...
Gathering /sys/block listing...
Creating report tarball in /root/ lvmdump-zakkhost.in-209456...
```

For more advanced data dumping, include the **-a** option, and then if you want to just collect the metadata for the LVM setup, use the **-m** option.

Finally, try adding the **--options** and **+devices** options to the end of your commands, and you'll see any device failure information and be able to troubleshoot that device more easily.

NOTE   Keep in mind that you don't need to know everything about troubleshooting LVM, just the basics of how to get the right information. Almost all the issues you'll encounter will require replacing a disk and possibly rebuilding the VG and even the LV.

Mount Option Issues

Unlike disks and partitions, filesystems have to be mounted to the system, and that operation can go wrong sometimes.

Mount Options Overview

Recall that mount options can be used both with the **mount** command and also in the **/etc/fstab** file when setting up a filesystem to be mounted automatically. For the **mount** command, the mount options are provided with the **-o** option. When specifying mount options in the **/etc/fstab** file, place the mount options in the fourth field of the file.

Causes and Symptoms of Mount Options Issues

The following are several possible causes of mount option issues:

- The **/etc/fstab** file is not set up correctly for a user to mount the filesystem.
- A filesystem has been set up to be mounted singularly.
- A filesystem has an error and cannot be mounted.
- The filesystem type is wrong or cannot be detected.

Symptoms of mount issues might include any of the following:

- A user cannot mount a filesystem.
- Only the user who mounted the filesystem can unmount it.
- A filesystem that should be mounted read-write is mounted read-only.

Diagnosing and Fixing Mount Option Issues

There is one main utility, the **mount** command (along with **umount**), that both mounts filesystems and displays information about them.

To view the mounted filesystems on your device, use the **mount** command by itself:

```
$ mount
sysfs on /sys type sysfs (rw,nosuid,nodev,noexec,relatime)
proc on /proc type proc (rw,nosuid,nodev,noexec,relatime)
udev on /dev type devtmpfs (rw,nosuid,noexec,relatime,size=19666
20k,nr_inodes=491655,mode=755,inode64)
devpts on /dev/pts type devpts (rw,nosuid,noexec,relatime,gid=5,
mode=620,ptmxmode=000)
tmpfs on /run type tmpfs (rw,nosuid,nodev,noexec,relatime,size=4
01104k,mode=755,inode64)
/dev/sda5 on / type ext4 (rw,relatime,errors=remount-ro)
securityfs on /sys/kernel/security type securityfs (rw,nosuid,no
dev,noexec,relatime)
tmpfs on /dev/shm type tmpfs (rw,nosuid,nodev,inode64)
```

You're very unlikely to see an error in the **mount** command output; any errors that occur either would be reported immediately if attempting to mount a filesystem from the command line or, in the case of **/etc/fstab**, would be masked mostly by the boot process events and only available in log files.

Understanding Mount Option Gotchas

A very common mistake is to fail to specify the **mount** command options properly.

A **mount** command must at least have the source device and target mount point, such as:

```
# mount /dev/sda7 /data
```

If the filesystem is set up in the **/etc/fstab** file, then this will work easily, give you no feedback, and enable you to then use the filesystem as you desired.

What Are All These UUIDs in My fstab?

A common issue is that someone doesn't understand mounting using the UUID of a filesystem, because they are used to using a plain partition path, such as **/dev/sda5**. When they see UUIDs and PARTUUIDs, they can get very confused as to what to do.

The problem that arises when using a plain partition path (a problem that has existed for a long time) is that device names are not totally stable—what was **/dev/ sda** on one boot may be changed to **/dev/sdb** on the next. In other words, your disks and partitions may not remain named as you thought they were.

To fix this issue, there is now the concept of the UUID, which is essentially a unique identifier that won't change like the device designation can and likely will.

In the following line, notice the **UUID**, **TYPE**, and **PARTUUID** keywords:

```
/dev/sda5: UUID="3df1294e-27da-4408-8a62-2b571efd8eb6" TYPE="ext4"
PARTUUID="1f305916-05"
```

A UUID is that unique identifier that is assigned to a filesystem by the creation tool, such as **mkfs.ext4**, and is supposed to be unique on this machine, on other machines, and across the galaxy. Well, maybe not the galaxy, but you get the intent.

A TYPE is the filesystem type.

A PARTUUID is mostly used for referring to raw or physical partitions, and it will stay the same even if you replace the filesystem on that partition. It's safest to use *both* of these UUID tags in case the filesystem is changed.

What Is This errors= Option?

Usually a filesystem will be mounted either read-only or read-write, such as a CD-ROM or DVD is usually read-only and a normal filesystem such as ext4 or BtrFS is usually read-write.

The following are your options when a filesystem has an error that is detected before or during the attempted mount:

- Ignore the error (dangerous!)
- Mark the filesystem as having the error (still dangerous!)
- Panic and halt the system (not always necessary)
- (Re)mount the filesystem as read-only

You may see a line in your **/etc/fstab** file that, instead of the usual "defaults" option, reads

```
errors=remount -ro
```

The reason you have this option in the **/etc/fstab** line is that having a filesystem mounted read-only is the first step to performing an **fsck** on it, so this is saving you a potential reboot, going into the emergency or rescue mode, and then trying to run **fsck** on this filesystem.

This will work fairly well on any of the filesystems, but there is still the strong chance that if a filesystem is broken or corrupted badly enough, you won't even be able to mount it read-only.

> **NOTE**   A seemingly infinite number of issues can happen during boot, and many of them result from someone messing with or misconfiguring the **/etc/fstab** file, so keep very close watch on it, back it up before every use, and have it available on another device just in case. I personally **cat** it out and mail it to myself as a backup.

In this chapter you learned all about troubleshooting storage issues, from Latency issues and why they can be a problem, to Low throughput issues and what causes them to what Input/Output Operations are and what makes them an issue in certain situations and how to recognize and troubleshoot Capacity issues, which includes Filesystem and I/O Scheduler issues.

Additionally, you learned about issues that affect Devices, Logical Volume Management issues that can affect systems and ended up with a few issues that affect users but are configured and managed by the administrator in Mount Option issues issues.

Exam Preparation Tasks

As mentioned in the section "Goals and Methods" in the Introduction, you have a couple of choices for exam preparation: the exercises here, Chapter 23, "Final Preparation," and the exam simulation questions in the Pearson Test Prep Software Online.

Review All Key Topics

Review the most important topics in this chapter, noted with the Key Topic icon in the margin of the page. Table 18-2 lists these key topics and the page number on which each is found.

Table 18-2 Key Topics for Chapter 18

Key Topic Element	Description	Page Number
Paragraph	High latency typically results from I/O wait time	623
List	Utilities that provide a good view of I/O wait times	624
Paragraph	Using the **watch** command to repeatedly run the **vmstat** command	626
Paragraph	Storage issues occur when hardware fails or its capacity is exceeded	627
Paragraph	IOPS are much less important now that a lot of disk is flash or memory	632
Note	Explanation of extents	637
Paragraph	Definition of the **fsck** command	640
Paragraph	Definition of filesystem mismatching	642
List	Newer and multiqueue-specific I/O schedulers	645
Paragraph	Setting a scheduler using the **echo** command	646
Paragraph	Verifying the currently set scheduler using the **cat** command	646
Paragraph	How NVMe differs from other flash storage management protocols	647
Paragraph	How a controller treats reads and writes and erasures differently	651
Paragraph	Definition of the SSD Trim function	652

Key Topic Element	Description	Page Number
Paragraph	Definition of the **smartctl** command	654
Paragraph	Description of what a UUID is used for	661
Paragraph	Reason to consider using the **errors=remount -ro** in **/etc/fstab**	662

Define Key Terms

Define the following key terms from this chapter and check your answers in the glossary:

high latency, input/output (I/O) wait, low IOPS, low throughput, IOPS, capacity issues, low disk space, inode exhaustion, filesystem corruption, filesystem mismatch, I/O errors, I/O scheduler issues, device issues, NVMe, SSD, SSD TRIM, RAID, LVM, mount option issues

Review Questions

The answers to these review questions are in Appendix A.

1. Which of the following is not considered a possible cause of I/O wait time?

   a. Storage system bottlenecks

   b. RAM shortage

   c. LVM configuration errors

   d. RAID array (I/O) errors

2. Which value of the output of the **top** command will provide you with useful information to diagnose high latency?

   a. ta

   b. Hostwa

   c. io

   d. la

   e. iops

3. _____ is how much data can be read or transferred across various system devices and the system bus to other devices, sustainably, over periods of time.

   a. Bandwidth

   b. Data rate

    c. Throughput

    d. Link Capacity

4. The _____ command can show you how much disk space you have used and is free in a filesystem, both in terms of absolute value and percentages to total disk space.

    a. df

    b. vmstat

    c. du

    d. iostat

5. You are concerned with the amount of space that a user is using in their home directory. Which command could you use to display a total of the amount of space that is being used in that directory?

    a. df

    b. find

    c. fsck

    d. du

6. The _____ daemon runs and uses system logging to let you know if anything is wrong with the RAID device

    a. mdadm

    b. smartctl

    c. hddtemp

    d. smartd

This chapter covers the following topics:

- Network Configuration Issues
- Firewall Issues
- Interface Errors
- Bandwidth Limitations
- Name Resolution Issues
- Testing Remote Systems

The exam objective covered in this chapter is as follows:

- **Objective 4.2:** Given a scenario, analyze and troubleshoot network resource issues

## CHAPTER 19

Analyzing and Troubleshooting Network Resource Issues

Network troubleshooting is a key part of any systems professional's life, if you can't get to the network, or something is wrong preventing your system from resolving names properly, your ability to function is severely limited.

In this chapter, we will explore different topics related to troubleshooting firewall issues. This will include network configuration issues, issues related to network interfaces, and issues that surround firewalls. We will also dive into how bandwidth limitations can impact network performance, how to test for name resolution issues, and how to perform testing on the connectivity to remote systems.

"Do I Know This Already?" Quiz

The "Do I Know This Already?" quiz enables you to assess whether you should read this entire chapter or simply jump to the "Exam Preparation Tasks" section for review. If you are in doubt, read the entire chapter. Table 19-1 outlines the major headings in this chapter and the corresponding "Do I Know This Already?" quiz questions. You can find the answers in Appendix A, "Answers to the 'Do I Know This Already?' Quizzes and Review Questions."

Table 19-1 "Do I Know This Already?" Foundation Topics Section-to-Question Mapping

Foundation Topics Section	Questions Covered in This Section
Network Configuration Issues	1
Firewall Issues	2
Interface Errors	3
Bandwidth Limitations	4
Name Resolution Issues	5
Testing Remote Systems	6

CAUTION   The goal of self-assessment is to gauge your mastery of the topics in this chapter. If you do not know the answer to a question or are only partially sure of the answer, you should mark that question as wrong for purposes of the self-assessment. Giving yourself credit for an answer you correctly guess skews your self-assessment results and might provide you with a false sense of security.

1. You are trying to reach a remote host that has recently been contactable, but are getting errors or and no response to any remote system. What is the easiest troubleshooting method to pursue first?

   a. Go find your DNS administrator

   b. Dig into the networking configuration files

   c. Check that your ethernet cable is connected

   d. Check the server room

2. You are trying to **ssh** to a remote host not long after a security audit but are not able to get a login prompt from the host. What may have been adjusted to disallow SSH access?

   a. The host firewall rules

   b. The organizational security policy

   c. Classless Inter-Domain Routing configuration

   d. Your host's VLAN location

3. Your office location has moved, and when you boot your Linux desktop, you are unable to connect to the network. You have already confirmed that your Ethernet cable is properly plugged in. What command with options is recommended to display your systems IP address information?

   a. **ifconfig -a**

   b. **netplan show**

   c. **sysconfig -v**

   d. **ip a s**

4. Your work partner has been testing a server's bandwidth usage, and when you use the server for your throughput testing, things seem very slow. Which of the following commands might your work partner have used to control the system's bandwidth? (Choose all that apply.)

   a. **tc**

   b. **ncat**

  c. **wondershaper**

  d. **ipfw**

  e. **trickle**

5. After spending a lot of time locally developing a website and then deploying it, you find that none of your updates are showing on what you assume to be the public site. What file should you check to ensure you are seeing the production site and not a local site?

  a. **/etc/sysconfig/network**

  b. **/etc/resolv.conf**

  c. **/etc/nsswitch.conf**

  d. **/etc/hosts**

6. Which of the following commands could you use to see if a remote system is available and the possible network path your traffic took to get to it? (Choose two.)

  a. **ifconfig**

  b. **ip**

  c. **netplan**

  d. **traceroute**

  e. **dig**

Network Configuration Issues

Linux includes a lot of auto-configuration tools, and most Linux distributions will walk you through a simple set of steps to get your network device connected either to wired Ethernet or to Wi-Fi.

Let's start simple by identifying the main causes of network configuration problems. We'll limit our focus primarily to the issues detailed in the Linux+ objectives, those related to the subnet and routing, but we'll also mention the default gateway, which in my opinion should be included in this objective.

Causes and Symptoms of Network Configuration Issues

The most likely causes of network configuration issues are

- Subnet issues
- Routing issues

Symptoms of *high latency* might include the following:

- Having a configured IP address but being unable to see any other hosts on the network, even if they can see each other
- Being able to see hosts on the local network but not being able to contact hosts outside of your local network

Diagnosing and Fixing Network Configuration Issues

You can use several utilities to see different aspects of your network configuration, but the main one is **ip**.

The **ip** command is a very versatile and complete command, featuring a number of subfunctions, but showing your overall network configuration is probably its most useful function.

Diagnosing Subnets with the **ip** Command

The **ip** command by itself is about all you'll need to see the majority of details about your IP addresses, subnets, and gateway information.

For example, the **ip** command can also display network configuration data, just like the **ifconfig** command (covered in Chapter 5, "Using Network Tools and Configuration Files"). If you execute the **ip addr show** command, the output looks like that shown in Example 19-1.

Example 19-1   Example of **ip addr show** Command Output

```
$ ip addr show
1: lo: <LOOPBACK,UP,LOWER_UP> mtu 16436 qdisc noqueue state UNKNOWN
 link/loopback 00:00:00:00:00:00 brd 00:00:00:00:00:00
 inet 127.0.0.1/8 scope host lo
 inet6 ::1/128 scope host
 valid_lft forever preferred_lft forever
2: eth0: <BROADCAST,MULTICAST,UP,LOWER_UP> mtu 1500 qdisc pfifo_fast
state UP qlen 1000
 link/ether 08:00:27:08:ea:ff brd ff:ff:ff:ff:ff:ff
 inet 192.168.1.22/24 brd 192.168.1.255 scope global eth0
 inet6 fe80::a00:27ff:fe08:eaff/64 scope link
 valid_lft forever preferred_lft forever
```

When the **ip** command displays its information, you have to parse the output to see what you need, so I recommend using the **grep** command to filter the output to get just what you want. Example 19-2 shows **grep** being used to filter for the word "inet."

Example 19-2   Example of **ip addr show | grep "inet"** Output

```
$ ip addr show | grep "inet"
inet 192.168.1.22/24 brd 192.168.1.255 scope global eth0
inet6 fe80::a00:27ff:fe08:eaff/64 scope link
```

What you are looking for in this situation is that the subnet mask (in this case a /24, or 24 bits long, aka 255.255.255.0) of this network interface means that it is on a standard Class C network in which the last octet (8 bits) is where the hosts are located.

On a Class C network with a standard subnet mask, you have 254 possible addressable hosts. Since the subnet mask is a /24 and the network being addressed is 192.168.1.0, the last address in the 255 available for hosts (.255) is also reserved for the use of broadcasting to all hosts on the subnet.

You can see in the output that "brd" is followed by the previously mentioned broadcast address of 192.168.1.255. The end of that line identifies the actual interface, which in this case is eth0, or the first Ethernet interface.

> **NOTE**   The real issue with subnet masks occurs when a mismatch exists between the actual subnet you're on and the configuration your system has. If your system has recently been moved, or perhaps it has a manually assigned IP address and other network configuration, those should be checked.

Diagnosing Routes Using the **ping** Command

You will sometimes need to troubleshoot the route that your system takes to reach a remote network location. One method of doing this is to use the **ping** command, as we will now explore.

> **NOTE**   If your subnet mask is improperly configured, you'll be trying to communicate on the wrong network, and that can cause your system to not know how to get out of the current network and cause routing issues.

The route your traffic will take is most important when that route involves another subnet, be it the very next one off your local router or all the way across the Internet.

One of the first tools you should use when you aren't sure if your system has a proper route is the **ping** command, which enables you to see if you can reach a remote host that you are pretty sure exists and will respond.

We covered the **ping** command in Chapter 5, and it's so simple to use that most every troubleshooting session that is about networking should start with a simple **ping** *otherhost* command, just to make sure that your networking *exists*.

You can also use the **ping** command to see if what you *think* is the default gateway out of your network is reachable; if not, there's probably a gateway problem.

Diagnosing Routes Using the **ip route** Command

The **ip route** command focuses on the route portion of your **ip** command and shows you the information that can be pulled from the **/proc** and probably **/sys** trees about the routing for your interface(s).

For instance, in Example 19-3 you see the output of the **ip route** command on a typical system with a local and eth0 interfaces.

Example 19-3 Example of **ip route show** Output

```
$ ip route show
default via 192.168.64.1 dev enp0s2 proto dhcp src 192.168.64.2 metric
100
192.168.64.0/24 dev enp0s2 proto kernel scope link src 192.168.64.2
192.168.64.1 dev enp0s2 proto dhcp scope link src 192.168.64.2 metric
100
```

What we are looking for in this output is the combination of items that will make for a properly configured route out of our network, starting with the first line that shows the default gateway, **default via 192.168.64.1**. This line also shows the device, the protocol, where the traffic comes from, and a metric.

The **ip route show** command's output is more complete than the **ip address show** command in that it focuses on the route and gateway address, and even shows the local host's IP address, 192.168.64.2.

Diagnosing Routes Using the **traceroute** Command

The final diagnostic tool is **traceroute**, a venerable and trusty tool that has sadly become less helpful across the wide area network or Internet due to the blocking of one of its main protocols, Internet Control Message Protocol (ICMP).

The **traceroute** command effectively sends out a series of packets to the first router and then subsequent routers it finds along the route to the remote host, each time reporting route information back to that router and building a set of routes that you can use to, well, trace where your packets have to travel. The reported route information includes the number of the hop and timings for each section of that route.

Partly because **traceroute** is *so* helpful in describing the route that has been taken and giving you statistics about the routers and timings, ICMP has been disabled on many public and private networks, since it can be used to gain a little too much information at times.

As an example, I did a **traceroute** from my local computer to the rossbrunson.com host, which produced the output shown in Example 19-4.

Example 19-4 Example of **traceroute rossbrunson.com** Output

```
$ traceroute rossbrunson.com
traceroute to rossbrunson.com (192.0.78.24), 30 hops max, 60 byte
packets
 1  _gateway (192.168.64.1)   0.161 ms   0.101 ms   0.092 ms
 2  www.webgui.nokiawifi.com (192.168.12.1)   2.544 ms   2.483 ms
    2.422 ms
```

```
 3   192.0.0.1 (192.0.0.1)   4.332 ms   4.248 ms   4.206 ms
 4   * 192.0.0.1 (192.0.0.1)   62.602 ms  *
 5   192.0.0.1 (192.0.0.1)   84.482 ms  84.430 ms  84.381 ms
 6   * * *
 7   * * *
 8   192.0.0.1 (192.0.0.1)   73.586 ms  80.029 ms  79.968 ms
 9   10.170.233.133 (10.170.233.133)  71.639 ms  71.975 ms  73.179 ms
10   10.164.176.237 (10.164.176.237)  68.158 ms  68.107 ms  79.140 ms
11   six.automattic.net (206.81.81.70)  77.953 ms  69.818 ms  69.747 ms
12   * * *
```

In Example 19-4, anywhere you see a set of three consecutive * characters instead of useful information, that identifies a router that has ICMP turned off, didn't respond in a timely manner, or is otherwise restricted.

Take note of the lines that *do* show good information—the three packets that are sent out report back the trip time for that packet, and therein lies a good amount of information; sometimes you'll see a router or two that are having issues or long trip times, a sure sign of heavy traffic or being overloaded.

NOTE   You should also try the **traceroute** command with the **-T** option (or "use TCP SYN for probes"). It often will show shorter and more complete output by avoiding the use of the much-restricted ICMP.

Firewall Issues

Chapter 10, "Implementing and Configuring Firewalls," covered firewall use cases, technologies, and features, so this section provides only a brief refresher and then focuses on what can go wrong with a firewall, mostly how a misconfigured firewall can affect appropriate or allowed traffic to a host.

Firewall Refresher

Keep in mind that a *firewall* exists so that a host can be protected from unwanted or harmful traffic. The challenge is for the firewall to differentiate between unwanted traffic that should be blocked and very similar-looking legitimate traffic that should be allowed to pass. After all, scammers and thieves attempt to make their traffic look as legitimate as possible to circumvent firewalls.

Consider a simple scenario in which a user's client computer wants to access a simple NGINX web server, and there is a firewall in between them, as shown in Figure 19-1.

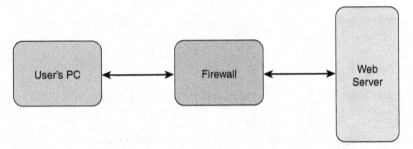

Figure 19-1 Diagram of simple firewall scenario

The user's computer needs to access the web server, but there is a firewall in the way that, by default, will not send the user's request traffic to the web server. To allow the user (or any host, for that matter) to access the web server or have it receive and respond to a request, there must be at least an exception added to the firewall rules that allows traffic on port 80 (for HTTP) and port 443 (for HTTPS), so that the firewall knows it's okay to forward requests on those ports to the web server.

Once those exceptions are made, and the rules are in effect, the user's computer will be able to make a request to the web server and get a response.

What Could Possibly Go Wrong?

Describing the numerous things that could go wrong with firewall configuration would fill a whole book in and of itself, but for purposes of the Linux+ exam, you should understand a couple of main things that can go wrong in even such a simple scenario as this. Those are covered next, followed by a discussion of how to fix them or avoid them.

Causes and Symptoms of Firewall Issues

The following are several possible causes of firewall issues:

- Service not running

- Incorrect ports being listened on

- Incorrect ports for the traffic being allowed or denied

- Nonstandard ports being used

Symptoms of firewall issues might include any of the following:

- Can reach the firewall, but not the destination server

- Can reach the gateway of the device's network, but not the device

- The connection happens, but the result is not what is expected

Diagnosing and Fixing Firewall Issues

There are several utilities that will give you a good view as to what may be the problem with your firewall:

- **ping:** As previously described, using a simple ping enables you to see if you can reach the remote target host, another host on that network, the firewall, the gateway on that network, your own gateway, and so forth.

- **telnet:** The **telnet** command is mostly deprecated, and your installation of Linux may not even have it available. It's a useful tool, something akin to using a stick to check if a turtle is sleeping, any response will be informative.

- **nmap:** The *nmap* command is used to scan IP addresses and ports in a network and to detect installed applications. We'll cover the **nmap** command in detail in the "Testing Remote Systems" section of this chapter.

While these tools are useful for finding firewall issues, you will still need to determine how to fix the issues. Consider the following techniques:

- Temporarily disable the firewall to see if it's causing the issue. This can help identify if the firewall is the root cause.

- Check firewall logs for any entries related to blocked or rejected traffic. Analyzing these logs can provide insights into potential issues.

- Modify firewall rules one at a time and test connectivity using the aforementioned tools (**ping**, **telnet**, and **nmap**) after you modify a rule.

- Note that these tools can help test the firewall, but the connectivity problem may be the service that listens to the network port. For example, if you can't connect to the web server, it could be a firewall issue, or it could be a misconfigured web server.

NOTE   A lot of networking utilities are already covered in Chapter 5, so we'll concentrate using them to troubleshoot services that aren't running properly and to test whether services are running properly on remote systems.

Diagnosing with the **ping** Command

You've seen the **ping** command before, it's important to know how to use it, no matter what your job is around Linux and open source, because the ping command sends a series of packets to a specific IP address and waits for a response. If the firewall is blocking the ping packets, the ping command will not receive a response.

The most basic step is to establish whether a host is accepting connections, or is alive at all, by pinging the device:

```
$ ping remotehost
```

Also consider that DNS (Domain Name System) may be busy or malfunctioning and use **ping** with the remote host's IP address, if you know it.

Once the host responds, then you can try higher-level connection requests. If the host doesn't respond, try another host on that same network, if you know of one.

Diagnosing with the **telnet** Command

The **telnet** command can be a useful tool for diagnosing firewall issues by testing network connectivity and identifying whether specific ports are open or blocked. The reason why you can use the telnet command for this purpose is that you can pass a port number to the command and it will attempt to establish a connection to the application that is listening to that port on the remote system. If a connection can't be established, this could lead you to the conclusion that there is a firewall issue.

Never use **telnet** for actual remote command-line sessions. It's stupendously insecure, so you really should only use it as a quick and dirty way to display the response you get to a query on a remote port.

For any connection that will contain any data of any import at all, always use the Secure Shell (SSH) suite of utilities rather than the Telnet and R-suite of utilities.

As a veteran of the operating system wars, I tend to use the **telnet** command first to poke a system on a particular port to see what responds, if anything. For example, I might want to see if a remote host has a web server configured on port 80, and although I could just use the **curl** command to do that, I might also want to just see if the port is responding at all, and with what.

NOTE   As a further point about the (possibly) puzzling use of a decades-out-of-date tool like telnet here, we do it because the **telnet** command when used this way is like sticking a straw into the target *service:port* and then looking at what leaks onto the screen as the output. It's very informative, and mostly *because* the **telnet** command is *so* leaky and open.

Figure 19-2 shows example results of poking a remote system with the **telnet** command.

```
ubuntu@primary:~$ telnet remotehost 80
Trying 127.0.1.1...
Connected to primary.
Escape character is '^]'.

HTTP/1.1 400 Bad Request
Server: nginx/1.18.0 (Ubuntu)
Date: Fri, 23 Dec 2022 03:53:52 GMT
Content-Type: text/html
Content-Length: 166
Connection: close

<html>
<head><title>400 Bad Request</title></head>
<body>
<center><h1>400 Bad Request</h1></center>
<hr><center>nginx/1.18.0 (Ubuntu)</center>
</body>
</html>
Connection closed by foreign host.
```

Figure 19-2   Example output of a **telnet** to a remote system

The response to the **telnet** command is the first block ending in the "Escape character is…" After pressing Enter (or any character and then Enter), the NGINX service responded to the invalid or bad request with a 400 return message.

Now that I know there is an open-source version of NGINX on that host, listening on port 80, I could try port 443 next because that is the port for HTTPS traffic, which NGINX also normally listens to.

Making Sure Services Are Running

What does ensuring services are running have to do with firewalls? I have seen some really embarrassing moments when someone reports a firewall issue and the actual issue is that the system is not running that service.

The **systemctl** command is the best way to ensure that a service is running, what its general configuration is, and some key log file entries that have happened (as covered in depth in Chapter 4, "Managing Processes and Services").

Figure 19-3 shows example output of the **systemctl status nginx** command.

```
ubuntu@primary:~$ systemctl status nginx
● nginx.service - A high performance web server and a reverse proxy server
     Loaded: loaded (/lib/systemd/system/nginx.service; enabled; vendor preset: enabled)
     Active: active (running) since Thu 2022-12-22 20:34:05 MST; 24h ago
       Docs: man:nginx(8)
   Main PID: 5452 (nginx)
      Tasks: 2 (limit: 1132)
     Memory: 4.8M
     CGroup: /system.slice/nginx.service
             ├─5452 nginx: master process /usr/sbin/nginx -g daemon on; master_process on;
             └─5693 nginx: worker process

Dec 22 20:34:05 primary systemd[1]: Starting A high performance web server and a reverse p
Dec 22 20:34:05 primary systemd[1]: Started A high performance web server and a reverse pr
```

Figure 19-3 Example output of the **systemctl status nginx** command

As you can see, the service is running, accepting connections, and everything seems to be okay, but you should also at least look at the log files to ensure that everything is being read and reported properly. For example, the **telnet** command and its 400 error previously shown in Figure 19-2 should be shown in the log files, which is confirmed in Figure 19-4.

```
ubuntu@primary:~$ cat /var/log/nginx/access.log
::1 - - [22/Dec/2022:20:35:15 -0700] "GET / HTTP/1.1" 200 612 "-" "curl/7.68.0"
127.0.0.1 - - [22/Dec/2022:20:36:13 -0700] "a" 400 166 "-" "-"
::1 - - [22/Dec/2022:20:38:18 -0700] "GET / HTTP/1.1" 200 612 "-" "curl/7.68.0"
::1 - - [22/Dec/2022:20:38:36 -0700] " " 400 166 "-" "-"
127.0.0.1 - - [22/Dec/2022:20:53:52 -0700] " " 400 166 "-" "-"
```

Figure 19-4 Example output of **cat** on the **/var/log/nginx/access.log** file

Oddly enough, you won't see the 400 error message in the actual **error.log** file for NGINX—it appears in the **access.log** file output.

So, as you can see, the service is running, accepting and rejecting connections, and throwing errors properly.

Interface Errors

An *interface error* refers to a problem or anomaly that occurs on a network interface, which is a connection point for devices within a network. Network interfaces can be physical ports on a networking device (like a router, switch, or computer) or virtual interfaces created by software. Interface errors can lead to disruptions in network communication and may result from various issues.

Since your network interfaces are how you contact, communicate with, and in general experience any other computer or resource, it's critical to understand what can go wrong with those interfaces and what you may be able to do about it.

Next we will explore common interface errors, including dropped packets, collisions, and link status. Because dropped packets and collisions are closely related, I will treat them as one topic in this section.

Dropped Packets and Collisions

Dropped packets are packets of data that are not successfully transmitted from one device to another on a network. A network collision is an event that occurs when two or more devices on a network attempt to transmit data on the same network segment at the same time. This causes the data to collide, which results in data loss and a degradation of network performance. In this section we will explore the causes and symptoms of these two issues, as well as how to diagnose and fix these problems.

Dropped packets refers to when a network interface is discarding or losing data packets, very often an indication of a damaged network cable somewhere, a firewall that is configured to not forward those packets, or even dysfunctional network card memory.

Collisions happen all the time on Ethernet, it's a fact of life. If you've ever had to move quickly down a long hallway filled with other people, you'll know how an Ethernet packet feels on its way down the wire.

Diagnosing and Fixing Issues Related to Dropped Packets and Collisions

The following utilities will help you diagnose and fix issues that may be causing dropped packets and collisions:

- **ethtool:** The **ethtool** command is versatile, reporting all kinds of good information for the network interfaces, both physical and virtual. It also can be used to set many parameters and control the interfaces, which is beyond the scope of the Linux+ exam.

- **netstat:** The **netstat** command can be used to show many things, including the kernel interface table, which shows details regarding the local network interfaces on the system.

- **/sys/class/net/<device>/statistics:** The raw statistics that are in **/sys** are the same general stats shown in the **ethtool** command output, with some minor differences, notably that there are more statistics in this directory set than are shown in the **ethtool -S** statistics.

> **NOTE** There is a *lot* that goes into understanding dropped packets, including knowledge of how Ethernet works overall, what packets are and how they collide, how packets are filtered, and so on. Linux+ objectives only expect you to know how to deal with an interface error reporting dropped packets.

Diagnosing with the **ethtool** Command

While you can view the raw statistics from the **/sys/class/net/device/statistics** directory and its files/contents, the **ethtool** command has a very useful statistics option, **-S**, that is very easy to use, an example of which is shown along with its output in Figure 19-5.

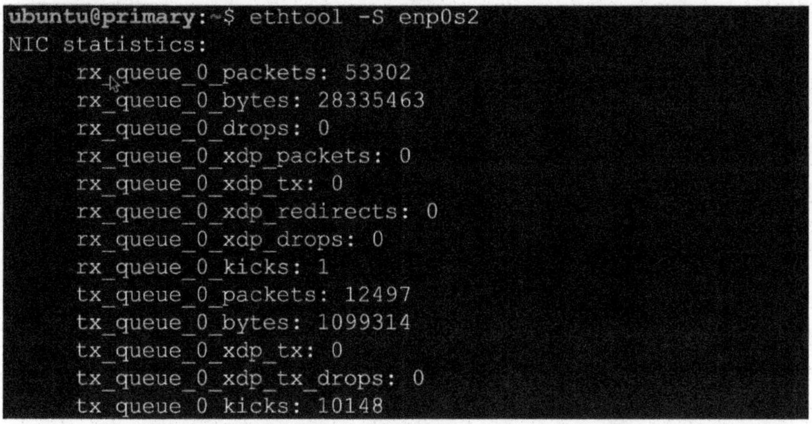

```
ubuntu@primary:~$ ethtool -S enp0s2
NIC statistics:
     rx_queue_0_packets: 53302
     rx_queue_0_bytes: 28335463
     rx_queue_0_drops: 0
     rx_queue_0_xdp_packets: 0
     rx_queue_0_xdp_tx: 0
     rx_queue_0_xdp_redirects: 0
     rx_queue_0_xdp_drops: 0
     rx_queue_0_kicks: 1
     tx_queue_0_packets: 12497
     tx_queue_0_bytes: 1099314
     tx_queue_0_xdp_tx: 0
     tx_queue_0_xdp_tx_drops: 0
     tx_queue_0_kicks: 10148
```

Figure 19-5   Example output of the **ethtool -S _<interfacename>_** command

You can use the **ethtool** command to view the network interface card (NIC) statistics, as shown in Figure 19-5, or you can filter those stats using the **grep** command, similarly to what is shown in Example 19-5.

Example 19-5   Example of **ethtool -S _<device>_** Output

```
$ ethtool -S enp0s2 | grep -i 'drop'
rx_queue_0_drops: 0
rx_queue_0_xdp_drops: 0
tx_queue_0_xdp_tx_drops: 0
```

Example 19-5 shows the **grep** command filtering for any instances of lines that contain the text "drop," and the output displays three lines that show no packets are being dropped currently.

Diagnosing with the **netstat** Command

You can also run the **netstat** command to identify drops and collisions, such as shown in Example 19-6.

Example 19-6   Viewing the Kernel Interface Table Using **netstat -i**

```
$ netstat -i
Kernel Interface table
Iface    MTU     RX-OK    RX-ERR RX-DRP RX-OVR   TX-OK    TX-ERR TX-DRP
TX-OVR Flg
enp0s2  1500    233716        0      0      0   80587        0      0
0    BMRU
lo       65536    5234        0      0      0    5234        0      0
0    LRU0
```

The kernel interface table shows you a lot of good information by interface. In Example 19-6, the enp0s2 interface is the eth0 equivalent on an Ubuntu virtual machine and the lo interface is the localhost. In example 19-7, there are no dropped packages. Unfortunately, this tool does not display collisions.

Diagnosing with the /sys/class/net/*<device>*/statistics Information

There is a more granular and less easy-to-read set of information you can consult for dropped packets and collisions, located in the **/sys** tree structure deep down in the **/sys/net/class/<device>/statistics** directory. It's a set of files that are intuitively named so that you can look at the filename and know what statistic you are viewing data for.

A great way to understand the structure of this directory is to run the **tree** command against it, such as shown in Figure 19-6.

It's incredibly difficult to find documentation for these values. You'd think that, being as important as these values are, there'd be a ready source that explains all you'd want to know about each one. Forgive me for being cynical in a historically informed manner, but lack of documentation is why I've been bugging the heck out of software engineers all my career. Documentation and explanation, while present in the software developer/software engineer community, is not as prevalent (or even nearly as complete) as you'd wish.

To get the most documentation that exists on these counters, visit the kernel.org documentation page for **struct_rtnl_link_stats64** (https://docs.kernel.org/networking/statistics.html?highlight=tx_dropped#c.rtnl_link_stats64) and follow the links to the **sysfs-class-net-statistics** page (https://www.kernel.org/doc/Documentation/ABI/testing/sysfs-class-net) for even more (slightly cryptic) information regarding these counters.

```
ubuntu@primary:~$ tree /sys/class/net/enp0s2/statistics
/sys/class/net/enp0s2/statistics
├── collisions
├── multicast
├── rx_bytes
├── rx_compressed
├── rx_crc_errors
├── rx_dropped
├── rx_errors
├── rx_fifo_errors
├── rx_frame_errors
├── rx_length_errors
├── rx_missed_errors
├── rx_nohandler
├── rx_over_errors
├── rx_packets
├── tx_aborted_errors
├── tx_bytes
├── tx_carrier_errors
├── tx_compressed
├── tx_dropped
├── tx_errors
├── tx_fifo_errors
├── tx_heartbeat_errors
├── tx_packets
└── tx_window_errors

0 directories, 24 files
```

Figure 19-6   Example output of the **tree** command on the **/sys/class/net/enp0s2** directory

Wrapping Up Dropping Packets

Detecting dropped packets and collisions is similar to panning for gold: most of the time you'll find a few little items here and there, but when you are least expecting it, you will hit the motherload and errors will crop up and be pretty obvious they are happening.

I recommend that, beyond replacing malfunctioning hardware and gathering information, you do not try to mess around with your networking, particularly using the **ethtool** command. If you do, you risk bollixing up your interfaces and how they function to the point of having to reinstall drivers, at the very least.

Link Status

Networking happens on several layers, so you need to know how to check the status of a link on those various layers. Determining that a network device or link isn't showing up properly or is not apparently working can be very helpful in pinpointing where an issue is located.

Diagnosing and Fixing Link Status Issues

We'll approach this by layer, starting with the lowest and going up, specifying the tools as we go.

> **NOTE** No longer is it as likely that you'll be able to find a blinking or steady green light on a NIC to let you know whether all is well in networking—so much is either not local or is completely virtual—so we'll skip the old-school method of checking link lights and go straight to checking link status via software.

Layer 1: Physical

At this layer, you're basically checking whether the cables or wires are actually present and conveying the signals they are supposed to be.

The primary way to find out if everything is working properly at the physical layer is to use the **ip** command and its **link** subcommand and options.

Example 19-7 shows example output from the **ip link** command.

Example 19-7 Example Output from the **ip link show** Command

```
$ ip link show
1: lo: <LOOPBACK,UP,LOWER_UP> mtu 65536 qdisc noqueue state UNKNOWN
mode DEFAULT group default qlen 1000
    link/loopback 00:00:00:00:00:00 brd 00:00:00:00:00:00
2: enp0s2: <BROADCAST,MULTICAST,UP,LOWER_UP> mtu 1500 qdisc fq_codel
state UP mode DEFAULT group default qlen 1000
    link/ether ca:3b:cc:0e:10:69 brd ff:ff:ff:ff:ff:ff
```

The key part here is to look at the non-lo interface, in this case the enp0s2 (eth0 equivalent), and see if "mode" is preceded by UP, which this interface does. This means the interface is up and connected.

Another method is to use the **ethtool** command to determine if the link is up, as shown in Example 19-8.

Example 19-8 Example Output from the **ethtool** Command

```
$ ethtool enp0s2 | grep Link
Cannot get wake-on-lan settings: Operation not permitted
    Link detected: yes:ff
```

There are other settings that can be seen in the **ethtool** output for a given interface, but we're looking only for the link information, so **grep** is used to show just that. You can safely ignore the wake-on-lan message.

Layer 2: Data Link

At this layer, we're not looking for whether the link is up but rather looking around to see if this device can see other devices on the network. If it can't, there might be a VLAN (virtual LAN) issue or the device could be literally on its own network.

Regardless, we can determine whether it can find its neighbors by using the Address Resolution Protocol (ARP), basically shouting "Hello? Anyone there?" on the local network, which will help us understand what else might be wrong.

The important thing is to query the ARP table, which you can do with the plain **arp** command, or by using the **ip neighbor show** command, as shown in Example 19-9.

Example 19-9   Example Output from the **ip neighbor show** Command

```
$ ip neighbor show
192.168.64.1 dev enp0s2 lladdr 3e:22:fb:91:6a:64 REACHABLE
```

This output shows that there is a host that is reachable by the example host, and given the IP address, it's probably a gateway (and in this case it is).

In Example 19-10 you see the **arp** command showing similar information.

Example 19-10   Example Output from the **arp** Command

```
$ arp -a
_gateway (192.168.64.1) at 3e:22:fb:91:6a:64 [ether] on enp0s2
```

As suspected, this is a gateway, and it's known that way to the ARP table and **arp** command. You can have it display the IP address instead of _gateway in the **Address** column by using the **-n** option to the **arp** command.

> **NOTE**   Keep in mind that the link status world has changed. The **ifstatus** command used to be a commonly used command, but **ip link show** has mostly taken over from that command, which is not even installed by default on many distributions.

Bandwidth Limitations

Bandwidth limitation refers to the restriction or capping of the maximum data transfer rate on a network connection. The rest of your computing environment can be operating at a very fast pace, but if your bandwidth or access to the rest of the world of computing is slow or has latency, it'll seem as if your network is slow.

Bandwidth and Latency

 Bandwidth is the maximum rate of data transfer across a given path. It is measured in bits per second (bps). Bandwidth is often used to refer to the capacity of a network connection. Network latency is the time it takes for a signal to travel from one point to another on a network. It is measured in milliseconds (ms). Latency is important because it determines how quickly data can be transferred between two points. A high latency connection will result in slower data transfer speeds.

Diagnosing and Fixing Bandwidth Limitations

Latency is usually determined by "feel," meaning the network response you are getting is not meeting your expectations of how quickly or responsive your session should be, or has been responsive but now is not. Ask hard-core gamers if their version of latency, aka "lag," is a factor in game performance and you'll get a resounding "Yes!"

The following utilities are helpful for troubleshooting latency issues on your system:

- **ping:** Described previously, use the **ping** command to see a very simple set of response times. Anything in the high two-digit millisecond range (80–99 ms) is pretty long, and anything above that indicates a fair amount of delay. The remoteness of the host can be a factor in this measurement.

- **traceroute:** Also described previously, use the **traceroute** command output to show you where delays are happening.

- **Bandwidth analyzers:** Several bandwidth analyzers are available online, perhaps the simplest of which is https://fast.com, run by Netflix, which will give you a quick speed indication, but not much else. This is somewhat akin to looking at the speedometer on your vehicle and assuming that since it *shows* 190 MPH, you can *go* that fast. Another, more informative bandwidth analyzer is www.speedtest.net, which gives you more metrics, including upload and download speeds, and you can typically choose a remote server to test against.

- **hping3:** Created by Antirez, the hping3 utility can be used to get more information than is possible with the **ping** command, and it also has some other interesting capabilities that include IP address spoofing and sending randomized traffic as a way to test a host.

NOTE Determining latency and its effect on bandwidth mostly involves using the previous list of tools to find out where the slowdown or throttle point is, and seeing if you can relieve it. However, often people will complain that they have latency, all while being in a location like a coffee shop where the people around them are viewing videos, downloading ISO and movie files, and so forth. You also have to be aware of what is going on around you to make a good determination as to what the problem is.

Name Resolution Issues

The resolution of host and domain names is so important that the Internet as we know it wouldn't really be possible without it. The centralization or the hierarchical organization of worldwide *name resolution* is a very good way to have all these names handled, not without a lot of work, but with much less work than constantly trying to manually update all the names attached to hosts you need to reach.

The Trifecta of DNS

As covered in Chapter 5, three files are used to configure how local and remote name resolution occurs via the ***Domain Name System (DNS)***: **/etc/hosts**, **/etc/resolv.conf**, and **/etc/nsswitch.conf**.

Effectively, if you are troubleshooting name resolution, it's because you are not able to use host or domain names to get to where you want to go.

Diagnosing and Fixing Name Resolution Issues

The process of troubleshooting name resolution issues may be as simple as the following steps:

Step 1. Ping the remote system by name, such as www.example.com.

Step 2. If you don't get a valid response, try pinging it by the IP address, which you may not have, but it might show up in the results of the failed attempt to ping the name.

Step 3. If that doesn't work (or you don't have the IP address), view your **/etc/hosts** file and look for an entry that would incorrectly resolve the remote host's name.

Step 4. If you find nothing in **/etc/hosts**, view the contents of the **/etc/resolv.conf** file and ensure those DNS servers are valid, can be contacted via **ping**, and will respond to a **dig** command.

Step 5. If the host is responding, look to see if there is an A record that corresponds to that host's name, such as the www host at example.com.

This can be done using the **dig** command as shown in Example 19-11.

Example 19-11   Example Output from the **dig** Command

```
$ dig www example.com
; <<>> DiG 9.16.1-Ubuntu <<>> www example.com
;; global options: +cmd
;; Got answer:
;; ->>HEADER<<- opcode: QUERY, status: SERVFAIL, id: 53331
;; flags: qr rd ra; QUERY: 1, ANSWER: 0, AUTHORITY: 0, ADDITIONAL: 1

;; OPT PSEUDOSECTION:
; EDNS: version: 0, flags:; udp: 65494
;; QUESTION SECTION:
;www.                           IN      A

;; Query time: 0 msec
;; SERVER: 127.0.0.53#53(127.0.0.53)
;; WHEN: Thu Dec 29 17:33:31 MST 2022
;; MSG SIZE  rcvd: 32

;; Got answer:
;; ->>HEADER<<- opcode: QUERY, status: NOERROR, id: 30864
;; flags: qr rd ra; QUERY: 1, ANSWER: 1, AUTHORITY: 0, ADDITIONAL: 1

;; OPT PSEUDOSECTION:
; EDNS: version: 0, flags:; udp: 65494
;; QUESTION SECTION:
;example.com.                   IN      A

;; ANSWER SECTION:
example.com.            3075    IN      A       93.184.216.34

;; Query time: 0 msec
;; SERVER: 127.0.0.53#53(127.0.0.53)
;; WHEN: Thu Dec 29 17:33:31 MST 2022
;; MSG SIZE  rcvd: 56
```

The output in Example 19-11 shows that we have requested the A or Address record type for the www host at the example.com domain or site. **dig** has gotten us a lot more than we truly need, but the lines highlighted in bold in the output contain the answer to our query: there is a host named www at the example.com domain and its IP address is 93.184.216.34, so now we can ping that directly.

NOTE If you can't ping by name a host on your local network but can ping by name a remote host, then it's a local network or DNS server issue, likely, but check the **/etc/ hosts** file. If you can ping a lot of other hosts, local and remote, but not a particular one, that system or its name resolution is the issue.

Testing Remote Systems

Testing (aka "probing") remote systems is a great way to get into a *lot* of trouble, as certain activities are considered at the very least inappropriate and at worst can constitute an attempt to hack or penetrate a remote system.

How (Not) to Break the Law

Checking your local laws before testing remote systems, using **nmap** in particular, is highly recommended. You'll also find many resources on the Web that will caution you to *not* use **nmap** and other tools to test remote systems.

The key is simply this: Secure *written* authorization before testing a system that you do not personally own. Period.

The *Open Source Security Testing Methodology Manual*, developed by ISECOM and freely available at its website (https://www.isecom.org/research.html#content5-a0), contains a very clear methodology that you can follow to make sure you are not breaking laws and causing yourself or others harm using probing tools like NMAP.

Purposes of Testing a Remote System

Why would you want to test a remote system? For security purposes, absolutely. But what else might you want to know about a system that is remote (i.e., other than the system you're using to test)?

The following are valid reasons to query or test remote systems (with written permission):

- Network mapping
- Port state discovery
- Ghost or shadow device detection
- Operating system inventory
- Service discovery
- Vulnerability inventory

Testing Remote Systems with NMAP

Note that the **nmap** command is also covered in Chapter 8, "Understanding Linux Security Best Practices." The focus of the coverage here is for testing remote systems for troubleshooting purposes.

On your own corporate network, using NMAP to conduct the previously listed tasks is quite reasonable; many examples of each are discussed and demo'ed in the NMAP official book, the online version of which is available at the NMAP.org site: https://nmap.org/book/toc.html.

Getting NMAP on your system is usually really easy—it's available in the package repositories for most of the major Linux distributions and many of the minor distributions.

Running NMAP is fairly easy, at least on the lower end of functionality. However, it can get extremely complex on the command line as you expand what you're asking NMAP to accomplish.

By performing various scans with the **nmap** command, you can identify open ports, blocked ports, and potential misconfigurations in the firewall rules. This section will explore which options you should use to determine if there is a firewall issue on a remote system.

Running a Simple System Scan

I own my own network and have access to many more networks for work, but I am incredibly aware of how quickly I could get into trouble areas with my organization, and even the ISP I use to get my data to my work networks, if I were to start port scanning without their knowledge and consent.

Let's run a simple scan on a local target host and see what NMAP can tell us about that host—you may be surprised at how much NMAP reveals about a supposedly secure Linux system. The results of our scan of the target host are shown in Example 19-12. Note the use of the -v option in this example, which provides more verbose output.

Example 19-12   Example Output of a Simple **nmap** Scan of the Target Host

```
$ nmap -v 192.168.64.2
Starting Nmap 7.80 ( https://nmap.org ) at 2022-12-31 19:04 MST
Initiating Ping Scan at 19:04
Scanning localhost (127.0.0.1) [2 ports]
Completed Ping Scan at 19:04, 0.02s elapsed (1 total hosts)
Initiating Connect Scan at 19:04
Scanning localhost (127.0.0.1) [1000 ports]
apsed (1000 total ports)
```

```
Discovered open port 80/tcp on 127.0.0.1
Discovered open port 22/tcp on 127.0.0.1
Completed Connect Scan at 19:04, 0.15s el
Nmap scan report for localhost (127.0.0.1)
Host is up (0.00073s latency).
Other addresses for localhost (not scanned): ::1
Not shown: 998 closed ports
PORT    STATE SERVICE
22/tcp open  ssh
80/tcp open  http

Read data files from: /usr/bin/../share/nmap
Nmap done: 1 IP address (1 host up) scanned in 0.24 seconds
```

In Example 19-12, scanning the target host quickly revealed that two ports are open out of the 1,000 scanned: ports 22 and 80 are open, so SSH and HTTP are allowing incoming traffic on this host. That's more information than we could have gotten with a simple **ping**.

Running a Service Discovery Scan

Now that we have a couple of ports that show as open, we can get more information on those services using nmap and its slightly more advanced scanning features.

The results of our scan of the target host are shown in Example 19-13. Note that the -V option in this example will display the version number of the software that is listening to the port. This can be used to determine if the software is out of date and may pose security concerns.

Example 19-13   Example Output from a Simple **nmap** Scan of the Localhost

```
$ nmap -sV -p 22,80 192.168.64.2
Starting Nmap 7.80 ( https://nmap.org ) at 2022-12-31 19:18 MST
Nmap scan report for localhost (127.0.0.1)
Host is up (0.0022s latency).
Other addresses for localhost (not scanned): ::1

PORT    STATE SERVICE VERSION
22/tcp open  ssh   OpenSSH 8.2p1 Ubuntu 4ubuntu0.4(Ubuntu Linux;
protocol 2.0)
80/tcp open  http nginx 1.18.0 (Ubuntu)

Service Info: OS: Linux; CPE: cpe:/o:linux:linux_kernel
```

```
Service detection performed. Please report any incorrect results at
https://nmap.org/submit/ .
Nmap done: 1 IP address (1 host up) scanned in 6.99 seconds
```

In the output shown in Example 19-13, we now have some information about the service that's running on each port, along with the version, and this is valuable information, as an attacker would want to know what version of OpenSSH or NGINX we are running, in case there are vulnerabilities that can be exploited in that particular version.

Running a Vulnerability Scan

Now the fun begins. Since we know the target host has a couple of ports open and we have identified the services running, let's do our final task in this section about NMAP, scanning the host and reporting back on vulnerabilities to those services.

The results of our vulnerability scan of the target host are shown in Example 19-14.

Example 19-14 Example Output from a Vulnerability Scan of the Target Host

```
$ nmap -P 80 -sV --script=vulners 192.168.64.2
Starting Nmap 7.80 ( https://nmap.org ) at 2022-12-31 19:53 MST
Nmap scan report for primary (192.168.64.2)
Host is up (0.0090s latency).
Not shown: 998 closed ports
PORT    STATE SERVICE VERSION
22/tcp open  ssh     OpenSSH 8.2p1 Ubuntu 4ubuntu0.4 (Ubuntu Linux;
protocol 2.0)
| vulners:
|   cpe:/a:openbsd:openssh:8.2p1:
|         CVE-2020-15778    6.8    https://vulners.com/cve/
CVE-2020-15778
|         C94132FD-1FA5-5342-B6EE-0DAF45EEFFE3    6.8    https://
vulners.com/githubexploit/C94132FD-1FA5-5342-B6EE-0DAF45EEFFE3
*EXPLOIT*
|         10213DBE-F683-58BB-B6D3-353173626207    6.8    https://
vulners.com/githubexploit/10213DBE-F683-58BB-B6D3-353173626207
*EXPLOIT*
|         CVE-2020-12062    5.0    https://vulners.com/cve/
CVE-2020-12062
|         CVE-2021-28041    4.6    https://vulners.com/cve/
CVE-2021-28041
|         CVE-2021-41617    4.4    https://vulners.com/cve/
CVE-2021-41617
```

```
|          CVE-2020-14145    4.3      https://vulners.com/cve/
CVE-2020-14145
|          CVE-2016-20012    4.3      https://vulners.com/cve/
CVE-2016-20012


|_         CVE-2021-36368    2.6      https://vulners.com/cve/
CVE-2021-36368
80/tcp open  http     nginx 1.18.0 (Ubuntu)
|_http-server-header: nginx/1.18.0 (Ubuntu)
| vulners:
|   cpe:/a:igor_sysoev:nginx:1.18.0:
|          OSV:CVE-2022-41742    0.0       https://vulners.com/osv/
OSV:CVE-2022-41742
|          OSV:CVE-2022-41741    0.0       https://vulners.com/osv/
OSV:CVE-2022-41741
|_         OSV:CVE-2021-3618     0.0       https://vulners.com/osv/
OSV:CVE-2021-3618
Service Info: OS: Linux; CPE: cpe:/o:linux:linux_kernel


Service detection performed. Please report any incorrect results at
https://nmap.org/submit/ .
Nmap done: 2 IP addresses (1 host up) scanned in 10.54 seconds
```

The great thing about a vulnerability scan is that it will not only show which vulnerabilities exist, but also give you the link to go see what needs to be fixed.

Hopefully you can see what a great tool NMAP is, even if only scanning a single target host for standard ports, associated services, and, of course, anything that could be used for an attack on those ports and services.

Testing Remote Systems with s_client

Running, maintaining, and accessing *OpenSSL* servers can be a lot to handle. Quite a few things could go wrong, so having a great tool like the s_client module to the **openssl** command can be very helpful in troubleshooting your OpenSSL servers and clients and their sometimes stormy relationships.

Verifying SSL Connection to a Remote System

The *s_client* module will perform a large number of test and connection functions, probably the first of which would be to confirm that the remote system has an SSL certificate and, if so, then view the contents of that certificate.

Running a simple verify query against a remote system is shown in Example 19-15.

Example 19-15   Example Output from an s_client Verification of example.com

```
$ openssl s_client -verify_return_error -connect example.com:443
CONNECTED(00000003)
depth=2 C = US, O = DigiCert Inc, OU = www.digicert.com, CN =
DigiCert Global Root CA
verify return:1
depth=1 C = US, O = DigiCert Inc, CN = DigiCert TLS RSA SHA256 2020
CA1
verify return:1
depth=0 C = US, ST = California, L = Los Angeles, O = Internet\C2\
A0Corporation\C2\A0for\C2\A0Assigned\C2\A0Names\C2\A0and\C2\A0Numbers,
CN = www.example.org
verify return:1
---
Certificate chain
 0 s:C = US, ST = California, L = Los Angeles, O = Internet\C2\
A0Corporation\C2\A0for\C2\A0Assigned\C2\A0Names\C2\A0and\C2\A0Numbers,
CN = www.example.org
   i:C = US, O = DigiCert Inc, CN = DigiCert TLS RSA SHA256 2020 CA1
 1 s:C = US, O = DigiCert Inc, CN = DigiCert TLS RSA SHA256 2020 CA1
   i:C = US, O = DigiCert Inc, OU = www.digicert.com, CN = DigiCert
Global Root CA
---
Server certificate
-----BEGIN CERTIFICATE-----
MIIHRzCCBi+gAwIBAgIQD6pjEJMHvD1BSJJkDM1NmjANBgkqhkiG9w0BAQsFADBP
MQswCQYDVQQGEwJVUzEVMBMGA1UEChMMRG1naUN1cnQgSW5jMSkwJwYDVQQDEyBE
aWdpQ2VydCBUTFMgU1NBIFN1QTI1NiAyMDIwIENBMTAeFw0yMjAzMTQwMDAwMDBa
Fw0yMzAzMTQyMzU5NT1aMIGWMQswCQYDVQQGEwJVUzETMBEGA1UECBMKQ2FsaWZv
cm5pYTEUMBIGA1UEBxMLTG9zIEFuZ2VsZXMxQjBABgNVBAoMOUludGVybmV0wqBD
<output truncated, it's extremely long>
```

We've connected to the example.com server and requested to see its certificate chain, which as you can see in the output is located in Los Angeles, California and is managed by the ICANN organization.

Other Useful s_client Commands

Because of the extreme length of the s_client module's query responses from any valid OpenSSL host, we'll just detail a couple of key commands and their explanations instead of spending many pages on the output you'll see if you try out these commands on your own system.

Commands to Use when Connected to a Host

You can use the following commands to perform various actions when connected via the s_client module to another host:

- **Q:** End the SSL connection and exit the command
- **R:** Renegotiate the SSL connection session, certain protocols only
- **B:** Send a heartbeat message to the system
- **k:** Send a Key Update message to the system
- **K:** Send a Key Update message to the system, and request a Key Update back from the system

> **NOTE** There are many other things you can do with the s_client module, some simple and a lot of them fairly complex. Read the s_client man page for more details than you probably want and certainly much more than you need for the Linux+ exam.
>
> ```
> $ man s_client
> ```

Opening an SSL Connection to a Host

To open an SSL connection to a host and get a lot of useful information back, use the command

```
$ openssl s_client -connect example.com:443
```

Parse through the copious output and notice how the query has been responded to; you can either use the commands or just quit the session.

Showing SSL Certificates on a Host

To show the entire certificate chain for a given host, use the command

```
$ openssl s_client -connect example.com:443 -showcerts
```

You'll see the certificate information listed; just parse through it to find out more about the host and its certifcate(s).

Testing a Particular TLS Version on a Host

There are times when you'll want to make sure that a given TLS version is available on hosts. To query just that information, use the command

```
$ openssl s_client -connect example.com:443 -tls1_3
```

The output displayed in Example 19-16 verifies that the proper TLS information is shown in the SSL-Session: block.

Example 19-16   Example Output from the **openssl s_client** TLS Version Query

```
$ openssl s_client -connect example.com:443 -tls1_3
SSL-Session:
    Protocol  : TLSv1.3
    Cipher    : TLS_AES_256_GCM_SHA384
    Session-ID: 84BF20BB5699F250177C680D4A074B9DB7E8976099C1C6C5D6AF
67A996D64
    Session-ID-ctx:
    Resumption PSK: 13005B8986AB6F6B74E89CE87B9497FBA20241110AA3F67D
4A58E9D83
```

Notice that the version of TLS we were querying for is present in the Protocol: portion of the query response.

Summary

In this chapter you learned all about troubleshooting networks, from subnets and routing, to firewall issues, to interface errors like dropped packets and collisions. You also learned about the relationship between bandwidth and latency issues, and about where name resolution system issues can occur.

Additionally, you learned about testing remote systems with **nmap**, as well as how to connect to remote SSL systems, query them for information, protocol support, show their certificates, and much more.

Exam Preparation Tasks

As mentioned in the section "Goals and Methods" in the Introduction, you have a couple of choices for exam preparation: the exercises here, Chapter 23, "Final Preparation," and the exam simulation questions in the Pearson Test Prep Software Online.

Review All Key Topics

Review the most important topics in this chapter, noted with the Key Topic icon in the margin of the page. Table 19-2 lists these key topics and the page number on which each is found.

Table 19-2   Key Topics for Chapter 19

Key Topic Element	Description	Page Number
Paragraph	The most likely causes of network configuration issues	670
Paragraph	Function of the **traceroute** command	673
Paragraph	Purpose of a firewall is to protect a host from unwanted or harmful traffic	674
List	Possible causes of firewall issues	675
Paragraph	Utilities for diagnosing causes of dropped packets	680
Paragraph	Diagnosing link status issues with **ip link**	684
Paragraph	Definition of bandwidth	686
Paragraph	Secure written authorization required before testing a system that you do not personally own	689
List	Reasons to query or test remote systems	689
List	Commands to perform various actions when connected via the s_client module to another host	695

Define Key Terms

Define the following key terms from this chapter and check your answers in the glossary:

high latency, firewall, **nmap**, interface errors, dropped packets, collisions, bandwidth limitations, name resolution, Domain Name System (DNS), OpenSSL, s_client

Review Questions

The answers to these review questions are in Appendix A.

1. Which of the following is an example of a standard Class C subnet? Choose the best answer.

   a. 255.0.0.0

   b. 255.255.0.0

   c. 255.255.255.0

   d. 255.255.255.255

2. When testing a remote system, which of the following tools can you use to test if any services are responding on particular ports? (Choose all that apply.)

   a. **ssh-connect**

   b. **nmap**

   c. **portscan**

   d. **telnet**

   e. **netbus**

3. Which of the following is a primary cause of dropped packets?

   a. RJ-11 error

   b. E-Sim error

   c. NIC error

   d. Port Error

4. When you suspect a latency issue, you run a simple website tool that shows your connection's current bandwidth capabilities. What website does this?

   a. Fast.com

   b. Lagging.com

   c. Speed.com

   d. Example.com

5. You've been developing a website locally and have pushed the code to production, yet when you push more changes, you don't see the results. Which file may contain a hint as to why this is happening?

   a. /etc/resolv.conf

   b. /etc/services

   c. /etc/nsswitch.conf

   d. /etc/hosts

6. What command to the **openssl s_client** command will send a Key Update to the remote system and request it to send a Key Update back?

   a. B

   b. Q

   c. R

   d. K

This chapter covers the following topics:

- Runaway and Zombie Processes

- High CPU Utilization/Load Average/Run Queues

- CPU Times and CPU Process Priorities

- Memory Exhaustion and Out of Memory

- Swapping

- Hardware

The exam objective covered in this chapter is as follows:

- **Objective 4.3:** Given a scenario, analyze and troubleshoot central processing unit (CPU) and memory issues

## CHAPTER 20

Analyzing and Troubleshooting CPU and Memory Issues

CPU and memory are closely linked, one feeding the other, and anytime you're experiencing memory issues, such as swapping or out of memory issues, that's going to affect the CPU.

This chapter will focus on tools and techniques that will help you analyze and troubleshoot CPU and memory issues.

"Do I Know This Already?" Quiz

The "Do I Know This Already?" quiz enables you to assess whether you should read this entire chapter or simply jump to the "Exam Preparation Tasks" section for review. If you are in doubt, read the entire chapter. Table 20-1 outlines the major headings in this chapter and the corresponding "Do I Know This Already?" quiz questions. You can find the answers in Appendix A, "Answers to the 'Do I Know This Already?' Quizzes and Review Questions."

Table 20-1 "Do I Know This Already?" Foundation Topics Section-to-Question Mapping

Foundation Topics Section	Questions Covered in This Section
Runaway and Zombie Processes	1
High CPU Utilization/Load Average/Run Queues	2
CPU Times and CPU Process Priorities	3
Memory Exhaustion and Out of Memory	4
Swapping	5
Hardware	6

CAUTION The goal of self-assessment is to gauge your mastery of the topics in this chapter. If you do not know the answer to a question or are only partially sure of the answer, you should mark that question as wrong for purposes of the self-assessment. Giving yourself credit for an answer you correctly guess skews your self-assessment results and might provide you with a false sense of security.

1. You see a process that is marked with a Z in the **STAT** column and realize that it's a zombie process. What phrase describes what has not happened at the parent process level for this process?

    a. Pausing

    b. Terminating

    c. Reaping

    d. Polling

2. You suspect that your system has overly high CPU utilization, as normal tasks are taking longer than usual and the system seems sluggish. Which tools will give you a quick overview of the system's CPU, memory, and other details on a refreshing display?

    a. **top**

    b. **tail**

    c. **stat**

    d. **uptime**

3. Which of the following commands displays the amount of time a process is taking up on the CPU?

    a. **cpuinfo**

    b. **syscpu**

    c. **procps**

    d. **iostat**

4. There is a quirkily named process in the Linux kernel that is invoked to free up memory when there is a danger of the system becoming bogged down or not allowing new processes to be created. What is the name of this process/component?

    a. Texas Chainsaw

    b. Chuckie

    c. The Thing

    d. OOM Killer

5. Swap for memory can be configured via what two methods?

    a. block

    b. disk

c. register

d. file

e. xrecord

6. Which of the following commands will display CPU information?

a. cpuinfo

b. list-cpu

c. display-cpu

d. lscpu

Foundation Topics

Runaway and Zombie Processes

Since we covered processes and how to deal with them quite thoroughly in Chapter 4, "Managing Processes and Services," we'll just recap what they are and how to understand the difference between a normally working process and a runaway or zombie, two very different extremes of process behavior.

Runaway Processes

A *runaway process* is a process that has either malfunctioned or is accidentally or maliciously creating copies of itself until the system becomes unresponsive or unusable due to the CPU load being taken over.

What Causes Runaway Processes?

Typically a program will be loaded, a process or processes will be created, and when the main program exits, the child processes of that main process will be ended by the parent or main process.

There are multiple schedulers in Linux, and an issue can occur with realtime or deadline processes where they can completely fence off or make useless any other process on the system by being a runaway.

Since about Linux kernel 2.6 or so, we have been able to set a couple of safety hatches for being able to kill off a runaway process that is using up all the CPU time and won't allow for a **kill** command from any process, aka the shell, that is running at a higher priority than the runaway process.

Yes, it is entirely possible to have a runaway process or processes hang the system so badly that you cannot correct the situation, because you can't start or use a shell that can issue the **kill** or other process-ending commands.

Reserving Some CPU for Non-Realtime Processes

There are two files that exist in **/proc** that allow you to reserve an amount of CPU time for non-realtime or non-deadline processes:

- **/proc/sys/kernel/sched_rt_period_us**
- **/proc/sys/kernel/sched_rt_runtime_us**

These two files contain integer values that are measured from -1, which means reserve no time, to whatever value you wish to set, all measured in microseconds.

This is very important, because unless you can reserve even a second or so, you won't be able to fit in a process that can kill a runaway process—no reserved time, no chance to run a non-realtime process such as a root shell to kill the runaway process!

For example, the default value for the **/proc/sys/kernel/sched_rt_period_us** file is **100,000**, or 1 second, which will allow you to try to squeeze in a command from the shell.

Identifying a Runaway Process

One of the ways to identify a runaway process is that the system is racing or unresponsive and you can hardly get a keystroke in.

Not all runaways take up the entire system, so if you have access to the command line, try using the **top** command, see what floats to the top of the chart of processes, and kill it.

It's also possible to find these processes using the **ps** command, but the output is nowhere as clear as with the **top** command. You can also use the very useful **htop** command, which gives you options that other tools don't and is visually easy to understand and use.

Ending a Runaway Process

To end a runaway process, you could use the built-in "kill" options that the **top** and **htop** commands offer. You would first highlight the offending process and then press the **F9** key, which would cause the program to send a SIGTERM or -15 signal to attempt to kill that process, all within those programs.

To have the most control over the kill of a process, use the **kill** command and specify the -9 or SIGKILL signal.

Zombie Processes

Processes have a parent process, and often child processes. Even the kernel or the **init** process will have an entry for its PPID, or Parent Process ID, which will point to its own process.

Occasionally you'll see a process marked in the output of commands such as **top**, **htop**, and **ps** with a "Z," which denotes it's a zombie process.

A *zombie process* is one that has exited, died, or been terminated, but its process descriptor in the process table (a location in RAM holding the information about processes) has not been updated.

What Causes Zombie Processes?

A zombie is not responsible for doing anything about its being killed, ended, or quit, other than sending notice to its parent process that it's been terminated, stopped by a signal, or resumed by a signal. The parent process is responsible for removing the child process's information from the Process Table, and if the parent process never uses the **wait()** syscall to retrieve the child process's termination information, the Process Table is not updated and a zombie exists.

When a child process is marked as a zombie, it hangs around "eating brains" or taking up a little bit of space in memory until it's cleaned up by the parent process.

There are also times when a parent process ends suddenly, and orphans all the child processes, which are then marked as zombies.

Are Zombie Processes Bad?

No, they just exist; they're not bad or harmful unless there are a lot of them. A zombie process takes whatever memory it was using, and having them now and then is fairly normal and to be expected.

However, if you are consistently getting them or are seeing a number of them consistently, it can be a sign of a malfunctioning program or corrupted code.

Removing Zombie Processes

A zombie process can be removed by sending a particular signal to the parent process, such as shown in Example 20-1.

Example 20-1   Example of the **kill** Command

```
$ kill -s SIGCHLD 12345
```

There may or may not be output from the command, but the signal SIGCHLD has been sent to the parent process, which will cause it to go and reap the zombies among its child processes.

High CPU Utilization/Load Average/Run Queues

The performance of the system CPU can have a significant impact on the usability of the system. You want to be aware of how much of the CPU is utilized and, if over-utilized, consider moving some services to other systems or upgrading your hardware. This section explores how to view CPU utilization and pinpoint performance issues.

High CPU Utilization

Since the CPU, memory, caching, and disk are all so interrelated (that is, x feeds y, which feeds z), a *high CPU utilization* situation can be any or all of several things:

- Resource-intensive processes
- Poorly written programs
- Memory leaks in programs
- Failing or overburdened disk

The fix for high CPU utilization is to find which process (or processes) is the problem and end it as previously described, such as by using the **kill** command.

High Load Average

Understanding the load average starts with understanding that the load of a Linux system is defined as what is currently the amount of CPU utilization, or what's running at that given moment in time.

You can think of a *load* as a numeric measurement of the number of processes being executed, or even waiting for execution. You'll see that a smooth and consistent set of loads over time is preferable to highly variable or spiky loads due to heavy system demands and then nothing for a while, then another heavy demand, and so on.

Because the number that indicates the current load changes from almost instant to instant, the really significant number we can view is the *load average*, or the average number of processes being executed or in waiting over a period of time.

A *high load average* indicates that the system is under heavy load, meaning there are many processes either actively running or waiting to run. However, the threshold for what constitutes a high load average can vary based on factors such as the number of CPU cores, the system's capacity, and the nature of the workload.

A high load average could be due to various reasons:

- **High CPU Utilization:** If the CPU is running at or near maximum capacity, processes may need to wait in the queue for their turn to be executed.

- **I/O Operations:** Heavy I/O operations, such as disk reads and writes, can lead to increased load as processes wait for I/O operations to complete.

- **Network Activity:** Network-intensive tasks can contribute to a high load average if processes are waiting for network responses.

- **Resource Intensive Processes:** Processes that require significant memory or other resources can lead to a higher load average.

Viewing System Load Details with the **uptime** Command

One of the easiest ways to get the load numbers is to run the **uptime** command, which will bring back a series of numbers and other information such as that shown in Example 20-2.

Example 20-2 Example Output from the **uptime** Command

```
$ uptime
16:28:23 up 13 min,  1 user,  load average: 0.47, 0.15, 0.08
```

First you see the current system time, then the length of time the system has been up (13 minutes). This is followed by the number of users, and then the three separate load averages, which break down as follows:

0.47: The load average for the last 1 minute

0.15: The load average for the last 5 minutes

0.08: The load average for the last 15 minutes

But the **uptime** command is sort of boring—it just outputs some text, and it only runs once (unless you use the **watch** command to make it run more often). Make sure you try **uptime** with the **-s** or **--since** option, which shows you the starting or specified time the system has been running since.

High Run Queues

A high run queue in Linux is a situation where there are a large number of processes waiting to be executed by the CPU. This can happen when there are too many processes running on the system, or when the CPU is not able to keep up with the demand for new processes.

High run queues can cause performance problems, as the CPU may not be able to respond to requests quickly enough. In some cases, high run queues can even lead to system instability.

There are several reasons why run queues might become high, including:

- **Too many processes running:** If there are too many processes running on the system, the CPU may not be able to keep up with the demand for new processes and the run queue will start to grow.

- **I/O bottlenecks:** If the system is experiencing I/O (Input/Output) bottlenecks, the kernel may not be able to schedule new processes until the I/O operations have completed.

- **Memory pressure:** If the system is under memory pressure (not enough available memory), the CPU may not be able to allocate memory for new processes.

- **CPU bottlenecks:** If the system is experiencing CPU bottlenecks, the system may not be able to schedule new processes quickly enough.

There are several actions that can be done to address high run queues including:

- **Reducing the number of processes running:** This can be accomplished by killing unnecessary processes or by using a process manager (like a crontab job) to control the number of processes that are running.

- **Improving I/O performance:** This can be accomplished by optimizing the system's I/O configuration or by adding more storage capacity.

- **Allocating more memory:** This can be accomplished by adding more RAM to the system or by using a memory management tool to optimize the memory usage of the system.

- **Improving CPU performance:** This can be accomplished by adding more CPU cores or by overclocking the existing cores.

In some cases, it may be necessary to upgrade the system's hardware in order to address high run queues. This is especially true if the system is experiencing CPU or memory bottlenecks.

If you are experiencing high run queues, it is important to identify the root cause of the problem so that you can implement the appropriate solution. By addressing the underlying issue, you can improve the performance of your system and prevent future problems.

Viewing System Load Details with the **tload** Command

Now let's go to the **tload** command, which I prefer over **uptime** because it has options to show some very useful information graphically, in a text method.

However, **tload** is initially just as uninspiring as the **uptime** command; running just the command itself yields even less information than the **uptime** output, the main difference being that there is no user or "up since" information, though it does refresh itself until you use **Ctrl+c** to cancel its operation.

To really get some good stuff out of **tload**, invoke it with the **-s** option and let it get rolling with a display of load via a side-scrolling graph made up of asterisks that represent the load on an ongoing basis.

To show the graphical chart, invoke **tload** as shown in Example 20-3.

Example 20-3 Invoking the **tload** Command with Options

```
$ tload -s 100
0.04, 0.03, 0.03
```

You'll quickly see a set of asterisks begin to appear at the bottom left of the display, and slowly march across the screen from left to right. You can open up applications and move windows around if you are on a graphical system, just to see the results in the graph, similar to my system shown in Figure 20-1.

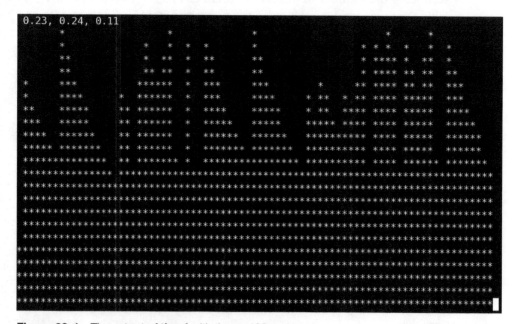

Figure 20-1 The output of **tload** with the **-s 100** option

The user's computer needs to access the web server, and there is a firewall in the way, which by default will not send the user's request traffic to the web server.

As you can see, the load is being shown at intervals (which you can specify using the **-d** *<value>* option) on the screen. It's good to experiment with the options for **tload** to get exactly what you want.

Notice the version of TLS we were querying for is present in the Protocol: portion of the query response.

NOTE Don't forget that the **top** command shows the same kind of information as **uptime** does: just look in the top few lines for that information.

CPU Times and CPU Process Priorities

The concept of *CPU time* requires us to realize that the real measurement of time is what time has elapsed since the start of a task to the present or the end of the task, or *elapsed time*.

As an analogy, think of the difference between CPU time and elapsed time as follows: elapsed time would be the length of time since you bought a vehicle, and CPU time would be the amount of time you actually drove the vehicle.

Additionally, elapsed time is real time, slivers of seconds to minutes, hours to days, and so on. Most computers have bursts of activity during which the CPU time represents being under load, or executing code, but that time is a relatively small fraction of the elapsed time.

As previously described, the fix for high CPU utilization is to find which process (or processes) is the problem and end it by using the **kill** command or another method.

Measuring CPU Time

To determine how much of the CPU time is currently being used—in effect, how much of the CPU is being utilized—you can use a couple of commands, one of which is **top**, which we have covered in detail elsewhere.

Another very important and useful utility is the **time** command, which measures the amount of time a command takes, and parses out what time was spent in what context or user or kernel space. Example 20-4 shows the **find** command being run and the time statistics being displayed.

Example 20-4   Example Output from the **time** Command

```
$ time find / -iname *.doc 2> /dev/null
/snap/gnome-3-34-1804/77/usr/lib/python2.7/pdb.doc
/snap/gnome-3-34-1804/72/usr/lib/python2.7/pdb.doc

real       0m6.997s
user       0m0.676s
sys        0m1.800s
```

What we are doing is timing a command to see how long it takes in real time, but also how much of that time is spent accessing, updating, or displaying in user or system space for that CPU time.

The number of output possibilities is *huge*, all of which you can see in the man page for the **time** command. The main thing you need to know about the **time** command is what it's measuring, and what the output shows you regarding the passage of real time (like the clock on the wall) and how much of that is taken up by the userspace and the system space for that command.

NOTE   Don't try to match the times up as a sum, but do read the man page for the **time** command. It'll teach you a lot about the system time and CPU utilization and how to report back on the characteristics you find most important.

Also keep in mind that running the exact same command multiple times may display shorter (in some cases, dramatically so) times after the first command is run. The system is caching from a disk block and filesystem perspective, and this will likely be the reason for the difference.

Important CPU Time Terms

The following terms related to CPU times are listed in objective 4.3, so be sure to familiarize yourself with them. Note that these times are displayed when executing the iostat command to display CPU utilization:

- **steal:** Steal time is the amount of time that a virtualized OS wanted to execute something but could not, as that time amount was being given to or used by another guest of the hypervisor.

- **user:** User time is the amount of time that is spent executing something that is located in the userspace or user-specific portion of the running operating system.

- **system:** System time is the amount of time that is spent executing something in the kernel portion of the system.

- **idle:** Idle time is the amount of time that the system spent not being busy, or running the System Idle Process. Effectively, this means that the CPU was not being used in any meaningful capacity.

- **iowait:** Iowait time is the amount of time that the system was idle, while an unfulfilled or in-process disk I/O request was pending.

See the "Diagnosing with the iostat Command" section in Chapter 18, "Analyzing and Troubleshooting Storage Issues" for more details about the iostat command.

CPU Process Priorities

CPU process priorities refer to the order in which the CPU allocates processing time to different tasks or processes running on a computer system. The concept of process priorities is crucial for efficient multitasking, as it determines which processes get more CPU time when there is competition for resources. Operating systems use various scheduling algorithms to manage process priorities and ensure fair and optimal resource utilization.

The CPU process priorities are managed using the concept of nice values and the priority scheduler. The nice value is a numeric value that determines the priority of a process, indicating how much CPU time it should receive compared to other processes. Processes with lower nice values are given higher priority.

The Chapter 4 section "Managing Process Priorities" covers process priorities and how to manage those priorities both for starting a command (via the **nice** command) and for remediating or altering a running command's priority (via the **renice** command), so we won't restate or rehash that topic here.

Memory Exhaustion and Out of Memory

The concept of *memory exhaustion* typically means that the system has run out of both physical RAM and *swap space*, which is a portion of the filesystem (a swap file) or a dedicated partition (swap partition) that becomes the overflow area for the actual system RAM and makes programs think the system has more RAM than it actually does.

Memory exhaustion doesn't happen in a vacuum; if you have very little memory and constantly load up available memory with running programs, eventually you'll reach a state where even a massive amount of swap won't help you and everything will grind to a halt, usually accompanied with many error messages, one of which is shown in Example 20-5.

Example 20-5   Logfile Entries Showing Memory Exhaustion

```
Allowed memory size of xxxxxxxx bytes exhausted (tried to allocate 62
bytes)
Allowed memory size of xxxxxxxx bytes exhausted (tried to allocate 39
bytes)
Allowed memory size of xxxxxxxx bytes exhausted (tried to allocate 62
bytes)
Allowed memory size of xxxxxxxx bytes exhausted (tried to allocate 39
bytes)
```

Receiving error messages usually isn't the first sign that something is going wrong, but rather the system will likely seem very sluggish and unresponsive, and there may be interface issues and service-response issues.

Memory exhaustion works hand in glove with out of memory, the topic of the next section.

Because a Linux system uses a multipart system for what it calls memory, swap (on disk or on the filesystem) and physical RAM, it can get a little confusing at times.

We'll get into all of this in the upcoming section "Swapping," where we talk about swap, caches and buffers, and virtual memory.

Another term mentioned in the exam objectives is file cache. The file cache is a region of memory that is used to store recently accessed files. This allows the kernel to access files more quickly, as it does not need to read them from disk each time they are needed. The file cache is also used to improve the performance of file systems, as it can reduce the number of times that the kernel needs to read and write data to disk.

What Is Out of Memory (OOM)?

The OOM Manager (Out of Memory Manager) is a Linux kernel component that manages memory allocation for processes. It is responsible for killing processes that are using too much memory, in order to prevent the system from running out of memory. It is not invoked except in certain cases of working with memory requests, (expanding heap and certain remap functions), so it's a bit of a niche player, but important, and of course, it's in the Linux+ objectives!

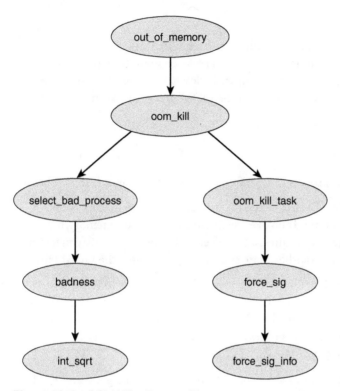

Figure 20-2   OOM Killer Process Diagram

The system attempts to avoid invoking the OOM Manager by harvesting old memory page frames, which may or may not be enough to handle the memory requests being made. The first thing that happens is that the system attempts to check if there is enough memory to fulfill a request for memory pages, and if the harvesting of old page frames isn't successful, the OOM Manager kicks in and performs the following:

■ Determines if there is enough available memory for a request

■ If not enough, verifies the system is really out of memory

■ Selects a process, according to a number of determinants, to kill to release memory page frames

NOTE   There exists a possibility that the system is *not* out of memory but rather has gotten ahead of the ability to process swap calls. The system goes through an extensive checklist once when the OOM Manager is called and, before the process selects something to kill, the OOM Manager will go verify the steps again.

Memory Leaks

As discussed earlier in this chapter pertaining to high CPU utilization, a memory leak can be from a malfunctioning program, bad code, or something malicious. Regardless, you'll find that the system memory is slowly being used up, then swap (virtual memory) is being used up, and then the OOM process kicks in. Eventually, failure may happen.

The Process Killer

The sequence for killing a process to start freeing up memory pages is shown below:

1. **Memory Exhaustion Event:** When the available memory in the system becomes critically low, the Linux kernel attempts to allocate memory for new processes or memory requests. However, if it's unable to satisfy memory requests and there are no other options available, it triggers the OOM killer.

2. **Selecting a Victim:** The OOM killer then selects a process to terminate. It aims to choose a process that is using a significant amount of memory and is deemed less critical or expendable. The selection process takes into account several factors, including the process's memory usage, its memory allocation behavior, and its priority.

3. **OOM Score Calculation:** Each process in the system is assigned an OOM score that reflects its likelihood of being terminated by the OOM killer. Processes with higher OOM scores are more likely to be selected as victims. The OOM score is based on various attributes, such as memory usage and resource consumption.

4. **Killing the Victim:** Once a victim process is selected, the OOM killer sends a signal (usually SIGKILL) to that process, instructing it to terminate immediately. This action releases the memory held by the terminated process and allows the system to recover from the memory shortage.

5. **Memory Reclamation:** After killing the victim process, the kernel releases the memory that was used by that process. This newly freed memory can then be used to satisfy memory requests from other processes.

The scenario for the **out_of_memory** kill process is fairly complex and completely beyond the scope of this discussion and the Linux+ exam. The Linux kernel documentation site has a great deal of useful information about how this works.

Swapping

Swapping refers to a technique used to manage memory when the physical RAM (Random Access Memory) becomes insufficient to accommodate all the running processes and the process data. When the system's RAM is fully utilized, the operating system transfers some of the less frequently used data from RAM to a designated portion of the hard disk called the swap space. This swap space may be a single large file on a filesystem or an entire partition designed as a swap partition.

Swapping frees up RAM for more active processes and helps prevent system instability or crashes due to memory exhaustion. Swap space is also commonly referred to as virtual memory.

You can run the **free** command and see what's going on with your system's RAM and virtual memory, and the combination of the two, which the system uses like a flexible pool for holding data for the processes and threads that are being executed currently (RAM) and those that have just gotten some time slices or are about to have a time slice of the CPU.

Swap, Caching, and Buffers

The **free** command is used to determine the amount of free memory on a system, not just by displaying the amount of unused system RAM but also by giving you more detailed information about how much free and in-use physical memory you have, how much swap space or disk-based fake memory is in use, and how much of the used system RAM is being taken up by buffers and caches. It's these buffers and caches that can produce a lot of confusion at times.

You can see what the **free** command shows in Example 20-6.

Example 20-6   Example Output from the **free -h** Command

```
$ ~ $: free -h
            total        used        free      shared   buff/cache
available
Mem:        3.8Gi       1.0Gi       1.2Gi       158Mi        1.6Gi
2.4Gi
Swap:       2.0Gi          0B       2.0Gi
```

In every Linux class that I've taught, there's always been at least one student who has viewed the output of the **free** command right after starting the lab system and asked me, "What is eating up all my system RAM?!"

This was always one of my favorite moments in class, and I have always taken the time to explain that system RAM on a lightly utilized system is like a bus that is only half full of passengers: Every passenger has room in the seat next to her for maga-zines, snacks, and drinks and ample room to stretch out a bit. I then make the cor-relation between the passenger and a running process.

I point out that the room the passenger has allocated to her is similar to the work-ing set (everything needed to run) for a process. The key here is that when lightly loaded, a system can allocate otherwise unused system RAM to handy and useful items such as cache and buffers, and the processes can stretch out a bit and have fully loaded working sets for efficient running of the processes.

Blocks and Buffers

Key to the running of processes and the speed of processing on a system are blocks and buffers. Block devices such as disks have an addressable unit called a *block*. This is typically (though not always) 512 bytes in size. System software also uses a con-struct called a block, but it's typically much larger than the physical size of a block on a hard disk or another block device.

When a disk block is read into system memory, it's stored in a *buffer*. A buffer is associated with one and only one block, and that buffer is used to address the data contained in that block while in memory.

Pages, Slabs, and Caches

The kernel uses *pages* to manage memory on a system. The processor can address very small units of memory (such as a "word" or "byte"), but the memory manage-ment unit uses pages and only addresses memory in page-sized chunks. The kernel addresses every single page of the memory in the struct_page table and includes in the table information that is critical to managing that page in each page's entry.

Pages are frequently populated with the same data, read from buffers and written back to *caches* for later reading. The system manages its own structure and marks pages as being used or free; the system can also use a number of other flags or parameters, but they are not important in this conversation.

Caches are made up of *slabs*; a slab is typically one page, though it can be multiple contiguous pages. To illustrate the relationship between a cache and a slab, we can say that a cache is like a city, a slab is like a neighborhood, and a page is like a block in that neighborhood.

To sum this all up, blocks are data locations on disk, blocks are read into buffers when a file or set of files is requested from disk, and then when those buffers are read into a page in memory, that page is a part of a slab or set of slabs that make up a cache.

To continue the bus and passenger analogy from earlier, remember that a lightly loaded system shows a large utilization of RAM but also a correspondingly hefty use of cache and buffers, while a heavily loaded system, with many processes running, shows a lot of RAM in use but relatively low cache and buffers. Effectively, as you load up the system with more processes, all the passengers/processes have to tighten up their working sets; put their magazines, snacks, extra luggage, and drinks in the overhead rack or under the seat; and be respectful of their fellow passengers/processes.

How Much Swap Is Enough?

In some ways this is like asking which car is better than another. I have been around Linux since its beginnings and have seen the answer to this question change more times than a YouTube influencer changes outfits for a video shoot!

Table 20-2 contains a simple guide to swap recommendations, adapted from an Opensource.com article regarding the Fedora Project's recommended size for a swap partition,".

Table 20-2 How Much Swap Is Recommended

Amount of RAM Installed in System	Recommended Swap Space	Recommended Swap Space with Hibernation
≤ 2GB	2 × RAM	3 × RAM
2GB – 8GB	= RAM	2 × RAM
8GB – 64GB	4GB to 0.5 × RAM	1.5 × RAM
> 64GB	Minimum 4GB	Hibernation not recommended

As you can see, even with a handy guide such as Table 20-2, how much swap is sufficient can be slightly unclear in some situations. The **Hibernation** column is primarily for systems that will be using the Hibernation option, which shouldn't be servers and high-end workstations.

Hardware

There are a couple of utilities, **lscpu** and **lsmem**, that you can use to gain more information about your *hardware*, especially the CPU and memory/RAM.

Viewing CPU Info

The **lscpu** command reads the CPU information from the **/sys** and **/proc/cpuinfo** locations and formats it for a human to read. The default produces a lot of output, so it might be better to pipe it to the **less** command as shown in this command line:

```
$ lscpu | less
```

Another extremely useful option that I use a lot is the caching display option, or **-C**, which shows information for the various levels of caches, an example of which is shown in Example 20-7.

Example 20-7   Example Output from the **lscpu -C** Command

```
$ lscpu -C
NAME ONE-SIZE ALL-SIZE WAYS TYPE         LEVEL   SETS PHY-LINE
COHERENCY-SIZE
L1d       32K      64K    8 Data          1     64      1       64
L1i       32K      64K    8 Instruction   1     64      1       64
L2       256K     512K    4 Unified       2   1024      1       64
L3        16M      16M   16 Unified       3  16384      1       64
```

Viewing Memory Info

The **lsmem** command reads the system memory information from the **/sys** and **/proc/meminfo** locations and formats it as well as it can, but it's pretty technical in nature. There isn't that much output, but at least it isn't cryptic, as you can see in Example 20-8.

Example 20-8   Example Output from the **lsmem** Command

```
$ lsmem
RANGE                                    SIZE   STATE REMOVABLE BLOCK
0x0000000000000000-0x00000000afffffff   2.8G online         yes  0-21
0x0000000100000000-0x000000014fffffff   1.3G online         yes  32-41

Memory block size:        128M
Total online memory:       4G
Total offline memory:      0B
```

Summary

In this chapter you learned all about troubleshooting the CPU and memory on a Linux system. We covered a lot of topics, including runaway and zombie processes, high CPU utilization, and the associated high load averages and high or long run queues. We looked at CPU times and CPU process priorities, as well as memory exhaustion and out of memory states.

Additionally, you learned about swap, its associated caches, blocks, and buffers, and how all this affects, and is affected by, the physical system RAM.

Exam Preparation Tasks

As mentioned in the section "Goals and Methods" in the Introduction, you have a couple of choices for exam preparation: the exercises here, Chapter 23, "Final Preparation," and the exam simulation questions in the Pearson Test Prep Software Online.

Review All Key Topics

Review the most important topics in this chapter, noted with the Key Topic icon in the margin of the page. Table 20-3 lists these key topics and the page number on which each is found.

Table 20-3 Key Topics for Chapter 20

Key Topic Element	Description	Page Number
Paragraph	Definition of a runaway process	706
Paragraph	Definition of a zombie process	708
Paragraph	The difference between CPU time and elapsed time	713
Paragraph	Definition of memory exhaustion	715
Paragraph	Definition of swap	719
Paragraph	Definition of blocks and buffers, and description of how they relate to each other	720

Define Key Terms

Define the following key terms from this chapter and check your answers in the glossary:

runaway process, zombie process, high CPU utilization, high load average, CPU time, CPU process priorities, memory exhaustion, out of memory (OOM), swapping, hardware

Review Questions

The answers to these review questions are in Appendix A.

1. Which of the following commands will show you a table of available and used system RAM, swap, buffers, and caching information?

   a. **meminfo**

   b. **bufflist**

c. free

d. lsmem

2. When a child process has exited but its entry in the process table has not been cleared by its parent process, what is that process called?

   a. Abandoned

   b. Orphan

   c. Zombie

   d. Loose

3. You've started a process and, through investigation, you find that it's consuming more than the usual amount of system resources. It's important and timely, so you don't want to just kill it and start over. Which of the following commands will allow you to affect the priority of this process as it's running?

   a. renice

   b. procadj

   c. sig

   d. ps

4. When your system needs to attempt to clear enough memory page frames to fulfill a request for memory usage and cannot, what overall process is called and used to attempt to fix this situation?

   a. select_bad_process

   b. badness

   c. force_sig

   d. out_of_memory

5. You're convinced that your system doesn't have enough swap space configured and you want to add some without interrupting the workloads that are in process. Your system has a single internal disk that is fully allocated but has free space on it. What method of swap can you safely add?

   a. Hardware-based swap

   b. Software-based swap

   c. Partition-based swap

   d. Filesystem-based swap

6. The **lscpu** command reads data from what **/proc**-based file?

   a. **cpustats**

   b. **cpudetails**

   c. **cpugrep**

   d. **cpuinfo**

This chapter covers the following topics:

- User Login Issues
- User File Access Issues
- Password Issues
- Privilege Elevation Issues
- Quota Issues

The exam objective covered in this chapter is as follows:

- **Objective 4.4:** Given a scenario, analyze and troubleshoot user access and file permissions

## CHAPTER 21

Analyzing and Troubleshooting User and File Permissions

Since everything on a Linux system is a file, right down to the filesystem objects, making sure your users have proper access to those files, and blocking improper access, is key.

"Do I Know This Already?" Quiz

The "Do I Know This Already?" quiz enables you to assess whether you should read this entire chapter or simply jump to the "Exam Preparation Tasks" section for review. If you are in doubt, read the entire chapter. Table 21-1 outlines the major headings in this chapter and the corresponding "Do I Know This Already?" quiz questions. You can find the answers in Appendix A, "Answers to the 'Do I Know This Already?' Quizzes and Review Questions."

Table 21-1 "Do I Know This Already?" Foundation Topics Section-to-Question Mapping

Foundation Topics Section	Questions Covered in This Section
User Login Issues	1
User File Access Issues	2
Password Issues	3
Privilege Elevation Issues	4
Quota Issues	5

CAUTION The goal of self-assessment is to gauge your mastery of the topics in this chapter. If you do not know the answer to a question or are only partially sure of the answer, you should mark that question as wrong for purposes of the self-assessment. Giving yourself credit for an answer you correctly guess skews your self-assessment results and might provide you with a false sense of security.

1. A new web designer who isn't familiar with how Linux works tries to sign on as the user nginx, and then sends you a request to reset the password. You explain to the user that no one is allowed to log in as a(n) _____ account.

   a. user

   b. login

   c. service

   d. access

2. A user has signed in with their usual account ID but needs to temporarily change over to a different ID. Which command would keep the user from having to log out and then back in again as that secondary account?

   a. su

   b. id

   c. ip

   d. df

3. A user has been migrated from another system and is having an issue with their password. Upon displaying the **/etc/passwd** entry for that user, you find the expected x in the second column, but in **/etc/shadow**, you find a(n) ___ character, showing the user has not set a password yet.

   a. #

   b. @

   c. %

   d. !

4. Which utility enables you to configure a regular user's ability to run various programs as if they were the root user, but not to have any knowledge of the actual password?

   a. **rootme**

   b. **newuser**

   c. **su -i**

   d. **sudo**

5. A user mentions they had expected to be restricted from using over a certain amount of disk space, but were able to save and store more than that, and wants to know why. What feature or option of quota management is responsible for this apparent lack of restriction?

    a. Weak save

    b. Soft limit

    c. Grace period

    d. Block restriction

Foundation Topics

User Login Issues

Nothing is more irritating to users than not being able to log in, and of course they'll share that irritation with the IT staff—it's all part of being a user!

Chapter 9, "Implementing Identity Management," covers the *user login* process, and much more about users, groups, and their management, so in this section we can move straight into the most common login issues that users experience and how to prevent them from happening, or fix them when they do happen.

Inspecting Account Details

Before you go running off in several directions attempting to troubleshoot why a user is unable to log in, it is important to first look at the user's account particulars and see whether there is a problem.

To truly understand what's going on with a user's login issues, you need to run at *least* three commands—**id**, **getent**, and **last**—to get enough information to have an informed and accurate picture of that user's situation.

ID Please

The **id** command displays a wealth of information about any user, as you can see in Example 21-1.

Example 21-1 Example of **id** Command Output

```
$ id
uid=1000(rossb) gid=1000(rossb) groups=1000(rossb),4(adm),20(dialout),
24(cdrom),25(floppy),27(sudo),29(audio),30(dip),44(video),46(plugdev),1
17(netdev),118(lxd)
```

The key values are as follows:

- **uid (User ID):** Shown matched up with the username, as configured in the **/etc/passwd** or other name services database.

- **gid (primary Group ID):** The group ID that would be used as the Group Owner if this account created the typical file or directory.

- **groups (Secondary Groups):** Lists the groups this user is a member of other than the Primary Group.

What you're looking for here is anything out of the ordinary, and especially if you don't recall making any changes.

Get Entity

The **getent** command also is quite useful since it will query a database such as the **/etc/passwd** or **/etc/shadow** file and return information like you see in Example 21-2.

Example 21-2   Example of **getent** Command Output

```
$ getent passwd rossb
rossb:x:1000:1000:RossB:/home/rossb:/bin/bash
$ sudo getent shadow rossb
rossb:!:19051:0:99999:7:::
```

The query to the **/etc/passwd** file shows data for the rossb account, which you will likely inspect and say to yourself, "But this is exactly what I would have gotten if I had run the **grep** command against the **/etc/passwd** file and searched for the user rossb." And you'd be right.

NOTE Also *very* important is that there be a valid shell as the last field in the entry in the **/etc/passwd** file. If there is not, the user can't log in. Take a look at the **/bin/false** and **/sbin/nologin** files in Chapter 9, which can be used to change the user's ability to log in dramatically.

The second query, to the **/etc/shadow** file, is necessary to run as root, since that file is *not* publicly accessible. If you were to run it without the **sudo** command, all you'd get is a blank return, no error.

In the **/etc/shadow** file you see what may indeed be a problem for this user trying to log in: there is an x in the **password** column in the **/etc/passwd** file, as there should be, but there is the all-important ! in the **password** column in the **/etc/shadow** file, which means this user has *not* had a password set!

NOTE Rather amusingly, I have had a student ask me why in a case like this the system doesn't just prompt the user to set a password when attempting to log in. As I gazed at him, contemplating how to answer, he suddenly nodded and said, "Oh, yeah, right, then anyone could set a password for that user." Bingo, he won the prize!

Case-Sensitivity

Let's face it, anyone who doesn't know about case-sensitivity in Linux will soon become very aware of how important even a single upper- or lowercase character can be.

Has the User Ever Logged In?

Sometimes you just know the user has never logged in, such as when the user is new, but there are times when you know the user logs in regularly and you'll need to know that information. Being able to determine if a user has logged in can help troubleshoot user login issues.

The last Command

The **last** command is used to show you a listing of output that lets you see what has happened last on the system, such as who has signed in, from what port, what they might have been running, and so on.

It's very helpful to see a reverse chronological order of things that could be important, in particular when the system was last booted, and who's still signed in, as you can see in Example 21-3.

Example 21-3 Example of **last** Command Output

```
$ last | head
ubuntu    pts/0         192.168.64.1     Sun Feb 12 20:31    still
logged in
ubuntu    pts/0         192.168.64.1     Sun Feb 12 20:29 - 20:31
(00:01)
ubuntu    pts/0         192.168.64.1     Fri Feb 10 15:28 - 17:00
(01:31)
reboot    system boot  5.4.0-99-generic Fri Feb 10 15:20    still
running
ubuntu    pts/0         192.168.64.1     Sun Jan 15 22:21 - 22:17
(23:55)
reboot    system boot  5.4.0-99-generic Sun Jan 15 22:09    still
running
```

The lastlog Command

Also quite useful but with some different information is the **lastlog** command, useful for a listing of users and their login status, the date and time they were logged in, the port from where they logged in and the IP address they logged in from, if discernable.

Example 21-4 shows the **lastlog** default output.

Example 21-4   Example of **lastlog** Command Output

```
$ lastlog | tail
tss                                           **Never logged in**
uuidd                                         **Never logged in**
tcpdump                                       **Never logged in**
sshd                                          **Never logged in**
landscape                                     **Never logged in**
pollinate                                     **Never logged in**
systemd-coredump                              **Never logged in**
ubuntu            pts/0      192.168.64.1     Sun Feb 12 20:31:34 -0700
2023
lxd                                           **Never logged in**
dnsmasq                                       **Never logged in**
```

This is very useful, but there is a trick you can pull using the **grep** command that will allow you to determine only who *has* logged in, screening out all those service accounts with the "Never logged in" message.

Example 21-5 shows the **lastlog** output filtered with the **grep** command to show only the accounts that have successfully logged in.

Example 21-5   Example of **lastlog | grep -v** Command Output

```
$ lastlog | grep -v "Never logged in"
ubuntu            pts/0      192.168.64.1     Sun Feb 12 20:31:34 -0700
2023
```

Now *that* is some seriously useful information to get. You don't have to sort through a couple dozen service accounts just to see what user accounts have successfully logged in, *and* you can look for service accounts that show up as having logged in, a sure sign of an error or a hack/crack on the system.

User File Access Issues

As a system administrator, you will sometimes be called upon to assist users who are not able access files. This can pose a challenge as there are several components that can affect a user's ability to access a file.

In this section you will explore these components, including issues with group membership, context issues, permission issues, and attribute issues.

Group Issues

Group issues can be even harder to track down and troubleshoot than user login issues. This is because group issues can affect multiple users in different ways while user login issues only affect a single user.

One of the issues that can evade casual inspection is if the user is in the proper *group* that has been assigned to have access to a resource.

The simplest way to find out what groups a user is a member of is to issue the **groups** or **id** command with that username as an argument, such as shown in Example 21-6.

Example 21-6   Example of **groups** Command Output

```
$ groups rossb
rossb : rossb adm dialout cdrom floppy sudo audio dip video plugdev
netdev
```

You should then inspect the **ls -l** output of the resource (or use **ls -ld** for a directory) and see if that group is listed in the middle three rwx positions as having at least r (read) permissions. You can read more about the other tools you may need to use in Chapter 2, "Managing Files and Directories," such as the **chmod** command, which you'd use to make any needed adjustments to the permissions for the group on the resource.

Context Issues

Context issues occur within the realm of AppArmor or SELinux, and can be complex to troubleshoot. Consult Chapter 12, "Understand and Apply Access Controls," for more information about how these two security context methods are applied and how you can troubleshoot them.

Permission Issues

Permissions are much simpler in Linux than they are in Windows, which is where a lot of confusion comes from—not Windows itself, but the difference between how Windows applies and manages permissions on files and directories and how Linux does.

In Chapter 2, you'll find a very full-featured discussion of permissions and how to view, change, and confirm them, all of which are the most likely actions you'd take to remediate a permissions issue.

ACL Issues

Once again, when it comes to *access control list (ACL)* issues, Chapter 12 is where you'll find the best discussion of how ACLs work, how they are used, and how to read and troubleshoot them.

Attribute Issues

File *attributes* are a kind of hazy situation where a special attribute has been set on a filesystem object, such as a file that has been set as being "append only" so that it cannot be overwritten, only added to. Another very common attribute that is set, especially on filesystems that undergo a very high set of read traffic, such as a web server, is the **noatime** attribute, where the reading of a file does *not* update the **atime** file information, which you can see along with the other two times, **mtime** and **ctime**, using the command shown in Example 21-7.

Example 21-7   Example of **stat** Command Output

```
$ stat file1
  File: file1
  Size: 0               Blocks: 0           IO Block: 4096    regular
empty file
Device: fc01h/64513d     Inode: 258226        Links: 1
Access: (0664/-rw-rw-r--)  Uid: ( 1000/  ubuntu)   Gid: ( 1000/
ubuntu)
Access: 2022-06-01 23:15:35.864502122 -0600
Modify: 2022-06-01 23:15:35.864502122 -0600
Change: 2022-06-01 23:29:41.424625649 -0600
 Birth: -
```

As you can see, the three times are toward the bottom of the output and are labeled Access (atime), Modify (mtime), and Change (ctime.)

To see the special attributes on a filesystem object, use the **lsattr** command against that object like you see in Example 21-8.

Example 21-8 Example of **lsattr** Command Output

```
$ laattr file1
------dA------e----- file1
```

As you can see, the "do not dump," "no atime updates," and "extent format" attributes are set on the humble **file1**.

The following are other attributes of note:

- **s (Secure Updates):** Means a secure wipe, where when that file is deleted, the filesystem mechanism overwrites its disk resources with zeros and writes those back to disk.

- **d (No Dump):** Means don't back up this file if the **dump backup** command is used.

- **i (Immutable):** Means the file is set to be unchangeable, and must be set to be mutable to make any changes.

- **e (Extents):** Means extents are being used for mapping the blocks on disk for this file.

Special attributes may not be obvious, and usually only show up on Ext filesystems; other filesystems may not allow the setting of any or all of these special attributes.

The best places to get more attribute information are the **chattr(1)** and **lsattr(1)** man pages.

Policy/Non-Policy Issues

Once again, the Linux+ objectives are not very specific, or even helpful, in determining what *policy* and *non-policy* user file access issues are potentially asked about on the exam.

What does occur to me, something that I have seen before, is what I term "silent access issues," which are usually related to having SELinux turned on and not getting anything from the logs about access being denied to a resource.

SELinux attempts to reduce the number of false positives that occur when a service "over-queries" its access, and as such uses something called the **dontaudit** policy rule, which results in a service being denied access but also being either misreported or, most importantly, not reported at all!

If you find yourself in such a situation, you can disable your **dontaudit** rule and cause such access attempts to be logged with the command

```
$ semodule -DB
```

This command disables the **dontaudit** policy rule with the **-D** option and rebuilds the policy via the **-B** option. This means you are using the "non-policy" feature listed in the exam objectives.

Now you can run the program, service, or command and watch the SELinux logs for more useful troubleshooting messages.

To re-enable the **dontaudit** policy, simply rebuild the policy overall with the command

```
$ semodule -B
```

Password Issues

Outside of the main issue, which is that users cannot seem to remember their *passwords* from day-to-day, there are a couple of password issues that occur that are relatively easy to fix.

When a user's password ages out, there are several opportunities to change it, or fail to change it, and I have rarely had a user admit they have put off changing the password until it was too late. Another issue, also rarely admitted, is that the user has bobbled the password change enough times that the system won't let them in.

The faillog Command

A utility that I highly recommend running every day, and even having it mail you the output, is the **faillog** command.

You can run the **faillog** command by itself or by specifying a user such as:

```
$ sudo faillog -u rossb
```

The **faillog** command can be very helpful, even allowing you to reset a user's failure counters after you get the problem fixed, with the **-r** or **--reset** option:

```
$ sudo faillog -u rossb --reset
```

> **NOTE** The **faillog** command may or may not prompt you to create the **/var/log/faillog** file, and if it does, just use the **touch** command as the root user:
>
> ```
> $ sudo touch /var/log/faillog
> ```
>
> This creates the file that **faillog** uses and allows it to commit any entries that occur to that log file.

/etc/security.access.conf

Another possible location that you might want to check is the PAM-related **/etc/security/access.conf** file, which is usually not used but contains a lot of very nice examples that seem to pick on the user john.

Ensure that the user in question is not configured to be limited in any of these circumstances, and if they are, comment them out or remove that entry and have the user attempt to log in again.

The **/etc/security/access.conf** file is not well known and, if misconfigured or mangled or corrupted, can cause a world of pain and hassle for users.

I highly recommend that you look at the man page for the **access.conf** file, which is very helpful in understanding what **access.conf** does, and that it affects all users who log in to the system. Just use the command

```
$ man access.conf
```

I also highly recommend that you look at the **pam_access** file man page:

```
$ man pam_access
```

Privilege Elevation Issues

The typical issue that a user experiences when attempting *privilege elevation* is that they don't know the difference between using the **su** command by itself and using the **su** command with the - option so that the login process is fully experienced, not just stepping in as the root user, but becoming the root user.

Another very likely issue is that the user is trying to use the **sudo** command and they are not configured properly or have insufficient privileges in the **/etc/sudoers** file.

You can refresh yourself about **sudo** and the **/etc/sudoers** files by referring back to Chapter 11, "Use Remote Connectivity for System Management."

Quota Issues

Quotas are outdated, for the most part. *Quotas* for disk usage were important back when disks were smaller, extremely expensive, and shared among massive numbers of users, such as at colleges and universities.

In my decades of experience, I have found quotas hard to enforce, difficult to maintain, and almost always misunderstood by sysadmins and users alike. I know quotas are in use still, but as a busy sysadmin, instructor and courseware developer, and author, I haven't seen a case of quotas in use in the wild (industry) for a decade or more.

Nevertheless, there is a big problem with quotas that is not related at all to how the quota system works but rather users' understanding of how quotas work.

Hard and soft limits are what cause the biggest problem for users, in that they are not very well defined from the outset, and when a user gets a message about having exceeded a limit, or grace period, the message never seems to make sense.

In Example 21-9, you see the output of the **edquota ross** command, which we'll use to try to make more sense of what is going on.

Example 21-9   The **edquota** Editor Window for the rossb User

```
$ sudo edquota rossb
Disk quotas for user rossb (uid 505):
   Filesystem                blocks    soft    hard   inodes soft hard
   /dev/VGroup01/MainVol01   106833       0       0    15120    0    0
```

The first column shows the filesystem that has the quotaon parameter, enabling quotas for this filesystem.

In the second column, you see the number of disk blocks the user is currently using. In the third and fourth columns, you see the soft and hard limits for disk blocks for the user on this filesystem.

The fifth column is the number of inodes that are in use for the files that the user is responsible for, and the last two columns are the hard and soft limits for the inodes the user is allowed on this system.

Possible Files or Entirety of Blocks?

The problem is that a lot of users, and even sysadmins or system managers, forget that there is an indirect linkage between the number of disk blocks in use by a user and the number of inodes. If you think of inodes as being the potential number of individual files, then that's however many files you want to let that user create, own, and maintain. It is *not* the entirety of the size of those files—that's the blocks quota soft and hard limits.

Converting to Usable Numbers

This was always the part of quotas that I hated the most. You need to know several things, in particular the size of the blocks on the disk in question, how many of those blocks make up a usable number like a gigabyte, and then how many of *those* you want the user to have for their quota.

I'm not about to do all that math here; you can figure out the block size of your disk in question by using the **stat** command and its **-f** option, like you see in Example 21-10.

Example 21-10   Finding Out a Filesystem Block Size Using **stat -f**

```
$ stat -f /dev/sda1
  File: "/dev/sda1"
    ID: 0          Namelen: 255      Type: tmpfs
Block size: 4096        Fundamental block size: 4096
Blocks: Total: 120761    Free: 120761    Available: 120761
Inodes: Total: 120761    Free: 120360
```

With a block size of 4096, and each file taking up at least one 4K block, you can do the rest of the math and determine how many blocks you want each user to have for their soft and hard limits.

Summary

In this chapter you learned all about troubleshooting user login issues, user file access issues, password issues, privilege elevation issues, and quota issues, with cross-references to other chapters where appropriate.

Exam Preparation Tasks

As mentioned in the section "Goals and Methods" in the Introduction, you have a couple of choices for exam preparation: the exercises here, Chapter 23, "Final Preparation," and the exam simulation questions in the Pearson Test Prep Software Online.

Review All Key Topics

Review the most important topics in this chapter, noted with the Key Topic icon in the margin of the page. Table 21-2 lists these key topics and the page number on which each is found.

Table 21-2   Key Topics for Chapter 21

Key Topic Element	Description	Page Number
Example 21-1	An example of **id** command output	728
Example 21-2	An example of **getent** command output	729
Paragraph	Definition of the **last** command and what it can do for the user	730
Example 21-6	An example of **groups** command output	732
Example 21-8	An example of **lsattr** command output	734
Paragraph	Why the **faillog** command can be very useful	735

Define Key Terms

Define the following key terms from this chapter and check your answers in the glossary:

user login, user file access, group, context, permissions, access control list (ACL), attributes, policy, non-policy, passwords, privilege elevation, quota

Review Questions

The answers to these review questions are in Appendix A.

1. If a user cannot log in after their account has been created, what file would you check to see if the user has a password that has been generated and set?

    a. **passwd**

    b. **security**

    c. **shadow**

    d. **nologin**

2. You are bewildered at the inability to make a change to a file in your user's home directory, and suspect the sysadmin has somehow marked it as being not just read-only, but not writable. Which of the following commands would you use to see special settings for this or any other file?

    a. **blattr**

    b. **chattr**

    c. **lsattr**

    d. **mattr**

3. One of your new Linux users is an experienced Windows user, but seems to have a lot of problems getting logged in consistently. What is the most common issue for transitioning Windows users in getting used to Linux system logins and files overall?

    a. Case-sensitivity

    b. Shared permissions

    c. Extended attributes

    d. **Ctrl-Alt-Del**

4. A user who you have allowed (foolishly, admittedly) to use privilege elevation keeps getting "command not found" messages when issuing standard root-level commands, and commands they are able to issue don't seem to work properly. What command and/or options should the user have used to directly become the root user?

    a. **suda**

    b. **su -x**

    c. **su**

    d. **su -**

5. You've trained your users to check on their quota statistics often in order to avoid problems with their space usage without any warnings. A user reports they cannot create new files, but they can add contents to existing files. Which of the following needs to be adjusted for the user?

    a. Repquota limit

    b. Grace limit

    c. Block soft limit

    d. Inode hard limit

This chapter covers the following topics:

- Unit Files
- Common Problems

The exam objective covered in this chapter is as follows:

- **Objective 4.5:** Given a scenario, use systemd to diagnose and resolve common problems with a Linux system

## CHAPTER 22

Analyzing and Troubleshooting Common Problems Using Systemd

The systemd method is somewhat complex, especially to newcomers, so having some good troubleshooting tips will help ease your transition to systemd, which is how the majority of Linux distributions handle their services these days.

Since systemd is relatively new, at least compared to SysV or the init scheme, there is a lot to be confused by and to go wrong, as systemd can be accurately described as both "progress" and "somewhat complex."

"Do I Know This Already?" Quiz

The "Do I Know This Already?" quiz enables you to assess whether you should read this entire chapter or simply jump to the "Exam Preparation Tasks" section for review. If you are in doubt, read the entire chapter. Table 22-1 outlines the major headings in this chapter and the corresponding "Do I Know This Already?" quiz questions. You can find the answers in Appendix A, "Answers to the 'Do I Know This Already?' Quizzes and Review Questions."

Table 22-1 "Do I Know This Already?" Foundation Topics Section-to-Question Mapping

Foundation Topics Section	Questions Covered in This Section
Unit Files	1–2
Common Problems	3–4

CAUTION The goal of self-assessment is to gauge your mastery of the topics in this chapter. If you do not know the answer to a question or are only partially sure of the answer, you should mark that question as wrong for purposes of the self-assessment. Giving yourself credit for an answer you correctly guess skews your self-assessment results and might provide you with a false sense of security.

1. What is a primary characteristic of a systemd service unit filename?

    a. Starts with **service_**

    b. Contains **_service_**

    c. Ends with the extension **.service**

    d. Has no extension whatsoever

2. In the transition of the majority of distributions to using systemd, what has replaced the concept of SysV runlevels?

    a. Targets

    b. Service levels

    c. ExecStarts

    d. Focuses

3. What systemd feature/function is designed to supplement and possibly supplant the use of cron and cron jobs?

    a. Ticks

    b. Tasks

    c. Todos

    d. Timers

4. What directive when used in a service unit will cause that service to not start until another service has started and is available?

    a. **Notyet=**

    b. **Requires=**

    c. **Until=**

    d. **After=**

Foundation Topics

Unit Files

This section focuses on the all-important unit files and issues regarding the keywords or directives found therein, as well as a few common problems that can affect systemd functioning.

Unit files are text files, but they are formatted in a certain way, with sections, such as [Unit], [Service], and many others. The man pages discuss unit files as being "ini-like," which means they are similar to **.ini** files, or are made up of directives with values separated by an = sign, such as you see in Example 22-1.

Example 22-1 Example of a Simple Unit File

```
[Section Name]
Directive=avalue
Directive=othervalue

[Other Section Name]
Directive=somevalue
```

You can find out much more about unit files and their contents in Chapter 4, "Managing Processes and Services."

> **NOTE** The goal of this chapter is to point out some of the possible issues or misconfigurations that will cause you to have to troubleshoot the issue. As the vast majority of unit files and even systemd files are editable text files, there is a lot that can go wrong, and human error and editing mistakes are at the top of the heap of trouble you can get into.

While there are many different unit files, only a handful of them are exam-testable. The next few sections will cover potential issues with the following key unit files: service, timer, mount, and target.

Service Unit File Issues

Keep in mind that a *service* unit file, such as **blahwoof.service**, is yet another text file that is broken up by sections containing directive=value configuration. Next we will explore some of the most common issues for service unit files that you need to be aware of for the exam.

Networking Services

One of the main issues with systemd is that seemingly all the services start at once, which is not usually true, but it sure seems like everything is up and roaring and available...but sometimes not networking.

Usually the issue will be that you want a firewall to start *before* networking configures your interfaces, but it could be any service that requires or needs the network to be functioning that can cause the issue.

Of the three network-related target units, only the network-online.target is an active unit, or one that will very specifically cause any other service to wait until the network is up before it starts. Including the **network-online.target** in any service unit file is convenient; you just specify that any unit that is dependent on the network be started after the network-online.target verifies there is a configured IP address and stack.

You can see in Example 22-2 the two configuration lines that should be included in any service unit file that depends on the network to be up and functioning before it runs.

Example 22-2   After and Wants Directive Usage

```
[Unit]
Otherdirectives=values
After=network-online.target
Wants=network-online.target
```

NOTE   Keep in mind that there are a couple of wait services that systemd can operate with, including the NetworkManager-wait-online.service (if you are using Network-Manager) and the systemd-networkd-wait-online.service. Whichever you choose, specify that service in the network-online.target file. You can find much more information about this in the systemd documentation, or you can run the **man** command and specify **systemd-networkd-wait-online.service**.

The other, and more passive, unit that can be used to order services that will rely on the network is the network-pre.target. The main method for using this target is to set an After=network-pre.target directive or Wants=network-pre.target directive in the service unit file that will depend on or want, respectively, the network to be present to function properly.

ExecStart and ExecStop

These two directives have *many* additional parameters, and getting something even slightly wrong will cause a lot of troubleshooting for you.

When *ExecStart* is used, the command (or commands) that follows the = symbol is executed at the time the containing unit service is started.

However, you can get into trouble right away by the type of service, because unless the service is **Type=oneshot**, you cannot have multiple commands or multiple ExecStart lines.

If the service is **Type=forking** or any of the others, you can have precisely one command on the **ExecStart=command** line, not multiple commands, and you can't have multiple ExecStart lines.

The *ExecStop* directive is tightly paired with the **ExecStart** directive and is used to specify how that command (or commands) is to be ended when the containing service is ended.

However, you cannot depend on just a **SIGTERM** signal to end those processes, because they may ignore it. You should consult the systemd.kill man page for the **KillMode=** and **KillSignal=** parameters and experiment with the various signals to ensure that the commands or processes that were ExecStart-ed are ExecStop-ped, as it were.

Before and After

Before and *After* are relatively simple ordering directives, useful in scenarios where you have a service that has to be started before a dependent service, or after a service that it itself depends on.

NOTE   There are two methods of dependencies in systemd: ordering and requirements. The Before/After directives are of the ordering dependency method. When starting a service, all of the dependencies are read, a matrix is constructed, and then the right services are started in that particular order.

When you are starting two or more services, there is no inherent order, but you can impose one by specifying Before=name.service and After=name.service.

One of the main characteristics of systemd is that when the system starts services, it will attempt to start as many of them in parallel as possible, and this can cause some confusion among services that depend on each other, or when a number of services depend on a particular service to be there for them to start properly and function.

The main thing here is that you can "over-configure" Before and After directives. You don't need to configure both; you just need to decide which service should contain a Before and the names of the other services, or configure the After in those services to point to the service they depend on. This can take a whiteboard and a few puzzling moments, so take your time and do it right!

If I were configuring serviceA to start Before serviceB, I would have two possibilities:

- Put a Before=serviceB directive line in the serviceA unit file, which will automatically put an After=serviceA entry into the dependency matrix for serviceB.

- Put an After=serviceA directive line in the serviceB unit file, which will cause the same order, but will put a Before=serviceB entry into the dependency matrix.

Either way, the order will be the same. If I were using three services, serviceA, serviceB, and serviceC, and wanted both serviceB and serviceC to be started after serviceA, I could do the same thing as shown, but just put the two service names in the After= or Before= line.

The real issue here is whether you want to order these services or want to have a requirement on them being available/unavailable in order to have another service(s) started or ended. That will be covered in the upcoming "Requires and Wants" section.

Type

As previously mentioned, all unit files are text files, and the unit *type* is usually indicated by the **.service** or **.socket** suffix. The focus of this section is the Type= directive and its options, such as the following (the latter two of which appear earlier in this chapter):

- **simple**

- **forking**

- **oneshot**

The main issue I have seen over and over is the misapplication of the Type=oneshot configuration, leading to extended waits and other issues.

A Type=simple or Type=forking setup will cause the unit to be processed and the service or executable to be started, and in the Type=forking case, it will immediately start a child process, but the system is *expecting* this and will keep track of what's going on.

The simple type will use something else like a similarly named **.socket** unit if the service communicates via a socket. Either way, it's a much simpler and more straightforward scenario if simple or forking is used.

The toughest issue is when Type=oneshot is used, and that is mainly because a one-shot will be very short-lived, but the system (systemd) is supposed to *wait* for the process to exit before it continues processing other units.

It's imperative to make sure that the proper Type= statement is used, or systemd may hang or wait an inordinately long time for a service to exit when it's supposed to keep running.

User

You can configure a systemd service to run as a given user by specifying something like you see in Example 22-3.

Example 22-3   Setting a systemd Service to Run as a Given User

```
[Service]
Type=simple
User=rossb
Group=staff
```

Specifying a user is usually done because there is a configuration wrinkle or reason to run that service as that particular user. This can affect most any service, but important and well-written services usually have their own given configuration that specifies the user they should be running as.

For example, NGINX has the user it should run as specified in the **/etc/nginx/nginx.conf** file, even though it typically runs as a systemd service on most distributions.

Requires and Wants

The main difference between the Requires= and Wants= directives is that if serviceA Requires serviceB, then it cannot run without serviceB, so serviceB *must* be running to allow serviceA to even start.

The concept of the Wants= directive is that although serviceA does not *require* serviceB to be running to start, it's a very good idea, and therefore it wants to have serviceB running. This difference is really important to know, because many a service *will* start without name services available, but they may not function properly without name services.

Timer Unit File Issues

Timer unit files are the systemd way of trying to replace cron jobs, with some limited success. The following will explore some of the most common issues for timer unit files that you need to be aware of for the exam.

OnCalendar

The *OnCalendar* setting defines a specific date and time for a timer event, which can cause some confusion if a timer doesn't occur at the specified moment. The clock needs to be accurate, so look at the AccuracySec setting for more information on ensuring the clock is accurate.

OnBootSec

Be certain that timers that have the *OnBootSec* setting are not in conflict with user settings. You can view any user-specific settings using **systemctl -*user***.

Unit

This setting indicates the unit that should be activated or turned on when the timer is reached, and having a configuration error or specifying a nonexistent unit are a couple of the most common problems.

If you accidentally set the unit to be another timer, it will not execute or activate that .timer unit, but default over to that same name.service, which can be very confusing (or alarming, in this case).

Time Expressions

The system method of *time expressions* is rather complex and can be quite confusing to the Linux newcomer. In addition, for those used to using @time notations in cron, you'll need to pay very close attention to what these mean in system time expressions.

Mount Unit File Issues

Mount units are designed to control and supervise systemd mounted devices and filesystems, including what can and cannot be mounted. Mount units are text files like the other units, and as such are subject to errors and typos that can complicate an already complex scenario.

Naming Conventions

The most sensitive and misconfigured part of mount units is the naming. ***Naming conventions*** means that the name of a mount unit *must* match the name of the file-system it controls, with one simple but important distinction: The mount point to be represented is matched up in the name not with **/mount/point/filesystem** but with **mount-point-filesystem**. You just replace the **/** characters with **-** characters, since **/** is a protected system character that only occurs between two file objects, typically a directory and another directory or file inside of it.

What

When reading a mount unit, systemd does not use the User= and Group= directives or settings; instead, it uses What= to show what is the source of the mount—that is, what is the type of device being mounted.

This setting is subject to typos, so you should check this setting very carefully in mount units that are manually created. The units that systemd auto-generates are less susceptible to (human) error.

Where

Working hand-in-hand with the What= setting is the Where= setting, which para-doxically for systemd is about as clear as you can get. Where= specifies where sys-temd is to mount what you have specified in the mount unit.

There are situations that can cause issues, such as having an existing mount point that is actually used for something else—mounting a filesystem over an existing directory as a mount point will obscure or make unavailable anything that was in that mount point and below until the new mount is unmounted.

Type

Usually systemd will detect the type of a filesystem when it's being mounted, but in some cases you may have to manually configure the type of the filesystem being mounted.

Keep in mind that root permissions are normally required to mount a filesystem, but systemd has provisions for non-root users to perform mounts, but that's out of the scope of the Linux+ objectives.

Options

There are times when you realize that the development team working so hard to make systemd an industry standard have thought about something pretty hard, and this is true of the Options= line in the mount unit files.

This is effectively to mimic the **Options** column in the **/etc/fstab** file, or to supplant it, depending on your point of view.

Of particular note is the fact that the Options= line doesn't support all the options in the **Options** column, and some experimentation will be necessary to see which of your desired options will work.

Target Unit File Issues

Target units are most similar to the SysV runlevels, and issues with targets will affect large amounts of other units being loaded or, in the case of errors, not being loaded.

Default

The default.target isn't really a target, remember, but a link to the target unit that was designated to be the default. To check that the default target is the one you thought it was, or that it ought to be, use the **systemctl get-default** command, like you see in Example 22-4.

Example 22-4   Determining the Default Target

```
$ systemctl get-default
graphical.target
```

The default is shown as it's known to the system. However, if you get a different result, you can see what the actual linked target is with the command shown in Example 22-5.

Example 22-5   Determining the Default Target via the **find** Command

```
$ find /usr -iname default.target -exec ls -l {} \;
lrwxrwxrwx 1 root root 16 Jun 27  2022 /usr/lib/systemd/system/
default.target -> graphical.target
```

As you can see, the default.target is really a symlink to the graphical.target. If you are getting strange target errors, check this first, then make sure the target is not masked, or cannot be run by systemd.

There are times when you will see that a target has been masked and cannot be run, such as the graphical.target in our previous examples. You can see if this is the case by listing the loaded target units, such as shown in Example 22-6.

Example 22-6 Viewing the Loaded Targets for Troubleshooting Purposes

```
$ systemctl list-units --type=target
  UNIT                     LOAD    ACTIVE SUB      DESCRIPTION
  basic.target             loaded active active Basic System
  cryptsetup.target        loaded active active Local Encrypted Volumes
  getty.target             loaded active active Login Prompts
  graphical.target         masked active active graphical.target
  local-fs-pre.target      loaded active active Preparation for Local
File Syst
  local-fs.target          loaded active active Local File Systems
  multi-user.target        loaded active active Multi-User System
  network-online.target    loaded active active Network is Online
  network-pre.target       loaded active active Preparation for Network
  network.target           loaded active active Network
  nss-lookup.target        loaded active active Host and Network Name
Lookups
  nss-user-lookup.target   loaded active active User and Group Name
Lookups
  paths.target             loaded active active Path Units
  printer.target           loaded active active Printer Support
  remote-fs.target         loaded active active Remote File Systems
  slices.target            loaded active active Slice Units
  sockets.target           loaded active active Socket Units
  sound.target             loaded active active Sound Card
  swap.target              loaded active active Swaps
  sysinit.target           loaded active active System Initialization
  time-set.target          loaded active active System Time Set
  timers.target            loaded active active Timer Units
  veritysetup.target       loaded active active Local Verity Protected
Volumes

LOAD   = Reflects whether the unit definition was properly loaded.
ACTIVE = The high-level unit activation state, i.e. generalization of
SUB.
SUB    = The low-level unit activation state, values depend on unit
type.
23 loaded units listed. Pass --all to see loaded but inactive units,
too.
To show all installed unit files use 'systemctl list-unit-files'.
```

If you inspect the line for the graphical.target, you'll see it's masked, and the way to unmask it is with the **unmask** subcommand:

```
$ sudo systemctl unmask graphical.target
```

Then you can inspect it with the command in Example 22-6, and see that it's unmasked and available. Reboot, if possible, to make sure things are loaded like you want them to be from this point.

Multiuser

My favorite issue of all is someone saying that their system doesn't load the graphical subsystem when booting up, only to find that the default target is the multi-user. target. This means that the system was *not supposed* to load the graphical subsystem, but rather the text-only interface. This is easily fixed by making the graphical.target the default target using

```
$ sudo systemctl set-default graphical.target
```

This configures the system to attempt to (if not actually) start and end up with the graphical subsystem as the interface default.

Network-online

As mentioned early in this chapter, one of the main issues with systemd is that seemingly all the services start at once—which is not usually true, but it sure seems like everything is up and roaring and available—but all of this takes time, and services that are all started at once will obviously load at different timings, due to their size or complexity.

One of the main things you can do to ensure that network services are online when needed is to configure either a Wants= directive or a Requires= directive that points to the appropriate network service management scheme for your system.

The "Networking Services" section near the beginning of this chapter has more information on how to determine what network management scheme you are using. This section includes a discussion of *network-online*.target, which is what the Linux+ exam objectives are referring to when mentioning **Network-online**.

Graphical

Because the graphical.target is just that, a target, a lot of things can keep it from loading how you expect.

In particular, if your system boots up, and you get the text login prompt, then you may have a dependency issue or problem loading some needed service or other target and need to inspect your log files and systemd configuration.

The first thing to do is to look at the After= line in the **/usr/lib/systemd/system/graphical.target** file, which may look like this:

```
After=multi-user.target rescue.service rescue.target display-manager.
service
```

This indicates what should be there for the graphical target to be loaded, so make sure that those services and targets are running using the following command:

systemctl list-units --type=target

Also look to see if there are any errors about gdm.service, the GNOME Display Manager, by running

systemctl status gdm

This will show a display that indicates if the gdm.service is running and a few log entries indicating its status.

If you need more information on this or any other service, use the journaling logs to get that with the following command:

$ **journalctl -b**

This will show the system journal entries from the latest system boot to the present. Earlier versions are available by referencing them in a backward chronological way, such as:

$ **journalctl --list-boots**

This will show a listing of the previous boots, with the current boot scenario referenced as 0, such as shown in Example 22-7.

Example 22-7   Example of **journalctl --list-boots** Command Output

```
$ journalctl --list-boots
-4 7702c4eb2f7d40f193b489b144c7b41e Thu 2022-07-07 12:41:15 MDT—Thu
2022-07-07 13:16:04 MDT
-3 8a9177df73c94980a4e30104d81e75c2 Mon 2022-07-18 07:42:28 MDT—Mon
2022-07-18 07:47:31 MDT
-2 05235a33547349c1a36facfefdf7a232 Mon 2022-07-18 07:47:37 MDT—Mon
2022-07-18 07:51:41 MDT
-1 89437fce32c24b95ba16aa8f5b3e7a84 Sat 2023-03-18 12:14:13 MDT—Sat
2023-03-18 12:16:33 MDT
 0 c9c983a4e4f7460a8fb5bd9d28824855 Sat 2023-03-18 12:16:39 MDT—Mon
2023-03-20 20:29:04 MDTnetdev
```

To see a previous boot log scenario, just specify that instance, in this case from **-1** to **-4**, with the command

```
$ journalctl -b -2
```

You also might try focusing on a single service at a time, such as looking at gdm.service (a common culprit in this type of scenario) with the command

```
$ journalctl -f -u gdm.service
```

This will display only lines related to the gdm.service unit and its operations.

Common Problems

This last section of the final chapter (phew!) is a bit of a catch-all for troubleshooting, hitting the highlights for some of the more common problems that can affect your Linux systems and cause you issues.

Name Resolution Failure

So much of our current systems and services depend on the resolution of friendly names to IP addresses that even a short outage of name services can wreak a lot of havoc.

In the context of systemd and Linux systems, "Name resolution failure" refers to the inability of the system to translate a hostname (such as a domain name) into an IP address using the Domain Name System (DNS). This failure can prevent the system from establishing network connections to remote hosts, accessing websites, or resolving domain names into their corresponding IP addresses. Systemd provides various tools and mechanisms for managing network configuration and name resolution. Since this topic was covered in Chapter 5, "Using Network Tools and Configuration Files," where we discussed the various *name resolution* components, and also in Chapter 19, "Analyzing and Troubleshooting Networks," where we discussed troubleshooting name resolution issues, we will count that topic as properly and fully covered and move on to the next common problem.

Application Crash

Just like a crime scene, an *application crash* can be difficult to investigate. Often there are not a lot of clues except a suddenly crashed application and, if you're lucky, an onscreen message that may or may not be helpful.

The first and probably easiest thing you can do is look in the system log files for any indication that something has happened. It's very likely that some sort of an error message(s) was committed to the logs or the journal in systemd-based systems.

Another great way to see where any entries have been placed on a syslog-based system is to use the **journalctl** command to view a timeframe of log entries over the past few minutes, such as the example output of the **journalctl --since "5 minutes"** command shown in Figure 22-1.

```
Mar 20 21:32:47 ubuntu-linux-22-04-desktop dbus-daemon[653]: [system] Activating via systemd: service name='net.reactivated.Fprint' unit='fprintd.service' r
Mar 20 21:32:47 ubuntu-linux-22-04-desktop systemd[1]: Starting Fingerprint Authentication Daemon...
Mar 20 21:32:47 ubuntu-linux-22-04-desktop dbus-daemon[653]: [system] Successfully activated service 'net.reactivated.Fprint'
Mar 20 21:32:47 ubuntu-linux-22-04-desktop systemd[1]: Started Fingerprint Authentication Daemon.
Mar 20 21:32:47 ubuntu-linux-22-04-desktop gnome-shell[2189]: JS ERROR: Failed to initialize fprintd service: Gio.IOErrorEnum: GDBus.Error:net.reactivated.F
                                                             asyncCallback@resource:///org/gnome/gjs/modules/core/overrides/Gio.js:114:23
Mar 20 21:32:49 ubuntu-linux-22-04-desktop gdm-password][165080]: gkr-pam: the password for the login keyring was invalid.
Mar 20 21:32:49 ubuntu-linux-22-04-desktop dbus-daemon[2043]: [session uid=1000 pid=2043] Activating service name='org.freedesktop.FileManager1' requested b
Mar 20 21:32:50 ubuntu-linux-22-04-desktop NetworkManager[60890]: <info>  [1679369570.0323] agent-manager: agent[225548ba5b56b3d2,:1.203/org.gnome.Shell.Net
Mar 20 21:32:50 ubuntu-linux-22-04-desktop ubuntu-appindicators@ubuntu.com[2189]: unable to update icon for software-update-available
Mar 20 21:32:50 ubuntu-linux-22-04-desktop ubuntu-appindicators@ubuntu.com[2189]: unable to update icon for livepatch
Mar 20 21:32:50 ubuntu-linux-22-04-desktop dbus-daemon[2043]: [session uid=1000 pid=2043] Successfully activated service 'org.freedesktop.FileManager1'
Mar 20 21:32:50 ubuntu-linux-22-04-desktop dbus-daemon[2043]: [session uid=1000 pid=2043] Activating service name='org.gnome.ArchiveManager1' requested by '
Mar 20 21:32:50 ubuntu-linux-22-04-desktop gnome-shell[2189]: Window manager warning: Overwriting existing binding of keysym 39 with keysym 39 (keycode 12).
Mar 20 21:32:50 ubuntu-linux-22-04-desktop gnome-shell[2189]: Window manager warning: Overwriting existing binding of keysym 32 with keysym 32 (keycode b).
Mar 20 21:32:50 ubuntu-linux-22-04-desktop gnome-shell[2189]: Window manager warning: Overwriting existing binding of keysym 33 with keysym 33 (keycode c).
Mar 20 21:32:50 ubuntu-linux-22-04-desktop gnome-shell[2189]: Window manager warning: Overwriting existing binding of keysym 34 with keysym 34 (keycode d).
Mar 20 21:32:50 ubuntu-linux-22-04-desktop gnome-shell[2189]: Window manager warning: Overwriting existing binding of keysym 35 with keysym 35 (keycode e).
Mar 20 21:32:50 ubuntu-linux-22-04-desktop gnome-shell[2189]: Window manager warning: Overwriting existing binding of keysym 36 with keysym 36 (keycode f).
Mar 20 21:32:50 ubuntu-linux-22-04-desktop gnome-shell[2189]: Window manager warning: Overwriting existing binding of keysym 37 with keysym 37 (keycode 10).
Mar 20 21:32:50 ubuntu-linux-22-04-desktop gnome-shell[2189]: Window manager warning: Overwriting existing binding of keysym 31 with keysym 31 (keycode a).
Mar 20 21:32:50 ubuntu-linux-22-04-desktop gnome-shell[2189]: Window manager warning: Overwriting existing binding of keysym 38 with keysym 38 (keycode 11).
Mar 20 21:32:50 ubuntu-linux-22-04-desktop dbus-daemon[2043]: [session uid=1000 pid=2043] Successfully activated service 'org.gnome.ArchiveManager1'
```

Figure 22-1   Output of the **journalctl --since "5 minutes"** command

You can modify this command to just about any time period, such as **"1 hour ago"** or **"2 days ago"**, to name just a couple of possibilities.

When an application crashes, you can configure the system to take a snapshot of the memory that system was using and commit it to disk, which is called a "core dump" or a "crash dump," depending on your background.

To enable core dumps on a systemd-based system:

Step 1.   As the root user, set the **ulimit** for crash files to **unlimited**:

```
# ulimit -c unlimited
```

Step 2.   Run the **sleep** command and crash it with

```
sleep 50 & ; killall -SIGSEGV sleep
```

Step 3.   This will either show a text mode message about sleep suffering a segmentation fault or kick off a graphical application (Apport) that will walk you through saving and possibly sending off a crash report.

NOTE To reset the core size limitation, use the same command you did to set it to **unlimited** as shown in step 2, but instead of **unlimited** use **0** (the number zero).

Step 4.   Depending on what distribution you are using, you may want to check if the core dump is in **/var/crash**. If it is, run a simple **ls** command to see its presence and size.

Step 5.   Your system may put the crash dump in your application's working directory, which you can confirm by looking at the **/etc/sysctl.conf** file for the line that contains kernel.core_pattern.

Step 6.   You can also view the kernel.core_pattern info with the **sysctl** command:

```
$ sysctl kernel.core_pattern
```

When an application is started by the system, systemd's service management capabilities manages the crashed application's behavior and potentially facilitates recovery. Systemd handles application crashes using the following:

1. **Service Units:** Service units define how the application is started, stopped, and managed by systemd. When an application crashes, the service unit associated with it comes into focus.

2. **Automatic Restart:** Many service units are configured to automatically restart the crashed application. This behavior is defined by the **Restart** directive in the service unit configuration.

3. **Restart Attempts:** The **RestartSec** directive in the service unit configuration specifies the delay between restart attempts. This helps prevent a situation where an application restarts immediately after crashing due to the same issue.

4. **Backoff Behavior:** If an application continues to crash repeatedly, systemd employs an exponential backoff behavior. This means that each time a restart fails, systemd increases the delay before the next restart attempt. This helps prevent excessive system resource consumption due to a continuously crashing application.

5. **Restart Limits:** To avoid an application causing excessive resource consumption, systemd can be configured with restart limits using directives like **StartLimitInterval** and **StartLimitBurst**. These directives define the number of restart attempts within a certain time interval.

6. **Custom Actions:** Depending on the scenario, administrators can customize actions taken when a service crashes. This might include sending notifications, executing scripts, or invoking specific recovery procedures.

Ubuntu has an automated routine that catches a crash that happens and pops up the aforementioned Apport program, which will walk you through inspecting the details of a crash.

NOTE   You can also use the **apport-cli** program, which will require a little reading and experimentation, but can be very helpful on nongraphical systems when investigating a crash.

Time-Zone Configuration

One of the less commonly understood but very important configuration items is the time zone. Even if a server is getting its time set from a valid time server, the time-zone offset can make it an hour or many more off of the correct time.

This is a critical issue when you have systems that are indexed on the exactly correct time, in particular database servers and anything else that requires exquisitely accurate timestamps.

A very quick way to see what your time zone is set to is to run the **date** command as shown in Example 22-8.

Example 22-8   Example of **date** Command Output

```
$ date
Mon Mar 20 22:53:09 MDT 2023
```

MDT, which represents Mountain Daylight Time, is the current value of the **$TZ** variable in the time configuration file **/etc/timezone**.

You can temporarily set this variable to anything you want, such as Pacific Daylight Time (PDT), by exporting a different value to the **$TZ** variable, as shown in Example 22-9.

Example 22-9   Example of Temporarily Changing the Time Zone

```
$ export TZ="America/Los_Angeles" ; date
Mon Mar 20 22:55:34 PDT 2023
```

You can, of course, permanently change your time-zone info by using the **/etc/localtime** symlink, an example of which is shown in Example 22-10.

Example 22-10   Example of **the /etc/localtime** Symlink Target

```
$ ls -l /etc/localtime
lrwxrwxrwx 1 root root 34 Mar 18 11:16 /etc/localtime -> /usr/share/
zoneinfo/America/Denver
```

You can investigate the **/etc/share/zoneinfo** directory contents and decide which of the other time-zone files you might want to change this symlink to point to, such as America/Los_Angeles in Example 22-9.

Configuring the time zone in systemd-based Linux systems should generally be a straightforward process, but problems can occur due to misconfigurations or issues.

If you're facing time-zone configuration problems, here are some common issues and solutions:

- **Incorrect Time Zone:** Solution — Update the time-zone configuration using the **timedatectl** command.

- **Time Zone Not Changing:** Solution - Check if the system clock is synchronized with a time server using the **timedatectl status** command. If not, synchronize it using the **sudo timedatectl set-ntp true** command.

- **Clock Drift Issues:** Solution - Make sure your system's hardware clock is correctly configured to UTC or local time, depending on your preference.

Boot Issues

Chapter 1, "Understanding Linux Fundamentals," covered the boot process and some resulting issues and troubleshooting steps, so we won't rehash that material here.

Journal Issues

"Journaling" used to mean a transaction log on ext filesystems, but since the introduction of systemd, journaling means "logging" in systemd.

Systemd's integration with the journaling system provides powerful tools for diagnosing and troubleshooting issues on Linux systems. The **journalctl** command allows you to access and analyze systemd journal logs, providing insights into various system events, services, errors, and more.

Some of the more common ways to use **journalctl** to diagnose problems include:

- View all journal logs using the **journalctl** command with no arguments.

- Use the **-u** option to view logs for a specific service or unit.

- Use the **--since** and **--until** options to view logs for a specific time range.

- Use the **-f** option to view "live logs" as they are sent to journald.

Services Not Starting on Time

The issue of services not starting on time is covered earlier in the chapter in the section "Networking Services" (in the context of troubleshooting service unit file issues) and relates mostly to making sure that services that everything depends on, in particular name services and the network, are in the Wants= or Requires= directives for those services.

Summary

In the first half of this chapter, you learned all about using systemd to troubleshoot issues with service, timer, mount, and target unit files.

You also learned about using systemd to troubleshoot common problems with a Linux system, though most of those problems were covered in detail elsewhere in previous chapters or earlier in this chapter and you were referred to the relevant coverage.

Exam Preparation Tasks

As mentioned in the section "Goals and Methods" in the Introduction, you have a couple of choices for exam preparation: the exercises here, Chapter 23, "Final Preparation," and the exam simulation questions in the Pearson Test Prep Software Online.

Review All Key Topics

Review the most important topics in this chapter, noted with the Key Topic icon in the margin of the page. Table 22-2 lists these key topics and the page number on which each is found.

Table 22-2   Key Topics for Chapter 22

Key Topic Element	Description	Page Number
Paragraph	Overview of unit files	745
Paragraph	Only the **network-online.target** file is an active unit	746
Paragraph	How you can get into trouble with the type of service	747
Note	The two types of dependencies in systemd	747
Paragraph	The Type= directive options	748
Paragraph	Difference between the Requires= and Wants= directives	749
Example 22-4	Determining the Default Target	752
Example 22-6	Viewing the Loaded Targets for Troubleshooting Purposes	753
Example 22-7	Example of **journalctl --list-boots** Command Output	755
Figure 22-1	Output of the **journalctl --since "5 minutes"** command	757
Example 22-8	Example of **date** Command Output	759

Define Key Terms

Define the following key terms from this chapter and check your answers in the glossary:

unit files, service, ExecStart, ExecStop, Before, After, type, timer, OnCalendar, OnBootSec, time expressions, naming conventions, network-online, name resolution, application crash

Review Questions

The answers to these review questions are in Appendix A.

1. In a systemd file, which setting prevents you from having multiple ExecStart lines?

   a. Type=single

   b. Type=onlyone

   c. Type=oneshot

   d. Type=reserved

2. You can configure a systemd service to run as a given user by specifying which of the following settings?

   a. User=

   b. RunAs=

   c. AllowUser=

   d. Exec=

3. The _____ setting defines a specific date and time for a timer event in a Timer unit file.

   a. OnDate

   b. AtTime

   c. EventDate

   d. OnCalendar

4. In a systemd unit file, the _____ will increase the delay before the next restart attempt of an application that has crashed.

   a. **Restart Limits**

   b. **Restart Attempts**

   c. **Delay Restarts**

   d. **Backoff Behavior**

## CHAPTER 23

Final Preparation

Are you excited for your exam after reading this book? I sure hope so. You should be. In this chapter we will put certification prep all together for you and take a more detailed look at the actual certification exam itself.

This chapter shares some great ideas for ensuring that you ace that exam. If you read this book to master Linux and you were not really considering certification, then maybe this chapter might even convince you to give it a try!

The first 22 chapters of this book cover the technologies, protocols, programming concepts, and considerations required to be prepared to pass the CompTIA Linux+ (XK0-005) exam. While these chapters supply the detailed information, most people need more preparation than just reading the first 22 chapters of this book. This chapter details a set of tools and a study plan to help you complete your preparation for the exam.

This short chapter has four main sections. The first section lists the CompTIA Linux+ (XK0-005) exam information and breakdown. The second section shares some important tips to keep in mind to ensure that you are ready for this exam. The third section discusses exam preparation tools that may be useful at this point in the study process. The final section lists a suggested study plan for you to follow now that you have completed all the earlier chapters in this book.

Exam Information

Here are details you should be aware of regarding the Linux+ exam:

- **Question types:** Multiple choice and performance based

- **Number of questions:** Maximum of 90

- **Time limit:** 90 minutes

- **Required passing score:** 720 (on a scale of 100 to 900)

- **Languages:** English (at launch); Japanese, Portuguese, and Spanish (coming soon)

■ **Exam fee:** US $358

■ **Exam ID code:** XK0-005

CompTIA Linux+ certification validates the skills of IT professionals with hands-on experience configuring, monitoring, and supporting servers running the Linux operating system. The new Linux+ exam has an increased focus on the following topics: security, kernel modules, storage and visualization, device management at an enterprise level, Git and automation, networking and firewalls, the server side and the command line, server (vs. client-based) coverage, troubleshooting, and SELinux.

The exam is broken up into four different domains. The following pages list those domains, the objectives in each domain, and the percentage of the exam devoted to each of the domains:

1.0 System Management (32% of the exam)

1.1 Summarize Linux fundamentals.

1.2 Given a scenario, manage files and directories.

1.3 Given a scenario, configure and manage storage using the appropriate tools.

1.4 Given a scenario, configure and use the appropriate processes and services.

1.5 Given a scenario, use the appropriate networking tools or configuration files.

1.6 Given a scenario, build and install software.

1.7 Given a scenario, manage software configurations.

2.0 Security (21% of the exam)

2.1 Summarize the purpose and use of security best practices in a Linux environment.

2.2 Given a scenario, implement identity management.

2.3 Given a scenario, implement and configure Linux firewalls.

2.4 Given a scenario, configure and execute remote connectivity for system management.

2.5 Given a scenario, apply the appropriate access controls.

3.0 Scripting, Containers, and Automation (19% of the exam)

3.1 Given a scenario, create simple shell scripts to automate common tasks.

3.2 Given a scenario, perform basic container operations.

3.3 Given a scenario, perform basic version control using Git.

3.4 Summarize common infrastructure as code technologies.

3.5 Summarize container, cloud, and orchestration concepts.

4.0 Troubleshooting (28% of the exam)

4.1 Given a scenario, analyze and troubleshoot storage issues.

4.2 Given a scenario, analyze and troubleshoot network resource issues.

4.3 Given a scenario, analyze and troubleshoot central processing unit (CPU) and memory issues.

4.4 Given a scenario, analyze and troubleshoot user access and file permissions.

4.5 Given a scenario, use systemd to diagnose and resolve common problems with a Linux system.

Be sure to visit CompTIA's web page at https://certification.comptia.org/certifications/linux to ensure that you have the latest information and exam objectives for the CompTIA Linux+ exam.

Getting Ready

Here are some important tips to keep in mind to ensure that you are ready for this rewarding exam:

- **Build and use a study tracker:** Consider using the exam objectives shown in this chapter to build a study tracker for yourself. Such a tracker can help ensure that you have not missed anything and that you are confident for your exam. As a matter of fact, this book offers a sample Study Planner as a website supplement.

- **Think about your time budget for questions on the exam:** When you do the math, you will see that, on average, you have one minute per question. While this does not sound like a lot of time, keep in mind that many of the questions will be very straightforward, and you will take 15 to 30 seconds on those. This leaves you extra time for other questions on the exam.

- **Watch the clock:** Check in on the time remaining periodically as you are taking the exam. You might even find that you can slow down pretty dramatically if you have built up a nice block of extra time.

- **Get some earplugs:** The testing center might provide earplugs, but get some just in case and bring them along. There might be other test takers in the center with you, and you do not want to be distracted by their screams. I personally have no issue blocking out the sounds around me, so I never worry about this, but I know it is an issue for some.

- **Plan your travel time:** Give yourself extra time to find the center and get checked in. Be sure to arrive early. As you test more at a particular center, you can certainly start cutting it closer time-wise.

- **Get rest:** Most students report that getting plenty of rest the night before the exam boosts their success. All-night cram sessions are not typically successful.

- **Prepare your body:** Don't forget to eat a banana (for the Niacin) and drink a good amount of water (hydrated brains take exams better!) before you go to the exam room.

- **Bring in valuables but get ready to lock them up:** The testing center will take your phone, your smartwatch, your wallet, and other such items and will provide a secure place for them.

- **Take notes:** You will be given note-taking implements and should not be afraid to use them. I always jot down any questions I struggle with on the exam. I then memorize them at the end of the test by reading my notes over and over again. I always make sure I have a pen and paper in the car, and I write down the issues in my car just after the exam. When I get home—with a pass or fail—I research those items.

- **Practice exam questions are great—so use them:** This text provides many practice exam questions. Be sure to go through them thoroughly. Remember that you shouldn't blindly memorize answers; rather, use the practice questions to really see where you are weak in your knowledge and then study up on those areas.

Tools for Final Preparation

This section lists some information about the available tools and how to access them.

Pearson Test Prep Practice Test Software and Questions on the Website

Register this book to get access to the Pearson IT Certification test engine (software that displays and grades a set of exam-realistic multiple-choice questions). Using the Pearson Test Prep practice test software, you can either study by going through the questions in Study Mode or take a simulated (timed) CompTIA Linux+ exam.

The Pearson Test Prep practice test software comes with two full practice exams. These practice tests are available to you either online or as an offline Windows application. To access the practice exams that were developed with this book, please see the instructions in the card inserted in the sleeve in the back of the book. This card includes a unique access code that enables you to activate your exams in the Pearson Test Prep software.

Accessing the Pearson Test Prep Practice Test Software Online

The online version of this software can be used on any device with a browser and connectivity to the Internet, including desktop machines, tablets, and smartphones. To start using your practice exams online, simply follow these steps:

Step 1.   Go to https://www.PearsonTestPrep.com.

Step 2.   Select Pearson IT Certification as your product group.

Step 3.   Enter your email and password for your account. If you don't have an account on PearsonITCertification.com or CiscoPress.com, you need to establish one by going to PearsonITCertification.com/join.

Step 4.   In the My Products tab, click the Activate New Product button.

Step 5.   Enter the access code printed on the insert card in the back of your book to activate your product. The product will now be listed in your My Products page.

Step 6.   Click the Exams button to launch the exam settings screen and start your exam.

Accessing the Pearson Test Prep Practice Test Software Offline

If you wish to study offline, you can download and install the Windows version of the Pearson Test Prep software. You can find a download link for this software on the book's companion website.

https://www.pearsonitcertification.com/content/downloads/pcpt/engine.zip

To access the book's companion website and the software, simply follow these steps:

Step 1.   Register your book by going to PearsonITCertification.com/register and entering the ISBN 9780137866885.

Step 2.   Respond to the challenge questions.

Step 3.   Go to your account page and select the Registered Products tab.

Step 4.   Click the Access Bonus Content link under the product listing.

Step 5.   Click the Install Pearson Test Prep Desktop Version link in the Practice Exams section of the page to download the software.

Step 6.   When the software finishes downloading, unzip all the files on your computer.

Step 7.   Double-click the application file to start the installation, and follow the onscreen instructions to complete the registration.

Step 8.   When the installation is complete, launch the application and click the Activate Exam button on the My Products tab.

Step 9.   Click the Activate a Product button in the Activate Product Wizard.

Step 10.   Enter the unique access code found on the card in the sleeve in the back of your book and click the Activate button.

Step 11.   Click Next, and then click the Finish button to download the exam data to your application.

Step 12.   You can now start using the practice exams by selecting the product and clicking the Open Exam button to open the exam settings screen.

Note that the offline and online versions sync together, so saved exams and grade results recorded on one version will be available to you on the other as well.

Customizing Your Exams

When you are in the exam settings screen, you can choose to take exams in one of three modes:

- Study Mode
- Practice Exam Mode
- Flash Card Mode

Study Mode enables you to fully customize your exams and review answers as you are taking the exam. This is typically the mode you use first to assess your knowledge and identify information gaps. Practice Exam Mode locks certain customization options in order to present a realistic exam experience. Use this mode when you are preparing to test your exam readiness. Flash Card Mode strips out the answers and presents you with only the question stem. This mode is great for late-stage preparation, when you really want to challenge yourself to provide answers without the benefit of seeing multiple-choice options. This mode does not provide the detailed score reports that the other two modes provide, so it is not the best mode for helping you identify knowledge gaps.

In addition to these three modes, you will be able to select the source of your questions. You can choose to take exams that cover all of the chapters, or you can narrow your selection to just a single chapter or the chapters that make up specific parts in the book. All chapters are selected by default. If you want to narrow your focus to individual chapters, simply deselect all the chapters and then select only those on which you wish to focus in the Objectives area.

You can also select the exam banks on which to focus. Each exam bank comes complete with a full exam of questions that cover topics in every chapter. You can have the test engine serve up exams from both banks or just from one individual bank by selecting the desired banks in the exam bank area.

There are several other customizations you can make to your exam from the exam settings screen, such as the time allowed to take the exam, the number of questions served up, whether to randomize questions and answers, whether to show the number of correct answers for multiple-answer questions, and whether to serve up only specific types of questions. You can also create custom test banks by selecting only questions that you have marked or questions on which you have added notes.

Updating Your Exams

If you are using the online version of the Pearson Test Prep software, you should always have access to the latest version of the software as well as the exam data. If you are using the Windows desktop version, every time you launch the software, it will check to see whether there are any updates to your exam data and automatically download any changes made since the last time you used the software. This requires you to be connected to the Internet at the time you launch the software.

Sometimes, due to a number of factors, the exam data might not fully download when you activate your exam. If you find that figures or exhibits are missing, you might need to manually update your exams.

To update a particular exam you have already activated and downloaded, simply select the Tools tab and click the Update Products button. Again, this is only an issue with the desktop Windows application.

If you wish to check for updates to the Windows desktop version of the Pearson Test Prep exam engine software, simply select the Tools tab and click the Update Application button. Doing so allows you to ensure that you are running the latest version of the software engine.

Premium Edition

In addition to the free practice exams provided on the website, you can purchase additional exams with expanded functionality directly from Pearson IT Certification. The Premium Edition of this title contains an additional two full practice exams and an eBook (in both PDF and ePub format). In addition, the Premium Edition title has remediation for each question to the specific part of the eBook that relates to that question.

Because you have purchased the print version of this title, you can purchase the Premium Edition at a deep discount. There is a coupon code in the book sleeve that contains a one-time-use code and instructions for where you can purchase the Premium Edition.

To view the Premium Edition product page, go to www.informit.com/title/9780137866885.

Chapter-Ending Review Tools

Chapters 2 through 22 each have several features in the "Exam Preparation Tasks" section at the end of the chapters. You might have already worked through these in each chapter. It can also be useful to use these tools again as you make your final preparations for the exam.

Suggested Plan for Final Review/Study

This section lists a suggested study plan from the point at which you finish reading through Chapter 22 until you take the CompTIA Linux+ exam. You can ignore this plan, use it as is, or just take suggestions from it.

The plan involves three steps:

Step 1. **Review key topics and "Do I Know This Already?" (DIKTA?) questions:** You can use the table that lists the key topics in each chapter or just flip the pages, looking for key topics. Also, reviewing the DIKTA? questions from the beginning of the chapter can be helpful for review.

Step 2. **Review "Review Questions" sections:** Go through the "Review Questions" section at the end of each chapter to identify areas where you need more study.

Step 3. **Use the Pearson Test Prep Practice Test software to practice:** The Pearson Test Prep practice test software enables you to study using a bank of unique exam-realistic questions available only with this book.

Summary

The tools and suggestions listed in this chapter have been designed with one goal in mind: to help you develop the skills required to pass the CompTIA Linux+ exam. This book has been developed from the beginning to not just tell you the facts but help you learn how to apply the facts. No matter what your experience level leading up to when you take the exams, it is my hope that the broad range of preparation tools, and even the structure of the book, will help you pass the exam with ease. I hope you do well on the exam.

Answers to the "Do I Know This Already?" Quizzes and Review Questions

Answers to the "Do I Know This Already?" Quizzes

Chapter 1

1. c
2. d
3. c
4. d
5. d
6. a
7. b

Chapter 2

1. b and c
2. c
3. a
4. c
5. c
6. a

Chapter 3

1. b
2. c
3. c
4. c
5. a and c
6. d

7. d

8. d

Chapter 4

1. a

2. b

3. c

4. d

5. c

6. a and d

7. c

Chapter 5

1. b

2. b and c

3. a

4. a, c, and d

5. a, b, and c

6. c

Chapter 6

1. c

2. a

3. d

4. a, c, d

5. b

6. c

Chapter 7

1. c

2. a

3. a and d

4. a and d

Chapter 8

1. b
2. a
3. b
4. a

Chapter 9

1. d
2. b
3. c
4. d

Chapter 10

1. d
2. b
3. c
4. d
5. d

Chapter 11

1. d
2. b
3. c
4. d
5. c
6. d

Chapter 12

1. c
2. b and c
3. b

    4. a, b, and d

    5. d

    6. d

Chapter 13

    1. c

    2. c

    3. a

    4. d

    5. b

    6. a

    7. a and d

Chapter 14

    1. c

    2. c

    3. a and e

    4. d

    5. a and b

    6. a

Chapter 15

    1. c

    2. b and d

    3. d

    4. a

    5. d

Chapter 16

    1. c

    2. a

    3. d

    4. a

    5. a, b, and d

    6. b and d

Chapter 17

    1. c

    2. a

    3. d

    4. a

    5. d

    6. d

    7. d

Chapter 18

    1. c

    2. a

    3. d

    4. a

    5. d

    6. b and d

    7. d

    8. d

    9. d

Chapter 19

    1. c

    2. a

    3. d

    4. a, c, and e

    5. d

    6. b and d

Chapter 20

1. c
2. a
3. d
4. d
5. b and d
6. d

Chapter 21

1. c
2. a
3. d
4. d
5. b

Chapter 22

1. c
2. a
3. d
4. d

Answers to the Review Questions

Chapter 1

1. **d**. D is correct because the file location is **/boot/grub2/grug2.cfg**, not some of the other choices, which refer to either incorrect distractors or previous versions of the GRUB configuration file location.

2. **b** and **c**. B and C are correct because they are the commands that will be the most helpful in getting information and pointing to a resolution of the issue. The other options are files, not commands.

3. **b**. Answer B is correct because the **/proc** directory contains a set of numbered directories that correspond to the running processes or the PID numerals.

4. **c.** Answer C is correct because the symptoms point directly to a kernel panic, where the system is rebooting repeatedly, and the log files support this conclusion.

5. **d.** Answer D is correct because one of the significant reasons to use a source code install is the ability to literally change any and all settings either in the code or in the processes of compiling and setting up.

6. **a.** Answer A is correct because the **dmidecode** command provides the capability to query and display the in-memory tables most directly and effectively.

7. **d.** Answer D is correct because the file method of storage allows you to change data at a deeply granular level, such as individual files, lines, words, and even single characters.

Chapter 2

1. **c.** Answer C is correct because **cd** is the fewest number of characters among the answers that will take the user back to their home directory. The other options are either longer (**cd**) or will not work.

2. **c.** Answer C is correct because the **file** command uses a reference set of data types and checks the target file contents and reports back the result.

3. **a.** Answer A is correct because a symbolic link is its own file with its own inode number. All the rest of the options describe characteristics of hard links.

4. **c.** Answer C is correct because the compression option **j** is used when the **tar** command compresses with the **bzip2** compression algorithm.

5. **b.** Answer B is correct because the **scp** command needs the **-r** option to properly copy directories and their contents between a local system and a remote system.

6. **b** and **e.** Answers B and E are correct because both **:wq** and **ZZ** accomplish the action of saving and exiting out of the **vi** or VIM editors.

Chapter 3

1. **c.** Answer C is correct because the **w** command will properly commit the configuration to the disk and exit the tool, also updating the filesystem information for the kernel.

2. **c.** Answer C is correct because **mdadm** is the correct command to set up a RAID configuration on your server.

3. **a.** Answer A is correct because a filesystem that supports resizing cannot be reduced in size while it's mounted; it should be unmounted first, resized, and then remounted.

4. **b.** Answer B is correct because the **auto** option causes the specified filesystem to be automatically mounted at system boot.

5. **d.** Answer D is correct because the **du** command with the **-sh** options will cause the directory tree in question to be measured and a summary of its space usage to be printed.

6. **c.** Answer C is correct because this command is a characteristic of the Ext filesystems, specifically in this case the Ext2 filesystem, and the **tune2fs** command is the only one in this answer set that can accomplish this action.

7. **b** and **e.** Answers B and E are correct because they are key characteristics of a network-attached storage device.

Chapter 4

1. **d.** Answer D is correct because it alone will cause the crontab command to run at the specified time consistently.

2. **c.** Answer C is correct because the **atrun** command can be used to set custom values for the **batch** command.

3. **a.** Answer A is correct because it properly sets the path so the shell instances used by cron can find the right commands in the path.

4. **a.** Answer A is correct because this is the proper location for user-related crontab files.

5. **b.** Answer B is correct because if both the **cron.allow** and **cron.deny** files exist, then only the **cron.allow** file is used.

6. **c.** Answer C is correct because **Ctrl+Z** alone of the answers will pause a foreground job.

Chapter 5

1. **a** and **d.** A and D are correct because **wget** and **curl** are the commands that will accomplish the download via the full URL.

2. **d.** D is correct because the **ssh** command is designed to replace the **telnet** command.

3. **c.** C is correct because the **scp** command is designed to provide secure copying over SSH.

4. **a** and **c.** A and C are correct because the **traceroute** and **mtr** commands both show the path that traffic takes to reach a destination host.

Chapter 6

1. **a.** A is correct because the description most closely matches source RPM packages, which contain source code that can be used to build binaries but don't contain actual application binaries.

2. **d.** D is correct because the process being described is the package manager downloading the most updated information about the package you are installing, its dependencies, and so on from the package repository.

3. **c.** C is correct because the **rpm -V** command will verify the specified packages or all packages for each of the nine different attributes.

4. **b.** B is correct because of all the options listed, **--allmatches** alone will work with the **rpm** command to remove all matches to a given package name.

5. **b.** B is correct because a sandboxed application typically needs to get permissions to access network (and disk) resources.

Chapter 7

1. **a.** A is correct because the service has replaced the existing config file with a new default one, and that is because the file was not marked with the "**noreplace**" attribute, and will therefore be saved with an **.rpmsave** extension.

2. **a and d.** A and D are correct because the DNF and YUM package managers are both based on using the YUM repos and underlying configuration files and directories.

3. **c.** C is correct because the **/etc/sysctl.conf** file is the proper file in which to put kernel parameters and values so that they are picked up at the next reboot.

4. **b.** B is correct because for some reason the objective writers included the **imsmod** command, perhaps as an overlooked typo of the insmod command.

5. **b.** B is correct because on a very recent distribution, the old NTP commands such as **ntpdate** have been replaced by the **chronyc** command, as well as the underlying chronyd daemon.

6. **c.** C is correct because the **debug** level of logging will give you the most verbose information about a particular category of logging messages.

Chapter 8

1. **d.** D is correct because the venerable (older) Secure Sockets Layer (SSL) security methodology is now a part of the newer Transport Layer Security (TLS) suite of security protocols.

2. **b.** B is correct because the client uses the public key of the remote system to mix with its own private key to properly encrypt and decrypt data.

3. **d.** D is correct because the **umask** command allows you to change the settings for the user mask or umask, affecting the effective permissions for files and directories.

4. **d.** D is correct because using self-signed certificates is less costly from a fee or outright costs standpoint, as public certificate authorities charge fees, which can approach large sums.

5. **c.** C is correct because the use of SSL/TLS on a web server means you are using HTTPS (Hypertext Transfer Protocol) Secure.

6. **a and d.** A and D are correct because they are two of the four valid control values, which are **required, requisite, sufficient,** and **optional.**

Chapter 9

1. **6.** The correct answer is the numeral 6, in that counting from the left to the right, the sixth column or field (as separated by the : character) is the number of warning days before the user's password expires.

2. **a.** A is correct because the user owner field contains an unassigned UID (1002) but the group field is assigned to an existing group, and the user's home directory apparently used to belong to the user snuffy.

3. **511.** The system does not go back and reallocate user ID numbers sandwiched between already assigned user ID numbers; therefore, adding ten users beginning with UID 501 and then deleting two users below UID 510 would not change the fact that the next user added would automatically be assigned UID 511.

4. The correct answer is the **/etc/skel** directory. Using **-m** (create the user home directory) and **-d** (use the user's login name as the home directory) copies the /**etc/skel** directory to **/home/username** during the user creation process.

5. **d.** The **chage** command is designed to help you adjust or set the password expiration, warning, and other parameters in the **/etc/shadow** file for a given user.

6. **newgrp** performs the described behavior. The issuance of the command will make it appear that the user has just relogged on, and issuing the **id** command will show the user's current group.

Chapter 10

1. **b and d.** B and D are correct because they are the options that are needed to create a rule that will filter as specified.

2. **-n.** The correct answer is **-n** because that shows port numbers and IP addresses instead of names. This can speed up the utilities' return of output.

3. **c.** The correct answer is C because it correctly describes the use of a DNAT.

4. **MASQUERADE.** The correct answer is **MASQUERADE** because it configures NAT for all client systems connecting to **eth0**.

5. **d.** The correct answer is D because it's the proper file to configure a Linux system to become an IPv6 router (and is the only valid file in the list).

6. **a** and **c.** A and C are correct because DROP and ACCEPT are built-in targets, whereas LOG and REJECT are extension targets.

Chapter 11

1. **b.** B is correct because the **pkexec** command should be used to execute a target command as another user that has the rights to execute that command.

2. **/etc/sudoers.** The correct answer is **/etc/sudoers** because that is the location and name of the file primarily used to configure the **sudo** command and the access it provides.

3. **a.** A is correct because in order to create an encrypted connection that will allow the use of a passphrase only, and not query you for your local user password on the remote system, you need to copy your own public key to the appropriate location on the remote system.

4. **/etc/ssh/sshd_config.** The correct answer is **/etc/ssh/sshd_config** because this file is where the configuration of users who are allowed and denied is kept for the SSH daemon.

5. **d.** The correct answer is D because using the **-X** option is designed to allow you to then run a command on the remote system and have it display locally on your X display.

6. **c.** C is correct because **sudoedit** is designed to allow users to edit while using elevated privileges, without the danger of enabling something like vi/vim, which can be shelled out of, to be used to gain access to the command line.

Chapter 12

1. **d.** D is correct because the execute (or x) permission on a directory means that it can be accessed or used as a step to get into a subdirectory.

2. **b.** B is correct because although the users group has all three permissions and the file owner ross has read and write, they are not additive, so the user owner ross only has read and write.

3. **a** and **c.** The correct answers are A and C because SELinux contexts are not applied to user accounts.

4. **b.** Answer B is correct because SELinux is not functional in disabled mode. Permissive mode does not disable SELinux, and the other answers are distractors (enforcing mode is the third legitimate mode).

5. **d.** The correct answer is D because the **chattr** command is designed to set or alter the file or directory attributes that exist for those objects. The other options are distractors and fake commands.

6. **c.** Answer C is correct because the **lsattr** command is designed to show you the state of the file attributes on this file, which has the i attribute set.

Chapter 13

1. **b.** Answer B is correct because the file descriptor for stdout is **/proc/self/fd/1**. The other options are valid descriptors, but not for stdout.

2. **c.** Answer C is correct because the use of the > output redirection before the supposed "sort" command actually writes a file named **sort** to the current directory. You'd have to use a | symbol to actually pass the output of the **find** command to the **sort** command.

3. **c.** Answer C is correct because the first line of a script should technically be **#!/ bin/<shell>**, aka the shebang or hashspling.

4. **b.** Answer B is correct because the test condition is not executing the command. Answer A checks to see if **/bin/foo** exists. Answer C checks if the return value is 0, which means there is not an error. Answer D is not a valid check.

5. **a.** Answer A is correct because only **seq** provides a list of integers.

6. **b.** Answer B is correct because the use of the **exit** command and a number to specify the exit code produces the result.

Chapter 14

1. **b.** B is correct because the **-i** (interactive) and **-t** (connect a pseudo tty) options are the ones you would use to immediately execute commands from the shell prompt.

2. **c.** C is correct because the **podman attach** *<container ID>* command will cause your terminal to attach to the container and act as if you were at the shell prompt on that container.

3. **c.** C is correct because the Image ID is generated when the container is built and stays consistent throughout operations. The Container ID will be different each time a container is invoked, and process IDs will be new or changed each time a process is invoked.

4. **b.** B is correct because the **podman logs** command will show you most directly the logging being performed on a given container.

5. **a and c.** A and C are correct because the most likely scenario would be to use a properly configured Containerfile and use the **buildah** build command to create that container.

6. **b.** B is correct because Podman is the method by which you'd most likely implement root-less containers for your developers who have most recently been using Docker.

Chapter 15

1. **a.** Answer B is incorrect because this command commits files from the staging area to the local repository, and the question asks what to do before taking this action.

2. **b.** Answer A is incorrect because this command creates a new repository.

3. **b.** Answer B is correct because the -m option is used to add a message. Answers A, C, and D are incorrect because they are not valid options when adding a message to a commit operation.

4. **c.** Answer C is correct because the command sends changes from the local repository test branch to the remote repository. Answers A, B, and D are incorrect because -l, -a, and -p are not valid options for the **git push** command.

5. **d.** Answer D is correct because **git status** determines whether any file's changes are in the working area and need to be committed. Answers A, B, and C are incorrect because **working**, **update**, and **changed** are not valid arguments to the **git** command.

6. **a.** Answer A is correct because you can add the filename to the **.gitignore** file to ensure that Git does not include the file in the repo. Answers B, C, and D are incorrect because these files have no meaning to the Git software.

Chapter 16

1. **c.** Answer C is correct because when you use the **terraform** command and the code file you have created, with the **.tf** extension, it will then generate the resulting plan file for use with a terraform deployment.

2. **b and c.** Answers B and C are correct because the two main data definition formats are JSON and YAML. These are text files formatted to certain specifications, typically key-value pairs expressed in text (not traditional code).

3. **c.** Answer C is correct because Ansible was created and is maintained by Red Hat engineers and is considered the prime IaC tool for managing Red Hat infrastructure.

4. **a.** Answer A is correct because the definition files for what should happen when a Salt minion receives its instructions are contained in a State file.

5. **d.** Answer D is correct because the **git rebase** command acts in the described way (the other options are distractors).

6. **d.** Answer D is correct because of the listed answers; JSON alone is a data definition format that does not allow comments.

Chapter 17

1. **c.** Answer C is correct because a Pod is the component of Kubernetes that contains at least one container when it has been deployed.

2. **b and d.** Answers B and D are correct because a host network and a bridge network are typically in use when a host system is running virtual machines or containers, and while there are other types, none of the rest of the choices are valid.

3. **c.** Answer C is correct because the situation being described is a sidecar container or sidecar proxy.

4. **a.** Answer A is correct because the type of storage described matches exactly the persistent volume concept.

5. **d.** Answer D is correct because a service mesh is what is being defined.

6. **d.** Answer D is correct because a container registry will enable the team to centralize all their container images, which will make it easier to find, retain, and catalog them.

Chapter 18

1. **c.** Answer C is correct because configurations have no impact on I/O wait time.

2. **b.** Answer B is correct as it is the only valid output type of the top command.

3. **c.** Answer C is correct because it matches the definition provided in the question.

4. **a.** Answer A is correct as the df command is designed to display space usage on a filesystem.

5. **d.** Answer D is correct because the du command will scan all of the files in a directory structure and provide a total of space used.

6. **d.** Answer D is correct because smartd is a daemon that provides the stated functionality. The other tools are commands, not daemons.

Chapter 19

1. **c.** Answer C is correct because a standard Class C subnet is 3 octets of 8 bits, or 255.255.255.0.

2. **b** and **d.** Both **nmap** and **telnet** can connect to a remote system and query or open up a port and get information from it. The **nmap** tool is much more comprehensive, but **telnet** will do the task well enough.

3. **c.** Answer C is correct because one of the prime causes of dropped packets is a NIC (network interface card) error.

4. **a.** Answer A is correct because the Fast.com website, maintained by the Netflix organization, helps users determine quickly and easily what their bandwidth capabilities are.

5. **d.** Answer D is correct because you have most likely added a local **/etc/hosts** name resolution entry for the website you are developing.

6. **d.** Answer D is correct because the **K** command alone will perform the Key Update send and request a Key Update response from the remote system.

Chapter 20

1. **c.** Answer C is correct because the **free** command shows all the information that is being requested.

2. **c.** Answer C is correct because a process that matches these conditions is known as a zombie process.

3. **a.** Answer A is correct because only the **renice** command out of this list will allow you to adjust the priority of a running process without killing and restarting it.

4. **d.** Answer D is correct because the **out_of_memory** process is the overall process for determining if the system is really out of memory, performing checks on processes, and selecting ones to kill to attempt to resolve the situation.

5. **d.** Answer D is correct because the only two methods you can use to add swap at all are filesystem-based and partition-based. The safest method here is to configure filesystem-based swap.

6. **d.** Answer D is correct because the file in question is the **/proc/cpuinfo** file, which contains volumes of information about the CPU(s) on the system and is used by the **lscpu** command to display that information to the requestor.

Chapter 21

1. **c.** Answer C is correct because the **/etc/shadow** file would normally contain the encrypted password for the user, or a ! in that field if the password has not been created yet.

2. **c.** Answer C is correct because the **lsattr** command will show any extended attributes that are set on a file, usually done using the **chattr** command.

3. **a.** Answer A is correct because Windows systems use and apply case-sensitivity differently and users who are used to that will struggle initially when trying to log in with mixed-case passwords and with case-sensitivity overall.

4. **d.** Answer D is correct because **su -** is the proper command and option to become the root user directly, including the root user's environment (which is the issue).

5. **d.** Answer D is correct because the problem being described and experienced is that of running out of inodes at the hard limit, not blocks, so the inode hard limit should be adjusted accordingly.

Chapter 22

1. **c**

2. **a**

3. **d**

4. **d**

Glossary

Numeric

$PATH A variable that contains a list of directories that will be searched for executable files when a user enters a command.

2FA See *two-factor authentication (2FA)*.

A

absolute path The location of a file or directory that starts from the root of the filesystem and therefore begins with a slash character (/).

accessibility options A feature provided on desktops that makes it easier for individuals with physical limitations to work with the desktop.

address class ranges The primary subnets of Class A, B, C, D, and E networks.

Advanced Package Tool (APT) A package management system for Debian-derived systems that wraps lower-level tools and provides easy searching of remote package sources, including downloading any needed dependencies.

agent In orchestration, a monitoring system that has been installed on the system or component that is being monitored.

agentless In orchestration, a monitoring system that has not been installed on the system but is performed remotely.

AppArmor A security feature that uses MAC (mandatory access control) to provide more secure access to files and directories.

append To write data to the end of current data in a file without overwriting the file. Appending is always *adding to* and not *replacing* content.

application data Any data that is associated with the operation of a software application.

archive file A collection of at least one file into a standardized type of container file such as a tar archive, which is a compressed file such as those produced by bzip2 and gzip.

ASCII (American Standard Code for Information Interchange)   A format for encoding letters, numbers, punctuation, spaces, and other characters into numbers between 0 and 255.

attribute   In orchestration, a parameter that is used to customize an automation procedure.

autoconfiguration   The process of automatically assigning network configurations such as IP addresses, hostnames, gateways, and subnet addresses.

B

back up   The process of copying a file or set of files to another location in order to memorialize them in some manner, either as a long-term or short-term backup copy.

bandwidth   The maximum amount of data that can travel through media.

Basic Input/Output System (BIOS)   The first software that is started when a computer starts on older IBM-compatible computers. Settings in the BIOS can be changed by using the BIOS setup program.

binary log   A **systemd** log that is not text based.

binary package   A collection of applications, documentation, libraries, and configuration files that can be downloaded and run without needing to be compiled from source.

BIOS   See *Basic Input/Output System (BIOS)*.

block   A contiguous chunk or amount of memory. Blocks can be of flexible size and contents.

blocks in   A value that represents how many blocks have been received from a block device (such as a hard disk).

blocks out   A value that represents how many blocks have been sent to a block device (such as a hard disk).

Boolean logic   Operations such as OR and AND that operate on the true and false primitives that computers understand rather than numbers that humans understand.

boot loader   A program that is called by the BIOS to start a computer and that takes care of loading the operating system kernel and **initramfs**.

boot logging   The process of logging and then investigating the logs that pertain to the boot portion of a system's logs.

boot process   The set of steps a system goes through from power on to full functioning.

broadcast address   A network address on an IPv4 network that is used to send network messages to all hosts on the subnet.

bus   A hardware component that allows other components to connect and talk to each other over a single shared connection rather than each component needing a unique connection to every other component.

C

cache   In memory management, the area of memory where recently used files are stored. Cache is an important mechanism to speed up reads on servers.

catenate   To use output from one command as input to another command, typically through the use of a pipe. The process of catenation creates what is known as a process output chain.

certificate authority   A commonly known organization that guarantees the reliability of PKI certificates. A certificate authority provides a certificate that can be used to sign public key certificates.

chain   A set of firewall rules that includes both the type and the filtering point.

check in   In version control, to send file changes to a repository.

check out   In version control, to get a copy of one or more files that are located in a repository.

Chef   Software that provides a relatively new method of configuration management; the logical successor to Puppet.

cloud-init   The initial bootstrap tool that prepares a VM environment for the more feature-full Chef, Puppet, and other software options.

coldplug   Describes a hardware device that needs the computer to be turned off and on to be recognized.

command substitution   A shell scripting technique in which a command is run and then injected into another command.

Common Unix Printing System (CUPS)   The software responsible for printing on most Linux systems.

conditional   A piece of shell code that tests for given conditions and executes different code, depending on the result of the test.

console   In Linux, the primary terminal where a user works. The console is also a specific device with the name **/dev/console**.

convert   To alter from one format to another, such as converting uppercase to lowercase or converting a set of characters to another set of characters, as with the **sed** or **tr** commands.

cron   A service that runs background jobs at scheduled times.

CUPS   See *Common Unix Printing System (CUPS)*.

CUPS back end   A piece of the Common Unix Printing System that is responsible for sending a processed print job to a printer.

CVE (Common Vulnerabilities and Exposures)   A system that provides information about publicly known vulnerabilities.

D

DAC   See *discretionary access control (DAC)*.

daemon   A process that runs in the background and provides some sort of service, either to the local machine or to remote machines.

DAG   See *directed acyclic graph (DAG)*.

database   In relational databases, a collection of tables that together are used to store data.

daylight saving time   A system by which in summer months, clocks are moved ahead an hour to take advantage of the longer nights. Daylight saving time is a source of frustration for developers and systems administrators.

default chain policy   The target to use when no rule in a chain is matched.

default gateway   The gateway used by default for a host. See also *gateway*.

desktop   A software program that acts as the interface between users and a GUI environment.

DHCP   See *Dynamic Host Configuration Protocol (DHCP)*.

directed acyclic graph (DAG)   A check-in technique used in third-generation version control systems.

discretionary access control (DAC)   The use of Linux file and directory permissions to limit access to items.

distributed version control system (DVCS)   A type of version control system in which an entire project is checked out.

DNAT (destination NAT)   A feature of a router in which inbound network packets are forwarded to another host. See also *NAT (network address translation)*.

DNF (Dandified Yum)   An updated version of YUM (Yellow Dog Modified).

DNS   See *Domain Name System (DNS)*.

Domain Name System (DNS)   A system that makes it possible to translate computer names to IP addresses and vice versa. DNS involves several domain levels, resembling a directory structure in a filesystem.

dotted-quad notation   An IPv4 address that consists of four octets.

driver   A piece of software that allows a kernel to understand how to communicate with a particular device or set of devices.

dual-homed   Describing a host that contains two network interface cards, each of which is on a different network for redundancy, performance, and other benefits.

DVCS   See *distributed version control system (DVCS)*.

Dynamic Host Configuration Protocol (DHCP)   A protocol that is often implemented by a server that takes care of providing an IP address and other related configuration information to clients. DHCP makes it possible to use systems in a computer network without the need to configure all of them with the required IP address configuration and related parameters.

dynamic linker (ld.so)   The library on a Linux system that is responsible for finding dynamic libraries and presenting them to the application that needs them.

dynamic linking   The process of sharing library code between applications rather than requiring each application to keep a copy of the library.

E

epoch time   In Linux, the number of seconds that have passed since midnight on Thursday, January 1, 1970. Some utilities write epoch time instead of real clock time.

extended partition   On MBR disks, a logical partition that performs just like a regular partition and allows a system administrator to exceed the usual maximum of four partitions that can be stored in the partition table.

extension module   An optional feature with iptables that allows more functionality than what the default iptables program provides.

F

File System Hierarchy (FSH)   A standard that defines which Linux directories should be used for which purpose. Read man 7 hier (the man page for hier in category 7 of the man pages) for a specification of FSH.

File Transfer Protocol (FTP)   A software program that allows users to copy files to and from a remote system. Unfortunately, FTP sends data in plain text, making it an unsecure method.

filesystem   Both the single virtual disk presented to a Linux system and the layout of files on the disks.

filtering point   A component of a firewall where rules are placed.

firewall   A software program designed to block or allow network packets.

firewalld   A front-end utility designed to make the process of configuring firewalls with **iptables** easier.

FSH   See *File System Hierarchy (FSH)*.

FTP   See *File Transfer Protocol (FTP)*.

G

gateway   A host that is used to allow hosts to communicate with other networks. Also known as a router.

GECOS   A field in the **/etc/passwd** file that can be used to store personal data about a user on the Linux operating system. Originally stood for General Electric Comprehensive Operating System.

GID (group identification number)   A unique number assigned to a group account.

Git   A third-generation version control system.

GMT   See *Greenwich Mean Time (GMT)*.

GNOME   A common desktop. See also *desktop*.

Gnu Privacy Guard (GnuPG)   A software suite that allows users to encrypt data and digitally sign files.

GPT   See *GUID partition table (GPT)*.

graphical user interface (GUI)   A Windows-based user interface.

Greenwich Mean Time (GMT)   The reference time zone by which all other time zones calculate their times. A time zone is defined as being a certain number of hours and minutes ahead of, or behind, GMT.

GUID partition table (GPT)   A modern solution for storing partitions on a hard disk, as opposed to using the older MBR partition table. A total of 128 GUID partitions can be created on a hard disk, and there is no difference between primary, extended, and logical partitions anymore.

H

hard link   A name associated with an inode, which is used for storing a Linux file and contains the complete administration of the file, including the blocks where the file is stored. A file that doesn't have at least one hard link is considered a deleted file. To increase file accessibility, more than one hard link can be created for an inode.

hardware   The physical components of a computer, such as CPU, RAM, disk, network card, and so on.

hotplug   A device that can be inserted and recognized while a computer is running.

I

IaC   See *infrastructure as code (IAC)*.

ICMP   See *Internet Control Message Protocol (ICMP)*.

infrastructure as code (IAC)   The use of software tools to perform orchestration tasks.

init   The first process started when the Linux kernel and initramfs have been loaded. From the init process, all other processes are started. In RHEL 7, the init process has been replaced by **systemd**.

init process   The program that is called by the BIOS to start a computer and that takes care of loading the operating system kernel and **initramfs**.

integrated peripheral   A piece of hardware that is part of the motherboard and is not removable or upgradable.

internationalization   A software method that involves allowing an application to change out the language used without needing separate versions of the application.

Internet Control Message Protocol (ICMP)   A protocol that allows networking devices, such as routers, to send error messages.

Internet Printing Protocol   A modern web-based protocol that allows printers to communicate with computers over a network.

Internet Protocol (IP)   A protocol that handles the addressing and communication between devices on a network. It defines IP addresses, subnetting, and routing.

IP   See *Internet Protocol (IP)*.

IP (Internet Protocol) address   An address used to direct network traffic to a specific host.

IPv4 (Internet Protocol, version 4)   An older version of IP that uses dotted-quad notation for IP addresses.

IPv6 (Internet Protocol, version 6)   A newer version of IP that uses larger IP addresses and enhanced features.

ISO-8859 standard   A series of standards that define standard 8-bit code pages for character encoding.

J–K

job   In a Linux shell, a task running in the current terminal. Jobs can be started in the foreground as well as in the background. Every job is also visible as a process.

KDE   A common desktop. See also *desktop*.

Kerberos   A computer network authentication protocol that uses tickets to allow nodes and users communicating over an unsecure network to prove their identity. It provides mutual authentication and on Linux is used for authentication of users as well as services.

L

latency   Any sort of delay in communication.

LDAP   See *Lightweight Directory Access Protocol (LDAP)*.

library   A collection of reusable software components that can be used by multiple applications.

Lightweight Directory Access Protocol (LDAP)   Originally, a protocol used to get information from an X.500 directory (which is a kind of address book). In modern computing environments, LDAP is also the service that provides centralized information that can be used for logging in and other purposes.

line printer remote   An older network printing protocol optimized for less powerful printer hardware.

link   A file, with its own inode, that points to another file.

Linux Unified Key Setup   See *LUKS (Linux Unified Key Setup)*.

load average   The average CPU usage over a specific period of time.

locale   In the context of internationalization and localization, the current language and country being used.

localization   The process of displaying numbers, monetary values, dates, and times in a manner appropriate for the given country and language.

log rotation   A service which ensures that log files cannot grow too big. Log files are monitored according to specific parameters, such as a maximum age or size. Once a specified parameter is reached, the log file closes, and a new log file is opened. Old log files are kept for a limited period and then are removed, often after only a couple weeks.

logging   The process of submitting log entries to a service running on the system that notes those entries into a file or files or sends those entries across the network to another server that is configured to be a central logging repository.

logical extent   The building block used in LVM to create logical volumes. It normally has a size of a few megabytes, which corresponds to the size of the physical extents that are used.

logical partition   A partition created in an extended partition. See also *extended partition*.

logical volume (LV)   The LVM component that represents a filesystem and that is composed of multiple physical extents.

logical volume manager (LVM)   A Linux component that abstracts the layout of filesystems from the actual disks, allowing filesystems to be grown without needing to be contiguous.

LUKS (Linux Unified Key Setup)   A disk encryption method commonly used on Linux systems.

LV   See *logical volume (LV)*.

M

MAC   See *mandatory access control (MAC)*.

mandatory access control (MAC)   A system that makes use of security groups or domains to limit access to objects, such as files and directories.

mangle   A firewall feature that modifies a network packet.

master boot record (MBR)   On a BIOS system, the first 512 bytes on the primary hard disk. It contains a boot loader as well as a partition table that gives access to the different partitions on the hard disk of the computer. It is the first block on disk that is executed on boot to launch the boot manager.

MBR   See *master boot record (MBR)*.

merge   In version control, to combine different versions of a file into a single result.

message of the day   See *MOTD (message of the day)*.

micro kernel   A kernel in which modules are used to extend the basic kernel code.

module   A piece of snap-in code. Modules are used by several systems on Linux, such as the kernel, GRUB2, and rsyslog. By using modules, Linux components can be extended easily, adding functionality without requiring a total rewrite of the software.

monolithic kernel   A kernel in which all of the code is embedded within a single executable chunk of code.

MOTD (message of the day)   A message that is displayed when a user logs in to a system.

mount point   A directory on disk to which another filesystem is attached.

multifactor authentication   A type of authentication in which a user is requested to provide multiple bits of evidence that prove the user's identity.

N

name server   In DNS, a server configured with a database that contains resource records used to answer DNS queries.

NAT (network address translation)   In firewalling, a configuration in which a computer on a private network uses the public IP address of the router to connect to computers on the Internet; also referred to as masquerading. The computer on the Internet sees only the public IP address and therefore cannot connect directly to the computer on the private network. Masquerading makes it possible to share one public IP address between many computers and at the same time is a security feature.

network   A grouping of hosts connected either by wireless signal or by cabling that can connect to each other and communicate in other ways.

Network File System (NFS)   A common Unix solution to export physical filesystems to other hosts on the network. The other hosts can mount an exported NFS directory in their local filesystem.

network mask   A dotted-quad notation used to define the network part of an IP address.

Network Time Protocol (NTP)   A service that allows a computer to query time servers for the purpose of keeping accurate time.

NFS   See *Network File System (NFS)*.

NTP   See *Network Time Protocol (NTP)*.

numeric mode   A method of setting object permissions that uses octal numbers.

O

octet   A portion of an IPv4 address consisting of 8 bits, each with a value of 0 or 1.

OS (operating system) data   Any data that is associated with the operation of an operating system.

OTP (One Time Password)   A password that only permits access for a single instance.

OVA (Open Virtual Appliance)   Effectively a bundling of one or more VMs together in an installable/runnable package such as a virtual appliance.

OVF (Open Virtualization Format)   A compressed package file format that contains any needed certificates and disk image files and that is similar in format to a TAR archive file.

P

package manager   A system such as APT or RPM that installs software and keeps track of what's currently installed.

packet drop   A process in which a remote system doesn't respond to an inbound network packet.

page   A page, memory page, or virtual page that is a fixed-length contiguous block of virtual memory, described by a single entry in the page table.

PAM (pluggable authentication module)   A collection of libraries designed to provide an administrator with the means to change how user accounts are authenticated.

partition   A subdivision of a hard disk on which a filesystem can be created to be mounted into the directory structure.

peripheral   A device, such as a printer or a monitor, that connects to a computer.

permission trio   A permission set for an object user owner, a group owner, and all other users.

physical extent   A component of logical volume management that forms the basis of a logical volume. A physical volume, such as a disk, is split into blocks called physical extents.

physical volume (PV)   The foundational building block of an LVM configuration that typically corresponds to a partition or a complete disk device.

PID   See *process identification number (PID)*.

pipe   A structure that can be used to forward the output of one command to be used as input for another command.

pluggable authentication module   See *PAM (pluggable authentication module)*.

port   A number associated with a service. The service listens for incoming network packets assigned to the port number.

Postfix   A mail transfer agent, originally built by IBM, that is split into separate components to enhance security.

primary group   The group owner of a file. Every Linux user is a member of a primary group.

primary partition   In MBR, one of a maximum of four partitions that can be created in the master boot record. See also *extended partition*.

print queue   A list of print jobs waiting to be printed.

print spooler   The component responsible for taking the next job off the print queue and sending it to the printer.

priority   In rsyslog, a level used to specify the severity of a logged event. Based on the severity, specific actions can be taken.

private key   A key used to decrypt data that has been encrypted with a public key.

procedure   In orchestration, the collection of steps that need to take place to complete an action.

process   A task running on a Linux machine. A process roughly corresponds to a program, although one program can start multiple processes.

process identification number (PID)   A unique number used to identify a process running on a Linux system.

public key   A key provided to other users and hosts that is used to encrypt data. This data, when returned to the original host, can be decrypted by the private key.

Puppet   An older and less capable method of providing configuration management that is being replaced by Chef.

PV   See *physical volume (PV)*.

Q–R

queue   In process management, the list of processes waiting to be executed.

RADIUS (Remote Authentication Dial-In Service)   A protocol that allows a client system to make use of a server to authenticate users.

RAID   See *redundant array of independent disks (RAID)*.

RCP   See *remote copy (RCP)*.

reboot   To cause a system to go from a running or halted state to not running and then back to properly running again.

redirect   To take content or output from a process and send that content or output to a file (either a device file or a regular file on disk).

redundant array of independent disks (RAID)   A method of using regular disks to build a larger and more reliable set of disks, such as by mirroring writes to two separate disks.

relative path   The location of a file, specified as an offset from the current working directory.

remote copy (RCP)   A software program that allows users to copy files to and from a remote system. Unfortunately, this process sends data in plain text, making it an unsecure method.

repo   See *repository*.

repository   In version control, a storage area that keeps track of different versions of files. Also known as a repo.

Request for Comments (RFC)   A publication that defines a standard, such as a protocol like IP.

RFC   See *Request for Comments (RFC)*.

root filesystem   The filesystem that contains the root (/) directory.

router   A device that transfers network packets from one network to another.

routing   The process of sending network data from one Internet Protocol network to another via a gateway.

runlevel   The services/daemons that will be running/stopped when the system is in a particular system state.

S

Samba   The Linux service that implements the SMB protocol.

saturation   A state in which throughput is often (or constantly) reaching the value of the bandwidth.

secondary group   A group to which a user belongs but for which membership is not defined in the **/etc/passwd** file. When creating new files, the secondary group does not automatically become the owner of those files. Users can access files via permissions when using a secondary group.

Secure Shell (SSH)   A solution that allows users to open a shell on a remote server, where security is implemented by using public/private key cryptography.

SELinux   A security feature that involves using MAC (mandatory access control) to provide more secure access to files and directories.

SELinux Boolean   A true/false value that can be used to configure an SELinux policy.

SELinux context   Metadata applied to an object, such as a file, directory, or process. This metadata is used to determine how the rules of an SELinux policy will be enforced on the object.

SELinux policy   Rules that determine how MAC is enforced on a system.

session   The presence of a user on a system after being authenticated until logging out.

SetGID (SGID)   A special permission set in which a command executes using the privileges of the group owner of the command.

SetUID (SUID)   A special permission set in which a command executes using the privileges of the user owner of the command.

SGID   See *SetGID (SGID)*.

Shadow Suite   A system function that allows for the encrypted passwords on a system to be kept in the much more secure **/etc/shadow** file instead of the less secure and often publicly available **/etc/passwd** file. Group passwords are also made more secure by being relocated from the public **/etc/group** file to the more secure **/etc/gshadow** file.

share   A directory to which remote access is configured using a remote filesystem protocol such as NFS or CIFS.

shared object   A library used by multiple applications and linked at runtime by the dynamic linker. Shared object files almost always end in .so.

shebang   A pair of characters used in a script to indicate which shell should be used for executing the code in the shell script. If no shebang is used, the script code is interpreted by the parent shell, which may lead to errors in some cases. A shebang starts with a #, which is followed by a ! and the complete path name of the shell, such as **#!/bin/bash**.

shell metacharacters   Characters such as *, ?, and [a-z] that allow users to refer to characters in filenames in a flexible way.

shut down   To close down a system properly.

signal   An instruction that can be sent to a process. Common signals exist, such as SIGTERM and SIGKILL, but the Linux kernel allows a total of 32 different signals to be used. To send a signal to a process, the **kill** command can be used.

Simple Mail Transfer Protocol (SMTP)   A text-based protocol that allows different mail transfer agents to send mail between themselves.

Simple Network Management Protocol (SNMP)   A protocol that allows for the management of network devices.

skel template   A directory used to populate a new user account's home directory with files.

slab   A cache that holds objects that are located in memory and managed by a slab allocator; effectively a memory allocator for use by the kernel.

SMTP   See *Simple Mail Transfer Protocol (SMTP)*.

SNMP   See *Simple Network Management Protocol (SNMP)*.

source format   A set of source files packaged up in an rpm or dpkg file that, when installed, populate a location and can be used to build a package from source.

source RPM   A package containing source code and the instructions on how to build the source into a binary.

SQL   See *Structured Query Language (SQL)*.

SSH   See *Secure Shell (SSH)*.

standard error   The default location to which a program sends error messages.

standard input   The default location from which a program gets its input.

standard output   The default location to which a program sends its regular output.

static linking   The process of taking code from common libraries and making it a part of a runnable application rather than something brought in from a shared library.

sticky bit   A special permission set that modifies the meaning of the write permission on a directory so that the only user who can delete a file in the directory is the file owner, the directory owner, or the root user. Historically, the sticky bit was used to keep a program resident in memory and prevent it from being swapped to disk.

strings   A collection of characters, such as **"hello"**, as opposed to a numeric type like an integer or a date.

Structured Query Language (SQL)   A language used to query and manipulate relational databases.

subnetting   The process of using a network mask to define the network part of an IP address.

SUID   See *SetUID (SUID)*.

swap space   Hard drive space used in place of RAM when available RAM runs low.

symbolic mode   A method of using symbols to set object permissions.

synchronization   The process of producing an identical copy of a set of files from one location to another, typically for the purpose of backup or safekeeping. During this process, a comparison is made between the two locations, and the differences are copied from the source to the target, in varying levels of atomicity, such as file by file or byte by byte, depending on the parameters and options specified.

syslog   A daemon that is the traditional logging service for Linux, recently supplanted in some instances by **rsyslog** and **systemd** logging.

system time   The time maintained by the operating system. When a Linux system boots, system time is set to the current hardware time, and while the operating system is running, it is often synchronized using Network Time Protocol.

systemd   The service manager on many distributions, which is the first process that starts after the kernel has loaded and takes care of starting all other processes and services on a Linux system.

T

table   A type of firewall rule, such as filter, nat, or mangle.

TACACS+ (Terminal Access Controller Access-Control System Plus)   A protocol that allows a client system to make use of a server to authenticate users.

tar command   An archival tool that allows a user to create archives and to use compression utilities to additionally compress the contents of an archive.

target   The action to be taken when a rule is matched.

TCP   See *Transmission Control Protocol (TCP)*.

TCP wrappers   A library designed to allow the administrator the means to secure network-based services by using the **/etc/hosts.allow** and **/etc/hosts.deny** configuration files.

Telnet   A software program that allows for connection to remote systems. Unfortunately, this connection is sent in plain text, making it an unsecure method.

throughput   The amount of data that passes through media.

time synchronization   A system which ensures that multiple servers are using exactly the same time. To accomplish time synchronization, it is common to use an external time server, as defined in the Network Time Protocol (NTP).

time zone   A set of locations that share a common time, measured in an offset from Universal Coordinated Time.

timeout   The use of a software component to determine whether a packet drop has occurred.

token   A unique value (typically either a number or an alphanumeric value) that is generated by either a hardware device or a software program.

Transmission Control Protocol (TCP)   A protocol that focuses on the transport of data packages. TCP differs from UDP in that the data packages are considered "reliable" because TCP performs error checking to make sure all data packages arrive at the destination.

two-factor authentication (2FA)   A process in which a user must provide two different forms of identification to be authenticated.

U

UDP   See *User Datagram Protocol (UDP)*.

UFW (Uncomplicated Firewall)   A front-end utility designed to make the process of configuring firewalls with **iptables** easier.

UID (user identification number)   A unique number assigned to a user account.

ulimit   A feature that allows an administrator to limit access to system resources for users and groups.

umask value   A value applied to the default permissions for files and directories when creating a new file or directory. The umask value modifies the permissions placed on the new file or directory.

Unicode   A universal encoding that defines each possible character as a *code point* (a unique number).

Universal Coordinated Time (UTC)   A time standard that is globally the same, no matter which specific time zone a user is in. Universal Coordinated Time corresponds to Greenwich Mean Time.

Universal Serial Bus   See *USB (Universal Serial Bus)*.

UPG (user private group)   A technique in which a new user is assigned to a private group that matches the user's username.

Upstart   The system used in RHEL 6 to start services during system initialization. It is similar in features to **systemd** and is an improvement over **init**.

USB (Universal Serial Bus)   An industry standard for external devices.

User Datagram Protocol (UDP)   A protocol that focuses on the transport of data packages. It is often contrasted with TCP, as they both perform similar functions. UDP differs from TCP in that the data packages are sent "connectionless," so no error checking is performed.

UTC   See *Universal Coordinated Time (UTC)*.

UTF-8   A character encoding format that encodes all characters in a variable width using blocks of 8 bits. That is, characters are from 1 to 4 bytes long. UTF-8 is also backward compatible with 8-bit ASCII.

UTF-16   A character encoding format that encodes all characters in a variable width using blocks of 16 bits. That is, characters are either 2 or 4 bytes each.

V–Z

variable   A label that corresponds to a location in memory that contains a specific value that can be changed dynamically. In scripting, variables are frequently used to allow the script to be flexible.

version control system   Software that tracks changes to files over time and can be used to see history or revert to older versions of a file.

VG   See *volume group (VG)*.

virtual memory   Hard drive space used in place of RAM.

virtualization   The process of running a client operating system on a host as if it were running on hardware.

VM template   A master version of a virtual machine that is used to make a copy that is then customized to become the VM that you want to spin up in your environment.

volume group   A collection of physical volumes in a logical volume manager system. You can split up a volume group into logical volumes on which you make filesystems.

window   A tmux or screen instance; a window is not necessarily a drawn window on the screen but may be a separate discrete instance of the BASH shell that contains a session.

Yellow Dog Modified (YUM)   The meta package handler that on RHEL 7 is used to install packages from yum repositories.

Zypper   The combination of ZYpp/libzypp and the **zypper** command, used to manage software mostly on SUSE systems and Ark.

Index

To receive your 10% off
Exam Voucher, register
your product at:

www.pearsonitcertification.com/register

and follow the instructions.